Comparative
Economic
Systems

Comparative Economic Systems

Richard L. Carson
Carleton University

Macmillan Publishing Co., Inc.
New York

Collier Macmillan Publishers
London

Macmillan Publishing Co., Inc.
866 Third Avenue, New York, New York 10022
Collier-Macmillan Canada, Ltd., Toronto, Ontario

Library of Congress Cataloging in Publication Data
Carson, Richard L.
Comparative economic systems.
1. Comparative economics. 1. Title.
HB90.C37   330   72–81652
ISBN 0–02–319510–X

Printing: 1 2 3 4 5 6 7 8   Year: 3 4 5 6 7 8 9 0

To the memory of my father

Preface

This volume follows an organizational approach to comparative economic systems—that is, it seeks to emphasize the ways in which different economies can organize themselves to solve the economic problems of what, how, and for whom.

Rather than focus on the traditional "capitalism vs. socialism" issue, however, I shall try to generalize this to derive "a spectrum of economic systems." In the process, I hope to shed light on the differences and similarities between economies that the capitalism–socialism dichotomy tends to blur, as well as to defuse the ideological issue. It is doubtful that there is such a thing as a unique "supersystem," best for solving the economic problem in every environment from India to Canada and regardless of the goals that a society or its leaders may determine.

The polar cases of the spectrum of economic systems are what we may call the "pure market" and "pure command" economies, respectively. Of course, all real-world systems combine markets with commands and indicators to solve their economic problems, and we shall therefore explore the comparative advantages of different combinations at some length. We shall also view systems from a property-rights standpoint and, in general, attempt a fairly rigorous classification of systems on the bases of both this and information flows. (At the same time, the book should not prove difficult reading to the student with a good grasp of principles.)

In addition, we shall find that we cannot ignore the political dimension of economic systems, which is therefore woven into the basic organizational framework from the start. I have also included discussions of the theories of Marx and Schumpeter—including the economic theory of history—along with special topics, such as moral incentives, workers' management, and the economics of democracy. Again, these are woven into the basic framework. We proceed largely on the basis of models rather than case studies, although we constantly seek to relate our analysis to real-world experience.

My thanks are due to numerous typists, working under the direction of Mrs. Evelyn Aldridge, who helped me through several laborious drafts of the manuscript: Dawn Archer, Judy Armstrong, Bette-Anne Berndt, Karen

Bouris, Joy Charlebois, Evelyn Irvine, Tina James, Edie Landau, Audrey McCallum, Nancy Daly, Barbara McClelland, Jackie Kellough, and Sandy Inglis. I am also indebted to Sheila Isaac for helping with the artwork.

In addition, I thank Horst Alter, Peter Yao, Marilyn Cayer, G. C. Trolley, and Aldyth Holmes, who worked for me as research assistants, and Professor Gilles Paquet for numerous ideas and inspirations. Finally, I thank my students, from whom I have learned a good deal.

Ottawa, Canada   R. L. C.

Contents

Part **TWO**

Part **SIX**

Part **One**

Chapter 0

Approaching the Study
of Comparative Systems

"L'Homme est supérieur au Rhinocéros."

Eugène Ionesco

0–1   Economic Systems in Competition

Nations have always competed for power, prestige, and wealth. In former times military might was the decisive factor in this contest. It constituted the best available indicator of a country's influence because war was the ultimate way of solving the most important international disputes. But today, one might argue that, although military power continues to be of utmost importance, the struggle for economic supremacy has stolen some of the show.

"We declare war on you, excuse the expression," ex-Premier Khrushchev is supposed to have proclaimed to an American diplomat one evening at a reception in Moscow, "We will bury you." [1] Khrushchev did not mean bury literally with bombs. He meant that the Soviet and other socialist societies would become so economically superior to Western capitalist nations that capitalism would be buried in much the same fashion as feudalism. In the same spirit, Soviet statisticians have proclaimed that "Statistics is a weapon

[1] See the text of the speech by Mayor Paulson of Los Angeles in *The New York Times*, Sept. 20, 1959.

in the class war," [2] meaning that the use of economic indicators is part of a new type of limited, economic war.

The importance of economic competition has been heightened in the years since World War I, especially since World War II, by the appearance of a variety of economic systems. Socialism, as a predominant economic form, did not really take hold in Russia until around 1930 and, in other socialist nations, until about 1950. Furthermore, within both socialist and capitalist camps there now exists an interesting variety of forms, much more so than prior to World War II or even, say, 1955.

France, for instance, is primarily a capitalist country, but her capitalism is of a species noticeably different from what we find in North America. China has a system clearly distinguishable from that of the U.S.S.R.—indeed, although both are planned economies, planning denotes a different process in one nation than in the other. The academic exercise of comparing different theoretical systems can be anchored to a contrasting of economies that must solve economic problems and function from day to day in the real world.

0-2 Rhinoceritis

Broadly speaking, it is the purpose of this book to put economic systems under the microscope. Realizing that any economic order is relative in the sense that it may evolve over time, we also want to explore the laws of motion of different forms of economic organization. We shall try to approach the study of comparative systems using the methods of scientific inquiry. To begin with, we wish to caution our readers against applying the very *opposite* of the scientific method.

If a label for this opposite approach were to be sought out, we might come up with "doctrinaire approach" or simply "dogmatism." Whatever one may call it, it is usually characterized by rigidity instead of flexibility and decision making based on ideology rather than analysis.

We now know, for example, that both the Soviet Union and the United States have passed through long periods of time in which there was a doc-

---

[2] Quoted by R. W. Campbell in *Soviet Economic Power* (Boston: Houghton, 1966), p. 112. We should distinguish at the outset between the Soviet Union (or the U.S.S.R.) on one hand, and Russia on the other. These terms are often used interchangeably, but strictly speaking, Russia is but one of the 15 constituent republics which make up the U.S.S.R. These reflect, to some extent, the multinational and multilingual nature of this giant nation (about 8.5 million square miles, more than twice as large as Canada or the United States, including Alaska and Hawaii). The Russian Republic does, however, cover nearly 78 per cent of the surface of the U.S.S.R. and contains more than half its population. (It is followed by Kazakhastan with about 12.5 per cent of the land area and the Ukraine with nearly 20 per cent of the total population.)

The old Imperial Russian Empire, which was overthrown during the 1917 Revolution, included most, although not all, of the present U.S.S.R. In addition, on the eve of World War I, the czars ruled over areas, including much of modern Poland, not comprised in the U.S.S.R.

trinaire unwillingness to experiment with any sort of economic reform. In the United States, adherents to the doctrine of laissez faire at one time refused even to allow input–output studies of the economy to be made on the grounds that one would only wish to perform them with a view to later control.[3] The same philosophy forbade constructive government effort during the early years of the Great Depression, insisting that there should be no deficit in the federal budget, regardless of the cost in lost output and employment.

In the U.S.S.R., Stalin maintained his overcentralized bureaucracy in power long after it had outlived its initial function of getting the economy on the road to industrialization, and brutally punished anyone who dared to suggest reform. These rigidities of economic doctrine have been relaxed in both countries—albeit cautiously—during the past decade or so, partly as a result of the competition between economic systems mentioned in Section 0-1.[4]

Yet events surrounding the war in Vietnam and the Soviet invasion of Czechoslovakia have reminded us that ideology remains a cruelly powerful force in the world. The student of comparative economic systems cannot ignore this. However, he must try to be as free as possible from personal bias. Ideally, he should approach his subject just as an engineer might approach a complex and intricate piece of equipment that he wanted to improve by redesigning.

In particular, the student of comparative systems is not, in any sense, a slayer of dragons. That the works of Marx, Keynes, Sismondi, John Bates Clark, and a host of other famous economists who have written on the subject contain inaccuracies, ambiguities, and inconsistencies is both true and uninteresting. The real task is to glean ideas from each author that are worthy of preservation and further development, while leaving the rest behind. It is in this way that any science must progress.

No economic system should be an end in itself. Rather, it is a means of increasing welfare, by some definition, and must be judged in this light. The very worst thing a comparative-systems analyst could do would be to unveil a given economic system as if it were a holy relic normally enshrined under glass and bearing a label "Do not touch." Yet it is often harder not to reveal one's doctrinaire leanings in the study of comparative systems than in any other branch of economic analysis. The study of comparative systems deals with topics that, historically, have been constant subjects of ideological dispute. These are issues on which virtually everyone (including the author of this book) has certain built-in norms and biases.

Playwright Eugène Ionesco prefaced his famous work *Rhinocéros* with a

---

[3] See *Business Week,* Aug. 29, 1953, p. 26.

[4] History moves in cycles, however, and during the period embracing the end of the 1960s and the beginning of the 1970s the clock was turned back somewhat in Eastern Europe and perhaps in North America as well. The long-run outlook, the author is convinced, is for less rigidity in practice, although it is likely to remain necessary to throw an ideological cloak around many measures that are taken.

story about a colleague attending a Nazi ra''y in Nuremburg just prior to the outbreak of World War II:

In 1938, Denis de Rougemont, writer and philosopher, was in Nuremburg, Germany, at the time of a Nazi demonstration. He tells us that he found himself in the middle of an immense crowd awaiting the arrival of Hitler. The people were beginning to grow impatient when someone caught a glimpse of the Fuhrer, a little man, and his retinue, appearing very tiny in the distance at the end of an avenue. From afar, Denis de Rougemont saw the crowd frantically acclaiming the sinister personnage as if overcome, bit by bit, with a kind of hysteria which was spreading and approaching him as Hitler advanced. He did not understand this frenzy, but when the Fuhrer came quite close to him and when the spectators all around him were swept away by hysteria, Denis de Rougemont felt that he, too, was being invaded by a passion or delirium which was electrifying him. He was about to succumb to the strange enchantment when something rose from the depths of his being to resist this collective storm. . . .[5]

It is a milder form of this collective hysteria that acts to build up and reinforce the biases that threaten to invade and suppress rational discussion and thinking when it comes to dealing with issues at the heart of comparative systems. And it is, as well, this kind of hysteria and its resultant dogmatic attitudes that must be resisted, intuitively, before creative discussion and study can begin. Ionesco called such a frame of mind "rhinoceritis." It is as if man were exchanging his existence for that of a rhinoceros, a huge, powerful animal that roams in herds and lives in the swamp. One of the principal symptoms of rhinoceritis is that the victim feels himself to be immune.

0–3   Why Study Comparative Systems?

Only an in-depth exploration of the structure and functioning of different types of economic systems, along with the causes and consequences of economic change within them, will enable us to reply to the individual who wants to settle economic issues on a purely ideological basis. This is one reason for studying comparative economic systems, but there are many more. From these, the following would appear to be worth emphasizing.

1. The study of comparative economic systems has a tendency to broaden and generalize our economic thinking. In the Western world, the institutional and organizational framework of laissez-faire capitalism is all too often an implicit and automatic assumption in discussions of economics. Yet many of the economic mechanisms that are crucial in the functioning of a laissez-faire economy would not work or would work rather differently in different organizational contexts. The course in comparative systems can draw the attention of the student to this relativism.

2. Comparative economic analysis, by enabling us to peer into the structure and functioning of systems fundamentally different from our own,

[5] Eugène Ionesco, "Préface de l'auteur," in Eugène Ionesco's *Rhinocéros,* ed. by Reuben Y. Ellison and Stowell C. Goding (New York: Holt, 1961).

provides us with a framework for exploring some of the most crucial socio-economic issues of the day. We can ask why consciously planned economies have been more successful at avoiding sharp cyclical swings in output and under what circumstances they are likely to achieve high growth rates. We may also ask what costs, if any, are associated with such built-in features.

3. Conscious central planning may replace freedom of decision making on the part of individual entrepreneurs. But planning and freedom can be complementary as well as mutually exclusive. We should not forget that giant corporations such as Alcoa, General Motors, and du Pont have to carry on efficient economic planning every day in order to survive. Certain problems that many socialist nations have encountered—for example, the question of how much decentralization to introduce into the structure of economic decision making—find their parallels in the organizational experience of these huge firms.

4. In an era in which international understanding is more important than ever before, the study of a variety of economic organizations and societies can, hopefully, enable us to better comprehend the motives and behavior of other peoples and nations. In this connection, it is worth noting that most countries of the world, in trying to solve their economic problems, have decided to chart a course that differs, in some respects, from that elected by North Americans. Few underdeveloped nations, for example, would benefit from an economic system patterned after the American one. For humane reasons, one should not try to force such a system on them. And, practically speaking, they probably would not accept it.

On the other hand, there does exist a variety of models which these nations might profitably study. The Japanese and Soviet paths to economic development are basically different, and the road currently being followed by Yugoslavia diverges in still another direction.

Finally, the author would not agree with the popular notion that all modern industrial or technology-based societies are fundamentally the same. This view holds that

Starting from the assumption of a basically similar pattern of technological evolution . . . industrial societies change in a common direction toward increasing occupational differentiation; the mobilization of the tradition-bound into markets, bureaucracies, and other institutions; an increase in state power; and the development of similar integrative mechanisms. . . . Technology is a unifying force because at a given time there . . . is only one best technology. The same technology calls for much the same occupational structure which in turn becomes the class structure. . . .[6]

[6] This passage is from Morris Bornstein, "East European Economic Reforms and the Convergence of Economic Systems," *Jahrbuch der Wirtschaft Osteuropas* (Yearbook of East European Economics), Vol. 2 (Munich: Gunter Olzog Verlag, 1971). Bornstein cites this position but does not advocate it. For advocates, see J. K. Galbraith, *The New Industrial State* (Boston: Houghton, 1967) and Clark Kerr, John T. Dunlop, F. H. Harbison, and Charles A. Myers, *Industrialism and Industrial Man* (Cambridge, Mass.: Harvard U.P., 1960), especially pp. 282–296. See other works cited by Bornstein.

These similarities appear, at best, to be overdrawn. It does make a difference, for example, whether markets or bureaucracies coordinate the bulk of economic activity, and both kinds of institution vary significantly from one country to another. Differences in the organization of economic activity in the U.S.S.R., China, Japan, Sweden, and North America are important and likely to persist and therefore are worthy of our study.

It is now time to begin our exploration of systems, and we start by refamiliarizing ourselves with the "economic problem," which summarizes in very general terms the tasks that every economy must solve.

0–4 The Economic Problem

Economic activity does not occur in a chaotic way. It is organized into a whole network of economic and semieconomic institutions, which, themselves, crystallize certain moments in the evolution of the economy in question. Markets are examples of such institutions—so would be the planning apparatus of a command economy. It is through these mechanisms that any society tackles its economic problem, that is, tries to efficiently allocate its resources among alternative ends. The question of efficiency arises because the resources of every economic system are scarce. There are many more uses to be found for these resources than they can possibly be made to serve. Thus the system has to choose those uses it considers most urgent and make its resources stretch as far as possible under current technological constraints.

In connection with this, each "economic actor" in society has a preference function which, roughly speaking, gives us the way he would rank the alternative uses to which he might put the purchasing power at his disposal. Presumably, for instance, food would come before a washing machine; a washing machine would receive priority over a television set; and so on. Like society as a whole, in other words, individual families and firms face problems of efficiently allocating their scarce resources. Yet such a problem as conceived from society's viewpoint is apt to be many times more complex, because individual preferences must somehow be synthesized into a social preference function, which ranks alternative uses of resources from society's point of view. We shall have a good deal to say about this later.

The economic problem is usually broken up into three subproblems, entitled *what, how,* and *for whom.* Let us briefly elaborate on each of these:

1. A decision must be made as to how much of each good to produce and, in particular, as to *what* goods to produce and which goods not to turn out at all. Some wants of virtually every individual in any society will have to go unsatisfied, and, in this sense, not enough can be produced. Where and how do we decide to draw the cutoff lines?

2. At least in the long run, there are a variety of ways of producing a ton of steel, a tube of toothpaste, an automobile, or a razor blade. Decisions must be made as to *how* inputs are going to be combined in the production of

goods and services. This involves, on the one hand, efficient management of complex production units. (The plans for the Novo Lipetsk steel mill in the U.S.S.R., for example, comprise "91 volumes totalling 70,000 pages.") [7] However, the most complicated aspect of all this is not the efficient running of given factories, farms, and mills but the simultaneous coordination of all their productive efforts.

Suppose that one were to try to program the entire producing sector of a single country on a computer or a series of computers. In other words, suppose that one were to try to coordinate, via a central "brain," every single productive effort both within factories and farms and from one producing enterprise to another. For the U.S.S.R., it has been estimated that several quintillion (that is, more than 1,000,000,000,000,000,000) relationships would have to be taken into account. Assuming that there are 1 million electronic computers each able to perform 30,000 operations per second available for the task, several years of continuous computation would be required.

Under the central problems of what and how to produce comes an important subproblem. What proportion of a society's productive resources should be diverted from the production of goods for current consumption toward investment or the production of capital goods? (A *capital* good or an *intermediate* good is an output of one firm and a productive input for another. A tractor is an intermediate good, as is a machine that helps to make a tractor).

The more consumer goods a society turns out in a given year, other things being equal, the fewer capital goods it can produce—thus the problem of capital formation is clearly part of the problem of *what* to produce. However, the principal reason for investing today is so that more efficient production can take place later. Farming is more efficient with a horse-drawn plow than when done almost entirely by hand. It is still more efficient with tractors and tractor-drawn plows. Hence, in the long run, the question, "How much shall be devoted to capital formation?" is, in part, a question as to *how* production shall be carried out.

3. Finally, the total output of the economy must be distributed among those who have helped produce it as well as those who, for a variety of reasons, did not participate directly in production. This problem of distributing or dividing up the social product is usually called the problem of *for whom* to produce. To a large extent, the problems of *what* and *for whom* are interrelated. In most Western economies, for instance, a redistribution of wealth, giving more to some and less to others, would eventually result in a different bill of goods being produced. Different individuals have different tastes, different propensities to save and consume, different preferences for work vis-à-vis leisure, and so forth.

[7] Leon Smolinski, "What Next in Soviet Planning?" *Foreign Affairs,* July 1964; reprinted in Morris Bornstein and Daniel Fusfeld, eds., *The Soviet Economy: A Book of Readings,* rev. ed. (Homewood, Ill.: Irwin, 1966).

An important problem subsumed under 1 and 3 is that of fully utilizing society's productive resources, especially labor. If laborers are willing to work at prevailing wage and salary rates but cannot find jobs, society's output may be less than it otherwise would be, and those who are unemployed will receive less in terms of consumer goods than they otherwise would. This unemployment may either be open or disguised. In many countries the farm labor force could be reduced without reducing farm output. Such disguised unemployment is often called *under*employment. Disguised or open, unemployment is a problem that all types of economic systems may have to face.

0–5   The Spectrum of Economic Systems

In the remainder of the first part of the book we are going to develop a searchlight to aid us in exploring the various models of economic systems to follow. Chapters 1 and 2 formulate an organizational model of economic administration that allows us to differentiate one kind of economy from another. In this way, it enables us to define a spectrum of economic systems and so forms a core for much of the succeeding work in the book. Chapters 3, 4, and 5 then probe questions related to the designing of economic systems. Finally, Chapter 6 will discuss problems involved in making economic comparisons.

Next, Chapters 7 through 21 will explore different subspaces of the spectrum of economic systems. At one pole we find a complete refraining from any conscious organization or control over economic activity except, perhaps, to lay down the rules of fair play and police them. This is an extreme form of what has come to be known as laissez-faire capitalism, the French words *laissez faire* meaning, crudely, "let alone." A modified version of this system prevailed in England and North America during much of the 19th century. At the other pole, we find an extreme form of command economy in which society, as embodied in the state, controls all material means of production and distribution.

Today all nations lie somewhere between these poles. That is, all nations contain recognizable elements of both the complete laissez-faire model and the extreme form of socialism just mentioned. Strictly speaking, "full communism" refers to a "state of bliss" prevailing *after* the economic problem has been solved, and most nations usually referred to as "communist" are really socialist, a distinction that we shall try to make clear below.

Finally, we shall close the book with two chapters on political decision making, planning, and democracy.

REFERENCES

Balassa, Bela A. "Success Criteria for Economic Systems." In Morris Bornstein, ed., *Comparative Economic Systems*. Homewood, Ill.: Richard D. Irwin, Inc., 1969, Ch. 1.

Grossman, Gregory. *Economic Systems.* Englewood Cliffs, N.J.: Prentice-Hall, Inc., 1967, Chs. 1, 2, 3.

Gruchy, Allan G. *Comparative Economic Systems.* Boston: Houghton-Mifflin Company, 1966, Pt. One.

Halm, George N. *Economic Systems: A Comparative Analysis.* New York: Holt, Rinehart and Winston, Inc., 1968, Ch. 1.

Koivisto, W. A. *Principles and Problems of Modern Economics.* New York: John Wiley & Sons, Inc., 1957, Chs. 1, 2.

Chapter **1**

The Spectrum
of Economic Systems

Under capitalism, man exploits man. Under socialism, it is just the reverse.
Anonymous

1–1 The Gains from Exchange

If nobody wished to exchange goods and services, there would be no need for economics or for economists. Fortunately for economists, a modern society is inconceivable without an intricate network of exchange relationships. But why is this so? What forces decree that economically as well as socially no man shall be an island unto himself?

Basically, exchange arises because it enables specialization in production to be combined with diversity in consumption. Variety is the spice of life in that most people are happiest when consuming a multitude of goods and services. But we are also most efficient in production, usually, when our work directly affects a far narrower range of goods. Witness the man who does nothing all day but inspect automobiles or teach economics to college students. In return for his efforts, he will receive many kinds of food and drink, clothing, housing, a refrigerator, stove, washing machine, automobile, and television set, plus a host of other products whose manufacture he does not even begin to understand.

Exchange contributes to material welfare, ultimately, by separating the activities of production and consumption. Without a vast complex of institutions to facilitate exchange, the standard of living that virtually every reader is currently enjoying would be beyond imagination. The process of exchange is a powerful force in shaping every community into a highly interdependent organism.

Exchange finds its justification in that it allows a pattern of economic cooperation to arise among the individual members of a community (and, we might add, among different communities, regions, or nations). Yet the process of exchange involves conflict over the terms at which trade is to take place. In the short run, the outcomes of these conflicts will depend upon the relative positions of the bargaining parties as well as the skill and intensity with which they bargain. But in the long run, the network of exchange relations in any society is, in part, shaped by and, in turn, helps to shape the entire institutional pattern of that society. Exchange is on quite a different basis in the U.S.S.R., for example, than in Canada or the United States, and quite different institutional frameworks have evolved in the two countries. This is far from being a complete coincidence. Exchange cannot be considered passive or neutral. It influences men's lives far beyond the realm of economics.

To make the role played by exchange easier to comprehend, it may be well to begin by examining a case in which exchange cannot take place because we have a man isolated from society. Robinson Crusoe, even though shipwrecked, will still try to allocate his scarce resources among competing uses so as to make himself as well off as possible.

1–2   Robinson Crusoe

The material well-being of our Robinson Crusoe will be determined by the amounts of goods and services that he produces or procures for himself and then consumes, along with the work needed to acquire these goods. Included will be leisure, provision for future consumption, and goods such as food and clothing which are to be consumed currently. Any index of Mr. Crusoe's material welfare or satisfaction (or "utility," as economists usually call it) will depend upon these factors. We often say that an individual's material welfare is a function of the goods he consumes plus his work effort.

In allocating his time among various activities, Mr. Crusoe, like all men, will face three broad choices: leisure, work for present consumption, and work for future consumption. Within these three categories he will have many more choices to make, but the important point is that his production possibilities are limited. During any specific time period he can produce or procure only so much for himself, and this acts as a constraint upon the level of material well-being that he is able to achieve. Indeed, his "economic problem" is to make his material welfare as high as possible given his limited production possibilities. This situation is described in Figure 1–1 with respect to two of the goods, numbers 2 and 3.

The production possibilities faced by Mr. Crusoe are described by the

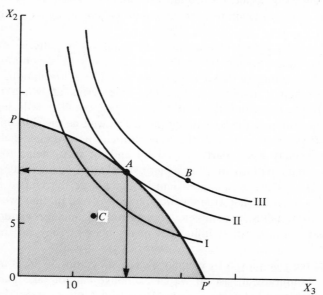

Figure 1-1. Robinson Crusoe's "economic problem."

shaded area of Figure 1–1 underneath the production-possibility (*PP'*) curve. All points in the shaded area represent combinations of goods 2 and 3 which he can produce or procure for himself and consume, given that the amounts of all other goods available to him are fixed. (We could graph his production possibilities or opportunities with respect to all of the goods that he consumes only if we had many-dimensional paper on which to draw the appropriate diagram.) A point such as *B* represents a combination of goods 2 and 3 that it is beyond Mr. Crusoe's capacity to procure for himself. Conversely, a point such as *C* would represent a combination of goods 2 and 3 that would not fully utilize Mr. Crusoe's capacity to produce.

The remaining curves—I, II, and III in Figure 1–1—are called indifference curves. They depict Mr. Crusoe's utility or welfare function. The entire set of indifference curves (including many that we have not drawn) is often called an indifference or preference map. Any given curve is drawn through all the combinations of goods 2 and 3 that provide the same level of satisfaction to Mr. Crusoe.

As these curves get farther away from the origin, they represent greater and greater levels of satisfaction. We may imagine a utility or welfare mountain that rises as we leave the origin going in a northeasterly direction. The indifference curves then become lines of equal altitude. Subject to his production possibilities, Mr. Crusoe would find his point of maximum satisfaction at *A*, where he is as high up the utility mountain as he can get, consuming, say, 5 units of good 2 and 10 units of good 3.

It is worth commenting on the shapes of Mr. Crusoe's production-possibility and indifference curves because we shall be encountering curves like this in later chapters. The indifference map (see Figure 1–1) is bowed in toward the origin, whereas the production-possibility frontier is bowed out away from the origin, reflecting the laws of *eventually diminishing marginal utility* and *eventually diminishing marginal productivity, respectively.* These laws, in turn, are special cases of the more general *law of eventually diminishing returns,* an assumption that is basic to all of economics.

Bowed-in indifference curves indicate that given levels of utility or welfare are easiest to attain when fairly heterogeneous mixes of goods and services are being consumed. This reflects the earlier remark that "variety is the spice of life." More precisely, it means the following: If an individual were to increase his consumption of any given good relative to all others, a point would eventually be reached beyond which the relative contribution of that good to material welfare would become less and less. For every good there is some point beyond which further specialization in consumption will make it more difficult for the consumer to achieve a given level of material well-being.

Similarly, a bowed-out production-possibility frontier implies that in order to keep on getting equal extra amounts of any one good, an economy must reduce its output of any other good by ever-increasing amounts. In the case of Robinson Crusoe, this may simply reflect the fact that any one task becomes increasingly tedious the longer he works at it. In the case of a more complex economy, most resources will be more efficient in the production of some goods than in others, and different resources will often be more effective in producing different kinds of goods. Consequently, we get diminishing returns as we shift resources out of the uses for which they are best suited.

The functions describing Mr. Crusoe's utility and the production possibilities open to him may turn out to be quite complex when written out in explicit form. Furthermore, his production possibilities are almost certain to change over time as he learns to make more efficient use of the island environment into which he has been cast, and as he builds durable goods, such as a house, a boat, and hunting and fishing equipment. These will enable him to increase his leisure time and to derive more pleasure from it while producing and consuming more. His tastes may change as well, meaning that the shapes of his indifference curves and the form of his utility function are changing. Thus, even if he were a brilliant scientist, he might not be able to set down the computations that would solve his own economic problem directly. Nor is this necessary.

Through trial-and-error experience, he will discover how to maximize his well-being. Consciously or unconsciously he will learn to work in such a way that the extra utility or satisfaction that he gets from the last quarter hour or so of every type of activity (including leisure) is approximately the same. In this fashion he will optimally divide his time among leisure, work for present consumption, and work for future consumption, and so better adapt himself in every way to his solitary condition.

The difficulties faced by a newly shipwrecked Robinson Crusoe are staggering indeed, but they are not part of the subject matter that economists usually study. There is no market on Mr. Crusoe's island. His problems are wholly those of consumption and production with no exchange intermediary. Later, when we discuss such ideal or pure forms of economic systems as laissez-faire capitalism, market socialism, the command economy, and so forth, it will be apparent that, in his case, these definitions boil down to the same thing. That is, differentiation of economic systems will largely depend upon the relations between different producers, consumers, and administrators that condition society's exchange processes.

There is potential for exchange inherent in the situation we have been describing. It can be realized when Mr. Crusoe meets someone whose production possibilities or tastes complement his own.

1–3   Exchange Between Two Individuals

Suppose that Mr. Crusoe has survived the first and worst months on his island, built himself a home, learned to hunt and fish, and constructed a crude boat that enables him to ply the waters around his island in search of better fishing. One day, to his surprise and delight, he is hailed by another shipwrecked Englishman also out fishing from a neighboring island.

This man, whose name turns out to be Alexander Selkirk, is equally surprised and delighted, and the two head back to Mr. Crusoe's island, where the latter presents gifts to his new-found friend. Mr. Selkirk, in turn, invites a return visit from Mr. Crusoe at which time another exchange of gifts will be made. Assuming that the two men maintain their friendly relations and remain marooned as well, let us try to describe the conditions under which we might expect them to trade with each other on a regular basis.

Assume that goods 2 and 3 are potential candidates for exchange. To be explicit, good 2 will be fish and good 3 arrows, suitable for hunting. The tastes of Mr. Selkirk and Mr. Crusoe for game vis-à-vis fish are not likely to be the same; for definiteness, let Mr. Crusoe be a game fan and Mr. Selkirk a connoisseur of fish. Likewise, their production possibilities will differ, and we shall suppose that Mr. Crusoe's island is better endowed with trees whose wood makes fine hunting arrows and that Mr. Crusoe himself is an expert at fashioning arrowheads. The fishing, on the other hand, will be assumed to be better around Mr. Selkirk's island, and Mr. Selkirk will be assumed to be an accomplished fisherman.

Given all this, before any exchange takes place, the behavior of each man is as described in Figure 1–2. The graph on the left applies to Mr. Crusoe; the right-hand diagram depicts Mr. Selkirk's circumstances. Without exchange Mr. Crusoe produces and consumes at A, while Mr. Selkirk maximizes his satisfaction at B. Each man has no choice but to consume exactly that bundle of goods and services which he produces for himself. Consumption is tied to production, and it is by removing this constraint that exchange enables both men to improve their material welfare.

Perhaps the first and most important thing to notice in this connection is that exchange may be able to enlarge each man's consumption possibilities beyond his production-possibility frontier. Whether or not exchange is possible, each man will be able to consume any bundle of goods and services that he is able to produce. However, when production is combined with exchange, each man may find that he can now consume combinations of goods —such as A_2 and B_2 in Figure 1–2—that he could never produce for himself.

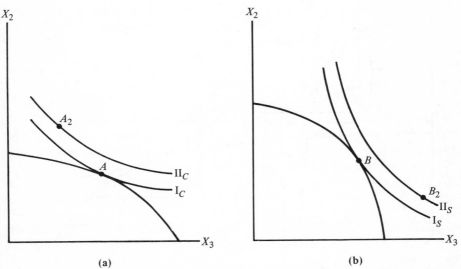

Figure 1-2. The production possibilities and tastes of Crusoe and Selkirk.

Let us therefore say that exchange can pay off if and only if *at least one* trading partner can improve his material welfare in the process while no other trading partner is being made worse off. This criterion will apply to any potential exchange situation, regardless of the number of trading partners or goods to be exchanged. If there are but two individuals and two commodities involved, the most favorable circumstances for trade will arise when each party prefers that good which the other is most efficient in producing. However, whenever any differences exist in tastes or production possibilities, some potential gains from exchange are likely to be present.

Diagrammatically, a trading partner becomes better off when he moves to a higher indifference curve. Therefore, Figure 1–3 gives us an example in which both traders can improve their lots through exchange, even though the most favorable conditions for trade do not prevail. Mr. Crusoe is more efficient in producing arrows, and he also has a general preference for game—and thus arrows—over fish; Mr. Selkirk is just the opposite in both respects. Nonetheless, through trade each gentleman can increase his specialization in production and then consume a more heterogeneous bundle of goods.

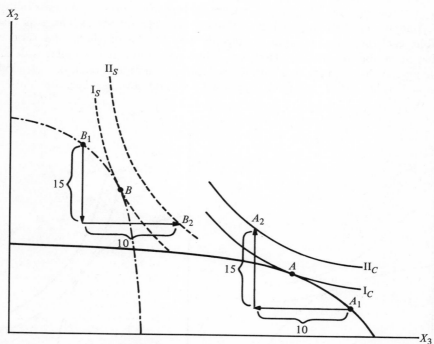

Figure 1-3. The gains from exchange.

Mr. Crusoe could first move from A to A_1 in Figure 1–3, turning out more arrows and catching fewer fish, and Mr. Selkirk could do just the reverse, going from B to B_1 in production. Mr. Crusoe would then give up 10 bundles of arrows to Mr. Selkirk in return for 15 catches of fish, allowing the pair to consume at A_2 and B_2, respectively. In the process, Mr. Crusoe would have advanced from the level of utility represented by indifference curve I_C to that represented by II_C and Mr. Selkirk would have risen from I_S to II_S.

The famous *law of comparative advantage* says that trade is likely to pay off whenever the production possibilities or tastes of two or more potential traders differ. This law applies either to individuals or to larger economic bodies, and it is worth nothing that, in our example, it could easily have paid Mr. Crusoe and Mr. Selkirk to divorce production from consumption via exchange, even though one of them was more efficient in producing *both* arrows and fish. The only requirement is that each man be relatively more efficient in producing one of the two goods. If Mr. Selkirk could make but five arrows or catch four fish in an average working hour while Mr. Crusoe was able to make ten arrows or catch five fish in the same period, some pattern of specialization and trade could probably still make each better off.

1–4   A Model of an Exchange Economy

Generalizing the above discussion to a community with many households and firms, we may say that as soon as there are differences in tastes or productive abilities, it pays to specialize according to ability and then to trade.[1] Indeed, within a large community, there is a powerful reason for specialization in production beyond the fact that productive abilities tend to differ from one person to another.

Along a modern assembly line, each worker may be able to do every task approximately equally well. Yet the specialization that an assembly line entails may be highly productive in the sense that, collectively, the workers involved can produce a far greater product than they could hope to produce separately. This division of the task of producing a *given* good or service into a number of smaller subtasks is called the division of labor. Division of labor is like exchange in that it enables individuals to specialize and cooperate, but in the production of one good rather than several.[2]

Without exchange, there probably would be no division of labor. At the same time, the division of labor conditions the exchange process. In a complex modern economy the most significant and familiar type of exchange does not involve one output traded against another, but rather the exchange of productive inputs for outputs such as consumer goods. It is because of the division of labor that we are able to distinguish between the roles played by producers or firms on one hand and households or consumers on the other. The latter sell primary inputs to firms that combine these to produce outputs which are then sold back to consumers.

---

[1] The classic articles on the gains from exchange are Wassily Leontief, "The Use of Indifference Curves in the Analysis of Foreign Trade," *Quarterly Journal of Economics,* May 1933, pp. 493–503; and Paul Samuelson, "The Gains from International Trade," *Canadian Journal of Economics and Political Science,* May 1939. Both articles are reprinted in the American Economic Association, ed., *Readings in the Theory of International Trade* (Homewood, Ill.: Irwin, 1950).

[2] The classic description of benefits from the division of labor is that of Adam Smith, *The Wealth of Nations* (New York: Random, 1937), Bk. I, Chs. 1–3.

It is worth noting that the producer would have basically no different part to play if suppliers of labor and natural resources were able to see each production task through from start to finish without having to cooperate with one another. In the Crusoe–Selkirk economy described above, there was exchange but no splitting up of the task of producing a *particular* good or service, and hence no separation of function between households and producers.

Both consumers and producers enter into exchange with a view to maximizing the satisfaction which they can get from playing their respective roles. Consumers will try to buy, sell, work, and save so as to make the net utility which they derive from this package of activities as high as possible. Their behavior will be conditioned by the terms upon which they can exchange their productive inputs for present and future consumer goods. Economists have traditionally assumed that producers maximize profit, although this will not always be so.

In addition to producers and consumers, one more sector is needed to complete our exchange-economy cast—that of direction and administration. The directors are the most elusive characters in the drama, playing a role that varies considerably from one kind of economic system to another. Under two models, extreme laissez-faire capitalism and full communism, there will be no such sector. The laissez-faire model is supposed to be self-regulating, and under full communism such an abundance exists of all goods, including leisure, that organization of economic activity is unnecessary. On the other hand, within a command-economy framework, directors and administrators may make most of the important decisions regarding what is to be produced, how, and even for whom. Normally, we can identify the sector of direction and administration as a part of a governing body.

With this background we can draw a circular-flow diagram of an abstract exchange economy, describing the way in which the value of the inputs supplied to production by the consuming sector eventually returns to it in the form of outputs. Primarily, the transformation of inputs into outputs is performed by the producing sector. This is shown in Figure 1–4 where the outer loop denotes the path followed by the flow of goods and services (both inputs and outputs) and the inner loop depicts the flow of payments for these goods and services going in the opposite direction.

The varying degree to which the sector of direction and administration is present from one type of economic system to another is indicated in Figure 1–4 by the use of dashed lines. Potentially, such a sector can siphon off both productive inputs and outputs from the flow around the outer loops of the diagram and pay for these, wholly or in part, with income from taxes. Taxes, in turn, must be differentiated from other payments flows because they do not *directly* compensate anyone for specific goods received or services rendered. They are, rather, a form of transfer payment, like old-age pensions, unemployment compensation, and so on, and are bracketed with these in the circular-flow diagram. Indeed, if we define a transfer to be any payment not

made to obtain a specific good or service directly, taxes would be those transfers paid to the sector of direction and administration.

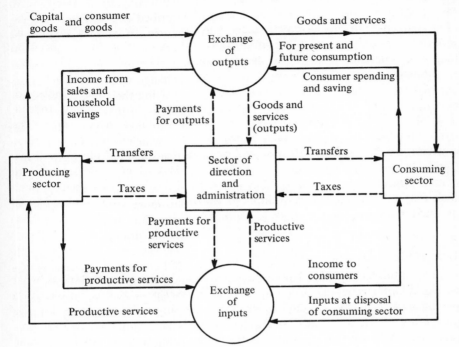

Figure 1-4. The circular-flow diagram.

When a consumer purchases the right to future consumption, we call this
an act of *saving*. Correspondingly, producers will turn out goods that are to
be sent to inventory or which, within the current time period, are to be put
to work in the production of still other goods and services. This describes the
activity we normally call *investment* or *capital formation*. In any exchange
economy with no taxes, transfer payments, or government spending, saving
and investment would have to be equal. Saving plus consumption must equal
total earned income (including profits), which, in turn, equals the value of
what is produced.

But this total value is also equal to investment plus consumption because
all goods produced are either sold directly to consumers or considered as
investment goods. If taxes and transfer payments are introduced and spending
on goods and services by all government agencies that are not part of the
producing sector is broken out as a separate category, net taxes (taxes or
transfers to government agencies minus transfer payments from them to the
rest of the economy) plus savings must equal investment plus government
spending. Net taxes may be thought of as involuntary saving.

In the Robinson Crusoe economy, an act of saving was the same as an act of investment. When Mr. Crusoe refrained from producing for present consumption during a portion of his working day, he simultaneously invested, that is, produced for future consumption. In an exchange economy, an act of saving, when performed by a producing unit, may at the same time be an act of investment, but any given producer may likewise invest with savings he gets from households and other producing units. A decision to save need no longer be a decision to invest, a phenomenon that underlies much of modern Keynesian macroeconomic theory.

Before leaving the circular-flow chart we should note that it does not portray all possible exchange opportunities that arise in an economy. Indeed, it completely ignores flows that occur entirely within a given sector. The latter may be just as important, especially in the producing sector, since enterprises will usually get their capital or investment goods from other firms. Capital goods are also called *intermediate* goods, in fact, because they are neither primary inputs, such as labor and natural resources, nor final outputs, such as goods for current consumption. Rather, they are the outputs of one production process and the inputs to another.[3]

1–5   Money, Prices, and the Terms of Trade

The little economy of Robinson Crusoe and Alexander Selkirk is what we call a barter economy. It has no *medium of exchange;* that is, no one good readily and regularly accepted in exchange for any other good. As long as only a few goods are traded at regular intervals and at one or two set geographical locations, that does not matter much. But when we switch the scene to an economy with several million commodities constantly being traded against one another, a new kind of situation emerges.

Let us define the terms of trade between any two goods—eggs and butter for instance—as the amount of one that may be exchanged against a given quantity of the other. Two dozen eggs, to give a specific example, might exchange for 1 pound of butter. As the number of different commodities that are subject to trade rises, the number of *different* possible terms of trade rises as well—at a multiplicative rate. By the time we get to a 1,000-good economy there would be no fewer than 499,500 potential terms of trade to keep track of, and, in addition, these would change over time. A 1-million-good economy —and most real-world systems produce an even wider variety of commodities —would contain 499,999,500,000 potential terms of trade.

If barter prevailed, chaos would result. It therefore becomes imperative to simplify matters by having one good accepted in payment for all others, and this good becomes a *medium of exchange* as well as a *unit of account*

---

[3] Only the barest description of national income accounting has been given here. The reader who wishes more should consult any good intermediate macroeconomics text, for example, Gardner Ackley, *Macroeconomic Theory* (New York: Macmillan, 1961), Chs. 2, 3.

or a *common denominator of value*. With a medium of exchange, there will be but 999 prices to consider in a 1,000-good economy. In general, there will always be one less price than the number of goods because the price of the medium of exchange is always unity.[4] The price of any other good equals the terms of trade between it and the exchange medium.

We therefore have a first glimpse at the way in which money and markets can simplify the coordination of exchange. Without an exchange medium, the costs of coordinating exchange would be astronomical. In fact, they would be so high that most of the gains from exchange would have to be forfeited.

The terms of trade between any two goods other than the medium of exchange are given by the ratio of their prices. If I earn $3 per hour and a salesman will let me "steal" a shiny new sports car for $6,000, the car is worth 2,000 hours of any labor or about 1 year's work on the basis of a 40-hour week.

We must often look at the terms of trade or at relative prices rather than at their absolute levels. If all prices were to exactly double in a severe inflation, for example, the terms of trade between nonmoney items would not change at all. Suppose that the price of the car in the preceding example went up to $8,000 but that my pay also rose, to $4 per hour. It still takes me 2,000 hours of work to buy the auto. The medium of exchange has lost half its value, but that is all. Indeed, whenever prices rise, it is just as if the *value* of the monetary unit has fallen or *depreciated.*

Sometimes economists and statisticians compute values in *real* or *constant* prices in order to avoid confusing inflation (or its opposite, deflation) with a growth in the bundle of goods and services actually produced. For example, suppose that Utopia had a gross national product of $200 billion in 1965 and $300 billion in 1970, both valued in current prices of those respective years. Then no real expansion of output took place between 1965 and 1970 unless prices rose, on the average, by less than 50 per cent.

Any complex economy will have a medium of exchange which we call money. In addition, since receipts do not usually coincide precisely with outlays for most economic actors in society, the same economy has to have a way of storing value as costlessly as possible. That is, since all sorts of time lapses or lags occur between paying and receiving, there must be a good that is commonly accepted as a store of value to tide over such intervals. It then becomes convenient to make this good identical with the one serving as the medium of exchange, these being the two principal roles that money plays in our society.

---

[4] If barter prevails, there will be $n[(n-1)/2]$ different terms of trade to take into account. To see this, suppose that we have a circle around which n goods are placed. Let us pick any of these goods as the medium of exchange and link it to each of the others. This gives us $(n-1)$ links. On the other hand, if we go around the circle and do the same thing for every good, we get $(n-1)$ links for each good with the others or $n(n-1)$ links in all. But we have now linked every good twice. Thus the total number of (single) links between goods must be $n[(n-1)/2]$.

1–6   Property Rights

The circular-flow diagram in Figure 1–4 is meant to apply to *any* economy characterized by exchange, the devision of labor, and the consequent specialization in production which these entail. We have briefly described what goes on in any exchange economy, but we have not yet found ways of distinguishing among different kinds of economic systems. The present section devotes itself to that task.

It has become popular to classify economic systems into two broad categories, *capitalist* and *socialist,* based upon ownership of the material means of production. Under capitalism these are privately owned; under socialism they are owned by the state. Sometimes a third form of collective or cooperative ownership is also singled out, and usually provision is made for *mixed economies,* in which more than one kind of ownership prevails to a significant extent. Unfortunately, however, this does not always turn out to be the most useful way of looking at economic systems when we wish to anatomize their structure and functioning. There are at least two important difficulties, in addition to those stemming from ideological overtones.

To begin with, the terms capitalism and socialism no longer conjure up unique and unambiguous images. So much admissible variety exists *within* each rubric that we can easily imagine two socialist economies—Yugoslavia and the U.S.S.R.—which are structurally further apart than a particular brand of capitalism on one hand and a particular brand of socialism on the other, say, France and Yugoslavia.

Preconceived notions about what constitutes "capitalism" and "socialism" can sometimes mislead us. We read, on occasion, that a laissez-faire economy, in which the government practices a hands-off attitude toward firms and households, is the purest form of capitalism. But the producing enterprises in such a system could just as easily be worker-managed and state-owned. Yugoslavia, in fact, has become a kind of laissez-faire economy with the decline of planning there. The public sector in West Germany is larger than that in Japan, but Japan is more likely to be a planned economy than is West Germany. These apparent contradictions disappear when we realize that "planning" or "nonplanning" is a characteristic of a nation's political and economic decision-making processes which need not refer to legal property ownership.

We get still another contrast between systems when we ask whether economic activity is principally coordinated by markets—as in Yugoslavia, the United States, Canada, the United Kingdom and probably Hungary—or by commands—as in the U.S.S.R., East Germany, Bulgaria, and Albania. As in the case of planning and nonplanning, this distinction cuts across the conventional capitalism–socialism dichotomy.

A second difficulty with capitalism versus socialism is best expressed by the Yugoslav economist Aleksander Bajt:

In analysing different economies and in categorizing them as socialist [or] capitalist, we are usually . . . too impressed by their institutional structure, that is, by their legal or constitutional structure. If this were not the case, we could discover elements of "socialism" in capitalist countries and of private property relations in socialist countries, and we would not be able to classify countries into black and white categories, but would have to measure the *degree of socialization* in [each] . . . we might even discover that the degree of socialization . . . is higher in some capitalist than in some socialist countries.[5]

The economist is not so much interested in legal or constitutional ownership as he is in the rights of individuals and firms to use property in the material means of production and consumption in different ways and to receive property incomes. He would argue that the distribution of these *property rights* is more important than legal ownership in determining the what, how, and for whom of the economic problem facing a particular society.

This is not to say that differences in legal ownership are unimportant. "Although [legal] ownership is not decisive in determining the character of an economic system, it is significant both as a factor in income distribution . . . and as a source of power in [social goal formation]." [6] But we need a more complete way of distinguishing economic systems. To generalize upon the capitalism versus socialism dichotomy, we shall first develop the notion of property rights a bit further by classifying property on the basis of the rights attached to it rather than on a legal or constitutional basis. There are three basic categories which, in their pure forms, may be described as follows: [7]

Private Property

A particular individual or group, called the owner, has the right to decide how private property shall be used, subject to his behavior as a good citizen. (This is defined by society's political decision-making processes.) Equally important, he can exclude others from using it, and he has a right to the income which it generates. He may also transfer his rights to another individual or group through gift or sale.

State Property

The government (or the sector of direction and administration) may use state property and distribute the income which this property generates as it wishes, subject to accepted political procedures. The government may also

5 See Alexander Bajt, "Property in Capital and in the Means of Production in Socialist Economies," *Journal of Law and Economics,* Apr. 1968.

6 Morris Bornstein, "An Integration," in Alexander Eckstein, ed., *Comparison of Economic Systems* (Berkeley, Calif.: U. of Calif., 1971), p. 345.

7 See Harold Demsetz, "Toward a Theory of Property Rights," *American Economic Review,* May 1967, p. 354. The above definitions depart somewhat from his.

exclude anyone from using state property in any given way and decides who shall manage (or act as custodian over) it and what rules he must obey.

Communal Property

All economic actors in a community have the right to freely use communal property as they wish and are able, subject to their behavior as good citizens. The government does *not* exclude anyone from using it, nor may one group exclude another. In a sense, this is the opposite of state property from a property-rights point of view.

We may similarly identify private, state, and communal property *rights*. A private property right, for example, is a right of a particular individual to use a particular piece of property in a particular way, to receive part of the income which it generates, to exclude others from using it, or to transfer one of these rights to someone else. The rights to consume a particular good, to produce it in a particular way, or to decide how much of it to buy or sell are private property rights, as is the right to enter into a specific type of contract.

A state property right is a right of the government (or the sector of direction and adminstration) to exclude a specific use of a specific piece of property, to distribute all or part of the income generated by this property, or to (help) make some or all decisions regarding its management. The rights to tax and to subsidize are state property rights. A communal property right is a right of all citizens to make a specific, unconstrained use of a specific piece of property (for example, to hunt but not necessarily to cut down the trees in a forest). While communal property rights in the means of production exist in every economy, they do not predominate except in primitive, tribal societies, for reasons that we shall explore in Chapter 12.

In practice, pure forms of property are rarely, if ever, found. Every piece of property probably has at least two kinds of rights attached to it, and the way we classify it depends upon the relative importance we assign to its private, state, and communal bundles.

For example, despite tax loopholes, it is rare when a particular individual or group in society can capture all the income generated by a particular piece of property, whether it be a uranium mine, the private plot of a Soviet collective farmer, or an electronic computer. Unless he can get away with it, a businessman does not have the right to destroy the material means of production used by a rival firm. He may or may not have the right to inflict costs on others via some form of pollution. By the same token, most managers are able to gain some freedom to produce as they like, independently of state control, even in the most highly centralized socialist economies.

Although a public park may be basically communal property, dog owners may not be permitted to walk their pets there because this interferes with others who want to watch the sky, the birds, the trees, or to smell the sweet scents of spring as they stroll.

In every economy, property rights govern the use of property, the nature of exchange, and the behavior of individual producers and consumers in ways that we shall examine. Nevertheless, property rights are relations between individuals that find their expression in the customs, laws, and mores of a community. (For this reason, they are sometimes called property *relations*.) More precisely, "property rights are an instrument of society and derive their significance from the fact that they help a man to form those expectations which he can reasonably hold in his dealings with others." [8]

1–7   Variations in Property Rights

If we can decide whether private, state, or communal property rights vis à vis the material means of production predominate, in some sense, within a particular economy, we can classify it as capitalist, socialist, or communist on that basis. Such a categorization may not correspond to that based on legal ownership, and even if it does, it may still conceal as much variation as it reveals. To show how subtler differences in property rights can alter the functioning of an economic system in important ways, we now wish to examine a few case studies. Our goal is to build toward a more general and detailed classifier of economic systems that will capture these variations.

To begin with, let us briefly compare Japan with the United States. We usually classify both of these countries as capitalist, and the bulk of the material means of production and distribution in each economy is privately owned in a legal sense and, probably, in a property-rights sense as well. [9] However, a close examination of the books of leading Japanese and American firms would reveal a stark contrast in the means of investment financing.

American companies generally prefer to finance their investments internally from retained earnings and depreciation. But, in Japan, bank loans are more important than these two sources put together. Correspondingly, firms there are heavily in debt to the commercial banks. By the technical standards of American accounting, many of the most important Japanese firms would be insolvent. The banking system, in turn, is in a state of overloan and illiquidity that would drive most Western bankers into permanent neurosis.

In these circumstances, the industrial and financial sectors of the economy are heavily dependent on one another. A financial squeeze on the banks—for example, a tight monetary policy—will translate fairly quickly into a squeeze on producers. A wave of bankruptcies among producers would quickly bring down many banks at the same time. The "out" for each sector, however, may come in the form of relief, ultimately financed by the government. The latter, in turn, often takes the form of cheap or easy credit chan-

---

[8] Demsetz, op. cit., p. 347.

[9] The property-rights classification of Japan is contentious. However, we shall see that its structure and functioning also depart in important ways from the socialist economies to be discussed later.

neled through the banking system to firms or banks in trouble.[10] This "safety net," as it has been called, can also be extended selectively, in that it can be withheld from inefficient enterprises, which would then be allowed to suffer financial distress, to fail or to be absorbed through merger.[11]

On the other hand, an efficient Japanese producer will be far more eager than his American counterpart to undertake high-risk investment, at least in areas believed to be important to future Japanese growth. Indeed, Herman Kahn argues that "very few American and hardly any European companies would risk, say 10–20 per cent of their capital on an investment that presented an equal chance of total loss or of tripling the money invested. Almost any large Japanese group would be willing to take such a risk." [12]

However, governmental approval or disapproval of expansion plans can be crucial. "When . . . a prominent [Japanese] steelmaker was complaining bitterly of the Government's interference in his plans for expansion, he was asked why he did not ignore the Government's wishes and go his own way. 'Because in that case I shouldn't get the money I want to finance the development,' he answered." [13] The Japanese firm has less freedom than its American counterpart to decide on the area of investment, but a greater incentive to undertake risky projects, at least in sectors with a relatively high growth priority.[14]

Consequently, the close interdependence between the banks and industry helps to give the Japanese government leverage to steer the economy along lines that it deems to be of national advantage. In this way, the Japanese have been able to achieve the most rapid economic growth in history, while avoiding many of the bottlenecks often associated with the development process.

[10] A commercial bank can be tided over a difficult period by credit from the central bank (in this case, the Bank of Japan).

[11] Because the banking system is so heavily loaned out to firms, it has an enormous incentive to scrutinize them and become informed about the competence of their managements and the nature of their operations. This makes the banks an effective check on enterprise efficiency. They can be relied upon to make intermediate to lower-level decisions about which sectors and firms should receive the financial resources to expand. Higher-level decisions of this nature would be the province of the government.

[12] See Herman Kahn, *The Emerging Japanese Superstate* (Englewood Cliffs, N.J.: Prentice-Hall, 1970) p. 108. Kahn's book gives an interesting insight into Japanese politics, economics, culture, and world relations. For more on government–business interface in Japan, see *The Industrial Policy of Japan* (Paris: OECD, 1972). The best introduction to the Japanese economy is G. C. Allen, *Japan's Economic Expansion* (New York: Oxford U.P., 1965).

[13] G. C. Allen, in the *Toronto Globe and Mail,* Aug. 26, 1971, p. B6.

[14] The counterpart of this is that year in and year out, the Japanese government provides some underwriting for a number of risky business ventures, probably more than in any Western market economy. This does not necessarily mean, however, that the government itself is in a financially dangerous position. Like an insurance company, it can diversify its risks so that losses in one sector, should they occur, are likely to be balanced by successes elsewhere. Indeed, the over-all success of the government in promoting growth has also led to an enormous expansion of its tax base. We shall return to this matter in Chapter 5.

The toolbox used by the Japanese government to steer the economy consists of taxes, subsidies, selective credit policies, and moral suasion, along with various other forms of government–business interface. These are the tools of planning in a mixed (and basically market) economy, a category that includes France, Sweden, and, perhaps, Hungary, as well as Japan. We shall see that, to an extent, they replace the detailed quantitative commands to the producing sector that back up centralized decision making in the U.S.S.R., Romania, or Bulgaria.

To complement the above analysis, let us pick three diverse economies that are all socialist in terms of legal ownership of the means of production. These are Yugoslavia, Hungary, and the Soviet Union. We wish to compare the roles of managers in the three systems.[15] As a point of departure, we would note that a North American enterprise management may buy, sell, and use its material means of production pretty much as it wishes, subject to those state property rights that define "good citizenship" (in practice rather than in principle). These correspond to a reasonably wide freedom to choose its product mix and its production methods. It also has a significant claim on the profits earned by the enterprise; and to the extent that managers hold ownership shares in the firm, they can normally pass the shares on to heirs or sell them to other individuals.

Finally, the freedoms to innovate and to start new firms and product lines, although not as great as they should be in many instances, are nevertheless higher than in most market economies. These freedoms are crucial because they are often the principal means through which competition can break up monopoly power.

In all the socialist economies mentioned above, managers cannot, in principle, hold ownership shares in the firm (which is nominally owned by the state). Neither, in principle, can managers inherit their positions. Otherwise, of these three countries, the freedom of management in Yugoslavia most closely corresponds to that of a North American firm. It has considerable latitude to decide what and how to produce, and the freedoms to innovate or to enter an industry are sometimes less and sometimes greater than in North America. On balance, Yugoslavia probably has higher barriers to competition than the United States, partly because the market is smaller (and barriers to international trade are even higher). Moreover, business interests have often been able to band together to preserve monopoly power on

---

[15] The U.S.S.R. and Hungary are clearly socialist from a property-rights standpoint as well. Yugoslavia becomes a unique case that does not classify easily as capitalist, socialist, or borderline. In particular, most Yugoslavia firms with more than five employees are nominally managed by the elected representatives of all the employees (which comprise a workers' council) together with a professional director and his staff. In the paragraphs to follow, references to "managers" in the Yugoslav context comprise both of these elements of enterprise management. (We shall discuss workers' management in Chapter 21.)

a regional basis. In addition, local governments appear to condone and even to encourage market-sharing and price-fixing arrangements, and there is little or no prosecution under the antitrust laws.

However, because of a phenomenon in Yugoslavia known as workers' management, which includes profit sharing, excess monopoly profits, where earned, are likely to be divided among many employees of the firm that makes them. In addition, widespread "temporary" price controls probably provide some check on the exercise of monopoly power.[16]

At the same time, there is no stock market in Yugoslavia and virtually no bond market. Furthermore, the behavior of banks and the government is such that savings often do not flow to those investment projects whose social yields are greatest. These restrictions on "capital mobility" are much greater than in North America and probably mean that the average yield on all investment in Yugoslavia is further below its potential than in most Western countries.

There are also important restrictions on the transfer of investment funds or capital goods between firms that may have a similar effect. One firm can lend money or sell capital equipment to another, but only with the understanding that it will not pay out interest earnings as higher wages and that it will replace the value of the equipment sold. Consequently, a Yugoslav enterprise cannot reduce its capital stock through sale, even when shifting patterns of demand and cost make a reallocation of equipment highly advisable on efficiency grounds.

The Hungarian manager faces many more restrictions on his freedom of choice. With some reservations, we can say that Hungary is a market economy, following the reform aimed at decentralizing economic decision making begun in 1968. However, managers have much less freedom to choose their product mixes and methods of production there than they do in Yugoslavia.

In particular, an enterprise cannot normally tool up to produce a good that is significantly different from one it has produced before without permission from above. A would-be manager cannot, generally speaking, start his own firm. The decision and the initiative for such a venture would have to come from a fairly high-level government authority. In this sense, barriers to new competition are extremely high. One student of the Hungarian economy has estimated that new firms are rarely started, perhaps no oftener than once a year or so.[17] The industrial structure of the country (which has an even

[16] Regarding the exercise of monopoly power in Yugoslavia, see Joel Dirlam, "Problems of Market Power and Public Policy in Yugoslavia," in Morris Bornstein, ed., *Comparative Economic Systems: Models and Cases* (Homewood, Ill.: Irwin, 1969), and Stephen R. Sacks, "Changes in Industrial Structure in Yugoslavia, 1959–1968," *Journal of Political Economy*, June 1972.

[17] Personal communication from David Granick. See his "The Hungarian Economic Reform," *World Politics*, April 1973. Together with Bela Balassa, "The Economic Reform in Hungary," *Economica*, Feb. 1970 (which should be read first), this gives reasonably good coverage of the Hungarian reforms. For Hungarian views (in English), see issues of *The New Hungarian Quarterly* and *Acta Oeconomica* for the years 1969–1972.

smaller market than Yugoslavia) is strongly oligopolistic to monopolistic. "Including industrial cooperatives, 291 enterprises employed 74 per cent of the country's labor force [in late 1970]." [18]

The effects of this monopolistic situation, however, are only partly what we would expect in most laissez-faire capitalist economies. For various reasons, the cutting edge of profits and other income differentials as incentives is less and, by the same token, the distribution of income is more equal. Because of the small number of firms, the government can more easily apply pressure on managers through moral suasion, and, once again, through direct price controls to prevent them from restricting output and raising prices. However, the weakened profit incentive has probably reduced the level of innovation and the motivation of managers to avoid waste in production vis-à-vis their counterparts in North America and Western Europe.[19]

Within their restricted freedom to change product mixes, enterprise managements do have a fair amount of choice in determining their investment programs. On balance, nearly half of all gross fixed investment in manufacturing appears to have resulted from managerial as opposed to higher-level government decision making in 1970. Nevertheless, the Hungarian government subsidizes or underwrites a much larger percentage of total investment than does the government in Japan, and it makes greater use of direct controls in determining where these funds will go and how they will be used. (Thus investment decision making is more centralized in the sense that more decisions are taken above the level of the firm.)

Moreover, for political reasons, the Hungarian government has been more willing than the Japanese to subsidize inefficient investments and to underwrite marginally competent managers. In the final analysis, the Hungarian manager has less freedom to take initiative, greater security against demotion, and stands to reap smaller rewards from successful risk taking than his Japanese counterpart. The Hungarian government's underwriting of industry helps to create this climate. Thus, while its program of financial incentives is structurally similar to that in Japan, the result is a smaller rather than a larger managerial willingness to bear risk.

The reduction in managerial freedom, or in the private property rights of management, as we move from Yugoslavia to Hungary goes hand in hand with a greater decision-making role for higher-level government authorities. From another point of view, the government contracts out fewer state property rights to managers whose own orbits close in toward what would become the realm of a divisional manager in the United States. When we switch to the U.S.S.R., the rights of a manager shrink still further toward those that we tend to associate with a plant foreman.

The most important feature of Soviet industrial planning is that each firm

---

[18] Granick, op. cit.

[19] In particular, the volume of unfinished construction has risen; the productivity of investment has fallen; the rate of growth of labor productivity has declined by one third; and the foreign trade deficit has spiraled since the introduction of the reform.

receives physical production targets that have the force of law. In addition, raw materials and intermediate goods are rationed among user firms, and managers must have authorizations (effectively ration cards) to get them through official channels. An enterprise will also receive a budget for wages and salaries, which it is not supposed to exceed, along with directives for the skill and white collar–blue collar mixes (among others) of its labor force. Like his Hungarian counterpart, a Soviet manager also faces important restrictions on dismissal and transfer of personnel between jobs.

This does not mean that managers in the U.S.S.R. have no room in which to make decisions. They can reorganize production to get more output from given inputs if they are able, and Soviet planners are constantly trying to pressure them into doing this. They have some freedom to vary product assortment and production methods. Particularly since the minireforms of the late 1960s, they have some freedom to determine their investment programs. Occasionally, they are allowed to market their goods. Considerable evidence has accumulated to indicate that they have more freedom to do all the above things in practice than they have in principle.

Nevertheless, basic production decisions in the U.S.S.R. are taken above the level of the firms by central planners who communicate their choices to managers in the form of input and output targets. This is why we have compared managers there to foremen in the United States. An American foreman does not have to worry about the financing of the firm or too much about the selling of the product, beyond the fact that it must meet certain specifications. He has limited freedom to change the mix of inputs that he uses or of outputs that he produces. His major problems are physical. He must put his allotted labor to work in a productive manner. He must see that the equipment is in good operating order and make sure that the production process functions more or less smoothly. Finally, he may have to get his output safely underway to a destination that has been dictated to him.

The Soviet manager's decision-making orbit is larger than this but closer to it than to the role of a Western corporate manager. The decisions that occupy most of the latter's time are made higher up the chain of command or planning hierarchy; in this sense, decisions about *what* is to be produced, *how,* and, to an extent, *for whom* are more centralized in the U.S.S.R. than in Hungary, Yugoslavia, or any developed Western country. They are even more centralized in Rumania and Bulgaria, and, at least until 1970, were more centralized in Cuba as well. Perhaps surprisingly, China is less centralized than the U.S.S.R.[20]

[20] Basic references for Cuba, China, and Rumania are (a) Carmelo Mesa-Lago, ed., *Revolutionary Change in Cuba* (Pittsburgh: U. of Pittsburgh Press, 1971), especially Pts. II and III. (b) Dwight Perkins, *Market Control and Planning in Communist China* (Cambridge: Harvard U.P., 1966). See Perkins's update, "Plans and Their Implementation in the People's Republic of China," *American Economic Review,* May 1973. (c) J. M. Montias, *Economic Development in Communist Rumania* (Cambridge, Mass.: M.I.T. Press, 1967). See, as well, David Granick, "The Orthodox Model of the Soviet-Type Firm Versus Romanian Experience," Indiana University Development Research Center Working Paper No. 18, Sept. 1972.

1–8   The Economy as an Information System

Our discussion indicates that a particular exchange of goods and services for money can take place between basically independent decision makers or be largely ordered by higher-level authorities. We label an economic system as *market* or *command,* according to whether the first or second type of exchange predominates within the producing sector. (Virtually every country uses markets of a sort to help allocate consumer goods and labor.)

Because decisions governing exchange are virtually inseparable from those that determine what and how to produce, a greater prevalence of commands usually implies a more centralized economic system. We would classify virtually all capitalist countries plus Yugoslavia and, perhaps, Hungary as market economies and the other socialist economies as command economies. Historically, capitalist command economies have arisen during emergency situations (for example, during wartime). The Soviet economy is, in fact, patterned after the German economy during World War I.

We would expect to find many differences between traditionally market and command economies. The legal system in a command economy, for instance, will probably be oriented more toward enforcing obligations to superior authorities; that of a market economy is more attuned to the enforcement of contracts. However, let us return for a moment to the circular flow diagram in Figure 1–4. In addition to money and goods, producers, consumers, and administrators also exchange messages. For example, prices, orders, invoices, and offers to buy and sell are constantly appearing in a market economy, whereas orders, responses, statements of plan fulfillment, and invoices are the information fare of command planning.

In a very real sense, an economic system is an information system, and it is the information flows that generate the physical flows. This suggests that we should try to differentiate economies along these lines. For example, we say that prices are the principal triggers of production and consumption activity in a market economy in the sense that quantities demanded and supplied depend upon the prices that are, or can be, charged. Orders to the producing sector play much the same role in a command economy.[21] Our distinction between these two types of systems must therefore rest on basic differences between prices and commands. In fact, we can identify two underlying dimensions along which they diverge, and these will become the first two dimensions of our spectrum of economic systems.

The first dimension revolves around the notion of a hierarchy or chain of command. Let us confine our attention to the production of a particular good or service, and suppose that a planner and a manager are both involved with this. More specifically, suppose that the planner can make decisions that

[21] Although virtually every command economy maintains markets for consumer goods, the production of these goods is largely governed by orders from the planning hierarchy, with consequences to be examined later.

directly require the manager to take some action, but the manager has no comparable authority over the planner with respect to the production of this particular good. For example, the planner can send production and productivity targets to the manager, and he can back up this authority with penalties or rewards based upon his assessment of managerial performance. (In this sense, the targets are "obligatory.")

We then say that the planner and producer (or, more generally, any pair of decision makers, A and B) occupy higher and lower levels, respectively, along a hierarchy or chain of command. In this fashion, we can proceed to order some of the decision makers in an economic system with respect to given economic activities. Those at the top of the ordering so defined will be said to occupy the top level in the chain of command, and so forth down the line. In a planned economy, the top level will be occupied by a central planner. Next in line might come industrial ministries (or agencies in charge of particular groups of industries), and finally we would work our way down to the producing enterprises at the bottom.

With the above in mind, we shall say that *vertical* channels of communication are those between different levels in the *same* chain of command. Any other channels of communication that appear will be called *horizontal* links. In particular, market links between independent buyers and sellers are horizontal. A completely centralized producing sector, insofar as the pattern of information flows is concerned, would be one with only vertical channels of communication. All messages would flow up and down various chains of command in the system, which would ultimately come together to form one giant hierarchy.

An oversimplified view of this system appears in Figure 1–5, with a central planner at the top and producers (P) at the bottom of the hierarchy. In all likelihood, a single planner cannot directly manage the entire producing sector, for this would comprise too many subordinates to be effectively supervised by a single superior. Consequently, we must have intermediate levels in the chain of command—a factor of some importance, as we shall see in the next chapter. Figure 1–5 shows a three-tiered chain of command; the Soviet economy apparently has six tiers.

We can introduce some decentralization into Figure 1–5 by adding horizontal communications links between planners and producers at the same levels. If we wish, this will then permit us to further reduce the degree of centralization by eliminating some of the vertical links. Within such a context, we can see that one important advantage of decentralized decision making is a shortening of communications routes. Some messages will no longer have to go up the chain of command, through the economic planning council, and back down again. Instead, they can be delivered directly. This may result in both a speeding up of the decision-making process and an avoidance of changes in information during its passage between the lower levels and the central authority. Or, more generally, one can hope for a reduction in the cost of decision making.

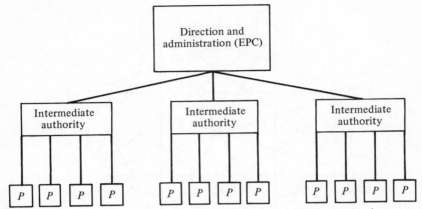

Figure 1-5. The pattern of information flows in a completely centralized economy.

This gives one reason why decentralized decision making tends to be preferable, provided that it can do the job. Both information theory and experience in Eastern Europe suggest, moreover, that an overly centralized network of information flows will be unstable, creating pressures for its own modification. Specifically, frustrated producers, bureaucrats, or administrators will try to short-circuit the official channels, and set up their own unofficial and more decentralized network.

On the other hand, a completely decentralized economy would have only horizontal channels of communication and no chains of command at all. If we imagine a (laissez-faire) system in which economic actors are linked only through markets and where all have the same transacting "rights," we shall probably come as close as we can to a completely decentralized system by this definition.

Figure 1–6 shows such an economy from two points of view. Part (a) depicts it as a circle of producers and consumers, each of whom has a communications link with every other actor. In reality, these actors will normally be linked through a system of markets that simplifies the exchange process, and this is shown in part (b). [However, the effects of market linkage are shown in part (a).]

The distinction between vertical and horizontal messages and the notion of a hierarchy relate to the *pattern* of information flows in an economic system. A second underlying dimension along which systems may diverge relates to the *nature* of the messages that producers, consumers, and planners exchange. Perhaps the most obvious thing about a price, considered as a message, is that it tends to be anonymous and impersonal. This contrasts sharply with a centrally planned economy, in which the planning authority guides exchange by addressing separate sets of orders to all trading partners.

Therefore, *anonymity* will be an important scale along which messages with economic content may be ranked. Let us adopt Hurwicz's formal defini-

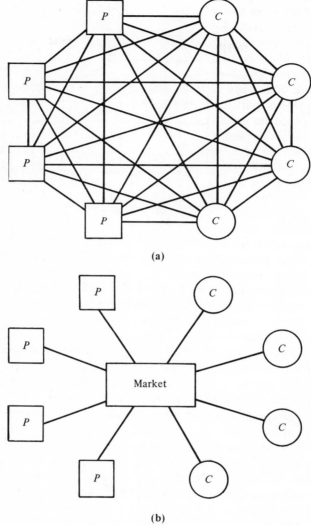

(a)

(b)

Figure 1-6. The pattern of information flows in a completely decentralized economy.

tion and say that a message must pass two tests before it is declared fully anonymous.[22]

1. It cannot differentiate in any way between potential receivers.
2. The response to the message must depend solely on its content, not on its origin or sender.

[22] Leonid Hurwicz, "Conditions for Economic Efficiency of Centralized and Decentralized Structures," in Gregory Grossman, ed., *Value and Plan* (Berkeley, Calif.: U. of Calif., 1960), pp. 169–170.

In a sense, a message is anonymous only when it is neither addressed nor signed. A summons, an order, a memo, and a personally addressed letter are all nonanonymous signals. A price is generally more anonymous than a command, since the latter violates both conditions 1 and 2. However, if price or wage discrimination is being practiced, condition 1 is violated because a given price applies to one group of buyers and not to another. Condition 2 might still be fulfilled, and, when it is, we have an intermediate case between the perfectly anonymous market system and the pure command-economy model.[23]

Other intermediate cases arise when just a few traders are involved in a given market. This applies to a modern industrial society, where there is only a small number of buyers and sellers for certain producers' goods, or to our island economy, where Robinson Crusoe and Alexander Selkirk will bargain over the terms of trade between goods such as arrows and fish. In each of these instances, strategy plays a role in the bargaining process. The buyer's reaction to a quoted price will depend, among other things, upon whether he thinks the seller is bluffing or is able to go lower.

Other things being equal, anonymity is a desirable quality. When a message is anonymous, just one will serve for all potential receivers—there is no need to send a separate communication to each one. It is, in part, the relatively anonymous character of prices vis-à-vis commands that simplifies the exchange process in a market economy. Later, we shall associate anonymity with certain requirements for economic efficiency.

We can now completely characterize a command as a message designed to trigger economic activity that is both vertical and nonanonymous, by 1 and 2 above. Within a perfectly competitive (or completely decentralized) economy, a price will be horizontal and completely anonymous. A greater degree of decentralization in economic decision making is signaled either by an increasing anonymity in the messages that generate economic activity or by an increase in the percentage of these messages that are horizontal rather than vertical. Nevertheless, the anonymity dimension is not completely redundant, as we may see by an example.

In the Soviet Union, once the yearly plan has been ratified by the Council of Ministers, it has the force of law. In theory, production and productivity targets are legally binding on enterprises, ministries, and regional bodies, even when they turn out to be mutually contradictory. In France, by contrast, production and productivity targets are not legally binding. Although affected producers cannot ignore them, the penalty for failing to meet them is far less than in the Soviet context. In this sense, they are less obligatory.

For this reason, we generally classify the quantitative targets of official French planning as indicators rather than commands. Both commands and indicators are nonanonymous, but the former are vertical, whereas the latter are horizontal. We would also classify as indicators many of the informal

---

[23] In fact, we can describe any exercise of market power as a violation of condition 1 above. We shall see how this works in Chapter 16.

targets that emerge in the government–business interface which characterizes unofficial planning in Japan, France, and other West European countries.[24] Because they are less binding, the value of indicators lies more in their usefulness as forecasts. When successful, they generally help the market to coordinate economic activity by helping to dovetail the long-range of plans of different sectors.

Finally, we should also distinguish between income tax forms, laws, and "no trespassing signs" on one hand and quantitative production-oriented targets on the other, since the former abound in any kind of economy. When we apply the terms "indicative" planning to the French economy and "command" planning to the U.S.S.R., we are thinking primarily of quantitative indices. These are likewise additive messages, inasmuch as it makes sense to add up the targets or forecasts sent to each individual actor to arrive at a meaningful number for the system as a whole.

By contrast, we have seen that the systematic use of *non*quantitative commands, such as credit controls, subsidies, taxes, licenses, building permits, and the like constitutes the steering mechanism of a market-planned or mixed economy. These change prices by altering the choices and the incentives of individual decision makers, thereby shifting demand and supply curves.

Indirectly, therefore, the steering instruments of market planning alter quantities of goods produced and consumed, which is what they are designed to do. However, these same instruments will often put some teeth into indicative planning, causing the emerging targets to become more binding than simple forecasts would be. In practice, the distinction between indicators and commands—and ultimately between centralized and decentralized decision making—is inevitably one of degree.

A second important quality that information flows may possess is *operationality*. We often say that a concept is "operational" if we can monitor or measure it. In this sense, gross national product is the outcome of an effort to operationalize material welfare.[25] In the same spirit we shall define a message to be completely operational when it describes a collection of events that is completely visible to *every* economic actor who receives it. This will imply that each receiver can conduct any necessary measurements or verify any details contained in the message for himself.

An example is given by housewives shopping in a supermarket. Each time a buyer passes the cash register she indicates to the clerk in charge what amount of each good she wishes—perhaps simply by placing her purchase on

[24] In France, this informal planning (called économie concertée) is more important than the formal planning process. It is also true in all command economies that the more-heralded, five-year horizon plans are more indicative than the one-year operating plans. Regarding the French economy, we refer the reader to Stephen Cohen, *Modern Capitalist Planning: The French Model* (Cambridge, Mass.: Harvard U.P., 1969).

[25] This is another term introduced by Hurwicz (op. cit., pp. 168–169). However, our definition is more restrictive than his and will enable us to make distinctions that his definition would not permit.

the counter. In this way, offers to buy and sell in most market economies are usually treated in economics textbooks as operational messages.

But suppose that we turn our attention once again to a command economy. The planners send a target of 100,000 tons to a steel firm for the year ahead. At the end of the year, we can imagine the producer telling the central planners that he has manufactured 105,000 tons, overfulfilling his plan by 5 per cent.

Such a message will be *non*operational whenever no representative of the planning authority monitors the steel, either as it rolls off the assembly line or during the period when it is being shipped or added to inventory. In practice, no government can closely survey all shipments and changes in inventory or internal production processes. Therefore, responses to a central planner's orders in a command system normally will not be completely operational.

Moreover, let us consider a rather different type of market economy than most readers will be familiar with. Here, prices of goods and services are not adjusted by those who sell or buy them, but by a central planner who tries to keep supply and demand in balance throughout the economy. Such a system could be one of the versions of market socialism to be discussed later. Within it, prices may retain at least part of their anonymous quality, but the responses to them in the form of quantities demanded and supplied will not normally be operational. Although a transaction may be visible to the partners in an exchange, it usually will not be to the central planners.

Indeed, economists are belatedly recognizing that our own type of system is less operational than the textbooks conventionally (and implicitly) assume. Consider the two messages from a buyer to a seller: "I am enclosing $10 in payment for my order," and "I will pay you $10 in one-dollar instalments over the next ten months." The first statement is unquestionably operational, but the second is not, in the sense that the receiver of the message cannot yet observe full payment. This may turn out to be of no consequence, inasmuch as the buyer is presumably legally obligated to pay. But the flourishing activity of collection agencies suggests that our distinction is far from irrelevant.

Moreover, an economy in which many purchases are made with promises to pay based on expected future earnings (for example, instalment buying) will sometimes differ markedly from a system in which payments usually accompany orders. For example, the former may be more prone to the boom and bust of business cycles.

We can also imagine an economic system that is operational but *non*-anonymous. In some kinds of feudal economies, flows of goods and money may be entirely visible to transacting parties, future promises to pay may be relatively unimportant, and the parties themselves may determine prices without any intervention from a central authority. But, at the same time, there may be a paucity of published prices and a considerable degree of secrecy surrounding the terms at which most exchanges take place. In this climate one would expect price and wage discrimination to flourish. In contemporary

North America the same climate is often fostered by the practice of discounting but not listing discount prices or quoting them over the phone.

It will often prove useful to distinguish two kinds of messages or information flows, which we shall call "triggers" on one hand and "responses" or "feedback" on the other. To grasp the motive behind this, let us examine an ordinary demand curve. Usually, we describe it by saying that quantity demanded is a function of (or depends upon) price. In other words, the sending of a price signal generates offers to buy, and we may think of the price as triggering economic activity. In response will come orders that explicitly or implicitly indicate payment for the good desired.

If payment is enclosed or else made currently in a fashion the seller can observe, the order will constitute an operational message. By the same token, a seller's invoice—which we may view as a response to the buyer's order—will be operational when it describes a flow of goods visible to the buyer. However, an order from a central planner in a command economy will often elicit a nonoperational response—for example, a simple confirmation or an attempt to bargain for an easier plan.

Generally, we shall be interested in the anonymity of triggers and the operationality of feedback rather than vice versa. (Sometimes, we may view a given message as both a response and a trigger and therefore be interested in both its anonymity and its operationality.) Whenever we speak of operational or anonymous economic systems we shall have this in mind.

The degree to which information triggers are anonymous and responses operational will therefore constitute the second dimension of our spectrum of economic systems. Evidently, this dimension could be expanded into many, for there will normally be many economic actors and often several types of communications between given pairs of actors. Fortunately, it will be sufficient for many purposes to simplify matters and consider the anonymity of a "representative" message from a class of information triggers. The same is true for operationality.

Despite our reservations, responses to market signals are likely to be more operational, by and large, than responses to commands or indicators. To be a bit more precise, the *cost* of operationalizing responses to commands will usually be higher and will grow with the length of a chain of command and with the average span of control of each planning authority.

In part, this is because goods and information tend to follow the same channels more often as markets come to predominate. In command economies, reports on performance must more frequently be sent to, and assessed by, superior authorities who are not normally the recipients of goods produced. Thus more decentralized economic systems tend to be more operational as well as more anonymous.

1–9 The Political or Power Dimension

Let us say that society's *political* decisions are those which collectively define or formulate its socioeconomic goals, including implicit and explicit decisions to extend the status quo. By contrast, a society's *economic* decisions are those which implement or carry out these goals.

For example, decisions by a manager or a central planner which set specific production and pricing targets or determine production methods are economic decisions. However, an income or sales tax law is a product of political decision making, as are a five-year plan (whose targets are normally expressions of intent rather than specific orders) and monopoly positions held by firms or labor unions.

When a firm takes advantage of its monopoly position to restrict output, raise price and advertising expenditure, and thereby increase its profit, it is making an economic decision. Likewise, a labor union's request for a wage hike results directly from an economic decision. But the size of the request depends, in turn, upon the union's ability to control access to jobs and apprenticeship programs. Society's tolerance of this manpower (or womanpower) monopoly is a political decision.

In the main, political decisions comprise many of those taken by the executive, legislative, and judicial branches of government, along with voting and lobbying. (These officials may also take a few economic decisions, notably in a command economy.) Matters such as referenda on whether to build schools and roads, passage or application of truth-in-lending, truth-in-advertising, and pure food and drug laws are all examples of political decisions. These often will include a simple failure to take any decision, thereby preserving the status quo (or allowing a law to expire, or the like).

Economic and political decisions are always interdependent. We cannot view one except in the context of the other, whether we are talking about Western corporations, professional associations and labor unions, or East European bureaucracies. We have just indicated that society's tolerance of a monopoly will often influence the amount of output it produces and the prices it charges. The existence of monopoly may be the consequence of effective lobbying or of an informal or formal agreement which restricts the range of choices open to the firm.

In this context, the nature and pattern of economic information flows indicate the loci of economic decision making. They show how the direct decisions governing what, how, and for whom are divided up among individuals and organizations in any society. They do not necessarily indicate whether the society in question is "dictatorial" or "democratic." Thus they measure economic rather than political (de)centralization.

Political decision making is more decentralized the more diverse elements in society are able to have a voice in goal formation. More decentralized political decision making is therefore more participatory, and more centralized political decision making more dictatorial, in the sense that a small group can more successfully impose its will upon the rest of society. Viewed as an economic dictatorship, its distinguishing feature is that the group in question has the power to determine society's basic economic goals. Similarly, we say that a monopoly firm or labor union has the power to raise prices or wages to its advantage. The exercise of this power is an economic decision, once again, but it is acquired and maintained through the political process, often by lobbying. Consequently, it becomes a part of society's political choice.

Political centralization or decentralization in any society is therefore reflected in its distribution of economic power. The measure of an actor's power in an exchange economy will ultimately be his ability to influence or manipulate the exchange process to his advantage. More precisely, this is his ability to alter the effective terms of trade between different goods and services, including all forms of productive inputs, as well as outputs.

This may take place directly, as when a central planner acquires the ability to control the flow of inputs into a firm's production process or when one major steel company gains control over the sources of supply for all other producers in the industry. It may also happen indirectly—for example, when a corporation like General Motors is large enough relative to the total market for a good or service to influence the terms of trade between its product and other commodities. Concentration of economic power, as we have defined the term, can refer to market power, but even in a market economy, it is broader.

Although seats of economic power may coincide with seats of ownership or wealth, the two need not go together. Witness the power of big corporate management or the wealth of some farmers who, as individuals, are still unable to influence the prices of agricultural produce. Economic power can be bureaucratic as well as monopoly power, and the structure often referred to as the "military–industrial complex" is an example of how the two can be effectively combined.

We shall call a system in which economic power is highly concentrated, a *power-centralized* economy (which is also an economy with centralized political decision making). In the extreme, only one economic actor, of necessity a dictatorial central planning authority, has power to influence the terms of trade between different goods and services. A completely *de*centralized system, by the same criterion, would be one in which the influence that any actor might have over *any* terms of trade would be so small that it would not be worth his while to take it into account. In this sense, power is completely diffused throughout the economy, implying, in particular, that no individual or organization has been able to acquire any through the political process.

Of necessity, the latter would be a laissez-faire economy, for even the government or sector of direction and administration could have virtually no power to influence the terms of trade, be it through spending, taxation, or direct manipulation. We would, in fact, be dealing with the perfectly competitive economy often encountered in elementary textbooks. Every actor would be a perfect competitor every time he bought and sold.

Finally, it is quite normal for a given economy to be highly centralized in some industries or geographical areas and highly decentralized in others. In the United States individual producers of aluminum, chemicals, and automobiles can significantly influence the (maximum) prices at which their products will sell, and thus the terms of trade between these and other goods, whereas paper and shoe manufacturers cannot. The distribution of power will be multidimensional in any event since there will be many pairs of goods and services and many terms of trade to take into account. Fortunately, it will often be sufficient to consider some sort of average distribution of power over all pairs of commodities entering into exchange.

Almost any kind of economic power can be competed or regulated away. For example, excess profits act like a magnet, pulling additional firms to enter an industry in which they are being made.[26] As they enter, they will expand industry-wide output and force prices down. This is how a competitive environment is supposed to lead to economic efficiency. Later we shall see that even the *threat* of new competition can force firms in the industry to keep output higher and price and profits lower. If a firm has a natural monopoly, so that competition is not feasible, regulation can encourage it to charge a lower price and produce a greater output than it otherwise would.

Similarly, when a labor union or professional association uses its economic power to raise wage or salary rates, these will attract more individuals seeking to enter the occupations involved or to acquire the necessary skills. If successful, their competition will reduce the earnings which the union can obtain in the long run without having unemployed members. On a completely different plane, a number of ways exist to introduce competition for posts in the sector of direction and administration—notably free elections. The need to face free elections periodically will reduce the costs that a would-be economic dictator is able to inflict upon the citizens he governs. A sharing of power among executives, legislative, and judicial branches—which can, in effect, regulate one another—will work in the same direction.

To protect their power and the benefits flowing from it, economic actors will therefore try to set up barriers to entry and to control.[27] Almost inevitably, these become the signposts of power. Thus a would-be dictator will try to abolish elections or restrict the number of contestants who may run. A labor union or professional association will seek to screen applicants for jobs or for the educational programs that provide professional or vocational skills. In this way it can restrict entry into the vocations or professions that it represents.

By the same token, established firms in an industry will try to raise the costs facing would-be competitors. For example, tariffs and import quotas increase the costs of foreign vis-à-vis domestic producers in supplying the home market. A qualified taxi driver or tobacco farmer may find that he cannot practice his profession without buying an expensive licence. A would-be pharmaceuticals producer will find that he needs a number of expensive

[26] We shall clarify the term "excess profit" in our discussion of laissez faire.

[27] Barriers may also arise naturally. For example, economies of mass production often lead to scale (or natural) entry barriers into an industry. We shall examine both kinds in Chapter 16.

patents plus a costly advertising campaign to establish his brand name.[28] A steel firm may find its access to essential raw materials and other supplies restricted.

Barriers to entry may be specific to a job or industry or they may be quite general, so that they become socioeconomic class barriers. Some societies will only permit a particular class or classes, to rule, to hold executive decision-making posts, or even to become professional or skilled workers. In customary societies, eldest sons may come under heavy pressure to follow in their fathers' professions.

Whatever form they may take, a network of barriers mirrors the distribution of power in any economy. We can measure the value of some barriers— for example, of certain market barriers to industrial or occupational entry —and thereby estimate the value to their beneficiaries of the economic power they protect. We shall give some examples in Chapters 17 and 23.

1–10   Economic and Political Centralization Contrasted

Our three-dimension spectrum of economic systems is now complete. All three dimensions are related, and all have been used by economists in the past when discussing the concept of centralization. In fact, we have tried to exploit the ambiguity in this idea. It is particularly important to distinguish between centralization in terms of economic power and centralization in terms of economic decision making.

For example, some economists argue that corporations in a laissez-faire economy should concentrate on maximizing long-run profits and forget about vague notions of "social consciousness" which many of their colleagues have recently been advocating. Firms following such a prescription would focus instead on minimizing their cost and maximizing their revenue functions, while planning to produce where long-run marginal cost and marginal revenue are the same. However, the cost-minimizing manager is supposed to concentrate on prudent organization of production within the enterprise. He is not supposed to phone his lobbyist to urge an even more diligent battle against pending antipollution and truth-in-labeling legislation.

Yet such lobbying may be one of the firm's most profitable activities. Economists who advocate profit maximization are referring only to the corporation's economic behavior. Within a workably competitive environment— containing several additional features to be explored later—profit maximization can produce a tolerably efficient result from an economy-wide standpoint. (The same economists have formulated guidelines advising society how to promote workable competition.) But firms may also have an incentive to raise

---

[28] A patent *need* not be a source of monopoly profit or power. But the patent laws often protect inventions long after those who have invested time and money into their discovery and development have recovered a competitive return on their investment. Thus the patent holders can often sell licenses to use inventions at a price that is high enough to include an allowance for some excess profit. This becomes a cost to the firm wishing access to the invention.

their profits through the political process by restricting competition and by shifting some of the costs of their activities onto others (for example, by polluting). This is demonstrably inefficient. Thus the efficiency claims for profit maximization presuppose a political process within which these inclinations are countervailed.[29]

Economic decentralization is measured by the nature and pattern of information flows between various economic actors in the process of carrying out decisions about what is to be produced, how, and for whom. Political decentralization is measured by the degree to which goal formation is participatory or power is diffused. Table 1-1 summarizes this. Poles of power need not coincide with the loci of economic decision making—witness the perfect competitor who may have the same range of economic decisions open to him as a monopolist.

However, consider the following example. We begin with an economy that is highly centralized in terms of both economic and political decision making. Thus it is necessarily a command economy and a dictatorship. Its principal economic decision makers are the bureaucratic elite who issue commands to the producing sector. This elite is also the center of economic power, so the seats of economic power and the principal economic decision makers tend to coincide.

The same phenomenon occurs in some laissez-faire economies. There the principal economic decision makers will be firms (or industries), labor unions, professional associations, and, conceivably, consumer cooperatives of one form or other. Through their lobbies these agents will also exert the greatest influence on political decision making. Thus they are the seats of economic power. It is for this reason that profit-maximizing monopolists or restrictive professional associations often shift the distribution of wealth in their favor, inflict some of the costs of their operations on others, or derive benefits for which they do not pay.

Table 1-1.   The spectrum of economic systems.

Dimension	Centralized	Decentralized
I. Political Decision Making		
(a) Goal formation	Dictatorial	Participatory
(b) Economic power	Concentrated	Diffuse
II. Nature of Information Flows	Nonanonymous triggers Nonoperational feedback	Anonymous triggers Operational responses
III. Pattern of Information Flows	Vertical (chain of command)	Horizontal

[29] We shall try to design a "democratic" political process in Chapter 23 with a reasonably good chance of doing this.

So far, the authority to implement goals is tied to the power to make them. Suppose, however, that as its production and distribution structure grows increasingly complex, the command economy becomes unacceptably inefficient to its planner–dictators. Consequently, they decide to delegate certain decision-making rights to lower levels of the planning hierarchy and to managers of producing enterprises. Firms may gain some control over investment decision making, and they could conceivably receive the right to buy inputs and sell outputs as they choose—which would mean that they were making the basic decisions about what and how to produce.

Still the central planners may have no intention of surrendering control over the economy. They wish to decentralize economic decision making without decentralizing power, that is, without decentralizing the political process of goal formation. Thus the center will try to manipulate the incentives of lower-level planners and producers and to retain power to overrule their decisions. It will also seek to keep these actors from acquiring monopoly power. Later we shall examine some of the practical limits on this kind of separation.

Finally, we can conceive of societies in which the political and economic decision-making processes are both *de*centralized but in which the authority to implement goals is separated from the power to make them. If such an economy is planned, the sector of direction and administration will charge itself with synthesizing a "will" of the people, determining a set of concrete goals that correspond to this will, and seeing to it that these goals are implemented within a framework of decentralized (economic) decision making. Some would argue that the ability to separate political and economic decision making in this way is an essential prerequisite for economic democracy, a matter to be considered in Chapter 23.

Yet to establish this separation is not as easy as it may look. A corporate manager, a labor leader, the president of a medical association, and an unemployed factory worker may each have one vote in an election. Nevertheless, those economic decision makers who have gained power or wealth will try to protect it by lobbying and otherwise influencing the decisions of elected representatives.

As we scan the various limited reform movements now progressing in Eastern Europe, the Hungarian experience also stands out in this regard. For it appears to be an effort to decentralize economic decision making without altering the economic power base, especially the political control of the Communist party elite. This is in sharp contrast to the aborted Czech reform, and for this reason the Hungarian decentralization appears to receive the sanction of Moscow, which might some day wish to emulate certain of its successful innovations.

In principle, any degree of political decentralization is compatible with any amount of economic centralization and vice versa. Limitations will arise in practice, however, and the extent of these will probably depend upon both economic and noneconomic factors. A strong dictatorship, for example, may be able to steer an economy, either by using commands or by delegating decisions and then manipulating the incentives of other decision makers. Thus it can combine centralized economic power with some decentralization in economic decision making. But a weaker dictatorship may need to base its power on the dead weight of bureaucratic mass to which highly centralized decision making inevitably gives rise. In any event, it will probably have fewer options as to the channels through which it can exercise power.

Finally, two important qualifications must be made concerning the nature of our spectrum of economic systems and its use as a classifier. First, and most important, it cannot begin to give us enough information to distinguish between two economies in every possible way. There will be a myriad of distinctive features attached to every system, and no three dimensional spectrum can ever hope to capture them all. Often we may leave out important features of any particular economy by restricting ourselves to this spectrum. Consequently, our three-way ranking of systems cannot be taken as exhaustive. Instead, it tries to be a systematic framework within which one may come to grips with some of the more important and oft-recurring differences among systems.

Second, it must be kept in mind when differentiating among economic systems that we are constantly referring to the economic actors—producers, consumers, and administrative units within them. But is U.S. Steel a single economic actor in the United States, or should we consider each plant of U.S. Steel to be an actor? Clearly, in some situations we might want to go one way, and in some situations the other.

Nevertheless, our choice will affect the position we would assign the American economy in the spectrum of economic systems. Messages among different plants of U.S. Steel will tend to be less anonymous than market signals. More generally, a partitioning or breakdown of the U.S. producing sector by plant would yield less anonymous signals than a partitioning by enterprise, because messages between different plants of the same firm are, on the average, less anonymous than market prices.

Unfortunately, there is no universal method that will always permit us to avoid this ambiguity. However, once we have decided upon a given partitioning, the way we classify an economic system depends solely upon relations between the various parts so chosen. It does not depend upon communications networks or relative power positions within General Motors or the Soviet Politburo should these be selected as single actors.

REFERENCES

Ames, Edward. *Soviet Economic Processes*. Homewood, Ill.: Richard D. Irwin, Inc., 1965, Ch. 14.

Bornstein, Morris, "East European Economic Reforms and the Convergence of Economic Systems." *Yearbook of East European Economics*. Munich: Gunter Olzog Verlag, Vol. 2, 1971.

————, ed. *Comparative Economic Systems: Models and Cases.* Homewood, Ill.: Richard D. Irwin, Inc., 1969, Chs. 20–23.

Boulding, Kenneth. *A Reconstruction of Economics.* New York: John Wiley & Sons, Inc., 1950, Pt. I.

Campbell, R. W. "On the Theory of Economic Administration." In H. Rosovsky, ed., *Industrialization in Two Systems.* New York: John Wiley & Sons, Inc., 1966.

Grossmann, Gregory. *Economic Systems.* Englewood Cliffs, N.J.: Prentice-Hall, Inc., 1967, Ch. 2.

Hurwicz, Leonid. "Conditions for Economic Efficiency of Centralized and Decentralized Structures." In Gregory Grossman, ed., *Value and Plan.* Berkeley, Calif.: University of California Press, 1960. See also the commentary by Joseph Berliner.

Pejovich, Svetozar. "Liberman's Reforms and Property Rights in the Soviet Union." *Journal of Law and Economics,* Apr. 1968.

Zielinski, J. G. "Centralization and Decentralization in Decision-Making." *Economics of Planning,* Dec. 1963.

Chapter **2**

The Whole and Its Parts

2–1 Completely Centralized and Completely Decentralized Systems

If ever they were to appear in the real world, both the completely centralized and completely decentralized systems emerging from Chapter 1 would be plagued with serious inefficiencies. Indeed, they could not last for long. But because existing systems do synthesize features from the polar forms, it will be worth our while to explore them briefly.

To begin with, all information triggers within a completely decentralized system must be fully anonymous. This, along with the absence of any chains of command, implies the existence of an all-pervasive market mechanism. Indeed, we have what might be called the ultimate "market model," not in the sense of efficient performance, but because markets perform the entire task of coordinating the economy.

Moreover, each buyer and seller will be a price taker, performing as if he had no power to influence prices. Every trader thus faces perfectly horizontal demand and supply curves each time he buys and sells, and a representative curve appears in Figure 2–1. Sometimes we call such a system an "all-around perfectly competitive economy" because the institutional form known as perfect competition implies, among other things, that prices are dictated to

49

individual buyers and sellers. It must likewise be a laissez-faire economy. Indeed, complete decentralization is a much stronger requirement, as we shall see.

Yet, despite the "dictatorship of the market," we say that a decentralized economy is governed by "consumers' sovereignty" because the votes of many consumers determine what and how much of each basic output or input shall be produced or used in production. If many consumers want more automobiles

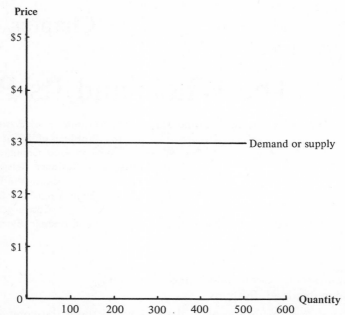

Figure 2–1. Demand or supply curve facing individual decision maker in a completely decentralized (perfectly competitive) economy.

and fewer bicycles, they can collectively bid up the price of the former and bid down the price of the latter, which will encourage producers to respond to these wants. If workers find a particular job to be especially distasteful, they can refuse to work for the going wage. Thus the wage will eventually rise or the job will be modified. Likewise, when a producer tries out a new product, the collective market votes of consumers decide whether it will continue to be offered and in what quantities.

Just as one voter cannot decide the result of most elections, a single buyer cannot set or even influence the price of toothpaste. But collectively, all buyers can have a powerful influence on the price at which toothpaste or any other commodity sells and on the quantities of these goods that are produced and sold. We show this through market demand and supply curves in Figure 2–2, which contrast with the individual demand or supply function of Figure 2–1. Economists say that prices are determined by market demand and supply, but dictated to the individual, who, in this case, is simply too small to affect the market when acting alone.

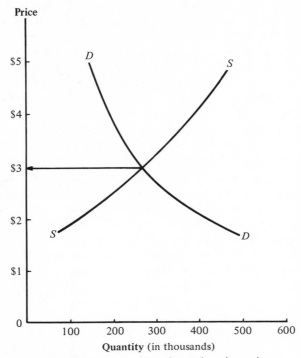

Figure 2–2. Market demand and supply.

Because the market price will not be independent of the buying and selling activities of many thousands of traders, market demand and supply curves will not be flat. It is their intersection which determines an equilibrium price for the product in question, $3 in Figure 2–2. Should the price exceed $3, suppliers will be trying to sell more of the good than buyers are willing to absorb. Either some frustrated suppliers will offer to sell for less, or certain buyers, sensing that sellers' plans are not being realized, will refuse to enter the market until the price falls. The opposite will occur if the price dips below $3.

Thus, when the market is functioning well, the price of toothpaste tends to remain fairly close to $3, regardless of the number of traders involved. Indeed, this last remark points up one more aspect of the market's ability to simplify exchange. It does not have to process millions of demand and supply votes in a complex way; it has only to balance them and enable price to respond to the net pressure that results. We should note, however, that the number of market votes granted to each household will be in proportion to its wealth. Thus the market resolves differences of opinion about how much of each good should be produced and who should receive goods on the basis of a definite, economy-wide distribution of wealth. Because individual tastes are different, a change in this distribution would probably raise the demand for some goods and lower it for others. Our claim of consumers' sovereignty should therefore be tempered by the observation that some households may be much more sovereign than others.

Finally, the completely decentralized economy is a frictionless model in which prices have the job of efficiently allocating inputs among society's various production processes and of efficiently distributing outputs among all potential users. For example, the demand for—and, therefore, the price offered—an input in each occupation would ideally reflect its (marginal) productivity there. When this happens, the highest productivity openings for the input will be able to offer the largest earnings to attract it.[1] We shall make these ideas a bit more precise in Chapter 3.

A completely decentralized system, then, constitutes one pole of the spectrum of economic systems. What about the other end? Returning to the circular-flow diagram (Figure 1–4), let us imagine that an agency, called the *economic planning council* (EPC), controls all economic activity. In particular, all production and distribution will be geared to the commands of this authority so that the producing sector acts like one giant firm. The central planners will also control the distribution of wealth in society, and, if we are really seeking the extreme, we might as well have consumption activity planned to the same extent as production, so that all messages run up and down one giant chain of command.

Therefore, we may aptly refer to this as the ultimate command model. It now becomes a central planner's job to allocate inputs efficiently among producers and to distribute the outputs of society's various production processes efficiently among users.

This does not imply, however, that the planners will specify exact amounts to be produced by every firm and consumed by every individual. Indeed, they will not be capable of doing this. Instead, they would tend to decree minimum acceptable performance levels. A producing enterprise, for example, might be given a planned level of output which it would be expected to reach or exceed, and planned levels of inputs which it would be expected *not* to exceed. A consumer would be given a maximum level of consumption and a minimum amount of work to do. In most cases, firms and individuals performing better than their minimum standards would get some kind of bonus; those falling short would receive a penalty. When this happens, we call these minimum standards or targets "success indicators" for lower-level decision makers.

In a completely centralized economy, therefore, the planning authority becomes the economic "dictator," and the constraints that the planners impose

---

[1] However, this may *not* happen if the private and social productivities of the input differ in a particular production process. We shall make this idea more concrete in the next section and in Chapter 3.

upon individual producers and consumers replace the market constraints present in a decentralized system. Goods are no longer rationed through the price mechanism. Instead, each household and firm receives ration cards which authorize it to consume or use maximal amounts of specific goods and services. Together with production and labor input targets, this comprehensive rationing system supplants the comprehensive market mechanism of the completely decentralized economy.

Finally, a central planner not only coordinates economic activity, as the market would do in a decentralized system, he also guides the economy in a definite direction. Perhaps his major tasks are to choose a path of economic development and to steer the system along this. Thus a command planning authority may consciously orient an economy in a way in which a market mechanism cannot be said to do. However, the cumulative weight of supply and demand votes by producers and consumers does direct a market economy, and a planner can reorient it through the market mechanism by altering the distribution of wealth and in ways to be explained later.

2–2   The Problem of Efficiency

Having briefly introduced the polar forms of economic systems, we now wish to examine a few defects of each of these extreme cases. As we proceed, we also want to begin asking whether by combining markets and commands, we may not be able to eliminate many of the major defects of each. We begin by considering the centralized model and drawing upon the experience of the manufacturing sector of the Soviet economy.[2]

In the mid-1960s, there were about 1.7 million enterprises in the Soviet economy, including at least 250,000 in the manufacturing sector. One central planner cannot directly supervise that many managers; the optimal span of control in such circumstances is said by some organization experts to be between 10 and 20 subordinates. Thus it is necessary to have intermediate planning authorities directly below the center, who, in turn, supervise lower-level planners, and so on.

Assuming there be six tiers in the chain of command (again, true by and large, for the Soviet economy in the mid-1960s), we may ask the following: If at each level of command about 95 per cent of all orders coming from above are satisfactorily obeyed, how successful will the center be in getting through to the producing enterprises at the bottom of the chain? More specifically, if the economic planning council, from the top of the chain, issued 100 orders designed to ultimately elicit action from individual firms, how many may be expected to result in the right sort of action being taken?

At the first level of the chain of command, we would expect to see 95 orders satisfactorily obeyed, resulting in a new collection of (less-aggregated)

[2] This example is taken from Edward Ames, *Soviet Economic Processes* (Homewood, Ill.: Irwin, 1965), Ch. 14. The number of enterprises counted as belonging to Soviet manufacturing sector does not include repair or work shops or construction firms.

commands being issued to the next level. These new commands will, on the average, be only 95 per cent satisfactory from the center's point of view. Furthermore, we would expect the orders issued by the next level to be only 90 per cent effective (95 per cent of 95) and so on until we get down to the firm. By now, performance can, at best, receive a 77 per cent rating from the center, 23 per cent of the gist of the original messages having been lost in filtering through the chain of command.

If we had started with a 90 per cent record of obedience and correct transmission, by contrast, we would expect the total information loss to average around 41 per cent. Finally, with an 80 per cent record, fewer than one third of the planners' orders will result in the desired performance by producers. If the economy were to use similar production techniques and produce similar assortments of the same goods and services year after year, this record would improve. The planners would have an opportunity to adjust to both the human and the technological constraints facing them. With better than 99 per cent obedience and correct transmission, the average total loss would be less than 5 per cent.

It is generally true that a command economy functions most efficiently when its production and distribution activities remain the same or grow along unchanging lines. By the same token, command planners will tend to resist the introduction of improved products or techniques, because this complexifies planning by upsetting old routines. The above record can also be improved if we allow lower levels in the chain of command to feed back information to their superiors in order to clarify commands. If we are to move in this direction of greater realism, however, we must also introduce the second aspect of the information cost of command planning.

Let us continue to think of the aspect illustrated above as the cost of *coordinating* producers. Conceptually, we may view the problem of coordination as one of allocating resources and tasks among different firms so as to maximize planners' welfare for any given productivity in physical terms of each firm. By and large, the cost of coordinating producers comprises the costs of gathering, processing, and sending information and of making decisions based upon the information at hand.

But this is not all that a command planner must do. He must also *supervise* his subordinates, who, in turn, supervise agencies or firms subordinate to them, and so on down to the bottom of the hierarchy. The problem of supervision arises because of a natural conflict of interest between higher- and lower-level decision makers. The latter are likely to prefer to do something other than what the former commands them to do. For example, employees may prefer to substitute leisure for work, to do their work more elaborately, to take longer doing it, or to somehow better express their individuality through their production activities. A division manager in a large corporation may wish to make a somewhat different product than his supervisors are calling for, to organize his work differently, or to qualify his secretaries on the basis of appearance as well as typing speed.

The list of ways in which goals may diverge is endless. This divergence may be reduced or mitigated by such things as charisma on the part of leaders, loyalty from below, a sharing of ideological beliefs or broad goals, and the desire of lower-level decision makers for advancement, but it is unlikely to disappear entirely. The ultimate aim of supervision, from the EPC's point of view, is to make each firm more productive. The cost of supervision becomes the second aspect of the information cost of command planning. It, in turn, breaks up into two component parts.

To begin with, supervisory costs will include the costs of monitoring and measuring the potential productive contribution of each firm in terms of physical goods and services. Once these goods have been evaluated in terms of their contributions to planners' welfare (a problem that is a major source of coordinating costs), it will be possible to get from this monitoring an indication of each firm's potential contribution to planners' welfare.

Ideally, the rewards and penalties administered to the management of each firm will then be geared to this contribution. (Enterprise managers will, in turn, have an incentive to tie the rewards of their employees to the same kind of measure.) The closer the correlation between a firm's contribution to planners' welfare and the rewards of its management, the greater this contribution is likely to be. The cost of designing incentives and disincentives that bring about such a correlation is the second component of supervisory costs. It notably includes the costs of enforcing commands, both in letter and in spirit.

From Chapter 1, we can say that supervisory costs will rise with the length of any given chain of command, and we would also expect them to increase with the average span of control. In some situations (for example, in many small to medium-size U.S. firms and, apparently, in the Romanian economy), superiors supervise by means of direct, subjective evaluations of subordinates. However, as the supervisory task grows more complex, this method may eventually no longer be feasible. Then, to reduce the costs of supervision, as well as to indicate in simple and intelligible terms to subordinates what kind of behavior is considered desirable, higher-level decision makers are likely to introduce the "success indicator" system outlined earlier.

Thus a manager will sometimes try to discourage his workers from shirking by putting them on piece rates. When they equal or exceed a given rate of output, they receive a bonus. Similarly, a planner may try to encourage production in a furniture factory by giving the manager a plan target based upon tons of output. Once again, a bonus would be scaled to fulfillment.

In both cases, the success indicator system may improve performance, from the viewpoint of the higher-level officials, for any given enforcement costs. It does this by blunting some aspects of the "natural" goal conflict just indicated. In the process, however, new conflicts of interest will almost certainly arise. The workers may find that they have an incentive to ignore quality in order to increase output, and the furniture factory may build a few heavy chairs rather than many light ones.

In each case, the lower-level decision maker is suboptimizing in the sense that he is behaving rationally from his own point of view while partially thwarting the goals of his superiors. Generally speaking, it will not be possible for the upper levels of a hierarchy to completely harmonize the goals of lower levels with their own. The problem of supervision will not disappear.[3]

Ideally, the economic planning council of a command economy will consider a number of different variants of each year's plan. That is, the planners should examine a variety of attainable production menus and select that combination of outputs which it prefers. At the same time, for each different combination of outputs, the EPC should examine several alternative production methods. In practice, the information costs of such a procedure, including both coordinating and supervisory costs, are so high that very few input and output combinations are actually compared. A bureaucratic routine has evolved which bases each year's plan on the preceding year's performance, with insufficient allowance for changes in planners' goals and negotiations between planners and producers over plan targets.

We would therefore expect an economy with centralized decision making to be more adept at hiking the output of a given bill of goods by, say, 10 per cent per year than in bringing about an expansion in the number and variety of products being produced or in designing and mass producing new goods to fulfill a wide range of production needs and consumer wants. The system would appear to be particularly insensitive when it comes to solving the last problem, because individual producers have a much greater incentive to respond to the commands of planners than to household preferences.

More generally, a command economy will encounter problems with success indicators, with bureaucratic inertia and rigidity, in comparing investment alternatives, in satisfying consumer wants, and with excessive autarky or self-sufficiency among different sectors of the economy. (The latter will often correspond to different hierarchies or subchains in the over-all chain of command.) We shall explore these matters in Chapters 5 and 7–11.

On the other hand, suppose for a moment that we were to be plunged into a completely decentralized world. Most of the vast industrial complex that has made high living standards possible in the Western Hemisphere would have to be ruled out because this implies large firms (which have to be large to be efficient), which tend to become poles of economic power. Imagine an automobile industry, for example, under conditions of perfect competition. Automobiles would have to be priced out of the reach of most people. Indeed,

---

[3] We may also think of this as a problem of incomplete centralization (or of creeping decentralization). If it were possible to specify every size, style, design, and quality of each individual input and output for every producer and to tie his salary uniquely to achievement of "perfect" plan targets in all these indicators, the problem of goal harmony between different levels of a hierarchy would not arise. However, such a procedure has not yet proved possible. We shall discuss this problem further in Chapters 9 and 10.

North America itself under such a constraint would probably have remained a continent of villages, handicraft shops, and agriculture.

It would not necessarily be a place where the distribution of wealth was considerably more equal than at present. Perfect competition requires only that each buyer or seller be small relative to the total size of the market. One seller or firm might still be several times larger than another, and a number of different firms in a variety of different industries might be owned by one family. One can be quite wealthy without being able to influence the terms of trade.

Furthermore, the government has no power to change the existing distribution of wealth or to alter national priorities in any other way. Priorities tend to be determined somewhat randomly or accidentally. Because of this, it would often be futile for an individual or group which feels that it has been oppressed, exploited, or treated unfairly to appeal to the government. This difficulty of political expression may then raise the level of violence in such a society.

When all economic decision making is decentralized, there is another extremely important, although somewhat less obvious problem. This relates to the concept of private versus social cost or benefit, and is captured in the following quotation: "The cost to society of producing some items may contain elements which can never be expected to show up in the books of the producing firm. If the production of some item causes soil erosion or pollution of water or leads to the growth of slums, these are matters which the economist must take into account in deciding whether, and in what quantity, the item should be produced." [4] Similarly, the production of the item may provide "spillover" social benefits which are not reflected in the revenues of the firm.

Thus society may want some more central authority to require standards that will move the economy toward pollution-free automobiles and smokestacks. It may also decide to prevent chemical or pharmaceutical companies and lumber mills from emptying untreated waste materials into rivers or lakes or oil drillers from fouling beaches. In each case, the management of a firm is barred from using any production process that causes spillover costs to fall upon other economic factors.

The same argument applies to individuals and governments. Some municipal authorities have become notorious water polluters because they have been unwilling or unable to buy sewage-treatment plants. Similarly, for various reasons, regional governments have often built airports too close to populated areas, thereby clogging ground transportation facilities and creating noise pollution, for which they do not have to pay the full cost.

Speaking generally, whenever private and social costs or benefits diverge,

---

[4] W. J. Baumol, *Economic Theory and Operations Analysis* (Englewood Cliffs, N.J.: Prentice-Hall, 1965), Ch. 16, p. 357.

leaving a component *external* to the producer or consumer in question, completely decentralized decision making will not lead to efficiency, expect through chance. The decentralized decision maker tends to reckon only the private or *internal* component, which is the only one relevant to him.

In such an event, economic efficiency requires us to centralize some decisions. The maximum *de*centralization consistent with efficiency is now one where every decision is taken at a level barely high enough to make negligible the external effects associated with it. Conversely, it is the failure to centralize these decisions and to take away some of the private property rights of management that permits externalities to arise in the first place. The culprit, in other words, is not the profit *motive,* but rather the fact that what is profitable to a firm may not be beneficial to the society in which it is located.[5]

In a command economy, the problem of externalities becomes one of recognizing how the production or consumption activities in one sector of the economy corresponding to one hierarchy affect other sectors corresponding to other hierarchies or under other jurisdictions. This adds in an important way to the complexity of centralized planning.

Not only will the resulting damages or benefits often be difficult to assess, but also considerable vertical flows of information may have to occur between officials before the matter becomes fully documented on the desk of a decision maker with enough authority to handle the problem. (He would presumably have to be high enough in the planning hierarchy to have some jurisdiction over both the polluter and his victims.) Repeated instances of this are likely to strain a centralized information system.

Water pollution, for example, has become a serious threat to wildlife, public health, and sanitation and even to certain industries in the U.S.S.R. and the United States. Its direct costs have been estimated at $6 billion annually in the Soviet Union.[6] Despite the repeated protests of Soviet conservationists, it may already be too late to save Lake Baikal, the world's largest freshwater lake and one of the ecological wonders of the world.

Nevertheless, the underlying causes of pollution in the two countries are probably somewhat different. In the United States, private enterprises did not have to pay the costs of pollution; thus they ignored its consequences. In the U.S.S.R. this was one cost factor among many that the planning bureaucracy tended to overlook or underestimate. In some cases as well, growth-oriented central planners have probably been willing to accept environmental disruption as part of the price of increased "output."

Finally, waste and pollution have been made worse by the pressure on enterprise managements to produce more, which command planning usually generates. This means that it is often in a firm's best interests to shift some of its costs onto others or to ignore costs. Even after a specific case of environ-

---

[5] This again becomes a question of social control of industry through the political process; it will be discussed in Chapter 23.

[6] This estimate is by a Soviet official. See *The New York Times,* Apr. 9, 1971, p. 12.

mental disruption has risen high enough in the planning hierarchy to receive the attention of the right official, the latter may therefore have an enforcement problem.

2–3   The Mixing of Markets and Commands

Because the polar forms are not interesting as practical economic systems, we must next ask how we may synthesize features from each into a useful design. Any intermediate form will combine markets with commands and, perhaps, indicators, and we can imagine two broad ways of doing this. On one hand, we may start with a basic command mechanism and use markets or quasi-markets to play roles in areas in which centralized decision making is especially inefficient. We may also insert commands into a basically market context, both to supplement the market mechanism and to take over the allocation of goods and resources in areas in which decentralized decision making is especially inefficient. In fact, the government of a predominantly market economy can use commands to supplement the market in three basic ways:

1. It may regulate prices directly. Here we include direct manipulation of prices to achieve market equilibrium, price ceilings to combat inflation or monopoly restrictions on output, and minimum wages to redistribute income.

We shall discuss each of these in subsequent chapters. However, we note now that most economists would recommend against this use of commands, except on a short-term or selective basis (when they may be able to alter expectations), or, possibly, within a small economy. A government is less likely to set an equilibrium price that balances supply and demand, and the resulting disequilibrium becomes a source of inefficiency.

For example, minimum wage laws are partly responsible for unemployment, because they price some less skilled or less fortunate labor out of the market. Price ceilings are often ineffective because firms find that they can replace price increases with reductions in the quality or servicing of their products. When ceilings are effective, they often create shortages, and some buyers may be willing to pay higher, black-market prices rather than go without the good.

In particular, price ceilings generally do not control inflation, except over short periods of time, because of the problems of quality monitoring and enforcement and because excess purchasing power will spill over into uncontrolled markets, including black markets. A problem of work disincentives, further aggravating shortages, may also arise. In the final analysis, the supervisory costs of these commands are likely to be quite high relative to the resulting benefits, with the possible exceptions noted above.

2. By altering the choices open to individual producers and consumers, the government may shift the demand and supply curves, thereby changing the price levels indirectly. In each case it effectively centralizes or decentralizes the decisions in question.

For example, it may invoke laws, regulations, and standards to deny firms the right to use production processes that pollute the air or water or to package their products unsafely. More generally it may seek to remove the rights of individual actors to produce and consume in such a way that external costs and benefits occur. If successful, the result will probably be higher prices for automobiles, fuels, steel, power, and chemical products in order to cover the costs of antipollution technology.[7]

3. It may also be able to shift demand and supply curves by altering the structure of rewards and penalties attached to different choices open to households and firms. Here it will not necessarily try to reduce or expand the range of choices available, but it will try to alter their relative attractiveness. A system of taxes and subsidies can sometimes make a production process which causes pollution less profitable than one which does not. The same is true of consumption. A motorist might be permitted to drive his car through Manhattan during rush hour without a filtration device, provided he pays a tax for doing so. This will discourage such behavior, and any resulting income can be used for a socially desirable purpose, such as improving public transportation.

Generally speaking, taxes and subsidies provide the most frequent example of method 3. In contrast to method 2, these do not usually seek to forbid certain activities altogether. Pollution, for example, will be consistent with economic efficiency in some cases, provided the polluters pay damages to injured parties.[8] Nevertheless, we should emphasize that the difference between methods 2 and 3 is one of degree. Laws prohibiting strikes or misleading advertising must be backed up by fines or other penalties, which are analogous to taxes. In some cases, firms, labor unions, and households will be willing to incur these in order to continue the forbidden practices.

In some instances it will be difficult to tell whether we are dealing with a basically marketized economy, where commands play a supplementary role, or vice versa. Nevertheless, purely from the standpoint of economic efficiency, we now wish to ask which of these two broad categories is likely to be preferable in most situations. That is, should commands form the core of an efficient economy, with markets atoning for specific failures, or should we reverse these roles?

In fact, we would usually opt for a market core, supplemented by commands, when efficiency is our *only* concern. We shall wait until Chapter 5 to detail most of the specific efficiency advantages of markets. For now, we note

[7] In effect, these firms are forbidden to use their least (private) cost methods of production because external costs are then inflicted on other producers or consumers. With higher costs, such a firm will wish to supply less of its product at each price. The market supply curve will shift up and to the left, resulting in a higher equilibrium price. The higher price will cover part of the increase in private costs.

[8] Indeed, it may be efficient for injured parties to bribe polluters to stop them from polluting. Many readers will object to this on grounds of fairness, however, and we shall encounter another objection in Chapter 15.

that these stem mainly from the ability of markets to break up and to otherwise simplify the economic problem and from the close links between producers and users of goods and services which they promote.[9]

To be a bit more precise, let us imagine a group of producers who are interdependent, in the sense that physical flows of goods and services are passing between them. We may further suppose that the size of the group grows over time, along with the number and variety of goods exchanged. The group will probably become more interdependent, as well, in the sense that each producer will develop more exchange links with a larger number of other group members. Finally, we assume initially that these actors must either be coordinated through an all-embracing chain of command, topped by a central planner, or through an all-embracing market mechanism.

As the size, complexity, and affluence of this economy increase, the information costs of command planning will multiply rapidly. This is true of the supervisory as well as the coordinating costs of planning. The problem of supervision is every bit as real in a market economy, but the market itself will provide some automatic supervision of the managements of most firms.

More than with other employees, the paychecks and promotion possibilities (or, more generally, the rewards) of managerial personnel are likely to depend upon the firm's profit residual, at least until what we shall later call a normal accounting profit has been earned. This residual is, in effect, what is left of the enterprise's revenues after it has paid its bills and, in most cases, met the bulk of its payroll. The stronger the influence of the firm's profit residual upon managerial salaries, the greater the automatic incentive of management to produce salable goods and to keep costs under control. (This influence need not be contingent upon the firm's being a profit maximizer, as we shall see in Chapter 17.)

While the market provides some discipline for management, the latter uses a combination of incentives, success indicators, penalties, controls, and direct supervision to enforce cost control within its own firm. Therefore, when the profit residual bites hard enough, the market goes a long way toward eliminating the need for success indicators from higher-level authorities. It also breaks the gigantic and intractable supervisory problem facing society as a whole into subproblems, most of which are comparatively tiny in scope and complexity. We shall later see that the coordinating problem can be broken up in the same way. The fly in the ointment comes when what is profitable for a firm is not profitable as well for society, a matter about which we shall shortly say more. But it then becomes the job of commands in a supplementary role to harmonize the two notions of profit.

Increasing the size and complexity of an economy does not necessarily make a market mechanism less efficient. When the problem is simple enough, command planning may work much more efficiently. That is, a command

[9] There are socialist-market as well as command economies, and present long-run tendencies within the socialist bloc point toward more rather than less marketization. Thus the issue we are considering is not the same as the capitalist–socialist dichotomy.

planner may be able to gather and process the necessary data, compute an optimal solution to the economic problem directly, and issue and enforce the proper plan targets more quickly and less expensively than the same solution could be found through simultaneous price adjustment.

For example, a network of computers may be able to find an optimal solution to a comparatively simple problem in less than a second when the appropriate data are fed into it, whereas a system of markets may take days or turn out a solution that is far from being optimal. We would therefore expect command planning to have its greatest advantage when the economy is small and simple and to progressively lose this as it grows larger and more complex.[10] The point at which the market mechanism begins to become more efficient will depend upon the managerial caliber of the planners as well as their enforcement means and the information-handling capabilities of the data systems under their control. The current revolutions in data processing and managerial technology should extend the comparative advantage of commands, although, at present, even large firms make some use of internal markets.[11]

In this context we note that an important theoretical result, bearing the grandiose title, Fundamental Theorem of Welfare Economics, forms the backbone of any discussion about market efficiency. This theorem says that the completely decentralized economy is efficient under highly implausible conditions. To wit, when external effects become too strong, when important scale economies go unrealized, when prices get too far from equilibrium levels, or when unemployment becomes too high, the fundamental theorem is no longer true, and the completely decentralized version becomes unattractive.

What keeps the Fundamental Theorem from becoming irrelevant, however, is the possibility of modifying a market economy, by means of a relatively small number of commands, so that it can deal with these phenomena and still operate with tolerable efficiency. Whereas the efficiency disadvantage of command economies lies in the information costs of operating complex systems, the disadvantage of a market economy lies in the difficulty that producers and consumers will sometimes have in cooperating through the market mechanism to their mutual advantage.

For example, let us imagine trying to find a market solution to a problem of social cost. Suppose that a soap producer is polluting the waters of a stream from which farmers' cattle drink. In effect, pure water is a scarce good in demand and, therefore, should have a positive price to ration its use. But

[10] This is a useful oversimplification. It would be more accurate to say that markets supplemented by relatively few commands become increasingly efficient relative to commands supplemented by markets as the economy grows and complexifies.

[11] Nevertheless, these firms use a basically command mechanism, and in some cases their value added approaches the net national products or national incomes of smaller command economies. The latter are far more difficult to coordinate with commands, however, because they contain many times the number of individual production units and turn out many times the number of individual products (indeed, several hundred to several thousand times as many products).

it is free to the soap company, which consequently uses it up by dumping wastes into it. The result is an increase in farmers' costs and, in all probability, some economic inefficiency as well. To solve the problem, the farmers could conceivably get together and decide to offer the soap company a "compensating payment" [12] for installing purification machinery. A new market, of sorts, would then be created for clean water, and it can be shown that, subject to some qualifications, the loss in efficiency could be restored.

Many readers will object to such a solution on grounds of equity or fairness. However, as later discussion will show, the presence of inefficiency implies that both parties can benefit. There will, in other words, be a net efficiency gain whose monetary value will be greater than zero. The farmers can theoretically offer a bribe which will make it possible for the soap manufacturer to purify the waters but which is still less than the total damages inflicted on them by pollution. Indeed, an entrepreneur, attracted by the possibility of claiming a part of the net efficiency gain as payment for his services, may offer to organize the farmers into an effective bargaining group.[13]

Logically, we can extend this analysis to almost any kind of inefficiency. Later we shall see that a monopoly firm—or, more generally, an imperfect competitor—may create inefficiency by charging a price that is too high and producing an output that is too low. If this monopolist were to expand output and lower price, his customers would benefit, as would some employees, whom he would hire at higher wages than they had been receiving. Many others would benefit indirectly. By the argument above, an entrepreneur could collect payment from the gainers and use this to induce the monopolist to expand, thereby eliminating the inefficiency.

The argument is not correct, but it is instructive to note where the analysis breaks down. There will always be *transactions costs* associated with carrying through an exchange to the satisfaction of both parties. In many cases, transactions costs will be low to negligible. However, they will rise whenever the product to be exchanged is difficult to measure and when prospective gainers from an exchange are difficult to identify or to organize into an effective bargaining group. They will also rise when the negotiations themselves are delicate or complicated or many-sided (multilateral) among numerous households or firms. In particular, transactions costs will be greater, the more scattered are the potential gains from an exchange among diverse beneficiaries and the more difficult it is to determine who the gainers are and by how much each one of them stands to benefit. This is the problem in the examples above.

Suppose, in fact, that we have a steel monopoly restricting output and setting its price at twice the efficient level. The potential gainers from an output expansion *cum* price reduction include the direct customers of the steel company—automobile producers, bridge builders, equipment manufacturers,

---

[12] Economeze for "bribe."

[13] If they do so, they may be able to use the threat of political pressure-group action to force the soap company to bear some of the costs of purification.

and so on. But these firms would pass on some of their reduced costs to their own customers, who could, in turn, cut prices. Because the economy is an interdependent organism, the benefits would spread through the system. In the end, millions of individuals would probably benefit, although by tiny amounts in most instances.

The situation becomes even more tangled in the case of externalities, such as air pollution from automobiles, factories, and homes, whose nature is such that millions of individuals inflict damages on one another. In the case of both air and water pollution, we must add the nearly prohibitive costs of monitoring the damages caused by each actor and computing their value. The upshot is that environmental agencies usually find it more effective to work through the political decision making process—seeking to modify society's laws, regulations, and enforcement procedures—than through the market mechanism. This is true even though they may be at some disadvantage in the political arena.[14]

There are several other factors that will often make transactions costs too high to permit effective market solutions. One of the most important is the *principle of exclusion.* As soon as our steel monopolist expands his output and lowers his price, there is no way to exclude anyone from the benefits of increased economic efficiency. Thus potential beneficiaries will have an incentive to understate the amounts by which they expect to gain, hoping, thereby, to shift the burden of compensating the monopolist onto others.

Because these benefits cannot be measured by any outside party, a private agency may be unable to collect sufficient compensation, even when it can discover who all the beneficiaries are. Knowing that compensation is unlikely, the monopolist would insist upon payment in advance as a price for relinquishing the exercise of its power, which is a much more certain way of shifting the distribution of income in its favor. A similar barrier often arises to market solutions of externality problems.

In other cases, the indivisible or difficult-to-measure nature of a commodity will make it too costly to transact. For example, it will often prove impossible to efficiently market methods and ideas unless they can be embodied in a usable product.[15] It is therefore efficient for most economies to subsidize basic research (for example, in universities) and to attach the majority of applied research laboratories directly to the firms they serve. Small firms may have to merge to realize scale economies in research and development as well as those in automated production or managerial decision making. Similarly, the problem of social cost will be best handled, on occasion, by merger.

Many independent and autonomous small producers may be unable to

---

[14] We shall see why in Chapter 23. Ironically, if such a group works through the political process, it may have to press for simplistic solutions, such as complete elimination of pollution, congestion, and pesticides, in order to attract attention and galvanize support. Yet the problem, when seen in all its ramifications, may be quite complex. Even in the best of circumstances, environmental disruption cannot be reduced or eliminated without cost.

[15] We shall examine this problem in Chapter 15.

realize the benefits of a finely honed division of labor if they insist on negotiating with one another through the market. Instead, they must agree to subordinate their efforts to coordination via a chain of command, internal to a
single firm. It is then no longer necessary for every producer to engage in many
separate contracts with each of the others. Every producer now makes just one
contract with the firm, in which he agrees to become its employee, accepting
certain conditions of work in return for a package of pay and fringe benefits.

Indeed, we may define a firm or enterprise to be a common party with
which employee contracts are made (or for which employees agree to work,
should these contracts formally be made with the government in a socialist
society). For the purposes of this book, we would add the condition that
firms cannot be largely administrative agencies.

When all is said and done, transactions costs play the major role in preventing market mechanisms from operating efficiently, a role that we assigned
to information costs in the case of commands. But information costs take their
computational toll when a basically command organization grows too large
and complex. Transactions costs are most serious when the producers in a
market economy grow too small and too unspecialized in their internal division of labor.

Let us therefore pick a hypothetical market economy with very small
producers, where the "size" of a firm is defined in terms of its scale of output and product range. The internal organization of each firm will be primarily, although not necessarily entirely, according to the command principle.
We then allow the average firm size to grow, through investment, bankruptcies, mergers, and absorptions. Neglecting the problem of monopoly
power for a moment, we may say that rising information costs of internal
operations will eventually determine maximum efficient firm sizes. Even in a
small economy, we would not expect to find any firm embracing the bulk of
the producing sector.

By the same token, let us now start with an all-embracing command
economy and begin introducing markets to reduce information costs. We
would probably not achieve our most efficient operation until we had crossed
the boundary into basically marketized systems. Sending fairly aggregated commands to the bulk of the producing sector, even in a small economy, probably
involves almost prohibitive information costs.[16] Should this not be so, however, we can be nearly certain that the smaller the economy, the more reliant
it must be on international trade and specialization according to comparative
advantage, if efficiency is its only concern. But the need to trade greatly complexifies command planning, partly because the world economy is basically
marketized.[17]

Finally, if we begin reducing firm sizes, within a market economy, we

---

[16] More precisely, given an acceptable investment in information gathering and
processing equipment, computers, and so on, it would probably take several years to
generate the optimal economic plan for a single year.

[17] We shall explore this problem in Chapter 7.

would expect rising transactions costs to eventually determine minimum levels consistent with efficiency. Beyond a point, potential scale economies would go increasingly unrealized, and external effects would also grow more costly.[18]

We therefore tend to associate static efficiency with markets, albeit markets adequately supplemented by commands and, perhaps, indicators. But no economy should be judged by efficiency alone, and in addition, individual actors will often have incentives to behave in ways inconsistent with economy-wide efficiency. This is the source of much pollution, congestion, and other external effects, since some households and firms will seek to inflict some of their costs upon others or to derive benefits for which they do not pay. It is also a source of monopoly power and of the wealth or prestige that this may embody. Where possible, the government of a market economy should therefore try to ensure the minimum, rather than the maximum, firm size consistent with efficiency—unless, perhaps, this power is largely exercised on international markets.[19]

Similarly, we may sometimes best be able to account for a command economy on grounds of ideological preferences or of a desire by its leaders for power or for a firm power base (in the command planning bureaucracy). These will override considerations of efficiency, on occasion, although the latter may dictate a command mechanism in special circumstances. But what is more interesting is that a command economy may prove advisable even when neither of the above considerations predominates. We cannot say anything about a "best" economic system until we know something of an economy's past performance and its present or expected future goals. The latter may override considerations of efficiency, even when goals are entirely phrased in terms of such mundane matters as production and income distribution. To see why, we must first probe a bit more closely into an economy's political decision-making processes.

2–4　Three Concepts of Rational Behavior

Lying behind the transformation of inputs into outputs by firms, households, and planners are the decision-making processes of these elements considered as economic actors or agents. A thorough analysis of economic

---

[18] This sentence, along with one or two others above, is redundant. It can be shown that unrealized scale economies are a special kind of externality, unless the market is too small to support a single minimum-sized efficient firm. Of course, many external costs and benefits can be eliminated (or "internalized") without increasing firm size. Because monopoly power is a real-world problem, this will normally be advisable where feasible. Our results on the optimal-size-of-the-firm problem, as it is known in the literature, are due to McManus. See John C. McManus, "The Organization of Production," Department of Economics, Working Paper 71–05, Ottawa, Carleton University, June 1971. There are, however, two sharp disagreements between McManus and the author. The first is over the nature of the information costs which determine an upper bound to efficient firm size. McManus would include only supervisory costs. The second is over the nature of centralized versus decentralized economic decision making.

[19] We are implicitly assuming here that most firms have pan-shaped average cost curves rather than the U shape found in textbooks. There is some empirical justification for such an assumption, and we shall take up the matter in Chapter 16.

decision making would involve us in a discussion of the concept of rational behavior in an economic system, and this is postponed to Chapters 3 and 4. Here, however, we want to introduce the idea and discuss its broad outlines without getting involved too deeply in detail.

We say that an economic actor is behaving rationally (or is rational) whenever he is as well off in terms of material welfare as he could be subject to the constraints on his aspirations. A consumer tries to maximize his utility subject to his budget constraint. Economics textbooks usually show producers trying to maximize profits subject to a cost constraint, but at the back of everyone's mind is a close link between the firm's profits and the material welfare of its owners. Modern theories of the firm often stress the divorce between ownership and control. In them, the material welfare of its management may depend upon factors such as sales or growth which are only partly related to the corporation's profitability. This requires us to rephrase the firm's goals in terms of a combination of growth and sales in addition to profitability.

Rational behavior is not defined except in the light of given goals. Moreover, if a change in these goals occurs, behavior that was previously rational need no longer be so. In the light of one set of goals, a given behavior—say, consumption of a certain bundle of goods and services—may appear quite rational. In the light of another set, defined by completely different tastes or preferences, it might appear terribly irrational.

There may be such a thing as rational behavior in situations in which goals are not well defined. But, if there is, we must be able to say that some activities are clearly less beneficial to the economic actor or group in question than others. Rational behavior would then comprise those activities which are not clearly less beneficial than some other. We may also talk about the degree of rationality. In this spirit, we may say that one act is more rational than another when it leaves the party in question better off, meaning at a higher level of utility. Both activities, however, may be irrational in the sense that neither leaves the economic actor as well off as he could be.

Finally, rational behavior is usually rooted in a psychological perspective. It is equated to a conscious or unconscious pursuit of satisfaction by one individual or group (such as a household) acting in unison and deriving utility in the same way under the same circumstances. In all likelihood, a trial-and-error approach will be the basic methodology of such an actor.

As economists use them, the terms "rationality" and "rational behavior" usually apply to individual decision makers and not to the economy as an organic whole. In our view, however, such an attitude is too costly to adopt. Accordingly, we shall reserve the expression *microrationality* for the usual notion of economic rationality—applying to the individual actors in a system —and turn our attention to the economy viewed as an entity. Like an individual, a society may choose between alternative courses of action. Over time, these become alternative paths of economic development. Any society will also have both political and economic decision-making processes which respectively define and implement its economic goals.

We have seen that an individual's utility or welfare may be viewed as an index of his success in achieving consumption goals. A firm's profits, sales, or growth may also indicate its success. It is therefore natural to define social welfare as an index of an economy's success in achieving the goals determined by its political process. Like an individual, society may grope toward an approximately optimal solution of its economic problem in trial-and-error fashion.

Unlike the well-being of an individual actor, however, social welfare need not be a psychological construct. It may refer to the psychological welfare of a planner–dictator who imposes his own goals for society on his subjects. However, it may also happen that an economic planning council tries to be guided by a synthesis of the preferences of individuals and groups in society. Then social welfare becomes more of a logical construct, and this must be true in an unplanned economy. Let us examine the planned case first.

We shall say that an economy is planned whenever there exists a particular agency, or small group of interacting agencies, able to define basic economic goals for society and to have these goals implemented. We shall continue to call this central planner or leading decision maker an economic planning council. (In any given country, the term *economic planning council* may, and usually will, refer to more than one body.) Such a definition of planning is independent of the means of plan implementation and allows for both market and command-planned economies. An economic planning council may also consider itself to be the voice of the people and make a serious effort to implement some version of the collective will, or it may try to run a dictatorship and impose its own priorities. In fact, we can imagine two polar kinds of EPC from this point of view, of which any central planner in practice will prove to be a combination.

In the first polar case, the EPC will be the dominant pole of economic power in the system and utilize its position to impose its own preferences. But planners may also play the role of intermediary between the origin of social goals and values on one hand and their implementation on the other. In the second polar case, the EPC contents itself to merely implement a set of social preferences synthesized from the microoriented preferences of individual members of society. Such a planner may be a kind of benevolent dictator. Alternatively, the citizens of a country may vest their collective power in the EPC, in more-or-less democratic fashion, as the instrument through which social goals are pursued.[20]

In either case, we can view the planner as trying to maximize a particular index of social welfare, thereby giving us the basic ingredients for a new concept of rationality. To the extent that it is rooted in the psychological perspective of the EPC, our new rationality is akin to microrationality. However, unlike microrationality, we now have an aggregate or social orientation, and "utility" depends, not on goods and services that are physically consumed

---

[20] In practice, any EPC will have some power to define the emerging consensus, thereby ruling out the second polar case. In either case, social goals may or may not be publicized.

or available, but on global indicators of economic performance. To have a name for this new kind of rationality, we shall borrow Alec Nove's term, *macrorationale*.[21] Let us try to draw the analogy between this and microrationality a bit more closely.

The ultimate goal of any economic actor is assumed to be welfare maximization. But, in itself, this is not terribly interesting. What we try to do, therefore, is to translate this abstract target into something more concrete. We have said that a household derives its utility from consuming goods and services. Thus an ordinary microeconomic utility function indexes a household's material welfare as a function of the goods it consumes. At the same time, it translates the goal of achieving maximum utility into more concrete goals relating to the household's consumption patterns. In the same vein, we have already noted that utility maximization may translate into profit maximization for a firm.

Returning to our economic planning council, let us suppose that its goal of utility maximization translates into a goal of growth maximization. This is still a bit abstract, but we can become even more concrete if we note that growth, in turn, depends upon such factors as the volume and assortment of current spending on new capital goods, the willingness of the labor force to work, and a host of other matters over which the EPC will normally have some control. After taking these into account we should be able to define a utility function or utility index that we shall call the *planners' preference function*—describing the social goals adopted by the EPC in terms of global indicators of economic performance.

Whether these goals are dictatorially imposed upon a people or an interpretation of their collective will, the planners' preference function plays exactly the same role in any discussion of the planners' macrorationale as the micro utility function plays in a discussion of microrationality. It poses the concrete goals that are needed before rationality can be defined. In this case the constraints on goal achievement are not individual budgets or costs but society's technological and human constraints or production, distribution, and welfare, Frequently, the economy's production possibilities are embodied in a frontier that resembles the production-possibility curve drawn for Robinson Crusoe in Chapter 1.

Of course, members of the EPC do not derive all their welfare from aggregate statistical indicators. They also consume goods and services like everyone else, and it would seem best to account for this by assigning them ordinary micro utility functions on top of the planners' preference function assigned to the council itself.

The notion of macrorationale introduces us to aggregate-oriented rationality and to social preferences. However, we can scarcely claim to equate macrorationale with aggregate-oriented rationality. The latter term must be

[21] A. Nove, *Economic Rationality and Soviet Politics* (New York: Praeger, 1964), p. 12.

broader because it is not useful to classify some economies as planned by any reasonable definition of the term. In these systems, social goals emerge primarily as syntheses of the microgoals of individual producers, consumers, labor unions, and so on, *without* being interpreted and implemented by a leading economic decision maker. Instead, social goals are synthesized directly, in mutual interaction, and many of them will remain implicit and ill-defined.

Because the diverse aims of various economic actors will often conflict, a synthesis of their preferences will yield something that may be labeled "net goals" and progress toward them as "net-goal achievement." A social preference function that phrases these net goals for society will be at least partly a weighted sum of individual preferences. The weights in question are outputs of society's political decision-making processes. They will indicate the relative importance of each individual's welfare in social welfare and his ability to acquire or have acquired for him the goods and services he desires.[22]

This ability will reflect the individual's power, but also his wealth and good fortune. A shift in the distribution of economic power will alter the weights attached to some actors and can thereby change the (net) goals of an unplanned economy. Such a shift, coupled with a subsequent goal reorientation, appeared to occur in the United States following the Great Depression and again after the peak of the Vietnam war.

When a social preference function arises directly, rather than through the intermediary of a planner, we shall say that it expresses the *macrorationality* of the system.[23] As in the case of macrorationale, the basic constraints on attaining social goals will be embodied in society's technological and human constraints. However, macrorationality is never rooted in the psychological makeup of an individual or in the sociopsychological characteristics of a small group or agency. The system as a whole cannot be assumed to consciously and purposefully try to maximize as an individual does. When one talks about the "rationality" of a system, it can only be with reference to a logical framework. In this framework, a system is completely rational when it makes as much progress toward achieving its social goals as is possible.

Yet the reader should not get the impression that the distinction between macrorationale and macrorationality (or between planning and nonplanning) is sudden and sharp. Every government in the world today engages in a substantial amount of economic policy making. Most countries are committed to full employment, have some antitrust laws, and seek to enforce certain

---

[22] More precisely and generally, each actor would have his own way of ranking various states of the economy in accordance with his own goals. If we then assign each actor or group of actors a weight, the net goals of the system will be the weighted sum of individual goals.

[23] The concept of macrorationality is broad enough to include the situation in which a would-be planner exists in the system, provided social goals are inconsistent with his macrorationale. That is, he tries to implement a certain set of social preferences, but he does not succeed. Prevailing social goals are likely to be syntheses of the goals of various micro decision makers in the system, along with the partly frustrated goals of the would-be leading decision maker.

standards regarding the quality of the goods that they produce. Such activities will determine or influence some social goals, partly by conditioning the environment within which micro decision makers operate. But we may still conclude that there is no economic planning council implementing most of society's major economic goals.

At the same time, no small group of decision makers in any economy will implement every social goal in complete detail. Even under command planning, production and productivity targets will be outlined in highly aggregated form by the EPC and then become more and more disaggregated as they move down the planning hierarchy toward individual firms. This inevitably leaves some room for lower-level decision making.

By our definition, some countries are pretty clearly planned and others are not. In the former category, we would probably place the U.S.S.R, China, and the Eastern European countries, excluding Yugoslavia. The United States, Canada, and the United Kingdom all probably fall on the other side of the division. But where would we put the French economy? France has a planning agency and appears to make an effort at democratic planning. But is this agency best viewed as the "leading decision maker" which actually steers the system along a particular path of economic development? We would classify the French economy as planned, but this is an empirical question to which different economists might give different answers. The same is true for the Japanese and West German economies. In the latter instance, the EPC, if it exists, is a hiding as well as a guiding hand. To identify it, we should first have to dig it out from the interlocking directorates of giant corporations and banks.

2–5 Social Welfare

Bela Balassa has suggested that we may apply some or all of five success criteria to a particular economic system.[24] These are static and dynamic efficiency, growth rate of national income, consumer satisfaction, and the distribution of income, insofar as this mirrors the distribution of welfare. The latter three criteria are partly value-oriented. Performance as judged by them depends not only upon the efficiency of the economy, but also upon the goals selected by the society in question. We now wish to discuss the nature of these goals, and to do so we first go back to the notion of individual welfare.

We have associated a utility or preference index with each economic actor in order to describe his utility (well-being, satisfaction, and so on) in relation to his work effort and the goods and services he consumes. Each household will prefer some combinations of goods and services to others. Indeed, we may say that its preference function ranks or orders all these combinations. Those that yield him the most utility will rank highest on his

[24] Bela Balassa, "Success Criteria for Economic Systems," Ch. 1 in Morris Bornstein, ed., *Comparative Economic Systems: Models and Cases,* rev. ed. (Homewood, Ill.: Irwin, 1969).

list. In the final analysis, his utility index is nothing more or less than such a ranking.

Similarly, a planners' preference function will rank various economy-wide solutions to the economic problem in terms of their desirability to the EPC or to the consensus it seeks to represent. In the case of an unplanned economy we can, at least in principle, rank each economy-wide solution in terms of net goal achievement. In both cases our ranking defines an index of *social welfare*, according to which the solutions ranking highest are said to provide the most welfare to society. Just as individual welfare or utility was linked to the concept of microrationality, we have now associated the notion of social welfare with social or aggregate-oriented rationality (macrorationale or macrorationality).

Continuing with this analogy, let us define a *social preference function* as the output of society's political decision-making processes. The social preference function will define economic goals for society in the same manner that an individual's utility function defines his consumption goals. Progress toward achieving these goals, on the other hand, is nothing more or less than an increase in social welfare. It follows that the social preference function will index social welfare and indicate society's preferences just as an individual's utility function defines the individual's preferences and indexes his welfare. As we spoke of maximizing individual utility above, we shall now speak of maximizing social welfare, whether or not this is done consciously.

We must bear in mind, however, that many different definitions of social welfare embodied in many distinct social preference functions and resulting in many contrasting social priorities are conceivable in any economy. The emerging social preference will notably depend upon the nature of the political process, in particular the extent to which it is dictatorial or participatory.

In Chapter 0 we described the economic problem facing each society as one of allocating scarce resources among competing ends. In Chapter 3 we shall learn that there are two component parts of an efficient solution to any economic problem. The first of these is the *production* aspect, concerned mainly with efficiently allocating resources among society's different production processes so as to approach its production-possibility frontier. The second is the *welfare* aspect, concerned not only with efficient production, but also with an efficient distribution of the fruits of production among society's members.

Correspondingly, we may consider the economic goals of any system to be, in the first instance, of two kinds, production goals and welfare goals. We shall therefore define three kinds of social preference functions according to the kinds of goals which they phrase:

1. First comes the famous social welfare function,[25] which defines social

---

[25] See A. Bergson, "A Reformulation of Certain Aspects of Welfare Economics," *Quarterly Journal of Economics,* Feb. 1938, pp. 310–334; and Paul Samuelson, *The Foundations of Economic Analysis* (Cambridge, Mass.: Harvard U.P., 1961), Ch. VIII, pp. 219–228.

welfare solely as a function of the welfare of each individual. We may think of it as a weighted sum of the welfares of each individual or household.

Let W index social welfare in a two-person economy (which we use for illustrative purposes). Then one simple example of a social welfare function arises when everyone's well-being always receives a weight of 1. This gives us $W = u_1 + u_2$. Social welfare is here defined as a straight sum of individual welfares or, in Jeremy Bentham's words, as the "greatest good for the greatest number." This function is historically associated with the utilitarian philosophical school, and we shall examine it in the Appendix to Chapter 4. Two other examples are $W = u_1 + 2u_2$ and $W = 2u_1 + u_2$. Here the first individual's well-being is half and then twice as important as that of the second.

Normally, the weights assigned to each individual will not be fixed but will themselves vary with the distribution of welfare. It is conceivable, for instance, that the weight of each individual would fall, the better off he was relative to everyone else. An extreme example of this is an "egalitarian" social welfare function, also to be explored in the Appendix to Chapter 4. It is even possible that some of the weights will turn out to be zero or negative. The higher the percentage of these, the less democratic is the social welfare function, according to criteria we shall outline later. Democratic or not, the weights indicate the relative importance of each individual in defining social welfare, and we are directly reminded of net goal achievement.

When we speak of a social welfare function that actually guides an economic system, the weights will be outputs of its political decision-making processes. However, we can also study the properties of various definitions of social welfare which we like, even though they have no current practical application. As private citizens we can argue that society ought to be guided by a definition that fits in with the ethical norms we consider to be "best." Then, we may compare actual economic performance with the result that we think would be achieved by a "just" reordering of priorities. Both the utilitarian and the egalitarian social welfare functions are drawn from this "If I Were King" file.

2. Second, what we shall call a *commodity preference function* phrases aggregate goals solely in terms of the quantities of goods and services produced or consumed, either on an aggregate or a per capita basis. A commodity preference function indexes social welfare as a weighted sum of quantities of goods and services. The weights will indicate the relative importance of each good in determining social welfare. In most cases they will also indicate the relative importance of each good to a central planner.

For example, suppose that we have a growth-oriented planning authority. Let X_1 be an index of aggregate consumer-goods output, X_2 an index of aggregate capital-goods production, and W represent the utility of the economic planning council. Since it is capital goods (or goods that can be used to produce other goods) that are essential to growth, we might describe such a set of planners' preferences by letting X_2 be twice as important as X_1. We would then write $W = X_1 + 2X_2$. The planners would aim to maximize $X_1 + 2X_2$, subject to the economy's production-possibility constraints, just as in one of the preceding examples, the goal was to maximize $(u_1 + u_2)$ subject to welfare constraints.

Any social preference function that synthesizes the microoriented preferences of individual economic actors will at least partly orient the economy toward the distribution of goods among these actors. We would therefore expect a commodity preference function to be the planners' preference function of a dictatorial EPC. By implication, the planners' sole interest in distribution stems from their opportunities to use goods as material incentives for still greater production. Consequently, they will try to achieve a distribution of wealth and welfare which they expect to maximize their production index and be willing to use coercion to the same end.

By contrast, we would tend to identify the social welfare function with a laissez-faire economy. However, the difference between the two is not quite as complete as it might, at first, appear. A dominating EPC could be distribution- rather than production-oriented. Moreover, suppose for a moment that we fix the distribution of welfare in a laissez-faire economy. Then social welfare can only be increased by expanding the scale of production or consumption. Our social welfare function can then take the form of a commodity preference function.

3. Finally, many, if not most, societies will have explicit welfare and production goals. When this happens, we say that the index of social welfare is defined by a social guide or social guiding function. A social guide is combination of the social welfare and commodity preference functions. If W indexes social welfare in a society in which a social guiding function applies, W is a weighted sum of individual welfares and aggregate or per capita quantities of goods and services available.[26]

An example of a social guiding function arises when a central planner

---

[26] Let u index the utility of any particular household. Let $(x_1, x_2, \ldots, x_m)$ be the quantities of goods and services that he consumes. Then we may write u as a weighted sum of these goods and services. That is,
$$u = w_1x_1 + w_2x_2 + \ldots + w_mx_m$$
where the w's are the weights. It can be shown that the relative weights (for example, w_1/w_2) are equal to the relative marginal utilities of the two goods. [For a derivation of the weights, see G. J. Stigler, *The Theory of Price* (New York: Macmillan, 1949), footnote, p. 141.]

Similarly, let W index social welfare as defined by a social welfare function. Let $(u_1, u_2, \ldots, u_n)$ index the welfares of the households in society. Then we may write social welfare as a weighted sum of individual welfares. That is,
$$W = a_1u_1 + a_2u_2 + \ldots + a_nu_n$$
where the a's are the weights indicating the relative importance of each individual's welfare in defining social welfare.

Finally, let $(X_1, X_2, \ldots, X_m)$ indicate aggregate or per capita quantities of goods and services available. In the case of a commodity preference function, we may write
$$W = b_1X_1 + b_2X_2 + \ldots + b_mX_m$$
where W again indexes social welfare. In the case of a social guide, we may write
$$W = c_1X_1 + c_2X_2 + \ldots + c_mX_m + d_1u_1 + d_2u_2 + \ldots + d_nu_n$$

first rises to power in a hitherto unplanned and traditionally distribution-oriented economy. If the planner seeks to impose his production-oriented preferences on the system, we would not expect him to be completely successful at first. Rather, a social guide would probably emerge as a synthesis of traditional and planner's goals. The course followed by the economy would then reflect this comprise. Once the new planner establishes control, the system may then become largely production-oriented.

Generalizing the above, we may say that the social guide will often arise as a consequence of two kinds of decision making from the point of view of the persons affected by the decision. The first kind, which we may call *individual* decision making, exists when an individual actor decides for himself and himself only. In such situations, the "common interest," even the individual's stake in the common interest, is not likely to be a salient motive in his behavior. He is unlikely to view his actions in a social context. Most market-oriented decision making would give us an example. If all economic and political decision making were like this, anarchy would prevail, and society would almost certainly degenerate into chaos. But if by some miracle it did not, a weighted sum or average of the preferences of individual actors would probably guide the economy. Each weight would indicate the relative importance of a particular actor's preferences in guiding production and distribution.

No society has ever existed for long in which all economic decision making was of a purely private nature. Some decisions always refer to the common interest and to the stake that various individuals have in this. Thus we are led to *collective* or *group* decision making, wherein one or several individuals in a group make a decision that they expect will bind others besides themselves to the course of action that the group decides upon. Some notion of the common interest of group members is then much more likely to be pushed to the fore.

When the group in question comprises the whole of society, we speak of "social decision making." Voting gives us an example of this, but so does a planner–dictator deciding to industrialize with savings forced out of agriculture or any government undertaking policies to stimulate output and employment. The adjective, "social" tells us only that a collectivity is affected by the decision taken. (The same is true of social welfare.) Because some decisions are social (or collective) whereas others are private, any basically market economy may have production in addition to welfare goals.

It need not be irrational for a man to vote for stiffer traffic fines and then run a red light on his way from the voting booth to an important engagement. In the first instance, he is participating in a collective decision in which his stake in the common interest is salient. The most productive way for him to raise his own welfare is by helping to raise social welfare in such a way that he can share in the increase. Afterward, he makes a purely private decision in which thoughts of the common interest are readily dismissed if they arise at all. The individual does not feel, in this instance, that his own welfare is tied to a concept of social well-being, although we might be able to dispute the matter with him.

Finally, a system could have many goals that are not easily expressed in terms of production or individual welfares. A planner may have a taste for power and, in consequence, seek to build a highly centralized, authoritarian system. The operation of such an economy may be virtually inexplicable until this factor is taken into account. By the same token, our analysis indicates that we sometimes confuse goals with means. For example, efficiency is not really an end in itself but a means of achieving other goals, notably the ones discussed above.

Similarly, the goal of full employment can often be identified with production and distribution goals. It only becomes a separate goal when the economy is willing to sacrifice production or the welfares of some individuals to provide employment for others. For example, "In Sweden, notice of a layoff must be given 60 days in advance. In the Netherlands, certain layoffs require the permission of the director of the local employment office. In West Germany, 30 to 60 days' notice must be given of a layoff exceeding a specified fraction of the firm's work force." [27] These countries are willing to pursue full employment even if some workers become temporarily redundant from time to time and have to live indirectly off the productive efforts of others. The same appears to be less true in North America.

By now the reader may feel that he needs a score card to keep track of rational behavior, and Table 2–1 provides this.

2–6   The Evolution of Systems

Not only is the fashion in which an economy evolves over time worthy of study in its own right, but it may be argued that the purely static features of a system can only be properly understood within a dynamic context. The usual sort of static economic analysis sometimes gives misleading results because it concentrates on just a part of the total picture. For instance, a common argument from macroeconomic analysis claims that a laissez-faire economy will always tend toward full employment when conditions are "right." However, it can be shown that, under these same right conditions, a system may not tend to follow a full-employment path of economic development over time. The usual discussion is phrased in purely static terms.

Another example relates to what might be called the general problem of entry. It is well known that the pricing and output policies of firms in many industries cannot be understood just by looking at the industry's present structure. The threat of entry by other firms or the threat of government regulation will tend to keep output higher and price lower than it otherwise would be. Similarly, one might not be able to explain a planner's behavior purely by

---

[27] Daniel B. Suits, *Principles of Economics* (New York: Harper, 1970), p. 140.

Table 2-1.   Three concepts of rational behavior.

Kind of Rationality	*Applying to*	*Embedded in*	*Basis*
Micro-rationality	Individual parts of the system	Individual preference function	Psychological perspective of household
Macro-rationale	System as a whole	Social preference function, here appearing as a planners' preference function and taking one of the following forms: 1. Social welfare function (welfare-oriented) 2. Commodity preference function (output-oriented) 3. Social guiding function (output- and welfare-oriented)	Psychological perspective of planner and/or a synthesis, by the planner, of micro-oriented preferences, "Utility," however, is defined as a function of statistical indicators of economic performance rather than of goods and services physically consumed.
Macro-rationality	System as a whole	Social preference function, here synthesized from individual preferences without going through a planning intermediary (same three preference functions as above)	A synthesis of micro- and, perhaps, macro-oriented preferences (i.e., of a would-be planner)

looking at what appear to be his basic goals in conjunction with the system's structure, technology, and resource endowments. The threat of replacement or, more generally, of the emergence or strengthening of unfriendly poles of power will inevitably influence his macrorationale. As the analysis switches from a static to a dynamic context, the notion of an economic system as a whole greater than the sum of its parts becomes increasingly important. Dynamic analysis draws our attention to the network of relations among the parts of a system and to the manner in which this evolves.

In this context we may distinguish two broad categories of economic change, which we label *outcome* and *process-oriented* change, respectively. The former refers specifically to the performance of the economy as measured by standard economic indicators. As such, it is an evolving what, how, and for whom through time. Of the two, outcome-oriented change comes closest to describing what we intuitively mean by "economic development," although within the boundaries of our definition, it could as easily mean increasing equality in the distribution of wealth as increasing GNP per capita.

On the other hand, process-oriented change refers specifically to the nature of an economic system. It comprises efforts to adapt an economy (or for the system to adapt itself) in order to pursue a particular set of goals more efficiently. This may follow a change in social goals or the discovery or emergence of new constraints on economic activity. For example, much of the concern over pollution stems from the discovery that fresh air and clean water are not free goods. They are scarce, like most other commodities, in the sense that their supply is limited and a cost must be paid to have more of them.

Similarly, in North America, access to the spectrum of radio waves has been allocated as if it were a free good to anyone who appeared to be qualified in the eyes of a custodial government agency. For awhile it may indeed have seemed so vast that the question of scarcity did not arise. But, at present, the consequence of this policy is a silent crisis in which (among other things)

Police and other public safety radio services in major metropolitan areas may be unable to obtain vital spectrum resources, while those resources allocated to others [for example, forestry services] go unused in the same area. [Consequently] electrical interference, congestion, and resultant spectrum scarcities threaten to make air, ground and sea travel slower and less safe; construction, distribution, mining, and manufacturing more costly; data transmission and information processing networks harder to develop for wide use; and some potential advances in education, law enforcement, and national security difficult to realize.[28]

The value to society of the entire radio spectrum is not nearly as high as it could be because, in many instances, no one really knows what are the relative social values of different uses to which parts of it might be put, or, within uses, the relative values of the services performed by different broadcasters. The prime function of a market here would be to provide reasonably precise answers to these questions while moving the spectrum into the hands of the highest-value users.

Still other examples of the need to adapt will arise in circumstances in which past performance has been deemed unsatisfactory in some respect. When firms do not meet their economic targets, when an economy's growth rate falls off or unemployment mounts, frictions will arise between economic actors, and pressure for streamlining the system will be created. Indeed, this is one way in which the structure and functioning of any economy interact. Poor performance will result in pressure for corrective action.

Such action may or may not require significant changes in an economy's institutions or information structure. When it does, an adaptable economy may be ill-suited to solve the underlying problems when they first appear, but its structure and institutions will then evolve so that it can cope within a rea-

----

[28] Quoted by Harvey J. Levin in "Spectrum Allocation Without Market," *American Economic Review,* May 1970, p. 209.

sonably short time period. In the case of pollution, this would mean supplementing the market with commands and incentives. In the case of a radio spectrum, it would imply replacing a command-allocating mechanism with a regulated market.

Ideally, the necessary structural adjustment would occur in semiautomatic fashion, much like a built-in stabilizer (such as a progressive income tax) is supposed to smooth out business-cycle fluctuations. A key feature of an adaptable economy is therefore a feedback mechanism, capable of automatically monitoring any problem and its apparent causes. The output of this device would include enough information to enable an administrator, or an automatic control mechanism, to bring about timely corrective action, including necessary structural change. Unfortunately, no economy in practice has yet approached this degree of perfection.

Sometimes, a government may be uncertain about the exact economic goals it wishes to pursue. These will then be ill-defined or emerge only gradually in the face of a turbulent environment. The behavior of an economic system and of its individual actors in the face of this turbulence and uncertainty constitutes a second dimension of process-oriented change. For an example, we invite interested readers to survey the literature on the economic turmoil in the Soviet Union during the 1920s, including the Soviet industrialization debates.[29]

Table 2-2 charts process-oriented change in the six socialist economies whose systems have undergone the greatest amount of evolution over the twentieth century.[30] We imagine each system moving through a spectrum of *socialist* economies whose center is the Soviet-type command economy (or the "Stalinist System") circa 1950. Pole Y is a highly decentralized market socialism (or the Yugoslav model). Pole X combines a command economy with a commitment to such things as continuing revolution, equality, ideological correctness, loyalty over expertise as the prime factor in selecting decision makers, moral over material incentives, and commitment to world revolution over peaceful coexistence.

In its extreme form, process-oriented change is a revolution in progress, but even when it is evolutionary we should distinguish those reforms which lead to fundamental systemic change, such as marketization of a command economy, and vice versa. (These are marked by asterisks in Table 2-2.)

2-7   Convergence

Let us loosely define the *environment* of an economic system to consist of its resource endowments, its geography, its prevailing culture and technology,

[29] See, in particular, Alexander Erlich, *The Soviet Industrialization Debate, 1924-28* (New York: Cambridge U.P., 1960). See, as well, M. Dobb, *Soviet Economic Development Since 1917* (New York, International Publishers, 1948); and Nicolas Spulber, *Soviet Strategy for Economic Growth* (Bloomington, Ind.: Indiana U.P., 1964).

[30] See Carmelo Mesa-Lago, "A Continuum Model to Compare Socialist Systems Globally," Pittsburgh, University of Pittsburgh, Oct. 1971 (mimeo).

Table 2-2. Cyclical and linear evolution of six socialist systems.

___

Cyclical Evolution in the U.S.S.R.

1918–1920	War communism (movement toward pole X) *
1921–1928	New economic policy (movement toward pole Y) *
1929–1953	Stalinist era (movement to center) *
1953–1964	Some moderation in Stalinist system of command planning (slight movement toward pole Y)
1964–1968	Economic reform (faster movement toward Y)
1968 on	Softening in the application of the reform (some movement back toward the center)

Cyclical Evolution in China

1953–1957	Application of Stalinist system (of command planning) *
1958–1960	Great Leap Forward (movement to pole X)
1961–1965	Return to moderation (movement back toward center } *, †
1966–1968	Great Proletarian Cultural Revolution (movement to pole X)
1969 on	Signs of moderation (movement toward center)

Cyclical Evolution in Cuba

1961–1963	Application of Stalinist system *
1963–1966	Testing some economic reforms (movement toward pole Y)
1966–1968	Revolutionary offensive (movement toward pole X) *
1969 on	Signs of moderation (slight movement toward center)

Linear Evolution in Yugoslavia

1947–1949	Application of Stalinist system *
1950–1953	First economic reform; abandonment of command planning (movement toward pole Y) *
1953–1961	Implementation of market socialism
1961–1965	New changes and discussion
1965 on	Second economic reform and reappearance of laissez faire (acceleration toward pole Y) *

Cyclical Evolution in Czechoslovakia

1948–1956	Application of Stalinist system *
1956–1961	Mild economic reform (movement toward pole Y)
1962–1966	Political liberalization, discussion of reform (further movement toward Y)
1966–1968	New economic model (approaching pole Y) *
1968 on	Soviet invasion (movement back toward the center)

(Largely) Linear Evolution in Hungary

1949–1953	Application of Stalinist system *
1953–1954	"New economic policy" of moderation and tolerance (some movement toward Y)

Table 2-2 (cont.)

1955–1956	Partial return to austerity and ambitious industrialization (movement toward center), culminating in the uprising of Oct. 1956; Imre Nagy, exponent of "softer" line, executed
1957–1961	Restoration and collectivization in agriculture (if anything, movement toward center)
1962–1967	Industrial reorganization, with some relaxation of central controls and decentralization of responsibility (probably slight movement toward Y)
1968 on	Transition to "new economic mechanism" (faster movement toward Y) *

Source (for all countries but Hungary): Carmelo Mesa-Lago, "A Continuum Model to Compare Socialist Systems Globally," Pittsburgh, University of Pittsburgh, Oct. 1971 (mimeo). This article is tentatively scheduled for publication in the July 1973 edition of *Economic Development and Cultural Change.*

* Major systemic change.
† In China, two distinct tendencies have been superimposed upon one another: Economic decision making (or administrative control) progressively centralized, following the end of the civil war in 1949, until 1957. With the Great Leap Forward in 1958, it began to *de*centralize and has more or less continued to decentralize since. But political control has oscillated between ideological extremism, notably during the Great Leap Forward and the Proletarian Cultural Revolution, and greater stress on expertise and production efficiency.

and its world position with regard to each of these factors vis-à-vis other economies. Then, one hypothesis says that, given sufficient stability in its environment and in its basic social goals, any economy has a long-run tendency to develop the most efficient information structure for translating these goals into reality. In cybernetics language, any system has a tendency to "learn," and we shall therefore call this the "learning hypothesis."

The learning hypothesis says, broadly, that under favorable conditions, any country's economic system will eventually evolve into something that depends only upon its economic environment and the social preferences that guide it. Under less favorable conditions, ideology, entrenched interests, inability to learn, and other factors will substantially impede this.

To our way of thinking, the learning hypothesis is a superior alternative to the famous convergence thesis. The latter says that, ultimately, all economic systems will converge along broad lines and become basically alike. In our terminology, all economic systems would come to have basically the same information structure. However, there appears to be no reason for this to occur unless one could design a sort of supersystem that was best for pursuing all kinds of goals in all kinds of environments from India to Canada.

Such a supersystem would be an economy capable of adapting instantly and costlessly to the efficient pursuit of any goals whatsoever without having to undergo additional major changes in its structure of information flows. From one point of view, the convergence thesis is similar to a strong learning hypothesis. The latter states that, in the very long run, every real-world economy will evolve to the point where it always adjusts rapidly to efficient goal pursuit, despite any changes in its goals or environment. This may require all economic systems to converge to a unique type of supersystem, but if supersystems are not unique, we should not be choosy.

The above ideas are important, if only because the notion of a best economic system is usually conveyed in purely static terms. But any economy must be at least partly judged on the way in which it evolves over time and, in particular, upon its ability to adapt and to learn. Other things being equal, more adaptable economies are better than less adaptable ones. When other things are not equal (as, in fact, they rarely are), adaptability remains one relevant criterion for assessing economic performance.

2–8 The Fundamental Question of Comparative Economic Systems

The idea of an economic organization adapting itself to pursue a particular set of goals more efficiently points to two fundamental problems that must be faced in any system. (We may also view these as two component parts of the over-all economic problem of allocating scarce resources among competing ends.)

To begin with, it has the task of functioning as efficiently as possible. We shall say in Chapter 3 that an organization is (completely) efficient whenever it is impossible to make one member better off without simultaneously making another worse off. Efficiency is a relatively weak criterion inasmuch as there is no way of comparing two efficient situations, one of which associates with, for example, a more equal distribution of welfare. Nevertheless, efficiency can be defined without reference to social goals or value judgements in most cases, and this is a principal reason for its appeal.

Efficiency likewise relates only to behavior at the level of the parts of an economic system. When we turn to systems as wholes, we find ourselves face to face with the second fundamental problem of economic organization—that of defining goals, adapting the system to pursue these effectively, and pursuing them. The second problem is not unrelated to efficiency—other things being equal, we can identify increased efficiency with more effective goal pursuit. But other things are not always the same. It will sometimes be desirable to neglect efficiency, at least temporarily, in order to anchor the system onto a new path of economic development.

With this in mind, we may now pose the fundamental question of comparative economic systems as follows: How should a particular economy be organized so as to maximize a *specific definition* of social welfare? Normally, such a question will have two variables—the definition of social welfare and the environment within which the social preference function is to be applied.

If we were to exclude the italicized words, we would get an entirely different question. For maximizing social welfare, as embodied in whatever goals a society happens to pursue, is really a question of maximizing efficiency only.

On the other hand, when we have two sets of social preferences to contrast, say the present set and a set advocated by a potential governing body, we can ask whether a best way exists of reorienting the system should the government change hands. This economics of goal pursuit breaks with the traditional emphasis on efficiency alone, but it is absolutely essential if we are to understand how some organizational forms arise at all.

We have said that market economies generally have a greater static efficiency potential than command economies.[31] By contrast, commands give a strong EPC direct leverage over the use and movement of large quantities of resources. If we were betting, we would not try to explain the emergence of command planning mechanisms on static efficiency grounds. Rather, we would emphasize their merits as vehicles through which a central authority can apply pressure when a market economy would tend to veer away from the path that an EPC is trying to maintain. A command economy is essentially a collection of readily accessible vertical channels through which a central planner can initiate orders, backed by incentives and penalties, to the producing sector.

Markets, on the other hand, allow for more individual initiative and break up the gigantic economic problem facing society as a whole into many infinitely smaller subproblems for each household and firm. However, there are limits on the extent to which a central planner can counter the collective preferences of many households and managers within a predominantly market context. Within any given time period there are also limits on a market economy's ability to shuffle resources from one industry or geographical region to another. These limits are more constraining the more likely is the reorientation to lead to bottlenecks in entrepreneurial talent, skilled labor, or plant capacity.

The ability of the market mechanism to serve as a vehicle for steering an economy depends upon the structure of priorities and also upon how radical are the proposed breaks with past performance. In those areas in which an abrupt re-orientation is required, it may be necessary to mobilize resources, to obtain direct leverage over their allocation, and even to use coercion. If we have a strong planning authority, this can best be done within a command framework of centralized decision making which is also able to stretch managerial talent over a wider variety of economic activities. The use of this framework will probably lead to a serious loss of efficiency, but it will still prove advisable if the proposed changes are urgent enough according to the social preferences being applied.

Later, once the economy is firmly anchored onto the new path, efficiency will become a more important consideration. Then, an increased use of markets coupled with greater decentralization in economic decision making suggests itself. A potential danger is that by then an entrenched bureaucracy may have a vested interest in preventing structural changes. If so, reform is likely

---

[31] However, if we consider dynamic efficiency, the first part of this statement only holds without qualification when we are assured that the government of a market economy can control the boom and bust of the business cycle.

to prove difficult, whether we are talking about reorganizing production and distribution activity in Eastern Europe, or reordering federal priorities for spending in the United States or Canada.

REFERENCES

Ames, Edward. *Soviet Economic Processes.* Homewood, Ill.: Richard D. Irwin, Inc., 1965, Ch. 14.

Balassa, Bela. "Success Criteria for Economic Systems," Ch. 1 in Morris Bornstein, ed., *Comparative Economic Systems: Models and Cases,* rev. ed. Homewood, Ill.: Richard D. Irwin, Inc., 1969.

Goldman, Marshall. *The Spoils of Progress: Environmental Pollution in the Soviet Union.* Cambridge, Mass.: MIT Press, 1972.

Greniewski, H. *Cybernetics Without Mathematics.* Elmsford, N.Y.: Pergamon Press, Inc., 1960.

Kuhn, A. *The Study of Society.* Homewood, Ill.: Richard D. Irwin, Inc., 1963.

Lange, Oskar. *Wholes and Parts.* Elmsford, N.Y.: Pergamon Press, Inc., 1965.

McManus, John C. "The Organization of Production," Working Paper 71-05, Ottawa, Carleton University, Department of Economics, June 1971.

Murphy, R. E., Jr. *Adaptive Processes in Economic Systems.* New York: Academic Press, Inc., 1965.

Nove, Alec. *Economic Rationality and Soviet Politics.* New York, Praeger Publishers, Inc., 1964.

Suits, Daniel B. *Principles of Economics.* New York: Harper & Row, Publishers, 1970, Chs. 7, 27.

Chapter **3**

Rational Behavior in an
Economic System: Efficiency

3–1   Introduction

Poets and philosophers may believe that man is basically irrational (and woman, too), but economists do not. By and large, they have tended to base their investigations on the premise that man behaves rationally. Perhaps surprisingly, this often turns out to be a useful assumption to make, and one reason for this may be what is known as the "law of large numbers." For it hardly seems unreasonable to think of much *ir*rational behavior as being essentially random in nature and canceling over large groups. This is why consumption for a whole country might be considered solely a function of personal wealth, although the amount that a particular family will want to spend in any year will depend partly upon such things as the buying mood of the household.

We shall not always assume that economic actors behave rationally in this volume, but we shall take rationality as a point of departure, whether we are dealing with decision making that applies to a whole economy or to one of its parts. Thus we need to investigate the concept of rational decision making, and the next two chapters are devoted to this.

The first step in our journey is to note that rational behavior has two faces, which must be kept separate. These are *efficiency,* to be examined in the present chapter, and *optimality,* to be explored in the next. As we shall soon discover, efficiency deals with the various parts of an economic system, and, in consequence, is closely linked with the concept of *micro*rationality introduced in Chapter 2. It refers only to the maximizing behavior of *individual* economic actors. Optimality, by contrast, is a stronger condition, applying to the system as a whole. As such, it is usually linked to a specific social preference function.

Consequently, we can normally talk about an *efficient* solution to the economic problem without specifying goals for the economy as a whole. But an optimal solution can only be defined with respect to given goals. Moreover, with respect to a particular set of goals, it is not always true that an efficient solution to the economic problem is preferable to an inefficient one. The reverse may easily hold.

3–2   The Concept of Economic Efficiency

In Chapter 0 we introduced the problem of allocating scarce resources among competing ends—the "economic problem." This problem has three parts, usually labeled "what," "how," and "for whom." Correspondingly, a *solution* to the economic problem can be defined in terms of a particular assortment of goods to be produced, a particular allocating or distribution of inputs among society's various production processes, and a particular distribution of goods among consumers. There are both efficient and inefficient ways of doing each of these things.

Efficiency in Production

Efficiency refers to *how* goods and services will be produced. Primarily, it deals with how such inputs as labor, land, and capital shall be allocated or distributed among the economy's various production processes. Production is efficient when it is impossible to produce more of one good or service without reducing the output of some other. If labor and capital could be reallocated among firms or industries so as to produce more of at least one good with no decrease in the output of any other, production would *not* be efficient.

Efficiency in production is the condition for any economic system to be on its production-possibility frontier. The reader may observe this in Figure 3–1 by picking a point inside the frontier, such as *B,* and noting that one may move toward it either in a completely horizontal or a completely vertical direction. By contrast, a horizontal or vertical move from a point on the frontier, such as *A,* will take us into the unachievable region.

Efficiency in Consumption

Loosely speaking, production efficiency asks how we should allocate and use available quantities of inputs so as to get the most output from them. Suppose, next, that we have produced a given bundle of goods and services. We may then ask how to distribute these among households so as to get the most

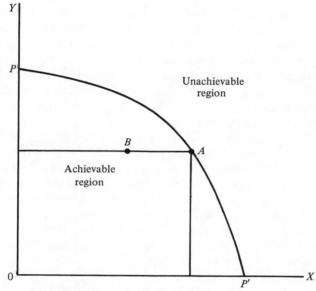

Figure 3–1. The production-possibility frontier (PP′).

welfare. In part, this is a question of what the distribution of welfare in society ought to be and, as such, is postponed until Chapter 4.

But we can also ask a more mundane question. Goods must be distributed among consumers whose preferences will normally differ. The bundle that each household receives, whether large or small, ought to match its tastes. Otherwise, a redistribution of a given economy-wide bundle of goods could make some households better off without making any others worse off. We shall say that consumption is efficient whenever it is no longer possible to do this.

Suppose, for example, that I have three bottles of wine and one loaf of bread; you have three loaves and one bottle. If we would be happier with two loaves and two bottles each, efficiency in consumption requires us to swap. We again consider leisure and savings to be "consumed," and we also take note of the fact that people derive positive or negative satisfaction from their work. (Generally speaking, Marxist economists tend to place more emphasis on conditions of work and less on goods consumed as a source of welfare than do most Western economists.)

Thus, if it is possible for some households to work and earn more while others work less and enjoy more leisure, and if this would make some people better off and no one worse off, efficiency in consumption does not prevail. Neither does it hold if individuals could switch occupations to their mutual benefit or arrange some package of changes in wages and working conditions that would make some better óff and none worse off.

Efficient Coordination of Production and Consumption

Suppose that production and consumption are both efficient. By reallocating inputs among production processes (which changes the *mix* of goods and services being produced) and simultaneously redistributing the fruits of production among society's members, it may still be possible to make someone better off in terms of material welfare without making anyone else worse off. We shall say, therefore, that efficiency in distribution prevails when such an improvement cannot take place. Distributive efficiency refers to the efficient *coordination* of production and consumption.

When all three kinds of efficiency prevail, we shall say that the economic problem is being efficiently solved. Economic efficiency will mean, in other words, that it is impossible to make one economic actor better off without making someone else worse off in the process. No redistribution of goods and services, no reallocation of productive inputs, no alteration of the mix of goods and services being produced will be able to bring this about.

Normally, there will be many efficient solutions to a society's economic problem, and the collection of all of them together constitutes its *efficiency* frontier. The efficiency frontier is analogous to a production-possibility frontier, except that the former presupposes efficiency in consumption and distribution, as well as in production. We have graphed two examples in Figures 3–2(a) and (b) for simple societies with only two people (all we can handle on two-dimensional paper). In each case the material welfare of the first person (U_1) is plotted along the vertical axis and the welfare of the second is measured on the horizontal axis. The efficiency frontier is the solid outer boundary.

Along it, neither individual can be made better off except at the other's expense. Thus the frontier must slope down, for if it was upward-sloping or horizontal, a movement along it would make at least one household better off without making anyone worse off. The efficiency frontier may slope down continuously from top to bottom as in Figure 3–2(a), but it may also stop, break off, and then start again further on as in Figure 3–2(b). In comparison with the production-possibility frontier, it may not be well behaved at all. Nevertheless, we can say that points inside it represent achievable but inefficient combinations of welfare for society's members. Welfare combinations beyond the efficiency frontier are not achievable, given current tastes, technology, and resource endowments.[1]

---

[1] Points along the dashed boundary in Figure 3–2(b) are *not* achievable. Otherwise this boundary would be part of the efficiency frontier, which would then slope upward. However, along with the efficiency frontier, it does separate the achievable from the unachievable regions.

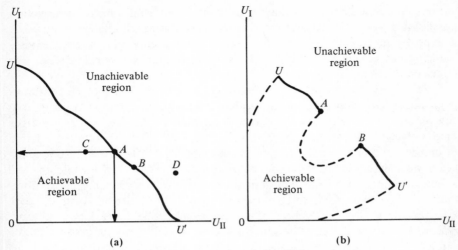

Figure 3-2. Two examples of the efficiency frontier.

Sometimes the efficiency frontier is called a *Pareto frontier,* after the Italian economist Vilfredo Pareto, who first described it. Likewise, economic efficiency is often labeled *Pareto optimality.* In the same vein, it is said that the economy is at a "Pareto optimum" or a "Pareto optimal" position when economic efficiency prevails. Probably no more unfortunate nomenclature could have been invented because many economically efficient positions will normally exist which are far from being optimal. As noted above, the distinction between efficiency and optimality is crucial.

Indeed, the very definition of economic efficiency rules out any *comparison* of individual welfares. Consequently, there is no basis upon which to aggregate or synthesize these welfares to get either a definition of social welfare or a social ordering of all the various mixes of goods and services that society might be able to produce. We are not able to define an optimal solution to the economic problem. The latter is only forthcoming when we pass from the parts of the system to the whole and orient the economy in a direction determined by a notion of macrorationale or macrorationality. Our immediate task, however, will be to explore the various aspects of economic efficiency in more detail.

To this end we shall now derive one rule for each of the three kinds of efficiency just described. These rules will not always ensure that the type of efficiency in question prevails, but they are well-known efficiency prerequisites.

3-3   Efficiency in Production

The natural starting point for a discussion of economic efficiency is the "how" problem. How should productive inputs be utilized so that production is carried on efficiently? At this stage we are not going to worry too much about producing efficiently *within* particular mines, mills, factories, and farms. Rather, we shall be concerned about how resources are allocated *among* the various production processes that, in the aggregate, define society's production possibilities. As indicated above, production will be called efficient only when it is no longer possible to produce more of one good without simultaneously reducing the output of some other by shifting resources around between different production processes.

We should also point out, in beginning, that the idea of moving resources from one production process to another has to be understood broadly. We can physically move inputs—or move production to the site of a plant. Over time, however, we can also increase the capital stock in one industry relative to that in another by concentrating our investment in the first industry. Similarly, we can allow the labor force in one industry to grow while that in another declines or remains constant. In practice this is probably, more often than not, how resources are effectively "shifted." For example, over the past 40 years or so the production of houses has become more labor-intensive *relative* to the production of automobiles, even though very few resources have actually been switched physically out of one industry and into the other.

To fix ideas, let us assume, at first, that we are dealing with a market economy. Here a certain kind of labor, L, and capital equipment, K, are both used to help make several goods, including wine, X, and bread, Y. The idea behind efficiency in production is that units of each particular input should always go to those production processes where they will be most productive. If labor is more productive in making bread than wine, some labor should be reallocated from wine to bread production. Before we can make this idea precise, however, we need a suitable measure of productivity.

Since we are not usually interested in shutting down or starting up whole industries, our productivity measure should indicate the effect of adding or subtracting a few units of any input to or from a given production process. This leads us to the idea of *marginal physical product*. The marginal physical product of any input is the increase (or decrease) in total output *per unit* of a small increase (or decrease) in the use of that input with the amounts of all other inputs held fixed.

Marginal physical products may be looked upon as physical measures of the productive values of inputs. We shall use the symbol MPP to denote marginal physical product. MPP_{LX} will be the marginal physical product of labor in producing wine, MPP_{KY} will be the marginal physical product of capital in producing bread, and so on.

Next we must convert our physical measure to a value measure of productivity. Let P_X and P_Y be the prices of wine and bread. Then the value of the marginal physical product of labor in producing wine is P_X times MPP_{LX}. This is the total amount of money for which MPP_{LX} will sell. For example, if an additional unit of labor can add five bottles of wine to each day's production, and the price of wine is $2.50 per bottle, the value of this marginal product is $12.50. We shall use the symbols VMP_{LX}, VMP_{KY}, and so on, to stand for values of marginal products. Each VMP equals the price of the product times the relevant MPP.

Figures 3–3(a) and (b) show curves relating the values of labor's marginal products in making wine and bread to the amounts of labor used in each, with the amounts of all other inputs held fixed. Because of the law of diminishing returns, such a curve must eventually slope down. As we add more and more of one input to fixed amounts of others, the value of the additional output produced eventually becomes less and less.

The reader may imagine a fixed plot of land to which we keep adding additional tillers or a given factory outfitted with machinery to which we keep adding additional workers. Eventually, the effect of this may even be to

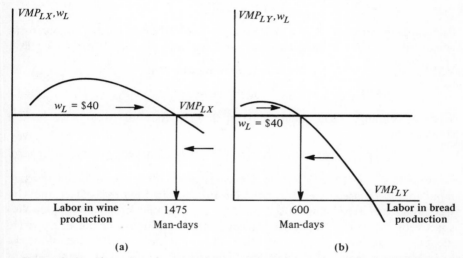

Figure 3–3.   The value of an input's marginal product and its efficient rate of use.

reduce output. That is, the value of labor's marginal product would become negative, and the same is true of other inputs and other production processes. It can be shown that the value of an input's marginal product is an appropriate measure of its benefit within each production process that uses it.

The price or wage paid to each input measures its cost. In Figures 3–3(a) and (b) this is $40 per day. Now suppose that the value of an input's marginal product in Figure 3–3(a) exceeds the wage rate being paid to it. A *cost-benefit analysis* then tells us to use more of the input, for the value that additional units will create exceeds their cost. The difference is a net gain to society. Similarly, when the value of an input's marginal product is less than its price, a cost-benefit analysis tells us to use less of it. The units of the input that are discharged were creating less value than it cost to employ them.

We therefore conclude that the input should be hired approximately to the point where its price equals the value of its marginal product. Let VMP_{LX} be the value of labor's marginal product in producing wine and VMP_{LY} be the value of labor's marginal product in producing bread. In each case we are dealing with the same kind of labor, whose wage we denote by W_L. Then efficiency in production requires that

$$\text{VMP}_{LX} = W_L$$

$$\text{VMP}_{LY} = W_L$$

However, efficiency does *not* allow there to be two different wage rates for the same kind of labor in two different industries. Therefore, VMP_{LX} and VMP_{LY} must be made equal since they must both be made equal to the wage rate, W_L, and this gives us

$$\text{VMP}_{LX} = \text{VMP}_{LY}$$

Generalizing, suppose that a particular type of labor is used in many firms where the values of its marginal products are labeled VMP_{L1}, VMP_{L2}, VMP_{L3}, . . . , VMP_{Ln}. Then, efficiency requires that

$$\text{VMP}_{L1} = \text{VMP}_{L2} = \text{VMP}_{L3} = \cdot \cdot \cdot = \text{VMP}_{Ln} = W_L \qquad (3\text{--}1)$$

There is nothing magic about labor in this respect. For capital, we have a similar result:

$$\text{VMP}_{K1} = \text{VMP}_{K2} = \text{VMP}_{K3} = \cdot \cdot \cdot = \text{VMP}_{Kn} = W_K \qquad (3\text{--}2)$$

Equalities (3–1) and (3–2) are rules that indicate *how much* of each input should be used in each production process. In Figures 3–3(a) and (b) we should use 1,475 and 600 man-days in wine and bread production, respectively. Of course, the VMP curves for a given input are not likely to be identical from one industry to another. However, they must be cut off at the same height in each industry [$40 in Figures 3–3(a) and (b)] by the price of the input if efficiency is to prevail.

These input prices must be the same from one industry to another, so wage discrimination is not compatible with efficiency. Unless there is enough labor relative to other inputs to drive labor's VMP to zero in all industries—as could conceivably happen in a developing nation—unemployment is inconsistent with economic efficiency. Nevertheless, the VMP of a particular input will never rise above its going price in many firms. These firms should not use the input at all.

More generally, our discussion tells us that additional units of any input should always be used in those production processes where the values of their marginal products will be highest. When applied to investments, such a rule states that investible funds should be used to create those capital goods (or in those projects) whose expected yields are highest, with allowance made for risk and other factors.[2] These yields, in turn, measure the VMP's of capital goods in producing other goods.

---

[2] The higher the risk surrounding a proposed investment project, the higher the expected yield that ought to be required in compensation. This is subject to qualification, however, since investment risk can sometimes be reduced in a manner to be indicated later.

Should the supply of any input be exhausted before its VMP falls to the level given by its price or wage rate, producers anxious to get more of the input will bid up its price. When the market is working well, input prices serve as rationing devices, allocating each factor of production to those occupations where their VMP's are highest. The highest VMP's translate into the highest wage offers. For example, if a specific type of labor leaves an industry in which its VMP is relatively low and responds to a higher wage offer by moving into an industry in which its VMP is relatively high, the VMP's of labor in the two industries move closer together. We move up one VMP curve in Figure 3–3 and down the other. It is this process that causes the VMP's of the same input in two different production processes to tend to equality.[3]

Finally, if we were trying to describe what anonymity means in symbols, we would use equalities just like (3–1) and (3–2). The VMPs relate specifically to the first, second, third, fourth, and so on, lines of production. But the market price signals, W_L and W_K, do not relate to a particular sender or receiver. If different messages were being sent to different producers, we would need to write $(W_{L1}, W_{L2}, \ldots, W_{Ln})$, and $(W_{K1}, W_{K2}, \ldots, W_{Kn})$, and our wage rates would lose their anonymity.

We now know a little bit more about why anonymous prices are desirable. The VMPs in (3–1) and (3–2), which may pertain to a multitude of diverse economic activities, must be brought together if economic efficiency is to prevail. This, in turn, suggests trying to coordinate them through signals which are not addressed to any particular receiver and which then form the common denominators of the efficiency rules.

The above cost-benefit analysis implicitly assumes that the costs and benefits of using an input are the same for society as they are for the user or the supplier of the input. If the employing firm or the supplying labor union is a monopolist, this may not be true, as we shall see later when we discuss laissez faire. In Chapter 2 we introduced the notion of external effects in production and consumption, along with the distinction between social and private costs and benefits. We said, for example, that the cost to society of producing some item might depart from private costs as recorded by the producing firm.

When this is the case, efficiency requires that the *social* costs and benefits

---

[3] The VMP's of a particular type of labor may not equalize across two different geographical regions. Workers will inevitably attach some cost to moving, and this gives us an exception to equations (3–1). Thus the VMP of labor is usually lower in depressed areas. One suggested remedy is often to transfer individuals to more prosperous regions, but many people will feel strong ties to their present location. This gives us an exception to the equalization of VMP's, but we can still say that efficiency requires them to differ by no more than their transfer costs.

A second exception to the equalization of VMP's as a prerequisite for efficiency may occur when an individual prefers a job in which he has a lower VMP. A man with a higher VMP as a carpenter may nevertheless accept a job as a professor. But then efficiency requires that the difference in VMP's be at least offset by the higher nonpecuniary benefits of professorship to the person involved.

of using an input determine whether or how much of the input to use. The existence of externalities affects the way in which the marginal physical product and thus the VMP of an input ought to be measured. Going back to our example, suppose that K no longer refers to machinery, but rather to fluoride being used by a chemical plant. Assume, furthermore, that part of the fluoride input is emitted in the form of waste by the producer and that this waste destroys crops and livestock in the surrounding area, increasing the cost burden on farmers. Then the marginal product of the fluoride will have a positive internal component and a negative external component.

Both components should be taken into account by society in allocating resources. If the negative component is sufficiently large, it might be necessary to prohibit the chemical firm from operating. However, the firm's manager will not use social costs in his own reckoning until they have been internalized— that is, until private and social costs have become the same. It is part of the task of nonmarket instruments in any market economy to see that social costs are internalized.

When externalities are present, rules (3–1) and (3–2) must be modified to read

$$\text{VMSP}_{L1} = \text{VMSP}_{L2} = \text{VMSP}_{L3} = \cdots = \text{VMSP}_{Ln} = W_L \qquad (3\text{-}1a)$$
$$\text{VMSP}_{K1} = \text{VMSP}_{K2} = \text{VMSP}_{K3} = \cdots \text{VMSP}_{Kn} = W_K \qquad (3\text{-}2a)$$

where VMSP stands for the value of marginal social product. More precisely, VMSP_{L1} is a measure of the increase or decrease in the outputs of *all* goods when an additional unit of input L is added to the first production process, and VMSP_{K1}, VMPS_{L2}, and so on, are defined similarly. It is the corresponding values of marginal *social* products that economic efficiency requires input prices to mirror.

3–4 Production Efficiency in a Nonmarket Economy

What about production in a *non*market economy? In 1920 the Austrian economist Ludwig von Mises wrote a famous article, "Economic Calculation in the Socialist Commonwealth," [4] in which he argued that it was logically impossible for a socialist economy to coordinate its production activities in a rational, efficient manner. Von Mises was referring to a command type of economic planning model in which there would be no markets for *nonhuman* factors of production (that is, natural resources and capital equipment of all kinds).

As a matter of fact, blueprints for a *market* socialist economy were first offered by Oskar Lange in 1936 as a reply to von Mises' criticism.[5] The reply, in other words, was formulated in terms of a socialist economy that would

[4] Ludwig von Mises, "Economic Calculation in the Socialist Commonwealth," in F. A. Hayek, ed., *Collectivist Economic Planning* (London: Routledge, 1920).

[5] Oskar Lange, "On the Economic Theory of Socialism," in Benjamin F. Lippincott, ed., *On the Economic Theory of Socialism* (New York: McGraw-Hill, 1964).

have "markets" for these inputs. Lange's position was bolstered by Abba Lerner, and von Mises received support from Halm and Hayek.[6] The result was one of the great economic debates of the period between World Wars I and II.

Here we want to postpone any questions relating to the adequacy of market socialism in dealing with this issue. Instead, we want to look at von Mises' criticism within the context to which it was intended to apply. At the same time, we should note that it is not only within a command economy that markets for natural resources and intermediate goods may be lacking. Modern capitalist societies are characterized by huge vertically and horizontally integrated firms. U.S. Steel, for example, does not simply make steel from pig iron—it makes pig iron and even owns many iron ore mines. Under capitalism it often happens that one branch, department, or plant of a huge, multiplant corporation produces a product for another branch of the same corporation. The nature of the problem of finding a rational or efficient value for such a product is the same as it would be in a command economy, where the producing sector may, for many purposes, be looked upon as a single giant firm.

Turning to a critical examination of von Mises' challenge, therefore, let us go back and divide each term in rule (3-1) by the corresponding term in (3-2) to get

$$\frac{\text{VMP}_{L1}}{\text{VMP}_{K1}} = \frac{\text{VMP}_{L2}}{\text{VMP}_{K2}} = \frac{\text{VMP}_{L3}}{\text{VMP}_{K3}} = \cdots = \frac{\text{VMP}_{Ln}}{\text{VMP}_{Kn}} = \frac{W_L}{W_K}$$

By definition, the value of any input's marginal product equals the product price times the relevant MPP. In each of the above ratios the product price therefore cancels. (For example, the price of the first product cancels out of the ratio $\text{VMP}_{L1}/\text{VMP}_{K1}$.) Thus we may rewrite the above equalities to read

$$\left(\frac{\text{MPP}_{L1}}{\text{MPP}_{K1}} = \frac{\text{MPP}_{L2}}{\text{MPP}_{K2}} = \frac{\text{MPP}_{L3}}{\text{MPP}_{K3}} = \cdots = \frac{\text{MPP}_{Ln}}{\text{MPP}_{Kn}} \right) = \frac{W_L}{W_K} \qquad (3\text{-}3)$$

Whenever external effects are present, finally, it can be shown that we must modify (3-3) to read

$$\left(\frac{\text{MSPP}_{L1}}{\text{MSPP}_{K1}} = \frac{\text{MSPP}_{L2}}{\text{MSPP}_{K2}} = \frac{\text{MSPP}_{L3}}{\text{MSPP}_{K3}} = \cdots = \frac{\text{MSPP}_{Ln}}{\text{MSPP}_{Kn}} \right) = \frac{W_L}{W_K} \qquad (3\text{-}3a)$$

where MSPP denotes marginal social physical product and is defined analogously to VMSP.

The part of either (3-3) or (3-3a) lying between parentheses constitutes a set of conditions for efficiency in production that does not involve any prices

[6] See Abba Lerner, "Statics and Dynamics in Socialist Economics," *Economic Journal*, June 1937; reprinted in Abba Lerner, *Essays in Economic Analysis* (New York: Macmillan, 1953). See, as well, the articles by Halm and Hayek in Hayek, *Collectivist Economic Planning*, op. cit.

whatsoever. As a matter of fact, we could show that these equations are really more basic than (3-1), (3-1a), (3-2), and (3-2a). A more rigorous and fundamental discussion of efficiency than the present one would first derive (3-3) and then show how (3-1) and (3-2) evolve from this within a market economy.

Thus it is logically possible for a command economy to be efficient in production. We may think of (3-3) and (3-3a) as sets of equations expressing the productive capabilities of every potential input into every potential production process—literally, every potential "turn of the screw." In principle it makes no difference whether these equations are solved by the market interplay of supply and demand—which is supposed to align each ratio of marginal products on a common price ratio—or by a complex of computers. In fact, when the latter are able to solve the problem, they will yield, as part of the solution, a set of efficient "shadow" prices for all inputs.

But could a network of computers solve the problem in practice? Many of the marginal productivities will turn out to be complex mathematical expressions, when written out in full, particularly if external effects are present. Even without these, it becomes necessary to compare the usefulness of each input in producing diverse goods and services (apples, oranges, haircuts, and machine tools, for example) without the help of rational prices to indicate VMPs. It is far from clear that the necessary data could be gathered from all over the economy, processed, and put into equation form within the brief time period that would be available to the central planners for this purpose. After this was accomplished, it would still be necessary to solve the equations and enforce the resulting commands. However, production possibilities and tastes are also changing constantly, and the solution would probably be obsolete before it was reached.

Not surprisingly, then, the high ground to which von Mises and his supporters have retreated is fortified with the proposition that the economic problem is far too complex to be efficiently handled in a basically nonmarket context. We have already indicated that the information costs of a command economy are likely to be relatively high, but that it may still prove to be justifiable. Von Mises' proposition relates to the fundamental question of comparative economic systems on which we shall have more to say in Section 3-9 and in subsequent chapters.

3-5 Efficiency in Consumption

Fidel Castro introduced rationing into Cuba in March 1962. At first, quotas existed only for a few commodities, but these were progressively extended until they covered nearly every consumer good. A partial list of rationed goods, over the decade of the 1960s, appears as Table 3-1. We would add that most individuals who worked could expect to get some meals at their place of employment. Nevertheless, the most striking thing about the Cuban mechanism for distributing goods is the uniformity of the package

Table 3-1. Monthly quotas of selected rationed consumer goods in Cuba, 1962–1969 (in pounds).

	1962	1965–1967	1969
Per capita			
Meat	3	3	3
Fish	1	1–8	2
Rice	6	3	4
Beans	1.5	3–9	1.5
Turkeys	9	3–10	9
Fats	2	3	1
Milk	nq *	2	2
Butter	0.125	0.125	0.125
Eggs (units)	4	12	15
Sugar	nq	nq	6
Coffee	nq	0.375	0.375
Bread	nq	nq	15
Per family			
Detergent	1	1	1
Soap	2	2	2.5
Toilet paper (roll)	nq	1	1
Toothpaste	1	1	1
Cigars (units)	nq	nq	2
Malt (bottle)	nq	nq	2
Beer (bottle)	nq	2	1

Source: Reprinted from *Revolutionary Change in Cuba,* Carmelo Mesa-Lago, editor, by permission of the University of Pittsburgh Press. © 1971 by the University of Pittsburgh Press.
* nq, no quota.

alloted to each consumer. To an extent, this undoubtedly stems from a desire by the Cuban leadership to promote egalitarianism.

But, egalitarian or not, it is inefficient to give the same package of goods to each individual when different people have different tastes. Referring to the figures for 1969 in Table 3-1, suppose that individual *A* likes Cuban cigars, whereas *B* does not smoke but enjoys beer with his rice and beans. Then, just as in the case of Crusoe and Selkirk, the two men can probably arrange an exchange that will make *each* one better off. The problem with any rationing scheme is that no official can simultaneously peer into the minds of millions of households to read their preferences. He will therefore not allocate goods efficiently among them. Unless individuals are then allowed to trade their ration allotments with one another, efficiency in consumption will not prevail.

In fact, Cuban authorities do tolerate some trading in ration allotments, and it is said that the price of rice is surprisingly uniform across Havana. Figure 3-4 shows why this probably raises material welfare. We may think of it as a generalization of the Crusoe-Selkirk case to many households, each endowed with a fixed allotment of goods and services.

As in the case of Robinson Crusoe (Figure 1-1), we describe each Cuban household's preferences by means of indifference curves. These include the curves labeled I, II, and III plus a great many more which we have not drawn in. Each curve represents all the combinations of sugar and rice which will provide the household with a particular level of utility. (Because we have only two-dimensional paper to write on, we must ignore the other goods for purpose of illustration.) As these curves get farther and farther from the origin, they represent greater levels of satisfaction and thus form the equal-altitude contours of a utility or welfare mountain.

Once again, our household will seek to achieve the highest indifference curve that it can reach. Its ration allowance (in 1969) is 4 pounds of rice and 6

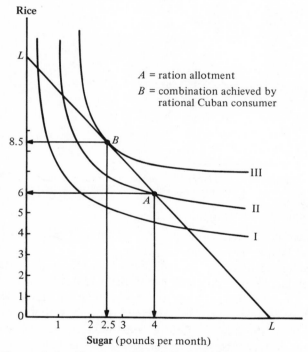

Figure 3—4. The gains from exchange under rationing.

pounds of sugar, described by the point, A, which leaves it on indifference curve II. By selling sugar and using the proceeds to buy rice, it can move upward along line LL'. By selling rice to buy sugar, it can move downward along LL'. Thus the line LL' describes all the combinations of rice and sugar that he can obtain, given his initial ration allotment and the market prices of rice and sugar.[7]

---

[7] Households may be able to buy additional quantities of sugar and rice on this market with money from their incomes. We ignore this possibility for the moment.

Because of his relative preference for rice, he would be rational to move from *A* to *B*, thereby improving his welfare from indifference curve II to III. Only by chance could a planner hope to put the individual at *B* to begin with. Once again, we see how the process of exchange can make people better off by matching their preferences more perfectly, even though no new goods are created. The only prerequisite is that tastes be complementary. Somewhere in Havana there must be a household willing to give up rice in exchange for sugar or for some other good that is available.

In a modern economy without rationing, it is possible to recast consumption efficiency in terms of what is called consumer choice. That is, we picture each household deciding upon an occupation, how to divide its time between work and leisure, and what assortment of goods and services, including savings or future consumption, to purchase with its income. If there is no price discrimination between households, if there is no problem with external effects, and if each household behaves rationally, the market will coordinate their behavior efficiently.

By implication, consumers are not fooled by advertising nor are they ignorant as to the nature of the goods they are buying. Instead, they are both informed and efficient in translating the information available to them into wise budget planning and occupational choice. However, even if they are not quite this good, the presence of a market mechanism will probably improve on the situation that would prevail otherwise.

The problem of consumer choice once again resembles that faced by Robinson Crusoe, with the notable difference that our household will now earn an income that he spends on goods and services. From all the combinations that he could buy, he must choose the one that maximizes his satisfaction. Returning to our wine-and-bread example, Figure 3-5 shows this. For simplicity, we suppose that he spends all his income on these two goods, although we shall relax this (obviously unrealistic) assumption shortly. Once again, he will try to reach the highest indifference curve. He is constrained in this endeavor by his limited income.

Line *LL'* in Figure 3-5 describes the household's income or budget constraint. More precisely, it passes through every combination of wine and bread that it can buy with the limited income available to spend on these goods. The farther the income constraint from the origin, the more the household can buy of all goods and services and the better off a rational household will be.

In Figure 3-5 it can afford the combination of 85 loaves of bread and 45 cases of wine at *A* and also the combinations indicated by *B* and *C*. It cannot reach the point *D*, however (representing approximately 85 cases of wine and 60 loaves of bread), within the time period in question. Subject to its budget constraint, therefore, the household maximizes its utility at *A*. We say that the household is rational whenever it moves to *A* rather than to another achievable point, such as *B* or *C*, which yields it a lower level of satisfaction.

We next draw attention to an important but not immediately obvious

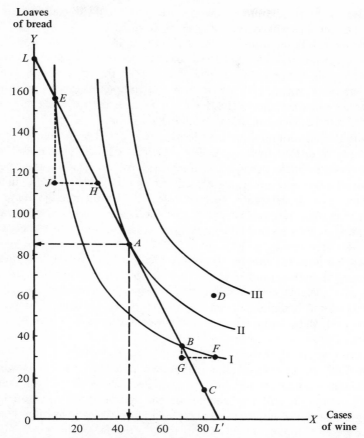

Figure 3—5. The rational consumer, subject to a budget constraint.

contrast between points *A* and *B* in Figure 3-5. At *B,* the budget line meets indifference curve I, and the two curves cross. At *A,* the budget line meets indifference curve II, and the curves meet but do *not* cross. Whenever curves meet without crossing, we say that they are *tangent.* Thus the household's budget constraint line is tangent to one of its indifference curves when and only when it reaches its highest achievable level of welfare.

At every other point, the budget line crosses an indifference curve, in-evitably one lower than II. We may therefore conceptualize the rational decision-maker-in-action as one who anticipates the welfare he will receive from alternative combinations of goods and services along his budget line. He moves mentally along this line, crossing higher and higher indifference curves by "trying out" different bundles, until he arrives at *A.* Should he move away from *A,* he will begin crossing lower curves, thus becoming worse off. This is his signal to move back.

At *A,* the steepness or slope of indifference curve II is the same as the slope of the budget constraint line. By contrast, indifference curve I is flatter than the budget line where the two cross at B and steeper where they cross at E. It is only at the point of tangency or greatest welfare that the two slopes are equal, and we now wish to investigate the meaning of this. To an economist the notion of slope is always bound up with the notion of tradeoff or of the terms of trade between two goods or goals. Here we are examining the tradeoffs between wine and bread, both on the market place and in providing satisfaction to the consumer. The former relates to the slope of the budget line, the latter to the slope of an indifference curve.

Suppose, then, that the household moves mentally down his budget line in Figure 3-5, trying to decide which combination of the two goods to buy. He is, in effect, giving up bread to get more wine. For example, when he moves from E to H, he exchanges the bundle of 10 cases of wine and 155 loaves of bread for 30 cases of wine and 115 loaves of bread. Conceptually, we may imagine that he first drops straight down to J by giving up 40 loaves of bread and then moves horizontally to H by receiving 20 cases of wine. For every 2 loaves of bread that he gives up, he can gain 1 case of wine, and we therefore say that the slope of the line equals -2. (The minus sign merely indicates that the line slopes down.) Formally, the slope of the budget line between E and H is defined to be (minus) the length of EJ divided by the length of JH, and the slope of the budget line remains the same from top to bottom.

On the other hand, if the household was able to trade 1 loaf of bread for 1 case of wine on the market, the slope of the budget line would be -1, and the line would be flatter. If 3 loaves of bread exchanged for 1 case of wine, the slope would be -3, and the line would be steeper. In all three cases the numerical value of the slope gives the market terms upon which the household can trade wine for bread, subject to a fixed purchasing power (or budget constraint). Consequently, the slope of the budget line must mirror the relative prices of bread and wine.

In fact, if 2 loaves of bread will exchange for 1 case of wine, wine must be twice as expensive as bread; if 1 loaf of bread exchanges for 1 case of wine, their prices are the same. Generally speaking, the slope of a budget line equals (minus) the price of the good plotted on the X axis divided by the price of the good along the Y axis, or

$$\text{slope of budget line} = -\frac{P_X}{P_Y}$$

To get an expression for the slope of an indifference curve, we must introduce the notion of *marginal utility*. The marginal utility of any good for a consumer is the increase (or decrease) in utility that the consumer receives per unit of any increase (or decrease) in consumption of the good in question with the consumption of all other goods remaining unchanged. It thus measures the consumption value of a good to a household in the same way that the marginal physical product measures the productive value of an input to a firm. Forgetting about the budget constraint for a moment, suppose that a household moves down one of the indifference curves in Figure 3-5. To be specific, suppose that it moves from B to F along curve I, consuming less bread and more wine in such a way as to remain at the same level of material welfare.

We may therefore say that the household is trading bread for wine in consumption. The terms upon which he can do this will be indicated by the slope of the indifference curve just as the market terms of trade are given by the slope of the budget line. We may conceptualize the move from B to F as a double move from B to G and then from G to F. When the household goes from B to G, it consumes less bread while keeping its consumption of other goods the same. Thus it loses an amount of welfare equal to the marginal utility of bread (written MU_Y) times the length of line segment BG, which measures the quantity of bread given up. In going from G to F, it gains an amount of utility equal to MU_X times GF.

Since material welfare is the same at B as at F, the amount lost between B and G will equal the amount gained between G and F. That is,

$$BG \text{ times } MU_Y = GF \text{ times } MU_X$$

As in the case of the budget line, the slope of the indifference curve between B and F is defined to be (minus) BG divided by GF. From the equalities above we derive

$$\frac{BG}{GF} = \frac{MU_X}{MU_Y}$$

And, generally speaking, the slope of an indifference curve mirrors the ratio of marginial utilities just as the ratio of market prices gives the slope of the budget line. We may therefore think of marginal utilities as consumption prices which mirror the household's internal tradeoffs between goods just as market prices mirror market tradeoffs. We have

$$\text{slope of an indifference curve} = -\frac{MU_X}{MU_Y}$$

At A and only at A, the slopes of the budget line and an indifference curve are the same, giving

$$\frac{MU_X}{MU_Y} = \frac{P_X}{P_Y} \tag{3-4}$$

An *irrational* consumer would stop at a point like E or B and achieve a lower level of welfare (indifference curve I lying below II). Conceivably, it could be forced away from A. Suppose for a moment that we are considering the tradeoff between leisure and work rather than wine and bread. Whether a household is permitted to take a particular job and how much labor it is allowed to supply at each wage rate may depend upon the approval of a labor union.

When there are many consumers, we may apply the above analysis to each of them to get

$$\left(\frac{MU_{X1}}{MU_{Y1}} = \frac{MU_{X2}}{MU_{Y2}} = \frac{MU_{X3}}{MU_{Y3}} = \cdots = \frac{MU_{Xn}}{MU_{Yn}}\right) = \frac{P_X}{P_Y} \qquad (3\text{-}5)$$

where the numbers index the consumers. Rule (3-5) is the condition for efficiency in consumption, and it shows how the market can coordinate thousands or even millions of rational consumers. Each household will have different tastes, and the diversity of preferences within a given city is likely to be enormous, yet a smoothly working market mechanism aligns each internal tradeoff in consumption on the anonymous price ratio. If we now expand our discussion to include many goods, then rule (3-5) must hold for every pair of goods and for all households that consume any given pair.

It is useful, in this respect, to compare rule (3-5) with (3-3). We may think of marginal physical products as internal production prices and ratios of marginal products as internal tradeoffs for each producer. When input markets are functioning smoothly, they align the tradeoffs for each producer on the anonymous price ratio.

Finally, when there are external components in consumption, these cannot be negelected in any discussion of efficiency. The nature of many goods— national defense, open-air concerts, and education, for example—is such that either the same units of the good may be consumed simultaneously by more than one individual (national defense, open-air concerts) or that consumption of the good by one individual can benefit others (education). When this happens the social utility or welfare yielded by the good in question is likely to be greater or less than the private utility enjoyed by any given member of society, and it can be shown that rule (3-5) generalizes to

$$\left(\frac{MSU_{X1}}{MSU_{Y1}} = \frac{MSU_{X2}}{MSU_{Y2}} = \frac{MSU_{X3}}{MSU_{Y3}} = \cdots = \frac{MSU_{Xn}}{MSU_{Yn}}\right) = \frac{P_X}{P_Y} \qquad (3\text{-}5a)$$

where MSU stands for marginal *social* utility and must be interpreted as follows: MSU_{X1} is a measure of the increase or decrease in the welfare accruing to *all* members of society which results from additional consumption of X by the first individual. A similar interpretation attaches to MSU_{Y1}, MSU_{X2}, and so on.

Although it is easy, in principle, to switch from rule (3-5) to rule (3-5a), the unaided market mechanism cannot normally bring about efficiency when external effects are present. Prices will have to be supplemented or replaced by other kinds of signals, a matter that we shall examine when we study laissez faire.

By the same token, the parts of (3-5) and (3-5a) between parentheses are rules for efficiency in consumption which do not involve prices at all. In principle, a dictator could align consumption tradeoffs for all consumers directly by using commands. But in practice this would require a far greater familiarity with the diverse preferences of many households than any ruler is likely to have. The only exception would be a 1984 world in which individual preferences have become alike or are molded and manipulated by the ruling powers.

As a corollary to the above analysis, let us consider the case where goods X and Y are not final outputs for consumption (such as wine and bread) but intermediate goods that are outputs of one production process, but also inputs for another—say, flour and grape juice. (In our economy, we suppose, nobody will touch the stuff until it ferments.) It can be shown that we must now replace the marginal utilities or consumption prices in rule (3-5) or (3-5a) with production prices or marginal physical products of users of X and Y. That is, we view X and Y as outputs which become inputs into production processes $(1, 2, \ldots, n)$. We then have

$$\left(\frac{\mathrm{MPP}_{X1}}{\mathrm{MPP}_{Y1}} = \frac{\mathrm{MPP}_{X2}}{\mathrm{MPP}_{Y2}} = \frac{\mathrm{MPP}_{X3}}{\mathrm{MPP}_{Y3}} = \cdots = \frac{\mathrm{MPP}_{Xn}}{\mathrm{MPP}_{Yn}}\right) = \frac{P_X}{P_Y} \quad (3\text{-}6)$$

$$\left(\frac{\mathrm{MSPP}_{X1}}{\mathrm{MSPP}_{Y1}} = \frac{\mathrm{MSPP}_{X2}}{\mathrm{MSPP}_{Y2}} = \frac{\mathrm{MSPP}_{X3}}{\mathrm{MSPP}_{Y3}} = \cdots = \frac{\mathrm{MSPP}_{Xn}}{\mathrm{MSPP}_{Yn}}\right) = \frac{P_X}{P_Y} \quad (3\text{-}6\text{a})$$

where a set of equalities such as the one in (3-6a) must hold for every pair of intermediate goods.

3–6 Efficient Coordination of Production and Consumption

To date, we have rules for efficiently coordinating consumption on one hand and production on the other. Suppose that these are, in fact, efficient. It may still be possible to improve over-all economic performance by simultaneously changing the mix of goods produced and redistributing the fruits of production among society's members. The latter implies a change in the distributions of wealth and welfare, and the former a move to a new position along the production-possibility frontier accomplished by reallocating inputs in production. The missing link, which we shall now provide, is a rule for efficiently coordinating consumption with production. It is, in fact, the most famous rule of all, which says that the price of each good should equal its marginal cost of production.

This is a rule for telling us how much of every good should be produced for any given set of prices. Once again, we employ a cost-benefit analysis to get the result. We assume that the price of any good, which is actually being produced and sold, always measures the benefit of providing an additional unit to at least one consumer. [More precisely, we assume that rule (3-5) or (3-5a) is always satisfied.] We then compare this with the good's marginal cost, which is the change in the total cost of production *per unit* of any small increase in the output of the good with the outputs of all other goods held fixed. Figure 3-6 shows this.

As long as the marginal cost of a good is less than its price, the benefit from increased production exceeds the additional cost and output should expand. When the marginal cost is greater than price, the benefit from increased production is less than the cost, and output should contract. When we put these two recommendations together, we get a rule which says that production of each good should be pushed approximately to the point where its price and marginal cost are the same.

When social costs depart from private costs, furthermore, it is the former with which society must reckon. Suppose, for example, that a pulp mill is dumping its waste products into a river and thereby polluting it. When we calculate the marginal cost of paper to society, we must include the cost of cleaning up the river, of eliminating the flow of waste, or of compensating those who are hurt in some way by the pollution. This gives us

$$P_X = \mathrm{MSC}_X \qquad P_Y = MSC_Y \qquad (3\text{-}7)$$

where MSC stands for marginal social cost. The same rule holds for *every* other good or service being produced.[8] If there is *no* rate of output at which the selling price of the good covers its MSC, the good should not be produced at all.

Of course, many goods are *intermediate goods,* which are the outputs of one production process and the inputs to another. These include durable capital goods, or plant and equipment, and material inputs such as flour used to make bread. The prices of these goods should equal their marginal costs of production and also the values of their marginal products in further production. If there is no rate of output of a particular intermediate good such that its VMSP—or benefit to society—exceeds its MSC, this good should not be produced.

Next, we divide the second part of rule (3-7) into the first part to get

$$\frac{\mathrm{MSC}_X}{\mathrm{MSC}_Y} = \frac{P_X}{P_Y} \qquad (3\text{-}7a)$$

and this may be combined with (3-5a) to get a complete set of conditions relating consumption to production:

$$\left(\frac{\mathrm{MSU}_{X1}}{\mathrm{MSU}_{Y1}} = \frac{\mathrm{MSU}_{X2}}{\mathrm{MSU}_{Y2}} = \cdots = \frac{\mathrm{MSU}_{Xn}}{\mathrm{MSU}_{Yn}} = \frac{\mathrm{MSC}_X}{\mathrm{MSC}_Y} \right) = \frac{P_X}{P_Y} \qquad (3\text{-}8)$$

For intermediate goods we have an analogous result:

$$\left(\frac{\mathrm{MSPP}_{X1}}{\mathrm{MSPP}_{Y1}} = \frac{\mathrm{MSPP}_{X2}}{\mathrm{MSPP}_{Y2}} = \cdots = \frac{\mathrm{MSPP}_{Xn}}{\mathrm{MSPP}_{Yn}} = \frac{\mathrm{MSC}_X}{\mathrm{MSC}_Y} \right) = \frac{P_X}{P_Y} \qquad (3\text{-}9)$$

[8] Neither rule (3-7) nor any of the other rules discussed above will hold exactly for every good or service produced and every productive input. It is possible to generalize these rules, but the generalizations become exceedingly complex to state.

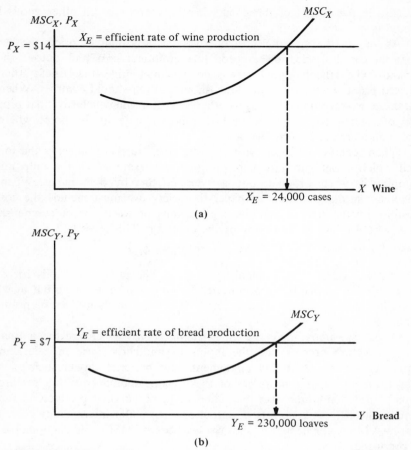

Figure 3-6. The efficient rate of production is the point at which the marginal social cost is equal to price.

Finally, it is possible to show that we may revise (3-8) and (3-9) to get rules that clearly do not involve any prices. Thus efficient coordination of production and consumption is at least logically possible in a nonmarket economy.[9]

3-7 X Efficiency

Up to now we have described inefficiency as misallocation of inputs *between* different firms or of outputs *between* different households or both.

---

[9] Suppose that L and K are two inputs, both used in producing X and Y. Then, if efficiency in production prevails, it can be shown that

$$\frac{\text{MSC}_X}{\text{MSC}_Y} = \frac{\text{MSPP}_{KY}}{\text{MSPP}_{KX}} = \frac{\text{MSPP}_{LY}}{\text{MSPP}_{LX}}$$

Consequently, we may replace the ratio of marginal costs in rules (3-8) and (3-9) with either ratio or marginal products above. Then the parts of (3-8) and (3-9) between parentheses do not depend upon any prices.

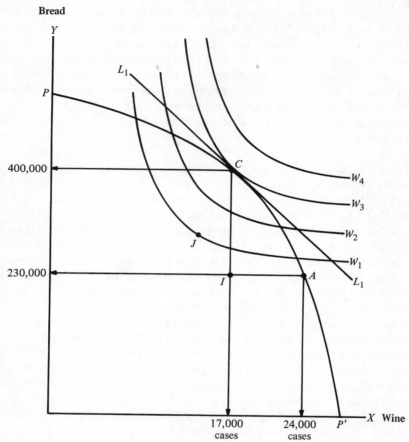

Figure 3–7. The production-possibility frontier and the pattern of aggregate demand.

We may label this "allocative inefficiency." We can extend the idea—for example, if we again think of leisure as a good, which is produced by not working and is consumed at the same time. Allocative inefficiency can then result from employee shirking or from any activity that results in too much or too little leisure relative to work.

Nevertheless, our conception of efficiency is still too narrow. It does not include all that the businessman has in mind, for example, when he talks about efficiency. He is apt to be concerned about the organization of production *within* a producing enterprise so that as much output as possible is obtained from given amounts of inputs. The second notion of efficiency is no less important than the first, but until recently, economists have tended to ignore it. When Harvey Leibenstein introduced the idea a few years ago, he called it "*X* efficiency." [10]

[10] Harvey Leibenstein, "Allocative vs. 'X Efficiency'," *American Economic Review,* June 1966.

More precisely, a gain in X efficiency occurs whenever a given firm is able to produce more of at least one output and no less of any other with the same amount of each input.[11] We now redefine efficiency to comprise X as well as allocative efficiency. The two kinds are clearly related and, indeed, are not mutually exclusive categories since quality of managerial effort (and, sometimes, more generally of "work effort") is classified under X efficiency. A gain in X efficiency is better management, in some sense, at the micro level, and thus X inefficiency may persist because society devotes too few resources to managerial education or research into organizational techniques. By the same token, a gain in X efficiency for one firm will probably raise several inputs' VMPs there. This may, in turn, lead to a reallocation of inputs.

But X inefficiency may also arise because a manager is not permitted or sufficiently motivated to organize his production efficiently. Here, X inefficiency stems either from faulty incentives or success indicators, and particularly from the fact that a firm's profit residual may not bite hard enough into managerial incomes (or, more generally, managerial "rewards"). The latter may happen, in turn, when markets are not sufficiently competitive (or when the firm is not regulated closely enough) or when there is a divorce between ownership and control of the firm. X inefficiency will prove to be a problem in both command and market economies, although "workably" competitive market economies probably have the best chance of keeping it low.

In the final analysis, any society has three potential ways of increasing its production of goods destined for present and future consumption. First, it can increase its level of production efficiency, comprising both X and allocative efficiency. The latter includes internalization of social costs and benefits and also realization of mass-production economies, broadly conceived. Second, it may be able to increase its inputs of labor and capital. And third, it can increase its level of technology, which would be embodied in new goods and services—such as an assembly line or a device to recycle waste products— which are superior to the old.

3–8 Families of Efficient Solutions

When we know only that efficiency prevails in a market system, we know that prices reflect marginal social costs or the values of marginal social products, as the case may call for. But we do not know the prices of eggs, apples, Cadillacs, borscht, caviar, or, for that matter, of any other good. Nor do we know how resources are allocated in production or how the fruits of production are distributed among society's members. The problem is that in either a market or a nonmarket society, many efficient solutions to the economic problem will exist that satisfy rules (3-1a), (3-2a), (3-3a), (3-5a), (3-8),

---

[11] Within a command economy, allocative efficiency recalls the costs of coordinating producers, while X efficiency recalls the costs of supervision, these being the two component parts of the information costs of command planning.

and (3-9). There is at least one solution for every point along the efficiency frontier in Figures 3-2(a) or (b).

We may be able to choose a particular solution, however, by selecting a particular position along either the efficiency or the production-possibility frontier. In the latter case, let us choose the point A in Figure 3-7, corresponding once more to 24,000 cases of wine and 230,000 loaves of bread. We assume that efficiency prevails, and, generally speaking, there will be, at most, a limited number of efficient ways of distributing this economy-wide bundle among households.

Under some conditions there will be just one way of distributing it. It might, for example, be necessary to give the first household 85 loaves of bread and 45 cases of wine, which puts him on indifference curve II in Figure 3-5. Under these conditions, his level of welfare is determined. When there is just one way to efficiently distribute the bundle of goods and services corresponding to a particular point on the production-possibility frontier, there will be a unique, efficient distribution of welfare corresponding to this point. That is, to a point such as A on the production-possibility frontier, there will correspond just one point along the efficiency frontier. (More generally, we would find only a limited number of efficient distributions of welfare corresponding to A.)

Let us next begin by choosing a distribution of welfare. Any one will do, and we therefore suppose that the second individual is twice as well off as the first. This puts us along the ray $U_I = \frac{1}{2} U_{II}$ (or $U_{II} = 2U_I$) in Figure 3-8. The only efficient combination of welfares is at B, where this ray crosses the efficiency frontier. However, let us move in and out along the ray for a moment on the assumption that efficiency in consumption always prevails. In doing so, we make everyone better off when we move out and everyone worse off when we move in. We can capture the same phenomenon in Figure 3-7 with the aid of indifference curves W_1, W_2, W_3, and W_4.

Because the distribution of welfare is fixed, the welfare of each and every individual can only be changed by expanding or contracting the economy-wide scale of production. A movement from D to E to B in Figure 3-8 is thus mirrored in a corresponding move from indifference curve W_1 to W_2 to W_3 in Figure 3-7. Each indifference curve represents a fixed level of utility for each member of society, given that the distribution of welfare lies along ray RR' (where $U_{II} = 2U_I$) in Figure 3-8. The highest level of welfare that can be reached is W_3, corresponding to B in Figure 3-8. The best achievable output assortment is therefore at C, representing 17,000 cases of wine and 400,000 loaves of bread.

Thus C is the only point along the production possibility frontier corresponding to B on the efficiency frontier, given the above assumptions. In general, there would be a limited number of points along the PP' frontier corresponding to C.

We may assign a further interpretation to Figure 3-7 which will be useful

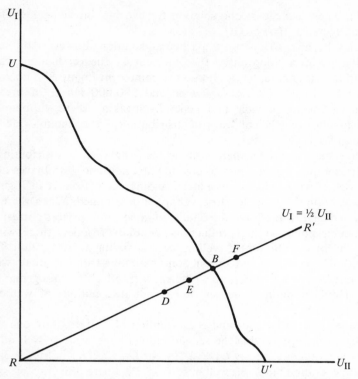

Figure 3–8. The efficiency frontier and a fixed distribution of welfare.

in later discussions. Efficiency in consumption implies that every household is equating its internal tradeoffs with price ratios. That is,

$$\frac{P_X}{P_Y} = \frac{\text{MSU}_X}{\text{MSU}_Y}$$

for all consumers. The slopes of indifference curves W_1, W_2, W_3, and W_4 are equal to this common ratio of marginal social utilities.

Now, suppose that the economy is at point D in Figure 3-8. It must therefore be somewhere along indifference curve W_1, although we do not yet know where. We can then zero in on an exact point by specifying a ratio of prices (or a common ratio of marginal social utilities for all households). If we specify that the prices of wine and bread are to be the same, we would select point J, the only combination of the two goods at which the slope of W_1 equals -1. Moreover, in trying to equate internal tradeoffs with price ratios, consumers will collectively try to consume the bundle of goods indicated by J. That is, J gives the quantity of each good that will be demanded when their prices are the same.

Generally speaking, the indifference curves of Figure 3-7 depict the economy-wide pattern of aggregate demand when efficiency in consumption prevails. This pattern depends upon the prices of all goods and the purchasing power that each household anticipates for itself (that is, upon its anticipated budget constraint). This determines its level of utility, as in Figure 3-5.

The production-possibility frontier gives the pattern of aggregate supply when each producer equates his prices with the corresponding marginal social costs. To see this, we shall first show that the slope of the production-possibility frontier equals the ratio of the marginal social costs of wine and bread. In our earlier manner, we imagine a move from C to A by first dropping down to I and then going horizontally to A. The first move lowers the total cost of producing both goods by an amount approximately equal to MSC_Y times the output reduction in Y, the latter being measured by the length of CI. The second move raises production costs by MSC_X times length IA.

However, the combined cost of producing both goods must be the same at C as at A since we are simply shuffling inputs from one production process to another without changing the total amount of any input in use. Therefore

$$\text{MSC}_Y \text{ times } CI = \text{MSC}_X \text{ times } IA$$

The slope of the production-possibility frontier between C and A is defined to be (minus) CI divided by IA. From the above equality we conclude that

$$\text{slope of } PP' \text{ curve} = -\frac{\text{MSC}_X}{\text{MSC}_Y} \tag{3-10}$$

Given prices for bread and wine, producers who are marginal-cost pricing will try to bring the economy to that position along the PP' frontier whose slope matches the ratio of prices. For example, if wine is twice as expensive as bread, producers will try to turn out the combination of wine and bread— 24,000 cases and 230,000 loaves—corresponding to A.

Only at C will the economy-wide demand and supply be equal for each and every good that is produced. And only at C will equations (3-8), necessary for efficient coordination of production and consumption, be satisfied. This is why we say that the market mechanism has the task of efficiently coordinating supply and demand so that the economy will reach C, or at least come close.

When this has been achieved, the slopes of an indifference curve (here W_3) and the PP' frontier must be the same. This common slope will, in turn, equal the ratio of market prices. We have tried to show this in Figure 3-7 by drawing in a budget line L_1L_1 for the whole economy. Its slope is the same as the ratio of market prices; its distance from the origin is a measure of economy-wide purchasing power. It is tangent both to the production-possibility frontier and to an indifference curve at C.

Finally, we should emphasize the assumptions underlying the discussion just concluded. The indifference curves in Figure 3-7 only give the pattern of economy-wide demand when efficiency in consumption prevails and when the distribution of welfare is fixed along the ray RR' in Figure 3-8. A change

in the distribution of welfare or in the efficiency of consumption would probably change the pattern of aggregate demand. Likewise, when producers fail
to equate prices with marginal social costs—as in the case of "monopoly
pricing"—the *PP* frontier will not show the pattern of aggregate supply.

To close this section we wish to point out that there are two separate ways
of thinking about marginal social cost. The more obvious is to view it as an
extra cost incurred in hiring more labor and more capital to produce more
output. In this spirit the price of a four-lane highway between Toronto and
Buffalo includes the cost of labor, asphalt, concrete, and wear and tear on
the bulldozers and cranes used to build it.

But since the total quantities of all inputs were fixed in the example
above, the extra cost of producing more *Y* could also have been phrased in
terms of the amount of *X* that had to be given up in changing positions along
the production-possibility frontier, and vice versa. Now, we are reckoning the
cost of a Toronto-to-Buffalo expressway as the opportunity passed up or de-
ferred to complete a four-lane highway between Montreal and Ottawa. Cuba
paid for its record 8.5-million-ton sugar harvest in 1970 with a reduced
output of shoes, clothing, toothpaste, and various industrial goods.[12]

It is in this way that the concept of *opportunity cost* arises in economics.
We have seen that economists like to think of individual economic actors and
groups as choosers. The idea behind a preference or utility function is that
actors will choose those courses of action which yield them the most benefit.
What could be more natural, then, than to view the cost of any course of
action taken as the (maximum) reward or benefit *not* received because this
course was chosen rather than some other? In our original example, a
decision to produce more *X* (wine) implies a simultaneous decision to produce less *Y* (bread), as long as we remain on the production-possibility frontier. One way of phrasing the cost of *X* is in terms of the output of *Y* foregone.

The concept of opportunity cost plays a fundamental role in economic
analysis.

3–9   Supersystems and the Fundamental Question Revisited

It is one thing to talk about an efficiency frontier as an ideal with which
we may compare performance in existing systems. But could we ever expect
a real-world economy to reach and roam its efficiency or production-possibility frontier at will? Unfortunately, the answer is "probably not." We can
think of these frontiers as applying to the supersystem introduced in Chapter
2, which can adapt instantly and costlessly to the efficient pursuit of any
consistent production and distribution goals whatsoever. Such an economy
would be able to shuffle resources in and out of different production processes

---

[12] Castro made this clear in his speech of July 26, 1970. See *Granma* (official organ
of the Central Committee of the Communist Party of Cuba), Aug. 2, 1970.

with ridiculous ease and would never be bothered with problems of bureaucracy or monopoly.

Thus, while the efficiency frontier remains a useful norm, we cannot fault existing economies for failing to perform like supersystems—at least until we have some evidence that the latter are, in fact, feasible. Any given economy will have frontiers representing maximal achievable levels of production and welfare, however, which lie at least partly inside its production-possibility and efficiency frontiers. Following tradition, let us call an economy's PP' and efficiency frontiers its *first-best* frontiers. These will depend solely upon its resource endowments, its technology of production and distribution, and the tastes (or micro utility functions) of its individual members. By contrast, the actually achievable frontiers will be called *second-best* frontiers. These depend upon tastes, technology, and resource endowments, but also upon the information structure of the economy.

Figure 3-9 contrasts the first-best production-possibility frontier facing a given society over—let us say—a five-year horizon, with two second-best frontiers that we have chosen for it. For definiteness, we suppose that it is now a particular kind of market economy and that A gives the actual assortment of production during the preceding five-year period. If its structure and partitioning remain unchanged, it will face the frontier labeled MM'. On the other hand, should it become a particular kind of command economy—with a strong planning authority—it will face CC'. The relation that we have drawn between these second-best frontiers is meant to suggest the comparative advantages and disadvantages of the two kinds of systems outlined in the last section of Chapter 2. (If a strong planning authority cannot emerge, CC' is likely to lie inside MM'.)

To follow this up, we should note that Soviet-bloc economists have gone to great lengths to stress the control the planners have over their system, its adaptability to rapid industrialization, and its relative freedom from cyclical fluctuations. Western economists have emphasized the static efficiency of their systems. Between the two, there has been much sound and fury, signifying little. But Western economies replace markets and prices with bureaus and commands whenever they need an urgent reordering of priorities, be it in wartime or in preparation for a space race. And whenever commands appear to be particularly inefficient, such as in distributing consumer goods among households, Soviet-bloc economies resort to some form of markets.

Thus, of the two frontiers, MM' passes closest to the (first-best) production-possibility frontier. We can think of this as indicating that, from a given bundle of inputs, a market system would enable the economy to produce a higher rate of output.[13] However, when a sufficiently "radical" reorientation

---

[13] See, for example, Joseph Berliner, "The Static Efficiency of the Soviet Economy," *American Economic Review,* May 1964; also, Abram Bergson, *Planning and Productivity Under Soviet Socialism* (New York: Columbia U.P., 1968), and "Comparing Productivity and Efficiency in the U.S.A. and the U.S.S.R.," in Alexander Eckstein, ed., *Comparison of Economic Systems* (Berkeley, Calif.: U. of Calif., 1971), pp. 180–181.

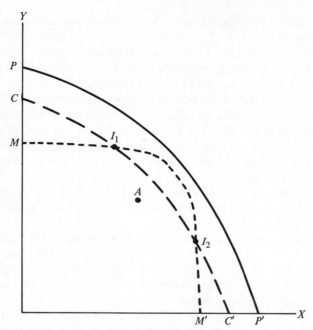

Figure 3–9. Possible second-best frontiers for market and command economies.

of priorities is called for—that is, outside the segments bounded by I_1 and I_2—
CC' will lie beyond the market frontier. We would hypothesize a similar situation relative to the efficiency frontier. In fact, some measures such as industrialization of an underdeveloped region, will cause a simultaneous reorientation,
both in production and in the distribution of welfare. This analysis is purely
static, moreover, and on some occasions rapid growth will require continuing
changes in relative priorities from one sector to another to prevent bottlenecks
from arising and as growth potential becomes relatively exhausted in some
sectors.

Nevertheless, it is not possible to say in the abstract just how big or how
rapid a reorientation must be before it becomes "radical." In addition, just
because we must draw our frontiers on two-dimensional paper, we should
not become a victim of two-dimensional mentality regarding economic systems. It will often prove feasible to combine commands and market signals
in a variety of ways, sometimes producing a planned market economy.

If we start with a command rather than a market economy, an additional note of complexity enters our analysis. Once the bureaucracy of a
particular command economy has solidified, an inertia tends to creep into
economic decision making that makes reorientation more difficult. Then a
radical reorientation may only be possible after a reorganization of the planning hierarchy.

Finally, we cannot ignore the costs of transforming one kind of system into another. In some cases, a revolution will be necessary, and revolutions often take time, in addition to the other sacrifices which they impose. To a planner, this factor may offset some of the advantages of switching to a command economy.

Henceforward, to simplify our diagrams, we shall not draw in second-best frontiers in most instances. Rather, when appropriate, we shall show solutions to the economic problem occurring inside the relevant first-best frontier.

Chapter 4

Rational Behavior in an Economic System: Optimality

4–1 Introduction

Near the end of Chapter 3 we saw that efficiency can tell us one but not both of the following things:

1. The "best" way(s) of distributing goods and services among society's members, *given* that a point has been chosen on the production-possibility frontier. Once we choose a particular assortment of final-use goods and services to be produced and consumed, there will be at most a limited number of efficient distributions of wealth and welfare that correspond to the assortment selected. Or, once we decide the *what* of the economic problem—for example, by choosing A in Figure 4-1(a)—there will be, at most, a limited number of efficient *for whom* solutions, such as B in Figure 4-1(b).

2. The "best" combination(s) of final-use goods to produce, given that a distribution of welfare has been selected along the efficiency or Pareto frontier. Once we select B in Figure 4-1(b), A may be the only efficient pattern of production corresponding to this.

To start by selecting a position along the production-possibility frontier as "optimal" is to phrase goals for the system as a whole in terms of the combination of final-use outputs that it "ought" to produce. This is precisely what a commodity preference function (introduced in Chapter 2) does. By contrast, each point on the efficiency frontier corresponds to a particular distribution of individual welfares among society's members. To start by choosing an optimal point along the efficiency frontier would be to phrase social goals in terms of the combination of individual welfares that "ought" to prevail. This is the role played by a social welfare function.

It follows that an economy may be oriented along an optimal path by anchoring it either to a social welfare or to a commodity preference function. The first chooses an optimal distribution of welfare, or position along the efficiency frontier which, by (2), corresponds to an optimal point or points on the production-possibility frontier. The second chooses an optimal assortment of final use production or point along the production-possibility frontier and, by (1), one or more optimal distributions of welfare along the efficiency frontier.

By contrast, a social guiding function tries to simultaneously orient an economy toward a point or points on the efficiency frontier and toward another point or points on the production-possibility frontier. Our discussion above tells us that this may not be possible because the two sets of points may not correspond to one another. When they do not, society's production and distribution goals will tend to collide, and there will be some loss of efficiency on that account. Nevertheless, the social guide is probably the most common type of social preference function in practice.

Finally, the above discussion remains essentially the same if we replace the first-best production-possibility and efficiency frontiers with second-best frontiers corresponding to some particular realizable economic system. The only additional point to make is that the link between production and distribution that we have established may depend upon the type of economic system under study.

As our analysis of optimality proceeds, it is worth bearing in mind that there can never be a uniquely optimal solution to the economic problem until social goals are defined for the economy as a whole. These goals will implicitly embody a particular set of value judgments about *what* goods to produce (and how much of each one), *how* to produce them, and how to distribute them among society's members. A change in values, and hence in goals, will generally reorient the system and determine a new optimal position.

4-2   From the Parts to the Whole

As indicated above, examples of particular commodity preference and social welfare functions, along with the optimal solutions to the economic problem which they determine, are depicted in Figures 4-1(a) and (b), respectively. In each case we make use of what are known as social indifference curves, along which social welfare remains constant. The objective of

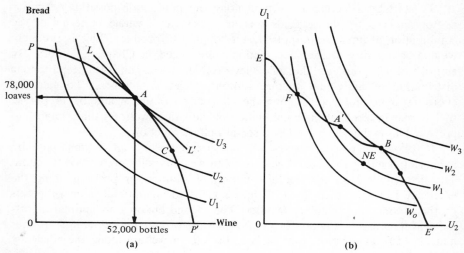

Figure 4–1. (a) The commodity preference function; (b) the social welfare function.

maximizing an index of social welfare translates graphically into the target of reaching the highest possible social indifference curve. Consequently, A and B are optimal.

However, optimality is strictly a relative concept. If we change the social goals of the two economies in these diagrams by introducing a new commodity preference function on the one hand and a new social welfare function on the other, points C and D could easily become optimal. This will mean both a new best pattern of outputs and prices, and a new best distribution of wealth and welfare.

In the case of a social welfare function, the slope of a social indifference curve measures the terms upon which the welfare of one individual or group can be substituted for that of another, with the index of social welfare remaining the same. (It can be shown that this slope also equals the ratio of the weights attached to the two individuals.) Similarly, the slope of a commodity indifference curve measures the terms upon which production (or importing) of one good can be substituted for production (or importing) of another if social welfare is to remain the same. (Once again, this will mirror the relative weights attached to the two goods.) Generally speaking, economists are more interested in these tradeoffs between different goals than they are in a simple listing of goals that a society may choose or say that it chooses to pursue. For example, a standard list of goals reads as follows:

1. A high rate of per capita current consumption.
2. A high growth rate (probably implying a high rate of saving and investment).
3. An equitable distribution of welfare, including in some cases development of particular, depressed geographical regions.

4. A high level of employment.
5. A low rate of inflation, implying among the things relatively higher welfares for pensioners and others on comparatively fixed incomes.
6. The development of new industries.

We might as well add the elimination of man-eating sharks and malaria. Insofar as the above really are goals, the important questions take the form: How much growth are we willing to sacrifice to get more current consumption or a greater equality of welfares? How much employment are we willing to sacrifice to get a given reduction in inflation? This does not deny that we may be able to restructure the economy, for example, to reduce both inflation and unemployment. However, at some point painful choices between desirable ends will have to be made, and these choices will indicate the relative importance or weight attached to each goal.

When social welfare is defined by a social welfare function, the optimal point [for example, B in Figure 4–1(b)] must lie on the efficiency frontier. Under most conditions, the optimum defined by a commodity preference function will also be efficient. Consequently, it is sometimes said that efficiency is a kind of "minimum requirement" to place on an economic system.[1] In general, however, such a contention is wrong. The point NE in Figure 4–1(b) is not efficient since it lies inside the efficiency frontier. Yet it corresponds to a greater level of social welfare than F which is efficient.

Because no government has ever figured out how to steer an economy without risking the introduction of some inefficiency, a move away from an inefficient position toward an efficient one may imply a *decrease* in a particular index of social welfare. The reason is that the economy has moved away from the path along which the social preference function in question seeks to orient it. This recalls our fundamental question of comparative economic systems, and in such a context, the following quotations are of more than passing interest. The first is by I. Kotov, a Soviet economist; the second is the most famous passage from Alan Smith's *Wealth of Nations:*

Apart from the essential difference in socioeconomic relations, the socialist mode of production is distinguished from capitalism in still one other important aspect. This distinction is that under socialism the objective laws of economic development are realized consciously within the framework of society as a whole. Productive forces and productive relations are under the control of men and consciously are developed and improved by them. The transition from capitalism to communism . . . [is] a leap from the realm of blind necessity to the realm of freedom, the freedom conceived of as comprehended necessity, as man's domination over social production and his economic relations.[2]

[1] See, for example, Leonid Hurwicz, "Conditions for Economic Efficiency of Centralized and Decentralized Structures," in Gregory Grossman, ed., *Value and Plan* (Berkeley, Calif.: U. of Calif., 1960).

[2] I. Kotov, "Some Problems in Applying Mathematical Methods to Economics, and the Political Economy of Socialism," *Problems of Economics,* Aug. 1966.

. . . every individual necessarily labours to render the annual revenue of the society as great as he can. He generally, indeed, neither intends to promote the public interest, nor knows how much he is promoting it. By . . . directing . . . [his] industry in such a manner as its produce may be of the greatest value, he intends only his own gain, and he is in this, as in many other cases, led by an invisible hand to promote an end which was no part of his intention. . . . By pursuing his own interest he frequently promotes that of the society more effectively than when he really intends to promote it.[3]

When we realize that Adam Smith was extolling the virtues of a basically laissez-faire capitalist economy, it appears that the two quotes are in part contradictory. However, this is not necessarily true. If Kotov's Marxist terminology is reinterpreted in terms of the tools we have been developing, his "objective laws" become a planners' preference function.[4] The "conscious realization" of these "laws" occurs when society, under the aegis of an economic planning council, consciously charts and follows a course embodied in such a function.

Under capitalism, according to Kotov, the path which the economy follows is determined blindly, in the sense that no central authority decides which way the system is to go. The path is determined by a synthesis of partly independent decisions of many economic actors, each of whom tends to push and pull in a different direction. National economic goals for a country like the United States always will reflect the nature of compromises that continually emerge between various poles of economic and political power in society, many of which focus solely on micro economic goals. This has two disadvantages.

1. No one has a clear, over-all picture of where the economy is going. When the distribution of power shifts in a decentralized economy or when significant changes in tastes occur, the system will reorient itself toward new goals. Over fairly long periods of time, we are by no means assured that any consistent set of goals will emerge, and, in this sense, the economy may work against itself. It could conceivably emphasize price stability at the expense of growth, for example, and then reverse this priority. This is partly why many economists maintain that it is meaningless to talk about the behavior of unplanned economic systems. Whether we agree with them or not, consistent pursuit of an explicit set of goals probably will be less feasible in North America than in Eastern Europe, in France, or in Japan.

2. Closely allied with the above, there may be paths of economic development which are not taken but which would leave many individuals better off and everyone at least as well off as the present course. This means that

---

[3] Adam Smith, *The Wealth of Nations,* ed. by Edwin Cannan (New York: Random, 1937), p. 423.

[4] In particular, most Western economists (including the author) would not agree that such things as objective laws of economic development exist. The path of development that any economy is to follow is necessarily subjective, in part, since it is dictated, subject to production constraints, by a concept of aggregate-oriented rationality that reflects human preferences, bargaining, and decision making.

the system is dynamically inefficient in a way to be made more explicit toward the end of the chapter.

In short, a laissez-faire economy risks following a path of economic development which, in a sense, is "haphazard" or "accidental" and which may be dynamically inefficient at the same time. Marxist economists are quite fond of leveling these charges at capitalist societies and of drawing unfavorable contrasts with the purposeful pattern of development in a planned socialist economy. No Marxist would accept macrorationality as a reasonable substitute for the macrorationale of a central planner. At the same time, Marxists do not take the trouble to point out that some kinds of economic planning are not incompatible with capitalism. In several countries "guided capitalism," as opposed to laissez faire, means precisely this.

Whether or not Kotov is correct, Smith's quote is not really a reply since he does not say how "public interest" is to be defined. His statement amounts to a claim that laissez-faire capitalism tends to be efficient under certain conditions but not necessarily effective in pursuing an explicit and consistent set of goals. We can therefore sum up this discussion by noting that Kotov and Smith are to an extent simply extolling the comparative advantages of different kinds of economic systems.

4-3   Changes in Goals and Production Possibilities

As noted above, a commodity preference function sets economic goals purely in terms of aggregate or per capita quantities of goods and services. Consequently, it is most likely to be a planners' preference function as well, describing the goals of an economic planning council which has become the dominant pole of power. Nevertheless, if we assume a fixed distribution of welfare, for purposes of illustration, the utility of each individual can only be increased by raising the volume of goods and services available to the whole of society. We may then rewrite the social welfare and social guiding functions in commodity preference form.

Assuming that this has been done, if necessary, we now wish to examine more closely how interaction between a commodity preference type of function (or aggregate demand) and the production-possibility frontier determines an economy's optimal output mix of goods and services and their optimal prices or terms of trade. We again confine ourselves to a simple two-good world and assume that, initially, a growth or investment-oriented planning council rules the roost. More precisely, if X_1 is an index of the total volume of consumer-goods production while X_2 indicates capital-goods output, we suppose that the planning council always assigns twice as much weight to X_2 as to X_1.

One way of expressing these preferences in symbols would be by writing $W_1 = X_1 + 2X_2$. W_1 thus indexes the social utility of the growth-oriented planning council, and the corresponding social indifference curves are the

dashed lines shown in Figure 4–2. The optimal combination of the two categories of goods is denoted by A. In a market economy, the optimal price of
capital goods will be exactly double that of consumer goods—a reflection of
the constant relative values assigned these two categories by the planning
authority.

To thicken the plot, let us also assume that the economy in question has
been following a growth-oriented policy for several years. One day, the planning power structure decides to take a goodwill tour abroad with a view to
obtaining increased economic aid. The planners wave goodbye at the airport,
but no sooner is their airplane safely out of the country than a palace coup
d'état replaces them. The new planners vow—and we shall suppose sincerely
intend—to reorient the economy toward current consumption.

In consequence, we shall assign them a commodity preference function
which is just the reverse of the old one in the sense that the consumer-goods
index X_1 receives twice the weight of the capital-goods index X_2. If W_2 indexes the utility of the second planning council, we write $W_2 = 2X_1 + X_2$.
Now the relevant indifference surfaces become the *solid* straight lines in
Figure 4–4, and the optimal product mix has shifted from A to B. The new
optimal terms of trade between the two kinds of goods have become just the

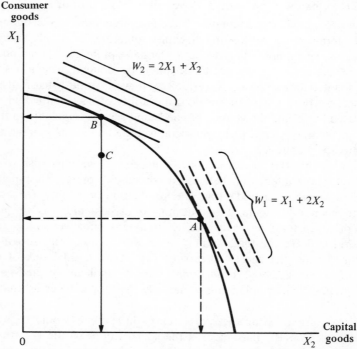

Figure 4–2. Growth (W_1) and consumption-oriented (W_2) commodity preference functions.

opposite of what they used to be, with the price of X_1 now twice as high as the price of X_2.

The economy will not be reoriented overnight. Nevertheless, when we compare the two optimal solutions, we see why we cannot talk about a universally best set of prices. The optimal price of a pound of butter might turn out to be $0.25, $1.50, or $0.75. That of a Cadillac could be $1,000, $6,000, or $3,175, depending upon prevailing social goals. However, when there is a shift of goals in a market economy, with no change in production possibilities, there will tend to be a *positive* relationship between optimal relative outputs and prices. In Figure 4-2, the relatively high price of capital goods at A corresponds to a relatively high output of capital goods, and vice versa for B.

To see why, suppose that the price of one type of good or service rises relative to others in a market economy and that this increase is expected to last. Then entrepreneurs will respond by moving resources out of the production of other goods and into the line whose price has become relatively higher. Given a market economy, therefore, the net impact of the switch in planners would be to raise consumer-goods prices relative to capital or investment-goods prices, thus encouraging a greater production of the former along with a lower production of the latter.

By contrast, Figure 4-3 shows the impact of a change in society's production possibilities on optimal prices with *no* change in social goals. This is just the reverse of the preceding example, and we again suppose there to be a growth-oriented planning board. It will emphasize investment relative to consumption, but, more particularly, investment in capital-goods industries over investment to produce consumer goods. One of the consequences will be a greater relative growth in the nation's capacity to produce capital goods. Figure 4-3 shows capital goods becoming cheaper relative to consumer goods over time. Broadly speaking, this is because supply is expanding more rapidly relative to demand in this industry. The general rule is that goods whose output potential is expanding most rapidly will tend to experience *relative* price declines.

In part, this is because investment has a direct scale effect on output. But in the above example increases in the efficiency of capital-goods production probably will exceed efficiency increases in the production of consumer goods. For one thing, more investment will go into research and development, and, for another, relatively large percentage increases in output will usually (although by no means always) permit a greater increase in the benefits from economies of mass production.

Indeed, in this respect, the phenomenon depicted in Figure 4-3 is one quite common to the 20th century. Automobiles, radios, television sets, telephone service, and a host of other consumer durables have become relatively less expensive than they were, say, forty years ago, largely through technological progress and the benefits of scale economies. Machine tools probably

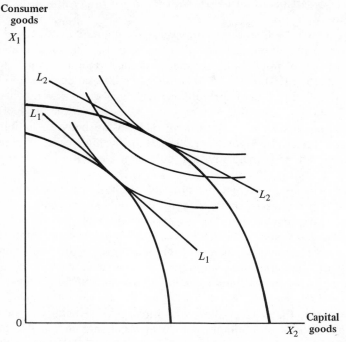

Figure 4–3. Changing optimal price relatives in response to shifts in relative production possibilities.

have undergone the same evolution in the U.S.S.R. Interestingly enough, the demand for these items probably did rise, but the price-increasing effect of the upward shift in demand was swamped by the price-reducing effect of larger increases in supply.

4–4 The Optimal Path of Economic Development

When we write social welfare as a weighted sum of production indexes and/or individual welfares, the relative values of the weights will indicate society's preferences. To expand upon a previous example, let X, Y, and Z be indexes of agricultural, light industrial, and heavy industrial output, respectively. Then, one particular planners' preference function is $3Z + 2Y + X$. Here Z has the highest priority, with Y second and X last, in the proportions $3:2:1$.

Suppose, on the other hand, that we do not know the planners' priorities and cannot discover what they are, except by observing economic performance. When the system in Figure 4–4 reaches A, we might conclude that the importance accorded X is $\frac{3}{4}$ of that given to Y. But this is probably false. It would be more accurate to say that the EPC attaches a higher relative weight to Y. The Soviet economy in 1930 would have presented an even more deceptive appearance to anyone looking only at production in that year. He would have concluded that agriculture was the priority sector, whereas steel and machine tools had nearly negligible importance. The higher priority for machine tools only reveals itself when we observe relative growth rates in different sectors of the economy over a fairly long period of time.[5]

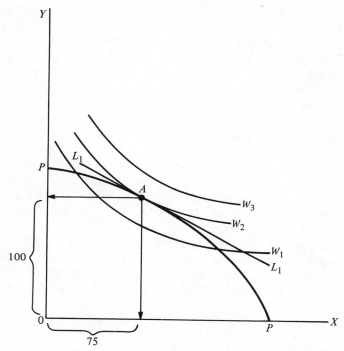

Figure 4–4. The production-possibility frontier and (unobserved) planners' preferences.

An EPC will also want to view the economy as an evolving entity. Any operational plan—covering, let us say, production over a one-year period—will be made within the framework of a longer horizon—for example, five years. A five-year plan may, in turn, be drawn up in the light of a still broader and looser twenty-year plan. Furthermore, these plans all interact. The five-year plan should be revised continuously in the light of current developments and the twenty-year plan as a consequence of revisions in five-year plans.

Hence a planners' preference function, which assigns current output targets, only makes sense when viewed within this wider perspective. The same thing is true in a more decentralized economy. Businessmen in a capitalist country will only set current goals in the light of a longer-run planned evolution or development of their enterprises. Even households appear to plan

[5] See, for example, Warren Nutter, *The Growth of Industrial Production in the Soviet Union* (Princeton, N.J.: Princeton U.P., 1962), especially Table 11, pp. 96-97.

present consumption in relation to expected future consumption and income. The net impact of such microplanning is to chart a course for the system as a whole over time.

As of a point in time, an economic planning council faces fixed production, consumption, and distribution possibilities. Over time, it can partly tailor the economy to its specifications by influencing relative growth rates and bringing about changes in the actual distribution of wealth and welfare. More generally a society's static choices between different distributions of welfare and production assortments become dynamic choices among alternative paths of economic development. The path ranked highest by the prevailing concept of social rationality becomes the optimal path. It is also here that social priorities will reveal themselves to an observer, provided these remain reasonably constant over time.

The idea appears in Figure 4–5(a) and (b), where we have graphed three different paths in output and welfare space. (A and A' are assumed to be images of the same path in the two spaces—similarly for B and B' and C and C'.) Each path represents, in the first instance, a set of directions or orientations open to the system. These are various combinations of goods and services and distributions of welfare that can be made available at different dates over the current planning horizon, perhaps accompanied by vaguer projections into the more remote future.

In this case, we have chosen a planning horizon of five years. The point shows the present position of the economy; the points labeled t_1 indicate projected alternative positions after the year to come, assumed to be the first year of the plan. If the point t_1 is attained along path A or A', the planners

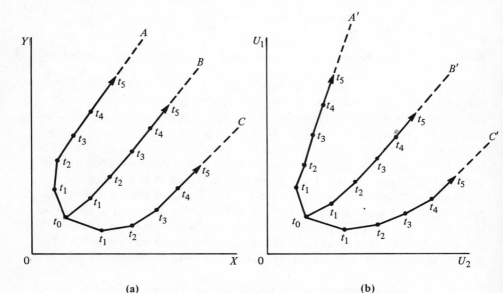

(a)   **(b)**

Figure 4–5. Paths of economic development.

expect to be able to reach t_2 along the same path during the second planning year. And so it goes. Each path is fully defined by points t_1 through t_5 and, perhaps, by a further projection beyond the five-year horizon, indicated by the dashed lines.

At least in theory, the total number of possible paths is virtually limitless. Moreover, there is no reason why any pair of paths cannot cross several times. Some paths may dominate others over fairly long planning horizons. We can define path 1 to dominate path 2 whenever path 1 yields more welfare for some individuals and more outputs of some goods in some years while path 2 yields no more output of any good or welfare for any individual in any year. No EPC would want to choose a path that was inefficient in this sense. However, any particular planners' preference function will then attach a social welfare weight to each path, and the planners' job will be to implement the path with the highest weight. In the same way, they can get a ranking of alternative economic systems. Let us examine this problem for a moment.

Just as different kinds of economic systems have different second-best utility and production frontiers, so they will give rise to different collections of feasible development paths. A switch from markets to commands in several sectors will alter the planners' options. This need not affect the variety of directions which it is possible for the system to take, but the *distances* that can be traveled in some directions over a given planning horizon will vary.

For example, suppose that the vertical and horizontal axes in Figure 4-5(a) represent industrial and agricultural production, respectively, in a predominantly agricultural economy. Consequently, we assume, rapid industrialization implies a radical reorientation of priorities in what is now a predominantly market economy. If the paths we have drawn correspond to a command economy, the effect of retaining markets would be to shorten the distance between t_0 and t_5 along path A and, perhaps, along path B as well. It might not be impossible to industrialize in a market environment, but the process would get off to a slower start in our example.

As a first approximation to a ranking of economic systems, the EPC may search through all the information structures it believes are feasible. (For example, it may decide to restrict itself to a basically command economy, but consider introducing or strengthening market and quasi-market mechanisms in certain sectors.) It could then choose a structure capable of yielding that path of economic development ranked highest by its social preference function.

Such an approach oversimplifies the problem, however, because it neglects the impact of uncertainty upon the EPC's task. No projected preformance levels to be attained over several years' time under different information structures can be more than guesstimates. There will always be some risk that any given path of economic development cannot be achieved under a particular information structure. Moreover, because goals of lower-level decision makers will not always harmonize with those of the EPC, some risk will always exist that structural reforms themselves cannot be implemented.

For example, intermediate planning authorities have been known to issue and enforce orders for some time after they were officially relieved of this function. By the same token, unofficial markets have been known to arise and persist in a basically command economy. Indeed, information theory suggests that some kind of "shadow" market mechanism will tend to emerge to short-circuit long information channels. Conceivably this system could become important enough to implement priorities contrary to those of the EPC (for example, in consumers' versus producers' goods).

Both kinds of risks will complicate the ranking of information structures (and thus of economic systems). We can further imagine the planners having a tradeoff between risk and expected performance which will influence both the structure that emerges and the course that the EPC tries to follow. A daring EPC might try to harness resources for a "great leap forward" during the upcoming five years, risking a virtual breakdown of the economy's production and distribution machinery as a consequence. A more conservative planning authority would settle for a slower, but surer advance, even though it, too, was basically growth-oriented.

From a purely economic standpoint, an EPC may then rank information systems on the basis of this kind of tradeoff. However, further considerations, such as ideology, political factors, and empire-building tendencies, will once again play a role. In the final analysis, they may well become the dominant choice criteria. Indeed, if we were political scientists, sociologists, or psychologists, we might well play down the economic criteria as relatively minor.

4–5 Some Major Additions and Qualifications

The core of our discussion of rational behavior in an economic system is now complete. Evidently, we could and should construct a long list of qualifications and additions to the foregoing analysis. From such a list, the following three items appear to merit the most urgent attention here and now.

1. So far we have depicted all equal-product and production-possibility surfaces as smooth curves entirely free of kinks and elbows. It is by no means obvious that this is always the best way of looking at matters. Suppose, for instance, that there are several production processes which can be used to make bread and several more to make wine, but that only four combinations of these two types of processes are technically efficient when both bread and wine are to be produced. Given fixed amounts of all inputs, and given that the economy is on its production possibility curve for bread and wine, one such combination might turn out 30,000 loaves of bread and 10,000 bottles of wine. Another might make 25,000 bottles of wine and 10,000 loaves of bread, and we shall assume that the final two manufacture 20,000 bottles of wine combined with 20,000 loaves of bread and 15,000 bottles of wine together with 27,500 loaves of bread.

Since these output combinations are all efficient, we now have four points on the production-possibility frontier for bread and wine. The remaining points are derived by asking ourselves what would happen if two or more different processes for making bread and two or more processes for wine manufacture were operated simultaneously. Then the economy would not wind up at any of the four points just derived. It would be operating somewhere between two of them—that is, on one of the dashed lines of Figure 4–6. These dashed lines, together with the four points, form the production-possibility frontier. It has an elbow at each point.

When this happens there will no longer be unique optimal price ratios between each pair of goods. Instead, there will normally be a range of price

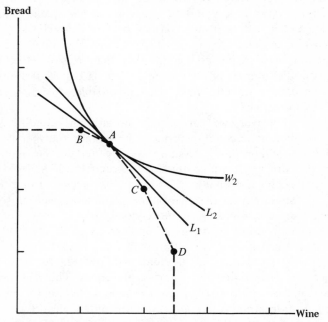

Figure 4–6. A kinked production-possibility frontier.

ratios which are optimal, and any price ratio in this range will be as good as any other. In Figure 4–8, A is the optimal point. However the production-possibility curve has no unique slope at A. There are no unique production prices and no unique production tradeoffs there.[6]

In practice there is some evidence to suggest that relative price changes do not always call forth changes in relative outputs by producers. That is, relative quantities of different goods and services being produced are some-

---

[6] Indeed, suppose that the slopes of line segments BA and AC are -1 and $-1\frac{1}{2}$, respectively. Then as long as the price of wine divided by the price of bread lies in the interval from 1 to $1\frac{1}{2}$, the two prices may be considered optimal insofar as this pair of commodities is concerned. The slopes of lines L_1 and L_2 are different, yet each represents an optimal price ratio at A. (If the reader will imagine L_1 tilting on the point A from the line segment BA to the line segment AC, he will get a good intuitive grasp as to why any price ratio between 1 and $1\frac{1}{2}$ is optimal.)

what, although not entirely, insensitive to relative price changes. If this is true, the task of the market system as a coordinator of production and distribution is simplified in comparison with the situation in which the production-possibility frontier was smooth. When the optimal value of any good or service relative to another is not uniquely defined but has only to fall within a certain range, the market system has a margin of error in which to operate. Absolute precision is not required as a prerequisite for the best mix of goods and services to be produced and then distributed in the best possible way.

2. Of the three concepts of social welfare proposed above, the social welfare function is the oldest and by far the most frequently discussed in the literature. Yet it suffers from a serious practical drawback. Suppose we have decided that a given economy is to be steered by an egalitarian social welfare function. The embarrassing question then arises: How are we to know when the distribution of welfare in society is equal? For utility is not something that can be directly measured, and in this sense a social welfare function is nonoperational.

Despite this, however, we can specify broadly the conditions that are favorable to promoting an equal distribution of welfare and thereby develop a usable notion of egalitarianism. Assume initially that we encounter a world in which every individual's utility function is precisely the same. If everyone consumes exactly the same bundle of goods and services and does exactly the same work, we would expect the distribution of material welfare to be equal.

To become more realistic, let us next violate one of these conditions by requiring some individuals to do more unpleasant work than others. Then inequalities in the distribution of welfare will reflect this factor alone. There will probably exist some unequal distribution of wealth, furthermore, which will just make the distribution of welfare again equal. Thus the first requirement of an equal distribution of welfare is income or wealth compensation which offsets or at least tends to compensate for differences in work disutility.

Next we introduce the additional wrinkle of jobs with different educational and skill requirements and, at the same time, allow individual preferences or utility functions to differ. Given the latter, a vastly unequal distribution of welfare could prevail even if everyone did the same kind of work and consumed the same basket of goods. However, rather than being asked to consume exactly the same bundle of commodities, we imagine that each individual is presented with a list of "menus" from which he may freely choose. His alternatives will include a wide variety of goods and services to consume along with a broad spectrum of occupations, differing not only in regard to disutility factors, but with qualitative differences and a variety of educational and skill requirements as well. In particular, it will be possible to postpone some present consumption in order to acquire the education and training that certain occupations require. The reward for this postponement will be higher incomes and higher consumption later.

Within such an environment, individuals will be able to compensate for differences in tastes or preferences and differences in native ability by selecting jobs they especially like or are adept at and also by consuming that bundle of goods which best suits their particular tastes.

In consequence, we would expect that the broader the spectrum of economic opportunities available in any given society and the more equally distributed these are among its citizenry, the more nearly equal the distribution of welfare will be, provided individuals have enough information and education to enable them to choose rationally. For then citizens will be more able to compensate for individual differences in taste and ability.

Thus the second requirement for an equal distribution of material welfare is an equal distribution of economic opportunity, coupled with as wide and varied a range of choices open to each economic actor as possible. Given this, the provision of enough education and information to permit rational individual decision making becomes the third requirement. By the same token, one way of producing an *un*equal distribution of welfare is to shut off opportunity in one form or other to certain individuals or groups. In the real world, this is one way it is often done.

The fourth and final requirement for an equal distribution of welfare will usually be some additional spreading of incomes from property (as opposed to wage and salary income) beyond that gotten by lowering barriers to equal opportunity. A capitalist society would achieve this, when it is achieved, by a program of taxes and income supplements designed to redistribute income. A socialist society would be more likely to disallow large property incomes to begin with. Because property income in the form of profit often serves as an incentive for innovation and efficient management, the price for either kind of equalization may be less of these desiderata.

3. Up to now we have been dealing with an economy's production-possibility frontier and a corresponding efficiency or Pareto frontier derived by methods outlined in Chapter 3. However, utility (or disutility) does not usually stem directly from production but from goods that are available for consumption, both present and future, and public and private. By this broad definition, the bundle of goods "consumed" within any nation's borders will differ from the bundle which it produces for final demand because of international trade. In Chapter 1 we saw how exchange could enlarge the consumption possibilities of an individual beyond his production possibilities, and the same holds for a nation.

Figure 4–7 shows this. The inner frontier is the economy's production-possibility curve. In the absence of trade, we shall suppose, the system would produce and consume at A. Trade then allows it to divorce consumption from production and exchange some of what it produces for goods that can be more cheaply manufactured abroad. Consequently, it is able to produce at B and consume at D, the latter representing a combination of outputs that otherwise would be unavailable to it. Moreover, its consumption possibilities may expand through increased trade possibilities (perhaps brought about by technical progress abroad) even though its own production possibilities remain unaltered.

Throughout the remainder of this volume we shall be interested in an economy's *consumption* possibilities, meaning its production *cum* international trade possibilities, as well as in its production potential alone. This does not

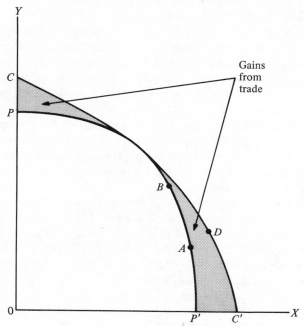

Figure 4–7. The consumption and production-possibility frontiers.

imply that we see no purpose in distinguishing between imports and domestically produced goods. Nations can and often do prefer to restrict domestic consumption by restricting imports and producing goods at home that could be purchased abroad more cheaply. In effect, they prefer domestic to foreign production. But unless they cut off trade altogether, we cannot assign a zero welfare weight to goods produced abroad.

4–6   Growth and Dynamic Efficiency

If we ignore distribution goals for the moment, we can say that any society has two broad alternatives pertaining to economic development. These might be labeled higher present consumption on one hand and growth on the other. A society could choose to consume most of its current income and thereby enjoy a relatively high level of current consumption, or it might opt to save and invest a larger proportion, thus trading some current consumption for growth and higher levels of future consumption. Some economists would argue, however, that such a choice is not really a choice at all—that is, all but the very poorest nations should sacrifice current consumption for additional growth whenever possible. Consider the following example.

Let two countries start from an initial national income equal to 100 rasbuckniks. Country I decides to save 30 per cent of its income or 30 rasbucknicks to start out with. Country II, though, chooses to live more for today and saves only 10 per cent of its income. As a consequence of these decisions, country I's national income grows at a yearly rate of 8 per cent while country II's grows by only 2 per cent. Consumption in country I, we shall suppose, increases less rapidly than investment, say at 7 per cent per year, while both consumption and investment in II go up by 2 per cent per annum. What will happen? After six years country I will not only be growing faster than II, it will actually have more to consume. In this sense it is having its cake and eating it, too.

The reasoning behind the above example is essentially as follows. To begin with, the law of eventually diminishing returns undoubtedly applies to savings and growth just as it does to most economic phenomena. Eventually, that is, given increases in the rate of saving will produce smaller and smaller additions to the long-run growth rate as the marginal efficiency of the additional investment from these savings declines.

Yet, before this happens, some would argue, it is possible and even likely that there will be a range where higher savings will actually bring increasing returns in calling forth higher long-term growth rates. This is implicitly assumed above, inasmuch as a trebling of the savings ratio could cause the growth rate to quadruple.

The reasons behind a range of increasing returns relate to economies of mass production in what is loosely called the "industry of invention." Basically, this industry encompasses research and development facilities, educational and training institutes of all kinds, and producers of capital goods as well, inasmuch as firms usually replace old pieces of capital equipment with improved models. Technological progress is the factor contributing the most to growth in practically every economy the world over and hence the importance of this industry. Unless facilities within it can operate at or above a fairly substantial minimum size, it may not be as efficient as it could be.[7]

Until this minimum scale is reached, additional savings and investment will generate additional expansion and increasing returns as more potential economies of mass production are realized in the industry of invention. Failure to reach this minimum scale may lead to inefficiency in the following sense. Over, let us say, a 10- to 15-year span, it would be possible to make some individuals better off while harming no one in terms of material welfare. This would require a higher level of economy-wide savings and growth. By the same token, once the range of increasing returns is past, the argument for growth emphasis becomes less persuasive.

Moreover, a policy of growth emphasis will not necessarily constitute a violation of consumers' sovereignty, particularly since future generations cannot vote on the percentage of national income that will be saved over the

---

[7] For a partially contradictory view, see Schumpeter's theory of capitalist development in Chapter 13.

immediate future. It can also be shown that external benefits arise from increased savings up to a point. That is, my savings will benefit others, and their savings will benefit me. If the economy-wide volume of savings is determined by the independent decisions of millions of individual households and firms, the result may be too little saving because savers do not fully take these external benefits into account. (This suggests that the decision about how much current income to save should be, in part, a collective one implemented through taxes and subsidies.) [8]

In the spirit of the above, we may say that *dynamic efficiency* prevails when it is no longer possible to make one economic actor better off, except at the expense of another, with the indefinite future taken into consideration. An implication of our discussion is that dynamic efficiency is a stronger condition than static efficiency. A decision to consume 95 per cent of each year's national income may well be statically efficient. But dynamic efficiency requires a minimal accent on savings, investment, and growth.

Conversely, dynamic efficiency requires that the accent on growth not be overdone. Additional investment can only generate additional growth up to a limit. When this limit is reached, there is no growth compensation for the sacrifice in consumption which further capital outlays require. Then the latter become dynamically wasteful even though the conditions for static efficiency may still be met.

Figure 4–8 sums this up. Each point on the consumption-possibility frontier will correspond to one or more statically efficient solutions to the economic problem. But only the segment AB can be considered dynamically efficient. A point like C is inefficient in dynamic terms, and any social preference function that leads the economy to C likewise will be dynamically inefficient. Indeed, efficient social preference functions can be defined in just this way. If an *in*efficient social preference function prevails, this may be a sign that the structure of the economy needs streamlining.

All in all, the arguments of the growth advocates can be compelling. They can also point to a number of success stories in the post-World War II era where high growth rates (by historical standards) have enabled nations to achieve prosperity or break out of the cycle of poverty. Yugoslavia, Japan, West Germany, Italy, France, Rumania, and Taiwan, for example, are all cases in point. Nevertheless, there are at least two major qualifications to their claims. The first concerns the measurement of growth; the second is a more basic philosophical objection.

The measurement problem, first of all, is one whose dimensions have only

[8] And, in this sense, it will not always be completely accurate to think of taxes as *in*voluntary savings. The best discussion of the optimal rate of saving of which the present author is aware is given by A. K. Sen in his article "Optimising the Rate of Saving," *Economic Journal,* Sept. 1961. See, as well, S. A. Margolin, "The Social Rate of Discount and the Optimal Rate of Investment," *Quarterly Journal of Economics,* Feb. 1963. Perhaps the staunchest advocate of growth maximization is Branko Horvat. See his *Towards a Theory of Planned Economy* (Belgrade: Yugoslav Institute of Economic Research, 1964). See, as well, Benjamin Ward's review of this book, "Marxism–Horvatism: A Yugoslav Theory of Socialism," *American Economic Review,* June 1967.

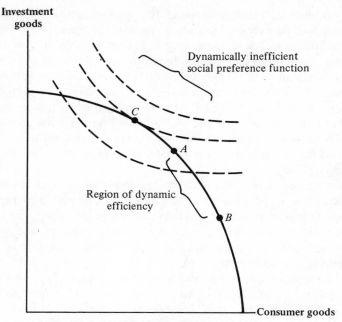

Figure 4–8.   Dynamic versus static efficiency.

lately come to be appreciated by the public at large. If a production process turns out both good and bad products—say, internal combustion engines and air pollution—the value added by this process will have two components. The engines should receive a positive price, reflecting their contribution to welfare, while the air pollution should receive a negative price, reflecting the fact that it detracts from welfare. In this sense, it is a cost rather than a benefit to society.

In calculating net national product or national income and growth, we ought to subtract the costs of pollution, congestion, and urban blight. But the latter are not traded on any market, and their value is practically impossible to estimate. In the case of an exhaustible natural resource, the value to society is likely to exceed the value to any private owner because the resource is being depleted for future generations. Consequently, a depletion charge for exhausting natural resources, similar to the depreciation allowance for wearing out capital equipment, should be deducted when computing the net value of goods and services produced during any given year. Once again, this charge would be practically impossible to estimate with precision, although in countries rapidly exploiting their reserves of oil and nonferrous metals, it should be significantly greater than zero.

The result is that we count the good products but fail to subtract the bad. Or, as Villard has pointed out, "national income is primarily the sum of private rather than social benefits." [9] When efforts to expand industrial out-

[9] H. H. Villard, "The Economic Implications of 3 Percent Growth," *American Economic Review,* May 1968.

put lead to increases in external costs as a percentage of national income, growth rates will be overstated. That is, recorded increases in the consumption of such items as housing, recreation, and transportation will exaggerate the resulting gains in social welfare. Japan may be the most likely candidate for growth overstatement on this account. However, the correlation between "development" and industrialization on one hand and increasing pollution and congestion on the other is marked in every kind of economic system.

All this is not to say that there is anything wrong with growth per se. However, because our measuring instruments are not as sensitive as we would like them to be, we will sometimes fool ourselves about how much growth we are really getting.

The second objection starts with the fact that there is likely to be a tradeoff between growth and equality at the outset of any period of rapid industrialization. This may last for some time, but more important, the process of growth in most countries has created positions of privilege and power that become vested interests. These interests can delay or even thwart any long-run tendencies toward equality.

When there is a tradeoff between growth and equality (or any other distribution goal), the ability of growth to raise human welfare must receive special scrutiny. The name "Bali" has become a symbol of paradise, although in North America, gross national product per capita is probably 20 to 30 times as high as in the Balinese Islands. Poets and philosophers have long emphasized that material welfare is only one side of total welfare, and some have also argued in favor of what we may call the "Thoreau effect."

Basically, this says that the more we have, the more we want. Or, more precisely, as our ability to acquire goods and services increases, it takes more of them just to keep us at the same level of welfare. In this sense, some growth is wasted, and the process of development becomes to some extent a merry-go-round. Increases in wealth raise living standards and thereby make at least some individuals better off. But these same increases raise aspirations and expectations, and this fact, in itself, reduces happiness. The two effects at least partly cancel.[10]

Consequently, some nations may want to reverse the usual development model. Instead of assigning an urgent priority to locking the economy onto a high-growth path, the first goal would be to achieve an approximately equal distribution of welfare. Then the planners (or the government) might try to raise the growth rate, but not at the expense of egalitarianism or of what is sometimes called the "quality of life." This means that they are willing to wait long periods of time, if necessary—while decision makers are educated to respond to moral incentives, including appeals to patriotism and other nonmaterial ideals—before high levels of per capita income and output are

---

[10] No student of economics should fail to read R. S. Weckstein's article "Welfare Criteria and Changing Tastes," *American Economic Review*, Mar. 1962. We have indicated his approach.

achieved. Various authors have argued that China or Cuba (or both) fall into this category.

Of course, there is no shortage of disagreement with any of the above specific claims. However, the important point for our purposes is that a society can legitimately pursue all-out equality instead of all-out growth or virtually any solution in between. Indeed, most economies will remain well within these extremes, seeking to combine a minimum acceptable growth performance with reasonably full employment and constraints to prevent the distribution of wealth from becoming too unequal. This still leaves plenty of room for variation, as we shall see in Chapter 6.

Appendix to Chapter 4

Utilitarianism and Egalitarianism

In this appendix, we wish to turn off the main path and briefly explore two social welfare functions which are of philosophical, ethical, and historical interest. These are the utilitarian and the egalitarian indexes of social welfare, and both are drawn from the "If I Were King" file. We shall say that social *equality* prevails whenever each individual's utility or material welfare is the same. In a two-person world, this will mean that $u_1 = u_2$. Social *inequality* (not necessarily social injustice) will then mean that u_1 and u_2 are not equal.[11]

Keeping these ideas in mind, we have displayed three straight lines in Figure 4–9. One, the 45-degree line, might be called the line of (absolute) social equality because the two individuals have the same welfare ($u_1 = u_2$) everywhere along it. Also shown are two lines of social inequality. The first line ($u_1 = 2u_2$) favors the first individual because his welfare is twice as great as that of the second everywhere along it. The second line ($u_2 = 2u_1$) similarly favors the second individual. These are but three of the infinite number of similar lines that one could draw.

By definition, social welfare is a weighted sum of individual welfares, and in simple cases these lines may be thought of as indicating what weight each individual is to receive. The social welfare function, $W = u_1 + 2u_2$, for example, treats the second individual as if he were twice as important as the first. Its indifference curves would, therefore, be centered on the line $u_2 = 2u_1$.

Let us now consider two definitions of social welfare, which focus on the line of social equality, $u_1 = u_2$. The first, $W = u_1 + u_2$, is closely associated with the early 19th-century philosopher, Jeremy Bentham, and Bentham's slogan, "the greatest good for the greatest number." Since the school of

---

[11] In an economy with many actors, social equality would mean that everyone was at exactly the same level of material welfare. In practice, this would never come to pass, if only because of chance considerations, and we would have to talk about more-or-less equal distributions of welfare.

thought that Bentham founded bears the label "utilitarianism," let us call this the utilitarian social welfare function. Its indifference curves [curves along which the level of social welfare ($= u_1 + u_2$) remains constant] are the straight lines of Figure 4–10(a).

Our second example of a social welfare function identifies to an extent

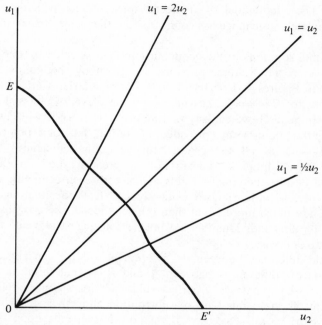

Figure 4–9. Lines of social equality ($u_1 = u_2$) and inequality.

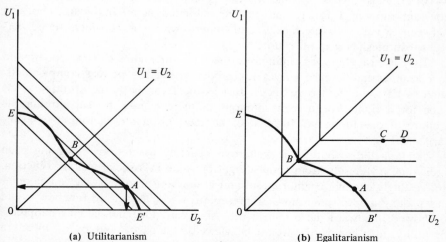

(a) Utilitarianism   (b) Egalitarianism
Figure 4–10. The utilitarian and egalitarian social welfare functions.

with the popular notion of "egalitarianism." It is difficult to put into symbolic form, but we may describe its indifference curves as follows: Social welfare (as defined by our egalitarian social welfare function) cannot rise or fall unless the level of material well-being rises or falls simultaneously for every member in society. These indifference curves have the kinked shape depicted in Figure 4–10(b). A movement such as the one from C to D which leaves some people (here individual 1) unaffected must also leave the level of social welfare completely unchanged, leaving us on the same social indifference curve.

The optimal solutions to the economic problem selected by our utilitarian and egalitarian social welfare functions are given by the points A and B, respectively, in Figures 4–10(a) and (b). The egalitarian function thus lives up to its name, for B is a point at which everyone's level of material well-being is the same. In general, we can say that an egalitarian SWF will always select a point along the line $u_1 = u_2$ (provided, of course, that some point along this line $u_1 = u_2$ satisfies all the criteria for economic efficiency). However, despite the ring of humanitarianism in "the greatest good for the greatest number" and despite the equal weights assigned to each economic actor by a utilitarian function, utilitarianism evidently can lead to situations in which some people are much more equal than others. Indeed, there is absolutely no reason why the first individual should not be starving at A while the second lives in the lap of luxury.

The basic difference between the two social welfare concepts, which, in turn, explains the differences between A and B, is that utilitarianism treats one individual's happiness as a perfect substitute for anyone else's, whereas egalitarianism disallows this kind of substitution altogether. If social welfare, W, is defined to be $u_1 + u_2$, then W in no way depends upon the relative values of u_1 and u_2. In moving along a social indifference curve in Figure 4–10(a), it is always possible to substitute u_1 for u_2, or vice versa, at the constant ratio of 1 for 1, and we are reminded of an individual choosing between two goods—say nickels and dimes—which he considers to be perfect substitutes (here in the ratio 2 for 1).

By contrast, the social indifference surfaces in Figure 4–3(b) correspond to consumer indifference curves for products that are perfect complements, such as left shoes and right shoes. Just as there can be no substituting a left shoe for a right shoe in consumption, so there can be no substituting the welfare of one individual for that of another, given our definition of egalitarianism.

An equal distribution of welfare is scarcely assured by assigning each individual or household an equal weight or value in a social welfare function. Interestingly enough, egalitarianism and utilitarianism may be viewed as polar cases along a spectrum whose "representative" social welfare function would be bowed in toward the origin in the usual way. One individual's happiness or utility, in other words, would be viewed as a partial but by no means a perfect substitute for someone else's.

Finally, when defined as equality of welfares, egalitarianism will not necessarily interfere with economic efficiency. But if we define it more narrowly to imply an equal distribution of wealth, the pursuit of egalitarianism may make economic efficiency unattainable. Unpleasant tasks will tend not to be done on one hand, and the level of education and skills of the labor force may be too low on the other. Furthermore, there would appear to be little or no moral or ethical grounds for using the narrower definition, since, in the final analysis, wealth is but a means to welfare.

REFERENCES

Bator, Francis M. "The Simple Analytics of Welfare Maximization." *American Economic Review,* Mar. 1957.

Baumol, W. J. *Economic Theory and Operations Analysis.* Englewood Cliffs, N.J.: Prentice-Hall, Inc., 1965, Ch. 16.

————. *Welfare Economics and the State.* Cambridge, Mass.: Harvard University Press, 1965, Pt. I.

Bergson, Abram. "A Reformulation of Certain Aspects of Welfare Economics." *Quarterly Journal of Economics,* Feb. 1938.

Drewnowski, Jan. "The Economic Theory of Socialism." *Journal of Political Economy,* Aug. 1961.

Ferguson, C. E. *Microeconomic Theory.* Homewood, Ill.: Richard D. Irwin, Inc., 1969, Ch. 16.

Graaff, J. de V. *Theoretical Welfare Economics.* New York: Cambridge University Press, 1967.

Horvat, Branko. *Toward a Theory of Planned Economy.* Belgrade: Yugoslav Institute of Economic Research, 1964, Chs. 4, 11.

Kohler, Heinz. *Welfare and Planning.* New York: John Wiley & Sons, Inc., 1966, Chs. 2, 3.

Lange, Oskar. "On the Foundations of Welfare Economics." *Econometrica,* July–Oct. 1942.

Lerner, Abba. "Statics and Dynamics in Socialist Economies." In Abba Lerner, *Essays in Economic Analysis.* London: Macmillan and Co., Ltd., 1953.

Lippincott, Benjamin E. "Introduction" to Benjamin E. Lippincott, ed., *On the Economic Theory of Socialism.* New York: McGraw-Hill Book Company, 1964.

Smith, Adam. *The Wealth of Nations* (Edwin Canaan, ed.). New York: Modern Library, 1937, Bks. I, II.

Villard, H. H. "The Economic Implications of 3 Percent Growth." *American Economic Review,* May 1968.

Weckstein, R. J. "Welfare Criteria and Changing Tastes." *American Economic Review,* Mar. 1962.

Weldon vs. Breton: "A Theory of Government Grants," A. Breton, *Canadian Journal of Economics and Political Science,* May 1965; "Public Goods (and Federalism)," J. C. Weldon, and "Reply" by Breton, *CJEPS,* May 1966.

Chapter **5**

Some Problems in the Designing of Systems

Our future may lie beyond our vision, but
it is not completely beyond our control.
Robert F. Kennedy

Equipped with more precise and robust notions of efficiency and optimality, we now wish to bring our knowledge to bear once again on the designing of systems. An important thesis implicit in our analysis thus far is that any nation has a series of organizational forms to pick from and that, depending upon its goals and constraints, some forms will be preferable to others. The present chapter therefore extends our exploration of some of the comparative advantages of different ways of organizing economic activity begun in the early sections of Chapter 2.

5–1   Some Boundaries

Economists generally divide all systems into three categories—centralized, mixed and decentralized—and we shall do the same.

Although the boundary lines are not precisely defined, the frontier between laissez-faire or decentralized and mixed economies is passed when we move from nonplanning to planning. An economic planning council emerges to implement society's major economic goals. The boundary between centralized (or command) and mixed economies is crossed when the greater part of production activity is no longer triggered by obligatory input and output targets. (Most activity in other words becomes generated by horizontal rather than vertical messages.) J. M. Montias once argued that

> The crucial test of the intensity of a reform is not whether what is "good for society" as esteemed by the planners has also been made profitable to the [producing] enterprise, but whether the [economic planning council] is willing to recognize as valid, and even as socially desirable, actions taken by enterprises that conflict with the detailed provisions of the plan or that are not comprehended by any plan at all.[1]

This is the acid test of whether we are dealing with a command or a mixed economy, which, in most cases, will be a market-planned economy.

It is harder to get an acid test of the dividing line between mixed economies and laissez faire. The completely decentralized economy discussed in Chapter 1 is evidently an example of the latter, but if we confine ourselves to this, laissez faire will be an empty category in this era and, one suspects, in every other. Virtually every society in the world today accepts some commitment toward full employment and some constraints on income inequality. Modern Keynesian theory stresses the public sector's obligation to maintain aggregate demand at a full-employment level, implying that the government must exert an important lever over economic activity.

In developed nations there have been few more striking phenomena than the rise in the government's share of aggregate demand after World War II. Charting the ratio of government spending to gross national product in the United States we find that it was 9 per cent in 1909. By 1925 it was only up to 11 per cent. However, it reached 19 per cent in 1947 and 20.7 per cent in 1954. After remaining constant until the mid-1960s, it jumped to a bit less than 23 per cent during the latter half of the decade.[2] In 1970 government *receipts* as a percentage of gross national product ran to 33 in the United Kingdom and to 29 in Canada and the United States, all of which we would classify under laissez faire. For market-planned economies, the same percentage was 41 in Sweden, 39 in France, and only 20 in Japan.

When the government undertakes to reduce unemployment and inequity, the result may be "laissez faire with a more human face." But it need not follow that the economy is planned. The standard Keynesian model speaks of a single composite index, X, of all goods and services produced within an economy and asks how we may raise this to a full-employment level. It does

---

[1] J. M. Montias, "Comment," in the *American Economic Review,* May 1968, p. 583.

[2] In Canada the same statistic shows a steady rise from 13.5 per cent in 1950 to 20.6 per cent in 1966. By 1970 it was 21.5 per cent.

not probe at all into the composition of output or the tradeoffs between production in different sectors of the economy. It has little to say about distribution.

The same "nonpriority" mentality has found its way into government policy making, which has often sought to raise or lower X in the most expedient way. Ironically, therefore, priorities have sometimes been decided on the basis of how well recipients of government spending or subsidies were able to plan ahead and line up a shelf of detailed projects ready to absorb additional funds. In addition, a number of government programs affecting the same problem areas have not been coordinated and have even worked against one another. This does not suggest planning at the economy-wide level, and it follows that a commitment to determine the *scale* of economic activity does not automatically constitute planning.

Rather, we cross the boundary into mixed economies when the government—acting through an agency or agencies that we call the economic planning council—is able to implement a set of weights attached to different goals which indicates their relative importance. These weights need not be determined in dictatorial fashion. But the government must have a whole-oriented framework of socioeconomic priorities and a definite idea of the terms upon which progress toward one goal can be substituted for progress toward another (with approximately no change in social welfare). Suppose, therefore, that we have an economy in which the government's leverage can prove decisive. Then we shall say that planning begins and laissez faire ends when the government controls the substitution, as well as the scale effects, of government policy making.[3]

Within a basically market system, planning is the coordinated use of *non*-market instruments to steer the economy, to make the market mechanism work better, and to supplement the market in "special" areas where it cannot coordinate economic activity efficiently. The instruments useful in planning include the complete range of fiscal and monetary policy tools, quantitative indicators and commands, antitrust laws, moral suasion and government–business interface, consumer-protection legislation, and measures to reduce the harmful effects of inflation. For the most part, these are commands of one kind or another, and their use is intended to help maximize some index of social welfare, however loosely defined.

For example, the efficiency of a market depends upon the environment within which it operates. It is the job of commands in the form of laws, regulations, and taxes, which collectively comprise a *market structure policy,* to create a favorable environment for efficient operation. To steer the economy, a government may draw on at least three different kinds of programs in addition to input and output targets and direct purchases of goods and services:

---

[3] Some economists would prefer to say that there is a gray area between mixed economies and laissez faire. Within this zone, the economy is not planned, but government participation does exceed some threshold level. In particular, it would include what we are calling a Keynesian laissez-faire economy.

1. *Manpower-retraining* programs seek to continually recycle individuals into productive employment by matching skills with demand.
2. *Income supplements,* such as unemployment compensation, old-age pensions, and a negative income tax, seek to put a standard-of-living floor under every household.
3. *A financial-incentive* program seeks to selectively stimulate the producing sector, to help realize scale economies of production, management, and research, and to internalize social costs and benefits. By and large, financial incentives (or subsidies) will have their impact on long-run, investment decisions. Depending upon circumstances, we would expect the program to directly influence 10 to 40 per cent of all investments made during a given year.

The financial-incentive program largely applies to firms, whereas the other two relate to households. If many economists had their way, a second major distinction would be that income supplements ought to be as consistent as possible with consumer sovereignty, whereas financial incentives are generally *not* consistent with complete producer sovereignty. The purpose of an income supplement is to raise the welfare of a household, and we generally start with the assumption that household members know better how to raise their own welfares than would a government official. The purpose of a financial-incentive program, by contrast, is to implement previously determined social—rather than individual—priorities.

Our first thought would therefore be to give income supplements in such a way as to make members of recipient households as liquid as possible. This requires us to give money and to let each household freely decide how to spend its allotment. Such a program would come in lieu of food stamps, free school lunches, or efforts to build special housing for the poor. The only exception to this rule would come when there was strong reason to feel that the money would be spent irrationally or in such a way as to generate external costs. Then the funds might be earmarked. However, many economists would still recommend, for example, giving a household rent or purchase money rather than building housing for it, because of the added freedom of choice that household members acquire.[4] In practice, of course, these recommendations are often disregarded.

On the other hand, we tend to view firms, not as entities which enjoy welfare themselves, but as means whereby individuals and households can increase their welfare. Financial incentives should therefore be tied to expanded investment, which satisfies some designated social priority. For ex-

---

[4] There may be other desirable effects. "Traditionally . . . Federal housing for the poor [has led to] . . . projects . . . where the congestion of human misery bred noise, filth, and crime." Many of these simply became new ghettoes. However, in a Kansas City experiment, over 200 poor families were handed rent money and told to find their own homes. In nearly every case, they were found to be content with their own choices, and many were able to lead more rewarding lives in one way or other. See "U.S. Helps Poor to Rent Own Homes," *The New York Times,* July 17, 1972, pp. 1, 40.

ample, they may be earmarked for production in selected industries or geographical regions. Once we have passed beyond the realm of the command economy and centralized economic decision making, the government will not usually take all the details of investment planning directly upon itself. But it will continue to sponsor a procedure that determines priority spending areas.

Financial incentives may also be used to encourage the expanded use of selected inputs, such as labor in a depressed area. Government policy makers can attempt to raise the aggregate demand for goods and services by means of financial incentives, as part of a contracyclical policy. But even the effects of a (temporarily) depressed aggregate demand will be felt differentially by region.

Essentially, planners who use financial incentives are applying social priorities by creating a two-price scheme. If he is a seller, the manager who is granted an incentive receives a higher price for his output, including the subsidy, than the users pay. The same is true if the incentive is granted to the buyer. Either way tries to encourage both the production and the use of the goods in question. Despite their name, financial incentives will be moral to the extent that the successful manager receives community recognition, a medal, or a title (such as "Hero of Socialist Labor") as his reward in place of expanded pay and promotion possibilities.

Finally, the above programs will not exhaust the economic activities of government. The latter will also concern itself with health, education, programs to internalize social costs and benefits, the use and conservation of natural resources, and, perhaps, with transportation and energy policies. All these programs could conceivably exist in a laissez-faire economy. But either many of them would be ineffective or else they would lack internal or external coordination, working against rather than complementing one another significantly often. To put the matter differently, suppose that we have an economy with a number of diverse special interests, each of which has some power. If such an economy is planned, there will be some mechanism to resolve disagreements between them before the stage of policy implementation is reached.

Or, to take another point of view, let us go back to the polar case of the completely decentralized economy. From there, each of the above measures can be seen as an effort to correct a weakness inherent in this system. The appearance of planning may then be the logical outgrowth of the systematic application of these measures.

5–2 Further Discussion of Markets and Efficiency

"What do you need prices for," a Soviet economist once asked, "if you already know what you are going to do?" If we freely grant him the benefit of any doubts, he is correct, although not entirely relevant. A major benefit from using prices and markets when they work well is that no one needs a detailed knowledge of the entire economy's capabilities and potentialities—

knowledge which, in any event, no single decision maker is likely to have.

This is one of the advantages of markets which permitted us to associate them with static efficiency in Chapter 2, provided they are properly supplemented with commands. To complete this association, we now wish to outline the four main efficiency advantages of the market mechanism. In more-or-less logical order, they are as follows.

Perhaps the most important advantage is the ability of a market system to break up the totality of the economic problem facing all of society into a multitude of subproblems facing each household and firm. These mini-problems are comparatively tiny, both in scope and in the number of variables which they involve. In Chapter 2 we emphasized this from the standpoint of supervisory costs, pointing to the disciplinary nature of markets under approximately competitive conditions. Here we wish to view matters a bit more from the angle of coordinating costs.

Within any economy, households and firms are *interdependent* in the sense that each actor trades with others and must rely upon the exchange network to supply the goods that he needs. Yet, within a market economy, each producer and consumer is largely an autonomous decision maker. He is free to make up his mind what and how to produce or consume and how much of each kind of productive input under his control he would like to supply. When it is working reasonably well, the market coordinates these autonomous decision makers with price signals that tell each one how to fit in with the system as a whole.

As long as prices remain fairly close to levels that balance supply and demand in a properly regulated and supplemented market system, each actor can solve his own problem largely independently of the others.[5] Then in "selfishly" pursuing their own welfares, individual households and firms will often produce a result that comes close to being statically efficient.

The entrepreneur who combines inexpensive inputs to produce an expensive output performs a social service, provided prices approximately mirror the values of these goods to society. If they do, enforceable *non*market signals (for the most part) are equating social and private costs and benefits, making the private profit earned by the entrepreneur a profit for society as well. In a society where self-interest is a strong—although not necessarily the sole—motivating force, markets and loose constraints on income distribution can harness greed and make it productive. In the words of J. M. Keynes, it can permit a man to "tyrannize over his bank balance [rather than] over his fellow citizens."

In practice, prices will normally depart from levels consistent with economic efficiency for many reasons. However, let us fix the distribution of welfare in society for a moment so that we define a unique, or, at most, a limited number of efficient solutions to the economic problem. In this context we shall

---

[5] For a more precise restatement of this claim, see Otto A. Davis and Andrew B. Whinston, "Welfare Economics and the Theory of the Second Best," *Review of Economic Studies,* Feb. 1965.

say that the percentage gap between the actual price of any good that is produced and its marginal social cost is the percentage by which the *lower* of
these two values departs from the higher. (Thus the maximum gap is 100 per
cent.)

Then, as it happens, this percentage gap is squared in computing the
efficiency loss due to monopoly, externalities, and other causes. If markets are
clearing and prices remain within 10 per cent of their efficiency values, by and
large, we can hope for an efficiency loss less than 1 per cent of the total value
of output. On the other hand, a gap of 50 per cent will lead to a loss of up to
25 per cent.[6]

If we imagine the price of a certain good or service starting from its efficient level and rising or falling at a constant percentage rate, the efficiency loss
is, at first, barely perceptible. This loss begins to rise more rapidly, however, as
the percentage gap increases. Insofar as prices do guide decision makers in an
economy where they bear little relation to marginal costs, the loss may be
great indeed. Nevertheless, we see another reason why markets need not give
precisely efficient results. They have some leeway within which to operate.

To show how coordination of decision makers may fail in the absence of
a market, let us return to the problem of efficiently allocating the radio spectrum among potential broadcasters—commercial, police, ham operators, airlines, the forestry service, and so on. The difficulty here is that at any time in
any particular geographical region, much of the spectrum will remain unused
even though there is an excess demand for another part. This means that those
users who find spectrum "space" scarce will need to buy expensive and
sophisticated equipment to conserve the bandwidths allotted them and to
rule out even the remotest chance of interfering with other users. A second class
of broadcasters may have an abundance of bandwidths—given their needs—
and use these wastefully.

Since access to a bandwidth costs nothing for those who have a license
and is prohibited otherwise, both classes of broadcasters are behaving rationally from their own individual points of view. But because the radio spectrum
is being misallocated, both are behaving irrationally from society's viewpoint.
The result of individuals pursuing their own welfares is not efficient, but could
become so if a regulated market were introduced to allocate the spectrum.[7]

To illustrate one of the complexities of centralized decision making, sup-

[6] The formula used to estimate efficiency losses due to misallocated resources, as a
percentage of national income or output, is

$$\tfrac{1}{2}\,\epsilon(\%P)^2$$

Here, $\%P$ is the average percentage gap across the entire economy and ϵ the average
elasticity of demand. The formula makes a number of assumptions, but it is likely to
overstate true efficiency losses unless too many important mass-production (or scale)
economies are not being realized.

[7] Harvey J. Levin, "Spectrum Allocation Without Market," *American Economic
Review,* May 1970.

pose that a planner wants to maximize growth and orders the machine-tools industry to produce all it can. Until a certain rate of output is reached, maximization of machine-tools production will be favorable to higher growth rates. But beyond this turning point, the economy's production resources would be more valuable to the planner working in other industries. In addition, whenever the machine-tools industry uses too many resources and produces too much output relative to other industries, the impact of its actions will reverberate through the system and cause the activity of other firms to become inefficient. Unfortunately, the critical turning point, as well as the optimal mix of different kinds of machine tools, may literally depend upon hundreds of thousands of variables.

Now let us introduce a market system whose prices reflect planners' priorities. *If* we can assume a reasonably elastic flow of resources into the machine-tools industry and exclude both monopoly and externalities within reasonable limits, a strong version of the invisible hand principle will hold. By maximizing their own profits, managers in the machine-tools industry will be furthering the over-all objectives of the planners at the same time.

Similar results hold under similar conditions in other industries. The prices of machine tools relative to the prices of other goods will then be good long-run guides to their relative values to the planner. In the long run, that is, these price relatives will properly allocate resources between different industries.[8] There is a problem, which we shall explore later, in getting prices to reflect planners' priorities. However, it is also worth recalling the comments of an East European official on trade between Soviet-bloc countries. After the world revolution, he said, a single capitalist country would have to remain. "For otherwise how would we know at which prices to trade?" East European countries have often valued their own producers' goods at world-market prices in order to determine the terms of international trade among themselves.

---

[8] Sometimes we call this the principle of suboptimizing. Suboptimizing "works" whenever pursuit of an over-all goal is furthered by pursuit of a subordinate goal. The best-known story about suboptimizing comes out of World War II. At the height of the German submarine menace, Allied specialists gathered to determine how an "optimal" convoy might be designed to get troops and supplies from North America across the Atlantic. The "optimum" was defined in terms of percentages of lives, ships, and materiel lost through submarine attack. The experts were aware that losses depended upon protection, but holding this factor fixed in proportion to convoy size, they found that the larger the convoy, the lower its percentage losses. The optimal size convoy would, on this basis, have consisted of every ship that could have been commandeered to sail the Atlantic. But because ships were scarce and had alternative uses, such a move would have been inconsistent with the over-all goal of winning the war.

Suppose, however, that we could insert a simulated market mechanism into the example. Specifically, let there be a (simulated) price for the use of each ship in the convoy, which will vary with such characteristics as speed, carrying capacity, armament, and armor. Let there also be prices for escort vessels and planes to protect the convoy and (simulated) monetary rewards for delivering men and materiel safely to Ireland. Finally, suppose that these prices reflect relative marginal productivities in reaching the over-all objective of winning the war. If the organizers of each convoy are told to maximize its (simulated) profit, their goals will tend to become consistent with the over-all objective.

These prices reflect preferences and scarcity relationships prevailing in the "capitalist" world and are often not entirely rational within an East European context. Yet they may be better than no prices at all.

The complexity of centralized decision making has three undesirable effects. First, it often causes planners to act according to rules of thumb that require less independent evaluation of each alternative. Second, it leads to large staffs and thus to the bureaucratization of planning, which, in turn, reinforces any other tendencies toward rigidity, inertia, and suppression of individual initiative.

Finally, it gives rise to a kind of "creeping decentralization" in command planning. Different decision makers tend to break up problems into component parts for each to solve, much as they would in a market economy. But in the absence of a market, no signals exist to tell each decision maker the cumulative results of decisions taken elsewhere. He has no simple way of knowing how to gear his own activities in with those of the rest of the economy. Thus interdependent decision makers are not properly coordinated. One manifestation of this is a persistent shortage of some goods, combined with surpluses of others.

In addition, without markets, no way exists to motivate households to consistently register their preferences as accurately as they are able. (This is a major reason why market prices of goods will often measure their relative marginal benefits tolerably well in the absence of significant externalities.) In particular, a command-economy EPC cannot simply send out consumption and labor input "targets" to each household. Experience shows that these are likely to be quite unrelated to individual tastes and, therefore, quite inefficient. Such a comprehensive form of rationing usually creates pressures for a market on which households can effectively redistribute their ration allotments among themselves.

A harsh EPC may set a low consumer-goods budget and try to control the rate at which this increases in order to keep rising expectations or preferences for leisure from "subverting" the system. But it will still want to ration any given budget efficiently among consumers, if only to maximize the material incentives available as rewards for productive effort. This explains why most command economies today maintain markets for labor and consumer goods, even though these often work quite inefficiently, as we shall see.

The advantages of a market system in transmitting and processing information divide naturally into two categories—one for triggers and the other for feedback.

1. Prices are anonymous information triggers. There must be one price for every commodity entering into market exchange but not one for each actor who uses or produces this commodity. To see how this simplifies matters, let us pick an intermediate good produced in 10 firms and used in 25 others as an input. Instead of one price, a command economy will need 35 input and output targets. When there are 100,000 intermediate goods used, on the average, in 25 firms and produced, on the average, in 10 others,

3,500,000 information triggers are required in a command economy as opposed to 100,000 in a market system. The number of additional commands rises multiplicatively with the number of goods or actors involved in the exchange of each good.

To make matters worse, the input and output targets are all interrelated. In the example above there are 250 possible links, on the average between the suppliers and users of each intermediate good, giving 250 X 100,000 = 25,000,000 possible links to consider. Each link is a variable subject to the planners' influence, and the value determined for it will affect the fulfilment of the EPC's preference function. The consequence is that an overwhelmed EPC may give the sectors with the highest priorities the attention they need, while the others are left to their own devices.

2. The information feedback prevalent in a market economy much resembles command-economy feedback. In the former we have quantities demanded and supplied as a function of prices and, in the latter, quantitative responses and counterproposals to plan targets. But the market processes this feedback in a particularly simple way without really giving individual attention to each message.

In effect, the market weighs total demand against total supply, with the weight of each supply or demand vote equal to the quantity demanded or supplied. It acts like a pair of scales with the price providing the balancing weight. When a market is working well, the balance shifts down in response to excess supply and up in response to excess demand, so that it automatically returns to a neighborhood of its equilibrium level.

In a command economy, by contrast, the planners should give some individual attention to every response from below. Suppose, in fact, that all this information is processed routinely—say by taking the midpoint between each original target figure and the corresponding countersuggestion and sending these midpoints out as new targets. This already amounts to considerably more computation than a market performs, but it will not be enough if the planners want to maintain effective control. Producers will soon guess any simple ad hoc rule being followed and manipulate their feedback to get second-round targets that are easy to overfulfill. They will consequently not produce to capacity, thus wasting their scarce plant and equipment. Generally speaking, feedback processing will become more complex as decision making centralizes.

It is worth noting, in this light, that economists often enjoy likening the market mechanism to an electronic computer. One author, getting a bit carried away, has called it a "giant IBM machine in the sky." [9] Analogies do exist between the way a computer will sometimes find a solution to a problem, conceptualized as a system of equations or inequalities, and the way a market would ideally guide the economy to an efficient solution to the economic problem. In each case a systematic trial-and-error procedure converges to the

[9] C. E. Ferguson, *Microeconomic Theory* (Homewood, Ill.: Irwin, 1966), pp. 350–351.

"best" position. Nonetheless, the basic characteristic of the market adjustment process is simplicity.

Even when markets do not work too well, information flows are less roundabout, on the average, because so many messages do not have to travel up one chain of command and down another. There is a cost saving just in shortening the lines of communication. In addition, innovation is encouraged and the distribution network becomes more flexible.

Within a market economy, producers have the power to initiate contacts with customers and suppliers. Either a firm or an individual can try to sell an improved product or a new idea and reap the rewards if it turns out to be profitable. This can lead to abuse, but there is much to be said for permitting initiative and attempting to channel this in the right direction by making innovations pay off to the firms or inventors which introduce them when and only when they are profitable for society. Innovation from below is apt to be seriously stifled in a command economy, which increases the danger that it may get into a rut.

By and large, command-economy firms will have relatively weak links to customers and suppliers and relatively strong ties up the planning chain of command. This will be particularly true when the customer or supplier firm comes under a different jurisdiction in the intermediate planning hierarchy. Consequently, managers will sometimes be more anxious to report statistical successes to their superiors than to tailor their production to user needs. There may be both excessive autarky within jurisdictions (which correspond to sub-hierarchies in the over-all planning chain of command) and external effects between them. Let us probe this problem a bit further.

Because a modern economy is highly interdependent, it will usually not be possible to put each group of firms which are interdependent in some way under the same immediate superior. Any attempt to do so would leave many administrators with spans of control that are too large. Consequently, it will frequently happen that there are two firms, A and B, such that firm A is a supplier for firm B or affects firm B's production process in some other way, while A and B have different immediate superiors and, in this sense, are in different subhierarchies. Often, it will be necessary to go up several links in the chain of command before a common superior for A and B is uncovered. For simplicity, let us assume that A and B are in two different ministries and that their only common superior is the EPC itself.

In this situation, orders for goods to be transferred between A and B will not usually go directly from A to B. Rather, they will follow a roundabout route through the EPC. From feedback information, including past production and projected growth, B's ministry will estimate the input needs of firms, including B, under its jurisdiction and transmit these requirements to the EPC. The latter will initiate the orders that eventually reach A. We would emphasize that many similar orders and responses are continually flowing through the chain of command, along with clarifications, corrections, and claims for recourse. Information channels are therefore likely to become fairly clogged as responses and orders converge on and depart from planning authorities.

Consequently, B will probably find that A is a somewhat unreliable supplier, even when A has the best of intentions. Goods may arrive late or not meet B's input requirements either because B's own superiors have deciphered its needs incorrectly or because the resulting commands were delayed in reaching A or rendered less than perfectly accurate somewhere along the route; B can then ask recourse, but this will mean another delay while information flows through many of the same roundabout channels as before.

Moreover, A may not have an incentive to be a particularly good supplier for B; A will be evaluated by its own ministerial superiors on the basis of statistical success indicators. When the plan is tight, A may sacrifice its required assortment of output in order to fulfill an over-all output index by producing more of those items which are easiest to turn out. (It will have some leeway to do this in any event because it is impossible to specify from above every detail of its production.) Firm A's ministry will have an incentive to encourage such behavior, or at least to not discourage it, because it is also likely to be judged on the basis of performance within its jurisdiction, which includes A but not B; A's ministry may, however, include firms C and D, which also use inputs produced by A. To ensure that C and D achieve their production targets, in turn, A's ministry may ask A to give C and D priority over B, even against the wishes of the central planner.

All this will make A an even less reliable supplier for B, and the degree of reliability will probably be lower, the further one must go up the planning chain of command to find a common superior for A and B. Let us alter the example so that B suffers from environmental disruption produced by A. (For instance, A may be a steel mill and B a fishery.) Then, we would predict that this externality would be more persistent, and more likely to arise in the first place, the further one must go up the planning hierarchy to find a common superior. (Hence, our discussion at the end of Section 2–2.)

As firms find that supplies from outside jurisdictions are faulty, uncertain, or otherwise unsatisfactory, they will take steps to ensure their own plan fulfillment. In many cases, they will undertake to produce some of their own inputs and to stockpile enough to get past supply breakdowns. In other cases, they will be prepared to alter incoming supplies to better fit their own specifications. Where possible, they will switch to suppliers with a closer common superior. Ministries will have an incentive to aid and abet this activity and, indeed, to steer a portion of their own investment credits toward the production of principal input needs of enterprises under their jurisdictions. On occasion, firms and even ministries may merge in an effort to integrate backwards. The final result is the excessive self-sufficiency or autarky, relative to the requirements of efficiency, referred to above.

A second consequence is that firms will undertake too many activities that are ancillary to their main lines of production. In so doing, they will often fail to realize scale economies or to acquire the expertise needed to produce these secondary lines as efficiently as could be done elsewhere. It follows that enterprises in a command economy will tend to be too unspecialized in this sense. The highly specialized firm, when it appears, will usually be the product of a market mechanism that permits development of dependable direct supplier–user relations.

On the other hand, market systems do increase the decision-making loads on producers and lower-level planners. It is not clear that these actors will have to handle a greater volume of data, but they must process a wider variety of information in more sophisticated ways. Likewise, they will have to assume greater risks and responsibilities and engage in functions like forecasting and marketing which are largely done for them—or not done at all—in a command economy. But the reason for breaking up the economy-wide task of optimizing in the first place is that the smaller decision-making chores are likely to prove manageable, whereas the larger one is not. Moreover, if an economy has a supply of competent managers, command planning may relegate them to tasks that will waste their talents. In this sense, the economy will have unused production capacity.

Although it may succeed in better utilizing managerial talent when this is very scarce, a command economy does not provide a good training ground for its top executives of the future. There will be too few positions with ranges of decision-making opportunity and responsibility comparable to that of the EPC, where future top-level planners can learn by doing. Consequently, there will be too much on-the-job training and too many mistakes made above, which should be ironed out below, where they would prove less costly. The shortage of managerial talent in a command economy will tend to perpetuate itself and become a factor prolonging the life of the command structure.

5–3 Commands and the Factory System [10]

Time is the ultimate constraint on all economic activity. If a technological innovation benefits society, it must shift out at least part of its efficiency frontier into previously unachievable space. Such a system achieves greater economy of time by being able to provide more welfare in a given time period or the same welfare in a shorter time period.

Here we wish to distinguish between technological innovations on one hand and economic innovations on the other. Economic innovations do not affect a society's efficiency or production-possibility frontiers. They are largely independent of the physical technology of production and distribution. Instead, they shift out one or more second-best frontiers corresponding to different kinds of economic systems. In this sense they enable society to better organize its economic activity. The introduction of money is an economic innovation that will shift out most second-best frontiers.

Even highly centralized command economies can benefit from a common

[10] This section has been adapted from Nicholas Georgescu-Roegen, "The Economics of Production," *American Economic Review*, May 1970.

denominator of value that becomes a unit of accounting and a store of value. But the principal function of money is as a medium of exchange that replaces barter. Hence more marketized economies will benefit most from its introduction. Indeed, without putting markets on a monetary basis, these economies probably could not hope to approach their production-possibility frontiers.

By contrast, the advantage of command planning lies in its merit as a vehicle through which pressure can be applied when this is the most effective way to steer the economy. The command mechanism provides readily accessible vertical channels from the EPC down to the firms in virtually every producing sector of any importance. Once these are established, they will often be the quickest and surest medium through which a strong planner can apply pressure on producers, mobilize them for priority tasks, or shift capital and labor resources from low- to high-priority sectors.

This is why command planning may best be able to achieve a radical change in social goals. The planners can try to steer the economy indirectly through the market mechanism, using financial incentives. For example, instead of directly allocating investment funds to priority sectors and ordering plants to be built and equipped there, while supplying the necessary technology, they can offer incentives to entrepreneurs who will step forward to build them. Instead of applying direct pressure on producers to utilize their resources intensively and to turn out the "correct" assortment of goods, the planners could rely upon competitive pressures, perhaps again backed by the tools of market planning.

But one of the problems encountered, for example, by a nation industrializing from the ground up is apt to be a severe shortage of entrepreneurs with the initiative and talent that legend assigns, for instance, to Henry Ford for his introduction of the assembly line. If so, financial incentives will do little to inspire the production and technological response that a dramatic takeoff into unfamiliar areas requires.

When a scarcity of entrepreneurs is complemented by shortages of technical personnel and a skilled, urban work force, the central government may have no choice but to play a direct, entrepreneurial role. This implies that the economy will become more like a single firm, and a major purpose in centralizing decision making is to spread scarce managerial talent. One of the basic tasks of the state as an industrializing entrepreneur, for example, will be to get labor out of agriculture and into priority sectors of manufacturing. To this end, it will not necessarily abolish all markets, but it will rely primarily on commands, exhortations, and even coercion.

The historical association between commands and rapid industrialization is by no means confined to Eastern Europe and mainland China. The industrial revolution in England went hand in hand with the enclosure movements in which small landholders were evicted. These became part of the urban work force, which formed the backbone of industrialization. In a different way, Russian peasants were obliged or encouraged to leave rural areas during the Stalin era and again became the backbone of industrialization. Finally,

Japan's pre-World War II industrialization was financed largely by taxes on agriculture, which also became a major source of urban labor.

In view of this, we wish to ask whether there is a major economic innovation that can sometimes enhance the potential of command planning in the same way that money improves the efficiency of the market mechanism. Indeed there is. We shall call it the "factory system," although, as will become apparent, it need not have anything to do with the physical structure called a factory.

To grasp the underlying idea, let us pick an arbitrary production activity. We shall divide its inputs into three categories—labor, stock inputs, such as natural resources and capital plant and equipment, and material inflows, such as cloth, into a dress-making factory. For definiteness, suppose that we are producing furniture and matchsticks, ultimately from trees in a forest. Our fixed inputs consist of logging plant, equipment, and machinery; an equipped factory to produce the final product; timberlands and forests; and a transportation network to move the logs to the factory. Our material inflows include seeds for reforestation, varnish, paint, and various chemicals.

In this context we can distinguish three separate production methodologies. These are (1) elementary production, (2) production in parallel, and (3) production in series or the factory system. To understand elementary production, suppose that we wish to make a chair. The lumberjacks cut down enough wood for this operation. The tree is trimmed and floated downstream to the furniture factory, where it is cut up into wood. Then the wood is fashioned into a chair, which is finally sanded and varnished. The entire operation describes elementary production. If we were to produce one dozen chairs, we would not cut down the tree for the second until the first chair was ready for shipment to market and so on.

Clearly elementary production is quite inefficient for two reasons. First, it takes a long time to produce chairs in this way, since two chairs are never being worked on at the same time. Second, most of the labor and stock inputs lie idle during most of the production process. The loggers and the logging equipment do nothing once the wood has gone to the factory. The joiners, carpenters, sanders, and varnishers do nothing until the logs arrive at the factory. Even after this, they are idle most of the time, and the same is true of most of their tools and machinery. We can register an improvement by letting the same men perform all trades—this is, indeed, the way of the home handyman—but it would be more efficient for them to specialize.

To speed things up a bit, we can start all our chairs at the same time. Now, woodsmen cut down enough trees for many chairs, which are then trimmed and floated downstream to the factory. However, we still do not start our second dozen until the first dozen is complete. Labor and fixed inputs again stand idle for most of the production process or else are not able to specialize sufficiently. In effect, we have taken many elementary processes and put them side by side in parallel. Agriculture in most parts of the world probably comes close to satisfying the conditions for production in parallel. Because of the weather, one crop is not usually started until the previous one has been completely harvested. Correspondingly, most equipment lies idle during most of the year, a major source of inefficiency in agricultural production.

Suppose, however, that we conquered the weather and could grow corn all year around as follows. Assuming a three-month growing season, we plant one fourth of the acreage allotted to corn each month. Thus our planting machinery is always in operation. After three months, we shall harvest one fourth of the acreage every month. Thus our harvesting machinery will operate continuously. The same is true of all our other equipment, which can now become even more specialized, and also of labor. We shall need less of these inputs to grow the same amount of corn, which is now truly being produced by the factory system.

A moment's reflection will show that this is precisely how an assembly line works. Assume that a line has four distinct operations. As soon as a batch of material has gone through the first operation and passes on to the second, a second batch starts the first operation again. Goods are constantly at each stage of the process from material input to finished output. In effect, we have broken up elementary production into its component parts and operated each component simultaneously with the others. This is one reason why an assembly line is so efficient and, more generally, why the factory system is the most efficient production methodology.

The use of commands becomes more effective when it is possible to satisfy social priorities by moving resources out of production in parallel and into production by the factory system. Such a development identifies closely with industrialization or, more precisely, with a change in the mix of output away from agricultural and toward industrial commodities.

This change need not involve any improvement in the technology of production. We sometimes call it *extensive* development, in contrast with *intensive* development, generated when improving technology shifts out a country's production-possibility frontier. (Extensive development is thus defined to be a shift along this frontier or along a lower second-best frontier to take better advantage of the factory system.) Intensive development may nevertheless lay the groundwork for extensive development, as when technical advances in agriculture permit a massive shift of labor to industry with nothing like a comparable loss of farm output.

A government that applies pressure through a chain of command to promote extensive development may sacrifice some of the efficiency of the market mechanism in the process. Then it is effectively trading one economic innovation for another, acquiring leverage and giving up precision.

To close our introduction to command economies, we briefly consider unemployment in command vis-à-vis market economies. Here we mean involuntary unemployment, whose hallmark is men willing and able to work at going wage and salary rates but unable to get jobs. We do *not* mean under-employment or "disguised unemployment" in the form of a redundant labor force, principally in agriculture. Table 5–1 gives figures for several market

Table 5—1.   Unemployment in market economies.

Country	1965	1968
United States	4.5	3.6
Canada	3.9	4.8
France *	2.1	3.3
West German	0.3	1.3
Great Britain	2.1	3.1
Italy	4.0	3.9
Japan	1.2	1.2
Sweden	1.2	2.2
Yugoslavia	2.8–2.9	About 4 (1970)

Sources: For all countries except Yugoslavia: U.S. Bureau of Labor Statistics, *Handbook of Labor Statistics,* 1970, Table 164, p. 383. These figures are adjusted to the definition of unemployment used by Canada and the United States. For Yugoslavia: Carmelo Mesa-Lago, "Unemployment in a Socialist Economy: Yugoslavia," *Industrial Relations,* Feb. 1971, Table 1, 4th col., p. 52. The 1970 estimate is from Andrew Borowiec, "Yugoslav Dilemma," *Toronto Globe and Mail,* Aug. 2, 1971, p. 3.
  * Based on incomplete data.

economies. The data for countries other than Yugoslavia have been reworked where necessary to make them comparable. Yugoslav data almost certainly *under*state unemployment in comparison with the other figures.

A principal advantage of command economies in lowering the unemploy-ment rate is the heavy demand pressures that are partly built into this kind of planning framework. Market economies have suffered unemployment in the past because the aggregate demand for goods and services was too low to absorb a full-employment level of output. Both kinds of economies may ex-perience unemployment that is seasonal, frictional (or workers between jobs), and structural (or a mismatching of labor-force skills and vacancies). Ex-tensive development coupled with urbanization can convert agricultural un-deremployment into structural unemployment in the cities, should industrial skills prove too difficult to acquire. Yet it is sometimes argued that compre-hensive planning will minimize all this, and most command economies officially claim that involuntary unemployment is zero.

A survey of the literature in these countries, however, reveals that un-employment does exist and may, in any particular country and year, reach the figures given in Table 5–1. (Except, possibly, for Canada in 1968, these correspond to a fairly high level of aggregate demand.) Comprehensive economy-wide estimates are rare, but official jobless numbered about 9 per cent of the labor force in Cuba in 1962. Subsequent estimates, by Carmelo Mesa-Lago, run from about 8 and 6.3 per cent in 1963 and 1964 down to approximately 2.2 per cent in 1969. (It may have risen again in 1970.)

Professor Mesa-Lago has also estimated unemployment in Poland at 2.6 to 3.9 per cent during 1965.

Chi-Ming Hou has made four estimates of nonagricultural male unemployment in China for 1949–1960. His lowest estimates include 1955, 16.8 per cent; 1956, 16.5 per cent; 1957, 19.5 per cent; 1958, .3 per cent; 1959, 12.4 per cent; 1960, 17.3 per cent. In interpreting these data we should keep in mind that unemployment is likely to be higher outside of agriculture. Nevertheless, except during the year of the "great leap forward," the comparison with market economies is unfavorable, even if we discount Hou's figures by 50 per cent. (Chinese unemployment has undoubtedly fallen since this time, however, although figures are unavailable.)

Finally, P. J. D. Wiles gives a range of estimates of unemployment in the U.S.S.R. over 1962–1963. The figure that appears most comparable to Table 5–1 is 1.8 per cent, although the possibility of significant error is high.

In nearly all command economies, the actual rate of unemployment varies inversely with the immediate concern of the regime over efficiency. When this concern is latent, *under*employment accumulates in the state bureaucracy and in industry where it serves managers as a reserve against failure in meeting plan targets. Actual *un*emplopment is then relatively low.

During the 1950s, the East European economies were much more interested in expanding production than in efficiency, and development was largely extensive. To all intents and purposes, full employment prevailed. Then, as growth rates slowed during the early 1960s, the concern with efficiency became more paramount. Profitability rose in importance as a success indicator for managers, and unemployment also rose. During 1965, which appears to be a transition year. Mesa-Lago estimates *non*agricultural *under*employment to be 9.7 per cent of the nonagricultural labor force in Poland.[11]

There are good reasons to believe that planning can reduce unemployment, but no particular advantage seems to attach to command vis-à-vis market planning.

5-4   Characteristics of Mixed Economies

Mixed economies comprise both market socialism and what is sometimes called "guided capitalism." By and large they seek to use nonmarket signals to move the economy into a broad neighborhood of its optimal position in

[11] References for the four preceding paragraphs are as follows: Chi-Ming Hou, "Manpower, Employment, and Unemployment," in Alexander Eckstein, Walter Galenson, and Ta-Chung Liu, eds., *Economic Trends in Communist China* (Chicago: Aldine, 1968), Table 17, p. 369; Carmelo Mesa-Lago, *Unemployment in Socialist Countries: Soviet Union, East Europe, China, and Cuba*, Ph.D. dissertation, Cornell University, 1968; P. J. D. Wiles, "A Note on Soviet Unemployment by U.S. Definitions," *Soviet Studies*, Apr. 1972; *Carmelo Mesa-Lago,* "Employment, Unemployment, and Underemployment in Cuba: 1899 to 1970," Pittsburgh, University of Pittsburgh, 1970 (mimeo); and Harry Shaffer, ed., *The Soviet Economy,* 2nd ed. (New York: Appleton, 1969), Pt. VII-B, especially the article "Problems of Labor Utilization" by E. Manevitch.

both output and welfare space. The job of markets is then to take the economy close to its actual optimum along the efficiency and production-possibility frontiers. This added precision cannot be embodied in commands, because planners no longer assume that they have sufficient knowledge of production possibilities.

Thus a mixed system substitutes prices and incentives for most quantitative commands. The EPC tends to look out over a collection of firms whose managers have considerable decision-making autonomy and responsibility. With a reduction in the stream of vertical controls, firms are more free to seek out their own buyer–seller relationships. Planning then becomes more a question of molding market structures and of designing an incentive system that will motivate managers to harmonize their goals with the center and produce efficiently.[12]

In short, when compared with the command-economy model, the mechanics of a mixed system are basically as follows:

1. The messages that trigger economic activity become more anonymous, and the responses to these messages generally more operational. Prices and, to a lesser extent, indicators tend to replace commands as guides for producers. At the same time, planners will tend to exercise more indirect controls over the system, and money will play a more prominent role as a medium of exchange.
2. Correspondingly, firms—and, to a lesser extent, households—will have more decision-making autonomy.

The manager who experiences a rapid transition to a command economy is likely to find the change traumatic. Under the old regime, he was mainly a foreman charged with meeting production targets and deadlines. Now he must decide what and how to produce, and he is also responsible for marketing his product, financing his operation, and staying abreast of technological progress. Some managers will fail to adapt to the new conditions and will succumb to their competitors. Hopefully, a new breed, which can flourish in an environment of expanded responsibility, will arise to replace them.

More generally, a mixed economy relies upon a division of function that is absent in the centralized model. The broad strategy of economic development is still defined by an economic planning council. But the operative decisions that make or break it are mostly made by the men on the spot. However, commands in the form of taxes will continue to mobilize additional savings when these are needed to finance development. Nonquantitative commands—such as truth-in-lending or antinoise legislation—will often define and enforce the rules governing good citizen firms and households.

In addition, the emergence of a mixed system to replace a command econ-

---

[12] However, the role of incentives is by no means unimportant in a command economy, as we shall discover in Chapter 9.

omy will probably imply one or both of two things: (1) the economy has grown so complex that an economic planning council can no longer decide what and how firms should produce more effectively (from the EPC's point of view) than the managers; (2) regardless of complexity, the EPC can no longer manipulate its actors via a system of commands for political, psychological, sociological, cultural, or other extraeconomic reasons.

One goal of a mixed economy, especially when the first point holds, will be to reduce the planning bureaucracy. Recalling the analogy between a command economy and a giant firm, we may state that decentralization of decision making in each case is often justifiable on many of the same grounds. Much has been written on the causes of decentralization in a corporation, and many of these reasons are relevant here. We would, in particular, cite the following passages by Gordon Shillinglaw:

The hallmark of the decentralized company is its subdivision into a number of smaller, relatively self-contained entities that are equipped to operate in substantially the same manner as independent firms dependent on their own profit performance for economic survival. The creation of these semi-autonomous units, often referred to as *profit centers,* has three major objectives:

1. To provide a basis for delegating portions of top management's decision-making responsibility to executives who have a close operating familiarity with individual products or markets.
2. To bring subordinate executives into more direct contact with the ultimate profit objectives of the firm.
3. To provide an integrated training ground for the top managers of the future.[13]

As the sphere covered by markets expands, many firms will become "profit centers" in the sense that profits will be a key managerial success criterion. But we may also speak in this sense of "growth centers" and "sales centers," inasmuch as these will sometimes reflect the principal goals of the firm. We shall discover later how an EPC can steer the economy by influencing entrepreneurial goals.

The "top management" of a mixed system will be its sector of direction and administration, which we continue to identify with the EPC. Between the EPC and the producing sector will lie a network of intermediate authorities. There will be a principal partitioning of all or part of the economy into geographical regions, groups of industries or products, or more complexly defined segments, and a minister of some kind will be responsible for implementing the EPC's goals within each. In comparison with a command economy, the minister's span of control should be greater and there should be fewer steps in the chain of command, on the average, before the individual

[13] Gordon Shillinglaw, *Cost Accounting: Analysis and Control* (Homewood, Ill.: Irwin, 1967), pp. 780–781.

firm is reached. This is another way of saying that the over-all planning bureaucracy should be smaller.[14]

Shillinglaw's second and third points apply to intermediate officials and managers of the economy's most important firms, with the social goals of the EPC replacing the ultimate profit objectives of the firm. As in a command economy, ministers may or may not sit on the EPC itself. In any event, as we replace vertical lines of communication with horizontal linkages, we reduce their authority to the degree that we spread decision-making autonomy and responsibility through the system. In comparison with a command economy, the planning hierarchy of a mixed economy should offer greater opportunity for future top planners to gain experience and make inevitable mistakes at lower levels.

Shillinglaw continues:

> To provide flexibility and adaptability to changing conditions, it has become increasingly necessary to delegate substantial powers to executives who can maintain a closer, more detailed familiarity with individual products or markets. In other words, decentralization aims to recreate in the large organization the conditions that give life and flexibility to the small company without sacrificing the advantages of size—diversification of risk, centralized financing, and specialization in the planning and advisory functions of management.[15]

These comments apply, as well, to mixed systems vis-à-vis command economies.

On the other hand, a mixed economy differs from a decentralized system in the existence of a leading decision maker who implements social priorities. Such an EPC exerts enough influence over the path of economic development that we decide to view the economy as being guided by the macrorationale of a planner rather than by a synthesis of microoriented preferences.

Yet the EPC could be nothing more than a grandiose version of the Council of Economic Advisers in the United States or of the Economic Council of Canada (although it would have to have considerably more power vested in it). Viewed as a staff agency, it could conceivably be a private planning board hired by the government. In some cases it may be difficult to say whether a given economy is being planned and, if so, who the planners are. At the other extreme, the EPC would constitute the central planning apparatus

[14] For example, the Hungarian decentralization or "reform," begun in the mid-1960s, had resulted in personnel cuts of at least 30 to 40 per cent at the ministerial level by early 1970. See Richard Portes, "Economic Reforms in Hungary," *American Economic Review,* May 1970.

[15] Shillinglaw, op. cit., p. 781. Gregory Grossman maintains that "The advantages of decentralization . . . [in] all economic organizations . . . and of the consequently shorter lines of communication are: greater speed and fidelity of transmission of information, lesser volume and cost of information processing, faster and better adaptation to changing conditions (demand, technology, resource position), resolution of conflicts at lower levels (hence a lesser politicization of economic conflicts), and a larger . . . realization of dispersed initiative for improvement and innovation." Gregory Grossman, "Notes for a Theory of the Command Economy," *Soviet Studies,* Oct. 1963.

of an economy such as Hungary, which has only recently evolved from the command form.

It follows from what we have said that mixed economies will tend to be more centralized in terms of economic decision making and thus less anonymous and less operational than laissez-faire systems. The reverse is true with respect to command-type economies. However, a mixed system could either be less power centralized than a particular laissez-faire economy or more power centralized than a given command economy, although the latter appears from historical evidence to be unlikely.

Important socialist writers like Lange, Taylor, and Dickinson identified the socialist market economy with "liberal socialism" and the command economy wth "authoritarian socialism." That is, they viewed the EPC in a socialist market economy as an intermediary rather than as the ultimate repository of power.[16] They also believed that the EPC would be more sensitive to public wants and needs under market socialism than within a command economy. Yet it is worth noting that nothing requires this to be so. The EPC could be authoritarian.

In the final analysis, mixed economic systems seek to combine the advantages of centralized and decentralized economies, as well as to realize a few special advantages of their own. However, in comparison with a command economy, the planners lose some leverage over the system. In comparison with laissez faire, the mixed economy may be more bureaucratic.

Yet in a world where the government necessarily plays a major role as a taxing and subsidizing agent and as a purchaser of goods and services, this will not always be true. Ironically, by streamlining and coordinating the economic affairs of government, planning may permit the same level of social welfare to be achieved with a smaller government participation in the economy. In particular, by enlarging the options of policy makers, planning can reduce their need to respond to contingencies of the moment.

Perhaps the biggest danger of any planned economy is that the planners will overconcentrate on production for the sake of production or growth for its own sake while neglecting the use value of production. There is ample evidence that Soviet planners have done this. (Ironically, neglect of use value was one of Marx's major criticisms of laissez-faire capitalism.) More recent indications are that some French planners may be developing a similar mentality.[17] We shall return to this problem in Chapter 23.

---

[16] See, for example, Fred M. Taylor, "The Guidance of Production in a Socialist State"; and Oskar Lange, "On the Economic Theory of Socialism," in Benjamin E. Lippincott, ed., *On the Economic Theory of Socialism* (New York: McGraw-Hill, 1964). See also E. Malinvaud, "Decentralized Procedures for Planning," in E. Malinvaud and M. O. L. Bacharach, eds., *Activity Analysis in the Theory of Growth and Planning* (New York: Macmillan, 1968); and H. D. Dickinson, *The Economics of Socialism* (New York: Oxford U.P., 1939), Ch. 1.

[17] For example, see François Perroux, Jean Denizet, and Henri Bourguinat, *Inflation, Dollar, Euro-dollar* (Paris: Editions Gallimard, 1971), especially Pt. I.

5–5   Mixed Economies and Efficiency

The best policy implementation under market planning tries to create and to channel initiative among producers. Initiative must often be channeled before we have any insurance that it will be socially worthwhile. An entrepreneur may earn a profit by bringing a useful product to market. But he can also improve his profits, sales, or growth performance, on occasion, by inflicting costs on society for which he does not pay. It is the task of *nonmarket* signals, including commands, to tie managerial success to social contribution.

To illustrate how planning can help to promote efficiency, consider the following situation. A major planning lever in any mixed economy is control over the terms upon which funds become available to producing enterprises for investment. A leading decision maker can steer by granting some sectors and projects more attractive credit than is generally available. This may be done directly through a banking agency or other lender or indirectly through such instruments as accelerated depreciation, which reward some—or all—investment with a tax advantage.

Any subsidy tied to long-run output expansion is basically of this nature. If a program of these "financial incentives" is handled properly, it can achieve a selective expansion of the economy or an income redistribution. Such a tool has found use all over Western Europe and in Japan.

For example, to aid the recovery from the devastation of World War II,

the [Japanese] government and the central financial authorities supplied funds lavishly to industry, both indirectly through the purchase of bank bonds and directly through subsidies. . . . The [Reconstruction Finance Bank] was founded in February, 1947 to furnish loans for the reconstruction of the "essential" or "basic" industries and to say that it made an important contribution to industrial recovery could be an understatement. In 1947, it furnished . . . 72 per cent and in 1948 69 per cent of the total funds applied to corporate fixed investment. The coal-mining, electric power, and shipping industries obtained nearly all of their new capital from this bank.[18]

Later, during the late 1950s and 1960s, Japan underwent perhaps the most rapid industrial transformation in history. Steel was at the heart of this growth, and steel production expanded from around 12 million tons annually in 1958 to almost 40 million tons in 1964 and reached 93 million tons by 1970. From a relatively modest producer of steel, Japan achieved third place in the world, producing over 15 per cent of global output, and far more on a per capita basis than either of the nations (the United States and the U.S.S.R.) that preceded her. As we have seen, this came about with government assistance, encouragement, and direction. In the process, economies of scale were realized, along with enormous technological progress. "The quality [of the product]

[18] G. C. Allen, *Japan's Economic Expansion* (New York: Oxford U.P., 1965), pp. 49–50.

was [also] improved and the range of products extended to take in special steels and highly fabricated goods." [19]

External economies played an important role in the expansion because Japan lacked a raw material base and had to import both iron ore and coal. Thus she relocated the industry close to the sea and "built large fleets of ore and coal carriers which greatly reduced the cost of transport from overseas . . . she [also] equipped herself with very efficient means of discharging the cargoes at the sites of the iron and steel plants." [20] This indicates how a planner on good terms with the producers he is guiding can use his vantage point to coordinate different industries which form a chain of buyer–seller relationships. (During the same period, autos became a principal user of steel. By 1970, passenger-car output reached 3,179,000 units, 67.5 times the 47 thousand units produced in 1957.)

Finally, the expansion involved considerable risk from many sources. For example, G. C. Allen wrote in 1965 that "not long ago it was commonplace to assert that [Japan's] lack of essential raw materials and the high cost of fuel would inevitably put narrow limits on her accomplishments in this industry." [21] This raises an interesting point. One way to make investment credit more attractive, of course, is to reduce interest rates on loans. But as businessmen are aware, the actual interest charge on a loan often represents a small part of its true "cost."

More important, on many occasions, will be the risk that the producer bears in contracting for the loan and in carrying out the capital-spending program for which it is intended. He will normally have to pay back principal and interest in regular instalments. If a year or two of low profits comes along, his repayments still fall due. In such circumstances the EPC can substitute a flexible repayment schedule in which interest and principal falling due are allowed to vary with profits. During bad years, these instalments would be reduced or postponed. The government would guarantee to make up lost repayments to the lender, thereby removing a risk burden from his shoulders as well.[22]

Guaranteed loans cannot be made without a careful weighing of social costs and benefits, and they should never be given out on a piecemeal basis. Yet there can be a net gain for the economy as a whole here when we take the entire financial-incentive program into account. That is, the EPC would hope to shoulder a smaller total risk burden than individual managers collectively give up. For its risk is effectively spread over diverse sectors of the economy so that failures in some areas are bound to be canceled by successes elsewhere. (This is the way that an insurance company or a mutual fund reduces its risk.) These risk reductions can then be passed on to firms in the form of more attractive credit. The net result is to realize what would otherwise often

[19] Ibid., p. 157.
[20] Ibid., p. 161.
[21] Ibid., pp. 157–158.
[22] However, the loan would usually have to be repaid eventually.

remain an external economy. Risk is a private but not a social cost to the extent that it can be diversified away.[23]

Nevertheless, a financial-incentive program will never involve all gain and no cost. We may view the borrowing costs of a loan, including an allowance for the repayment terms, as a price to be paid just like the prices of food, clothing, and medical care. Because taxes and subsidies change the prices that buyers pay or sellers receive, they may cause any of these prices to depart or to depart further from their efficient values. When this happens, an efficiency loss will be created.

The potential price-distorting effects of a financial-incentive program will, if realized, become costs to society. The potential benefits to be weighed against these are efficiency gains—such as those from reducing unemployment, realizing scale economies, or internalizing external effects—and the leverage that the EPC gains over the path of economic development. Our earlier discussion reveals that the losses from price distortion are likely to be small, provided managers respond to incentives with initiative and skill. And if they do not, a greater reliance on command planning may be necessary to achieve a desired reorienting of the economy.

Several estimates of the efficiency with which resources are allocated under market and command planning tend to bear out parts of our discussion above. The famous Soviet mathematical economist L. V. Kantorovich once maintained that the U.S.S.R. could raise its national income by 30 to 50 per cent through a better allocation of resources. However, he presented no calculations. Abram Bergson, on the other hand, used elaborate calculations to estimate that Soviet national income per unit of factor inputs was between 34 and 69 per cent of the U.S. level in 1960.[24] Part of this gap results from differences in the efficiency of resource allocation, but part is also due to differences in the quality of inputs and in levels of technology. The net impact

---

[23] Some risk will be diversified away in almost any market economy, but an EPC will be better equipped for the task than any other actor. To see how diversifying risk can reduce it, suppose that we have a small investor who purchases shares in two or three small oil and uranium prospecting companies. His money is now in great danger of being lost altogether, but he could also become enormously wealthy, and this is what he is gambling on. Let us suppose his gamble pays off and he strikes it rich. To celebrate, escape income taxes, and establish a perpetual income stream, he buys shares in 2,000 companies—1,000 diversified blue chips and 1,000 widely diversified, but highly uncertain, "growth" stocks.

What will happen? It is quite possible that the return from each category, averaged, let us say, over a 15- to 20-year period, will be about the same. Yields from specific stocks in the second category will show more ups and downs, and firms in it will either tend to fail or succeed spectacularly more often than in the "blue-chip" category. But when the averaging process is allowed for, there will be no reason for yields from the two categories to differ by much.

In diversifying, the investor has cut the risk to himself, even though a number of his holdings may still be perilous ventures.

[24] Abram Bergson, "Comparing Productivity and Efficiency in the U.S.A. and the U.S.S.R.," in Alexander Eckstein, ed., *Comparison of Economic Systems* (Berkeley, Calif.: U. of Calif., 1971), pp. 180–181.

of these and other studies indicates that the efficiency cost of command planning is often high, but it is not possible to say just how high.

At least until late 1969 or early 1970, the Soviet planners reinforced their control through the command mechanism with what amounted to a financial-incentive program. To qualify for a loan or grant from the state budget, proposed investment projects had to have a much higher yield in light industry, on the average, than they did in heavy industry. This channeled funds into heavy industry, which had a high priority in the planners' preference function. Table 5–2 shows the entire structure of effective interest rates prevailing in

Table 5–2. Effective interest rates in Soviet industry, 1964.

Industry	Per Cent Yield Expected	Per Cent Subsidy or Incentive *
Coal	5.36	9.59
Petroleum	9.15	5.80
Electric power	4.63	10.32
Ferrous metallurgy	8.72	6.23
Machine building and metal working	16.48	−1.53
Chemicals	17.82	−2.87
Forest products, paper, and woodworking	8.26	6.69
Building materials	4.67	10.28
Light industry	31.97	−17.02
Food industry	30.78	−15.83
Average for all industries	14.95	

Source: Judith Thornton, "Differential Capital Charges and Resource Allocation in Soviet Industry," *Journal of Political Economy,* May–June 1971.

* Average yield less actual yield. A minus sign (−) denotes an effective additional tax rather than a subsidy.

the U.S.S.R. as of 1964. There can be little doubt that they reflect planners' priorities through most of the era since the first five-year plan began in 1928.

We shall see later why the Soviets had to reinforce command planning in this way. For now let us assume briefly that they could have caused the economy to produce the 1964 assortment of goods and services solely with the aid of the differential interest charges—amounting to differential expansion incentives—found in Table 5–2. These would be superimposed upon a common managerial success indicator, such as maximization of the enterprise's long-run profitability. In place of a comprehensive network of commands, we would find a comprehensive network of markets directly linking buyers and sellers. We have therefore transformed a command into a mixed-economy scenario.

There will be an efficiency loss from steering this mixed economy due to the price distortions that the differential incentives in Table 5–2 create. Specifically, too much capital will be concentrated in the high-priority sectors and not enough in the low-priority sectors, in comparison with the completely efficient supersystem. To ensure that priority sectors do, in fact, expand, the planners grant them lower-cost loans.

Referring to Table 5–2, managers in the building-materials industry can make investments that yield only 5 per cent, pay back the interest charges, and still have some profit left over. Managers in light industry, on the other hand, could have in mind a project yielding six times as much. However, such a project would still be unprofitable after deducting interest charges. It follows that capital will have a lower yield—or a lower value of marginal product—on the average in higher-priority sectors. The reverse is true of labor, because manpower in higher-priority sectors has more capital to work with.

In theory, output would be higher if more investments had been concentrated in lower-priority sectors—where capital is more productive—and if more labor were concentrated in higher-priority sectors. From Chapter 3 we know that efficiency requires the value of each input's marginal product to be the *same* in all industries. The differential rates in Table 5–2 prevent this. If we could somehow equalize marginal products across industries and yet steer the economy, we could increase the output of *every* good and maintain the same output mix. However, the total gain would have been no more than 2 to 4 per cent of national income. This is the maximum price-distortion cost of using incentives to steer the economy.

In fact, by redesigning the incentives in Table 5–2 along lines to be suggested later, we could probably reduce this cost still further without sacrificing steering power. In the Soviet context, however, there would doubtless be some leverage loss in comparison with the command mechanism.[25]

5–6   Classification of Some Real-World Economies

At this point it may be helpful to the reader if we place real-world economies into some of the categories we have created. The exercise is speculative, but we would suggest the classification in Table 5–3.

Such a scheme is bound to conceal many important distinguishing characteristics. For example, within the mixed category, Yugoslavia is the only country whose enterprises are at least nominally governed by the workers themselves through their representative on workers' councils. Both France and Japan rely to some extent upon indicative planning. An important difference between Eastern Europe and the U.S.S.R. on one hand and China and Cuba on the other is that the latter have relied more heavily on moral incentives to achieve national goals. It is also true that administrative control over industry has never reached the degree of centralization in China that it

---

[25] The reference for the preceding discussion is Judith Thornton, "Differential Capital Charges and Resource Allocation in Soviet Industry," *Journal of Political Economy,* May–June 1971. See, as well, the references cited by Thornton.

Table 5–3

Kind of System	Country
Decentralized (laissez faire)	Canada; United Kingdom; United States
Between laissez faire and mixed	West Germany; Yugoslavia
Mixed	Sweden; Japan; France; Hungary *
Between mixed and command	
Command	U.S.S.R. and East-bloc countries, except Yugoslavia and Hungary; Cuba; People's Republic of China *

* Either Hungary or China may lie in the category "Between mixed and command."

did in Eastern Europe. Perhaps surprisingly, markets of one kind or other have usually played a more important role there.

National goals differ radically within as well as between categories. For example, Sweden is more distribution-oriented than Japan, which has achieved the world's highest growth rate. China has put less emphasis on heavy industry than has the Soviet Union and more on agriculture. China has also shown less interest in growth per se or in production for the sake of production, and more in the use value of production. Managerial performance in China is graded on loyalty, ideological purity, and product quality as well as sheer volume of production. The pressure to report statistical "successes" is considerably lower there.

Perhaps the most contentious classification is that of China, which is in many ways unique and defies easy categorization.

REFERENCES

Grossman, Gregory. "Notes for the Theory of a Command Economy." *Soviet Studies,* Oct. 1963.

Tinbergen, Jan. *Central Planning.* New Haven, Conn.: Yale University Press, 1964.

————. "The Theory of the Optimum Régime." In Jan Tinbergen, *Selected Papers.* Amsterdam: North-Holland Publishing Company, 1959.

Chapter 6[*]

On Making Economic Comparisons— Income, Wealth, Welfare

6–1   Introduction

We live in a materialistic age. Such is our preoccupation with "growth" and "development" that there can be no dancing on the village green, it seems, while the gross national product is tapering off. The importance assigned by our society to production was illustrated during the post-Sputnik era, when it

---

[*] If the reader is as bored by comparisons as I am, he can skip this chapter altogether without missing any essential ideas. If he is interested in the results of the comparisons, but wishes to skip the underlying (revealed preference) theory, he should skip sections 6–5 through 6–8. I am indebted to Sheila Isaac for the artwork and to G. F. Trolley and P. C. Yao for many of the computations in this chapter.

became apparent that the Soviet economy was growing faster than that of the United States. Panels, discussions, and congressional hearings were convened at which political and economic sages debated ways of preventing this awful event from occurring. Very few were the voices asking "so what?" or "what for?" and those who did cried strictly in the wilderness.

Nor were such preoccupations confined to the West. Political jokes in the U.S.S.R. are sometimes attributed to a fictitious "Armenian Radio." A few years back the Armenian radio reportedly told of a Soviet schoolteacher who asked her best pupil to describe life in America. The pupil replied:

"All American workers are unemployed. Only the capitalists can eat. Negroes are lynched every day, and no one is happy."

The teacher then asked about Soviet life:

"We have full employment. The state provides everything. Schools are free. No one is unhappy."

"Good," the teacher said, "and what is our party slogan?"

"We must overtake and surpass the United States." [1]

In such an age, making economic comparisons has come to be a popular indoor sport, and our basic goal in this chapter will be to discuss and evaluate ways of making comparisons. The ultimate criterion for comparing will be some concept of social welfare, as expressed in one of the social preference functions developed in Chapters 2 and 4. Thus the dimensionality of our comparisons will reflect the dimensionality of social welfare. When we take account of data availability, we are normally left with three broad kinds of comparisons:

1. The distribution of income or wealth.
2. Aggregate or per capita gross national product.
3. The growth of GNP.

In two of the three measures, GNP is the predominate variable. It is essentially a measure of the total volume of goods and services produced within a particular economy during any given year.

There is prestige value for the United States in maintaining a higher per capita GNP than the Soviet Union and for Japan in maintaining the world's fastest rate of growth of GNP. However, at best, GNP can only be an ordinal index of welfare. A doubling of GNP per capita in the United States during a short time period might well raise the material welfares of many citizens. But we have no a priori way of knowing whether this welfare more than doubles or less than doubles on the average. Sometimes we read that an extra dollar provides more additional welfare to a poor man than to a rich man because the marginal utility of income obeys the law of diminishing returns. If so, a doubling of everyone's purchasing power—and a doubling of production to match—would less than double the welfares of most citizens.

Moreover, there are several drawbacks specifically to using GNP as an

[1] Retold from C. L. Sulzberger, "The Deadliest Radio of Them All," *The New York Times,* Aug. 22, 1962, p. 32.

index of welfare. To begin with, GNP includes depreciation on plant and equipment, which does not contribute to welfare but is rather difficult to estimate precisely. Subtracting depreciation, we get net national product. This is still a measure oriented toward goods produced rather than consumed. Country *A*, which runs a surplus of exports over imports year after year, may on that account show a higher level of per capita NNP than country *B*, whose exports and imports more nearly balance over the long haul. Yet per capita consumption in the two countries may be virtually the same on a year-in year-out basis.

Moreover, suppose that Japanese or Americans place a high marginal value on leisure—perhaps because they wish more time to enjoy some of the goods being produced and made available. Then a program to keep GNP and NNP high could imply an actual sacrifice of welfare. In fact, a price tag— a wage or salary rate—can be placed on leisure. One "buys" an hour of leisure by not working during that hour. In principle it is possible to estimate a total value for all the leisure consumed each year within a given economy and include this in our measure of social welfare. Nevertheless, we can probably rest assured that national-income accountants will continue to value automobile production in the billions of dollars while leisure continues to be valued at nothing.

Consequently, although we can take a major step or two beyond the usual comparisons that are made under measure 2 above, we shall have to rely upon GNP as our principal index of well-being. Before doing this, however, we shall discuss one pioneering effort to estimate a more comprehensive welfare measure.

6–2   Income and Wealth Comparisons

Income is a *flow* concept as opposed to a *stock* concept like wealth. Any flow always has a time dimension that is missing from a stock. If the amount of money in my bank account is $2,000, for example, this refers to a portion of my wealth. However, my income might be $5,000 *per year*. Similarly, the GNP of the United States in constant dollars of 1958 purchasing power was $724.1 billion in 1970, or $3,535, on the average, for every man, woman, and child. Depreciation charges ran about 62.5 billion 1958 dollars, leaving a net national product of approximately $661.6 billion. Thus during 1970 the U.S. economy turned out about $661.6 billion worth of goods and services at 1958 prices.

During the five-year period 1966–1970, U.S. GNP averaged 697.7 billion per year in constant 1958 dollars.[2] GNP, then, is an amount per year, per quarter, and so on—that is, a flow. By contrast, the total wealth of the United States in 1968 was estimated to be between 2.5 and 2.6 trillion 1958 dollars,

[2] Sources: U.S. Department of Commerce, Bureau of the Census, *Business Conditions Digest,* Mar. 1969, Table 1, p. 5, and Apr. 1971, Table 1, p. 5 (Washington, D.C.: G.P.O.).

with $1.9 trillion of this in the form of reproducible assets. In terms of current dollars, these figures were $3.1 trillion and $2.4 trillion, respectively.[3] These indicators give the total stocks of goods, both capital and consumer goods, in the country as of 1968. As such they have no time dimension.

Although it is usually much easier to estimate *flows,* such as GNP or NNP, than *stocks,* such as aggregate wealth, comparisons in terms of wealth are usually more meaningful. As a measure of welfare, income concentrates largely on current consumption possibilities. Ideally, welfare measures should also give some indication of future consumption possibilities, suitably discounted. Wealth does this better than income.

Let us go back for a moment to the Robinson Crusoe island economy and again change the plot a bit so that Mr. Crusoe and Mr. Selkirk inhabit separate islands and do not trade. Then, in terms of present satisfaction, Mr. Crusoe and Mr. Selkirk may be equally well off and approximately equally well equipped with the means of obtaining current well-being. But if Mr. Crusoe's island was much more capable of providing him with an increased store of wealth over the forthcoming years of his isolation, and consequently more in terms of future consumption prospects, we would want to say that he was better off than Mr. Selkirk. Income comparisons sometimes neglect this kind of growth potential.

Even comparisons of current well-being may be grossly misstated by contrasting incomes alone. If the Robinsons own a family mansion and a Rolls-Royce while maintaining a bank account on the order of $500,000 or so, they are bound to have a higher living standard than the Prescotts, who own a $20,000 home with a $10,000 mortgage, a Volkswagen, and a $2,000 bank account, even though Mr. Prescott may have earned a slightly higher after-tax income last year for one reason or another. A less extreme form of the same thing may happen when aggregate levels of income are being considered.

This does not mean that we should avoid income comparisons altogether. Indeed, because of data limitations, comparisons are almost always made in terms of income flows. Nevertheless, we should realize that we are using income as a proxy or substitute for wealth. An even better approximation to welfare would be a measure of present and *potential* wealth, which we could then convert to a flow of sustainable income or consumption over long periods of time. There has been one pioneering effort, due to Nordhaus and Tobin, to derive a measure of this kind, relating to the U.S. economy for selected years over the period 1929–1965. Before proceeding to actual comparisons, we shall explore it briefly. We would emphasize its highly tentative and experimental nature at the outset.[4]

[3] Sources: U.S. Department of Commerce, Bureau of the Census, *Statistical Abstract of the United States, 1967* (Washington, D.C.: G.P.O., 1971), Tables 524–525, pp. 328–329. The implicit price deflator for reproducible assets was applied to total tangible assets.

[4] James Tobin and William D. Nordhaus, in *Economic Growth, Retrospect & Prospect,* National Bureau of Economic Research Fiftieth Anniversary Colloquium V (New York: Columbia University Press, 1972).

6–3   Sustainable Measure of Economic Welfare

We have already pointed out several ways in which a country's GNP must be adjusted to determine a level of aggregate or per capita consumption which it could reasonably hope to sustain over long periods over time. Following Nordhaus and Tobin, we shall derive a related concept called "sustainable measure of economic welfare" or "sustainable MEW." We would caution the reader that this computation allows only for the more obvious discrepancies between GNP and economic welfare. The adjustment from GNP to sustainable MEW appears in Table 6–1. The top figures are aggregate (Table 6–1A; the bottom figures are per capita (Table 6–1B). In an unplanned economy, the latter are more meaningful.

Going through the tables, our first adjustment is simply to subtract depreciation or capital consumption as per the national income and product accounts to arrive at net national product in line 3. Depreciation should not count as part of any measure of sustainable consumption. (Depreciation is rather a *cost* of production.) Some depreciation, however, is not included in the national accounts. This includes depreciation on automobiles and other consumer durables, certain government capital, and on the educational and medical capital embodied in individuals. Whatever expenditures a family may make just to maintain its health should not be classified as consumption. We must subtract these just as we subtract expenditures needed to maintain the stock of physical capital. Likewise, when an individual acquires a productive skill we say that he is investing in himself. Expenses to maintain occupational competence should not count as consumption. This completes our explanation of line 4.

Line 5 makes a second subtraction from NNP to compensate for population increase. Suppose that an economy with a zero rate of technological progress has a population growth of 1 per cent per year. It must therefore invest to build up its stock of physical capital just to maintain its standard of living. If its productive capacity remained the same, consumption per capita would fall as it became less able to provide for each member of a growing population. When technological progress is positive, this statement is no longer true, because technical advance alone could keep living standards at the same level or even permit them to rise. However, we can then subtract that amount of investment just needed to keep sustainable consumption per capita growing at the rate of technological progress. Such a deduction forms the substance of line 5.[5]

Regrettables and intermediates covers a pot pourri of items, notably defense spending. We must subtract defense expenditures to arrive at a meaningful measure of economic welfare, because "No reasonable country (or household) buys national defense for its own sake. If there were no . . . risk

---

[5] In 1947 this deduction turns out to be an addition. Apparently technological progress was negative during that year. That is, for some reason output per worker appears to have declined.

of war, there would be no need for defense expenditures, and no one would be worse without them." [6] Thus defense spending is a "regrettable" whose size largely reflects the steeply increased cost (from $500 million to $50 billion over the period 1929–1965) of providing a given level of security. The result of an arms race or a deterioration in international relations is that very few gain and many lose. For similar reasons, we also classify expenditures on police protection as a regrettable. The intermediate in line 6 includes such outlays as those for public health and sanitation, which we think of as enabling a given level of welfare to be maintained.

Finally, the subtraction for pollution and congestion appears as line 7. Nordhaus and Tobin tackle the almost impossible task of estimating these costs by assuming that they collectively appear as an item making urban life less agreeable than living in rural areas. To the extent that rural dwellers also bear the costs of pollution and congestion, for whatever reason, line 7 understates the true loss to society. Moreover, the Nordhaus and Tobin estimates are based on the 1960 U.S. Census, from which they derive a "disamenity premium" attached to life in urban areas. The increase in urban disamenity costs over time reflects no rise in this premium—only the fact that the American population became increasingly urban between 1929 and 1965, so that more people had to pay. If the premium, itself, rose, line 7 understates the urban disamenity loss.

In addition, many writers have suggested that there are costs of environmental disruption and natural-resource exhaustion which are cumulating now but will have to be borne by future generations. Some "pessimists" have even maintained that the planet will eventually become uninhabitable from past air pollution, regardless of future efforts to clean up. There is no way of allowing for this loss. Consequently, line 7 may understate pollution and congestion on three counts and correspondingly lead us to an overestimate of sustainable MEW.

There are likewise general items that we must include in a comprehensible measure of sustainable welfare but which fail to appear in the national accounts. The biggest of these is leisure (line 8), whose value actually exceeds GNP in every year. This is not so surprising, however, when we consider that people spend more time in leisure activities than they do at work—even after subtracting essential time for sleeping, eating, housework, child care, school attendance, and so forth. We attempt to value this time at the wage or salary rate that could be earned while working, which is therefore foregone by not working.

Line 8 does *not* allow for a concept that Marxist economists claim to be important but which Western economists largely ignore. This is work alienation. Whereas Western economists tend to think of individuals as deriving their welfare from consumption during nonworking hours, Marxists emphasize the potential welfare gains from work at least as much. Work is

---

[6] Tobin and Nordhaus, op. cit., p. 12.

Table 6–1. Gross national product and sustainable MEW.

A. Aggregate figures
(in billions of 1958 U.S. dollars)

Year	1929	1935	1945	1947	1954	1958	1965
1. GNP	203.6	169.5	355.2	309.9	407.0	447.3	617.8
2. Capital consumption	−20	−20	−21.9	−18.3	−32.5	−38.9	−54.7
3. NNP	183.6	149.5	333.3	291.6	374.5	408.4	563.1
4. Additional capital consumption	−19.3	−33.4	−11.7	−50.8	−35.2	−27.3	−92.7
5. Growth requirement	−46.1	−46.7	−65.8	5.4	−63.1	−78.9	−101.8
6. Regrettables and intermediates	−17.0	−16.6	−155.5	−31.7	−74.2	−76.3	−94.1
7. Urban disamenities	−12.5	−14.1	−18.1	−19.1	−24.3	−27.6	−34.6
8. Leisure	339.5	401.3	450.7	466.9	523.2	554.9	626.9
9. Nonmarket activity	85.7	109.2	152.4	159.6	211.5	239.7	295.4
10. Service of public and private capital	29.7	24.2	31.0	36.7	48.9	54.8	78.9
11. Sustainable MEW	543.6	573.4	716.3	858.6	961.3	1,047.7	1,241.1

B. Per capita figures
(1958 U.S. dollars)

Year	1929	1935	1945	1947	1954	1958	1965
1. GNP	1,671	1,392	2,528	2,142	2,497	2,557	3,175
2. Capital consumption	−164	−157	−155	−126	−199	−222	−278
3. NNP	1,507	1,174	2,372	2,015	2,298	2,335	2,894
4. Additional capital consumption	−158	−262	−83	−351	−216	−156	−199
5. Growth requirement	−378	−367	−468	37	−387	−451	−523
6. Regrettables and intermediates	−139	−130	−169	−219	−455	−436	−484
7. Urban disamenities	−103	−111	−129	−132	−149	−158	−178
8. Leisure	2,787	3,152	3,208	3,227	3,216	3,173	3,221
9. Nonmarket activity	704	858	1,084	1,103	1,297	1,370	1,518
10. Services of public and private capital	243	190	220	252	300	314	405
11. Sustainable MEW	4,454	4,504	5,098	5,795	5,897	5,990	6,378

Source: "Is Growth Obsolete?" James Tobin and William D. Nordhaus, in *Economic Growth, Retrospect & Prospect*, National Bureau of Economic Research Fiftieth Anniversary Colloquium V, New York: Columbia University Press, 1972, Tables A-16 and A-17.

potentially an expression of man's need to create, as well as a means of self-expression and realization.

However, two phenomena in modern society may prevent this. An advanced division of labor and consequent specialization in production decree that an individual is but a part of a team which, itself, may produce only a component of an entire assembly. He may repeatedly bolt one end of an automobile fender onto the body, for example. Many experts and nonexperts alike have argued that this kind of work—which characterizes nearly all modern industrial societies—is dehumanizing. Marx also argued that, under capitalism, the products created by workmen belonged not to them but to their employer. This was his second form of alienation (the product is alienated from the workers, in other words), and we would argue that it may characterize noncapitalist economies as well. The importance of alienation as a source of lost welfare appears virtually impossible to estimate and it is not provided for in Table 6–1.

Next, the old story about the man who married his cook and thereby caused GNP to fall is true. The national-income accounts do not add in the services of housewives—even though their "outputs" are consumed by millions of happy husbands—nor any other goods and services that fail to pass through the market place. Line 9 therefore estimates them and adds them into the computation of sustainable MEW.

Finally, individuals use all kinds of durable goods—roads, schools, automobiles, stereos, television sets, clothing—which were built or originally purchased during previous years. Let us have another look at the Robinsons, who own a family mansion and a Rolls-Royce plus a $500,000 bank account, vis-à-vis the Prescotts with their mortgage, Volkswagen, and $2,000 account but slightly higher current income. The Robinsons enjoy a higher living standard because they can consume the services of the Rolls-Royce, mansion, and bank account (which presumably provides security, if nothing else). That is, they can consume the services of goods acquired during previous years. Yet the national-income accounts would include only the rental value of services yielded by the mansion. Line 10 is, therefore, a final addition that tries to place a value on the services yielded by all other durables.

We then arrive at sustainable MEW, which is more than twice as high as GNP in every year, principally because of the contribution of leisure. However, the average annual rate of growth of NNP is higher than that of sustainable MEW. Over 1929–1965 and 1947–1965, sustainable MEW grew at only 1.0 and 0.5 per cent per annum, respectively, on a per capita basis. Per capita NNP grew at 1.9 and 2 per cent over these periods. Once again, this stems largely from the contribution of leisure, which has been growing more slowly than NNP. If MEW is a better measure of economic welfare than NNP, growth in the latter probably overstates the true increase in average well-being.

Moreover, let us return to a comparison paradox raised in Chapter 4. The name "Bali" has become a symbol of paradise, although in North

America, GNP per capita is probably 20 to 30 times as high as in the Balinese Islands. However, suppose that we value Bali leisure time at an average North American wage rate. We shall see below that this is appropriate if we are to make the comparison from the viewpoint of a Canadian or American. Then Bali MEW will quite likely be half or more of MEW in the United States or Canada.

Of course, even MEW fails to capture many dimensions of human welfare. Some economists have suggested that we must average such "social indicators" as crime, death, suicide, and infant mortality rates, incidence of disease, average levels of population density and schooling, and several others in with NNP (or MEW) to get a more comprehensive welfare measure. But so far no one has been able to derive a formula that would enable us to combine such diverse measures convincingly.

6–4   Comparisons in Terms of Distribution

Of the three kinds of comparisons that we can make—distribution, output, and growth—distribution comparisons are the most underdeveloped. It is easy to get GNP and growth-rate comparisons for many different countries possessing a variety of forms of economic organization. But good wealth-distribution data are nearly impossible to come by.

So much is this the case that we must despair, for the most part, of getting direct country-to-country comparisons of wealth distributions. Even our income-distribution figures are highly imperfect. Ideally we should compare income distributions *after* all taxes have been paid to the government and all goods and transfer payments (such as parks and schools, old-age pensions, unemployment insurance, and farm-owners' subsidies) are received from it. An expressed goal of every non-Communist nation's program of taxes, transfers, and government expenditures is to equalize the distribution of income and, ultimately, of wealth. Despite tax loopholes, most succeed to some extent, although the amount of equalization achieved varies widely.

After-tax incomes will be more equally distributed than pretax incomes in most Western countries, and when we count government services, the distribution becomes more equal still. Moreover, the ranking in terms of equality will change from one country to another. Unfortunately, we must largely confine ourselves to comparisons of pretax income distributions. Table 6–2 gives these distributions for Brazil, Canada, Czechoslovakia, Denmark, Finland, France, India, Japan, Sweden, Taiwan, the United States, the United Kingdom, West Germany, and Yugoslavia in the years indicated. (These were chosen in an effort to make the data as comparable as possible.)

To read the table, note first that the figures under column A refer to percentages of income receivers or households. These are cumulative. Thus "10" refers to the bottom 10 per cent of all income receivers, and "40" to the bottom 40 per cent of all income receivers. The figures under each country give cumulative percentages of income received. Looking under Canada we

Table 6–2. Pre-tax income distribution in selected countries (cumulative per cent of income received).

A *	Canada 1965	Brazil 1960	Denmark 1963	Finland 1962	France 1962	India 1961
10	—	—	1.7	0.5	0.5	—
20	6	6	5.0	2.4	1.9	8
40	16	14	15.8	11.1	9.5	20
60	30	26	32.6	26.5	24.0	36
80	56	44	56.8	50.7	47	58
90	—	59	72.9	67.5	64	73
95	80	69	83.1	79.0	76	—
100	100	100	100	100	100	100
Top 20 ÷ Bottom 20	7	9	9	25	27	5

Japan 1962	Sweden 1963	Taiwan 1964	U.S. 1968	U.K. 1964	West Germany 1964	Yugo-slavia 1963	Czecho-slovakia 1965
—	1.6	—	—	2	2.1	3.2	2.9
5	4.4	8	4	5	5.3	7.9	6.3
15	14.0	20	15	15	15.4	19.5	20.3
31	31.4	37	32	32	29.1	35.2	40.0
54	56.0	59	57	56	47.1	58.1	65.6
70	72.1	74	73	71	58.6	74.6	79.8
—	82.4	84	83	81	66.3	84.8	—
100	100	100	100	100	100	100	100
9	10	5	11	9	10	5	5

Sources: For Canada: Paul Samuelson and Anthony Scott, *Economics* (Toronto: McGraw-Hill, 1971), p. 150. For Czechoslovakia: See footnote 9. For Brazil, Taiwan, India, and U.S.: D. J. Turnham, "Income Distribution: Measurement and Problems," paper presented to Society for International Development, 12th World Conference, Ottawa, May 18, 1971, Table 1. For others: See U.N. Economic Commission for Europe, "Incomes in Post War Europe: A Study of Policies, Growth and Distribution," *Economic Survey of Europe in 1965*, Pt. Two, Geneva, 1967.

* Cumulative per cent of income receivers or households.

note that the bottom 20 per cent of all income receivers received just 6 per cent of all income. (We could not discover what percentage of all income was received by the bottom 10 per cent of all income receivers.) The next highest 20 per cent received 10 per cent of all income, so that the lowest 40 per cent of income receivers received 16 per cent of all income. The lowest 95 per cent of income receivers received 80 per cent of all income, so that the top 5 per cent got 20 per cent of all income, before redistribution through taxes, transfers, and government expenditures.

Looking under Denmark in 1963, we discover that the bottom 10 per cent of all income receivers got 1.7 per cent of all income, the next 10 per cent got 3.3 per cent, and so on. A country with a perfectly equal income distribution would duplicate the percentages under column A. That is, the bottom 20 per cent of all income receivers would receive 20 per cent of all income; the bottom 40 per cent would receive 40 per cent of all income, and so on. We can derive a crude measure of income inequality by taking the ratio of the total income going to the top 20 per cent to the income received by the bottom 20 per cent.

In Canada, the top 20 per cent of income receivers got seven times as much income as the bottom 20 per cent. The same ratio in Brazil and Denmark was nine. By this measure, France and Finland had the most unequal income distributions, and the distributions of Yugoslavia, India, Czechoslovakia, and Taiwan were most equal. If we were to split all countries into three groups on this basis, we would designate Yugoslavia, India, Taiwan, Czechoslovakia, and Canada as countries of low inequality; the United Kingdom, Brazil, Denmark, Japan, West Germany, Sweden, and the United States as countries of medium inequality; and France and Finland as countries of high inequality. The problem with this kind of comparison, of course, is that it depends entirely upon the ends of the income distribution and ignores the middle.

To get a more comprehensive comparison, we have drawn pictures of these distributions in Figures 6–1(a) and (b). The results are called Lorenz curves. Let us plot the cumulative percentage of income received on the vertical axis and the cumulative percentage of income receivers along the horizontal. If the distribution of income were perfectly equal, the lowest 20 per cent of income recipients would get 20 per cent of the income. The lowest 40 per cent of recipients would get 40 per cent of the income, and so on until we reach 100 per cent on both axes. When we plot this, we get the diagonal 45-degree lines in Figures 6–1(a) and (b), which we consequently christen "the line of perfect equality."

To get a line of perfect inequality, consider what would happen if 99.9 per cent of citizenry had nothing while 0.1 per cent had it all. In plotting this state of affairs, we would follow the horizontal axis from the origin virtually to the 100 per cent mark. Then, to capture the rajahs in our midst, we should have to undertake a nearly vertical ascent from the bottom of the diagram to the upper right-hand corner. It follows that the broken lines composed of the bottom and right-hand sides of the boxes in Figures 6–1(a) and (b) constitute lines of perfect inequality. Actual income distributions will be neither perfectly equal nor perfectly unequal. They will lie between the broken line of complete inequality and the 45-degree line. Those closest to the latter will be most equal.

Utilizing the Lorenz-curve concept, we have again classified all countries except Czechoslovakia and West Germany into three categories, based on income inequality. Again, India, Taiwan, and Yugoslavia are countries of low inequality. Their Lorenz curves lie within band 1 in Figure 6–1(a), which is closest to the 45-degree line. The United States, Canada, Denmark, Japan, the United Kingdom, and Sweden become countries of medium in-

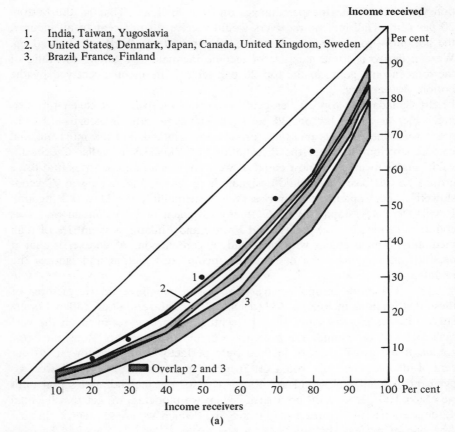

Figure 6–1. Lorenz curves giving pretax income distributions in (a) selected countries, (b) West Germany and Czechoslovakia.

equality whose Lorenz curves are encompassed by the middle band, 2. Finally, France and Finland are now joined by Brazil as countries of high inequality. Their Lorenz curves span the widest band, 3. However, Czechoslovakia shows up as the country with the least income inequality of all those listed in Table 6–2. West Germany falls between the countries of medium and high inequality. Both countries are impossible to classify in Figure 6–1(a) and are graphed separately in Figure 6–1(b).

When we turn to posttax income distributions, we find more meager fare, but we can also hope to get some better East–West comparisons. Socialist nations tend to make less use of their tax systems for income redistribution than do capitalist countries. Therefore, we shall retain the pretax distribution data for Yuogslavia and Czechoslovakia already presented, and supplement it with posttax distributions for Poland, the United States, Sweden, and West Germany. All six countries are compared in Figure 6–2, but before drawing any conclusions, we should note that our comparison is probably biased some-

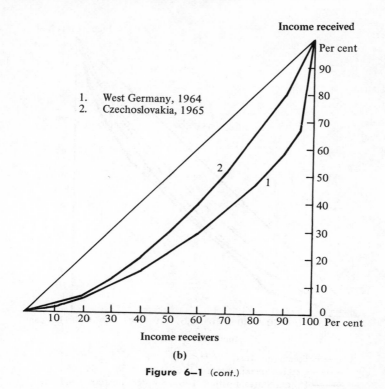

1. West Germany, 1964
2. Czechoslovakia, 1965

(b)

Figure 6–1 (cont.)

what in favor of Poland and the United States and against Sweden and West Germany, along with Yugoslavia and Czechoslovakia (to the extent that some redistribution does take place in the latter countries through the tax mechanism).

The U.S. and Polish distributions incorporate more public or social benefits, which tend to be equalizing factors. The U.S. distribution, for example, includes expenditures on "national defense, international affairs, general government, transportation (excluding highways), commerce and finance, housing and community development, health and sanitation, civilian "safety," and a miscellaneous category.[7] The other distributions do not allow for these items, which are provided collectively to some or all citizens in kind. The U.S. distribution may also fail to allow adequately for well-publicized tax loopholes.

[7] Quoted by Henry Aaron and Martin McGuire in "Public Goods and Income Distribution," Brookings Reprint 202, The Brookings Institution, Washington, D.C., 1971, from (U.S.) Tax Foundation, Inc., *Tax Burdens and Benefits of Government Expenditures by Income Class,* 1961 and 1965 (New York: 1967). The data provided for the United States in Figure 6–2 are taken from the tax foundation study. It is reasonably consistent with the income distribution after federal, but not state and local, taxes given by Joseph A. Pechman and Benjamin A. Okner in "Applications of the Carter Commission Proposals to the United States: A Simulation Study," *National Tax Journal,* Mar. 1969. State and local taxes, transfers, and public benefits probably do not make the distribution of income more equal in the United States.

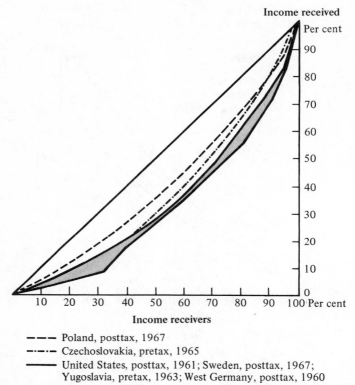

— — — Poland, posttax, 1967
—·—·— Czechoslovakia, pretax, 1965
———— United States, posttax, 1961; Sweden, posttax, 1967;
        Yugoslavia, pretax, 1963; West Germany, posttax, 1960

Figure 6–2. Posttax income distributions in selected countries. Source: See footnote 9.

However, a check made against tax data for 1972, which do incorporate loopholes, reveals that this would not be enough to render Figure 6–2 incorrect as drawn.[8]

In addition, the Polish sample is entirely *non*agricultural. The inclusion of rural families, who are poorer, on the average, than urban dwellers in nearly every country, would almost certainly have made the Polish distribution less ⸤qual. It would probably have bowed out the lower half of Poland's Lorenz curve and could have made up the entire difference between the Polish and Czech distributions (which are the first and second most equal in Figure 6–2). Following this pair comes a band comprising the United States after tax (1961), Sweden after tax (1967), West Germany after tax (1960), and Yugoslavia (1963), along with India and Taiwan.[9]

---

[8] See Joseph A. Pechman and Benjamin A. Okner, "Individual Income Tax Erosion by Classes," Brookings Reprint 230, The Brookings Institution, Washington, D.C., 1972.

[9] The various sources are as follows: Poland and the United Kingdom: P. J. D. Wiles and Stefan Markowski, "Income Distribution under Communism and Capitalism: Some Facts about Poland, the U.K., the U.S.A., and the U.S.S.R.," Pts. I and II *Soviet Studies,* Jan.–Apr. 1971. Czechoslovakia: Estimate made by Večernik in Pavel Machonin ed.,

The most unequal band in Figure 6–2 corresponds to the most equal band in Figure 6–1(a). It appears reasonable to argue that redistribution in the United States, Sweden, and West Germany takes these countries from band 2 or 3 there to band 1. As we shall see, redistribution in the United Kingdom may well take it *inside* band 1.

Indeed, after a fairly exhaustive survey of income redistribution in Sweden, Schnitzer concludes that "the ratio of income inequality between the highest and lowest income groups [in Sweden]—is certainly much lower than that which exists in either the United States or the Soviet Union." [10] This statement is probably strong, but there is some suggestion (to be examined below) that income distribution in the U.S.S.R. is a bit less equal than Poland and Czechoslovakia. Let us say that the zone of lowest income inequality (among the nations considered thus far) is roughly bounded by the posttax and post-income redistribution Lorenz curves of these three countries.

Then, even if we discount Schnitzer's claims a bit, Sweden's Lorenz curve would be almost entirely in this zone, once the full impact of her redistributive efforts is taken into account. It seems fairly clear that neither the United States nor Canada would achieve this zone. From the exhaustive treatment given by Wiles and Markowski, it is doubtful that the United Kingdom reaches it either, although net inequality there appears to be less than in North America.[11] Regarding West Germany, we cannot really say. France and Brazil probably remain as countries with the highest income inequality of those surveyed.

If we wish to include numerical estimates of income inequality in Hungary and the U.S.S.R. among our comparisons, we must turn to a somewhat cruder methodology. In every country there will be some level of income below which 25 per cent (or one fourth) of all households fall and above which 75 (or three fourths) per cent of all households fall. This level of income is usually called the *first quartile* (Q_1). There will be a higher income which just divides the population in half, with half of all households receiving incomes below this level and half above. This level is called the *median* income or *second quartile* (Q_2). Finally, there will be a still higher level of

et al., *Československa Společnost (The Czechoslovak Society)*, Bratislava, 1969; quoted by Jan Michal in "Size Distribution of Incomes under Socialism in Czechoslovakia," Research Memorandum 57, Institut für Höhere Studien, Vienna, June 1971. United States: Tax Foundation, op. cit., via Aaron and McGuire, op. cit., or Pechman and Okner, "Applications of the Carter Commission Proposals," op. cit. Sweden: Martin Schnitzer, *The Economy of Sweden* (New York: Praeger, 1970), Table V-1, p. 129, quoted from Skattebetalarnas Förening, *Fakta för Skattebetalare*, Stockholm, 1969, pp. 4–5. The author has estimated an income distribution from the after-tax table quoted by Schnitzer. Yugoslavia: UN Economic Commission for Europe, "Incomes in Post War Europe: A Study of Policies, Growth and Distribution," *Economic Survey of Europe in 1965*, Pt. Two, Geneva, 1967. West Germany: Klauss-Dieter Schmidt et al., *Die Umverteilung des Volkseinkommens in der Bundesrepublik Deutschland*, 1955 and 1960, J. C. B. Mohr (Paul Siebeck), Tubingen, 1965, Table 58, p. 198.

[10] Schnitzer, op. cit.

[11] Wiles and Markowski, op. cit.

Table 6–3. Distribution of income in selected countries, measured by dispersion ratios.

Ratio	U.S.S.R. 1965	Poland Posttax, 1967	Czechoslovakia 1965	U.K. Posttax, 1969	Hungary 1967	West Germany Posttax, 1960	Sweden Posttax, 1967
1. Quartile	1.80	1.80	1.85	1.75	1.75	2.17	1.74
2. Decile	3.85	About 3.05	3.15	3.3	3.0	About 5.9	—
3. Semidecile	6.20	—	4.52	4.6	About 4.1	—	—

Sources:
U.S.S.R., Poland, United Kingdom, and Hungary from P. J. D. Wiles and Stefan Markowski, "Income Distribution under Communism and Capitalism, Some Facts about Poland, the U.K., and the U.S.S.R.," Pt. II, *Soviet Studies*, Apr. 1971, Table 29, p. 507.
Sweden from Martin Schnitzer, *The Economy of Sweden* (New York: Praeger, 1970), Table V-I, p. 129.
West Germany from Klaus-Dieter Schmidt et al., Die Umverteilung des Volkseinkommens in der Bundesrepublik Deutschland, 1955 and 1960, J. C. B. Mohr (Paul Siebeck), Tubingen, 1965, Table 58, p. 198.
Czechoslovakia from Jan Michal, "Size Distribution of Incomes under Socialism in Czechoslovakia," Research Memorandum 57, Institut für Höhere Studien, Vienna, June 1971, Table 8, p. 61.

income below which three fourths of all households fall and above which lie just one fourth of the nation's households. This level is called the *third quartile* (Q_3). The ratio of the highest to lowest quartile (Q_3 divided by Q_1) is a measure of income inequality. It is called the *quartile ratio*.

Similarly, we can divide the population of any nation into tenths. There will be a very low level of income below which one tenth of the population will lie. We call this the first decile (D_1). There will be a very high level above which just one tenth of all households lie and below which 90 per cent of households are to be found. We call this the tenth decile (D_{10}). The ratio of the highest to lowest deciles (or D_{10} divided by D_1) is another measure of income inequality. It is called the *decile ratio*.

To get our final measure we shall divide a country's population into 20 categories. There will be an extremely high level of income above which only 5 per cent of all households will lie and an extremely low level below which just 5 per cent of all households will fall. The ratio of this extremely high level to the extremely low level is called the *semidecile ratio*. The reader should note that the semidecile ratio will be larger than the decile ratio and the quartile ratio will be the smallest of all. For any given country, lower ratios imply greater equality.

Table 6–3 gives all three ratios for the U.S.S.R., Hungary, and Czechoslovakia (pretax), along with Poland, Sweden, the United Kingdom, and West Germany (posttax), where this information is available. The table indicates that Hungary would belong among the countries of low inequality in Figure 6–2, and, on a posttax basis, the same may well be true for the United Kingdom. (In particular, the income tax seems to have a greater equalizing effect in the United Kingdom than in the United States.) We do not know how representative is the sample for the U.S.S.R. However, the rather high semidecile ratio there (6.2) in comparison with Hungary and Czechoslovakia indicates the presence of some quite poor (presumably peasant) households.

Of course, our comparisons are limited strictly to the countries included in Tables 6–2 and 6–3, along with Figure 6–2. Notably missing are such countries as China, Cuba, and Israel, and the Arab states. These omissions are by necessity rather than choice. Samuelson asks, "which country today has the greatest equality? No one knows how to compare the inequality in the Soviet Union or China with that in mixed economies. If we confine ourselves to the noncommunist world, it has been suggested that Israel may lead the list." [12]

As we have seen, Samuelson is not quite right about the U.S.S.R. However, some observers do suggest that China has the world's most equal income distribution. (It has been said, for example, that one rarely encounters an income differential of more than $4:1$ there.) It is certainly possible that either Israel or China have Lorenz curves lying inside the "most equal" curve in Figure 6–2. But we are unable to make the computations that would confirm or deny this.

[12] Paul Samuelson, *Economics* (New York: McGraw-Hill, 1970), p. 112.

Although there are variations and exceptions, socialist countries appear, by and large, to have more equal income distributions than capitalist nations. The reason is *not* that wages and salaries are more equally distributed under socialism. Indeed, there appears to be little difference here, if any. Property incomes tend to be more spread out in socialist countries, where the populace, in principle, owns the material means of production collectively. In the United States the distribution of pretax property incomes contrasts sharply with the pretax wage and salary distribution, as Figure 6–3 shows. We have considered two types of property income: capital gains, realized when stocks, bonds, and other assets go up in value, and dividends.

Both distributions are more unequal than anything we have encountered so far. Although taxation undoubtedly levels them a bit—despite the presence of loopholes—the contrasts between the three curves in Figure 6–3 would undoubtedly remain. A staunch defender of laissez faire would defend these inequalities by arguing that they are necessary to produce a rational allocation of resources and to encourage innovation. If he is a follower of the late J. A. Schumpeter, he would argue that the generally higher rate of innovation observed under capitalism results from the presence of dynamic entrepreneurship. Entrepreneurs are willing to take the risks of innovation upon their shoulders, but only when there is some prospect of earning large profits in consequence, according to this doctrine. By leveling the gap between the highest and lowest income levels that can be achieved, a socialist economy—or any economy, for that matter—would discourage innovation.

If property incomes are largely a reward for risk-bearing innovation, we would expect them to be distributed unevenly. A few entrepreneurs would succeed in a big way, realizing large profits and large increases in the values of their properties, while many would be unsuccessful and go bankrupt. According to Schumpeter, those innovators who do become rich make a far greater contribution to society than the enormous profits which they earn. Thus income inequities are not too high a price to pay for innovation.[13]

But while this argument may stand up in explaining the divergence between wage and salary incomes and capital gains, it scarcely accounts for the departure of dividend earnings from capital gains. Dividends are, if anything, less risky and, we suspect, more likely to manifest differences in inherited wealth. Neither will Schumpeter's doctrine explain the departure of the French income distribution from that of Sweden or the United States.

Finally, what evidence we have regarding changes in income distributions over time suggests that they have become more equal since the late 1940s or early 1950s. Wiles and Markowski find this to be true for the United Kingdom, the U.S.S.R., and the United States. Figure 6–4 shows their calculations for pretax income distribution in the United States. Evidence for Poland indicates that income distribution for 1967 is more equal than that for 1965 or

---

[13] Joseph A. Schumpeter, *Capitalism, Socialism, and Democracy* (New York: Harper, 1950), Pt. II.

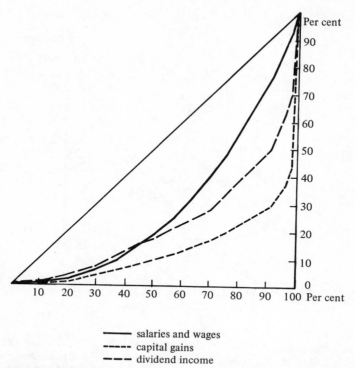

salaries and wages
capital gains
dividend income

Figure 6–3. Distribution of wages and salaries, capital gains, and dividend income in the United States in 1968. Source: United States Internal Revenue Service, *Statistics of Income, 1968, Individual Tax Returns,* Washington, D.C., 1970, pp. 4, 10.

1962. Michal finds evidence to indicate that income distribution in Czechoslovakia became more equal over the period 1945–1948 to 1959–1967. Both the posttax and the pretax income distribution appear to have equalized in West Germany. The Senate Committee on Poverty in Canada reported a somewhat more equal distribution of pretax income among urban families in 1967 as opposed to 1951. Its findings appear in Figure 6–5.

6–5 Values and Value Judgments: The Background for Income and Growth Comparisons

Without prices or value weights of some kind to attach to quantities of goods and services that are produced or consumed, income or output comparisons usually cannot be made at all. Suppose that we observe a country producing a variety of goods and services in each of two separate years. (We could illustrate the point equally well using two different countries in the same year.) In which year was production greatest? Certainly, if the output of every good or service was higher in the second year, one could say that production was greater in that year, although he could not say by how much.

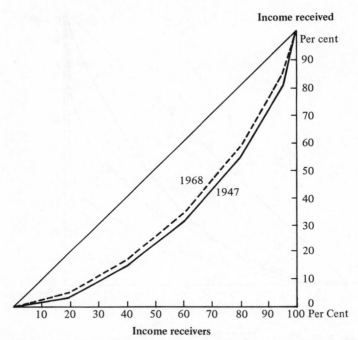

Figure 6–4. Pretax income distributions for the United States in 1947 and 1968. Source: P. J. D. Wiles and Stefan Markowski, "Income Distribution Under Communism and Capitalism, Some Facts about Poland, the U.K., the U.S.A., and the U.S.S.R., Part I," *Soviet Studies* (Jan. 1971), Table 6.

But assume that more of just one good—potato chips—is turned out during the first year. Since production of every other commodity rises in the second year, we would like to say that total output is higher then. However, let us define "output" in such a way that the price of potato chips is astronomically high and that of everything else exceptionally low. Then it will look as if total output fell during the second year in comparison with the first.

This example is rather far-fetched, but it does emphasize a crucial fact. Unless we are talking about just one good, there is no such thing as "output," until we have chosen prices for all goods. We can talk about the output of apples, but we cannot add apples to oranges to get total output until we assign prices to each commodity. Similarly, when we say that "production" in the United States is twice as high as the U.S.S.R., we must be referring to a particular set of prices. At some other set, Soviet output could be higher. We know, for instance, that the Soviet Union mines much more iron ore each year than does the United States and that it is the world's leading producer of coal.[14]

[14] During 1968, to give an example, the iron ore figures were about 92 million tons (U.S.S.R.) and 50 million tons (United States). The higher Soviet figure reflects the fact that the U.S.S.R. is the principal iron ore supplier for Eastern Europe. Source: *U.N.*

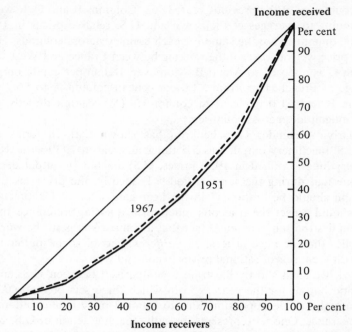

Figure 6–5. Pretax income distribution of nonfarm families in Canada in 1951 and 1967. Source: *Poverty in Canada,* Report of the Special Senate Committee on Poverty, Ottawa, Information Canada, 1971.

Table 6–4.   Per capita GNP of France, Italy and West Germany in three different sets of prices (1964 quantities).

A 1963 Own Price Relatives		B First Average of Own and U.S. Relatives		C Second Average of Own and U.S. Relatives	
1. France	$1,730	1. France	$2,010	1. West Germany	$2,150
2. West Germany	1,720	2. West Germany	1,980	2. France	1,950
3. Italy	910	3. Italy	1,140	3. Italy	1,110
$\frac{I}{F} = 52.6\%$		$\frac{I}{F} = 56.7\%$		$\frac{I}{F} = 61.0\%$	

Sources: Columns A and B are reproduced from Table 1 in Maurice Ernst, "Postwar Economic Growth in Eastern Europe," in U.S. Congress, Joint Economic Committee, *New Directions in the Soviet Economy* (Washington, D.C.: G.P.O. 1966), Vol. IV, p. 877. Column C comes from Stanley H. Cohn, "Soviet Growth Retardation," in Vol. II-A of the same study, Table 7, p. 108.

Table 6–4 shows the differences resulting from a ranking of the per capita GNPs of France, West Germany, and Italy for the same year (1964) in terms of three different sets of prices. Column A uses the relative prices prevailing in each country as of the previous year, 1963. Columns B and C, however, use what amounts to averages of their own and U.S. relative prices in 1963 and 1964. The quantities are the same for each country across columns. However, different price weights reverse the ranking between France and West Germany in column C as opposed to A and B. Moreover, Italian per capita output, as a percentage of French, rises from 52.6 per cent in column A to 56.7 per cent in column B and 61.0 per cent in column C. (We cannot directly compare absolute magnitudes across countries.)

Similarly, Alexander Gerschenkron has shown that, in terms of 1899 prices, U.S. machinery output was 5.5 times as great in 1939 as in 1899. But when everything is valued in 1939 prices, U.S. machinery output declined by almost one half during the same period.[15] Evidently, the prices used for any comparison should be "rational" in the aggregate sense of Chapter 4. (That is, they should reflect the tradeoffs inherent in a social preference function.) But herein lies the rub. The mere fact that a comparison is in the works probably implies that we have at least two *different* sets of social preferences and thus two different sets of rational prices to contend with.

Indeed, we shall shortly illustrate a comparison between U.S. and Soviet income and output for the year 1955 in which three sets of "rational" prices (or, accurately, crude approximations to rational price configurations) make their appearance. One set represents, broadly, the interaction of U.S. consumer preferences with U.S. production possibilities; another, the interaction of Soviet planners' preferences with Soviet production possibilities; and the third, Soviet consumer preferences interacting with Soviet production possibilities. Each set of prices yields a separate comparison, no two comparisons give exactly the same result, and there is no rule that says conclusively that one result is universally preferable to another. As we shall see, each comparison answers a different question, and some questions are only answered by looking at more than one comparison. Indeed, the theoretical basis for making valid income and output comparisons rests on a double-comparison technique.

6–6   The Basis for Income Comparisons: Revealed Preference [16]

Let us first consider the simplest sort of comparison situation that can arise. Suppose that a single household spends all of its income on two goods— bread and wine. We shall assume that it consumes two different combinations or bundles of these goods during two successive time periods labeled year 1 and year 2. We want to ask whether this household is better off in year 2 or in year 1. For simplicity we shall suppose at first that the household's welfare

[15] See Alexander Gerschenkron, *A Dollar Index of Soviet Machinery Output, 1927– 28 to 1937*, Report R-197, Santa Monica, Calif., Rand Corp., Apr. 6, 1951, p. 53.

[16] For a more complete discussion of revealed preference, see C. E. Ferguson, *Microeconomic Theory* (Homewood, Ill.: Irwin, 1972), Sec. 3.6, or another good price-theory book. The theory of revealed preference is also called the theory of index numbers.

is entirely determined by the wine and bread it consumes in each year. Later, we shall relax this obviously restrictive assumption.

We shall also suppose, at the outset, that the household's tastes do not change from one year to the next. Otherwise we should have no way of determining when it is better off. If, for instance, the household consists of one person who progressively acquires a craving for bread and wine, it might eventually take much more of each good to keep him at the same level of satisfaction. The assumption of constant tastes is nevertheless a rigid one, which we shall also eventually relax.

Given constant tastes, suppose that we observe the household consuming more wine *and* more bread in the second year as opposed to the first. (Or, more generally, suppose that we observe him consuming more of every good or service in the second year.) Then, since his tastes have not changed, we can conclude that he is better off during the second year. In Figure 6–6 he must have advanced to a higher indifference curve. On the other hand, if he consumes more of every good during the first year, he is certainly better off then.

Indeed, we can say more than this. Figure 6–6 shows how a rational household would behave when its income changes with *no* change in prices or its tastes. As the rational household's income expands, its budget or expenditure line shifts out, enabling it to purchase more of both goods—or, more generally, more of many goods. Consequently, it becomes progressively better off, moving up the path in Figure 6–6 to higher and higher indifference curves. Conversely, as its income contracts, it moves down this path, becoming worse off.

In a way, this result is the most important in all of economics because it translates a nonmeasurable quantity, utility, into a measurable quantity, income. Provided tastes and prices remain the same, and that there is no change in the household's comsumption of leisure, household income and utility rise and fall together. (More generally, household utility and a measure of present and prospective future wealth would rise and fall together if prices, tastes, and consumption of leisure remained the same.) Under these conditions, an increased income in Figure 6–6 would always imply an increase in welfare, even though the household eventually consumes no more bread. All we need assume is that there is at least one good whose increased consumption will raise household welfare.

Nevertheless, the most interesting comparisons in revealed preference arise when prices change so that the budget lines relating to two different time periods cross. This is shown in Figure 6–7. What may be surprising is that we can still use the above analysis in some cases to determine in which year a rational household is better off. Suppose that it chooses the combination of bread and wine denoted by *A* during the first time period. Then, because it is rational, it reveals a preference for *A* over *every* other bundle along the budget line for time period 1. If it were to face instead the dashed budget line through *B*, it would have an even more restricted selection of bread and wine available. It could not make itself as well off as it is at *A*.

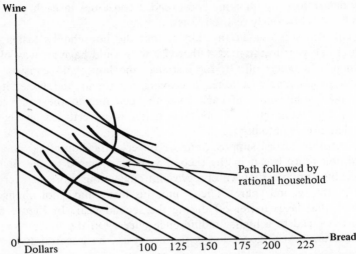

Figure 6—6. The rational household responding to changes in income with no changes in tastes or prices.

Assume that the household chooses A in time period 1 and B in time period 2. Then it is better off in time period 1. We can shift its budget line for period 1 backward in parallel fashion, indicating no change in prices, until it passes through B. Since B lies on a lower budget line (the dashed one) the household is better off at A.[17] By exactly the same reasoning, if the household consumes the bundle, D, in period 2 and C in period 1, it is better off in the second period.

On the other hand, suppose that it consumes at A in period 1 and at D in period 2. Then we cannot say in which period the household is better off. To do so we should have to "see" whether the indifference curve through A passes above or below D. But we never see indifference curves. This is why we need revealed preference.

Note that it is not correct to say the following. We could shift the budget line through D outward, in parallel fashion, until it passes through A. Therefore, A is preferred to D. If the household were to receive the increase in income that such a shift implies, we do not know that it would then decide to purchase the bundle indicated by A. It has not revealed its preferences at this level of income and it may consume a quite different combination. Whatever bundle it does choose would indeed be preferred to D, but we do not know whether A is preferred to D.[18]

---

[17] If the household were to face the dashed budget line, it might or might not choose to consume the combination of goods represented by B. Thus there may be another bundle along this dashed line which would leave it better off, but still not as well off as it is at A.

[18] We could also perform the exercise of shifting the budget line through A outward, in parallel fashion, until it passes through D. This would be fruitless for the same reason.

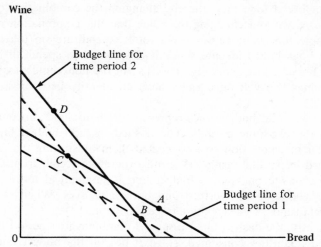

Figure 6–7. Price changes and intersecting budget lines over time.

Finally, suppose that we observe the household consuming at *C* in time period 1 and at *B* in time period 2. In which period is it better off now? By our above discussion, we can shift each budget line backward in parallel fashion to reveal that the household is better off at *B* than at *C* and at *C* than at *B*. Tastes must have changed on us, or else the household is more rational in one time period than in the other.

It follows that there are three cases and four possibilities in all to consider. Case 1 occurs when the household does reveal itself to be better off in one time period or the other, given rational behavior and constant tastes, along with a constant division of time between work and leisure. Case 2 arises when we cannot reach any conclusions—in effect, because the household does not sufficiently reveal its preferences by its market behavior. In case 3 we get a clear-cut contradiction, either to the assumption of constant tastes or to the supposition that the household is as rational in one time period as it is in the other. The fourth possibility is taken care of by noting that, in case 1, the household may reveal itself better off either in period 1 or in period 2.

Let us view the × made by the budget lines in Figure 6–7 as a scissors with its handles toward the origin and its blades outward. Then case 1 arises whenever the household consumes on a blade of the scissors during one time period and on a handle during the other. Case 2 emerges when the household consumes on both blades, and case 3 results when it consumes on both handles.

To make use of these ideas we must translate the graphics of Figure 6–7 into numbers. Specifically, we must give a numerical interpretation of the two budget lines and two pseudo-budget lines (that is, the dashed lines) appearing there. Each of these four lines represents a constant level of expenditure on wine and bread. As we move along any line, we simply substitute wine for bread—or bread for wine—thereby changing the combination of the two goods purchased without changing the value that this combination represents. In our example this value represents a total expenditure on the two goods and also the household's income, since it is assumed to spend all its income on wine and bread. More generally, if we list all the household's expenditures, including savings, we will once again have an identity between income and expenditure.[19]

Thus the two solid budget lines represent the household's income and expenditure in the two time periods. The dashed, pseudo budget lines have a slightly subtler interpretation. We concocted them by shifting the real budget lines backward in parallel fashion. We must therefore recall, from Chapter 3, that the slope or steepness of a budget line is uniquely determined by the prices of the goods on the vertical and horizontal axes. When we shift the line in parallel fashion, we leave these prices unchanged.

Consequently, the dashed line through *B* combines first-period prices with second-period quantities consumed, since *B* lies on the budget line for time period 2. Suppose that the household does purchase the combination of wine and bread represented by *B* in period 2. Then the dashed line through *B* gives the total expenditure that the household would have made had it purchased these quantities at first period prices. (Alternatively, it gives the value of *B* in first-period prices.) The dashed line through *C* gives the total value of this (first-period) bundle in second-period prices. We may now restate our cases as follows.

Case I (a) The household is better off in the first time period if its total income and expenditure exceed the total value of the goods consumed in the second period, valued in *first*-period prices. This would be the situation described by *A* and *B* in Figure 6–7. We shall call this *result* 1. (b) The household is better off in period 2, when its total income and expenditure exceed the value of the goods consumed in the first period, valued in second-period prices. This is the possibility illustrated by *C* and *D* in Figure 6–7. We shall call this *result* 2.

Case II If neither result 1 nor result 2 holds, we can not tell in which period the household is better off. This possibility is shown by *A* and *D* in Figure 6–7.

Case III If both result 1 and result 2 hold, we have a contradiction, as when the household consumes *C* during time period 1 and *B* during period 2.

Table 6–5 gives one illustration of each of these possibilities. Since we are no longer confined to two-dimensional graphical analysis, we allow our house-

---

[19] When we list *all* a household's expenditures, we must be exhaustive, even to the point of taking account of the net savings that the household puts into a strongbox or under the mattress at home during any given time period.

Table 6–5. The four possibilities of revealed preference.

Case	Goods Consumed	First-Period Price	First-Period Quantity	Second-Period Price	Second-Period Quantity	Value Columns * (1)	(2)	(3)	(4)
Ia (a)	Bread	0.15	15	0.20	14	2.25	2.10	3.00	2.80
	Wine	0.40	10	0.30	12	4.00	4.80	3.00	3.60
	Beef	1.00	14	0.70	10	14.00	10.00	9.80	7.00

Total values $20.25 $16.90 $15.80 $13.40

$20.25 is greater than $16.90. A rational household with constant tastes would therefore be better off in period 1.

Case	Goods Consumed	First-Period Price	First-Period Quantity	Second-Period Price	Second-Period Quantity	(1)	(2)	(3)	(4)
Ib (b)	Bread	0.15	5	0.20	6	0.75	0.90	1.00	1.20
	Wine	0.40	8	0.30	13	3.20	5.20	2.40	3.90
	Beef	0.60	15	0.70	14	9.00	8.40	10.50	9.80

Total values $12.95 $14.50 $13.90 $14.90

$14.90 is greater than $13.90. The household is better off in period 2.

Case	Goods Consumed	First-Period Price	First-Period Quantity	Second-Period Price	Second-Period Quantity	(1)	(2)	(3)	(4)
II (c)	Bread	0.15	5	0.08	20	0.75	3.00	0.40	1.60
	Wine	0.40	8	0.30	14	3.20	5.60	2.40	4.20
	Beef	0.60	15	0.70	10	9.00	6.00	10.50	7.00

Total values $12.95 $15.60 $13.30 $12.80

$12.95 is less than $15.60. $12.80 is less than $13.30. We do not know when the household is better off.

Case	Goods Consumed	First-Period Price	First-Period Quantity	Second-Period Price	Second-Period Quantity	(1)	(2)	(3)	(4)
III (d)	Bread	0.10	20	0.08	10	2.00	1.00	1.60	.80
	Wine	0.40	8	0.35	5	3.20	2.00	2.80	1.75
	Beef	0.65	12	0.70	15	7.80	9.75	8.40	10.50

Total values $13.00 $12.75 $12.80 $13.05

$13.00 is greater than $12.75. $13.05 is greater than $12.80. Either the assumption of constant tastes or that of equally rational behavior is contradicted.

* Column 1 gives first-year expenditures (or the value of first-year quantities at first-year prices). Column 2 gives the value of second-year quantities at first-year prices. Column 3 gives the value of first-year quantities at second-year prices. Column 4 gives second-year expenditures (or the value of second-year quantities at second-year prices).

hold to consume three goods: bread, wine, and beef. In particular, it can now make beef sandwiches. Opposite the prices and quantities consumed of bread, wine, and beef in each time period, we give the four possible ways of combining these prices and quantities. Column 1 displays first-year expenditures (or the values of first-year quantities at first-year prices). Columns 2 and 3 give second-year quantities valued at first-year prices and first-year quantities valued at second-year prices, respectively. Column 4 shows second-year expenditures (or the value of second-year quantities at second-year prices).[20]

Consequently, the total values in column 1 correspond to the first-period budget line in Figure 6–7. Column 4 corresponds to the second-period budget line. The pseudo budget line through B represents second-period quantities in first-period prices. These are the totals given in column 2. The pseudo budget line through C represents first-period quantities at second-year prices. These are the totals given in column 3. In the spirit of Figure 6–7, we shall compare column 1 with column 2 and column 3 with column 4.

When the total value of column 1 exceeds that of column 2, the household is better off during the first time period (case Ia). This is the condition for us to be able to shift the first-period budget line *backward* in parallel fashion until it passes through the second-period quantities. In Figure 6–7 this is analogous to the household consuming at A during period 1 and at B during period 2. When the total value of column 4 exceeds that of column 3, the household is better off during the second period (case Ib). This is the condition for us to be able to shift the second-period budget line backward until it passes through the first-period quantities. In Figure 6–7 this corresponds to consumption at C and then D.

We leave the remaining cases in Table 6–4 and correspondences with Figure 6–7 to the reader.

6–7 A Weaker Version of Revealed Preference

Revealed preference in its original form is not very useful because we cannot usually assume constant tastes or preferences. This is most obvious when we are comparing two different households, but it arises in comparisons across time as well—particularly, comparisons across long periods of time. For example, we think that, in 1965, U.S. real per capita income (that is, income per capita after price changes have been accounted for) was six times the corresponding value in 1865.

However, in 1865 wealthy individuals ate "venison, buffalo meat, and passenger pigeon eggs" and enjoyed the care of personal servants "on a scale not open to the rich in 1965." [21] The latter traveled in Rolls-Royce and private airplanes and enjoyed air conditioning and color television—all products not available in 1865. These vastly different environments probably led to important differences in tastes. And even if they did not, we probably could not carry out a revealed preference type of comparison because we do

---

[20] To illustrate from the very top line in Table 6-5, the household consumes 15 loaves of bread during the first period. At a price of 15 cents a loaf, this represents an expenditure of $2.25, entered in column 1. At a second-period price of 20 cents, this represents a value of $3.00. During the second period it consumes 14 loaves. At a 20-cent price, this gives a total expenditure on bread of $2.80. At the first-year price (15 cents), the 14 loaves are worth $2.10.

[21] H. H. Villard, "The Economic Implications of 3 Percent Growth," *American Economic Review*, May 1968.

not have prices for automobiles or airplane rides in 1865, nor do we have prices for passenger pigeon eggs in 1965. Thus, even if the distribution of income did not change between 1865 and 1965, there is little or no basis for claiming that rich people in 1965 were six times better off—or, for that matter, were better off at all—than wealthy individuals in 1865.

As a matter of fact, any comparison between households consuming vastly different collections of goods is likely to be nearly meaningless. When the only problem is a difference in tastes, on the other hand, we can continue to use a modified form of revealed preference. This will not permit us to say whether one household is better off than another during a particular time period or whether a single household is better off in time period 1 or time period 2. But it will often permit a weaker result, which will be sufficient, given our purposes in making the comparison.

Let us reconsider Figure 6–7, under the new assumption that the flatter budget line is faced by household 1 while the steeper budget line applies to household 2. (The respective time periods may be the same or different.) We still cannot "see" indifference curves, but we suppose the preferences of the two households to differ, giving us two separate sets of indifference curves to contend with.

Corresponding to case Ia in the previous section, we assume that household 1 consumes the combination of wine and bread indicated by A, while household 2 consumes at B. As before, we shift 1's budget line backward in parallel fashion until it passes through B. This tells us that the first household is better off with its own bundle (A) than it would have been with the bundle (B) consumed by household 2. Its own bundle leaves it on a higher indifference curve—supposing it to behave rationally—and given a choice, it would prefer A to B.

This shows the kind of question we can still hope to answer when we allow tastes to differ or change. We cannot know whether household 1 or 2 is better off. Yet we can hope to tell whether household 1 would trade his bundle for 2's or whether household 2 would trade his bundle for 1's. Our three cases and four possibilities now become as follows.

Case 1a Household 1's expenditure on the combination of goods it consumes exceeds the value of the bundle consumed by household 2, valued in prices faced by household 1. Household 1 is then better off with its own market basket than it would be with the basket consumed by household 2. Call this result 1.

Case 1b Household 2's expenditure on the combination of goods it consumes exceeds the value of the bundle consumed by household 1, valued in prices faced by household 2. Household 1 consumes at C in Figure 6–7, for example, and household 2 consumes at D. Household 2 is then better off with its own market basket than it would be with the basket consumed by household 1. Call this result 2.

Case 2 If neither result 1 nor result 2 holds, we can draw no conclusions. In particular, we can *never* say that one household would have been better off with the *other's* bundle. Suppose that the bundle consumed by 2 is worth more than 1's bundle, valued in prices faced by 1. This is indeed the case when the first household consumes at *C* or *A,* while the second consumes at *D.* For we can shift out the budget line through *A* and *C* until it passes through *D.*

However, if the first household were to face such an expanded budget constraint, we do not know that it would choose to consume at *D.* It has not revealed its preferences under these conditions, and we must allow for the possibility that it would select a quite different bundle. Thus it may prefer either *A* or *C* to *D.*

Case 3 If result 1 and result 2 both hold, *each* household is better off with its own market basket than it would be with the basket consumed by the other.

Note that the contradiction previously inherent in case 3 disappears because we have already allowed tastes to differ. Instead, we get what could be described as the best of all four possible worlds. It is quite possible, for example, that the "representative" Canadian family is better off with the bundle of goods and services presently available to it than it would be with the bundle available to the representative Swedish family, and vice versa. If so, both families "win" the comparison, and no one loses.

Finally, we would remind the reader that we are still supposing both households to behave rationally.

6–8   From the Parts to the Whole

We have been discussing the theoretical basis for comparing the material well-being of one individual or household in two different time periods or of two individuals in the same or in different time periods. In this section we want to move from the level of the parts of an economic system to the level of the whole, where, it may be argued, the most interesting economic comparisons usually arise. We want to know whether the Soviet Union is "better off" than or "catching up with" the United States. Alternatively, we might want to compare the standard of living of a representative Soviet household in 1970 with its 1960 counterpart, meaning that we really want to know whether the standard of living in the U.S.S.R. has "risen" during this decade.

Fortunately, we can apply revealed preference to problems involving aggregate comparisons. However, we cannot usually make the direct and sweeping sort of comparisons that the statements of the preceding paragraph suggest. We must rather be content with weaker conclusions, such as those discussed in Section 6–7. The kinds of questions we can hope to answer are indicated by the following:

the Soviet economy can be judged either by the avowed goals of those who led the Revolution or by the ends people hope to achieve by capitalism. We should judge communism both by whether it has done what it claimed to do and by whether it is the type of economy we would like for ourselves. If the system gives the Russians what they desire, it cannot be considered a failure in the Soviet Union. If, however, it does not give what we would want, it must be adjudged a poor system for [North America] no matter how the Russians view its accomplishments.[22]

Given certain qualifications, we can ask whether a representative American household would have preferred its own market basket of goods to that consumed by a representative Soviet household of the same size in 1965, provided we know what we mean by "representative" in each case. We can also ask whether a Soviet planner would have preferred his own productive capacity or that of the American economy in the same year. But we cannot say whether a representative American household was worse or better off than its Soviet counterpart because the Russian household has different tastes and is probably content with less. This will reflect itself in two distinct indifference or preference maps.

Yet, as we have already said, the kinds of comparison questions we can answer will often prove sufficient for the purposes we have in mind. The basic idea in making aggregate-oriented comparisons is to use the weak version of revealed preference. Each comparison situation—say, between country I and country II—is split into two comparisons. We never ask whether country I was better off than country II. Rather, we ask whether country I was in some sense better off with its own bundle of goods and services than it would have been with II's. Then we repeat, reversing the roles of I and II.

In these comparisons, the household's price line, whose position indicates the income or wealth constraint on its spending, is replaced by a consumption-possibility frontier—or, more accurately, by a corresponding second-best frontier—which constrains society as a whole. This is shown in Figure 6–8. Formally, it is quite similar to the household's problem illustrated earlier. Like the individual, we imagine society, guided by a (social) preference function, rewritten, if necessary, in commodity preference form, trying to "choose" a best combination of goods and services. To begin with, let us assume that we are making comparisons between two countries from the viewpoints of representative households in each. When we have sufficient information, we may proceed as follows.

First, we define the "representative" economic actor in a particular country—say country I—to be a composite household whose expenditure pattern conforms to the national average. Such a household may not actually exist, but this is no obstacle as long as we can locate it as a position within a nationwide income distribution. We shall say that the basket of goods and services consumed by the representative of country I is the entire basket of goods and services available to I divided by the country's population. For comparison purposes, investment goods are treated like savings. Then the

[22] Alfred Oxenfeldt and Vsevolod Holubnychy, *Economic Systems in Action* (New York: Holt, 1965), p. 143.

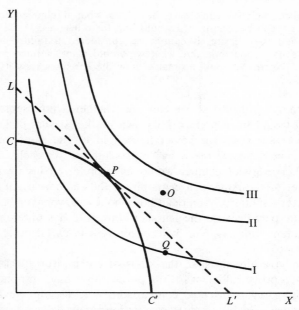

Figure 6–8. The weak version of revealed preference applied to the economy as a whole.

bundle consumed by the representative household in country I becomes a standard to compare consumption in some other country—call it country II —against, and vice versa.

Suppose that 75 per cent of the households in country I have incomes exceeding the value of the representative bundle for country II, valued in country I's prices. Then we may wish to say that these households were better off with their own bundles than they would have been with the combination of goods and services consumed by the "representative" household in II. A similar analysis holds with the roles of I and II reversed. Moreover, it is quite possible both for a substantial majority of the residents of I to prefer their own baskets to the representative bundle for II and vice versa since tastes are almost certain to differ between the two countries.[23]

Sometimes, however, sufficient data on income distributions will not be available to carry out the comparison suggested above. Even when it is, the man in a hurry may wish to shortcut it, and perhaps the most obvious way to do so is as follows: We may assign to the representative household in each country a preference function which is the economy's social preference function put on a per capita basis. As above, we assume that we have prices for

---

[23] We may view the above comparison as a shortcut for a procedure that computes and compares the entire income distribution of both countries in both sets of prices. Such a procedure would be somewhat costly and time consuming. Moreover, it would require more data on income distributions and consumption patterns of "representative" households in different income categories than is ever likely to become available, except in a very few countries.

each country reflecting the interplay between these preferences and a second-best frontier. Then we ask whether the representative household in country I would have preferred the bundle of goods actually available to it over the bundle available to the representative of country II.

By the definition of these bundles, such a procedure amounts to valuing the goods and services available to each country both in its own and in the other country's prices. After adjusting for population differences, a weak revealed-preference type of comparison is carried out between them.

Thus we would compute per capita national income or GNP (or, preferably, net national product with depreciation subtracted) for both countries. Each nation's per capita output would be valued both in its own and in the other country's prices. In a table analogous to Table 6–5, we would enter, for example, the per capita GNP of country I in column 1 and the per capita GNP of country II in column 4. Column 2 would give country II's quantities in country I's prices; column 3 would give country I's quantities in II's prices. We would compare columns 1 and 2 in an effort to determine whether the representative household in country I was better off with its own bundle of goods and services. We would compare columns 3 and 4 to investigate a similar result for country II. The basic thing to remember is that the comparison in, for example, Swedish crowns is relevant to Swedish households, while that in Canadian dollars is relevant to Canadian households.

Once again we can never say definitely that the representative household of one country would have been better off with the other country's "representative bundle." However, if the value in column 2 is very much greater than column 1, we may conjecture such a result. Note, in any event, the contrast between the standard comparison technique and the double comparison suggested by the weak version of revealed preference. The former would contrast, for example, the GNPs of two countries on an aggregate or per capita basis. That is, it compares column 1 with column 4 and declares one country to have a higher living standard or to be somewhat "better off" on this basis. Such a comparison makes no sense except as an approximation to those between columns 1 and 2 or columns 3 and 4. As Table 6–5 shows, this approximation may be considerably off. Even if it isn't, we can never say that one country is better off than another.

Assume that a weak revealed preference comparison indicates the representative household in country I to have preferred its own bundle to the representative bundle available in country II. For this statement to have any significance, we must be able to suppose as well that at least a majority of the residents of I would have preferred their own bundles. In this sense, either the representative of each country being compared must be truly "representative," or the gap between the values of the bundles being compared must be large. If country I is inhabited by a few extremely wealthy households and many extremely poor ones, its "representative" will be an average of extremes and thus not really representative at all. It might be difficult to say more than that the wealthy households in I are better off with their own baskets. Thus distribution considerations still make their appearance through the back door.

This discussion assumes that we are making comparisons from the viewpoint of consumers. Suppose instead that we are interested in success as measured by the goals of a planning authority which is a dominant pole of economic power. In this case we assume that we have prices reflecting the interaction of this planner's preferences with his economy's (second-best) consumption or production possibilities. Then we ask whether he would have preferred the basket of goods and services produced or consumed at home to that produced or consumed in some other country. This leads us to make the same kind of (weak) revealed preference comparison outlined above, except that the planners' goals may be phrased either in aggregate or per capita terms, and our comparison should utilize whichever figures are appropriate.

Once we have rewritten our social preference function in commodity preference form and subject to the considerations outlined above, we face still other problems presumed not to exist in individual comparisons. To begin with, suppose our economy has found the optimal position on its consumption or production-possibilities frontier. Moreover, let prevailing prices reflect the common slope of this frontier and the social indifference surface that is tangent to it. In Figure 6–8, P is such an optimum, and the slope of LL' gives the relative prices of goods X and Y at P.

In the case of individual comparisons, we assume that each household possesses no economic power whatsoever over the prices of any of the goods it buys. Consequently, if Figure 6–8 applied to a household, we would calculate the latter's price line (which gives us its consumption possibilities) as the line, LL', through the optimal combination, P, whose slope reflects the prices prevailing at P. We would then divide all combinations of goods and services into two categories. Those inside the triangle bounded by the line LL' and the axes would be available to our economy during the year in question. Those outside, like O, would lie beyond our reach.

Unhappily, it is not LL' but CC' in Figure 6–8 which bounds society's consumption possibilities. There are points, like Q, which lie inside LL' but which represent output combinations that society cannot have even if it wants them. What we must assume, therefore, if we want to use revealed preference, is that it would *not* have wanted them. Every point inside LL' must lie on a lower indifference surface representing a lower level of social welfare than is available from the output combination at P. This amounts to assuming that the indifference surface (II in Figure 6–8) passing through P lies beyond LL' or, at worst, coincides with LL'. This indifference surface must be bowed in toward the origin *or* a straight line, therefore, like all the indifference curves we have drawn up to now.

Unfortunately, it is not so easy to argue that social indifference surfaces have this property as it was for individuals. We have no choice, however, but to make such an assumption.

Finally, regardless of the definition(s) of social welfare in any country that we may choose for comparison purposes, we cannot assume that economic actors in one will prefer a market basket of goods and services consumed in the other, except within their own cultural, psychological, and social environment. In some cases, this environment will affect the technical specifications of the goods themselves.

By now the reader is tired of theorizing, and we therefore turn to case comparisons.

6-9   Income Comparisons [24]

For reasons already explored, we must make our aggregate and per capita income comparisons in terms of GNP, although this is far from being an entirely satisfactory index. We shall choose the years 1955, 1964, 1966, 1967, and 1970 for comparison purposes, partly because data are available and partly because these appear to be reasonably good benchmark years. Given the comparison technique recommended in the last section, the best data of all are for 1955. Experts did go to the trouble of computing the GNPs of several countries in U.S. prices and U.S. GNP in Soviet prices for that year. But such a procedure is troublesome, costly, and time consuming. Consequently, for the other years, we must content ourselves with approximations.

For our first example, we shall compare U.S. and Soviet GNP in 1955. We incur a problem at the outset because prices in the U.S.S.R. do not, generally speaking, reflect either scarcity relationships or planners' priorities. However, Abram Bergson has "adjusted" Soviet prices in an effort to make them more rational from the planners' point of view. And Peter Wiles has argued that actual ruble prices may reflect consumer or household priorities much better than those of the planner.[25]

We shall therefore assume that Bergson's "adjusted" ruble prices were more rational from the planners' point of view, while actual ruble prices were more rational from the viewpoint of a representative Soviet household. This gives us three sets of prices—representing three separate social preference functions—and thus three separate comparisons of U.S. and Soviet GNP in

[24] For reasons discussed above and because of limitations on data availability, we have used U.S. prices (or their approximations) to carry out most of the comparisons below. That is, we compare the GNPs of the United States and France or the U.S.S.R. by first trying to value the goods and services produced in *each* country in U.S. prices. Most comparisons do not do this. Instead, they compare the GNPs of the United States and of France by, in effect, first valuing U.S. goods at U.S. prices and then valuing French goods at French prices or at averages of U.S. and French prices. There is no scientific basis for such a procedure that the author is aware of.

[25] The references for this paragraph are A. Bergson, *The Real National Income of Soviet Russia Since 1928* (Cambridge, Mass.: Harvard U.P., 1961); A. Bergson, Hans Neyman, Jr., and Oleg Hoeffding, *Soviet National Income and Product, 1928–48: Revised Data*, Santa Monica, Calif., Rand Corp., Nov. 15, 1960; and P. J. D. Wiles, "Are Adjusted Rubles Rational," *Soviet Studies*, Oct. 1955, and "A Rejoinder to All and Sundry," *Soviet Studies*, Oct. 1956, along with the references cited in the latter work.

1955. The first will use U.S. prices; the second will use "adjusted" ruble prices representing planners' preferences, and the third will use actual ruble prices, which we assume to mirror the preferences of a "representative" Soviet household.

Morris Bornstein has calculated Soviet GNP by sector of end use in both actual and adjusted ruble prices for the year 1955. He has also calculated U.S. GNP in actual ruble prices and Soviet GNP in U.S. dollar prices. We can add to this a crude, rough-and-ready calculation of U.S. GNP in Soviet adjusted ruble prices by assuming, in effect, that sales taxes, which are quite large in the U.S.S.R. and constitute the principal difference between actual and adjusted ruble prices, would be applied by the Soviet planners to the U.S. economy just as they were applied in the Soviet Union.[26] Thus we arrive at a double comparison of Soviet and American GNP in all three sets of prices and in both aggregate and per capita terms. This is shown in Table 6–6.

Turning first to the aggregate figures, we see that total GNP for the U.S.S.R. as a percentage of U.S. GNP was 28.2 in terms of Soviet planners' (or adjusted ruble) prices, 26.8 in Soviet consumers' (or actual ruble) prices, and 53.4 in U.S. dollar prices. If we look across the row for consumption, we can see that, in terms of ruble prices, the U.S. basket received a value nearly five times as great as the Soviet, while in dollar prices U.S. consumption was only 2.5 times as great. The contrast in the GNP figures reflects the similar, although even more pronounced, contrast in the consumption figures.

A similar story is reflected in the per capita data. As a percentage of the U.S. GNP, Soviet per capita GNP was 23.4 in adjusted ruble prices, 22.2 in actual ruble prices, and 44.2 in dollar prices. In terms of per capita consumption, the indexes are 17.3 in ruble prices and 32.3 in dollar prices.

Thus the representative American consumer would have preferred his own basket of goods to the representative Soviet basket. Valued in dollars, Soviet per capita GNP was about 1,062, and we would like to locate this standard within the American income distribution. Such a procedure is difficult because after-tax U.S. income distribution statistics for 1955 are published in terms of personal disposable income per household. The latter differs from GNP per capita along two dimensions. First, most households have more than one member, and, second, disposable income is always smaller than GNP. We must translate the figure for Soviet GNP per capita into a corresponding figure which we can compare with disposable income per household in the United States.

To do this we multiply $1,062 times the average size of a U.S. household in 1955 (3.15) and then multiply the result by the ratio of personal disposable

---

[26] In other words, if sales taxes (called "turnover" taxes by the Soviets) constitute *x* per cent of Soviet consumption spending, we assumed they would likewise constitute *x* per cent of consumption spending in the United States. Similarly for investment, defense, and government administration. This is, admittedly, quite an arbitrary assumption, although data limitations precluded something more sophisticated. The basic reference is Morris Bornstein, "A Comparison of Soviet and United States National Products," in F. D. Holzman, ed., *Readings on the Soviet Economy* (Chicago: Rand McNally, 1962).

Table 6–6. Three comparisons of U.S. and Soviet GNP in 1955.

A. Aggregate comparisons

Type of Income Flow	(A) Adjusted Ruble Prices (billions)			(B) Actual Ruble Prices (billions)			(C) U.S. Dollar Prices (billions)		
	(1) U.S.	(2) U.S.S.R.	(3) (2)÷(1) per cent	(1) U.S.	(2) U.S.S.R.	(3) (2)÷(1) per cent	(1) U.S.	(2) U.S.S.R.	(3) (2)÷(1) per cent
Consumption	2,123.1	566.4	20.8	4,045.5	840.8	20.8	269.7	105.1	39.0
Investment	495.5	241.8	48.8	540.4	263.5	48.8	77.2	52.7	68.3
Defense	166.3	125.2	75.3	192.0	144.6	75.3	38.4	36.2	94.3
Government administration	18.1	27.6	152.5	24.2	36.9	152.5	12.1	18.4	152.1
Total GNP	3,403.0	961.0	28.2	4,802.1	1,285.8	26.8	397.5	212.4	53.4

B. Per capita comparisons

Type of Income Flow	(A) Adjusted Ruble Prices (in rubles)			(B) Actual Ruble Prices (in rubles)			(C) U.S. Dollar Prices (in U.S. dollars)		
	(1) U.S.	(2) U.S.S.R.	(3) (2)÷(1) per cent	(1) U.S.	(2) U.S.S.R.	(3) (2)÷(1) per cent	(1) U.S.	(2) U.S.S.R.	(3) (2)÷(1) per cent
Consumption	16,404.2	2,832.0	17.3	24,370.5	4,204.0	17.3	1,632.2	525.5	32.3
Investment	2,984.9	1,209.0	40.5	3,255.4	1,317.5	40.5	466.2	263.5	56.7
Defense	1,001.8	626.0	62.5	1,156.6	723.0	62.5	232.4	181.01	78.3
Government administration	109.0	138.0	126.6	145.8	184.5	126.5	73.2	92.0	126.2
Total GNP	20,499.9	4,805.0	23.4	28,928.3	6,429.0	22.2	2,405.0	1,062.0	44.2

income to GNP (70 per cent). We get a corresponding per household disposable income of $2,336. About 21 per cent of all U.S. households had after-tax incomes below this Soviet standard in 1955. (Therefore, about 79 per cent had higher disposable incomes.) It has been alleged that Soviet goods were of lower quality. If so, our comparison may be biased against the United States, but other sources of error were probably present as well.

Because of the magnitude of the comparison gap between Soviet and U.S. statistics in (actual) ruble prices, the "representative" Soviet consumer would probably have voted for the American market basket had it been embedded in a Soviet cultural milieu. We have seen that the distribution of income in the U.S.S.R. is more equal than in the United States, largely because of the spreading of property incomes. In 1960, for example, the top 10 per cent of households in the United States apparently received fifteen to twenty times as much income as the lowest 10 per cent.[27] For the U.S.S.R. around the same period, the highest 10 per cent of households are crudely estimated to have received only six or seven times the share going to the lowest 10 per cent. Given that the Soviet income distribution is relatively bunched up around its per capita mean of 6,429 rubles (Table 6–6), it is likely that very few Soviet households achieved the American standard of 28,928.3.

It also appears reasonable to conjecture that the Soviet planners would have preferred the American human and physical capital plant, if this were embedded in a Soviet institutional and cultural setting. By every standard of comparison the U.S. economy outperformed the U.S.S.R. in each sector (except government administration), and this would probably have counted doubly inasmuch as the planners get satisfaction from statistical indicators per se, in addition to actual performance.

Strictly speaking, however, the weak version of revealed preference does not allow us to say that either Soviet consumers or Soviet planners would have preferred the corresponding American "bundle." Moreover, we have neglected a number of significant factors. For one thing, we followed the national-income statisticans in working entirely with goods produced rather than consumed. Yet both the United States and the U.S.S.R. did little international trading relative to their GNPs, so any error introduced here would be small.

More importantly, the Soviet economy was more pliable to the wishes of its planners than the American economy would have been, and this helps to explain the important higher Soviet growth rate. Looking at matters from the perspective of 1971, the Soviet economy has continued to grow at a faster rate than the American, although the margin has shown some tendency to narrow. Thus we pay a price here for neglecting *future* income and output potential.

With this beginning we now extend our 1955 comparisons brazenly to other countries, both East and West, in Table 6–7A. Our results rest on the works of many scholars listed as sources there, notably those of Gilbert and

---

[27] The Soviet estimate is from Murray Yanowitch, "The Soviet Income Revolution," *Slavic Studies,* Dec. 1963. The U.S. estimate is from Aaron and McGuire, op. cit.

Table 6–7. Estimated per capita GNPs of selected nations in U.S. dollars and placement in U.S. income distribution (current dollars).

A. 1955

Country	Per Capita GNP	Equivalent Disposable Income per Household	Approximate per Cent of U.S. Households Below
United States	$2,400	$5,280	60
United Kingdom	1,450	3,190	30
West Germany	1,340	2,970	30
Denmark	1,300	2,860	25
France	1,300	2,860	25
East Germany	1,150	2,530	20
U.S.S.R.	1,050	2,310	20
Hungary	800	1,760	15
Italy	800	1,760	15
Poland	750	1,650	15
Cuba	600	1,320	10
Yugoslavia	450	990	10

B. 1964

Country	Per Capita GNP	Equivalent Personal Income per Household	Approximate per Cent of U.S. Households Below
United States	$3,250	$8,547	70
Sweden	2,750	7,232	60
West Germany	2,650	6,969	60
France	2,300	6,049	55
United Kingdom	2,000	5,260	45
East Germany	1,850	4,865	45
U.S.S.R.	1,700	4,471	40
Italy	1,650	4,339	40
Hungary	1,350	3,550	30
Japan	1,300	3,419	30
Poland	1,100	2,893	25

C. 1966

Country	Per Capita GNP	Equivalent Personal Income per Household	Approximate per Cent of U.S. Households Below
United States	$3,800	$9,766	70
Sweden	2,950	7,581	60
West Germany	2,900	7,453	55
France	2,750	7,067	50
United Kingdom	2,150	5,525	40
East Germany	2,050	5,268	40
U.S.S.R.	2,000	5,140	40
Italy	1,900	4,883	35
Japan	1,550	3,983	30
Hungary	1,450	3,726	30
Poland	1,250	3,212	25

Table 6—7 (cont.)

D. 1967

Country	Per Capita GNP	Equivalent Personal Income per Household	Approximate per Cent of U.S. Households Below
United States	$4,000	$10,520	75
Sweden	3,150	8,284	60
West Germany	3,000	7,890	55
France	2,950	7,758	55
United Kingdom	2,300	6,049	45
East Germany	2,150	5,654	40
U.S.S.R.	2,100	5,523	40
Italy	2,100	5,523	40
Japan	1,800	4,734	35
Hungary	1,550	4,076	30
Poland	1,300	3,419	25

E. 1970

Country	Per Capita GNP	Equivalent Personal Income per Household	Approximate per Cent of U.S. Households Below
United States	$4,750	$12,350	70
Sweden	4,100	10,660	60
France	4,000	10,400	60
West Germany	3,950	10,270	60
Canada	3,750	9,750	55
United Kingdom	2,800	7,280	40
Japan	2,800	7,280	40
Italy	2,800	7,280	40
U.S.S.R.	2,750	7,150	40
East Germany	2,700	7,020	40
Israel	2,200	5,720	35
Hungary	2,050	5,330	30
Poland	1,750	4,550	25
Yugoslavia	1,350	3,510	15
Cuba	750	1,950	10
China	150–200	390–520	About 2

Sources:
Statistical abstracts of countries involved and *U.N. Statistical Yearbooks.*
Authors' computations.
S. H. Cohn, "Soviet Growth Retardation," in Pt. II-A of U.S. Congress, Joint Economic Committee, *New Directions in the Soviet Economy* (Washington, D.C.: G.P.O., 1966); "Comparative Growth Record of the Soviet Economy," in U.S. Congress, JEC, Soviet *Economic Performance,* 1966–1967 (Washington, D.C.: G.P.O., 1968).
"The Economies of Eastern Europe," in U.S. Congress, Joint Economic Committee, *Soviet Economic Performance,* 1966–1967 (Washington, D.C.: G.P.O., 1968).
U.S. Congress, JEC, *Economic Developments in Countries of Eastern Europe* (Washington, D.C.: G.P.O., 1970), articles by Thad P. Alton and Paul F. Myers.
Agency for International Development, Statistics and Reports Division, *Gross National Product, Growth Rates, and Trend Data.*
Harry T. Oshima, "A New Estimate of National Income and Product of Cuba in 1953," *Stanford University Food Research Institute Study,* Vol. II, No. 3, p. 214 (for Cuba).
The New York Times, Jan. 26, 1970, p. 82 (for Cuba).

Kravis for Western countries and Pryor and Staller for Eastern Europe. Per capita GNPs range from a high of $2,400 for the United States to a low of $600 for Cuba.

We have also transformed the per capita GNP for each country, including the United States, into a per household disposable income, as outlined above. Then we have inserted the per household figures into the U.S. posttax (disposable) income distribution. The final column in Table 6–7A gives the approximate percentage of U.S. households lying below the standard for each country. Ideally, we would next compute the per capita GNPs for each country in British prices, German prices, and so on down the line. Unfortunately, data for these comparisons are not available.

Therefore, we proceed instead to repeat the 1955 exercise for 1964, 1966, 1967, and 1970. These results appear in Tables 6–7B, 6–7C, 6–7D, and 6–7E, respectively. We do not have studies possessing the scope and dimention of the works by Bornstein and Gilbert and Kravis for these years. Consequently, we must rely on estimates, particularly for 1970. (And for 1970, we would add, the estimates for China, Cuba, and Yugoslavia are particularly risky.) The calculations for 1964, 1966, and 1967 are largely the work of S. H. Cohn and Thad Alton, who in some cases were updating the Gilbert study.[28] Moreover, we do not have suitable posttax income distributions for the United States relating to those years. Consequently, we have had to use the less-satisfactory pretax (personal) income distributions.

The United States clearly ranks first in terms of dollar per capita GNP during each comparison year.[29] However, the percentage gaps between the United States and several other countries did close over the period 1955–1970. Although the 1960s were not as good as a growth decade for the

---

Ta-Chung Liu, "The Tempo of Economic Development of the Chinese Mainland, 1949–1965," in U.S. Congress, JEC, *An Economic Profile of Mainland China*, Vol. I (Washington, D.C.: G.P.O., 1967).

"The Canadian Economy in 1971," Canadian Imperial Bank of Commerce Commercial Letter, Toronto, Sept. 1971 (for Canada).

Frederic L. Pryor and George J. Staller, "The Dollar Values of the Gross National Products in Eastern Europe, 1955," *Economics of Planning*, 1966, No. 1, p. 16.

Milton Gilbert and associates, *Comparative National Products and Price Levels*, Paris, Organization for European Economic Co-operation, 1958; see Table 3, p. 23. (This volume extended an earlier work by Gilbert and Irving Kravis.)

United Nations, *Statistical Yearbook*.

OECD, *National Accounts Statistics*.

[28] The references are: S. H. Cohn, "Soviet Growth Retardation," in Pt. II-A of U.S. Congress, Joint Economic Committee, *New Directions in the Soviet Economy* (Washington, D.C.: G.P.O., 1966); "Comparative Growth Record of the Soviet Economy," in U.S. Congress, JEC, *Soviet Economic Performance, 1966–1967* (Washington, D.C.: G.P.O., 1966). Thad Alton, "Economic Structure and Growth in Eastern Europe," in U.S. Congress, JEC, *Economic Developments in Countries of Eastern Europe* (Washington, D.C.: G.P.O., 1970); "General Growth Performance of the Soviet Economy," in U.S. Congress, JEC, *Economic Performance and the Military Burden in the Soviet Union* (Washington, D.C.: G.P.O., 1970).

[29] However, there is probably at least one country in the world which ranks higher than the United States in terms of per capita GNP. This is the Arab kingdom of Kuwait, once described as "a desert floating on a sea of oil." There, housing, education, and many social services are free to citizens.

U.S.S.R.—and for command economics generally—as the 1950s had been, U.S.S.R. GNP per head as a percentage of U.S. GNP did rise from 44 in 1955 to 58 by 1970. West Germany rose even more, from 55 per cent in 1955 to 83 per cent by 1970. Japan's GNP per capita was only 36 per cent of the U.S. level in 1964, but it rose to 40 per cent in 1968, 44 in 1967, and 59 by 1970. At the same time, the Japanese standard moved up through the U.S. income distribution during each year. In 1964 only 24 per cent of all U.S. households had pretax incomes below this standard. Just two years later, 27 per cent were below; 29 per cent were below in 1967, and about 37 per cent were below by 1970.

We would add that only one country experienced an absolute reduction in real (or constant-dollar) per capita GNP. This was Cuba, which suffered a decline of 10–15 per cent between 1955 and 1970 (and of 15–20 per cent between 1958, the year of the revolution, and 1970).[30] The same period saw the introduction of comprehensive rationing—the only country in Table 6–7 experiencing this phenomenon—but the distribution of income and wealth undoubtedly becomes more equal as well.

6–10   Growth Comparisons

We shall close by comparing growth rates of income and output. Whether we are advocates of zero population growth or enthusiasts for all-out economic expansion or somewhere in between, growth-rate comparisons appear to be more popular and to attract more headlines and attention than do comparisons of income distributions or of GNP per head. Table 6–8 describes and contrasts the post-World War II growth of per capita GNP in several nations from different parts of the world and with diverse socioeconomic systems. We take 1950 as our starting point because, by that year, most countries had at least regained their prewar levels of production.

To keep the table in perspective, we should note that the worldwide growth of output per head since, let us say, the dawn of civilization in 5000 B.C., is far less than 0.1 per cent per year. For better or worse, the period 1950–1970 is probably the era of most rapid growth in world history. It would surprise the present author if many of these growth rates could be sustained until the end of the 20th century. Whether present levels of income and output per head are even sustainable in the more developed nations is currently a lively controversy, but also one based largely on speculation that we shall not explore here.

To complement our growth comparisons, Figure 6–9 contrasts the percentages of GNP that several of the same nations devote to gross investment.

[30] See Harry T. Oshima, "A New Estimate of National Income and Product of Cuba in 1953," *Stanford University Food Research Institute Study*, Vol. 2, No. 3, p. 214, and *The New York Times*, Jan. 26, 1970, p. 82. We have assumed that no change in real per capita GNP occurred between 1967 and 1970.

Table 6–8.   Per capita growth rates of GNP.
(alphabetical order)

Country	1950–1955	1955–1960	1960–1965	1965–1970	Rank 1965–1970
Australia	1.5	1.7	3.1	3.1	14–15–16
Belgium	2.9	1.7	4.2	3.9	11–12
Bulgaria*	5.4	6.4	5.8	6.6	2
Canada	1.8	0.6	3.7	2.9	17
Czechoslovakia*	2.3	5.5	1.6	4.3	10
East Germany*	7.6	5.8	2.7	3.1	14–15–16
France	3.6	3.8	3.8	4.9	6–7–8
Hungary*	4.4	3.5	3.9	4.9	6–7–8
India	2.1	2.3	0.8	1.9	21–22
Israel	5.7	4.9	6.1	5.2	4
Italy	5.4	5.1	4.1	5.1	5
Japan	N.a.	8.0	8.6	11.2	1
Netherlands	4.5	2.8	3.6	3.9	11–12
Pakistan	−0.5	1.3	3.1	2.5	18–19
Poland*	2.6	2.9	3.2	4.9	6–7–8
Rumania*	6.0	3.2	5.4	5.6	3
Sweden	2.5	2.8	4.3	3.1	14–15–16
Switzerland	3.8	2.5	3.0	2.5	18–19
United Kingdom	2.5	1.9	2.6	1.5	23
United States	2.6	0.6	3.2	2.1	20
U.S.S.R.	4.1	4.8	3.6	4.4	9
West Germany	8.2	5.1	3.6	3.8	13
Yugoslavia*	2.9	6.2	4.6	1.9	21–22
China				2.0 †	N.a.

Sources:
Statistical abstracts of countries involved and *U.N. Statistical Yearbooks.*
Authors' computations.
S. H. Cohn, "Soviet Growth Retardation," in Pt. II-A of U. S. Congress, Joint Economic Committee, *New Directions in the Soviet Economy* (Washington, D.C.: G.P.O., 1966); "Comparative Growth Record of the Soviet Economy," in U.S. Congress, JEC, *Soviet Economic Performance, 1966–1967* (Washington, D.C.: G.P.O., 1968).
"The Economies of Eastern Europe," in U.S. Congress, Joint Economic Committee, *Soviet Economic Performance, 1966–1967* (Washington, D.C.: G.P.O., 1968).
U.S. Congress, JEC, *Economic Developments in Countries of Eastern Europe* (Washington, D.C.: G.P.O., 1970), articles by Thad P. Alton and Paul F. Myers.
Agency for International Development, Statistics and Reports Division, *Gross National Product, Growth Rates, and Trend Data,* Apr. 1970 and May 15, 1971.
Harry T. Oshima, "A New Estimate of National Income and Product of Cuba in 1953," *Stanford University Food Research Institute Study,* Vol. II, No. 3, p. 214 (for Cuba).
The New York Times, Jan. 26, 1970, p. 82 (for Cuba.)
Ta-Chung Liu, "The Tempo of Economic Development of the Chinese Mainland, 1949–1965," in U.S. Congress, JEC, *An Economic Profile of Mainland China,* Vol. I (Washington, D.C.: G.P.O., 1967).
"The Canadian Economy in 1971," Canadian Imperial Bank of Commerce Commercial Letter, Toronto, Sept. 1971 (for Canada).
Frederic L. Pryor and George J. Staller, "The Dollar Values of the Gross National Products in Eastern Europe, 1955," *Economics of Planning,* 1966, No. 1, p. 16.
Milton Gilbert and associates, *Comparative National Products and Price Levels,* Paris, Organization for European Economic Co-operation, 1958; see Table 3, p. 23. (This volume extended an earlier work by Gilbert and Irving Kravis.)
   * 1965–1968.
   † Approximate figure for 1949–1969.

(India and Pakistan, not included in Figure 6–9, would have lower gross-investment ratios than any of the countries that are included; the same is true of most developing countries with the notable exception of China.) Other things being equal, higher gross investment ratios mean higher growth rates. The nation in question is sacrificing present for future consumption. Thus, while Soviet GNP per capita has been on the order of 44–52 per cent of the U.S. figure during the latter 1950s and 1960s (in U.S. dollars), per capita consumption has been only 32–38 per cent as great (see Table 6–9). The

Table 6–9. U.S. and Soviet per capita GNP versus per capita consumption (in U.S. dollars).

		Per Cent		
Ratio	*1955*	*1964*	*1966*	*1967*
1. Soviet GNP per capita / U.S. GNP per capita	44	51	52	52
2. Soviet consumption per capita / U.S. consumption per capita	32	36	37	38

Sources: Table 6–7 and David W. Bronson and Barbara S. Severin, "Consumer Welfare," in U.S. Congress, Joint Economic Committee, *Economic Performance and the Military Burden in the Soviet Union* (Washington, D.C.: G.P.O., 1970).

U.S.S.R. now spends about as much on investment and probably more on defense than the United States in absolute terms even though total Soviet GNP is only around 70 per cent as great in U.S. dollar prices.

Nevertheless, the gross-investment ratio is far from being the sole determinant of growth. To begin with, much of *gross* investment—in some cases more than half—simply goes to replace capital equipment or productive capacity which had worn out or become obsolete. A comprehensive ranking of countries by *net* investment as a percentage of *net* national product (unfortunately unavailable) would show some changes, although probably only a few. More importantly, different nations have different growth potentials for reasons largely unrelated to social goals or to the organization of their economies. Both goals and the manner in which production and distribution are organized will also influence the amount of growth that a given sum spent on investment can "buy."

For example, during the 1930s the U.S.S.R. concentrated its investment rubles on basic industries such as steel, electricity, coal, and machine tools, where they could generate a relatively large amount of growth. Transportation, housing, and other kinds of social overhead capital, where the growth payoff was not nearly so large, were avoided. However, the Soviets did not allocate their investment funds very efficiently among alternative uses. Had they done so, their growth rate would have been even higher. Several East European countries present an even more extreme picture of misused investment resources, causing a large sacrifice of present consumption to result in a small increase—perhaps even a decrease—in growth. The persistence of a

Per cent

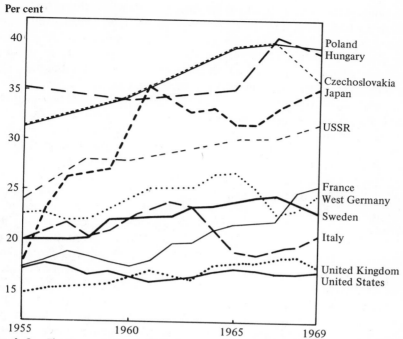

Figure 6–9. The percentage of GNP devoted to gross investment in selected countries.

rigid command planning mechanism has undoubtedly played a role in this.[31]

Sweden, on the other hand, probably achieves a more rational allocation of investible resources, but growth is not an overriding objective. (Sweden leads the world in percentage of GNP devoted to public consumption.) Finally, Japan presents a rather unique picture of a country facing a high growth potential during the early 1950s and achieving this in record time. Systemic features, once again, are partly responsible. The Japanese relied upon a basically market economy to achieve a reasonably efficient allocation of investible resources. But the government also both directly and indirectly encouraged the adoption and improvement of foreign technology, helped to find imaginative solutions to natural-resource shortages, and provided coordination of rapid expansion in diverse sectors of the economy.

Speaking generally, the share of GNP devoted to investment; the efficiency with which this is allocated; social tradeoffs between growth and other goals; changes in labor-force participation rates; the availability and mobility of resources, including labor; the flow of new ideas and the ease with which technology can spread; the ability of the economy to employ its resources— all these factors work together to determine the per capita growth rate of in-

---

[31] For further discussion of the Czechoslovak case by two Czech economists, see J. Goldmann and J. Flek, "Economic Growth in Czechoslovakia," *Economics of Planning,* 1966, No. 2.

come and output. There is an additional, less obvious determinant. Figure 6–10 shows the actual upward evolution of total GNP in the United States measured in dollars of constant 1958 purchasing power from 1952 to 1970. (This is the jagged line.) This is contrasted with a trend line depicting the potential GNP that would have been produced in each year had all the resources that were actually available been fully employed.[32]

In most years over the period 1952–1970 full employment did not prevail in the United States. The shaded area between the lines describing actual and potential gives the output that was not produced because some productive inputs were idle. As it happens, the average annual growth rate of GNP in 1958 dollars was about 3.4 per cent during these years. But as Figure 6–10 shows, this is an average of lows and highs; it is not necessarily a rate actually achieved during any particular year.

Suppose, for the sake of argument, that the rate of unemployment was about the same in 1970 as in 1952. Then, instead of following the jagged line in Figure 6–10, let us assume that the economy had achieved full employment in every year from 1952 through 1970 inclusive. This would have meant more goods and services produced during most years of this period. But would it have meant a higher rate of growth over the period as a whole?

In fact, it would have. If the shaded area in Figure 6–10 had been produced, the economy would have turned out more capital goods, or goods that help make other goods, as well as more consumer goods. By 1970, therefore, America's productive capacity would have been significantly greater than it actually was. Consequently, her full-employment level of output would have been greater; members of the labor force would have had more capital to work with, on the average, and would have produced more. Thus the 1970 level of GNP would have been higher *relative* to the 1952 level than it actually was, implying an increased rate of growth.[33]

It follows that cyclical fluctuations in output and employment reduce an economy's long-run rate of growth. By smoothing out their business cycles and making fuller use of available resources, the United States, Canada, and perhaps some other Western countries would improve their growth performance relative to economies—including those of Eastern Europe—where cycles have historically been less severe.

---

[32] In fact, the line of potential GNP does not assume a zero rate of unemployment because this is, in practice, unachievable. Instead, it presupposes a low rate which is slightly greater than the actual in very good years. (Presumably, the potential rate is the lowest that could possibly be maintained under ideal conditions over fairly long periods of time.) The actual will, on occasion, exceed the "potential."

[33] In fact, the unemployment rate was much higher in 1970 than in 1952, 5.0 per cent as opposed to 2.7. This explains why the economy was further below its potential in 1970 and was an additional factor depressing the average growth rate over the period.

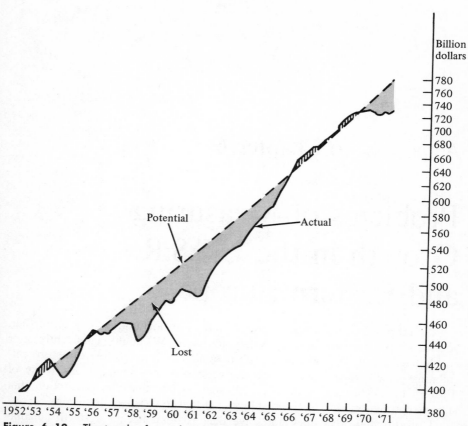

Figure 6–10. The trends of actual and potential GNP in the United States (in dollars of 1958 purchasing power). Source: *Business Conditions Digest* (Apr. 1971), p. 56.

Appendix to Chapter 6

Problems of Measuring Growth in the U.S.S.R. and Eastern Europe

As the reader may suspect, growth rates are not unique, any more than are the output measures on which they are based. We could significantly alter Table 6–8, simply by computing each nation's GNP in U.S. prices before calculating growth rates. Instead, we use each country's own prices—those of Eastern European economies are "adjusted"—reflecting the assumption that a particular nation's growth is most pertinent to its own rulers or citizens.

Unfortunately, this does not solve the problem, because growth calculations usually cover a time span during which relative prices change. This is why it was impossible for us to say unambiguously whether U.S. machinery output declined or increased between 1899 and 1939. Valued in 1899 prices, we recall, the 1939 output was 5.5 times as great, while in 1939 prices, 1899 output was nearly twice as high. During this period, far-reaching changes occurred in the structure of physical flows in the U.S. economy, causing major changes in relative prices.

Whether one is contrasting two economies over space (the U.S. and Soviet economies in 1970) or over time (the Soviet economy in 1928 and 1970), the basic conceptual problems are the same. In either instance, the wider the differences in tastes, in structure, in the organization of the economy, in social goals, and in comparative production possibilities, the greater the potential discrepancy in results when one set of candidate prices is used rather than another.

At the same time, one could assert that there is considerably increased "sport" in making comparisons when vast differences in tastes of production possibilities are involved. Suppose, for example, that we do not like either extreme result obtained from measuring the growth of U.S. machinery output.

We then simply denounce the use of 1899 *and* 1939 prices as extreme and proceed to choose a year in between as being more "representative." If we are careful, we can probably pick just the year whose prices will give us the growth rate we wished to proclaim in the first place.

Because of this, one suggested way of "avoiding bias" in calculating growth rates is to use a method known as "chaining the links." It works on the principle that rational prices change slowly enough over time that one can ignore the effects of this evolution by always comparing time periods sufficiently close together. The method is generally accepted among Western statisticians and has found increasing acceptance in Eastern Europe since World War II.

To illustrate it, suppose we wish to calculate an average annual growth rate for GNP in Canada over 1950–1970. First, we simply calculate GNP for 1950, using prices that we feel are rational for that year. Next we calculate GNP for 1951 using 1950 prices, which we hope are also very close to the *relative* prices prevailing in 1951. By comparison, we get a growth rate from 1950 to 1951.

We then proceed to calculate GNP for 1951 and for 1952, both in 1951 prices. This will give us a growth rate from 1951 to 1952. And so the process goes, right on up to 1970. By taking the (geometric) average of these rates, we arrive at an average growth rate for the entire period. (Similarly, we can find growth rates for any subperiod such as 1950–1955.) Usually, this will yield about the same results that we would have gotten by using prices pertaining to some intermediate year, although we cannot know in advance which year to use.

Although the link-chaining procedure is "scientific" and often appropriate, given the questions that our growth calculations are intended to answer, this is not always true. Sometimes, it is actually more appropriate to use prices from an early or late part of the period to which our growth calculations apply. To show what we mean in a "real-world" context, let us turn to the dispute over growth in the Soviet Union and Eastern Europe.

Table 6–10A shows per capita post-World War II growth rates for Eastern Europe, both as calculated from the official statistical yearbooks [columns (1)] and as recalculated by Western experts so as to be more comparable with the West [columns (2)]. Table 6–11 gives official Soviet estimates of growth covering selected periods since the inception of the five-year plans in 1928. We contrast this with two Western estimates and, for good measure, with an independent estimate by two Soviet economists. In nearly all cases, the official estimates are highest of all, and Soviet statisticians have spiced the debate by proclaiming that "statistics are a weapon in the class war." Our approach, however, will be to ask whether the two sets of figures in columns (1) and (2) of Table 6–11 do not give better answers to two different questions.

Three basic differences in calculating growth separate the Eastern and Western estimates. The first relates to the pricing problem discussed above. It induces a gap between the two estimates which we shall call the "pricing" gap. Second comes the use of prices, which include turnover taxes, in cal-

Figure 6–10

A. Per capita growth rates for Eastern Europe: Official (1) versus
Western recalculation (2)

Country	1955–1960 (1)	(2)	1960–1965 (1)	(2)	1965–1968 (1)	(2)
U.S.S.R.	7.5	4.8	4.9	3.6	7.1	5.0
Bulgaria	8.6	6.4	5.6	5.8	8.3	6.6
Czechoslavakia	6.3	5.5	1.3	1.6	7.3	4.3
East Germany	10.6	5.8	3.2	2.7	4.9	3.1
Hungary	5.7	3.5	4.1	3.9	5.7	4.9
Poland	5.0	2.9	4.9	3.2	5.7	4.9
Rumania	5.7	3.2	8.3	5.4	5.3	5.6
Yugoslavia	7.5	6.2	6.9	4.6	6.1	1.9

B. Per capita growth rates for Western countries: Official (1) versus
recalculation (2) in East-bloc net material product

Country	1950–1957 (1)	(2)	1958–1966 (1)	(2)
France	3.8	3.9	3.8	4.0
West Germany	6.6	8.0	5.2	4.7
Italy	5.1	6.1	4.5	5.0
United Kingdom	2.0	2.3	2.2	2.4
United States	1.9	1.8	2.9	2.9

Sources:
Robert W. Campbell, "The Dynamics of Socialism: Problems and Reforms," in *Papers and Proceedings of the McMaster Conference on Current Problems of Socialist Economies,* Hamilton, Ontario, McMaster University, Spring 1971.
S. H. Cohn, "National Income Growth Statistics," paper prepared for Duke University Conference on Soviet Statistics, Nov. 1969, rev. Dec. 1969.
U.S. Congress, Joint Economic Committee, *Economic Developments in Eastern Europe* (Washington, D.C.: G.P.O., 1970).
U.N. Demographic Yearbooks.

culating income and output. (For example, the Soviets use actual ruble prices, whereas Western experts prefer adjusted ruble prices.) We shall call this the weighting or turnover tax gap. Last comes the fact that most socialist countries professing to follow a Marxist philosophy do not include the value of services in their measure of national output. The resulting concept is called "net material product," in contrast to the GNP used by most Western nations and induces a gap that we shall call the "coverage" gap.[34] Table 6–10B shows the effect on Western growth rates of replacing GNP with net material product.

[34] Following Adam Smith and other economists of the Classical school (roughly 1750–1870), Marx considered labor in service sectors to be unproductive. This leads to some rather odd results. For example, the output of the Ministry of Ferrous Metallurgy in the U.S.S.R. consists largely of administrative services. The income and output of a typist, a clerk, or an accountant working there does not count as part of net material product. But the same kind of work done for a coal-mining firm is included.

Table 6–11. Western and Soviet growth estimates for the U.S.S.R.

Period	Official Estimate (1)	First Western Estimate (2)	Second Western Estimate (3)	Estimate by Soviet Economists (4)	Estimation Gaps		
					(1)–(2)	(1)–(3)	(1)–(4)
1928–1932	16.2	2.0	2.0	—	14.2	14.2	—
1932–1937	16.2	6.6	6.6	—	9.6	9.6	—
1937–1940	10.0	3.6	3.6	—	6.4	6.4	—
1950–1955	11.3	6.9	7.7	—	4.4	3.6	—
1955–1958	10.2	7.4	8.2	—	2.8	2.0	—
1958–1961	7.5	5.8	6.2	—	1.7	1.3	—
1961–1966	6.7	5.6	6.0	—	0.9	0.7	—
1950–1958	10.5	7.1	7.9	8.7	3.4	2.6	1.8
1958–1963	6.3	4.9	5.3	4.4	1.4	1.0	1.9
1950–1963	9.1	6.2	6.9	7.0	2.9	2.2	2.1

Sources:
S. H. Cohn, "National Income Growth Statistics," paper presented for Duke University Conference on Soviet Statistics, Nov. 1969, rev. Dec. 1969.
Abraham Becker, Richard Moorsteen, and Raymond Powell, "The Soviet Capital Stock: Revisions and Extensions, 1961–1967," New Haven, Conn., Yale University, Economic Growth Center, 1968.

In most cases they go up because the service sector grew more slowly than the economy as a whole.

The sum of the three gaps will equal the divergence between Western and Eastern estimates. S. H. Cohn has shown the size of each gap in reconciling the official Soviet with the first Western estimate in Table 6–11. We have reproduced his work as Table 6–12.[35] The reader should start with the Western per capita estimate in column (1) and progressively add columns (2), (3), (4) and (5) to arrive at the official estimate, column (6), of growth of total net material product. We must now explain why, from a Soviet planner's viewpoint, each adjustment may be justifiable.

To begin with, Soviet planners have historically been more interested in growth of total production capacity than in growth of output per head. This was especially true during the 1930s when the Soviet leaders feared—correctly, as it turned out—that they would eventually be attacked by one or more capitalist powers. The "catch-up" mentality that prevailed on into the 1960s and probably still is not dead was usually couched in aggregate rather than per capita terms.

Prior to World War II, the pricing gap accounted for by far the largest part of the total estimation discrepancy. The chief cause of this gap lay in the application of what were known as "1926–1927 constant prices" to compute net material product for each year. In other words, Soviet growth computa-

[35] S. H. Cohn, "National Income Growth Statistics," paper prepared for Duke University Conference on Soviet Statistics, Nov. 1969, rev. Dec. 1969.

Table 6-12. Reconciliation of official and Western growth rates for the U.S.S.R.

Period	Western Estimate (per capita) (1)	Population Growth (2)	Estimation Gaps			Official Estimate (6)
			Pricing Gap (3)	Weighting (Turnover Tax) Gap (4)	Coverage Gap (5)	
1928–1932	0.5	1.5	10.2	5.0	-1.0	16.2
1932–1937	6.0	0.6	8.5	0.8	0.8	16.2
1950–1955	5.2	1.7	0.9	2.3	1.2	11.3
1955–1958	5.8	1.6	1.2	0.1	1.5	10.2
1958–1961	4.2	1.6	0.6	1.0	0.1	7.5
1961–1966	4.2	1.4	0.4	0.5	0.2	6.7
1928–1932	0.5	1.5		14.2		16.2
1932–1937	6.0	0.6		9.6		16.2
1950–1955	5.2	1.7		4.4		11.3
1955–1958	5.8	1.6		2.8		10.2
1958–1961	4.2	1.6		1.7		7.5
1961–1966	4.2	1.4		0.9		6.7

Sources:
S. H. Cohn, "National Income Growth Statistics," paper prepared for Duke University Conference on Soviet Statistics, Nov. 1969, rev. Dec. 1969.
Warren W. Eason, "Labor Force," in A. Bergson and S. Kuznets, eds., *Economic Trends in the Soviet Union* (Cambridge, Mass.: Harvard U.P., 1963).

tions used price weights which prevailed just before the start of their drive for industrialization. During the period 1928–1940 the Soviet industrial structure underwent a rapid and radical transformation. The set of rational relative prices of different products altered considerably. In particular, the output of heavy industry increased at a rate spectacularly exceeding the rise in light industry. The output of industry as a whole rose much faster than that of agriculture, which actually fell between 1928 and 1936 and was only 8 per cent higher in 1937 than in 1928.

At the same time, and also due to the large amounts of investment capital poured into it, heavy industry increased in efficiency much more rapidly than did light industry. Heavy industry was likewise able to achieve more scale economies, and the rate of technical progress was faster there. These statements hold for industry as a whole vis-à-vis agriculture and services. Consequently, the products of heavy industry became cheaper relative to those of light industry, and industrial products as a category became cheaper relative to agriculture and services.

Given this, someone who wanted to show a high statistical growth rate of output would naturally tend to chart growth using prices that prevailed at or near the beginning of the period in question. In this way he would give the highest price weights to those products whose outputs grew the most. If he wished to show a low statistical growth rate of output, he would use price weights prevailing near the end of the period, which would emphasize least those products having expanded the most rapidly. This explains the striking contrast obtained by Gerschenkron, and it was indeed to emphasize this very principle that he carried out the double comparison we described.

Returning to the Soviet case, there was an added growth booster that was partly endemic to the kind of command-planning mechanism that prevailed there. As the industrialization drive gathered momentum, many goods began to come out of Soviet factories which were not produced at all in 1926 or 1927. These products had no "constant 1926–1927 prices." Officially, they were to be introduced at prices that might reasonably be expected to have prevailed during the 1926–1927 period. However, the Soviet Union was strongly output-oriented. Rewards of officials, managers, and workers from the apex of the planning hierarchy all the way down to the individual workshop depended upon expansion of production.

Consequently there was a tendency to report as much "production" as possible and hence to introduce new products at "1926–1927 constant prices," which were as high as possible. It is even believed that slight alterations were introduced into the design of items already in production so that they could receive higher 1926–27 constant prices. Since 1950 the U.S.S.R. has adopted a link-chaining procedure, thereby reducing the pricing gap drastically, although not causing it to vanish completely.

Because of the way in which they are applied, inclusion of the large Soviet turnover (or sales) taxes in prices also increases the weight of industry and reduces that of agriculture in net material product. It also has several other less important effects, but the weighting or turnover tax gap (column D) results largely from the fact that industry-wide output has grown more rapidly than agricultural production. Finally, the growth of services has normally been slower than the growth of the rest of the economy, explaining the coverage gap in column E. The only exception, during 1928–1932, marks the birth of the five-year plans and may be due to a rapid expansion of planning (or administrative) services then.

The basic argument for including all three columns (C)–(E) in the official index is that the Soviet planners have historically attached the highest priority of all to the growth of defense-oriented and heavy industries. Next has come light industry and last, agriculture and services. On these grounds one could argue that the official index gave a better assessment of the economy's performance than did most Western recalculations. Nonetheless, the official growth claims of the nine years from 1928 to 1937—when economy-wide output supposedly became nearly four times as large as it had been —are unquestionably exaggerated, even from the planners' viewpoint. The same cannot necessarily be said for the period since 1950.

Part **Two**

The Social Technology
of a Command Economy

It will soon be half a century since the establishment of the U.S.S.R. State Planning Committee and the beginning of planned economy on a countrywide scale. It seems to me that mankind ought to mark this date . . . as a historical event, signifying man's attainment of a basically new stage in human development. . . . Today, it is hard to name a country, regardless of political orientation or economic system, that does not try to develop long-range economic plans.

Alexander Birman
(a prominent Soviet economist)

7–1 Introduction

In the early days of the space race when the Soviet cosmonaut Yuri Gagarin had just become the first man in space, a story circulated in Moscow about a visitor who came to call at the Gagarins' apartment. After knocking and waiting for some time, he was about to leave when a neighbor appeared.

"I would like to see Comrade Gagarin," the visitor said.

"I am sorry," the neighbor replied. "He is presently circling the Earth in outer space. He will be back in about two hours."

"Oh, then, may I see Mrs. Gagarin?"

"I am sorry, she is gone to the butcher's. She will return in five hours."

A command economy's rulers are best equipped to determine a few overriding priorities and to see to it directly that these sectors get the best men and materiel while the others do without, if need be. The Soviet performance in heavy industry, space, and defense is much more impressive than its record in textiles, food processing, housing, and agriculture.

In the light of achievements by priority sectors—including space feats and the ability of steel production to at long last surpass the U.S. level in 1971— and, perhaps in the light of a more equal income distribution, the Soviet leaders were probably consoled over setbacks elsewhere. Among the latter we would include obsolete production methods by Western standards and a general lag in the growth of consumer goods production and in the over-all standard of living behind that of the "leading links" of the economy. Housing was a notable sore spot, and the average per capita living space in urban areas probably did not surpass the 1928 level until the early 1960s.

As we write these words, however, old priorities appear to be undergoing somewhat of a change, and more emphasis may be placed on consumption and on improving production techniques in years to come.[1] However, we are getting ahead of our story. To begin with, we should review the basic definition of a command economy and how it differs from more marketized systems.

Perhaps its most important distinguishing feature is centralized economic decision making. Society's basic production decisions are taken above the level of firms and translated into obligatory quantitative targets for enterprise managements. In effect, the bulk of the producing sector becomes more like a single firm than would be the case in a market economy. The economic planning council is the top management of this firm, and most managers of enterprises assume roles analogous to foremen or, at best, division managers in market economies. (In agriculture, the most important targets have traditionally been for *deliveries* to the state rather than production, for reasons that we shall examine in Section 7–7.)

Because they do not expect this much authority to be delegated by the "people" to an economic planning council, most Western economists treat

---

[1] These changes in priorities are probably due more to shifts in production possibilities (in a way to be made clear below) than to changes in social preferences. We would also note that, although the Soviet income distribution is more equal than the American, it is not necessarily more equal than that in Sweden or, perhaps, in Yugoslavia or West Germany. See the discussion in Section 6–6. Finally, in terms of *over-all* per capita consumption, the Soviet Union had at least trebled the 1928 level by 1970, a rise that was far less spectacular than accomplishments in the economy's leading links. See Janet Chapman, "Consumption," in A. Bergson and S. Kuznets, eds., *Economic Trends in the Soviet Union* (Cambridge, Mass.: Harvard U.P., 1963). See David W. Bronson and Barbara S. Severin, "Consumer Welfare" in U.S. Congress, Joint Economic Committee, *Economic Performance and the Military Burden in the Soviet Union* (Washington, D.C.: G.P.O., 1970).

command-economy EPCs like dominant poles of economic power. Certainly, it is improbable that a command economy would arise spontaneously, because spontaneity in production and distribution tends to go hand in hand with many independent decision makers who find it to their advantage to specialize and exchange. This inevitably leads to markets for the outputs and inputs, including labor, of society's production processes and thus to the coordination of economic activity through the market mechanism.

Nevertheless, it is quite conceivable for a society to take a fundamental, "democratic" decision to industralize and then delegate broad powers to an EPC. The planners might select a command mechanism, in turn, as the best way of carrying out their assignment. However, we would then predict a tendency for the planning bureaucracy to stay in power and for the command structure to remain intact after both have fulfilled their purpose.

7–2 The Markets That Should Remain in a Command Economy [2]

Although it is theoretically possible to centralize decision making in both production and consumption, virtually every country on earth maintains at least limited markets for labor and consumer goods. So much is this the case that some economists have argued for convergence of different kinds of economic and social systems on these grounds. As consumer-goods production becomes relatively more important in communist nations, these economies would inevitably become more marketized. At the same time, a relatively higher priority for provision of social services and control over the economy would lead to a greater role for the public sector in capitalist societies. Such a move would bring a greater bureaucratization of the economy along with it.

This convergence thesis is probably overdrawn, although it may receive a test during the 1970s in the Soviet Union, Poland, and one or two other East European countries. These have promised both to do a much better job in satisfying the consumer and to retain their essentially centralized economic decision-making structures.

Yet, assuming that individuals have not become semiautomatons, their preferences will be both nonoperational and unstable. No outside party can hope to peer into their minds and forecast the wishes of each individual on a consistently accurate basis. The best we can hope for are good predictions of aggregate or region-wide consumer demand and labor supply. For this reason, even the harshest EPC wanting growth at any price would be wise to maintain markets for consumer goods and labor in the interests of efficiency.

The alternative is a severe kind of rationing in which households receive obligatory consumption and labor input targets, thus placing them on a footing exactly analogous with producers. Each household would be given ration cards to turn in for fixed amounts of each consumer good allotted to it.

[2] Before reading this section it may be useful to examine Section 7-8.

Once individuals had obtained the quantities rationed to them, they could *not* then trade among themselves so that each household would give up goods it did not want in exchange for goods that it preferred.[3]

An enormous misallocation of labor resources and maldistribution of consumer goods among households would result. No command economy has ever attempted such a comprehensive form of rationing. In Cuba, which still has rationing, the labor market is relatively free, and individuals are able to trade rationed quantities among themselves. The fact that they do, and usually have in similar situations throughout history, reveals that consumer goods are not efficiently distributed to begin with. Outside of Cuba, no command economy today allocates a large percentage of its available consumer goods through any formal rationing scheme.

Where formal rationing has been resorted to, in fact, its goal has not been to accommodate individual preferences more perfectly. Rather, it has been to ensure a distribution of scarce necessities, which prevents any member of the population at large or of a particular group from living below a minimal material standard. This is true both of the U.S.S.R. during the bitterest years of its industrialization drive (that is, the 1930s) and of North America during World War II.

For example, Stalinist Russia had the motto, "He who does not work, neither shall he eat." Nonetheless, a reasonably healthy urban labor force was a prerequisite to industrialization, and its members were generally guaranteed a minimum ration. The rural peasantry was not. Indeed, grain and animal products were extracted from them at nearly confiscatory prices, and many starved.

Even during the 1930s, markets for consumer goods and labor continued to play an important allocative role, which has since expanded. The existence of labor markets will mean that the planners must occupy themselves with forecasting and influencing the supply of various components of the labor force. They may encourage population migration, for example, or offer larger subsidies for some kinds of education or professional training than for other kinds.

More important, the usual top-down planning in a command economy should be largely supplanted with bottom-up planning in consumer-goods production. In order for consumer votes to direct production, the initial sequence of orders must go *up* the chain of command. Retail stores should first try to forecast demand and then gear their own orders to meet this. It would be most efficient for these orders to go directly to consumer-goods producers. After aggregation the latter would send them up the command hierarchy toward the EPC or a regional planning authority.

In reply, the planners could tighten or ease up on the budget constraints of producers. But, in most instances, they would not seek to adjust the production

[3] This discussion recalls Section 3–5. See also Pts. VII and IX, Ch. 1, in F. D. Holzman, ed., *Readings on the Soviet Economy* (Chicago: Rand McNally, 1962).

targets of specific goods. (Producers and retail outlets would also receive some leeway to change prices.) To enforce the reliability of demand estimates, the planners can award managerial bonuses for good predictions and attach penalties to bad ones, whether the forecast turns out to be above or below the actual figure. Similar penalties should discourage the excessive accumulation of consumer goods in inventory. The planners can also aid demand forecasting by supplying their own predictions of economy or region-wide income and population growth.[4]

All this says nothing at all about whether the EPC is harsh or benign or oriented toward consumer-goods production or growth. The central planners continue to fix the over-all consumer-goods budget. A harsh EPC would set a tight budget, assigning higher priorities to investment, defense, or certain prestige projects. But even the severest of EPCs has a stake in consumer welfare if he wants to maintain his power. A better matching of consumer-goods production with consumer wants increases household satisfaction just as an increase in real income would do.

In addition, the prospect of higher incomes in a command economy should motivate managers and workers to produce more. Historically, material incentives have probably been the most important "work motivators" in command economies. That is, they have probably been more important than coercion, mass mobilization, moral incentives, or the work ethic—which all command economies strive to instill in their youth. But higher incomes may not serve as incentives if households cannot use this money to buy goods they want (a problem to be discussed in greater detail below). Thus, within the consumer-goods budget that he determines, even a harsh central planner should try to respond to household demand.

Nevertheless, principle does not always coincide with practice. With the notable exception of China, the EPCs of most real-world command economies have been reluctant to encourage this kind and degree of initiative from below. They have feared a loss of decision-making power which might grow out of it, and they appear, as well, to have been unwilling to rely on managers to make good forecasts. One result has been freedom of consumer choice among goods already stocked in retail outlets, but not true consumer sovereignty over consumer-goods production.

In other words, Soviet and other East European households have historically possessed only a limited and roundabout ability to determine the composition of consumer-goods production. Where unsold goods have piled up on store shelves and become virtually unsalable, word has sometimes gotten far enough up the chain of command for an authority to alter production or distribution targets. But often when excess demand or supply has been less visible, no price or quantity adjustment has been forthcoming until

---

[4] We shall say more about the broader problem of managerial incentives in Chapter 9.

after long delays. The bureaucrats have customarily failed to react to a shift in consumer preferences and ordered more of the same.[5]

The costs of this are inevitably difficult to measure. However, in 1970, shortly after achieving the diplomatic triumph of his career, in the form of a treaty renouncing West Germany's claim to Poland's western regions, Wladyslaw Gomulka was deposed as first secretary of the Polish Communist Party. The basic reason was consumer dissatisfaction, culminating in the Gdansk riots of that year. There are also less spectacular instances in which shortages of consumer goods have helped to thwart planners' intentions, and we shall consider one such case.

Most of the natural resources of the Soviet Union are found in its Asiatic regions, notably in Siberia and the Far East. For climatic and historical reasons, most of the population has traditionally lived in European Russia and in other Western Soviet Republics. Therefore, an important priority has been attached to moving the population eastward. "With 90 per cent of the country's coal, 60 per cent of its hydroelectric power resources, 75 per cent of the forests, and enormous deposits of oil and gas located in Siberia and the Far East, it has long been the Soviet goal to achieve the necessary movement of the population to these sparsely settled areas." [6] To this end, higher salary rates, exhortations, and even coercion have been used. For example, university graduates have often been required to spend at least three years in remote areas immediately after receiving their diplomas.

Nevertheless, the desired (net) migration of labor into the area has not been achieved, and the area has always suffered from a rapid labor turnover, especially among skilled workers, who are in acutely short supply. One reason often mentioned is that the flow of consumer goods, especially housing and associated amenities, did not keep pace with the higher wages and salaries being paid there.[7]

As a result, Siberia acquired for young Russians something of the image that Alaska possesses for many young Americans. It was a place to live temporarily while earning and saving money, but not a place to settle down permanently. As a consequence, some Soviet planners have recently argued in favor of a change in priorities to place less emphasis on bringing people into Siberia and more on automating the industries there. It is far from

---

[5] See Morris Bornstein, "The Soviet Price System," *American Economic Review,* Mar. 1962, Pt. I; Alec Nove, *The Soviet Economy* (London: G. Allen, 1968), pp. 141–143; and Philip Hanson, *The Consumer in the Soviet Economy* (New York: Macmillan, 1968), Ch. 8. For Soviet sources, see M. Darbinyan, "Demand, the Supplying of Commodities, and Cybernetics," *Ekonomicheskaya Gazeta,* Apr. 2, 1968, and *Current Digest of the Soviet Press,* Mar. 30, 1966, p. 27, and Apr. 28, 1970, pp. 1–5.

[6] Janet Chapman, "Labor Mobility and Labor Allocation in the U.S.S.R.," paper presented to a joint session of the Association for Comparative Economics, Detroit, Dec. 29, 1970, pp. 14–15.

[7] "The differentials in per-capita family income are widely recognized as insufficient to compensate for the harsh climate, isolation, poor working conditions, inadequate housing, shortage of shops, child care facilities, schools, movies, and other cultural facilities typical of so much of the eastern regions." Ibid., p. 27.

obvious, however, that this solution is the best one in a country where capital is still relatively scarce.

Moreover, the Chinese threat has recently raised the desirability of East-ward migration to the Soviet leaders. Nonetheless, "in the past eleven years (1959–1970), the population increase in Siberia and the Far East was only 12.4 per cent, less than the national average . . . . This apparently represents a net outflow, at least for East and West Siberia." [8]

7–3   An Outline of the Planning Hierarchy

The most common and best known commands in a command economy are (additive) orders from the EPC to lower-level planning organs and thence to producers expressing output and input targets. In this section we wish to out-line the planning organizations and procedures, to pave the way for discussion in the remainder of Part 2.

When broken down in compete detail, an almost infinite number of ways of organizing a command economy becomes conceivable. However, we can evolve a more or less standard organizational format, and this appears in Figure 7–1, where the solid arrows denote the principal routes followed by

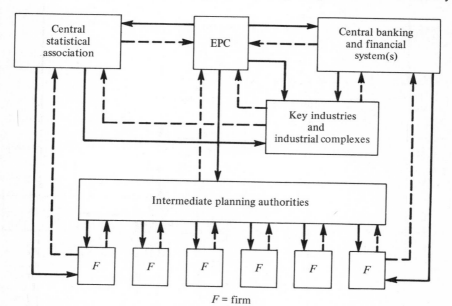

F = firm

Figure 7–1. A typical organization chart for a hypothetical command economy.

information triggers and the dashed arrows refer to feedback. For good measure, we have also included an organization chart of the Soviet economy (circa 1966) for comparison. This is Figure 7–2, in which feedback arrows

[8] Ibid, p. 15. See also the Soviet sources cited by Chapman.

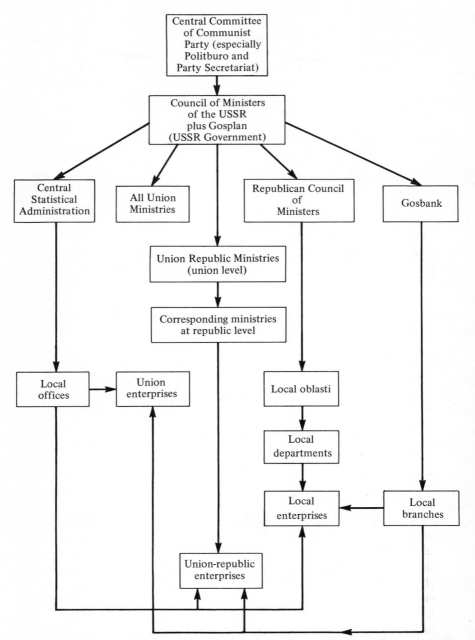

Figure 7–2. The organization of the Soviet economy (circa 1966). The All-Union Ministries include those for medium, heavy, and general machine building, machine tools, defense, transportation, communications, and electronics. The Union-Republic Ministries include light industries, meat and dairy products, food, agriculture, trade, chemical, and ferrous and non-ferrous metallurgy. Source: Eugene Zaleski, *Planning Reforms in the Soviet Union 1962–1966* (Chapel Hill: U. of North Carolina Press, 1967), Ch. 2 (especially Chart 2, p. 18).

have been omitted for clarity. Every planning hierarchy will feature an EPC (or planning arm of the sector of direction and administration) at its apex and producing enterprises at the bottom. In the Soviet Union, the duties of the EPC are shared by the Central Committee of the Communist Party and by the Council of Ministers. However, no central planner can begin to manage the producing sector of an entire economy directly so that a network of intermediate planning authorities is also necessary.

The presence of such a network means that, to administer the plan, most of the producing sector has been divided up vertically into groups of industries or horizontally into geographical regions. In fact, we would expect to find several intermediate layers in any planning hierarchy with both industrial and regional partitioning occurring at least once. We can, however, define the *principal* partitioning to be that division just below the EPC. We may call the relevant administrative organs *ministries* and their directors ministers. Ministers take their orders directly from the EPC and send feedback directly to the EPC. Although we often speak of exchanges between an EPC and its producers, the existence of ministries and other intermediate authorities implies that the actual route followed by the relevant information flows is longer and more complex.

Most production targets for example, will start out in aggregated form and be progressively disaggregated as they filter down through the intermediate hierarchy toward the firms below. A ministry of petrochemicals might get a target for each broad product group along with a few guidelines indicating how this should be broken down into targets for each individual product. The minister will use these guidelines, along with his own prognosis of EPC preferences, to delineate product-by-product targets more finely. Then he will divide each product's quota among the sectors under his control.

Ideally, by the time targets reach individual producers, they will be completely disaggregated. Each firm should receive a minimum amount of each output to produce and a maximum amount of each input to use. In practice, because of the work load involved, targets will not be completely disaggregated when they reach the firm level, with consequences that we shall explore a bit later.

A wise EPC will then allow firms and intermediate officials to make counterproposals to the original targets. These will travel up the planning hierarchy, becoming progressively aggregated, until they return to the EPC. It follows that lower-level decision makers will have at least one vehicle through which to gain some decision-making authority for themselves. A command economy will not be a carbon copy of the completely centralized model, even when we confine our attention to the producing sector.

Moreover, the tasks of aggregating and disaggregating production targets will give enterprising intermediate authorities a chance to use some discretion and consequently shift more decision-making power into their hands. In the final analysis, we may attribute this decentralization to the complexity of the economy, which makes perfectly centralized decision making impossible. As a result, the EPC will also have the problem of motivating managers and intermediate authorities to harmonize their goals with the priorities embodied in its social preference function. When the wrong incentives are given, lower-level decision makers may work against the center, a phenomenon that we shall examine below.

For some firms, information routes to and from the EPC will be considerably shorter than the average as one or more links in the chain of command are bypassed. These are likely to be firms deemed to be as important as whole industries in other sectors of the economy. They are also producers who must be able to respond flexibly to changing circumstances and do much more than the average amount of innovating.

In extremely high priority sectors, these enterprises may be largely mission-oriented (toward putting a man on the moon, for example) and entitled to major cost overruns, provided certain priority targets are achieved. In the past, firms connected with defense, space, and atomic energy production are believed to have occupied such key positions in the U.S.S.R.[9] Because of their special status, many of the criticisms concerning rigidity, inertia, routinization, bottlenecks, and a lack of technological progress under command planning may not apply to them.

The economic planning council will also need a number of staff agencies to gather and process the information necessary for decision making, to help implement the plan, and to aid in controlling plan performance. It will have to rely upon a central statistical association to gather data on past performance and to assist in outlining future possibilities. It will need a central planning staff (implicitly lumped in with the EPC in Figures 7–1 and 7–2) and a central banking and financial system. These agencies will be duplicated at the ministerial level and, in all likelihood, further down the chain of command as well.

Each ministerial staff agency will have ties both with the ministry and with its corresponding superior agency at the level of the EPC. Thus a conflict between the EPC and a minister is likely to lead to a conflict of interest within ministerial staff agencies. The center will want to tie the latter more closely to its own staff so that it has a built-in network to report on the activities of lower-level decision makers. But because ministers are likely to do more business and have more daily contact with their own staffs, they are in a good position to win any struggle for their loyalty.

Consequently, if it is felt necessary to directly check up or "spy" on intermediate authorities, a completely independent chain of command will probably be established. In every command economy today, the Communist Party plays such a role. Its members are inserted into each planning or producing organization to protect the interests of the sector of direction and administration to whom they owe sole allegiance. They are supplemented by special organizations, such as communist youth groups, who roam from

[9] On this subject see Nove, op. cit., Ch. 2; Eugene Zaleski, *Planning Reforms in the Soviet Union, 1962–1966* (Chapel Hill, N.C.: U. of N.C., 1967), Ch. 2; and Phillippe Bernard, *Planning in the Soviet Union* (Elmsford, N.Y.: Pergamon, 1966), Ch. 6.

factory to farm to construction site, urging the workers to greater achievement, publicizing idleness and waste, and occasionally forming their own work brigades. Communist Party membership is a great national honor, and party members are supposed to be motivated by a combination of patriotism and ideology rather than material rewards.

Nevertheless, bureaucrats or managers and local party representatives are sometimes able to come to a "mutual understanding" because all are judged by the same success indicators. That is, all have a strong interest in higher levels of production within the enterprise, region, or other organization to which they are attached. This understanding may be to produce more output from fewer inputs, but it may also be to conceal poor performance or to deviate from the plan in some way.[10]

Aside from this, the banking and financial systems will play an important, although indirect, watchdog role. Banks in a command economy, for example, will accept household savings and pay interest on savings accounts as one (probably minor) way of raising savings for investment. They will make short-term loans to enterprises to cover working-capital requirements, charging interest on these to discourage their use for unauthorized purposes. But their major role is likely to be what is known in the U.S.S.R. as "control by the ruble."

7–4   Control by the Ruble [11]

Lying behind the input and output targets that comprise a command economy's plan will be a network of authorized flows of intermediate goods from producing to using firms. Because prices will continue to be common denominators of value, even though their medium of exchange function will be restricted, these physical flows will translate into money flows. Likewise, the planners can assign monetary values to broad aggregates such as consumption, saving and investment, defense, and government administration. All this suggests trying to enforce a plan through the money flows that it generates.

If the system of administrative controls was completely comprehensive, no monetary controls would be needed. In practice, the former will always permit some freedom of managerial decision making. Consequently, "Money confers the power to influence economic decisions and thus for firms . . . to frustrate the will of central authority in some degree." It is the task of monetary controls to minimize this.[12]

---

[10] See, for example, Joseph S. Berliner, "The Informal Organization of the Soviet Firm," *Quarterly Journal of Economics,* Aug. 1952, reprinted in Holzman, op. cit. A more recent work by the same author is "Managerial Incentives and Decision-making," Ch. 9 in Morris Bornstein and Daniel R. Fusfeld, eds., *The Soviet Economy,* 3rd ed. (Homewood, Ill., Irwin, 1969).

[11] The discussion below is vastly simplified. In particular, we are not differentiating between the complementary roles of the state bank and the state budget in control by the ruble.

[12] Donald R. Hodgman, "Soviet Monetary Controls Through the Banking System," in Holzman, op. cit., p. 584.

Danger of unauthorized physical flows will arise when a firm has difficulty getting the inputs it needs to fulfill the production program its management has decided upon. This may be because it has been wasteful, because its plan is unrealistic, because it is engaging in some kind of unauthorized production, because of supply failures, because it wants to build a reserve against contingencies, or simply because it is overfulfilling its production targets by a large margin.

It may, for example, produce its own spare parts or do more of its own repair and maintenance work than the plan foresees because past experience has taught it that spare parts will not arrive on time and that maintenance will be poorly handled by others. It may hoard scarce inputs, including labor, in reserve against possible shortages. Or, it may wish to use money and gifts to bribe other managers for above-quota quantities of scarce inputs. We shall see later what can motivate this kind of activity. Now we ask what the banks and other financial institutions can do to limit it.

Ideally, the first step in "control by the ruble" (or the yuan, forint, zloty, or whatever) would be to establish two categories of money, which we shall label *credit* and *currency,* respectively. Credit would be used exclusively in transactions between firms within the formal command hierarchy in Figures 7–1 and 7–2. It will consist almost exclusively of checking accounts. By contrast, currency will only be available for transactions in which at least one party is a firm or household outside this hierarchy, including collective farms and small handicraft and other retail shops in most command economies today. This is likely to consist primarily of cash.

Finally, each firm's credit account would be divided into a short-term account, for current expenses, and a long-term account, which could only be used for additions or alterations to plant capacity. A separate investment bank, called the stroybank in the U.S.S.R., may administer long-term credit accounts.[13]

If it is successful, the immediate consequence of this tripartite segregation of accounts will be to reduce the ability of firms to spend funds for unauthorized purposes. For example, managers will be unable to use excess credit to buy labor over and above their planned allotments or to purchase any sort of goods on a black market. They will also be unable to use part of their allotments for wages or workers' housing and recreation to buy extra supplies of intermediate goods or to build new production capacity. Nor will it be possible to invest short-term working capital or to use capital-construction allowances to buy goods-in-process.

Beyond this, the state will have a number of goals for each category. With respect to currency, a principal aim will be to strike a balance between the

---

[13] In fact, the U.S.S.R. does not use the terms "credit" and "currency" in quite the same way that we are using them. However, it does try to segregate and to keep separate track of money flows remaining within the state sector on one hand and flows whose origin or destination is outside this sector on the other. Likewise, it tries to segregate the funds remaining within the state sector into long-run and short-run accounts.

purchasing power of households and the planned value of goods available for them to buy. Our first expectation is that planners will try to avoid repressed inflation in the form of a household purchasing power that exceeds this value. Otherwise, some goods are bound to be in excess demand. People will want to buy more of them at going prices than are available, and some would be buyers will go home empty-handed. (This becomes even more likely when the composition of consumer-goods production is ill-adapted to consumer demand.[14])

Under these conditions, workers will eventually begin to notice that increases in their paychecks do not always translate readily into a higher purchasing power over goods and services. The result will be a work disincentive —or, as in the case of Siberia, an incentive to emigrate—which the planners will wish to avoid. In Eastern Europe, including the U.S.S.R., the authorities have indeed nominally sought to equalize household buying power with the value of consumer goods offered for sale.

They have likewise permitted ideologically undesirable institutions whose purpose is partly to mop up excess household purchasing power, while providing an increased flow of goods and services to households at small cost to the state. These include private savings accounts which earn positive interest and peasant markets where collective farmers sell the produce from their private plots and privately owned farm animals. Prices of these markets respond freely to the forces of supply and demand. In particular, they can rise to absorb an increase in household purchasing power relative to the value of goods in state stores. In areas served by peasant markets, prices will be higher there than prices of corresponding items in state stores. The differential will provide some measure of excess household purchasing power. (Analytically, the peasant markets play the role of a black market in absorbing excess demand.)

Nevertheless, if we survey the historical records of East European economies, there has been a constant tendency (albeit one somewhat reduced in recent years) for total household incomes to exceed the total value of consumer goods and services available. This has come on top of frequent mismatches between the pattern of consumer demand and the assortment of consumer goods in supply. Regarding the Hungarian experience, Janos Kornai writes: "Although there may be a regular supply of some products, the quantity [available] is insufficient, meaning that the consumer may wait for months or even years for a flat, telephone, car, or foreign exchange allocation for a trip abroad." [15]

[14] If the composition of consumer-goods production (plus net imports of consumer goods) does not match household preferences, individual markets may be badly out of equilibrium even though overall purchasing power matches the total value of goods available. In the U.S.S.R., significant surpluses have coexisted with shortages at least since the late 1950s.

[15] Janos Kornai, "Pressure and Suction on the Market," Indiana University Development Research Center Working Paper 7, Bloomington, Ind., 1971, p. 1. Kornai continues (p. 2): "on a number of markets, shortages are *continuous*."

We therefore suspect that planners in East Europe have often been willing to tolerate some excess of household purchasing power, and there are several possible reasons for this. First, the government may wish to keep prices low for propaganda or morale purposes. Second, and more important, socialist countries have often been reluctant to shift workers from one job to another, even within the same factory, against their will. This is consistent with the greater emphasis in the writings of Marx on conditions of work, rather than goods and services consumed, as a determinant of individual welfare. However, the resulting labor immobility probably makes it even harder for command planners to adjust the composition of consumer goods production to household demand. In these conditions, excess household purchasing power keeps down the size of stocks that can only be sold at heavy loss.

Third, some command planners have probably felt that workers are afflicted with money illusion—that they respond to the money values of their paychecks, in other words, rather than to their real purchasing power over goods and services.

Yet, Cuban economists have noted that "High wages can be an incentive to better work only when more money automatically means more consumer goods," and Castro himself has asked, "[How] are we going to stimulate the people with money with which they can buy nothing?" [16] Along with the Soviet problem of populating Siberia and experience elsewhere in Eastern Europe, this suggests that, for a specific family in specific circumstances, money illusion is apt to be short-lived.

On the other hand, a partial rationing of goods by queueing will sometimes equalize the effective distribution of purchasing power. Lower-paid families will often have the same chance to obtain scarce, but inexpensive items as others higher up the income ladder in regular state stores. In fact, the more highly paid an individual is, the more often he will choose to avoid queueing by purchasing goods in peasant markets, in artisan or private shops, and, if he is sufficiently important, in special state stores. Except in the latter, he will pay higher prices to avoid the unpleasantness of waiting.

As long as the cumulated excess of household purchasing power does not become too great, moreover, a partial rationing of goods by queueing will not destroy the incentive power of additional earned income. If there is a fairly good chance that workers can eventually spend higher pay on goods that they want, they will have an incentive to raise their earnings by maintaining or increasing their work effort. In the Soviet Union today, a worker can put money into a savings account and sign his name to a waiting list for such relatively expensive durables as a car, a refrigerator, or even a better apartment. To an extent, the work incentive of his income will depend upon the lengths of these lists, along with the normal gap between supply and demand for such nondurables as fresh meat, eggs, butter, milk, vegetables, and fruit.

[16] Quoted by Carmelo Mesa-Lago in "Ideological, Political and Economic Factors in the Cuban Controversy on Material vs. Moral Incentives," *Journal of Interamerican Studies and World Affairs*, Feb. 1972.

Economists would normally argue that it is more efficient to redistribute income directly, via taxes on the rich and income supplements for the poor, rather than indirectly, by queueing. However, this argument presupposes that individual preferences, weighted by their respective incomes, will then be better able to guide the production of consumer goods. In a command economy, this is unlikely.

At the same time, it may be easy for bureaucrats to underestimate the cost in frustration and lost leisure time of standing in line for long periods or of repeatedly failing to obtain goods that are nominally available. The excess household purchasing power in most command economies has probably combined with the poor assortment of goods available to serve as a work disincentive.[17]

As an additional step in control by the ruble, the banking system would ideally be able to supervise every transaction involving firms within the command hierarchy, constantly looking for warning signals that the producing sector was not operating according to plan. We can imagine two kinds of warning signals. First, some firms may not be able to meet their output targets without using more inputs than the plan permits. These extra inputs must be paid for, regardless of whether the enterprise buys them from outside the state sector or applies to its superiors within the command hierarchy. They must also be paid for when the firm buys them on some kind of black market. A need for extra inputs will often translate into a demand for additional funds above the quotas allotted to the firm by the plan.

A second kind of alarm signal should go off whenever there is a supply breakdown. Let us focus our attention upon short-term credit transactions (between firms in the command hierarchy). An ideal procedure here would be as follows. Just prior to each scheduled exchange of goods, the banking system would grant the buyer sufficient credit for the purchase, and the seller would receive a corresponding deficit. Within a specified period of time after the transaction, the buyer would be required to indicate whether the goods have arrived on time in the proper amounts and meet all quality standards. If he indicates that they do, the buyer's account would be debited and the seller's account credited back to their previous levels.

Otherwise, the buyer's claims would be examined, the case would go to court if necessary, and the seller would be required to make good any damages if he was found at fault. In addition, his account would remain below its

---

[17] This problem appears to have been especially acute in Cuba. See A. R. M. Ritter, "Development Strategy in Revolutionary Cuba," unpublished Ph.D. thesis, Austin, University of Texas, 1972, Ch. 7. A much shorter version is contained in Section VI of Ritter's "The Political Economy of Revolutionary Socialism in Cuba," *Canadian Perspectives in Economics* series (Toronto: Collier-Macmillan, 1972).

Queueing to buy goods is like paying higher prices for them in the sense that the average net welfare derived from each kopek spent, after subtracting the displeasure of waiting, is less. Thus the effects of open and repressed inflation on an average household will be similar. However, an open inflation will tend to redistribute purchasing power away from families on relatively fixed incomes. A repressed inflation may do the reverse.

previous level until the order was filled satisfactorily. Firms can then be fined for carrying negative balances, either because they fail to meet users' requirements or because they must purchase or be allocated above-plan input quotas in order to meet their output targets. In effect, they would have to borrow funds to cover the shortfall at an unusually high interest rate. These interest charges or fines can then be translated, in some way, into reduced managerial bonuses. "Excessive" borrowing of currency can be penalized in the same way.

In practice, however, command-economy financial plans are universally less detailed than the physical plans which they underlie. No less than several hundred million transactions are likely to occur every year within the command hierarchy. The cost of issuing a separate credit and debit to cover everyone— while supervising the system to ensure that credit is not used for unauthorized purchases—will be prohibitive. This approach can therefore be used, at most, for transactions with an especially high priority.

For other transactions, firms will have to be allowed bank deposits, much as in a market economy, which they can potentially spend on unauthorized purchases. Aside from increased supervision to enforce the segregation of accounts, the state has two basic ways of combatting this. First, it can try to minimize the sizes of the credit and currency balances permitted each firm, while still enabling the firm to meet its obligations. A tightening of short-term monetary controls has, in fact, been a principal goal of post-World War II Soviet monetary policy.[18] Second, it can rely upon what are called "mutually offsetting" short-term credit accounts.

During the normal course of a year's operations, most firms' planned money inflows, including both credit and currency, will largely balance its money outflows. The major difference will normally come because a firm's revenues consist largely of payments for goods received and will correspond to the firm's deliveries of goods, with some lag. Costs, on the other hand, will more nearly correspond to the firm's cycle of production over the year.

Whenever an enterprise threatens to become illiquid because its planned inventories are rising or its planned sales receipts lag behind its planned payments for inputs, the state bank must tide it over with working capital loans of currency and short-term credit. Whenever the enterprise becomes overly liquid, the state bank must quickly siphon off this potential source of unauthorized purchases. The speed with which it can do so, without impairing the firm's ability to meet authorized obligations, is the crucial test of the state's short-term monetary controls.

The state bank, together with the state budget, will also transfer funds between enterprise accounts. Suppose that we have a firm producing entirely for other firms within the state sector. Its receipts will come entirely in the form of credit, which we may view initially as short-term credit. Some of

---

[18] See Hodgman, op. cit. According to Hodgman (p. 586), "The problem [of Soviet monetary policy], essentially, is to determine the minimum amount of money required to effect the planned real processes of the economy at established price levels."

this will probably be switched into the long-term credit account to be earmarked for various investment projects. In addition, some of it will be transferred into the enterprise's currency account, largely for wages and salaries. Some receipts will go to the state treasury as taxes. In return, the firm will receive grants, mainly in the form of additional long-term credits in most instances.

Once all these adjustments are made, each firm will ideally have just enough money in each kind of account throughout the year to meet authorized expenditures. The ideal will not usually be realized, but a regime of mutually offsetting short-term credit accounts can add a partial second line of defense. Under it, the seller's account is automatically credited and the buyer's account debited at the same time within a specified grace period after each scheduled transaction. Suppose that the grace period is two days. Then the banking system will be continually adjusting each firm's short-term credit balance to net out transactions that were supposed to have occurred two days ago. (The other kinds of adjustment described above will also be made.)

There are two advantages to mutually offsetting credit accounts. First, they are easier to supervise against unauthorized spending than ordinary checking accounts. A firm cannot withdraw funds from an offset account. Hence it cannot easily translate excess liquidity into additional purchasing over items, notably labor, which must be paid for with currency or long-term credit. Second, mutually offsetting accounts minimize the amount of working capital that the state bank must grant. The seller receives payment immediately when the buyer pays—there is never any need for loans to tide the seller over between disbursal and receipt.

The only official exception to the automatic debiting and crediting of offsetting accounts occurs when the buyer makes a point of complaining about the goods he does or does not receive. In effect, such a complaint is now one of the warnings that alerts authorities to a malfunctioning of the producing sector. At least in principle, a procedure will then exist whereby the buyer can claim recourse. Once recourse is granted, the seller will lose any credit he may have received for selling the goods until he makes amends. This forces him to take out an "extraordinary" short-term loan from the state bank, a procedure that can be penalized in a variety of ways. (Likewise, the banking system can penalize loans to finance above-plan input requirements which a manager needs to fulfill his own output quotas.)

In the meantime, the state may try to re-route production, perhaps taking advantage of the fact that some potential suppliers are exceeding their planned targets, so that the buyer does not have to wait too long for deliveries. This is especially likely if the buyer's own outputs have a high planners' priority so that the latter attach a high cost to any slowdown of his production process. (Later we shall see that the art of command-economy planning is in no small measure an ability to confine bottlenecks and slowdowns to low-priority sectors.)

Because a manager may pay dearly in lost bonuses for failing to meet his own output targets, he will have an incentive to alert the bank whenever a serious supply breakdown occurs. Yet the *automatic* debiting and crediting of accounts does tend to favor the seller over the buyer. Under the ideal scheme, in which every transaction is individually supervised, a warning is sounded automatically when the buyer does not routinely approve the transfer of goods. Now he must go to the trouble of complaining.

Built-in favoritism for the seller will be greater the shorter the grace period allowed before automatic debiting and crediting of accounts take place. After once having adjusted them, the banking system will be somewhat reluctant to go back and undo its work. Yet there will also be pressures to keep the grace period short. Since the seller must meet current expenses, he will sometimes be eligible for a credit or currency loan to tide him over all or part of this time. As long as there is a positive probability that he can spend a portion of these funds on unauthorized purchases, the bank will want to minimize them by minimizing the length of the grace period. (We must remember that not all short-term credit funds will be in the more easily supervised offsetting accounts.[19]

Favoring the seller is consistent with the mobilization spirit of a command economy and the resultant pressure for greater production. But it will also reinforce the distortions to which these pressures sometimes lead. For example, firms will have added incentives to start producing their own inputs when supply sources prove especially unreliable. On occasion, the banking system will discourage innovation if the resulting new products take longer than usual to find a buyer for and must be financed with "extraordinary" (or above-plan) loans in the meantime.

Beyond this, it is interesting to speculate on the extent to which failures in control by the ruble have sometimes actually aided the Soviet planners. For example, there is a kind of underground supply network, or series of black markets, which supplements the official one. Firms can sometimes obtain needed supplies on the underground network of goods which they otherwise could not get for bribes in money or in kind. There is some indication that this distribution system improves the allocation of resources—and, in particular, gives managers a disincentive to hoard scarce goods in their inventories —at least as long as it does not get out of hand.

Moreover, during the 1930s, the segregation of accounts was incomplete, and firms were able to spend receipts from deliveries to other firms to hire more workers. Labor was both scarce, and to most managers, the chief source of short-run production increases. Consequently, enterprises accumulated excess spending power, which they used to bid up wage rates and to raid

---

[19] The reader wishing to compare finance and banking as it is actually practiced in a particular command economy with our discussion is invited to examine George Garvy, "Finance and Banking in the U.S.S.R.," Ch. 8 in Bornstein and Fusfeld, op. cit., and Hodgman, op. cit.

one another's work force. It is at least plausible that these higher wages made it appear more attractive to farm youth to move to the city and join the urban labor force. This speeded up a migration necessary to the rapid industrialization which the planners so earnestly desired.[20]

Table 7–1 compares rural–urban migration and average percentage wage increases in industry for the period 1929–1936. Two peaks in net migration occurred. The first, in 1931, can be assigned to the rigors of the collectivization drive in agriculture, which reached its highest pitch during 1930 and 1931, when most Soviet peasants joined or were forced onto collective farms. The second peak in 1936 may then be due to urban wage increases, mostly unplanned.[21]

7–5   An Outline of the Planning Procedure

Now that we have identified the actors in our drama, let us see how they interact in plan formation. We shall first make the conventional distinction between horizon or long-term planning, which does not result in specific orders for production to take place, and operative or short-term planning, which does.

Horizon planning concerns itself with the basic strategy of economic development. The best known examples of this are the Soviet five- and seven-year plans, although similar constructs appear in the planning of every contemporary communist nation, along with France, India, and several other countries not clearly in the socialist camp. The EPC will fashion a broad set of priorities relating to relative expansion between different industries and geographical regions and paying special attention to such matters as prestige industries, the institutional environment for research and development, and the nature of incentives to lower-level decision makers. Intermediate planning levels will fill in the details of the EPC's strategy and advise their superiors as to which goals are or are not achievable.

Short-term plans are then drawn up in the light of these long-range goals, and current achievements, in turn, will reveal new opportunities and obstacles that may cause the long-run goals to be changed. The horizon plans should be

[20] F. D. Holzman, "Soviet Inflationary Pressures, 1928–1957: Causes and Cures." *Quarterly Journal of Economics,* May 1960,   especially pp. 175–177; reprinted in Pt. VIII of Holzman, *Readings on the Soviet Economy,* op. cit.

[21] Yet urban prices were increasing even more rapidly during this period so that workers' purchasing power actually fell. (The price of consumers goods increased by 70 per cent more over 1928–1936 than did the average wage rate in urban areas. See Holzman, "Soviet Inflationary Pressures, 1928–1957: Causes and Cures," op. cit., Table I.) This does not take into account the sharp decline in per capita living space during the 1930s, so that the urban standard of living undoubtedly fell on balance during the period in question. However, it is plausible to assume that peasants suffered from temporary money illusion which helped to bring many of them to the cities in the first place. The fact that rural living standards were falling even more rapidly probably kept many from going back to the country.

Table 7–1. Urban–rural migration and average percentage wage increases, U.S.S.R., 1929–1935.

Year	Arriving in Urban Areas (in thousands)	Leaving Urban Areas (in thousands)	Net Change (in thousands)	Percentage Wage Increase		
				Planned	Unplanned	Total
1929	6,958	5,566	1,392	—	—	14
1930	9,534	6,901	2,633	—	—	17
1931	10,810	6,710	4,100	7	13	20
1932	10,605	7,886	2,719	N.a.	N.a.	27
1933	7,416	6,644	772	7	3	10
1934	11,856	9,404	2,452	4	14	19
1935	13,732	11,176	2,556	9	12	22
1936	N.a.	N.a.	Approx. 5,000	9	16	26

Sources:

Migration from Table 1 of Janet Chapman, "Labor Mobility and Labor Allocation in the U.S.S.R.," paper presented to a joint session of the Association for the Study of Soviet-Type Economics and the Association for Comparative Economics, Detroit, Dec. 29, 1970, except 1936 figure. This is crudely derived from Warren Eason, "Labor Force," in Abram Bergson and Simon Kuznets, eds., *Economic Trends in the Soviet Union* (Cambridge, Mass.: Harvard U.P., 1963), Table II.10. According to Eason, the nonagricultural labor force increased by 1.2 million between July 1, 1934, and July 1, 1935; by another 1.5 million between July 1, 1935, and July 1, 1936, and by 4 million between July 1, 1936, and July 1, 1937. We have used the ratios implied by these magnitudes.

Wage Increases from F. D. Holzman, "Soviet Inflationary Pressures, 1928–1957: Causes and Cures," *Quarterly Journal of Economics*, May 1960, Table II.

modified on a continuing basis and also kept as flexible as possible. For example, when these targets first appear, they may be stated as intervals (15 to 20 million tons of steel) at a time when the target date is several years distant. As it approaches, these intervals can be shifted up or down and their limits narrowed until they become specific numbers to be passed down to producers during the preceding year. This completes the transition to operative planning.

The short-term planning period may be either more or less than a calendar year, but to simplify matters let us refer to it as a "year." During any given "year," planners and firms will be planning for the year ahead at the same time that they are carrying out the preceding year's plan. It is customary to use the term "planning year" to indicate the year in which the plan is drawn up and "operating year" to indicate the year of plan implementation. During the planning year, input, output, and financial targets travel down the system's various chains of command in the manner outlined earlier. Feedback in the form of counterproposals will then flow in the opposite direction, and the bargaining that results is often said to play much the same role as bargaining between buyers and sellers in a market economy. Indeed, we may view firms and lower-level planners as "sellers" and the EPC as a "buyer" of goods to the extent that it derives satisfaction from the economy's performance.

As a minimum requirement, we would hope to get one full round of exchanges between planners and producers during the planning year. That is, preliminary targets from the EPC should reach firms, and the latter should have a chance to make counterproposals before the final plan targets are issued, which then have the force of law. Of course, more than one exchange of preliminary figures, meaning that firms will have more than one chance to make counterproposals, is conceivable. Economic models of the short-term planning process often speak of n rounds of exchanges during the planning year, as the operative plan is progressively fashioned and refashioned in response to the reactions of lower-level decision makers.

As n tends to infinity, these models show the plan being hammered into optimal form. But insofar as any workable plan in the foreseeable future is concerned, this is pure science fiction. Because the process of formulating proposals and replies is time consuming, the planning hierarchy is fortunate if it can circulate a plan twice and then get consistent final targets to producers on time.[22] This gives us a deeper insight into the nightmare that might result were markets for consumer goods and labor inputs to be replaced by commands. The number of households is many times the number of firms, and the average consumer will need more targets than the average producer. Yet, first-round figures for households are apt to be considerably farther from the mark, and there will be little, if any, chance to correct these before the operating year begins.

[22] For a discussion of Soviet practice in this regard, see Herbert S. Levine, "The Centralized Planning of Supply in Soviet Industry," in Holzman, *Readings on the Soviet Economy,* op. cit, especially pp. 156–162 and p. 168.

From a producer's standpoint, additional problems with the planning process are likely to arise. It is not unheard of for a firm's output, input, and productivity targets to turn out to be mutually inconsistent or for its physical plan to contradict its financial plan. For example, a manager might be ordered to manufacture at least 1 million units of a given product and to use no more than $\frac{1}{2}$ labor hour in the manufacture of each unit. He ought then to receive a wages fund allotment for 500,000 labor hours. However, it is quite conceivable that his allotment will only cover 400,000 labor hours at going wage rates. Or it may happen that the firm starts its operating year without having received all of its final plan targets.

In these circumstances enterprise managements will face a series of stresses and strains which require them, in effect, to psychoanalyze their superiors. The former will not be able to meet all of their norms, and a crucial test of a manager's survival-ability will be his ingenuity in finding out quickly which targets can be underfulfilled and by how much. This will have a number of secondary effects. For example, if production targets are viewed as more important than financial targets, control by the ruble will be weakened. Managers and bureaucrats will have an extra incentive to establish an understanding with banks to get financing for increased output, which the EPC seems to desire above all else.

In connection with the above, the EPC will communicate with managers and bureaucrats through the planning hierarchy concerning the entire range of incentives, which are rewards for satisfactory to outstanding performance. Usually these are referred to as "success indicators" or "success criteria" because they nominally tell lower-level decision makers what to do to succeed. Except in a regime of purely moral incentives, success indicators will be buttressed by the promise of increased pay and promotion possibilities for those who succeed.

If a manager's pay and promotion possibilities depend upon the gross monetary value or total weight of his output, he will have an incentive to maximize the relevant index. On a subtler plane, he may have observed that the gross value of his output means more to his superiors than cutting down on waste or improving labor productivity whenever these goals collide. The entire structure of (implicit and explicit) success indicators will be both extensive and overlapping, and it will sometimes take a clever manager to figure out exactly what he should do when he can not simultaneously fulfill all his plan targets.

Managers can add to social welfare in two basic ways by achieving their plan targets. First, if a part of their output goes to final demand (or final use), it will enter directly into the index of social welfare. We should also include special direct contributions, such as the psychological satisfaction that central planners may derive from statistical performance indicators—for example, the growth in steel production.

Second, by fulfilling their own targets, one set of managers can make the plans of other firms easier to fulfill. Suppose that industry B supplies inputs for industry C—say steel being supplied to automobile producers. The ability of industry C to meet its plan clearly depends upon the performance of B. Likewise, assume that B uses an input also required by industry A (for example, the machine-tool industry). The less of the input used by B, for any given level of output, the more that may become available for A, and vice versa.

Let us think of any set of input and output targets as an information document. In this light, input targets for industry C become not only a constraint, but a forecast about the quantities of inputs that will become available to C. Similarly, output targets for B constitute not only a statement of expectations, but also a set of forecasts about the quantities that demand will absorb. Provided the plan is consistent, its predictive power for any one firm is greater, the better other firms conform, on balance, to their input and output targets. By conforming to plan, one firm creates an external benefit for other firms. By violating the plan, at least in certain ways, it inflicts external costs. One purpose of material incentives is to internalize these social costs and benefits.

The same is even more true, interestingly enough, in a mixed economy (such as France) characterized by indicative planning. Here the coercion of the plan is inevitably less. Consequently, its accuracy as a forecaster of changes in the composition of market supply and demand, in technology, and in regional development becomes even more crucial if it is to play a useful role insofar as producers are concerned.

Finally, prices will enter as guides to lower-level decision making, even in a command economy, although often through the back door. A manager paid to maximize the gross value of his output will concentrate on the more expensive items even though command-economy pricing is likely to be completely irrational. Where prices do not guide managerial decision making in this way, other common denominators of "value" will inevitably emerge. A manager paid to maximize the weight of his output will emphasize production of the heavier items. The relative weights of different goods serve as prices insofar as he is concerned.

We have now identified four types of signals sent down the planning hierarchy to guide the behavior of firms below. They are:

1. Commands in the form of quantitative targets.
2. Decision rules telling managers which behavior is most desirable. These define their success indicators.
3. Material rewards for successful performance.
4. Prices or other common denominators of "value."

A regime of moral incentives is characterized by absence of signal 3. We shall explore each of these categories in Chapter 8.

7–6   Command Planning and International Trade

Historically, command economies have tended to view foreign trade as an evil, necessarily for rapid industrial expansion. Because of this and because command planning creates special problems in the foreign-trade sector, we wish to spend the last section of our introductory chapter exploring some of these problems. We may cite four important features of command economies' behavior in international trade.

First, command economies generally trade less than market economies at comparable levels of development or with similar resource endowments. Second, at least until quite recently, command economies have preferred bilateral or two-way trade to multilateral trade arrangements. The former have often been embodied in prearranged barter deals. Third, command economies trade primarily to obtain imports with a high planners' priority whose home production costs would be prohibitive. Ironically, they are far less export- and more import-oriented than market economies.

Finally, because command-economy prices do not reflect true production costs, command planners have had great difficulty specializing in the world economy according to comparative advantage, even to the extent that they have wanted to do so. In part, this loss of potential gains from trade has been compensated for by the fact that trade is carried on within a framework of economy-wide planning and may serve national priorities better than it would under a regime of laissez faire. In addition, foreign trade is monopolized by state trading corporations, which often have more power on world markets than do most producers. We shall explore each of these four features briefly.

Table 7–2 ranks selected market and command economies according to. their dependence on, or openness to, world trade in 1964. There (M) denotes market and (C) command economy; the initials (SB) stand opposite those smaller East European countries often said to form the Soviet Bloc. (There appears to be some disagreement over whether Rumania belongs in this category.) The table indicates a clearly higher propensity of market economies to engage in international trade.[23]

We would note in addition that, although command economies comprised 28.6 per cent of the world's geographical area, 35.5 per cent of its population, and produced 38 per cent of its industrial output in 1967, they accounted for only about 11 per cent of world trade turnover. With 26.4 per cent of the world's area, 21.5 per cent of its population, and 55 per cent of industrial output, developed market economies accounted for more than 69 per cent of

---

[23] In order to get a comparison between market and command economies, we have had to restrict this table to merchandise trade, ignoring trade in services (such as tourism). This inevitably alters the ranking of some countries in the table. However, communist countries generally do not indicate the value of services exchanged, regarding these as "unproductive." (See the discussion of this point in the Appendix to Chapter 6.)

Table 7–2. The openness of selected economies to merchandise trade in 1964   (the average of merchandise imports and exports as a percentage of GNP).

1. Netherlands (M) *	38.3
2. Belgium (M)	30.1
3. Denmark (M)	26.6
4. Canada (M)	16.8
5. West Germany (M)	15.4
6. United Kingdom (M)	15.1
7. Hungary (C) † (SB)	14.1
8. Italy (M)	13.3
9. Czechoslavakia (C) (SB)	12.3
10. Greece (M)	12.0
11. East Germany (C) (SB)	11.6
12. France (M)	10.9
13. Bulgaria (C) (SB)	9.8
14. Rumania (C)	8.6
15. Poland (C) (SB)	7.6
16. India (?)	5.4
17. United States (M)	3.6
18. U.S.S.R. (C)	2.6

Source: Carl McMillan, Jr., "Aspects of Soviet Participation in International Trade," unpublished Ph.D. thesis, Johns Hopkins University, 1972, Table III-1.
* M, market economy; C, command economy; ?, difficult to classify.
† In 1964, Hungary was still a command economy.

international trade turnover. Even less developed countries, producing only 7 per cent of world industrial output, accounted for more than 19 per cent of world trade.[24]

Nevertheless, because two command economies, China and the U.S.S.R., are vast and heterogeneous, the above figures understate their trading propensities. Whereas trade between France and her former African colonies shows up as world trade, exchanges between Eastern Siberia and the Moscow area count as in*tra*national trade, even though many of the same purposes will be served. The more diverse are the resource endowments of different regions within the same country, the more she can realize the benefits of specialization according to comparative advantage and exchange without going beyond her own borders. (This probably also explains, in part, the low propensity of the United States to engage in international trade.)

Despite this, in the period just before World War I, the export volume of Imperial Russia rose to more than 10 per cent of her GNP. By 1970 the Soviet export ratio had probably not yet gone this high in any single year, although GNP per head had reached a level 4 to 5 times as great. Moreover,

[24] See J. Wilczynski, *The Economies and Politics of East-West Trade* (New York: St. Martin's, 1969), p. 24.

the unweighted geometric average of market-economy ratios in Table 7–2 is about twice as high as the average for command economies.[25]

Both economic and political reasons lie behind this. Historically, the planners have been willing to sacrifice material consumer welfare for greater self-sufficiency and thus greater economic independence from capitalist nations deemed potentially unfriendly. We shall see that the same phenomenon has persisted in Western market economies, but other priorities have been able to assert themselves more firmly.

The consumer-goods content of exports from the Soviet Bloc to the West has always been much higher than the consumer-goods content of imports. The reverse has been true with respect to equipment, essential to the building of heavy industries. (Machinery and equipment appear to have accounted for over one third of all imports to the U.S.S.R. since 1928.) In addition, because of her wealth of natural resources, the U.S.S.R. is probably more capable than any nation on earth of supporting autarky, although the same is by no means true of Eastern Europe. These countries have paid a much higher premium for autarkic development.

Command-economy trade participation has suffered, as well, from the U.S. embargo on selling "strategic" goods to "enemy" countries. Some of these commodities have had extremely high central planners' priorities—for example, computers and other sophisticated electronic equipment. Political factors have also caused command economies other than China to trade mainly with one another. The U.S.S.R. regularly conducts 60 to 70 per cent of her total trade with other command economies, including 50 to 60 per cent with Eastern Europe. In 1938, by contrast, the latter trade accounted only for about 5 per cent of the Soviet total.[26]

Even if self-sufficiency were not an important priority, the organization of economic activity by means of commands would probably decrease reliance on international trade. The world economy is basically coordinated by a system of markets, upon which even command economies buy and sell from one another. The immediate effect of foreign trade is to complexify an already difficult central planning task and, more precisely, to render an uncertain supply situation even more uncertain.

[25] The inclusion of additional market economies, such as Yugoslavia and the Scandinavian countries, would probably raise the market average. The inclusion of China would lower the average for command economies. (Indeed, she would fall below the U.S.S.R.) However, the per capita income of China is much lower than any other country in the table, save India, and trade participation as a percentage of output usually rises with the level of development or affluence.

[26] See Alan Brown and Paul Marer, "Foreign Trade in the East European Reforms," International Development Research Center, Bloomington, Ind., Indiana University, 1970, especially Appendix Table C; Wilczynski, op. cit.; and H. W. Heiss, "The Soviet Union in the World Market," in Pt. IV of U.S. Congress, Joint Economic Committee, *New Directions in the Soviet Economy* (Washington, D.C.: G.P.O., 1966). A later report in the same series is R. S. Kovach and J. T. Farrell, "Foreign Trade of the U.S.S.R.," *Economic Performance and the Military Burden of the U.S.S.R.,* 1970.

Because future world market prices cannot be forecast with certainty, command planners do not know how much they will have to export to be able to purchase a particular bill of imports, unless every exchange is included in the plan at prearranged prices. If they find that they must export more than previously foreseen, the plan may be disrupted, causing hardship or shortages on one hand and bottlenecks on the other.[27]

For example, a feature of the worldwide Great Depression during the 1930s was that agricultural prices dropped much more sharply than prices of capital equipment and other manufactured items.[28] This coincided with the launching of the U.S.S.R.'s drive for rapid superindustrialization, to which the central planners had made a long-range commitment. The first and second five-year plans required fairly large imports of machinery and equipment, owing to the lack of technology and industrial base that might have allowed for production of these goods at home. In addition, peasants were resisting the collectivization drives by slaughtering draft animals, requiring the importing of tractors. All these items were largely paid for with farm produce, even as farmers were starving at home.[29]

The uncertainty surrounding future terms of trade means that a command-economy EPC prefers to import only the most scarce and essential items to plan fulfillment and to export only low-priority items to get these. Trade planning therefore focuses upon the bill of goods to be imported, trying to find ways of minimizing this, both in the long and short runs. During the 1930s, for example, it appears that the Soviet Union imported capital as much to copy the technology embodied in it as to use it in production. Over time, most command economies prefer to run deficits in the sense of importing more than they export. This contrasts with the somewhat mercantilist views of market economies, which prefer an export surplus—partly because this is presumed to be employment-generating.

The net result for most command economies has been a fairly extreme policy of import substitution in the sense of replacing imports by expanding production of the same goods at home. Import substitution is a fairly common practice, as well, among growth-oriented market economies. It ties in closely with the infant-industry argument, saying, in effect, that some factors, such as realization of scale economies or gaining production and marketing experience, will turn a comparative *dis*advantage today in certain lines of production

---

[27] We shall see more precisely how this may come to pass when we explore the interdependency of an economy in Chapter 8. We would add that, because the planners lack reliable cost data on goods produced at home, they will sometimes not know which particular goods they will be best off exporting or even to which countries.

[28] Holzman has estimated that the commodity terms of trade fell to a low of 71.5 in 1932 and 1933, taking 1927 as 100. (That is, they fell by nearly 30 per cent.) See F. D. Holzman, "Foreign Trade Behavior of Centrally Planned Economies," in H. Rosovsky, ed., *Industrialization in Two Systems: Essays in Honor of Alexander Gerschenkron* (New York: Wiley, 1966).

[29] See the Appendix to this chapter.

into a comparative advantage tomorrow. What is unique about the command-economy experience, once again, is that it is also a policy of export suppression. Command economies cannot allow foreigners to buy home-produced goods freely, because this activity is as likely to disrupt a plan, and to create bottlenecks in some cases, as is unchecked importing.

Consequently, market economies will often ration available supplies of foreign exchange to producers and consumers whose import needs are assumed to be most urgent, especially if they are having balance-of-payments problems. But they will usually do everything possible to promote exports, and consider rationing of their own currencies to be a kind of heresy.

However, command economies usually ration both their own currencies and foreign exchange, thereby maximizing the insulation of the domestic economy from world market fluctuations. One consequence is that Eastern Europe has become a sheltered market, of sorts, upon which command economies trade with one another. This protection has probably helped some countries, notably Bulgaria, during the takeoff period of industrialization by providing an outlet for goods which could not have them sold on the world market except at unacceptable losses. But the same protection has continued to foster production and exchange of outdated producer goods and inferior consumer goods by world standards. Aside from inefficiency, which affects every economy in the area, this has created a kind of "dependency trap" for the smaller countries, who would be hard put to sell their products elsewhere.

Ideally, all foreign trade will be included in the operational one-year command-economy plans and a fairly detailed outline of expected trade will appear in five-year horizon plans. To ensure fulfillment, the EPC will prefer to negotiate as much trade as possible well in advance. To simplify planning it will try to arrange (future) exchanges of goods at present or past world prices (which are effectively frozen for several years). If these are unsatisfactory, it may try to barter specific low-priority goods for the high-priority imports it needs. Moreover, the planners will usually prefer *bilateral* to *multilateral* trade agreements, again to reduce the complexity of planning.

Consider for a moment four command economies—Czechoslavakia (A), Bulgaria (B), the Soviet Union (C), and Rumania (D). Assume that A has a comparative advantage in precision instruments and sophisticated machinery, B in steel production, C in iron ore and coal mining, and D in petroleum drilling and oil refining. If each specializes to some extent according to comparative advantage, a rational pattern of trade among them might find A dividing exports comparatively evenly among all three other countries. However, B would be likely to export relatively more to A and D; C would probably send most of its exports to B; and D would export relatively more to A and B.

Under these conditions, the total exports and imports of each country could exactly balance without a balance occurring between any two nations considered in isolation. This is what we mean by multilateral trading. Each economy considers only its own comparative advantage within the world as a whole, and if exports and imports from any other country balance, this is simple coincidence. Specialization according to comparative advantage usually requires multilateral trade. When markets are working reasonably well, a nation will automatically specialize according to comparative advantage and participate in multilateral trade by producing those goods in which it has a cost advantage.

For command economies, however, multilateral trading is more difficult. The easiest way to balance the supply and demand for each good is to send exports directly to those countries from which the essential imports are obtained. Multilateral trading implies more-or-less simultaneous interdependent multilateral negotiations involving each of a command economy's major trading partners. In the extreme, all the world's important nations would become involved. Each command-economy negotiator would also have to accept a long-run constraint to cover a given percentage of all his imports with exports, even though he is running surpluses and deficits with many different countries.

In the final analysis, extensive multilateral trading is impractical; a command economy must limit both the number of countries and the number of goods involved in such agreements. Bilateral trading, by contrast, focuses on long-run balances between the imports and exports of two countries signing bilateral trade agreements. It therefore sacrifices comparative advantage for planning simplicity.

A bloc of command economies could probably specialize according to comparative advantage in comprehensive fashion, only by subordinating national economic plans to a supranational planning authority. This world EPC would treat the whole bloc like a single, interdependent economic organism within which each nation would appear as a particular region.

At present, an agency exists (Comecon) which is intended to promote trade, cooperation, and development among the economies of Eastern Europe, including the Soviet Union. In principle, Comecon could eventually serve as a vehicle for comprehensive supranational planning, and an associated bank, the International Bank of Economic Cooperation (IBEC) started operations in 1964. (Its main declared function is to settle member countries' trade balances on a multilateral basis.) However, since then the percentage of multilateral trade within the bloc of command economies has actually declined.[30]

A major problem with supranational planning is that some countries, notably Rumania have not yet been willing to make the required sacrifice of national sovereignty. Whereas the Common Market is now beginning to coordinate national financial incentive programs, partly to reduce their canceling effect, Comecon has yet to develop a supranational planning institution of any consequence. Even if the requisite sacrifices of sovereignty were forthcoming, the problem of insulation from the rest of the world would remain.[31]

---

[30] Wilczynski, op. cit., p. 209.

[31] In principle, a supranational planning body could be "democratic" in the sense discussed in Chapter 23 or, better, in the sense of Horvat's worker-managed firm to be discussed in Chapter 21. Practically speaking, however, China or the Soviet Union would dominate goal formation in any command-economy bloc which included one of them.

Recent years have seen a relaxation of tensions between East and West, coupled with overtures by the U.S.S.R. and other Eastern European countries for more East–West trade. This goes hand in hand with an apparent general change in priorities, noted at the outset of this chapter, and a realization that foreign trade must play a broader role in future command-economy growth. (Indeed, it may be a prerequisite to continued growth, even at a moderately rapid pace.) Command-economy trade has also been growing, since the early 1960s, at a rate above the 7 to 8 per cent characteristic of world trade as a whole, although East–West trade has grown less rapidly than trade within the "socialist group of nations." [32]

But if the watershed toward a wider role for foreign trade is truly to be crossed, command-economy planners must again face the problem of how to specialize according to comparative advantage when internal prices are irrational and do not reflect home production costs. (If they did, a nation would specialize according to comparative advantage, simply by exporting those goods in which it has its biggest cost advantage and importing those goods in which its cost *dis*advantage is greatest, vis-à-vis other nations.)

C. H. McMillan has discovered that, in 1964, the U.S.S.R. did indeed specialize according to comparative advantage in a very broad sense. That is, it tended to trade primary, natural resource intensive products to the more industralized countries in return for manufactured goods. It also tended to trade manufactures for primary products from developing nations.[33] Yet, aside from imports of technology and raw materials not obtainable at home, trade apparently failed to push the Soviet Union beyond its production-possibility frontier. McMillan notes:

In 1959, an average million rubles of Soviet exports embodied both more capital and more labor than would have been required to replace, through domestic production, one million rubles of Soviet imports. Thus foreign trade does not appear to have permitted the Soviet Union, in that year, to economize in terms of either of these two major categories of productive resources.[34]

Some Western experts maintain that the U.S.S.R. often uses trade for political advantage, but it is doubtful that this factor alone accounts for trade inefficiency. Rather, at a more detailed and less obvious level than that indicated above, a failure to specialize according to comparative advantage has taken its toll.

The cost has probably been higher in Eastern Europe. When the socialist nations there adopted central planning after the war, the only available model

[32] Wilczynski, op. cit., p. 55, and Kovach and Farrell, op. cit.

[33] More precisely, McMillan found that relatively more capital was embodied in Soviet exports to developing countries, while exports to the developed countries embodied more labor relative to capital. Upon extending the two-input model to include natural resources, McMillan found that Soviet exports to the developed nations embodied more natural resources than did Soviet exports to developing countries. See C. H. McMillan, "Factor Proportions and the Structure of Soviet Foreign Trade," Working Paper 72-04, Ottawa, Carleton University, Department of Economics, 1972.

[34] Ibid., p. 7.

was the one developed by the U.S.S.R. during the 1930s. Each nation copied this, despite its lack of suitability for local conditions. Thus, at first, all East European economies had similar goals which they translated into similar planned compositions of output, completely heedless of comparative advantage.

For example, each country started a major iron–steel complex and specialized in the construction of heavy industry, especially heavy machinery and electric power generation. As a result, nations invested in uneconomic projects for which they had a comparative disadvantage. Each country had short production runs and parallel investment. There was even large capital investment in projects that were uneconomical from the view of *absolute* advantage, the best known example being the Hungarian steel industry. The foreign exchange spent to import iron and coke to produce steel at home actually exceeded the cost of buying an equivalent amount of steel imported directly.[35]

Without an unlikely degree of supranational planning, command economies cannot specialize extensively according to comparative advantage and remain command economies. The interesting question is therefore to what extent the tail can wag the dog. Will yearning after the potential gains from trade force some remaining command economies to decentralize until they are basically marketized? At present, this appears unlikely. The Soviet Union has relatively less to gain than the smaller economies of Eastern Europe (China probably has less still to gain), and the U.S.S.R. must effectively approve any major reform there along these lines.

At this point the reader has two choices. He may go on to the "functioning of a command economy" in Chapter 8 or he may stay awhile for the appendix to this chapter, "Special Topics in a Command-Economy Setting." First, we shall consider a case history of the use of commands to achieve economic development—in Imperial Russia and later in the U.S.S.R. This is followed by explorations of planners' versus consumers' sovereignty and the problem of moral incentives.

[35] Frederic Pryor, *The Communist Foreign Trade System* (Cambridge, Mass.: MIT 1963), p. 28.

Appendix to Chapter 7

Special Topics in a Command-Economy Setting

7-7   The Russian Strategy of Economic Development

Everyone knows now that the revolution which Marx envisioned as bursting the workers' chains asunder in an advanced capitalist nation occurred first in one not far beyond the first stages of capitalist development. The Russian Revolution did not bring Marxists to power in a highly industrialized country whose government could then proceed to wither away. Instead the Soviet rulers faced an urgent task of industrializing, which they pushed with excessive zeal. What is most interesting is that the model of economic development exploited by Stalin bears many basic similarities to the one used by Czarist authorities all the way back to Peter the Great. An important difference is that the Soviets pushed the basic idea more efficiently and more ruthlessly than the Czarist authorities ever did.

The key elements of what we shall call the "Russian industrialization model" are simple enough. Suppose that we are in a predominantly agricultural country, decidedly lacking in entrepreneurial talent, whose leaders fervently wish to industrialize rapidly. If such a nation wishes to reach her goals while remaining relatively free of foreign controls, agriculture must become the source of industrial growth. Moreover, the state will have to step in and play an entrepreneurial role. This need not imply a command economy, however, and, if pushed, we would probably classify the later Czarist era (circa 1860–1914) as a mixed economy or as a borderline case.[36]

We sometimes hear that agriculture is at once the least and the most important sector of the Soviet economy. It has been least important, historically, in the sense that the Soviet planners have attached a higher priority to in-

---

[36] Peter the Great's economy (1682–1725) would probably fall into the command category. Within the last 50 years or so before the Russian Revolution, however, there was a fair amount of variation. There was greater use of commands during the Witte era (1892–1903) than before or after.

258

dustrial growth. But without largely forced savings from agriculture to finance rapid industrial growth, the latter would not have occurred, and the same is true of Imperial Russia under the later Czars. Inasmuch as the Czars favored the landed gentry, and those nobles who did not emigrate were liquidated as a class by the Soviets, it was ultimately the peasants, the poorest class of all, who had to bear the burden of economic development.

When we say that agriculture is the source of industrial growth, therefore, we mean in part that rural savings are financing industrialization. But there is another crucial factor which the Soviets made use of, but which Czarist officials never seemed to fully comprehend. The peasantry also had to serve as the source of migration to the cities so that a large urban labor force could arise. Under the Czars, Russia's rural population never fell below 85 per cent of the total. By 1928, on the eve of the first five-year plan, there was an excess supply of rural labor. At the same time, many Soviet industries were either technologically backward or virtually nonexistent. Conditions were therefore ripe for extensive development.

Thus, during the decade, 1929–1939, of rapid extensive development, the urban population nearly doubled, from 29.2 million (19.1 per cent of the total) to 56.1 million (32.9 per cent of the total). Table 7–3 shows the percentage of the population living in urban areas during selected years from 1722, when Peter the Great organized the first census, to 1970. 1960 was the first year in which the population was more than 50 per cent urban.[37]

The industrial development of Russia came in a series of growth spurts and, more than with most countries, we can identify each spurt with the policies of a key governmental figure. Peter the Great was the first leader to have a vision of an industrialized Russia, and Table 7–4 matches three other men with the approximate growth rates and periods of growth attributable to their policies. In evaluating the record under Stalin, we should keep in mind that territorial additions to the U.S.S.R. during 1939–1940 inflate the recorded achievement for 1928–1940.

The table may also understate the growth contribution of Count Sergei Witte, the most famous Czarist finance minister. One reason recorded growth for the 1890s was not higher relates to the kinds of investments that Witte undertook. They were much more capital intensive than Stalin's, meaning that for every ruble invested, the immediately resulting increment to output was less. Witte built a transportation infrastructure and a heavy industrial base, and he was, first of all, a builder of railroads. Because Russia is a country whose natural resources lie far from traditional population centers, it is fair to say

[37] To give comparisons, the United States was 56.2 per cent urban by 1930. Canada, which is climatically more comparable with the U.S.S.R., achieved 54.3 per cent urbanization by 1941 and 62.1 per cent urbanization by 1951. Sweden was 56.3 per cent urbanized by 1950, and France was 53 per cent and 55.9 per cent urban by 1946 and 1954. By contrast, the United Kingdom, which was the first nation to industrialize, achieved 77 per cent urbanization by 1901. The reader is cautioned that the definition of an urban area will vary somewhat from country to country and time to time. Source: *U.N. Yearbook of Demographic Statistics.*

Table 7–3. Percentage of population living in urban areas, Imperial Russia–U.S.S.R.

Year	Per Cent Urban
1722	2.3
1796	3.6
1859	5.7
1897	12.6
1914	14.6
1918	18.2
1929	19.1
1939	32.9
1950	38.4
1961	50.3
1970	56.3

Sources: Until 1900: P. I. Lyashchenko, *The History of the National Economy of Russia to the 1917 Revolution* (New York: Macmillan, 1949). From 1900 to 1950: Warren Eason, "Labor Force," in Abram Bergson and Simon Kuznets, *Economic Trends in the Soviet Union* (Cambridge, Mass.: Harvard U.P., 1963), pp. 72–73. From 1961 on: Murray Feshbach, "Population" in U.S. Congress, Joint Economic Committee, *Economic Performance and the Military Burden in the Soviet Union* (Washington, D.C.: G.P.O., 1970).

Table 7–4. Spurts of Russian and Soviet growth.

Period	Leading Figure	Growth Rate of Industrial Output (%)
1890–1899	Sergei Witte	8
1907–1913	P. A. Stolypin	6.25
1928–1940	J. Stalin	8.5–13
1950–1961	J. Stalin	9–10
	N. S. Khrushchev	

Sources: The periods 1890–1899 and 1907–1913 are cited by Alexander Gerschenkron in "The Rate of Growth in Russia Since 1885," *Journal of Economic History*, Suppl. VII, 1947. The latter two periods are given in R. W. Campbell, *Soviet Economic Power* (Boston: Houghton, 1966), p. 124. We have omitted the official Soviet index (for reasons given in the appendix to Chapter 6) as well as the lowest Western estimate.

that there could have been no major industrialization without a railroad network.

During 1928–1940, Stalin added relatively little mileage to the former Czarist lines. Instead, he organized freight transportation in paramilitary fashion and utilized the existing infrastructure with unheard-of intensity. Likewise, Stolypin's reforms (1906) and earlier measures of a similar kind finally freed the peasantry from bondage to the land. But the growth of this era—

based largely on individual initiative—also benefitted from the earlier forced industrialization under Witte.

Still, the growth achieved under Stalin stands out, both as the most remarkable and as the costliest in human sacrifice. By 1950 the U.S.S.R. was firmly established as the second largest industrial power on earth. This was a stature that she had not enjoyed since the middle of the 18th century when she produced more cast iron and more copper than any other nation and more linen than France or Germany. Peter the Great had given the direct stimulus to Russia's earlier surge, but despite his ambitions the long-run legacy of Peter was industrial stagnation. In pig-iron production, for example, Russia fell way behind England in the early 19th century. By 1860 she was eighth worldwide behind Austria and Prussia despite an almost sixfold expansion in population and a considerable enlargement of territory since Peter's reign.

Paradoxically, the very modernization of the state administrative machinery under Peter made the government better able to enforce serfdom. When subsequent Czars proved relatively weak and unable to dominate the nobility, the latter became the most powerful force in Russia. The nobles believed it to be in their interest to preserve the status quo, meaning a nation made up of landed estates worked by a peasant class whom they could exploit. They imitated everything Western that they were able to, except economic progress. Rather than entrepreneurship, they turned to conspicuous consumption. Only the declining efficiency of serfdom and the shock of Russia's backwardness— revealed in the Crimean War defeat—combined with political pressures eventually forced a change in priorities.

Rapid growth came again, beginning in the late 1880s, but even then the Czarist regime did not demonstrate a *long-run* tendency to catch up with the industrialized nations of the West. Table 7–5 shows this. (Of course, it is useless to speculate about what would have happened if the 1917 Revolution had never occurred.) We add that in 1913 the output of large-scale industry in Imperial Russia was about 6.9 per cent of the U.S. level and 4.8 per cent on a per capita basis. By 1938 the former figure was probably around 32 per cent; by now it may well be above 85 per cent if we value the outputs of both countries in U.S. prices.[38]

In the discussion surrounding Figure 1–4, we divided the economy into three sectors—producers, consumers and administrators—and described the flows of goods and money among them. The consuming sector, for example, supplies labor and other inputs to producers in exchange for incomes. Most of the latter are recycled to the producing sector in the form of purchases of goods and services and savings which become loans to enterprises. Our opening

[38] The other percentages should be viewed as crude averages of dollar and ruble ratios. See Alexander Gerschenkron, "The Rate of Industrial Growth in Russia Since 1885," *Journal of Economic History,* Suppl. VII, 1947, especially pp. 155, 166, 168. In 1963, the ratio of Soviet to U.S. industrial output was 77.2 in dollar prices and 60.4 per cent in ruble prices. See Alexander Tarn, "A Comparison of Dollar and Ruble Values of the Industrial Outputs of the U.S.A. and the U.S.S.R.," *Soviet Studies,* Apr. 1967.

Table 7–5. Position of Imperial Russia among world economies.

A. National income per capita

(in rubles)

	1894	1913	Per Cent Growth
1. United Kingdom	273	463	70
2. France	233	355	52
3. Germany	184	292	58
4. Italy	104	230	121
5. Austria–Hungary	127	227	79
6. European Russia	67	101	50

B. Comparative industrialization per capita

(ranking of leading countries)

	Rank in 1860	Rank in 1910
1. United Kingdom	1	2
2. Belgium	2–3	3
3. United States	2–3	1
4. Switzerland	4	4–5
5. France	5	6
6. Germany	6	4–5
7. Sweden	7	7
8. Spain	8	8
9. Italy	9–10	9
10. Russia	9–10	10

Source: Alec Nove, *An Economic History of the U.S.S.R.* (London: Allen Lane The Penguin Press, 1969), pp. 14–15. Reprinted by permission of Allen Lane The Penguin Press.

remarks suggest that, to understand the Russian development strategy, we should now consider a different division of the economy—into a relatively large agricultural sector and a relatively small industrial one—and study the flows of goods and money between these as in Figure 7–3.

We can, in fact, identify four important kinds of flows between rural and

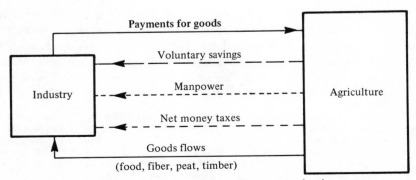

Figure 7–3. The Russian strategy of economic development.

urban areas. The latter cannot hope to feed themselves, so a food supply must be maintained for the industrial labor force. When we add productive inputs, such as cotton and other fibers, timber, and fuels we get the complete set of commodity flows. These include goods that are sold for the return flow in Figure 7–3, as well as taxes collected in kind. We can also identify money taxes and voluntary savings as historically of minor importance. Finally, rural areas are potentially the major source of growth in the urban labor force. Urban migration was probably not very important at the time of Peter the Great (1682–1725) when the scale of production was small enough to permit efficient manufacturing in rural areas. But it became an increasingly important ingredient of growth during the first half of the 19th century, and it was of paramount importance under Stalin.

Whenever voluntary savings are low, the first key to making the model work efficiently is either (1) to tax agriculture effectively or (2) to raise agricultural productivity rapidly. These approaches define two distinct strategies of industrialization which can be combined to an extent.

The first tries to force additional savings out of the peasant, which will then be invested to industrialize the country. It is therefore called the "forced industrialization model." The second gives emphasis to expanding and improving efficiency in agriculture as prerequisite to or at least concomitant with industrialization. Suppose for a moment that it works. Then rising agricultural productivity will make some rural labor redundant and available for siphoning off into the urban work force. Rising rural incomes would probably lead to increasing voluntary savings, which could be tapped for investment in industry.[39] Finally, with an increased agricultural surplus, the flow of food and industrial raw materials to the cities would rise and cause the prices of these goods to fall.

The great Soviet industrialization debate of 1924–1928 was partly about which of these strategies to concentrate on. Stalin rose to power by first siding more or less with the moderates, who favored the second plan. After helping to oust the forced industrialization advocates (Trotsky, Preobrazhenskii), he turned on the moderates and purged them. In the meantime he was applying an "improved" version of the forced industrialization model.[40]

Without justifying the tactics used by Stalin or by some of his Czarist predecessors, we may nevertheless ask whether the voluntary plan could have produced *immediate* rapid industrialization in the Russian context. Russian peasants were not traditionally innovative. Modernization of agriculture would

[39] However, rising rural incomes relative to those in the city can also act as a deterrent to urban migration.

[40] Actually, Stalin took a bit more of a middle ground between the forced industrialists and the moderates during the debates, favoring collectivization as a way out of the industrialization dilemma. However, this was a much more benign industrialization than he ultimately pursued. We again refer the readers to Alexander Erlich, *The Soviet Industrialization Debate, 1924–1928*, (Cambridge, Mass.: Harvard U.P., 1960). An extremely short version of the debate appears in R. W. Campbell, *Soviet Economic Power* (Boston: Houghton, 1966).

have involved a substantial investment effort, and might have had to be imposed upon some farmers. In order to coax agricultural surpluses from them, there are indications that an abundant supply of industrial consumer goods would have had to be offered in exchange to ensure that the peasants' material welfare was clearly tied to their output. Then the risk of conspicuous consumption would have arisen as a substitute for voluntary savings.

On the other hand, the peasants have always resented and resisted efforts to raise their tax burden. They are in a relatively good position to resist because, unlike city dwellers, farmers can be entirely self-sufficient. By consuming what he produces, the individual peasant can survive and also deprive the cities of food and raw materials. The tax collector who tries to take the farmer's produce before he eats it will find the latter particularly adept at concealment and evasion. Moreover, there are always many more peasants than tax collectors. In fact, Peter the Great did rely on excise and direct per head taxes. He had to, because the nobles or *boyars* were his chief tax collectors from the peasants living on their feudal estates. Only later, when the peasants and then the state owned the land, could a more sophisticated method of taxation be used.

In seeking a more effective means of taxation, let us again study the flows of Figure 7–3. There we may imagine that some of the voluntary and involuntary savings collected from the peasants are ultimately used to buy their agricultural produce. It is possible to short-circuit this flow by paying a lower price to farmers in the first place, provided they can be made to sell at such prices. In this way we would directly worsen the terms at which rural areas can trade with the cities so that a large flow of goods from the countryside exchanges for a much smaller return flow.

Both the later Czars and the Soviets have had communal organizations at the village level which were capable both of taxing in kind and of forcing the peasantry to market on unfavorable terms. For the Czars, this was the *mir* or peasant land commune whose members worked their own strips of land but had a collective fiscal responsibility.[41] Most *mirs* also had the right to reallocate land among peasant families, and allotted land could not be sold, mortgaged, or inherited by the peasant households.

Under Stalin, the *kolkhoz* or collective farm and, to a much lesser extent, the state farm replaced the *mir*. An important difference was that individual land holdings were now merged and worked collectively, while tools and implements were held in common. It could be argued that both the mir and the kolkhoz, while nominally under the control of their members, were actually run for the benefit of the state. Both probably retarded peasant initiative and the overall development of agriculture in the interest of decreasing the share of peasant income that was consumed. Under Stalin, however, indirect taxation became more ruthless and effective than ever before. Ironically, it was

---

[41] See Lazar Volin, "The Peasant Household Under the Mir and the Kolkhoz in Modern Russian History," in F. D. Holzman, ed., *Readings on the Soviet Economy* (Chicago: Rand McNally, 1962).

peasant resistance to his drive to put them into collectives that accounted for the large part of this effectiveness. Let us trace a bit of the relevant history.

We have said that a need to supply the peasants with consumer goods in exchange for their food and raw materials was a major weakness of the voluntary industrialization plan. For ideological reasons, the Soviet government tried to enforce prices that were below equilibrium levels during the comparatively marketized era of the late 1920s.[42] This policy applied to the prices of goods peasants bought as well as the ones they sold. However, an especially low price was set on grain. This was the "staff of life" of Russia, to which over 80 per cent of all cultivated land was sown. In addition, the generally low prices of industrial consumer goods meant that they were in short supply; lines formed at stores, and the peasants, who lived farther from retail points of sale than city dwellers, were hardest hit by the shortages.

The incentive to market agricultural produce fell, and the incentive to market grain fell most of all. Peasants reacted by feeding their grain to livestock, by hoarding it in expectation of higher prices, or by selling it to private buyers who transacted at prices above official levels. They also substituted other crops for grain. By early 1928, a crisis in grain deliveries was developing and it appeared that the government might not have enough food to feed the urban population and the Red Army. Stalin resorted to direct requisitioning by force, but these measures turned the wealthier peasants or *kulaks* and many of the "middle" peasants against the regime. (It was they who marketed the largest percentages of their produce.) Moreover, forced requisitioning could only work efficiently as a "shock" tactic in a country with 26 million separate peasant farms.

When the first five-year plan was launched in October 1928, the proportion of the population not engaged in agriculture was increasing, and it was planned to increase by much more. This made a solution to the procurement difficulties extremely urgent. By 1929 Stalin had decided that agriculture must be collectivized and that the kulaks as an independent class would have to be wiped out.

Both tasks were then carried out, almost overnight, in a campaign whose terror and tempestuousness is unrivaled in modern peacetime. Collectivization was literally forced down the throats of middle income and of relatively wealthy peasants (most of whom were poor, however, by Western standards). The poorest peasants were turned against their better-off neighbors, whose property, tools, livestock, and even personal effects were simply confiscated.

Perhaps 1.5 million kulaks and other resisting peasants and members of the families were deported to remote regions of the U.S.S.R., chiefly Siberia.

---

[42] This was especially true under the New Economic Policy, which prevailed from 1924 to 1928. For a discussion of this program within a historical framework, see Alec Nove, *An Economic History of the U.S.S.R.* (London: Allen Lane The Penguin Press, 1969), and Harry Schwartz, *Russia's Soviet Economy* (Englewood Cliffs, N.J.: Prentice-Hall, 1960). Much of the discussion below is taken from these sources, along with Volin's article.

There was widespread famine in 1932–1934, during which period $5\frac{1}{2}$ million people may have starved to death. (Soviet death statistics for this era have never been published.) Many of these were peasants living in grain-surplus areas, who had to watch their crops being carried away to feed the urban population or to export. (Thus the famine was, in part, official government policy.)

In 1928 individual peasants were farming 97.3 per cent of the sown area. Collective farms occupied only 1.2 per cent, and most of these were of a rather loosely knit variety. In November 1929 the Central Committee of the Communist party ordered 25,000 trusted industrial workers into the country-side to lead the collectivization drive. On July 30, 1930, the *mir* was liquidated by decree. By July 1, 1931, there were 211,100 kolkhozes, including 52.7 of all peasant households and nearly 68 per cent of all crop area. Two years later, these figures were 64.4 per cent and 83.1 per cent, respectively. Resisting peasants slaughtered nearly half of all the livestock in the U.S.S.R. and destroyed much of the other forms of agricultural capital. Without importing large numbers of American tractors (partly financed from grain exports), Stalin might have been unable to prevent a catastrophic drop in grain harvesting. As it was, the 1928 harvest level was not achieved again until 1935.

But herein lies the irony. By slaughtering their draft animals, the peasants forced the government to import and then to produce tractors, combines, and other complicated machinery which mechanized agriculture. Instead of selling this equipment to the collective farms, the government kept them in state-controlled machine-tractor stations (MTS). From February 1933 the collectives, had to pay for MTS services in kind, normally with a percentage of the harvest.

Thus each year at harvest time, representatives of the MTS, who owed their allegiance to the government, were right on the spot to collect grain deliveries —as taxes, as payments for the services of the MTS, or as "obligatory deliveries" at almost confiscatory prices. If members of any kolkhoz offered resistance, the MTS could threaten to withhold its services and impoverish the collective even more. The peasant had become the last in line to claim the fruits of his own labor.

There can be no doubt that the MTS raised agricultural efficiency because each station could serve several collectives with the same machinery. However, the chief advantage to the state appears to have been the additional control which the MTS provided. Lazar Volin writes: "It is an interesting paradox that the peasants, by slaughtering their horses during the early years of collectivization, made the tractor more vitally necessary, thus unwittingly helping the course of agrarian regimentation to which they were opposed." [43]

With the decline of incentives the official index of gross agricultural output actually fell over 1928–1939, and other indexes show a rise of, at most, 1 per cent per year. (By contrast, industrial production was rising anywhere

[43] Volin, op. cit., p. 137.

from 8.5 to 13 per cent per year.) However, the deliveries of cheap food and raw materials to the cities soared. For example, the vitally important grain collection increased from 12 million short tons in 1928 to 32 million in 1937 while total production rose from 73.3 million to only 97.4 million. (And 1937 was an extraordinarily good year weather-wise.) The rural population declined but slightly, so that most peasants were eating less and also enjoying it less.

Consequently, a vast urban migration took place whose dimension we have already indicated. This was the second key to making the forced-industrialization model work. With notable exceptions, the Soviets did not order workers off the farm and into factories and mines as Peter the Great and his successors had often done. Instead, they relied upon differential living standards created through the command mechanism. Previous to this, the Czars had tied the peasants to the land, first as serfs and later by means of what were called "redemption payments."

When Alexander II officially freed the serfs with the Emancipation Act of 1861, the practical effect was to tie them more closely to the land than before. The former serfs did not receive land free from the state. Rather, they had to pay an often outrageous price for it, which, when converted into annual mortgage instalments, became a series of redemption dues. As the instrument for enforcing payment, the *mir* (or village collective), rather than the individual peasant, actually owned the land. Sometimes, the redemption dues, together with taxes, actually exceeded the entire income from the land.

To meet these claims, the *mir* organized its own internal system of taxation and had power to refuse anyone permission to leave the village. This it generally did, whenever there was a good chance that his marginal product would be positive, given the inefficient and labor-intensive strip farming that the *mir* enforced. Even after taking a job in the city, the former peasant would often have to continue with his redemption payments.[44]

The effect was to stagnate urban migration until after Stolypin's land reforms of 1906 broke the power of the *mir*. This era signaled the end of Czarist reliance on the specific model of forced industrialization that we have outlined. Stolypin sought to create a class of prosperous peasant entrepreneurs who would be productive and loyal to the Czar. His reforms favored the most efficient individual peasant proprietors and encouraged many others to leave for the cities.

Along with other measures around the turn of the century, they greatly expanded the independent, and relatively prosperous, peasant class, the kulaks, which Stalin was later to wipe out. Interestingly enough, Stolypin's reforms came after Witte's forced industrialization drive during the 1890s had created bottlenecks and disproportions in industry. Capacity was built to

[44] The marginal product of labor in agriculture was probably zero or negative in many areas by 1861 in the sense that agriculture could have been reorganized so as to render much of the rural labor force redundant. But the communal and feudal traditions of the *mir* barred any such reorganization.

produce goods that could not be absorbed by the domestic market, so the economy was extremely vulnerable to worldwide depression, and badly needed social and cultural services were being curtailed.

Nearly 50 years later, the Soviets would begin abandoning the model under similar circumstances. By the mid-1950s, forced industrialization under Stalin had created the most sustained period of rapid growth that the world had ever seen. But it had also created disproportions, including the relative stagnation of agriculture, and severe hardships. By the time of Stalin's death in 1953, the Soviet standard of living had barely regained the level reached in 1928. The period of 1954–1958 saw a rise in agricultural procurement prices and, in the first half of 1958, an end to the machine–tractor stations whose equipment was then sold to the collectives. For ideological reasons, collectivism could not be abandoned, but the peasant's welfare did become tied somewhat more closely to his output.

Of course, long-run reliance upon forced agricultural savings is limited by the ability of a declining rural population to supply the needs of a growing industrial establishment and a rising number of city dwellers. Eventually, other sources of development financing must become more important, and productivity improvements will have to replace volume input increases as the prime source of industrial growth. Successful exploitation of the model thus breeds the conditions in which it becomes less and less appropirate.

7–8 Planners' and Consumers' Sovereignty

If the economic planning council is a dominating pole of economic power, does this rule out consumers' sovereignty? Many economists and noneconomists alike have said "yes" and have substituted the term "planners' sovereignty" to indicate that the social preference function originates with the EPC. Unfortunately, the sought-after distinction is not so clear-cut as it might seem, partly because different authors have assigned different meanings to these terms. To begin, therefore, we shall try to give a "reasonable" definition of consumers' sovereignty.

The basic idea is that individuals, in their roles as consumers and suppliers of human productive effort, rather than as planners and producers, should ultimately direct the production and distribution of goods and services. The micro votes of households choose quantities of toothpaste, automobiles, radios, bridges, and national defense to be produced and consumed. Through the mechanism of derived demand, these choices translate into votes for concrete, plastic, transistors, rubber, and a host of other intermediate products and natural resources.

Ultimately, these votes determine what the optimal solution to the economic problem will be. Many solutions are possible, depending upon the prevailing distributions of wealth and economic power, and some writers would not apply consumers' sovereignty to those situations in which power or wealth is too concentrated. Others would probably maintain as a *necessary* condition for consumers' sovereignty that society be completely distribution-oriented—in other words, that the social preference function be a social welfare function. Any increase in production would "count" as a part of social welfare only to the extent that individual welfares rise in the process.

There is also the problem of how individuals' votes are to be cast. In Chapter 4 we saw that the method of choice could influence the amount a community was willing to save and the volume of goods with public properties that it was willing to produce. More precisely, we would expect collective decisions to lead to more savings and more collective consumption than independent, private decisions. Conceivably, a planner could impose a higher or lower saving rate than the citizenry would pick by any method of voluntary choice. Yet some forms of forced saving and investment will exist in almost any society. The separation of ownership from control in giant corporations may lead managements to emphasize expansion at the partial expense of profits—a move the shareholders would not approve—if they had the information to act rationally and the power to control managerial behavior. Clearly, it is a matter of degree before we decide to say that consumers' sovereignty has been abandoned. Moreover, forced saving is not entirely the antithesis of consumers' sovereignty.

A weak version of the doctrine is what we shall call "consumers' sovereignty over consumer goods." Within a fixed consumer-goods budget, households may choose freely among the goods they wish to consume, and their votes will direct production and consumption activity. There need be no contradiction between this and planners' sovereignty, for an EPC could still decide how to allocate resources between consumption and investment and to some extent between investment in heavy and light industries. We have already pointed out how even the harshest of economic planning councils would view consumer goods as potential material incentives to work longer and harder. This, in turn, puts priority both on efficient production of the goods consumers want most, and on an efficient distribution of goods among consumers (that is, efficiency in consumption). It also penalizes the production of items that are going to remain unwanted on store shelves.

In short, consumers' sovereignty over consumer goods goes under the heading, *What Every Good Planner Should Do,* although command-economy planners have not often followed this advice. In most of Eastern Europe, they have usually allowed consumers to choose freely among goods already on store shelves—this is called "free consumer choice"—but they have rarely gone far beyond this.[45] The variety and assortment of commodities available has not been what households wanted most because household votes were not predominant in guiding the efforts of producers. With a smaller consumer-goods budget, the planners might have been able to produce the same amount of consumer satisfaction.

But most writers would not equate consumers' sovereignty with consumers'

---

[45] Yugoslavia and China would provide us with exceptions to this rule.

sovereignty over consumer goods. To them some kind of democratic decision on the breakdown of income into savings and consumption, and some say over the investment opportunities into which these savings are channeled are also prerequisites. Moreover, there is another problem. "Let's make consumers like what we produce" a former president of U.S. Steel is supposed to have said. Or consider the slogan, "Let us all go to the Donbass. To be a coal miner, it sounds glorious," used by the Soviets in their industrialization drive of the 1930s. The problem is that consumer preferences are subject to manipulation by planners or producers, and this is what many people have in mind when they contrast producers' or planners' sovereignty with consumers' sovereignty. The sovereign consumer is supposed to make up his own mind and form his own preferences. In this sense, the preference molders are the actors we call "sovereign."

Galbraith has argued that the net effect of advertising in the United States is to shift household preferences away from saving toward purchases of goods for current consumption.[46] In this sense we might speak of "forced consumption" of particular goods whose advertising campaigns were unusually successful. But now we have opened a Pandora's box. Everyone's personality and preferences are strongly influenced by his cultural environment. If I buy my wife a fur coat because every other wife in my country club has one, is this "forced consumption"? Am I a sovereign consumer? It is true that much advertising is directed toward peer-group leaders, but it seems rather irrelevant whether I am manipulated directly or follow the dictates of a group which has, itself, been "manipulated."

The list of interpretive tangles can be extended. Surely, my sovereignty has to be restricted whenever I do direct injury to others, no matter how much sadistic pleasure it may bring me. In fact, any society finds that it cannot survive unless it limits the economic sovereignty of its members in countless ways with laws, regulations, and customs. Many court suits and appeals are challenges to this social code, which is constantly changing.

In some cases social decisions will simply be more efficient than private ones and, on these grounds, we can take the results of the former when the two collide. But more often it will be a matter of denying some people their sovereignty in order to grant sovereignty to others, and it is the task of the social code to prescribe how this "should" be done. Some codes we would no doubt feel to be so restrictive or otherwise "undemocratic" as to suppress consumers' sovereignty. Yet others, perhaps restrictive in different ways, we would regard to be actually promoting it. On the other hand, were we products of an altogether different environment, we might change our classification. Thus we are not entirely "sovereign" in deciding what consumers' sovereignty is.

Before we throw out the idea, however, let us reflect a bit on what we might do with concepts such as "liberty" or "freedom." Apparently, we could

---

[46] J. K. Galbraith, *The New Industrial State* (Boston: Houghton, 1967), especially Chs. 18, 19.

also assassinate them with the same kind of overanalysis used above.[47] Indeed, consumers' sovereignty is basically economic freedom. To do so would be a mistake because we should be giving up something which, however incomplete and ambiguous, is still valuable while getting little or nothing in return. As economists concerned with opportunity cost, we should recognize this to be a bad bargain. The eradication of such amorphous and subjective norms as "consumers' sovereignty" is a blanket invitation to violate *everyone's* conception of what these norms should be. Consequently, it may be worth our while to lay out a few minimal requirements which many will feel any doctrine of consumers' sovereignty ought to include.

To begin with, there should be freedom of choice in most economic activities which does not violate the freedom of other economic actors to choose. There may be exceptions during emergencies, but normally individuals should have the right to opt in or out of particular occupations as well as to choose among goods to be consumed. It follows that consumers' folly and consumers' sovereignty may coexist, and most people will prefer the right to be wrong once in a while. Nevertheless, measures designed to make buyers better informed and more rational in their choices will generally be desirable. If economic actors are basically irrational most of the time, in fact, it becomes virtually impossible to argue in favor of consumers' sovereignty.[48]

The use of labor cards to prevent workers from changing jobs in the U.S.S.R. during the late 1930s and early 1940s would be a violation of consumers' sovereignty by the above criterion. The practices in the same country of requiring college students to serve after graduation for several years in remote regions, in exchange for scholarships, or in North America of tying professional athletes to particular teams, are borderline cases. Finally, participation as a buyer or seller in any given market may be purely voluntary and thus consistent with consumers' sovereignty. But an urban dweller in a market economy has no real choice between participating and not participating in the market mechanism as a whole if he wants to survive. Freedom of choice implies the right to at least a minimum subsistence level of living consistent with survival.

Second, whenever an individual chooses to express them, his preferences should count in determining the mix of goods and services to be made available to society.[49] Households must have the right to register their tastes to

---

[47] The development here is due to W. J. Baumol. See W. J. Baumol, "Discussion," under the topic "Reappraisal of the Doctrine of Consumer Sovereignty," *American Economic Review,* May 1962. The entire discussion of consumers' sovereignty there is worth reading. A portion is repeated here.

[48] A consumer research and information service, such as The Consumers' Union in the United States (but with a vastly augmented budget), and a protection service, such as a governmental Department of Consumer Affairs, may be necessary to make consumers' sovereignty work. We shall return to this issue in our discussion of mixed economies.

[49] This point is made by Abram Bergson in, "Reappraisal of the Doctrine of Consumers' Sovereignty," op. cit.

producers, and no household's vote should receive a zero weight. In particular, the EPC cannot take an action to which everyone (save its own members) is indifferent or opposed. Thus the harshest forms of forced saving are outlawed.

Finally, it will sometimes pay an EPC to produce a good called "coercion," which attaches punishment to various actions or to the failure to engage in certain activities. Unlike persuasion, coercion tries to influence choices without altering preferences in order to make individuals work longer hours, choose different jobs, consume different combinations of goods, or remain in a more restricted geographical location than they would otherwise do. Some kinds of coercion tend to be associated with the commodity preference function because they are designed to raise productive effort, regardless of the effect on individual welfare. On the other hand, no society is possible where coercion is nonexistent. Correspondingly, we could probably agree that it will sometimes aid in enforcing consumers' sovereignty. However, if coercion is not to violate this doctrine, we shall at least require that its use be sanctioned by a social decision in which individual preferences are allowed to count.

These three requirements are not overly stringent, and yet there are reasons to believe that many command economies will not be able to satisfy them. In Eastern Europe, as we have seen, it has even been difficult for the planners to adjust to consumers' sovereignty over consumer goods.

7–9   The Problem of Moral Incentives

There are not a few people who are irresponsible in their work, preferring the light to the heavy, shoving the heavy loads onto others and leaving the easy ones for themselves. . . . In fact such people are not true Communists . . . we must all learn the spirit of absolute selflessness. . . . A man's ability may be great or small, but if he has this spirit, he is already noble-minded and pure, a man of moral integrity and above vulgar interests, a man who is of value to the people.

Mao Tse-Tung
("In Memory of Norman Bethune")

The difference between reliance on moral and material incentives is that, in the former case, the pay and promotion possibilities of the manager, worker, or planner do not depend upon meeting production, cost, or profit targets. A manager or a worker entirely on moral incentives may win a medal for fulfilling his targets or a newspaper story which praises him for "serving the people with his whole being." But he would not also receive a bonus.

Interestingly enough, command economies have not relied primarily on moral incentives for the most part. (In the broadest sense, material incentives are nearly always *present* because firing and promotion will depend, in part, upon expected or past performance.) Stalin mixed moral with material incentives to a greater degree than have his successors to the Soviet leadership. There has likewise been a progression toward greater use of material incentives in other East European countries, although the future in both the U.S.S.R. and Eastern Europe is now somewhat uncertain in this regard.

The most notable exceptions to reliance upon material incentives are

Cuba and, to a lesser extent, China, North Korea, and North Vietnam. But while the record of Cuba in expanding social services is good, its output expansion has been poor, especially when measured against the achievements of other command economies during their first decade of economy-wide planning. It has proved necessary to introduce comprehensive rationing, which continues into the 1970s. As a result, the Cubans now appear to be sharply reducing their reliance on moral incentives.[50]

The economic history of the People's Republic of China since the end of the civil war in 1949 is largely one of oscillation between ideological extremism and managerial and technical expertise. This is often summarized in the phrase "Red versus Expert." Favorable economic performance, under the control of the experts, generates concern about revisionism in ideology. A slogan such as "Politics Takes Command" eventually becomes the theme of an intensive ideological campaign stressing correct political thought as the key to building a Communist society. Equality is a cornerstone of such a society, as is the notion of building the "new Communist man" who has learned to work solely because his labor contributes to the good of all people and to the state. Thus moral incentives come to the fore during periods of ideological extremism.[51]

We can cite two such intervals to date—the Great Leap Forward and its aftermath (1958–1961) and the Cultural Revolution (1966–1969). Each followed a period of satisfactory to outstanding economic performance. Each caused a decline in output which helped bring about a return to emphasis on expertise and material incentives. (A nearly disastrous 30 per cent drop in industrial production occurred in 1961.)[52] Similarly, Mesa-Lago noted in

---

[50] Mesa-Lago writes that "In the socialist world, there are three groups of countries taking part in the [material versus moral incentives] controversy: Yugoslavia [is] the leading proponent of material incentives; the Soviet Union and most of Eastern Europe [are] also in favor of material incentives, but in a more moderate position; and Cuba and the Chinese group stress . . . moral incentives" (see Carmelo Mesa-Lago, "Ideological, Political, and Economic Factors in the Cuban Controversy on Material vs. Moral Incentives," *Journal of Interamerican Studies and World Affairs*, Feb. 1972). The present author would not entirely agree with Mesa-Lago. Yugoslavia is the leading proponent of workers' management, which may result in a dominance of material incentives, although the two are not per se the same. Moreover, in China, moral incentives have been dominant only during the periods cited below and, in Cuba, only since 1964 or 1965, at the earliest.

[51] We would remind the reader that equality of individual welfares is not the same thing as an equal distribution of wealth. (See Section 4–5.) However, suppose that we rotate the more unpleasant tasks (as is done to some extent in China) and provide free schooling. Then equality of welfares should correspond to moderate wealth inequities, especially when differences between individual utility functions have been obliterated. This homogenization of individuals is, however, an aspect of the "new Communist man" which will not likely appeal to many Western readers.

[52] Part of this undoubtedly resulted from the Soviet pullout of scientific, technical, and economic experts in 1960, along with various blueprints and equipment. However, to put matters in perspective we should note that industrial output grew 16 per cent annually during the first five-year plan (1953–1957) and, apparently, even more rapidly during 1958 and 1959. In 1958 the U.S. CIA was forecasting a 14 per cent annual industrial growth over 1959–1965. In fact, industrial output had probably not recovered to its 1959 level by 1965.

1972 that "the policy of moral incentives in Cuba has not [yet] succeeded . . . in transforming the mass consciousness [into one oriented toward Communist values] and . . . may have contributed to the decline in production, particularly in agriculture." [53]

According to Marx, both Guévara and Mao were jumping the gun in applying moral incentives. For Marx, the transition from capitalism to full communism was to take place in two stages. In the first stage, characterized by "dictatorship of the proletariat," income differentials would remain, reflecting the rule that each person was to be paid according to his productive contribution. Only much later, after the state had gradually withered away amidst a growing material abundance, would full communism appear. Then the rule "From each according to his ability; to each according to his needs" would come to prevail. But by then the economy was supposed to be so superproductive that all material wants could be satisfied without any danger of scarcity. Barry Richman has maintained that: "Mao's vision of the pure Communist Chinese society has long been a nation of selfless, altruistic, classless, equal and completely dedicated citizens. This may be an admirable society from a philosophical viewpoint, but it seems to be unworkable in terms of industrial progress." [54]

We could ascribe a similar idealism to Guévara. Our purpose in this section, however, is to find out why Richman and many other Western authors regard this idealism as incompatible with rapid industrial development.

For any particular individual, a moral incentive may simply be a form of recognition that he prizes highly—such as winning a medal or the Red Banner in some kind of "socialist competition" to produce more. Nearly all socialist countries make some use of this kind of moral incentive. The Chinese press often lauds workers who "serve the people with their whole being" and prints stories whose basic message is that doers of good deeds are rewarded by the respect and admiration of their fellows.

The strength of such an incentive is not clear, but if Red Banners, medals, and laudatory newspaper articles do become highly prized for their own sake, the state will have found a way to maintain high performance levels at small cost in terms of wage and salary differentials. From this point of view, it is also cheaper when managers are content to accumulate pennants instead of profits.

However, we should also note that these "moral" incentives may really be material incentives in disguise. Winning the Red Banner in production may be important to a manager and to his immediate staff, including the Communist

---

53 Mesa-Lago, op. cit., p. 101.

54 Barry Richman, "Ideology and Management: The Chinese Oscillate," *Columbia Journal of World Business,* Jan.–Feb. 1971. It is noteworthy that when Lenin came to power in the U.S.S.R. following the (second) 1917 Revolution, he quickly attempted to reduce wealth inequities. By 1921 he was arguing that "Personal interest elevates production" (quoted by Mesa-Lago, op. cit., p. 53).

Party representative always attached to a firm, because it enhances their chances of future promotion and higher incomes. They may also be willing to use coercion or to withhold income as a means of extracting higher productivity from their workers.

In any event, the image of a selfless, altruistic man evokes a different conception of moral incentive. Here a moral incentive for one individual is an increase in the affluence or, more generally, in the welfares of neighbors, fellow workers, or other citizens of his country or community. Such an incentive will only work when individuals have become "selfless." Specifically, this means that they have been educated or indoctrinated (depending upon your point of view) to become better off themselves when others receive increases in income or other benefits. The same "education" would reduce each individual's own acquisitive instincts.

This idea is not new. The ancient Greek philosopher, Plato, described what such an education was supposed to accomplish in Book VII of his dialogue, *The Republic*.[55] There he likens self-seeking men to prisoners chained in a cave who are never exposed to the light of the sun and who never see anything at all that is real, only the shadows of images. The slow tortuous process by which they are brought up into the light of the sun is the process of transmuting the selfish nature of man into one that regards pursuit of wealth and power as a totally petty and unworthy goal. Instead, he dedicates himself to a pursuit of truth, justice, social improvement, and other noble ideals.

Nevertheless, Plato described this transmutation as the "upward progress of the soul into the intellectual world," and prescribed it only for society's leaders, whom he left materially well provided for. His ideal state would come to pass when, to paraphrase him, leading decision makers become philosophers and philosophers become leading decision makers.

Mao and Guévara, on the other hand, have at times taken an almost anti-intellectual view of this transmutation. With them it becomes an emerging social mass consciousness, communication, and leveling, exemplified by a respect for manual labor, rather than abstract science or art.[56] White collar workers are supposed to go periodically among the workers and peasants and perform manual tasks with them. Either the Maoist or the Platonic transformation of human nature would require an enormous investment in high-risk human capital, which is probably why Richman and others have felt that China could not have rapid growth at the same time.

What is, perhaps, more surprising is that even if the "New Communist Man" sought by Mao and Guévara arises from the ashes of a self-seeking

[55] Plato, *The Republic*, in William Lowe Bryan, and Charlotte Lowe Bryan, eds., *Plato the Teacher*, translation by Jowett (New York: Scribner, 1897).

[56] Neither would Plato's vision of the "upward progress of the soul into the intellectual world" be attractive to most graduate schools of business administration in the West. His vision does not embrace Creative Marketing Strategy, Planning and Controlling Production, or Advanced Computer Applications. Chronologically, the how-to-do-it studies were to come after the study of abstract subjects such as pure mathematics, philosophy, fine arts, and dialectics had transmuted human nature.

society, it may still not be possible to achieve both rapid growth and equality
by using moral incentives. To see why, let us first try to contrast the selfish
with the selfless individual, using ideas developed above. Figure 7–4(a) shows

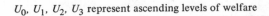

U_0, U_1, U_2, U_3 represent ascending levels of welfare

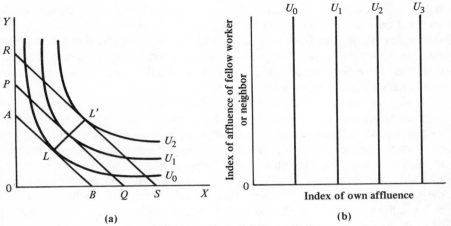

(a)   (b)

Figure 7–4. Indifference maps for the selfish household.

the selfish individual, once again, consuming two goods, X and Y, from which
he derives welfare. The line AB represents his initial budget line. Increases in
the individual's income shift this budget line out and enable him to reach
higher levels of consumption and welfare. Not only will he consume more of
given goods, he will also be able to afford a bigger car, a color-television set, a
trip abroad, or even a villa in Spain, which he could not have before.

This is the basic argument behind the use of material incentives. They
convert striving for higher consumption levels, including certain kinds of
prestige and the right to leave wealth to heirs, into higher productivity. Historically, the result has often been unequal incomes.[57] Thus, according to one
Chinese official, "Material incentives are like rat poison. They may look
attractive, but they are fatal to the system." In countries where the profit
motive and wide income differentials are not officially sanctioned, the problem
of providing individuals with a sufficient incentive to raise the income level of
the society as a whole may become serious. In part, this is why Mao linked
the transmutation of human nature with the economic transformation of China.

[57] However, it is difficult to say to what extent income differentials are due to differences in work effort and in productivity on one hand, and to differences in economic
power on the other. (Alternatively, we do not know to what extent unequal distributions
of wealth result from unequal distributions of monopoly rent.) The problem is further
complicated by the fact that in most societies it pays individuals who acquire wealth to
invest a part of this to acquire economic power.

To show the impact of selflessness, we must modify Figure 7–4(a) to get Figure 7–4(b). There we plot the income or wealth of the individual (or household) along the horizontal axis and a measure of the material affluence of a neighbor or a fellow worker along the vertical. According to traditional economic theory, the individual's indifference curves on such a diagram would be vertical lines. One cannot make him either better or worse off by raising the well-being of his neighbor or fellow worker. But as we have just seen, he will become better off as his own income rises and his consumption expands along path LL' in Figure 7–4(a).

Any good advertising or sales manager knows that Figure 7–1(b) does not describe the real world very well. In fact, a neighbor's or fellow worker's welfare may affect the individual's own level of utility in two ways. Few households would feel content if neighbors or fellow citizens with whom they come into contact are starving. To an extent, households will cut back on their own consumption levels to relieve the poverty of others. (This gives us an economic theory of charity.) "If, however, the neighbor's income is comparable to its own, the households compete for social status—the familiar process of 'keeping up with the Joneses.' If the Joneses increase their consumption, a household with comparable income may feel dissatisfied unless it, too, increases its consumption." [58]

To take advantage of this, the astute auto salesman will ask his prospective customer to take the new car home and drive it for a day or two. Thereby, he hopes to capture both the prospect and the bestowers of any admiration or envy. We show the indifference curves for such a household in Figure 7–5. Once again, we plot own income or wealth along the horizontal axis and the affluence of a neighbor or fellow worker along the vertical. We may divide the household's indifference map into two segments, one above line NN' and the other below.

Below NN', increases in the other household's affluence make the household whose indifference curves we have drawn better off at the same time. (If we start at A on the diagram and move straight up, we cross higher and higher indifference curves.) By giving money to his neighbor or fellow worker, his own happiness increases. This is because he sympathizes or identifies with the object of his giving. Above NN', on the other hand, the household begins to feel competitive, and its utility actually falls because of an increase in the affluence of a neighbor or fellow worker. (If we start at B on the diagram and move straight up, we cross lower and lower indifference curves.) This is the region that the auto salesman was exploiting.

As the individual becomes more selfless, he shows more sympathy for, identification with, and understanding of others. The selfless individual becomes better off, by and large, when the affluence of his neighbors or fellow workers rises, perhaps provided they are not already much more affluent than

[58] Joseph McKenna, *Intermediate Economic Theory* (New York: Holt, 1965), p. 132.

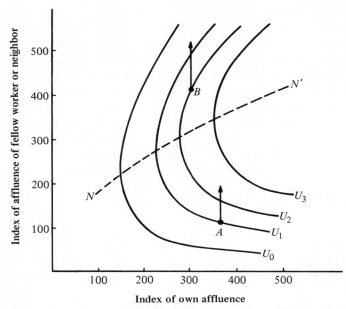

Figure 7–5. Alternative indifference map for the selfish household.

he is. The line NN' shifts upward to its position in Figure 7–6. By the same token, the selfless individual eventually reaches a point where he can no longer be made better off by an increase in his own affluence relative to that of his neighbors or fellow workers. This is the line MM' in Figure 7–6. Beyond MM', an increase in own income with no increase in the affluence of others leaves the household worse off. (If we start from C in Figure 7–6 and go to the right, we shall cross lower and lower indifference curves.)

Thus in a land of selfless households, we can only use material incentives to improve productivity up to the point where individuals reach their ridge lines MM'. From there, they will only raise their work effort when they have some assurance that others are benefitting as well as or instead of themselves. A selfless manager, for example, might work harder or assume additional risks of innovation simply to make the workers in his plant better off. If we extend the notion of others' "welfare," he may be willing to hold political discussions or mass meetings with his workers if he feels that they will be made better off thereby.[59]

The difficulty is that most individuals cannot have more than a negligible effect on the GNP of their country, region, or municipality. A manager, a peasant, or a worker may become imbued with the Maoist spirit of self-sacrifice and the notion of laboring only for the good the society and the

[59] There is, however, a fly in this ointment. One man may develop a faulty notion of what makes another "better off." Medieval torturers sometimes thought that they were doing their victims a favor by exorcising evil spirits. Or one man may decide that he knows what *should* make another better off.

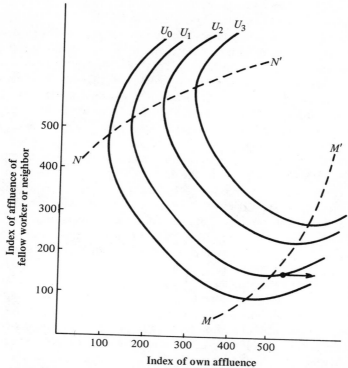

Figure 7–6. An indifference map for a more selfless household.

state and not for his own benefit. But the fact is that he personally cannot perceptibly affect this good. An assembly-line worker in the Loyang tractor plant may not even affect the output of his factory by much when he personally decides to work harder and more diligently. The knowledge that his extra effort won't make much difference can easily blunt his incentive to work harder. In Figure 7–6 the household may be willing but unable to move up the ridge line MM'.

Thus the central problem with moral incentives in a land of selfless men is that the benefit of one worker's increased productivity is spread among many people. In the extreme, no single other individual will benefit very much. This contrasts with material incentives, which concentrate the benefits of one person's increased productivity upon himself.

Of course, a manager may be able to benefit his workers by increasing his own effort, so that the plant becomes more productive and profitable—with the increased profits being shared among the employees. But the profit-sharing fund may also benefit when the firm is able to raise its price or reduce the quality of its product or service at a given price. This penalizes users of the good and causes a net efficiency loss for society. The manager may genuinely wish to help society, but he may feel closer to his workers than to the users of his product. Moral incentives are therefore no substitute for the various checks and controls that can subdue these tendencies.[60]

It follows that a central authority wishing to rely on moral incentives must do more than transmute human nature. It must also demonstrate to each citizen that serving the desires of the central authority is also helping to measurably improve the welfare of fellow workers, neighbors, or other citizens. Some combination of three potential ways of doing this suggests itself.

First, the authorities can reduce the size of the work unit upon which performance is evaluated and give each work unit definite tasks, such as planting rice or fabricating auto bodies, whose output is comparatively easy to measure. Ideally, the work unit would act as a team whose members help one another. Because it is small, the effect of one member's effort on the productivity of the team need not be inconsequential. However, if one worker's effort is to appreciably raise the incomes of other members of the unit, the unit itself will have to be put on material incentives. (Within the team the distribution of earnings would presumably be egalitarian.) This may defeat the purpose of moral incentives on an individual basis because an unequal income distribution may develop among teams.

More generally, the smaller the work unit, the more akin are material incentives for work units to material incentives for individuals. The larger the work unit, the less can one individual's work effort affect the average earnings of the team. To get around this problem, we may try to organize work within a factory, at some possible loss of efficiency, so that each team serves as a potential bottleneck. Then it may be possible to argue that the effort of each work unit significantly raises the output of the factory and that the effort of every member raises the productivity of his work unit.

Each worker might be more easily convinced on that account of the importance of his own effort within the enterprise. We should then have to put the enterprise itself on some kind of material incentive if this work effort is to result in higher incomes for fellow workers. While the distribution of income may be quite equal within firms, therefore, it could remain quite unequal between them.

Our second approach involves a concession to Plato's view, but it may still be able to combine long-run growth with egalitarianism. Its prescription is to use strictly material incentives for the least well-paid members of society, who ought likewise to have the least decision-making responsibility, by and large. As individuals gain authority to make decisions and, thereby, to affect

---

[60] In sharp contrast to the U.S.S.R. and Eastern Europe, the Chinese have tried to control all aspects of individual managerial behavior rather than to concentrate strictly on production targets. Managers receive (both moral and material) bonuses based upon their loyalty to the regime, the correctness of their ideological outlook, and their helpfulness to workers, which may be more important than their rewards for production performance. They also have some incentive to worry about the use value of their products. See Barry Richman's articles, "Capitalists and Managers in Communist China," *Harvard Business Review,* Jan.–Feb. 1967, and "A Firsthand Study of Marketing in Communist China," *Journal of Retailing,* Summer 1970.

the productive contributions of others more decisively, they are switched toward moral incentives. The most important economic decision makers in society would be entirely motivated by moral incentives. Although the Chinese do not profess to follow this policy, it may describe the net effect that sometimes emerges.

Finally, we can try to make the decision to be more productive a group rather than an individual choice. The entire work force of a factory may reach a decision to produce more at a mass meeting. If each employee has faith in his fellows, he knows that his own decision is linked to similar and simultaneous choices by many others. In effect, each agrees to raise his own contribution if the others will follow suit. Collectively, they can raise output significantly, and each worker has therefore tied his decision to contribute more to a measurable improvement in the whole factory's performance. Of course, the collective agreement may have to be selectively enforced later, but, in principle, each worker can gain strength, or leverage over the outcome, through collective action.

This decision can then be linked to a similar one at a higher level in which the managers, Communist party cadres, or revolutionary committees of many firms in an industry or region collectively pledge to try to raise output or growth. We may repeat this, in principle, up to the level of the EPC, again with allowance for selective enforcement of collective decisions taken. The entire procedure may be linked to a mobilization campaign to raise production of important goods, such as sugar in Cuba.

However, society is not likely to benefit from vague promises to increase one's productive contribution. There will have to be some agreement at each level to follow guidelines or success indicators from above, which become a catalyst for and a measure of performance. Moral incentives are no substitute for efficient organization.

The third approach best matches the mass social consciousness that Mao has said he wants to build in China. Yet, without becoming too cynical, we may note that a kind of material-incentive insurance can be built into it. A few activists may whip up enthusiasm at a mass meeting (or in a work unit). This is fine insofar as it goes, but the result may be an intimidating climate for reticent workers. The promotion possibilities of the activists may depend upon their ability to whip up enthusiasm. If the latter results in a kind of coercion, it is not clear how to separate these two impacts from the purely moral incentive effect in reaching the collective decisions referred to above.

Similarly, with work rotation. Reportedly, a general in the Chinese Army will often have to take his turn at cleaning latrines, and most managers are nominally required to spend at least one day per week in physical labor. Many bureaucrats must spend a month or more at periodic intervals working on agricultural communes. We may view this as part of the effort to build mass consciousness, and it can also serve as a substitute for providing material incentives to do undesirable work—at a cost of using skilled and professional labor inefficiently.

But it also reminds the upper economic strata of how the lower half lives. This is particularly true because one punishment for officials and managers whose behavior or attitude has been judged especially unsatisfactory is an extended, or even permanent, period of unskilled labor.

Nevertheless, for whatever reason, there is some evidence that the long-run trend of incomes in China is to become irregularly more equal. Following the cultural revolution, moreover, a fairly rapid growth rate appears to have resumed. Only time will tell whether either or both of these tendencies can be maintained.

REFERENCES

Baykov, Alexander. "The Economic Development of Russia." *Economic History Review,* Dec. 1954.

Campbell, R. W. *Soviet Economic Power.* Boston: Houghton Mifflin Company, 1966, Chs. 1, 2, 6.

Carson, G. "Russia, 1890–1939." In H. G. Aitken, ed., *The State and Economic Growth.* New York: Columbia University Press, 1959.

Erlich, Alexander. *The Soviet Industrialization Debate, 1924–1928.* Cambridge, Mass.: Harvard University Press, 1960.

Gerschenkron, Alexander. *Economic Backwardness in Historical Perspective.* New York: Praeger Publishers, Inc., 1965, especially Chs. 6, 7, 9, 10, 11.

———, "The Rate of Industrial Growth in Russia Since 1885." *Journal of Economic History,* Suppl. VII, 1947.

Goldsmith, R. W. "The Economic Growth of Russia, 1860–1913." *Economic Development and Cultural Change,* Apr. 1961.

Lyaschenko, P. I. *The History of the National Economy of Russia to the 1917 Revolution.* New York: Macmillan Publishing Co., Inc., 1949.

Nove, Alec. *An Economic History of the U.S.S.R.* Baltimore: Penguin Books, Inc., 1969.

Rimlinger, G. V. "The Expansion of the Labour Market in Capitalist Russia: 1861–1917." *Journal of Economic History,* June 1961.

Rosovsky, H. "The Serf Entrepreneur in Russia." *Explorations in Entrepreneurial History,* May 1954.

Schwartz, Harry. *Russia's Soviet Economy.* Englewood Cliffs, N.J.: Prentice-Hall, Inc., 1960, Chs. 2, 4, Appendix.

Volin, Lozar. "The Peasant Household under the Mir and the Kolkhoz in Modern Russian History." In F. D. Holzman, ed., *Readings on the Soviet Economy.* Chicago: Rand McNally & Company, 1962.

Von Laue, T. H. "The Witte System in Russia." *Journal of Economic History,* Fall 1953.

Chapter **8**

The Functioning of
a Command Economy

Most of the remainder of our discussion of command economies will deal with problems of command planning. To simplify our task, during this chapter we shall concentrate upon the dialogue between planners and producers and in Chapter 9 treat the planning bureaucracy, excluding firms, as a single bloc. Sometimes this is called a two-level model of planning. In Chapter 10 we shall probe inside the planning bureaucracy and consider the EPC and its intermediate authorities to be two distinct actors. This gives us a three-level command planning model (EPC, intermediate authorities, firms), and the generalization to more levels simply picks apart the intermediate planning hierarchy.

8-1 The Complexity of Command Planning

It was the fashion among Western intellectuals not too long ago to talk about "programming" an economy and finding an optional solution to the economic problem on a series of computers. Usually, the words "linear programming" were liberally sprinkled through discussions of computer-opia as if this were a magic tool for solving all the major difficulties that a quantities approach to optimizing presents.

Unfortunately, life is not that simple. A Soviet cybernetician once estimated that to completely program a year's operation of the Soviet economy would require 1 million high-speed computers operating nonstop for several years.[1] These were "high-speed" computers circa 1961 or 1962, capable of doing 30,000 operations per second. Today's space-age computers do anywhere up to 10 million operations and beyond per second, so the problem, although not yet solvable on a practical basis, no longer seems so utopian.

Nevertheless, command economies have been laggard in developing computer technology, and the planning process has had a low priority in gaining access to the best available computers. Even if there were virtually no limit on computer availability, the planners would still have to gather information and put this into a form that is digestible for decision-making purposes. Because there are (at least) billions of possible solutions to the economic problem which should be considered, the cost of this is prohibitive and likely to remain so for some time. The cost of dehumanizing the planning process to the extent that a full programming model suggests is also likely to be high because it will reduce the reliability of feedback information from lower-level decision makers.

Linear programming is an optimizing technique which presupposes that the "optimal" prices, or prices of all goods and services that would prevail, were a market system to guide the economy to its optimum, are known in advance. We have already indicated that this is highly unlikely. If we cannot make such an assumption, a more sophisticated programming technique must be called in. But then we are no longer even assured that an exact method can be found to solve the problem, and if a satisfactory method is found, it will probably require a greater number of more difficult computations plus a greater computer information-handling capacity than linear programming. The same is true when we switch from static programming (linear or otherwise) to dynamic programming.

It seems paradoxical, at first, that programming techniques should be more widely used in Western industry than in Soviet planning. The paradox disappears, however, when we realize that such techniques can often be used profitably within a much smaller producing unit turning out a much narrower range of products, even when ill-suited to whole economies.

On the other hand, computers and modern information retrieval technology probably do have a bright future in command-type planning. But their greatest potential lies less in finding optimal solutions from given data than in processing more information more rapidly and in more complex ways so that a greater number of more efficient exchanges between planners and producers becomes possible.

Nevertheless, it is a major problem in any command economy to compare the social rates of return on alternative investment projects. In particular, no

---

[1] Leon Smolinski, "What Next in Soviet Planning?" *Foreign Affairs,* July 1964. Reprinted in Morris Bornstein and Daniel R. Fusfeld, eds., *The Soviet Economy: A Book of Readings,* rev. ed. (Homewood, Ill.: Irwin, 1966), Ch. 20, p. 335.

one has a good comparison between the yields from further automating the planning process and capital expenditures elsewhere in the economy. The ultimate irony of command planning is that the EPC is likely to lack even a vague notion of the optimal planning technology.

8-2   Economic Interdependence

A natural starting point for a discussion of command planning problems is the notion of economic interdependence. The complexity of any economy is just as much a creature of its interdependence as of its multiversity. By and large it is the former that can be most devastating in making command planning a managerial nightmare. To understand why, we now want to probe a little more thoroughly into the physical structure of a system—its commodity flows, in other words— and the way in which this interacts with the production activities going on within individual firms. The topic is not an easy one, but we shall only go far enough to get a rudimentary understanding.

To begin with, let us enumerate *every* good or service available in a hypothetical command economy and assign an official "price" to each good. This price will serve as a common denominator of value, enabling us to add, subtract, divide, or multiply amounts of dissimilar goods. It may or may not indicate the terms upon which the commodity in question can be traded, and, in any event, it will not be a price in the full sense in which Western readers understand this term.

Consumer goods can normally be bought at "official" prices when they are available, but to get a producer's good of any consequence through official channels, the buyer will need a requisition from a higher authority charged with allocating it. Even when prices serve the medium of exchange role, they will not usually be "rational" nor will they be designed to equate supply and demand, which would imply decentralized decision making.

With this in mind we suppose there to be n goods available to our command economy, where n quite possibly runs into the millions. If the reader wishes a concrete figure, he may think of n as equaling 1 million. The amounts of these goods, in value terms, will be written as $(X_1, X_2, \ldots, X_n)$. If P_1 is the official price and Q_1 the physical volume of good 1, $X_1 = P_1 Q_1$, and similarly for the other goods. We shall assume that the EPC has enough information about future prices to allow us to translate physical targets into value targets. (In practice this will mean some reluctance by the planners to change prices.)

The first step in analyzing interdependence is then to distinguish different units of any good by their various destinations after they are produced or imported. Some will be used up again in additional *current* production, some will go to inventory, and some will go to other final demand uses, including public and private consumption, net capital formation, and export. Within the intermediate-use sector, we can further designate the particular industry, geographical region, or even production process to which various units of each good go. Thus some steel will go into the fabrication of bridges, some to the automobile industry, some to machine tools, some to defense, and some into the production of more steel. Since we are enumerating every good at this stage, we shall assume that every production process is taken into account.

Symbolically let X_1 be the total amount of good 1 available, and similarly, for X_2, X_3, X_4, and so forth. Also, let x_{11} be the amount of the first good going back into the production of itself, x_{12} be the amount of good 1 currently used up in producing the second good, and so on with x_{13}, x_{14}, on down to x_{1n}. The sum $x_{11} + x_{12} + \cdots + x_{1n}$ gives the total amount of good 1 used up currently as an input in making other goods. If Z_1 represents this total amount, $Z_1 = x_{11} + x_{12} + \cdots + x_{1n}$. The *difference*, $X_1 - Z_1$, is the amount of the first good left over for final demand. Letting Y_1 denote the amount available for final demand, we have

X_1: the total amount of good 1 available, $= Z_1 + Y_1$

$x_{11}, x_{12}, \cdots, x_{1n}$: the amounts currently used up in producing goods $(1, 2, \cdots, n)$

$Z_1 = x_{11} + x_{12} + \cdots + x_{1n}$: the total amount of good 1 going to intermediate use

$Y_1 = X_1 - Z_1$: the total amount of good 1 going to final demand use

Any of the numbers Y_1; $x_{11}, \cdots, x_{1n}$; or Z_1 may be zero. The same holds for every other good, and we may write the following relations to cover the entire economy:

$$X_1 = Z_1 + Y_1 = x_{11} + x_{12} + \cdots + x_{1n} + Y_1$$
$$X_2 = Z_2 + Y_2 = x_{21} + x_{22} + \cdots + x_{2n} + Y_2$$
$$\cdots \cdots \cdots \cdots \cdots \cdots \cdots \cdots \cdots$$
$$X_n = Z_n + Y_n = x_{n1} + x_{n2} + \cdots + x_{nn} + Y_n$$

Each row in the above array stands for a particular good, and so does each column of the small x's. The column $(x_{11}, x_{21}, \cdots, x_{n1})$, for example,[2] gives us the entire assortment of material inputs used up in making good 1. We often say that the rows refer to industries or firms viewed as *producers* while the columns refer to the same entities viewed as *users*. (Alternatively, the columns classify goods according to sector of *origin* while the rows classify goods by sector of *destination*.) Sometimes the small x's are called *intersectoral flows* or flows of goods from one production process (or "sector" of the economy) to another. The array of these numbers is then called the array or matrix of intersectoral flows. Table 8–1 shows such an array for China

---

[2] We must be careful not to confuse the rows with columns. $(x_{11}, x_{21}, \ldots, x_{n1})$ gives the first *column* of the array. The *second* number of the subscript is always 1. By contrast, $(x_{11}, x_{12}, \ldots, x_{1n})$ gives the first *row* of the array. The *first* number of the subscript is always 1.

in 1956. Here the sectors, industries, or groups of industries are numbered 1 through 22.

Within any time period, the basic task of the EPC is to get the "optimal" final use quantities from its producing sector. Aside from certain prestige goods, social welfare ultimately depends upon the Y's rather than the X's. It is the former which make up at least part of the basis for ranking alternative solutions to the economic problem and, over time, for deciding between alternative paths of economic development. For the most part it is the final-demand quantities which should appear in the commodity preference or social guiding functions. If we use the total outputs instead, the implication is that we have a formula (to be discussed shortly) for deriving the X's from the Y's, and are making use of this link.

Prestige considerations aside, the intermediate quantities (Z_1, Z_2, $\cdots$, Z_n) have no value beyond the value they impart to the goods which they assist in producing. Indeed, an economy is conceivable whose total outputs are high and increasing but where the amounts left over for final use and, in particular, for consumption are zero! Every good produced would be entirely used up in producing other goods. No social welfare would be generated by such a system, and it could not survive for long, even though its industries might look physically impressive.[3]

But while the EPC (or "society") derives its welfare from the Y's, its orders to the producing sector tell managers how much of each output to produce, how much of each input to use, and where to send the goods after they are produced. The commands of a command economy thus relate to total outputs, to the matrix of intersectoral flows, and to the various technologies of production used in each firm. A virtue of the famous input–output theory is that it forges the necessary link between each of these variables and the final outputs.

To see how this works, let a_{12} be defined as the input of good 1 used, on average, to make one unit of good 2. Or, a_{12} equals x_{12} divided by X_2. We may call a_{12} the technical coefficient *directly* linking input 1 to output 2. For every intersectoral flow, there will be a corresponding technical coefficient, and the complete array of all these fractions gives us one way of portraying an economy's technology as of any point in time. The technology of the Chinese economy in 1956, so described, appears as Table 8-2. The lowercase a's are

---

[3] This is not the wildest fantasy. The percentage of the value of output of intermediate-goods industries in the Soviet Union which was available as inputs into domestic consumer-goods production had fallen from 28 per cent in 1950 to 18 per cent in 1964. The year 1964 also marked the conclusion of the slowest growth period the Soviet Union has yet encountered and the fall of Khrushchev from power as well as the beginning of a somewhat hesitating reform movement (the "Kosygin reforms") to introduce increased decision-making autonomy for enterprise managements. The corresponding percentage for Canada in 1949, to give a Western comparison, lay between 50 and 62 per cent, depending upon how much of government spending went for consumption. Source: Dominion Bureau of Statistics (Government of Canada), *Supplement to the Inter-Industry Flow of Goods and Services, Canada, 1949*, Publication 13-513 (Ottawa: Queen's Printer, 1960), Table 4, "The Primary Input Content of Final Output."

Table 8–1. China intersectoral flows, 1956 (in millions of 1952 yuan).

	1	2	3	4	5	6	7	8	9	10	11	12	13	14	15	16	17
1. Agriculture products for food (including fishery)	2,492.2	207.8	0.8	0.2	0.0	0.0	0.0	2,712.0	9.8	7.6	2,079.1	0.3	0.2	0.0	11.3	23.6	0.0
2. Agriculture products for textile material	0.0	0.0	0.0	0.0	0.0	0.0	0.0	0.0	1,355.8	0.1	0.4	0.0	5.9	0.0	182.0	27.2	0.0
3. Forestry	1.7	0.2	0.0	114.2	0.2	4.2	6.0	6.9	0.2	721.5	3.8	3.3	1.3	0.0	64.2	10.4	0.0
4. Coal and allied products	0.2	0.0	0.0	340.7	0.2	0.0	16.2	38.5	25.5	61.2	37.0	125.7	4.5	4.3	17.4	13.2	10.5
5. Crude petroleum and allied products	60.5	5.0	10.0	18.5	860.8	11.3	42.0	33.9	41.6	73.3	40.4	71.4	38.6	73.4	43.0	67.0	3.3
6. Iron ore	0.0	0.0	0.0	0.0	0.0	0.0	0.0	0.0	0.0	0.0	0.0	600.9	0.0	0.0	0.0	0.0	0.0
7. Other mining and non-ferrous metals	8.1	0.6	0.0	0.0	0.3	0.0	310.3	8.7	2.6	181.8	182.9	78.5	503.9	35.7	30.8	20.9	0.0
8. Foodstuff manufactured	26.1	2.1	0.3	6.1	0.9	0.0	0.6	2,195.1	50.7	12.1	70.2	6.6	2.4	9.7	8.8	5.2	0.0
9. Textiles	39.6	3.2	2.7	1.7	0.3	1.3	5.5	116.0	7,936.7	27.1	13.7	0.9	29.4	26.8	254.4	142.9	0.1
10. Construction materials	8.5	0.6	0.0	18.9	1.4	1.3	20.5	347.5	22.3	613.7	32.1	52.7	5.6	104.3	26.9	292.2	1.3
11. Chemicals	927.5	77.5	0.0	40.8	11.2	17.9	43.1	683.0	591.2	146.2	1,143.3	5.7	10.0	68.0	280.5	784.8	0.2
12. Iron and steel	0.4	0.0	0.3	69.8	0.0	31.6	56.8	6.2	20.4	75.7	3.8	4,693.9	982.5	2,024.4	34.4	51.6	0.6
13. Metal working	7.8	0.6	3.8	42.7	15.3	33.9	62.2	450.0	30.0	29.3	94.4	21.7	168.5	483.9	10.8	83.8	0.2
14. Machinery (including arms production)	70.2	5.8	0.4	17.0	0.1	0.4	1.1	2.0	71.7	1.6	1.6	20.1	4.5	1,546.9	1.1	17.8	0.0
15. Other producer goods (paper, pulp, etc.)	9.8	0.8	1.0	4.8	1.5	6.6	12.1	231.1	243.0	93.5	46.1	9.5	8.7	85.8	760.0	776.4	0.1
16. Other consumer goods	2.5	0.2	0.3	1.6	1.1	1.1	2.8	27.1	52.3	3.6	11.2	4.6	2.5	29.1	23.4	197.4	0.2
17. Gas	0.0	0.0	0.0	28.5	0.0	0.0	0.0	2.3	0.6	4.1	0.1	0.0	0.4	1.4	0.1	1.0	0.0
18. Electricity	4.6	0.3	0.1	98.9	14.3	13.9	39.5	40.3	140.0	39.0	58.2	107.7	62.3	33.0	67.1	37.9	1.3
19. Transport and communications	235.5	19.7	17.8	96.3	7.9	10.0	43.4	654.5	259.9	400.7	176.4	88.2	49.9	118.2	209.9	221.8	7.7
20. Construction	156.9	13.1	1.1	36.5	4.6	3.2	25.5	92.8	101.4	11.8	48.3	20.3	6.2	27.8	25.1	78.1	11.4
21. Other services	627.9	52.5	3.9	31.5	5.1	9.2	165.6	456.2	766.4	126.5	162.2	476.7	200.5	152.7	162.0	315.3	0.3
22. Not classified	0.0	0.0	76.8	162.9	137.9	8.9	195.5	1,515.1	737.3	480.8	341.4	239.0	443.9	417.1	329.8	774.8	16.3
Total 1–22	4,680.0	390.0	119.3	1,131.6	1,063.1	154.8	1,048.7	9,619.2	12,459.4	3,111.2	4,546.6	6,627.7	2,531.7	5,242.7	2,543.0	3,944.2	53.5
Gross value added	35,180.0	3,120.0	2,700.0	787.3	628.3	445.2	2,046.3	4,056.4	5,045.5	1,081.2	1,097.6	3,147.5	1,437.0	3,609.7	512.4	1,968.9	51.2
Gross input	39,860.0	3,510.0	2,819.3	1,918.9	1,691.4	600.0	3,095.0	13,675.6	17,504.9	4,192.4	5,644.2	9,775.2	3,968.7	8,852.4	3,055.4	5,913.1	104.7

Source: Haruki Niwa, "An Outline of the Compilation Work on the Input–Output Table for Mainland China (1956)," Kwansei Gakuin University Annual Studies, Vol. 18, Dec. 1969.

sometimes called *direct* input–output coefficients, and the entire array of them forms an *input–output matrix* which we label A. Thus Table 8–2 gives us the A matrix for China in 1956.

Because a_{12} equals x_{12} divided by X_2, it follows that $x_{12} = a_{12}X_2$. Similarly, $x_{11} = a_{11}X_1$, $x_{13} = a_{13}X_3$, and so on. We shall now use these results to get ways of expressing the Y's in terms of the total outputs (X's) and of the economy's technology. We have already seen that

$$X_1 = x_{11} + x_{12} + \cdots + x_{1n} + Y_1 \quad \text{or} \quad Y_1 = X_1 - x_{11} - x_{12} - \cdots - x_{1n},$$

but this now becomes

$$Y_1 = X_1 - a_{11}X_1 - a_{12}X_2 - \cdots - a_{1n}X_n,$$

and an analogous result holds for each of the other Y's. Knowing both the direct technical coefficients and the total outputs will enable a command-economy planner to determine quantities available for final use.

Unfortunately, however, this is not good enough. It is far more important, and far more difficult, to turn things around and determine the total output requirements (X's) corresponding to each bill of goods for final use (Y's). Or, since commands to the producing sector are based on total outputs, we can think of this procedure as one that helps to determine the best set of commands corresponding to each final-use bill. Assuming the EPC to be maximizing some index of social welfare which depends upon the Y's, its exchange with the producing sector would *ideally* go something like the following.

First, the center will rank different sets of final-use quantities based upon the social welfare it attaches to each. Then it will choose a desirable target set which it thinks is a bit beyond the system's capacity to provide. The idea is, on one hand, to prevent firms from producing below their output potentials and, on the other, to refrain from making the plan so hard that there is substantial incentive to falsify reports of achievement. These final demands must then be translated into commands to the producing sector, which will respond with feedback relating to their feasibility. Essentially, managers will either agree to turn out the minimal output assortments called for by the plan with the maximal amounts of inputs allowed them or they will argue that the planners have overoptimistically assessed their technical capabilities. In the latter event firms will ask to be allowed more inputs or to have some output targets reduced. (Either way they are asking for less output per unit of input.) Subsequently, the planners will probably scale down some of their requests, while attempting to confine any major reductions to low-priority sectors. A new set of commands relating to a new set of output targets and a less ambitious technology will then go out to producers to be followed by a second set of responses. And so it goes until the EPC deems it necessary or desirable to stop.

8–3   Direct and Indirect Technologies

However, the procedure just outlined can only operate if EPC is able to compute the total output requirements that correspond to any given bill of

Table 8–2. Direct input coefficients, China 1956.*

	1	2	3	4	5	6	7	8	9	10	11
1	0.06252378	0.05920227	0.00028375	0.00010422	0.00000000	0.00000000	0.00000000	0.19830942	0.00055984	0.00181280	0.36836045
2	0.00000000	0.00000000	0.00000000	0.00000000	0.00000000	0.00000000	0.00000000	0.00000000	0.07745254	0.00002385	0.00007086
3	0.00004264	0.00005698	0.00000000	0.05951326	0.00011824	0.00699999	0.00193861	0.00050454	0.00001142	0.17209714	0.00067325
4	0.00000501	0.00000000	0.00000000	0.17754960	0.00011824	0.00000000	0.00523424	0.00281523	0.00145673	0.01459784	0.00655540
5	0.00151781	0.00142450	0.00354697	0.00964093	0.50892740	0.01883333	0.01357027	0.00247886	0.00237647	0.01748402	0.00715778
6	0.00000000	0.00000000	0.00000000	0.00000000	0.00000000	0.00000000	0.00000000	0.00000000	0.00000000	0.00000000	0.00000000
7	0.00020321	0.00017094	0.00000000	0.00000000	0.00017736	0.00000000	0.10025840	0.00063616	0.00014852	0.04336419	0.03240494
8	0.00065479	0.00059829	0.00010640	0.00317890	0.00053210	0.00000000	0.00019386	0.16051214	0.00289633	0.00288617	0.01243754
9	0.00099347	0.00091168	0.00095768	0.00088592	0.00017736	0.00216666	0.00177705	0.00848225	0.45339870	0.00646407	0.00242727
10	0.00021324	0.00017094	0.00000000	0.00984938	0.00082771	0.00216666	0.00662358	0.02541022	0.00127392	0.14638394	0.00568725
11	0.02326893	0.02207976	0.00000000	0.02126217	0.00662173	0.02983332	0.01392568	0.04994297	0.03377339	0.03487263	0.20256191
12	0.00001003	0.00000000	0.00010640	0.03637500	0.00000000	0.05266664	0.01835217	0.00045336	0.00116538	0.01805648	0.00067325
13	0.00019568	0.00017094	0.00134785	0.02225232	0.00904575	0.05649998	0.02009692	0.03290532	0.00171380	0.00698883	0.01672513
14	0.00176116	0.00165242	0.00014187	0.00885923	0.00005912	0.00066666	0.00035541	0.00014624	0.00409599	0.00038164	0.00028347
15	0.00024586	0.00022792	0.00035469	0.00250143	0.00088683	0.01099999	0.00390952	0.01689871	0.01388182	0.02230226	0.00816767
16	0.00006271	0.00005698	0.00010640	0.00083381	0.00065034	0.00183333	0.00090468	0.00198163	0.00298773	0.00085869	0.00198433
17	0.00000000	0.00000000	0.00000000	0.01485225	0.00000000	0.00000000	0.00000000	0.00016818	0.00003427	0.00097796	0.00031771
18	0.00011540	0.00008547	0.00003546	0.05153994	0.00845453	0.02316666	0.01276251	0.00294685	0.00799775	0.00930254	0.01031146
19	0.00590817	0.00561253	0.00631361	0.05018499	0.00467068	0.01666666	0.01402261	0.04785896	0.01484726	0.09557771	0.03125332
20	0.00393627	0.00373219	0.00039016	0.01902131	0.00271964	0.00533333	0.00823909	0.00678580	0.00579266	0.00281461	0.00855745
21	0.01575262	0.01495726	0.00138332	0.01641565	0.00301525	0.01533333	0.05350564	0.03335868	0.04378202	0.03017365	0.02873746
22	0.00000000	0.00000000	0.02724080	0.08489233	0.08153009	0.01483333	0.06316637	0.11078852	0.04211962	0.11468368	0.06048686

	12	13	14	15	16	17	18	19	20	21	22
1	0.00003068	0.00005039	0.00000000	0.00369836	0.00399113	0.00000000	0.00000000	0.00025302	0.00205932	0.00909430	0.50898504
2	0.00000000	0.00148663	0.00000000	0.05956666	0.00459995	0.00000000	0.00000000	0.00000000	0.00000000	0.00000000	0.08101189
3	0.00033758	0.00032756	0.00000000	0.02101197	0.00175880	0.00000000	0.00074810	0.00047442	0.00385714	0.00066850	0.00000000
4	0.01285907	0.00113387	0.00048574	0.00569483	0.00223233	0.10028648	0.15934592	0.01536077	0.00001307	0.00116771	0.01948240
5	0.00730419	0.00972610	0.00829153	0.01407344	0.01148298	0.03151861	0.00523671	0.12075650	0.01484019	0.00109826	0.00000000
6	0.06147187	0.00000000	0.00000000	0.00000000	0.00000000	0.00000000	0.00000000	0.00000000	0.00000000	0.00000000	0.00000000
7	0.00803052	0.12696850	0.00405539	0.01008050	0.00353452	0.00000000	0.00000000	0.00027411	0.01802396	0.00026045	0.09482401
8	0.00067517	0.00060473	0.00109574	0.00288014	0.00087940	0.00000000	0.00181682	0.00248808	0.00000000	0.03115069	0.00000000
9	0.00009206	0.00740796	0.00302742	0.08326238	0.02416668	0.00095510	0.00085497	0.01002614	0.00162430	0.00217481	0.00000000
10	0.00539119	0.00141104	0.01178211	0.00880407	0.04941571	0.01241641	0.01271774	0.00834984	0.18775784	0.00244395	0.00000000
11	0.00058310	0.00251971	0.00768153	0.09180462	0.13272225	0.00191021	0.00170994	0.00246700	0.01413413	0.01379989	0.00000000
12	0.48018437	0.24756217	0.22863376	0.01125875	0.00872638	0.00573065	0.01464144	0.02057942	0.10666632	0.00048184	0.00786080
13	0.00221990	0.04245722	0.05466314	0.00353472	0.01417192	0.00191021	0.02522175	0.01697381	0.10458081	0.00591672	0.00000000
14	0.00205622	0.00113387	0.17474353	0.00036001	0.00301026	0.00000000	0.00406112	0.02298317	0.01372881	0.01424701	0.00000000
15	0.00097181	0.00219215	0.00969228	0.24873989	0.13130170	0.00095510	0.00106871	0.00669463	0.00417094	0.00544355	0.00000000
16	0.00047057	0.00062992	0.00328724	0.00765856	0.03338351	0.00191021	0.00106871	0.00529245	0.01358498	0.01497195	0.28783553
17	0.00000000	0.00010078	0.00015811	0.00003272	0.00016911	0.00000000	0.00000000	0.00001054	0.00001307	0.00026045	0.00000000
18	0.01101767	0.01569782	0.00372780	0.02196111	0.00640949	0.01241641	0.02532862	0.00088559	0.00284382	0.00065548	0.00000000
19	0.00902283	0.01257338	0.01335231	0.06869798	0.03750994	0.07351342	0.03216842	0.03485428	0.04776318	0.04414317	0.00000000
20	0.00207668	0.00156222	0.00314039	0.00821495	0.01320796	0.10888248	0.01068718	0.01939414	0.00268038	0.01961243	0.00000000
21	0.04876626	0.05052031	0.01724956	0.05302087	0.05332227	0.00286532	0.01485518	0.02770630	0.06936967	0.06464546	0.00000000
22	0.02444962	0.11185020	0.04711715	0.10793995	0.13103109	0.15568274	0.07247591	0.07948166	0.00802154	0.10850214	0.00000000

Source: Haruki Niwa, "An Outline of the Compilation Work on the Input–Output Table for Mainland China (1956)," *Kwansei Gakuin University Annual Studies,* Vol. 18, Dec. 1969.

* Column and row numbers refer to industries in Table 8–1.

final demands. The direct input–output coefficients will not enable the planners to do this, and an example will readily show why. Suppose that the EPC wishes to increase automobile production for final use by 2,000 units over the current-operating-year's target. Using the matrix A, it finds that this will require 1,000 tons of sheet steel, 10,000 tires, 4,000 upholstery units, and so on as inputs for the auto industry. But this is only the beginning. The steel, upholstery, and tire industries will likewise require more inputs and so will their suppliers in the rubber, leather, coal, and plastics industries. The impact will then spread to the suppliers of these industries. Thus the impact of any change in the bill of goods produced to meet final demands will spread like a shock wave through the entire economy.[4]

Nor does the process stop here. The first wave begets a second, the second a third, and so on. Somewhere between five and 12 of them will be generated before they die down, and it can be shown that, the more interdependent the economy, the greater the number of reverberations that will occur.[5] The second wave may begin in our example if the tire or upholstery industries need steel implements or machinery in order to expand production, eventually resulting in a second increase in the demand for steel. (Indeed, steel will probably be an input into its own manufacture.) This, in turn, will be transmitted to suppliers of the steel industry and thence through the system. The third wave could begin when the leather, rubber, or coal industries need more inputs made of steel. Because the economy is an interdependent organism, an initial increase in the final demands for some goods will set off a wave of derived demands for inputs. These input industries will now raise their own derived demands, and, eventually, the widening circle of increased demand will reverberate back and restart the entire cycle. To capture this process, we need a much more sophisticated notion of technology than the one displayed in the direct input–output coefficients.

To be definite, suppose that steel is good 1 and autos good 2. Based upon our discussion above, we may divide the increase in the demand for steel resulting from an increased final use production of automobiles into two parts. The first part consists of the extra steel going *directly* to help make more cars and is captured by the direct technical coefficient, a_{12}. The second part consists of the extra steel that is not needed to make cars directly, but which is generated by the increased production of other inputs into the manufacture of automobiles. We may call this the *indirect* input of steel into auto production. The indirect input is precisely what a_{12} *fails* to capture.

When we add the two increases in steel demand, we can derive a new coefficient, call it b_{12}, whose value will exceed a_{12} whenever there is a positive indirect input requirement. The coefficient b_{12} is the *entire* increase in steel output generated by a unit increase in auto production. Similarly, we get a

<hr/>

[4] Herbert S. Levine, "The Centralized Planning of Supply in the Soviet Union," in F. D. Holzman, ed., *Readings on the Soviet Economy* (Chicago: Rand McNally, 1962), especially footnotes 45 and 46, p. 165. See, as well, the sources cited by Levine.

[5] Ibid.

complete array or matrix of *b* coefficients—one for every *a*—and we label the entire matrix *B*. Such an array, again for China in 1956, appears in Table 8–3. (The reader should compare each entry in this table with its opposite number in Table 8–2.) These are the coefficients which a command-economy planner will need to know in order to compute the total outputs required by a given bill of final-use commodities. They alone summarize the combined impact of an economy's production technology and its structure of commodity flows.

It is also here that the interdependence of an economy takes its computational toll. *B* is, in fact, a function of *A* because the *b* coefficients are determined entirely from the *a*'s. But to compute each *b* coefficient requires a massive number of multiplications and additions, and this number rises both with interdependence and with the number of goods being produced and used up.

Given the computing facilities available to them circa 1970, there is no way that the Soviet planners could have computed the *B* matrix for 1 million commodities with acceptable accuracy. They probably could not have computed the *b* coefficients corresponding to the 20,000 or so centrally planned goods without tying up much of their personnel in several months of solid computation.[6]

Nevertheless, the principal bottleneck is likely to lie in the gathering and processing of necessary information. If one fourth of the entries in an array of 1 million by 1 million intersectoral flows (analogous to Table 8–1) are not zero, the planners must compile data on 250 billion (250,000,000,000) flows. Most goods will be produced by several different enterprises, each operating with a somewhat different technology. Moreover, while the central planners will have a summary vision of the pattern of final-use production which they want, they will not know this in great detail—especially in consumer-goods-producing industries.

Consequently, massive amounts of detailed information must be gathered at local levels and aggregated as they move up the planning hierarchy. Later, millions of aggregated targets would start back down again, and so it would go until the final targets appeared. Such a procedure is presently impractical,

[6] By "centrally planned" goods here we mean those commodities planned for the economy as a whole rather than on a regional basis. The difficulty of computing *B*, given *A* and given no change in the degree to which an economy is interdependent, rises approximately with n^3, where *n* is the number of goods. If it takes three hours to compute *B* for 1,000 goods, it will take more than eight times as long, or more than 24 hours, when the number of goods rises to 2,000 ($2^3 = 8$).

To write *B* in terms of *A*, suppose that *X* is the column of total outputs, *Z* the column of quantities available for intermediate use, and *Y* the column of final-use quantities. We then have the following matrix equation:
$$X = Z + Y \qquad \text{or} \qquad Y = X - Z$$
However, $Z = AX$, so $Y = X - AX = (I - A)\ X$, where *I* is the (n x n) identity matrix.

Therefore, $X = BY$, where $B = (I - A)^{-1}$. That is, *B* as defined in the text, is simply $(I - A)^{-1}$, and it can be shown that this inverse will exist, provided it is possible to produce a set of final-use quantities such that none is less than zero, while at least one is greater than zero. (Otherwise, the economy would be completely unproductive.)

Table 8–3. Direct plus indirect input coefficients, China, 1956.*

	1	2	3	4	5	6	7	8	9	10	11
1	1.08482837	0.08032894	0.01917315	0.11130790	0.11994462	0.04762752	0.07267060	0.40083933	0.12213776	0.14866256	0.57675108
2	0.00099217	1.00092393	0.00299783	0.01509666	0.01721938	0.00623994	0.01026268	0.02066648	0.15547974	0.02210670	0.01252416
3	0.00060638	0.00058335	1.00034381	0.07974325	0.00300694	0.00984652	0.00643979	0.01086139	0.00435963	0.20737894	0.00609993
4	0.00101510	0.00094876	0.00118207	1.24091544	0.01052173	0.01065487	0.01580455	0.01543742	0.01321146	0.03545301	0.01953571
5	0.00699311	0.00659517	0.00993512	0.05694767	2.04676970	0.05298112	0.04395451	0.03790196	0.02887557	0.08825787	0.04207382
6	0.00027835	0.00026124	0.00018704	0.00819959	0.00135512	1.00841789	0.00398060	0.00270453	0.00174238	0.00457891	0.00203226
7	0.00289713	0.00271496	0.00395471	0.02836564	0.02650423	0.01841118	1.12983507	0.03559966	0.02076231	0.08616132	0.06539704
8	0.00220505	0.00206359	0.00040029	0.00825934	0.00304270	0.00264671	0.00420666	1.19679918	0.01261809	0.00904976	0.02262435
9	0.00292861	0.00271745	0.00285048	0.01077243	0.00699609	0.01012183	0.00933481	0.03240084	1.84146767	0.02937759	0.01499793
10	0.00222448	0.00206902	0.00103763	0.02887109	0.00900811	0.00843853	0.01581684	0.04622013	0.01265854	1.18306190	0.01817439
11	0.03341996	0.03169507	0.00305732	0.05300357	0.03490412	0.04795670	0.03366782	0.10927888	0.10351634	0.08052038	1.28746393
12	0.00452821	0.00424979	0.00304277	0.13338772	0.02204457	0.14181923	0.06475486	0.04399628	0.02834439	0.07448798	0.03306011
13	0.00222615	0.00209032	0.00219129	0.04140541	0.02414738	0.06505306	0.02953040	0.05064346	0.01246607	0.02097298	0.03091119
14	0.00311794	0.00166010	0.00060272	0.01837486	0.00208922	0.00337642	0.00373214	0.00584867	0.01376947	0.00736095	0.00550286
15	0.00176375	0.00166010	0.00247393	0.01721293	0.01439053	0.02022250	0.01430224	0.04289691	0.04556950	0.05097851	0.02434159
16	0.00296968	0.00280559	0.00976864	0.05097683	0.05926397	0.01823720	0.03418726	0.06118006	0.04504532	0.06444220	0.04003298
17	0.00002528	0.00002372	0.00002190	0.01849159	0.00018546	0.00018886	0.00028260	0.00051682	0.00031679	0.00172280	0.00036475
18	0.00089309	0.00081601	0.00051563	0.07105255	0.02064829	0.02924447	0.01860399	0.01009049	0.01972348	0.01932721	0.01821869
19	0.00986365	0.00935240	0.00797412	0.08463059	0.01996564	0.02903237	0.02937534	0.08328800	0.04845863	0.13840062	0.05934408
20	0.00537701	0.00509601	0.00101138	0.03192786	0.00897404	0.00906486	0.01364622	0.01639401	0.01769206	0.01265269	0.01829302
21	0.02119974	0.02010894	0.00371214	0.04878272	0.02069173	0.03633037	0.07862216	0.07352021	0.10694276	0.06847630	0.06638770
22	0.00778772	0.00736017	0.03186276	0.15968644	0.19144262	0.05020489	0.10472318	0.18807325	0.1227337	0.20284905	0.11838781

	12	13	14	15	16	17	18	19	20	21	22
1	0.06000096	0.11329945	0.07848584	0.21812990	0.22669005	0.13464452	0.08120310	0.08744093	0.08299234	0.11967554	0.63344953
2	0.00864051	0.01925284	0.01255557	0.11634202	0.04255093	0.02015214	0.01199763	0.01467561	0.01177680	0.01501491	0.09516951
3	0.00778789	0.00553500	0.00715355	0.03607010	0.02115135	0.01788950	0.01837088	0.00663740	0.04589406	0.00482496	0.00866946
4	0.04033370	0.02249697	0.01827333	0.02924249	0.02020940	0.13717093	0.20847974	0.02709201	0.01754222	0.00902683	0.03240223
5	0.04812464	0.04879687	0.04736839	0.08350743	0.06525860	0.10481730	0.03617265	0.26688582	0.07556274	0.02487219	0.02853314
6	0.12049707	0.03238836	0.03610309	0.00402839	0.00379485	0.00454453	0.00483217	0.00508234	0.01825477	0.00199795	0.00273954
7	0.03181251	0.17542240	0.03728751	0.05225713	0.04846818	0.03388194	0.02261216	0.02277058	0.06491395	0.02240677	0.12358360
8	0.00677691	0.00627976	0.00583341	0.01390561	0.01046136	0.00335204	0.00537285	0.00616632	0.00708568	0.04167603	0.00491374
9	0.00629575	0.02230060	0.01595558	0.21585214	0.08532984	0.01208085	0.00830601	0.02642786	0.01677320	0.01351134	0.02741625
10	0.01927077	0.01419537	0.02743030	0.02966782	0.07659082	0.04930161	0.02664960	0.02140648	0.23093185	0.01576730	0.02555918
11	0.02048540	0.02869037	0.03167962	0.19648284	0.22815519	0.03228658	0.02291979	0.02449650	0.04920192	0.04160956	0.08963529
12	1.96019862	0.52688100	0.58731090	0.06553231	0.06173322	0.07392866	0.07860797	0.08267763	0.29696146	0.03250197	0.04456585
13	0.01876120	1.05753419	0.07899498	0.02096061	0.03083930	0.02567673	0.03900136	0.02958854	0.12259664	0.01647379	0.01393311
14	0.00908550	0.00693441	1.21656850	0.00947834	0.01043951	0.00806451	0.01061654	0.03178083	0.02333770	0.02183556	0.00561286
15	0.01247392	0.01793360	0.02724270	1.35598377	0.20284977	0.01878048	0.01218005	0.02113911	0.02562463	0.02241051	0.06120918
16	0.03030364	0.05732640	0.04097877	0.08275914	1.10810536	0.07061034	0.04102969	0.04846362	0.04904241	0.06339916	0.32525039
17	0.00065912	0.00049675	0.00052749	0.00057128	0.00061154	1.00211563	0.00314774	0.00046729	0.00055992	0.00045877	0.00058305
18	0.02943640	0.02927335	0.01704623	0.03974636	0.01959321	0.02505277	1.04060403	0.00827630	0.01528051	0.00438546	0.00953870
19	0.03594700	0.03706535	0.03845868	0.12705784	0.08617346	0.10547707	0.05735690	1.05241844	0.09306175	0.06310353	0.03529876
20	0.01041666	0.01006343	0.01016642	0.02350357	0.02543258	0.11813442	0.01930426	0.02559886	1.01167619	0.02567858	0.01246796
21	0.11572629	0.10726172	0.07091307	0.11946390	0.10629161	0.03647492	0.03797620	0.05100002	0.12102986	1.08855124	0.05232930
22	0.08937781	0.18045660	0.11588648	0.22744594	0.23078573	0.21887308	0.12812703	0.13702138	0.10534822	0.15200316	1.08473235

Source: Haruki Niwa, "An Outline of the Compilation Work on the Input-Output Table for Mainland China (1956)," *Kwansei Gakuin University Annual Studies,* Vol. 18, Dec. 1969.

* Column and row numbers refer to industries in Table 8–1.

largely because the economy's information-gathering and processing facilities would be overwhelmed. Serious errors would creep into compilations of the final-use quantities, of the (aggregated) intersectoral flows, and therefore of the array of direct input–output coefficients. Many of these would be exaggerated further in computing the B matrix of full input–output coefficients.

When we pass from operative to horizon planning and investment decision-making problems, the above difficulties are magnified even further by changing technology over time. Not only will there arise new ways of producing and distributing already-existing commodities, but, probably more important, new products and whole new industries will become candidates for adoption and expansion within the system. We can show the first kind of technical progress on a graph just by shifting out a production or consumption possibility frontier. Thus we are getting more output from fixed amounts of inputs. But to show the second kind we should have to add new dimensions to this frontier.

The way an economy's technology evolves over time will depend upon the investment decisions that the planning hierarchy is currently making, including its research and development programs. As part of its problem of choosing the optimal evolution of final-use quantities (that is, the optimal path of economic development), the EPC must cause the full technology matrix, B, to evolve in the best possible way. On one hand, this means reducing technical coefficients to get more output per unit of input. Perhaps more importantly, however, it means deleting and adding the right columns and rows of B so that the product mix evolves in the optimal way. In any event the planners will have to contemplate a panorama of B matrices—B_1, B_2, B_3, and so forth—over the planning horizon. Each succeeding technology evolves out of the former, and every technical coefficient in each future array is likely to be affected by current decisions.

8–4 Planning in Theory and Planning in Practice

By now the reader will probably not be surprised to learn that the B matrix of full technical coefficients is currently of little practical use, either in long- or short-term plan construction. The costs and time needed to compute such an animal mean that it is only likely to appear on an economy-wide basis once in several years. Moreover, when it appears, it will probably be too outdated for use in planning, and will still apply to fewer than 200 or so highly consolidated commodity groups. (That is, it will apply to steel and textiles rather than to 10- by 30-ft cold-rolled sheets or size 3 overalls.)

The same is true for the complete A matrix, although various rows and columns from it are kept up to date and used in centralized planning.[7] (Cur-

---

[7] Canada has the most advanced intersectoral accounts and input–output tables in the world. Yet the accounts compiled for 1961 comprise only 110 industries and 197 commodities or commodity groups, and did not appear until 1969. As planning tools, these data can, at best, be of indirect use. See Statistics Canada (Government of Canada), *The Input–Output Structure of the Canadian Economy, 1961* (Ottawa: The Queen's Printer, 1969), Vol. II.

rently, about 20,000 commodities are planned centrally in the U.S.S.R., using the materials-balance method to be discussed below.) Consequently, much of our discussion above must be catalogued under "command planning in the future," with "command planning in practice" yet to come. But the retreat from using full technical coefficients represents a setback to the EPC, which must now do without a comprehensive knowledge of the link from total outputs to final demand quantities.

This represents a second step away from computeropia. We would expect it to reinforce any emphasis on production for the sake of production and the consequent deemphasis of use value which the command economy may generate.[8] Historically, the need to do without the B matrix, in both short-term and horizon planning, has helped a number of "simplifications" to creep into command planning process. These simplifications, which have had far-reaching consequences, are as follows:

1. With limited information-gathering and processing capacity, the EPC and its staff agencies will not be able to plan every good and service that is produced. In the U.S.S.R., fewer than 20,000 commodities out of several million have ever been planned centrally. The rest are handled by industrial ministries, by regional authorities, or even locally. Furthermore, at any particular level in the planning hierarchy, it is not unknown for one agency to concern itself with the production of a particular good while another is responsible for allocating it among its various intermediate and final uses.[9]

The upshot is a fragmentation of decision making among different levels and agencies in the planning hierarchy, giving rise to serious problems of coordination and goal harmony between different levels. It is quite possible for an agency to allocate more of a good than is being produced or for a ministry to plan to produce certain inputs for important firms under its jurisdiction when these could be manufactured more efficiently elsewhere.

Because there is no device in a command structure analogous to a market mechanism, decision makers cannot act independently of one another. Instead, the best decision rules or guidelines for any particular actor to use will depend upon what other decision makers are doing. The best way for the EPC to allocate key material inputs among producers will depend upon the allocation of inputs by intermediate authorities and vice versa. Similarly, the planning activities of different ministries will be interdependent and require close

---

[8] However, in the absence of technological change, the planners may automatically gain a reasonably satisfactory approximation to the B matrix over time, just through ordinary supply planning with materials balances. (See the discussion below.) The interested reader should consult Michael Manove, "A Model of Soviet-type Economic Planning," *American Economic Review*, June 1971. Manove assumes a constant technology (that is, a constant A matrix) over time. In these conditions, one could hope that plans would become consistent after three to five years, even with extremely limited computing capacity. However, if technology changes rapidly—particularly, if many new products appear and old ones depart—Manove's conclusions may not hold. In practice, the difficulty of accommodating new commodities has led planning hierarchies to resist this kind of technical change.

[9] See Levine, op. cit.

coordination within some kind of over-all framework. However, both the framework and the coordination are likely to be inadequate.

2. During the planning year the planners are likely to find very little time for optimizing in the sense of choosing among alternative paths of economic development on the basis of the desirability of each. Instead, they are likely to be preoccupied with making the plan consistent. The result will be a tendency to use a fairly rigid formula to derive each year's plan from the preceding one.

3. As we have already indicated, instead of dealing with individual goods, planners from the EPC on down will tend to phrase goals and perform most of their calculations in terms of aggregates. It becomes impossible for them to deal directly with every possible size, shape, style, design, and quality variation of each product. (On this basis, there would not be millions, but billions of "different" goods and services produced in an economy like the Soviet Union.) This tends to shift decision-making authority down the chain of command and also to introduce implicit and explicit "prices" as guides to decision making at both the intermediate and managerial levels.

For example, if firms try to maximize the gross values of their outputs, they will concentrate on goods with the highest official prices. If the manager's paycheck is tied to weight, he will emphasize the heaviest goods and may even increase the weight of his output artificially. In any event, neither prices nor weights reflect the contributions of given goods to social welfare in a command economy. Thus the manager may have an incentive to behave in a way that is quite detrimental to the interests of his superiors.

8–5 Operative Planning and Materials Balances

We have already said that operative planning will tend to focus on "balancing"—or making the yearly plans consistent—rather than on optimizing. In practice, the emphasis of year-to-year planning in Eastern Europe has been almost exclusively on plan consistency. In fact, what optimizing has been done has emerged as a kind of by-product of failures to make over-ambitious plans as consistent in practice as they were in the offices of planning bureaus. The focal point of short-term planning is what the Russians call "material balances." Every orthodox Soviet writer eulogizes materials-balances planning, and we shall begin our discussion by inquiring into it.

Basically, a materials-balance sheet is an accounting statement showing the quantity of any good produced or transacted during a particular period of time. On one side of the ledger, the good is broken down by its sources of supply—production, import, or reduction of inventories. On the other side, it is listed by current use—as an input for further production or for final demand, including export.

We can think of such a statement as a historical record, but materials-balances planning also refers to projecting balances for the year to come. The plan is consistent when the projected supply matches the projected demand for every good. Figure 8–1 shows a materials-balance sheet for a centrally allocated commodity in the U.S.S.R. The symbols in parentheses attempt to relate the various categories of the sheet to our discussion of intersectoral flows above.

Suppose that, in the ordering of things, we find ourselves dealing with "good" 2. This may be a single good, but in the light of paragraph 3 near the end of the last section, it may also be an index of several goods or even the output of an entire industry. The left-hand side of the materials-balance sheet for good 2 will give us all the sources of supply for the product. Adding the amounts from each source, we get the total available supply, X_2. On the right-hand side we list the total uses or total demand for the good. These comprise the amounts destined for intermediate use, broken down by destination, and also the final-use quantities. All in all, we get $x_{21} + x_{22} + \ldots + x_{2n} + Y_2$, which we may rewrite to involve the direct technical coefficients as $a_{21}X_1 + a_{22}X_2 + \ldots + a_{2n}X_n + Y_2$. We next suppose the planners to have found a set of final demand quantities $(Y_1, Y_2, \ldots, Y_n)$ with which they are sufficiently happy that they will finalize the plan, provided it is "consistent."

Consistency here, however, means nothing more nor less than paper equality between total supply and total demand for every good. It means that the two sides of every materials-balance sheet will, in fact, balance. At this stage the EPC is only preparing to send production targets to the producing sector. Consistency has nothing to do with whether the system can actually produce the quantities $(X_1, X_2, \ldots, X_n)$ that may be ordered, and we would expect further adjustments later based on the responses of the producing sector to these commands. If the EPC had the full B matrix at its disposal, it could compute the total output targets (the X's) directly from the final-use quantities (the Y's) as in the last section and the plan would automatically be consistent.[10]

However, if full technical coefficients are not available, it is quite possible that supply and demand will be out of balance for a number of goods when the plan is first drawn up. Normally, we would expect command-economy planners to compose an overambitious first draft in which demand often exceeds supply. (In other words, the right-hand sides of many materials-balances sheets will be greater than the left-hand sides.) If this is true for good 2, for example, the plan will not work in its present form even if producers can make the target output (X_2 units) available. There simply will not be enough of the good to go around among its various intermediate and final uses.

In a market economy the initial excess demand for good 2 would cause its price to rise. Decentralized decision makers would respond by supplying more and buying less of it, thereby returning the market to equilibrium (assuming the market mechanism to be working smoothly). At the same time, they would

[10] Recall that $X = BY$ (see footnote 6).

demand less and supply more of goods complementary to good 2, while buying more and supplying less of substitutes for 2. This will trigger a complex reaction in prices and quantities of other goods.

However, if prices remain reasonably close to their equilibrium levels—so that they accurately signal the values of each input and output for all producers and consumers—the structure of independent decision makers will respond accurately. Within a command economy, the planners must duplicate at least a part of the chain reaction by manipulating quantities directly (again on paper) to achieve a balance.

To trace this through, suppose, at first, that no changes are contemplated in the direct technical coefficients or in the final-use quantities. If the quantity of machine tools supplied is X_s (say 9 million units) while the amount demanded in all uses is X_d (say, 10 million units) we might guess that the planners could achieve a paper balance simply by raising supplies or lowering demands by the amount of the discrepancy (here 1 million units). This is wrong. If we cut the demand by 1 million units, it will become impossible for some firms who are scheduled to receive machine tools to meet their delivery quotas. Therefore, a second set of industries is left short, and a wave of input shortages has begun to spread through the system. Eventually, this will reverberate back to affect the machine-tool industry itself, and force it to cut back production, setting off a second round of shortages among users. On the other hand, if we raise the supply of machine tools by 1 million units, the machine-tool industry will use more inputs, eventually forcing cutbacks in other areas. Again, several waves of shortages will chain-react through the economy.

The situation we are describing here is exactly analogous to that depicted in the last section. We can only correct an imbalance between planned supply and demand completely by taking account of both the direct and indirect technical coefficients. In short, we must derive the necessary corrections by using the matrix, B, of full input–output coefficients which earlier enabled us to derive the total outputs corresponding to a particular collection of final demands. Ironically, if the planners had this matrix, the problem of plan inconsistency would not have arisen in the first place.[11]

Consequently, the planners will sometimes balance the plan partly by changing either its technology or its bill of final-use quantities, including changes in inventory. In the former case, they can "tighten" the plan by lowering direct technical coefficients in an effort to get more output per unit of material input. Alternatively, they can try to provide more labor by increasing overtime and labor-force participation.

However, in a market economy, unforeseen increases in demand are met not only by increasing production and prices, but, in the very short run, by letting inventories temporarily run down below optimal levels. To an extent, the same procedure applies here. Referring to Table 8–4, these are actually two

[11] Levine, op. cit., p. 165, ftn. 45.

Table 8–4. Materials-balance sheet.

Sources (X_2) *	Uses
1. Production, broken down by major industrial complexes	1. Current production and construction needs, broken down by industrial complexes using the good as an input $(x_{21} + x_{22} + x_{23} + \ldots + x_{2n})$
2. Imports	2. Export
3. Reduction of inventories in hands of suppliers	3. Current consumption ⎫
	4. Increase in inventories ⎬ Y_2
4. Reduction in reserves and other sources	of suppliers
	5. Increase in reserves ⎭

Source: Herbert S. Levine, "The Centralized Planning of Supply in Soviet Industry," in F. D. Holzman, ed., *Readings on the Soviet Economy* (Chicago: Rand McNally, 1962), Pt. V, Ch. 2.
* X_2 (supply) $= Y_2 + x_{21} + x_{22} + \ldots + x_{2n}$ (demand).

kinds of inventories—one in the hands of producers and the other held in reserve by the government. Although the latter may be more in the nature of "reserves for contingencies," they can be varied somewhat from year to year, and it is entirely possible that specific shortages can be at least partly met from them.

Nevertheless, both reserves and inventories will play a primarily shock-absorber role. The EPC cannot go on drawing them down year after year. Similarly, labor input can sometimes be stepped up above previously planned levels to cut down on waste or increase the tempo of production and construction. The planned rate of introduction of new technology can also be speeded up on occasion. But, again, these are not measured that the EPC can take year after year or rely upon every time an inconsistency arises.

If we are going to reduce available quantities in some other area of final demand, the natural thing to do is to take a close look at priorities. If consumer goods rank relatively low on the list of a growth-oriented EPC, cutbacks may well occur here. Households can be made to bear the brunt of shortages in coal, electricity, and other forms of fuel and power or in certain kinds of spare parts. A crucial assumption, however, is that such shortages will not decrease the motive to work hard or to do the kinds of work the planners need done.

There is also a short- versus long-run problem here. An individual's first reaction to unrealized aspirations may actually be to work harder and more obediently. But a continued failure to achieve consumption goals is likely to result in frustrations and reduced productive effort or even hostility. It may still pay a planner to cut final demands for household use, even if he has to resort to coercion in consequence. But the link between the availability of consumer goods and the supply of labor can scarcely be ignored.

Of course, some goods have very little household use, and in these cases the planners may have no choice but to correct imbalances by reducing direct technical coefficients. They can still apply the spirit of the preceding paragraph, however. Suppose that there is a shortage of machine tools of a type that finds little use around the home. They may still serve as inputs for low-priority industries, and the idea would be to reduce the allotment for these sectors or to make part of it contingent upon the machine-tool industry exceeding its production targets. If these low-priority sectors actually produce more efficiently than foreseen, they might achieve their own targets with fewer machine-tool inputs. But the best managerial resources will also be concentrated in high-priority sectors, so we would rather expect to find some low-priority targets being underfulfilled.

This can be viewed as a price to pay for plan inconsistency, but it also represents the kind of optimizing that we associate with materials-balance supply planning. The idea is to make an overly ambitious plan, then retreat from these targets, if need be, by starving the low-priority sectors. It is a dangerous game because when a few sectors fail to achieve their targets, a shock wave may reverberate through the economy and affect high-priority sectors indirectly. The EPC has the job of confining any shock waves to low-priority firms by continually ensuring that high-priority producers get the inputs they need. The same is true once the plan gets under way. The effective EPC will shunt all unexpected shortages into low-priority areas and prevent bottlenecks from interfering with production elsewhere.

This is to no small extent the art of command-economy planning in the short run. In what appears to be an example, the Soviets in 1966 set a 1970 production goal of 750,000 automobiles. By early 1970, this target had been revised downward to less than half that number. Many other goals of this five-year plan (1966–1970) were not met. However, the over-all plan for industrial production was fulfilled, suggesting a spectacularly above-plan performance in defense-oriented industries.

The planners will also adjust technical coefficients, of both high- and low-priority firms, in a genuine effort to make the economy more efficient by setting high standards for managers. Loosely speaking, more efficient production means more output per unit of input or lower values for the entries in B. Consequently, some aspects of technical progress will show up as declining b coefficients over time. Since B is not computed often enough, we shall have to substitute A. Let us recall that a_{11} is the amount of good 1 used up directly in producing a unit of itself, a_{21} is the amount of good 2 used up in producing a unit of 1, and so on down to a_{n1}. The column of fractions

$$a_{11}$$
$$a_{21}$$
$$.$$
$$.$$
$$.$$
$$a_{n1}$$

will describe the technology for sector 1. If we look back to Table 8–2 or 8–3, the first column gives the technology for industry 1, the second for industry 2, and so on. When we put all industries side by side we get the complete matrix, A or B.

A common goal in any nation or region planning with input–output data is to continually align the entire economy on the most efficient producers. When one firm has technical coefficients that are lower than most others it is held up as an example for all to follow. Beyond any medals or monetary rewards that its directors or workers may receive, it will pay the EPC to spread information about efficient production methods to less efficient producers. It will also pay the planners to impose lower target coefficients upon these firms after a "sufficient" time period has elapsed. Remembering that managers can be heavily penalized in a command economy for using more input or producing less output than the plan calls for, this can be viewed as the stick to spur the spread of technology.

The carrot might then come in the form of a plan to let producers who adopt new methods soon enough operate for a time under the old production targets and keep the substantial rewards that result. The EPC can also vary its incentive program to systematically compensate for the expected tightness of the forthcoming plan. Finally, if successful, such measures can be tied in with a "model-firms" program which seeks to develop and try out new techniques in enterprises under especially close supervision by the planning bureaucracy.

Beyond this, we have to view the input–output coefficients in any plan as subjects of an ongoing game of strategy and bluff between planners and producers. It is often said that a major advantage of planning with materials balances is that it requires constant negotiation between planners and producers (and between higher- and lower-level planners) and thus keeps the channels of communication open between decision-making levels within the planning hierarchy. Consequently, decision makers are prevented from operating in individual ivory towers isolated from economic reality.

Even if a magic computer capable of programming an economy of any complexity in minute detail were suddenly to appear one day, we would not want to do away with this dialogue. For the computer could not give a better solution than the data on which it is based. In a command economy, most of this information comes from lower level decision makers and is nonoperational. While this will never be entirely reliable, constant negotiating and compromising can help to keep things in check.

But if the bargaining between planners and producers is to yield useful feedback information, the former must constantly challenge the latter with plan targets that are difficult but not impossible to meet. The reaction of managers to expected plan tightening will be to try to hoard inputs. That is, they will seek to build themselves a safety reserve of labor, production capacity, and other inputs beyond what is needed to meet production targets.

Ironically, therefore, when managers get the best of bargaining with planners, the very phenomena which these negotiations are designed to prevent will flourish, leading to excessive input inventories, inflated factory payrolls, and excess capacity. In trying to get more productive effort out of the system, the EPC may actually cut down on its ability to produce and grow.[12] It follows that managers need additional incentives to get the most efficient use out of scarce resources which have been overcommitted to development or growth. Later, we shall see what forms these incentives can take.

For now, we note that additional problems arise because materials balances often do not provide a good negotiating format. It would be better to compute the full technical coefficients, even if we could only break the economy down into 1,000 or so commodity groups, and bargain over these. For not only does materials balancing rely on direct rather than full technical coefficients, it also misplaces the emphasis of planning. In effect, it focuses upon the *rows* of an input–output table rather than the columns.

We have seen that each column in Table 8–2 or 8–3 describes the technology of a particular sector of the economy. Each column gives the (direct or full) amounts of all inputs per unit of that sector's output. If one entry in a particular column is changed, several others should normally be altered at the same time. The firm is being told, in effect, to change its method of production. On a per-unit-of-output basis, the second-best technology would probably require increases in some inputs, which are substitutes for the one originally cut back, along with decreases in others. Still others would remain unchanged.

But this, in turn, would have a complex effect upon the rest of the system which the planners are unable to evaluate without the full technical coefficients. Indeed, because planning is fragmented, with the EPC balancing some inputs and various intermediate officials balancing others, no planning authority will have a comprehensive view of either the direct or indirect technologies of most firms or industries. Just as each sector's technology is detailed by the column of an input–output table, so the rows give the supply and demand for each sector's outputs. It is here, therefore, that materials-balances planning concentrates.

The result is a piecemeal approach in which direct technical coefficients are altered to make the plan consistent, while too little attention is given to the consequences of these changes on the over-all technologies of industries and firms. Such an approach will work to the extent that the EPC imposes upon managers whenever they are hoarding inputs or otherwise using them less efficiently than they could. However, to the extent that managers are forced to cut back on inputs where no slack exists, they are likely to be forced into using less efficient production methods.

This suggests that we attempt to switch from materials balancing to the input–output planning described earlier, where required total output targets are computed directly from desired final output quantities using the full input–output coefficients. Neither method resembles the full computer-opia model

---

[12] This point has been made by Robert W. Campbell. See his "Economic Reform in the U.S.S.R.," *American Economic Review,* May 1968, especially pp. 556–558.

with its unimaginable number of simultaneous equations. Furthermore, because it leaves the optimizing to be hammered out in bargaining between planners and producers, the switch to input–output planning should eventually be aided by the current revolution in computers, information storage, and transmitting capacity.

If a decentralization is infeasible or undesirable to the EPC, the best alternative route may lie in the direction of a more computerized, and more efficient, dialogue between different decision-making levels. But computers can also replace bureaucrats, leading us to expect some resistance to or subversion of this kind of change as well.[13]

8–6   The Problems of Investment Decision Making and Growth

Let us return to horizon planning and investment-decision-making problems. The value of natural resources and intermediate goods always depends partly on their marginal productivities in making other goods. An EPC cannot assign the proper priority to steel production without knowing how useful steel is as an input into automobiles, bridges, cranes, and literally thousands of other items. It must also know how productive cranes and bridges are; indeed, one can use cranes to make bridges, further complicating the picture.

Generally speaking, the whole question of assigning priorities to goods used to make other goods cannot be divorced from an understanding of the interdependency of the economy. In this connection it may be helpful to make a conceptual division of the production and distribution tasks facing a command-economy EPC into two categories.

On one hand, the planners must keep the existing plant and equipment operating smoothly at the optimal tempo and combined optimally with other inputs to produce the best combination of outputs. But they must also continually alter and expand the capital stock, often to produce new goods in new ways. Normally, the number of investment projects that could conceivably be undertaken in any year will vastly exceed the number that actually get under way. Somehow, the planners must choose, and their goal will be to select those yielding the most social welfare over the long run. To better grasp this problem, let us pursue the analogy in a market economy.

A Western corporate management serving the sole interests of its stockholders should undertake only those projects that will add the most to owners'

---

[13] Thus in the Soviet Union the expansion of computing equipment has sometimes gone hand in hand with a simultaneous increase in the personnel that such equipment was supposed to replace. For a complaint, see *Current Digest of the Soviet Press,* Mar. 31, 1970, p. 5. According to this source, the "staffs of managerial agencies" (apparently at the intermediate and enterprise levels of the planning hierarchy) grew from a total of 1,460,000 in 1965 to 1,749,000 in 1968.

One can see a possible double motive in this. First, officials have the short-run objective of keeping their jobs and expanding their jurisdiction (see the discussion of bureaucracy below). In the long run they would hope to convince higher-ups that the social return from computerizing their jobs is low.

welfare. This will be measured by the per share value of the firm, and the management should undertake an investment project when and only when the enterprise's per share value goes up in consequence.

But the per share value of a corporation is measured by its long-run profitability. Therefore, a proposed capital expenditure must be expected to raise the firm's long-run revenues by at least as much as its long-run costs. The difference between the two, divided by long-run cost and put on an annual basis, is the expected (percentage) yield of the investment. A new plant initially costing $100 million which is then expected to raise annual profits by $8 million on the average over the relevant future has a yield of 8 per cent.[14]

Naturally enough, corporations will prefer projects with higher expected yields, but they will also pay attention to the risk that these yields might fail to materialize. Any investment project can fail to live up to expectations, and, by the same token, it may perform beyond what had been hoped for. By and large, firms will examine expected yields, riskiness, and third factors, not always wholly economic in nature, before ranking investment proposals according to their attractiveness. The cutoff point for acceptance is then determined by the cost of raising finance. When the expected yield from a project, with allowance for risk and third factors, exceeds the cost of financing, the project is deemed "profitable" and given a green light. Otherwise, it is delayed or forgotten altogether.

When money for capital spending is raised by borrowing, the interest rate paid on the loan constitutes at least part of the financing costs. Likewise, when the firm sells more stock, the financing costs will include the increased dividend burden on future profits plus any decrease in the price of the stocks occasioned by the increase in supply. Even when the money for investment comes directly out of the firm's own profits, financing costs will not be zero. For the management could purchase bonds with the same money or pay it out to stockholders. The "opportunity cost" of investing in any particular project is never zero. It always reflects the yield from the best alternative use of funds.

The above ideas carry over fairly directly into a planned market economy, whether capitalist or socialist. The planners would want to see those projects undertaken which have the highest social yields. It is crucial, therefore, that prices be rational—that they reflect the interaction between social preferences and the economy's consumption-possibility frontier. Otherwise, the cost and revenues that go into the calculation of investment yields will not indicate the

---

[14] Under certain assumptions, the project would be expected to require about $12\frac{1}{2}$ years to return the company its $100 million cost price. We therefore speak of an expected "payoff" or "payback" period of $12\frac{1}{2}$ years to go with the 8 per cent yield. A dollar invested at a yield of 8 percent or 8 cents, on the average, each year will just be entirely returned over a $12\frac{1}{2}$-year period.

Generally speaking, the payoff period times the yield equals 1. Thus we can associate a unique average yield with each payoff period, one being the reciprocal of the other. However, yields may vary considerably from year to year, and this can affect the desirability of a particular investment project. The payoff period does not reflect this variability. Thus it is not always a satisfactory measure of a project's profitability.

"true" sacrifices and benefits that an investment and its associated act of saving require. The calculated yield will not be the true one, and, as a result, society will undertake some projects with lower true yields than other projects, which are rejected. It will build steel mills, for example, when it should construct aluminum factories, cement plants, and textile mills. The average yield realized over all its investment projects will be correspondingly reduced.

Switching back to a command economy, suppose, for the moment, that no monetary investment yields are computed. The planners must nevertheless evaluate capital projects in order to determine an optimal investment strategy. The only procedure left open to them is to try to directly compare the physical consequences of all possible investment projects without using a common denominator of value in the process.

In some cases this will prove to be quite manageable. Much of the growth history of the Soviet economy during the 1930s revolved around a number of key industries or "leading links," such as steel, coal, and electric power, and machine tools. A basic decision was made to develop these as a prerequisite to industrialization, and one can easily defend the grand strategy that the Soviets followed.

Moreover, the process of industrial development continually creates bottlenecks as the capacities of different industries get out of line with one another and make synchronization of various production processes difficult. Either too much or not enough of one input is produced relative to others, or else industries that use the input have too little or too much capacity to absorb the quantities of it that can be made available. In order for development to proceed, the bottlenecks must be eliminated, and a high priority can be attached to this without making elaborate "payoff" calculations. However, the very process of eliminating bottlenecks will often create new ones.

Nevertheless, the above criteria will provide partial, but rarely complete and unique answers to questions about how much to invest in each sector of the economy, how much of each specific capital good to produce, and what methods of production to use.

Thus, whatever the merits of the Soviet grand design for industrialization, many of their specific tactics appear to have been irrational. For example, high-priority sectors often used too much capital and too little labor in production, while other areas of the economy were forced to do just the opposite. Often, the wrong mix of capital goods was used.[15] In addition, factories were sometimes planned or maintained too large or too small to operate at the peak

---

[15] For example, one author estimated that, with a "proper" network of highways, the Russian Republic could have moved all its truck freight in 1966 with 500,000 fewer trucks. The implication is that it would have been more efficient to build fewer trucks and more roadway, but without rational prices, no one really knows for sure. See V. Zaluzhny, "Highway Construction and a Developing Economy," *Voprosy Ekonomiki,* Jan. 1968. The classic article on Soviet investment decision making is Gregory Grossman, "Scarce Capital and Soviet Doctrine," *Quarterly Journal of Economics,* Aug. 1953; reprinted in Holzman, op. cit., Pt. II, Ch. 3, and Wayne Leeman, ed., *Capitalism, Market Socialism, and Central Planning* (Boston: Houghton, 1963), Ch. 13.

of efficiency.[16] It seems fairly clear that their methods of depreciation were unsound and that their decisions about when to repair and when to replace were often questionable.[17] Machines were frequently neglected or run too intensively, so that they wore out before they should have. Shortages of spare parts were (and are) commonplace and the unsuitability of equipment, notably farm implements, to the specific tasks which they were called upon to perform was also more prevalent than it probably would have been in a market economy.

On ideological grounds, rent and interest charges have at least until recently been far too low so that planners and managers figuring on this basis were always demanding more investment credits than were available. For the same reason, the volume of unfinished projects has generally been much too high. Historically, the capital tied up in this way has often been as high as 70 to 75 per cent of total investment, and by 1970 was quite likely greater than this.[18]

In a market economy, the firm that drags out an investment project has money tied up in it. If these funds are borrowed, it must pay interest charges on them. If they are internal funds (from the company's retained earnings) the firm foregoes the earnings it could get by completing the project and investing the funds elsewhere. The heavy volume of unfinished projects in the U.S.S.R. indicates that managers did not have to pay the entire opportunity cost to society of the resources that were thereby immobilized. This cost should appear in the form of rent and interest charges to finance the projects in question.

Finally, we pointed out earlier that managers would try to hoard inputs in order to build a safety margin into their ability to meet plan targets. The government effectively raises the incentive to board—and defeats its own purposes—by not reducing the paychecks of managers who accumulate inventories and production capacity or who fail to complete capital-spending projects on time. One way to penalize these managers is to raise interest and rent charges while tying managerial incomes to the profits earned by their enterprises. The problem, in other words, is partly one of managerial success indicators, to which we shall return in Chapter 9.

---

[16] See *Current Digest of the Soviet Press,* Jan. 27, 1970, pp. 19–20. Also, M. Gardner Clark, *The Economics of Soviet Steel* (Cambridge, Mass.: Harvard U.P. 1956), Pt. 2.

[17] R. W. Campbell, *Accounting in Soviet Planning and Management* (Cambridge, Mass.: Harvard U.P., 1963), especially Ch. 11.

[18] See Harry Schwartz, *The Soviet Economy Since Stalin* (New York: Prentice-Hall, 1965), especially p. 136; and Scot Butler, "The Soviet Capital Investment Program," in U.S. Congress, Joint Economic Committee, *Economic Performance and the Military Burden in the Soviet Union* (Washington, D.C.: G.P.O., 1970), p. 44. For Soviet comments on investment decision-making problems, see, for example, the *Current Digest of the Soviet Press,* Feb. 25, 1970, p. 28; and Ya. Varentsov, "How Much Do Imperfections Cost?" (letter to the editor), *Komsomolskaya Pravda,* Apr. 25, 1968, p. 2. See also *Current Digest of the Soviet Press,* May 12, 1970, p. 19; July 14, 1970, p. 23; July 21, 1970, pp. 26, 28, July 28, 1970, pp. 5–6, 9–10.

When the Soviets launched their grand design for industrialization during the late 1970s, it definitely represented a radical restructuring of priorities. But once in motion, the industrialization drive tended to develop an inertia and an inner logic of its own. The economy got into a rut of doing more of the same—in particular, of expanding the same old heavy industries without really considering alternative uses of investment funds. As one Soviet economist put it.: "Literally everything is anticipated in these blueprints [of a Soviet steel mill], the emplacement of each nail, lamp, or washstand. Only one aspect of the project is not considered at all: its economic effectiveness." [19]

In other words, the only thing that remains unknown about the steel mill is whether it should have been built and, if so, what its capacity should have been, given the alternative uses of the resources involved.

Unless yields are calculated (as in our example above), a comparison of investment alternatives becomes staggering beyond all imagination. Literally millions of uncertain, dissimilar, and multidimensional physical flows—the outputs or yields in physical terms of proposed capital projects—would have to be evaluated over at least five-to-ten year planning horizons. Direct comparisons will be especially difficult to make in four crucial areas:

1. Where capital goods are useful in making other capital goods, themselves at least one or two stages removed from any final use.
2. When competing projects are in diverse sectors of the economy.
3. Where completely new products and production and distribution methods are proposed that do not readily compare with those in current use.
4. In other areas where uncertainty and other intangible factors often play a major role—for example, in research and development.

In fact, the mere cataloguing of alternative investment projects may become a virtually impossible task, without any thought given to comparing and choosing among them. The need to compare will therefore almost inevitably give rise to computation of investment yield or payback periods. Most command economies have evolved toward using such yardsticks on an increasingly comprehensive basis.

Unfortunately this is not likely to solve the problem completely. Because a command economy operates without a rational price system, it lacks the basis for computing "true" investment yields. An increasing need for more rational prices will create pressure for more decentralized decision making. It is in such a fashion that a command economy which is successful year after year in generating rapid growth will eventually begin to create the conditions for its own demise.

As the system complexifies and the most obvious high-yielding investment opportunities disappear, the EPC will find it increasingly difficult to keep the over-all yield on investment high without rational prices to rank the available

[19] Smolinski, op. cit., p. 331.

alternatives by. In the U.S.S.R., the average yield on investments began falling, at least by the late 1950s and apparently has continued along a long-run downward path ever since. To compensate for this, the planners began raising the total volume of investment. (That is, they tried to maintain the growth rate by investing more rubles when the additional future output generated by each invested ruble declined.) From around 20 to 24 per cent in 1951–1955, the investment share of GNP reached 30 per cent in 1958–1961. It has continued to rise and is now probably more than one third.[20]

Nevertheless, this has, at best, kept the Soviet growth rate from declining very much below the levels achieved during the early 1950s. It is quite possible that the declining efficiency of investment played a role in Khrushchev's ouster in 1964 and subsequent measures aimed at decentralization. These have since proved somewhat abortive.

And yet the basic task of planning *is* changing. In the early period of industrialization, the crucial job of the planners is to reorient the economy. It may be fairly obvious in which broad areas investment must be concentrated to earn the highest yields and from whose earnings the necessary savings will have to be generated. Similarly, it may not be difficult to discover what basic resource shifts are necessary. The charisma, exuberance, and potential of a command economy for naked harshness may be decisive in launching an industrialization drive.

But once the drive is well under way, it grows increasingly necessary to be able to discover and compare long-run investment alternatives fairly precisely. There will be a continual need to change directions, often in subtle ways, as the system evolves.

For example, the U.S.S.R. continued to strongly emphasize the traditional heavy industries, such as steel, machine tools, metallurgy, mining, electric power generation, and defense during the late 1950s and early 1960s. Her leaders would probably have been better off allocating more investment and research funds to plastics, petrochemicals, electronics, peaceful uses of atomic energy, housing and other consumer durables, and, not least, data-processing equipment, including computers. (This, in particular, would have made planning more efficient.) By so doing, they might have avoided the semicrisis in the middle 1960s when the marginal productivity of investments temporarily fell nearly to zero and the heavy industrial sector was consuming most of its own output.[21]

[20] Of course, the yield on investments has not fallen in every single year, but the long-run trend appears to be distinctly downward. See Richard Moorsteen and Raymond Powell, *The Soviet Capital Stock* (Homewood, Ill.: Irwin, 1966), Pt. II, and the *Supplement* to this volume put out by the Yale University Economic Growth Center in 1968. See, as well, U.S. Congress, Joint Economic Committee, *Economic Performance and the Military Burden in the Soviet Union* (Washington, D.C.: G.P.O., 1970), pp. 9–17, 43–53. Finally, see T. S. Khachaturov, "The Economic Effectiveness of Capital Investments," *Problems of Economics*, Sept. 1967.

[21] See footnote 3. There are numerous discussions of what might be called "problems of centralized decision making" in the Soviet press. See, for example, the *Current Digest of the Soviet Press*, Apr. 28 and July 21, 1970, p. 17 and p. 29, respectively.

As investment alternatives become more difficult to compare, the EPC will have some incentive to reorient toward markets and prices. Two potential countervailing forces may offset this, however. [The center may fear that any decentralization of decision-making risks eroding its power base.] The intermediate planners will share these fears, and the jobs of many of their subordinates will be threatened by the reduced demand for supervisors which the increase in horizontal links between producers implies. Ideological considerations may then bolster any resistance to which these factors give rise. We shall have a final word on this subject in Chapter 10.

Chapter **9**

The Problem
of Success Indicators

Our top management likes to make all the major decisions. They think they do, but I've just seen one case where a division beat them.

I received for editing a request from the division for a large chimney. I couldn't see what anyone could do with just a chimney, so I flew out for a visit. They've built and equipped a whole plant on expense orders. The chimney is the only indivisible item that exceeded the $50,000 limit we put on the expense orders.

Apparently, they learned informally that a new plant wouldn't be favorably received, so they built the damn thing. . . .

Quoted by **Joseph L. Bower**

9–1   Incentives and Interaction Between Planners and Producers[1]

A now-classic cartoon in *Krokodil,* the Soviet humor magazine, once showed a factory fulfilling its output target for nails by making one gigantic

---

[1] The first section relies heavily on the following papers: Joseph Berliner, "Innovation and Economic Structure in Soviet Industry," unpublished paper delivered at American Economic Association meetings, New York, Dec. 30, 1969. Schumpei Kumon, "A Contribution to the Theory of a Command Economy," unpublished paper delivered to the Workshop on Economic Organization and Development, Ottawa, Carleton University, Feb. 1970. See also M. Iwata and S. Kumon, "A Reconsideration of the Centralized System of Management," *Shiso,* Sept. 1969. Alec Nove, "The Problem of 'Success Indicators' in Soviet Industry," *Economica,* Feb. 1958, reprinted in F. D. Holzman, ed., *Readings on the Soviet Economy* (Chicago: Rand McNally, 1962); *The Soviet Economy* (London: G. Allen, 1968), pp. 171–186.

nail hanging from an overhead crane all the way from one end of the shop to the other. The firm's quota was phrased in tons, and the bonuses of the manager, along with numerous other employees, depending upon how heavy its output was. The fact that no one could use such a nail—and that valuable resources were therefore squandered—became of secondary importance in the circumstances. Weight was the enterprise's "success indicator," and the firm was rational, in the micro sense, to maximize the weight of its output even though its behavior was socially irrational.[2]

In Chapter 2, we saw that command-economy planners have two basic ways of supervising their subordinates. In some countries—notably China and Romania—an effort is made to subjectively evaluate managerial performance and to issue rewards on this basis. But for one reason or another, most command economies, including the U.S.S.R., find this method infeasible or undesirable. These countries—the ones that will interest us in the present chapter —use the success-indicator system. According to this, the input and output targets that characterize all command economies become standards for determining managerial salaries and promotion potential.

However, because command-economy planners cannot specify every size, style, design, and quality of each individual input and output for every producer, the latter's targets will usually be aggregated to some extent. The upshot is that managers gain some freedom to decide what and how to produce, and this freedom is increased by the costs of monitoring managerial performance.

The need to aggregate plan targets also implies the use of common denominators in which goods must be measured before they can be added together. Sometimes physical measures such as weight, length, height, area, or volume will do, but when goods are less similar, their monetary value must be used. In each case the common denominator becomes both a "success indicator" and a decision variable for the recipient of plan targets, who is rewarded for fulfilling them and punished for failing to meet them.

To illustrate the impact of this on managerial decision making, consider the following case history from a recent issue of *Pravda,* the Communist Party newspaper in the Soviet Union. A producer of metal pipe, call it firm *X,* received an order for 115 kilometers (about 72 miles) of pipe to be delivered to Leningrad Province during 1970. According to user's specifications, the pipe was to have a diameter of 325 millimeters and its walls were to be 8 millimeters thick. The estimated weight in these dimensions was 7,200 tons.

As it happened, firm *X*'s plan target was also phrased in tons. Soon after receiving the order through channels, firm *X* gave notice that it could only deliver pipe with walls 1 millimeter thicker. When the 7,200 tons was delivered, it was found to be more than 8 miles too short! The customer then

---

[2] Discussions of behavior that is microrational but socially irrational are legion in the U.S.S.R. The following from the *Current Digest of the Soviet Press,* are representative: Mar. 30, 1966, pp. 3–5; July 24, 1968, p. 27; Aug. 7, 1968, p. 14; Nov. 20, 1968, pp. 5–6; Dec. 11, 1968, p. 24; Aug. 13, 1969, p. 30; Aug. 20, 1969, p. 16; Feb. 24, 1970, p. 6; May 5, 1970, p. 5.

appealed for an order to firm X to provide the extra length of pipe—some 313 tons worth with the thick walls. Speculating that this appeal would be granted in the normal course of events, *Pravda* asked, "Who stands to gain from this?"

The management of firm X would be delighted because the additional production counts toward plan overfulfillment. Indeed, ". . . because it is easier to make thick-walled than thin-walled pipe, labor productivity in terms of tonnage will rise at the plant; the volume of sales and of profits will increase. Ultimately, the plant will receive larger allocations for its incentive funds . . . ." In this case users would also gain.

> By laying . . . pipe worth a larger sum of money, they will overfulfill the plan for construction and installation work. . . . Their labor productivity will also increase. . . . The railroad workers will not be injured either. The transportation of those tons is not planned, and this means it is above the plan. . . .
>
> But after all, it is impossible that everyone will gain from this obvious managerial slip. Someone has to lose. The loser is the state! As well as some other enterprise or construction project, which will be deprived of the aforementioned 313 tons of steel—a quantity sufficient to make 150 tractors, for instance. . . .[3]

When a pipe factory receives its output targets in tons, and the manager's salary depends upon plan performance, the relative weights of different kinds of pipe become "prices" that guide the manager in his production decisions. He will therefore have an incentive to concentrate on the heaviest items in an assortment and to design new products whose only "virtue" may be that they are heavier than the old.

Any common denominator contains such an implicit set of price guides. If a collective farm is commanded to increase its "output" and output is measured in rubles—the relative procurement prices of peas, carrots, corn, and potatoes will influence its production plans. If a firm receives its labor-input norms in value terms, its methods of production will depend upon relative wage rates for different kinds of labor. The same is true for material inputs and for human vis-à-vis material inputs if some of the latter are purchased outside the state sector or if the currency and credit accounts are not kept separate. Unfortunately, neither the weight of a good nor its length nor its price in a command economy is likely to give an accurate index of its value to users or planners. Official prices and wages will usually not even balance supply and demand.

Historically, the reactions of command economies to this phenomenon have been basically twofold. First, upon the failure of one set of success indicators, the planners have simply introduced another. This did not solve the basic problem, however, because the implicit price weights were generally no more rational in the second case than in the first.

Regarding the Soviet economy, Nove writes that

---

[3] *Pravda,* June 29, 1970, p. 2. Parts of the article are reprinted in the *Current Digest of the Soviet Press,* July, 28, 1970, pp. 7, 52.

Cloth was measured in linear metres for many years, with the result that it was made narrower than was desirable from other points of view. Consequently, from 1959 the basis was changed to square metres. But this is . . . [not] . . . always satisfactory since other desirata tend to be sacrificed . . . for instance, quality or workmanship. Roofing metal which was too heavy when the plan was in tons becomes too thin when the plan is in square metres. If a plan for nails was expressed in quantity . . . they would tend to be too small, if in tons they would be too large. . . .[4]

Similarly, when firms are asked to maximize the gross value of current output (historically the predominant target) they respond, in part, by maximizing the value of inputs used, including labor, upon which output valuation is based. When the bonus depends upon value added, firms tend to turn out some of their own inputs, which could be more efficiently produced elsewhere. If the situation becomes serious enough, the "wild-goose chase" will be broken by direct central pressure. For the firm this will mean some combination of more detailed plan targets, more interference in the firm's internal affairs by higher authorities, and more direct enforcement of the plan.

We shall later encounter a form of market planning in which the EPC tries to balance the supply and demand for each good by manipulating prices. The basic rule is to raise the prices of goods in short supply (so as to encourage production and reduce demand) while lowering prices of goods in surplus. With luck and good management, the EPC may succeed in getting most prices close to their equilibrium values, provided it builds some flexibility into the operation and does not try to manipulate too many prices at the same time.

But suppose that the planners decided to adjust prices with scarcely any reference to shortages and surpluses. Only by good fortune would their quest for a balance between supply and demand ever be fulfilled. Yet this is, in effect, just what command-economy planners have done by changing success indicators since the latter contain implicit price tags.

The second reaction to performance deemed "poor" by superior authorities in a command economy has been to question the loyalty of the manager involved or his dedication to the goals and ideals of the regime. It will be worth our while to spend a few moments examining this phenomenon.

9–2   Planners and Magicians

In a famous short story, an old man receives a monkey's paw and is told that it will grant him three wishes. At the same time, he is more or less warned that a kind of evil curse attaches to the paw. Nevertheless, he wishes for 200 pounds. The next day a representative of the company where his son works arrives to announce that the son has fallen into the machinery. A compensation of 200 pounds will be paid for his death.[5]

[4] Nove, *The Soviet Economy,* op. cit., p. 176.

[5] W. W. Jacobs, "The Monkey's Paw," in W. Somerset Maugham, ed., *Tellers of Tales* (Garden City, N.Y.: Doubleday, 1939).

An economist might ruin this story by analyzing it thus: Given the paw's "evil intentions" and magic power, it was impossible to hand it a sufficiently detailed set of commands so that it would have no room to bring harm to its "master."

We can scarcely imagine anyone admonishing the monkey's paw for not obeying the rules of Christian charity, but command-economy managers who deviated from the plan have been reprimanded for "unsocialist" behavior. As a remedy they have been asked "to make a more careful and devoted political study of . . . the resolutions of the central committee [of the Communist Party] . . . the classics of Marxism-Leninism," or the thoughts of Mao Tse-Tung.[6] Their factories may receive the "benefit" of visits by the Communist Youth League or the Red Guards, who try to "encourage" managers and workers to be more productive. The same factories may be criticized in the press, which has the task of publicizing plan failures. Finally, since the plan has the force of law, it is by no means inconceivable that managers will receive prison sentences. Until several years ago, minor prison terms were much more common for Soviet than for Western managers and carried a lesser social stigma.

Yet punitive measures are only appropriate when the behavior of managers is really "antisocialist," and even then, they will not be enough. Just as we suppose the money's paw to be evil, so the planners would be assuming that managers really know the socially best combinations of outputs to produce and inputs to use in production. In fact, managers do deviate from their plan targets simply because (irrational) bonus schemes make such behavior profitable. But they also deviate out of sheer ignorance. Similarly, one interpretation of the monkey's paw is that it was ignorant of the relative values to the old man of his son and the 200 pounds and simply chose the most expedient way of gaining him the latter.

One function of prices in a market economy is to inform producers about users' wants and needs. The more users want a particular good, the more they are willing to pay for it, other things being equal. Within a completely centralized economy, quantitative targets would entirely fill the void left by prices. They would specify exactly what and how to produce for each firm, and, ultimately, where to send each unit of every good a service that it turns out. Thus its behavior is exactly determined if it obeys its production goals.

However, in any practicable command economy, firms will have decision-making leeway and be in need of rational prices or other guidelines upon which to base their choices. Studying political resolutions or the thought of Mao Tse-Tung is likely to prove an imperfect substitute for such guides in telling managers what and how to produce. Indeed, suppose that managers wish only to harmonize their goals with the EPC. Then, failing rational price-

---

[6] The quoted passage is from Kumon, op. cit., p. 21. See, for example, Joseph Berliner, "Managerial Incentives and Decision-making: A Comparison of the United States and the Soviet Union," in Morris Bornstein and Daniel R. Fusfeld, ed., *The Soviet Economy: A Book of Readings,* 3rd ed. (Homewood, Ill.: Irwin, 1970).

type weights to guide them in areas where quantitative targets are incomplete, they are effectively asked to become magicians.

First, the dedicated manager must psychoanalyze his superiors to find out exactly what the latters' goals are. Then he must respond to his plan targets in the way most likely to please his superiors and ensure his own survival—or in the way most likely to benefit the "state," should a conflict arise between this and some other goal. In particular, because the EPC of such a system is apt to be overambitious, managers may have to be magicians in fulfilling unrealistic plan targets. Finally, the lack of communication between producers and users means that the former may have to be magicians to keep up with the latters' requirements.

Even with dedicated managers, we may have the problem of furniture that is too heavy to get up the stairs (plan targets phrased in tons); of cloth produced in strips that are too long and too narrow (plan targets phrased in meters); of tractors that are ill-adapted to the soil and crops of the regions that receive them, and of managers who are penalized for improving the distribution of goods to customers (plan targets phrased in amounts produced rather than delivered). (The latter is perhaps best exemplified by the one-time dilemma of the Leningard Power Company, which was punished for reducing power losses in transmitting electric current.)[7] When managers are less than completely dedicated, of course, difficulties may be compounded.

9–3   Demand Pressures and Supply Inertia

We cannot isolate the problem of managerial success indicators from the other factors which determine the environment of a command-economy firm and condition the dialogue between planners and plannees. Of these factors, three stand out as being important, both in a historical sense and because they are to an extent built into the functioning of a command economy. The first is the pressure resulting from command planning, particularly supply planning with materials balances. (This and the emphasis on the gross-output plan have historically been opposite sides of the same coin.) The second is a defective supply network in the sense that goods may arrive late or fail to meet user specifications in some way. The third, not yet mentioned, is a kind of supply inertia that complements the other two.

The existence of demand pressures and consequent supply deficiencies is partly historical, owing to the emphasis on raising production which has characterized most command economies. High output targets for one set of production activities—say, those geared to final use production—become high demands for inputs. Because the economy is an interdependent organism, these demands, and the stresses and strains that go with them, can easily transmit themselves throughout the system when some firms fail to meet their input or output targets or produce assortments of goods that are unsatisfactory

---

[7] Nove, *The Soviet Economy,* op. cit., p. 176.

from users' points of view. The latter is an especially severe casualty of the success-indicator approach and the emphasis on reporting statistical successes up the chain of command at the expense of close supplier–customer relations.

However, demand pressures and supply deficiencies are also partly inherent in supply planning with materials balances and in the success-indicator method of evaluating subordinates. We have seen that the plan is often tightened at the upper and intermediate levels of the planning hierarchy in order to give it paper consistency. Unfortunately, these "technological advances" cannot always be realized in the real world of the wheat field and the assembly line and therefore lead to demand pressures.

Furthermore, during the planning year, a conflict of interest naturally arises between planner and producer. The latter, if he considers only his own interest, will try to build some slack into his plan to ensure overfulfillment. To do this, he will continually give a slight overstatement of his input needs, while understating his production capacity, in reports to authorities. His superiors will then find it to their interest to countervail this by challenging him with input and output targets that attempt to push him to the limit of his production capacity.

Managers will tend to respond to these demand pressures, in turn, by hoarding key inputs. The net result of the conflict of interest is to further tighten the supply situation and to partially thwart the planners' intentions by tying up valuable resources in excess capacity. As a part of this, the surviving manager will overfulfill his current output plan by 5 per cent, but rarely by 25 per cent, even if he is able, because he knows that next year's plan targets would then be set even higher in consequence. (The need for routinization of planning means that this year's performance will strongly influence next year's plan.) A proper restructuring of incentives can blunt the conflict of interest, as we shall see, although it is not likely to disappear entirely.

Supply deficiencies between firms attached to different jurisdictions, corresponding to different subhierarchies in the over-all planning chain of command may also arise because of autarkic tendencies within these jurisdictions. The principal reason for supply *inertia,* on the other hand, has been the limited powers of command-economy managers to market their products and to seek new customers and suppliers. The planning bureaucracy is responsible for the basic distribution of goods and resources.

Because it is a bureaucracy, with an immense number of intersectoral flows to manipulate, it will adjust most easily to a stable network of flows. When the need for new links arises, it is likely to be generally slow in responding, and to become slower the greater the number of jurisdictional lines that must be crossed. To a manager, therefore, supply inertia is another microreflection of the tendencies of a command toward excessive routinization and autarky.

To see how the three phenomena—supply inertia, demand pressures, and supply deficiencies—can reinforce one another, let us briefly consider the problem of innovation, long a sore spot for command economies.[8] Supply inertia tends to impede innovation because managers aren't sure when or if new products, will be marketed, even though they may be useful to potential customers. Likewise, they cannot count on getting all the resources, including research inputs, needed to develop new products and techniques if they have not been habitual users of these inputs. A lack of contact between customers and suppliers makes the latter inadequately informed about the kinds of inventions that can be most helpful to the former.

The U.S.S.R. has tried to bridge the "innovation gap" by relying on research and development institutes. However, firms have not been free to shop among institutes, and bonuses have been geared, characteristically, to number of inventions made rather than number adopted. The result is a monopolistic position of research and development institutes vis-à-vis industrial enterprises and a large volume of inventions that are of little practical use. This, in turn, makes managers reluctant to patronize the institutes, thereby isolating them from the real world of production which they are supposed to serve.

Demand pressures also work against innovation since production must usually be halted in order to install new equipment or to change to new products or methods. More importantly, innovation invariably involves risk and time-consuming experimentation. Thus the short-run loss in output may prevent a firm from fulfilling its annual plan. Historically, the impact of demand pressures has been aided and abetted by an ethical bias toward strong egalitarian constraints on the distribution of income. Command-economy planners have often been unwilling to pay managers, scientists, and engineers the incentives necessary to make innovation more attractive than maintaining some kind of current routine.[9]

9–4   The Optimal Degree of Centralization

Because complete centralization is not achievable, the EPC should not try for this. Instead, it should concentrate on enforcing those targets which have highest priority, while allowing managers considerable decision-making latitude in other areas. This, in turn, implies a relaxation of controls from above, including control by the ruble.[10] The *potential* saving from such a relaxation

---

[8] The discussion below is due to Berliner. See Joseph Berliner, "Innovation and Economic Structure in Soviet Industry," op. cit.

[9] In the U.S.S.R., the official prices of new products are often too low vis-à-vis older substitutes to encourage producers to make them. For example, ". . . in a number of branches of machine building . . . prices for individual machines were set in conformity with [costs] during the machines' initial period of production, while the unit cost of output declined markedly as production expanded. As a result . . . enterprises have lost their economic incentive for replacing output in production with more advanced types of output, inasmuch as the old-type products are yielding a good profit." *Current Digest of the Soviet Press*, Aug. 25, 1970, p. 12.

[10] The U.S.S.R. and other East European command economies have loosened short-term monetary controls in recent years and also permitted some desegregation of currency and credit accounts.

includes both reduced enforcement costs and a better allocation of any given bundle of productive resources from the EPC's point of view.

From a purely economic standpoint, the optimal degree or centralization probably involves sending the minimum number of binding production targets which the EPC feels absolutely must be fulfilled. These values would ideally become fixed points around which economic activity revolves. In fact, assume for a moment that, as far as they go, aggregate plan targets are "optimal" from the EPC's point of view. In this sense, infinite wisdom guides decision making above the level of the firm, but does not guide it far enough to take all of the necessary decisions about production and distribution. Suppose, once again, that every manager is trying to harmonize his own goals with those of the leaders.

Then, within aggregate plan targets, the socially best assortments of goods are determined by user preferences interacting with cost considerations of producers—by supply and demand, in other words. The best combination of different kinds of nails to be produced at a given level of cost to suppliers should be that which enables furniture makers and house builders to produce most efficiently. The assortments of peas, carrots, meat, and potatoes should correspond to household preferences for these goods.

This, in turn, requires each enterprise to bypass the command economy's labyrinth of bureaucrats and officials to maintain close contacts with customers and suppliers. User firms, whether they be retail stores or members of the construction industry, will need the authority to negotiate enforceable contracts with suppliers. Any agreements reached must fall within the constraints of the plan, but the idea would be to allow users to specify their exact requirements to producers. To back these up, no manager should be allowed to collect his full bonus until his products are completed, delivered, and in the case of complaints, shown to satisfy "reasonable" customer requirements.

All this means nothing less than implanting a market or semimarket mechanism within the command structure. To improve their bargaining power, users must be permitted limited freedom to seek out alternative suppliers.[11] (This freedom should also work in reverse.) The role of this market would be greatest in the production of consumer goods and diminish as we move toward heavy industry. Except in determining the assortment of consumer-goods production, the command mechanism would remain dominant because the first requirement of managers is that they fulfill plan targets, with the added condition that their goods be marketable. The aim is to use commands to implement the planners' most basic priorities and markets or quasi-markets to pursue these more efficiently.

Yet, except possibly in China, command-economy planners have not pur-

[11] The planners will have to permit and even to promote competition among suppliers. In addition, users will sometimes be able to develop countervailing power against their suppliers as follows: Suppose that firm A supplies firm B with parts. Then B may be under aegis of an intermediate authority who also has jurisdiction over firm C, which supplies A. A multilevel intermediate planning hierarchy could be designed, in part, with this in mind.

sued such a strategy. Instead they have tended to suppress direct links between firms. Customers have had little power to dictate quality and assortment to users, and the legal systems of command economies have been geared toward enforcement of obligations to superior authorities rather than contracts between trading partners viewed as equals. Finally, arrangements within the state banking sector for handling transactions between firms have normally favored the supplier for reasons discussed in Chapter 7.

In part, the suppression of direct links has stemmed from a fear by planning officials that these would get out of hand and subvert their control over production and distribution. Partly, too, the planners have often derived welfare from statistical indications of success and have not wanted production held up or slowed down by too many difficulties with user requirements. But the cost of not allowing a dialogue between customers and suppliers, who are partly decentralized decision makers, has often been high, even outside the consumer-goods sector.

The most obvious cost stems from the fact that each firm's output performance depends upon its ability to acquire the kinds of inputs it needs. The failure of one set of firms to meet user requirements becomes a supply deficiency insofar as user firms are concerned, causing work stoppages, waste, and low-quality output. To prepare himself for these difficulties, the surviving manager will carefully stockpile key inputs (or substitutes). They will also acquire spare production capacity and hang on to a surplus labor supply. In some cases, where breakdowns or defects in the supply network can prove critical, firms will begin producing their own inputs, even though it would normally be more efficient to produce these inputs on a larger scale elsewhere. Such behavior is ultimately detrimental to the goal of raising economy-wide output.

And in the final analysis, producers and users will get together anyway whether the planning hierarchy wishes them to or not. For example, in the U.S.S.R. a kind of shadow market has sprung up on which purchasing agents or *tolkachi* seek to procure scarce supplies from potential producers through illegal barter agreements or outright sale. "The most recent outburst against them reports that the number of *tolkachi* who annually visit the typical large enterprise runs into the thousands and their expenses into the hundreds of thousands of rubles." [12]

The activities and the existence of these salesmen in reverse is quite outside the plan and therefore the law. Yet it appears that they are officially tolerated to some extent because they improve the distribution network. One author argues that "It is probably only because of the use of these extralegal and semilegal expedients that the supply system manages to work with tolerable satisfaction." [13] If so, it would work even better if direct supplier–user relations were officially sanctioned and even encouraged.

[12] Joseph S. Berliner, "Managerial Incentives and Decision-making: A Comparison of the United States and the Soviet Union," op. cit.

[13] Harry Schwartz, *Russia's Soviet Economy* (Englewood Cliffs, N.J.: Prentice-Hall, 1960), p. 201.

The most effective incentive program is one that harmonizes the goals of each lower-level decision maker with those of his superiors. In particular, the success indicators that such a program embodies should not relate to factors over which the lower-level decision maker has virtually no control. And they should not encourage perverse behavior in connection with choices that he can make. An optimal incentive program (or success-indicator package) will therefore depend upon the degree to which economic decision making has been decentralized, as well as environmental factors and the priorities of the central planner.

In designing an incentive package to go with the optimal degree of decentralization outlined above for a command economy, we would first try to drastically reduce the impacts of the three kinds of problems we have been discussing. To improve the supply network, for example, we would attempt to operationalize planning by basing managerial rewards on the value or volume of goods delivered and accepted by customers, rather than on producers' on bureaucrats' production claims. In particular, we would try to tie rewards for innovation to adoption of new methods and products.[14]

The most famous proposals along the lines we have in mind come from the Soviet economist Yevsei Liberman. Writing in *Pravda* on September 9, 1962, he unleashed the most penetrating economic controversy in the Soviet Union since the great industrialization debates of the 1920s. (His proposals ultimately helped spark the limited and now somewhat aborted reforms begun in the Soviet Union in 1964.[15])

9-5 The Liberman Success Indicators

Good plan targets should carry a reward for fulfillment and a penalty for underfulfillment. Our first thought, therefore, is to grant the manager a bonus for each target that he meets and to deny him the relevant bonus whenever he uses too much of a particular input or produces too little of a particular output. A more interesting question is: What do we do when he overfulfills a target—that is, when he produces more output or uses less of an input than the plan calls for?

Traditionally, command economies have unhesitatingly rewarded the over-

---

[14] For reasons we shall encounter in Chapter 15, it will probably be necessary to attach most applied research institutes to the firms they serve.

[15] See Yevsei Liberman, "The Plan, Profits, and Bonuses," in Bornstein and Fusfeld, op. cit., Ch. 18. Replies to Liberman by the Soviet economists V. S. Nemchinov, A. Zverev, and G. Kosiachenko occupy Chapter 19 of the same book. Finally, Chapter 20 contains Premier Kosygin's actual proposals for limited decentralization presented to the Central Committee of the Communist party in Sept. 27, 1965.

These proposals did not go as far as Liberman recommended, and they were considerably watered down, even as the Soviets adopted them at a pace exceeding their own plan targets over the years 1966–1969. In particular, Soviet managers did not receive the contractual rights (or decision-making freedom) that Liberman foresaw. See Svetozar Pejovich, "Liberman's Reforms and Property Rights in the Soviet Union," *Journal of Law and Economics*, Apr. 1968.

fulfilling manager or worker and held him up as an example for others to emulate. A typical structure of incentives would give nothing when a target is underfulfilled and a significant bonus—perhaps 20 per cent or more of base pay—when it is just fulfilled. (Paraphrasing Dickens, Nove describes this as 99.9 per cent, misery, 100.1 per cent, happiness.[16]) The bonus then rises steeply, up to a certain limit, as the percentage of overfulfillment rises. Moreover, it has often been quite rewarding to overfulfill some parts of the plan—notably the value, weight, length, and so on, of current production— at the expense of efficiency or of turning out the planned assortment of goods.[17] Many managers have doubled their base salaries on this kind of incentive scheme. Truly spectacular overfulfillment has earned medals and titles such as "Hero of Socialist Labor."

But this is not always rational. If a manager is underfulfilling targets with lower bonus rates while overfulfilling higher-bonus norms, his performance may be much less beneficial to the EPC than if he were to just meet all targets. In Eastern Europe, overfulfillment of the output plan has come at the cost of wasting all kinds of inputs from labor to forest preserves to scrap metal and of producing the right assortment of outputs. It has often been unprofitable to manufacture spare parts, for example, because a tube, a spark plug, or a voltage regulator counted more toward plan fulfillment as part of a radio, truck, or tractor. The result: a shortage of spares and a need to cannibalize.

In addition, there has sometimes been little or no incentive to service what the company sells. Anyone who has ever worked in an office building with permanently sealed windows when the air conditioning broke down will appreciate the plight of their counterparts in the U.S.S.R., where, at least until recently, such occurrences were so common that the buildings could not be closed for repairs.

Perhaps the chief problem with incentives based entirely on overfulfillment is that they magnify the demand pressures of command planning. The drive to overfulfill the plan becomes almost a religious rite. During the early part of a production period, the factory goes slowly, then increases the pace as time goes on. By the end of it, workers are "storming," to use the Russian expression—literally going flat out to overfulfill their quotas before it is too late. Then the cycle repeats itself.

The costs of this are numerous. We have already mentioned the effect on innovation. We also read, for example, that Krivoi Rog, a city of 500,000 people, which produces about half of the iron ore in the U.S.S.R., is in danger of collapsing because of mine tunnels. "Immediate production aims prevailed over long-range considerations in building the city. The situation is the same in the Kuznetsk Basin where some towns are literally suspended over an

[16] Nove, *The Soviet Economy,* op. cit., p. 205.

[17] Ibid., Chs. 6, 7; Berliner, "Managerial Incentives and Decision-making: A Comparison of the United States and the Soviet Union," op. cit.; Gregory Grossman, "Soviet Growth: Routine, Inertia, and Pressure," *American Economic Review,* May 1960. There have been numerous articles in the Soviet press on the subject—for example, *Current Digest of the Soviet Press,* Dec. 11, 1968, p. 24; Feb. 24, 1970, p. 6.

artificial abyss." [18] Pollution may thrive and quality control suffer in these conditions because time and effort spent in cleaning up or reducing waste can also be used to produce more output. A leading Soviet scientist has estimated that Soviet industry wastes an amount of steel equal to the total production of Italy (17.5 million tons in 1971 of a total Soviet output of about 120 million tons).

Consequently, although the idea is not likely to be popular right away with command-economy planners, nothing prevents us from trying an altogether different approach. If the EPC has any confidence in its plan targets, it should penalize managers for producing too much of each good as well as too little. (Managers would not be penalized for using too little of any input, however, unless there was a chronic economy-wide surplus of this good.) The output bonus will protect the planned assortment of goods until *every* target is fulfilled. The manager's total bonus should equal this output bonus, B_1, plus another bonus, B_2, for staying within his input norms. However, we should note that, once input targets are fixed for the year, B_2 simply depends upon how much of each input is used. B_2 rises as the firm uses fewer inputs, and vice versa.

Suppose, however, that we have a manager who can achieve every output target by October with no overexpenditure of inputs. He will have a vested interest in slowing down so that he just reaches his goals in December. There will still be some incentive for each manager to try for an easy plan, and success will encourage him to under- or overfulfill his output plan by from 0 to 5 per cent when he could do much better. If he could overfulfill by 25 per cent, for example, his inputs might as well be idle for three months of the year.

The suggested correction is to break the managerial bonus into three parts rather than two. The third part, B_3, will rise with the absolute amount of each output produced. The managerial incentive scheme now depends upon two broad factors: deviation from the output plan and actual performance without explicit reference to the plan.

Innovation incentives can be paid as a special bonus (B_4) or they may be built into the above scheme. For instance, suppose that a new type of automated assembly line appears feasible. A high bonus paid to the producer and developer for each line installed, coupled with a low charge to initial users, will encourage its adoption. (Producers and users should also be required to get together over exact specifications.) Similarly, charges can be levied for polluting, or it can be prohibited altogether. We may view such charges as "prices" to be paid for using up pure air and water. These disincentives can be built into B_2.

In final form, the total bonus now equals an amount, B_1, for conforming to the planned output targets, plus performance incentives, B_2 and B_3, for

---

[18] V. Tavinsky, "The Mines and the City," *Literaturnaya Gazeta,* Mar. 6, 1968. Subsequent discussion of the topic appeared in the July 31, 1968, issue. Various officials admitted the problems described by Tavinsky, but claimed he had exaggerated.

using fewer inputs and producing more output, respectively, plus (in some cases) an innovation incentive, B_4.

Forgetting for the moment about the incentive to conform to the plan (B_1), let us concentrate on B_2 and B_3 in order to see more precisely just what they reward. Suppose that we have a firm producing tables and chairs. If it raises production of both, B_3 will rise. But what happens when it produces more chairs and fewer tables? The answer here will depend upon the relative weights attached to the outputs of tables and chairs in calculating B_3. These weights act like prices. If we multiply the "price" of each output so obtained by the amount of the good produced or delivered, we get a measure of the "revenue" earned by the firm on that good. Adding up the revenues on all goods produced or sold by the firm gives us its total revenue. B_3 is therefore a bonus whose size increases with this definition of total revenue.

By the same token, assume that the firm uses less of one type of material input and more of a certain kind of machinery. The effect of this on B_2 depends upon the relative weights attached to the two inputs, which we again view as prices. Thus B_2 is a bonus whose size increases as the costs of the firm— calculated with the "prices" just defined— go down. We have now defined costs and revenues for each enterprise, and if we take revenues minus costs, we get a measure of its profitability. Together B_2 and B_3 tie a manager's income to the "profits" earned by his firm and encourage him to maximize these.

The entire Liberman bonus scheme ties managerial income to profitability and to the output assortment specified in the plan. We can easily specify variations on its basic theme. For example, in the case of some goods, we may wish to make the penalty for plan overfulfillment less than the penalty for underfulfillment. We have also seen that managers will not strive for a spectacular plan overfulfillment this year when they will automatically receive sharply increased output targets or reduced input targets next year in consequence.

One way to reduce this effect is to introduce realistic rental and interest charges. These will penalize the inefficient use of any resources by raising the costs, and lowering the profits, of the offending firm. A second way is to make the performance bonuses a larger percentage of the total. Indeed, this could be done by offering managers a chance to overbid their initial plan targets— that is, to set higher output or lower input norms than the plan originally demands—and then raising the performance bonus for those who take the offer. Such an arrangement has been tried out in East Germany.[19]

Liberman's central thesis was, in fact, that managerial incentives should be tied to enterprise profits. The EPC was to retain "the basic levers of centralized planning," meaning that the major output goals of the center had to be protected. Nevertheless, managers were to be given more freedom of

---

[19] Michael Keren, "Concentration and Efficiency in Eastern European Reforms," paper delivered at a Research Conference on Reform in Eastern Europe, Ann Arbor, Mich., Nov. 1970, pp. 27–28.

choice than before, especially in deciding how to produce and how to invest a portion of the funds available to them. Liberman also stressed direct contacts between customers and suppliers, along with the requirement that goods be sold before counting toward plan fulfillment.

The advantage of profit, he noted, is that it summarizes in a single index all the basic variables that a manager has to consider. A producer can neglect neither the cost nor the revenue side of his operations without being penalized by a lower bonus. Thus it potentially replaces many separate incentive payments geared to efficiency, output, and assortment. Traditionally, Soviet managers have faced a maze of bonuses, often overlapping and sometimes working directly against one another. Quite often a manager who overfulfilled his gross value of output target could count on being forgiven the others.

In addition, profit-oriented managers will have less of an incentive to conceal production capacity and hoard inputs—provided, once again, that interest and rental charges are deducted from profits and not set much too low. In the Soviet context, the importance of meeting the output plan to the detriment of everything else has even led managers to falsify their production achievements when their targets have become too unrealistic. Generally speaking, Liberman hoped to make the dialogue between planners and plannees more instructive to the former by reducing the incentive of producers to feed back false, inadequate, or misleading information.

Under his incentive plan, both planners and producers have an interest in setting realistic targets. Nevertheless, suppose that a manager receives one or more output targets which are unrealistically high. Then, in trying to fulfill them, he will incur a heavy cost and so reduce his bonus (B_2) for cost reduction. Similarly, in failing to overfulfill unrealistically low targets, he would sacrifice part of his revenue bonus (B_3). Not only does he have a smaller incentive to build slack into the plan, but when output targets are unrealistic, the result is more likely to be a deviation between plan and performance. This year's performance becomes a more reliable base upon which to build next year's plan.

Generally speaking, the EPC can expect more useful and reliable feedback information than under alternative incentive schemes. The planners should therefore be less isolated from the system's true production possibilities. Moreover, because managers have a chance to compensate for a few unreasonable targets, the Liberman incentive scheme is less likely to snuff out any patriotic or revolutionary fervor which helps them to identify with the central planners' goals. The scheme is quite consistent with moral incentives, for managers need not be paid on the basis of the indices of profitability and plan conformance which they are asked to maximize. Complete reliance on overfulfillment seems justifiable only when managers are extremely unsophisticated from a technical point of view.

The chief disadvantage of using profits as a "success indicator" in a world where prices are irrational (that is, do not reflect production scarcities or use values) is that the profitability of a particular production activity in a particular firm may be a poor guide to its contribution to social welfare. Because of irrational prices, a manager may find it profitable to expand his capacity to make ball bearings or steel girders when the same resources could create more welfare by constructing sheet steel or plastics capacity or building houses. In general, inputs will be misallocated among producers—a point that Western critics of Liberman have hammered relentlessly into the ground.

But no one has ever designed a command-economy incentive system capable of completely overcoming these defects. We have seen that non-profit-oriented incentive schemes always contain a built-in irrational price system. Sooner or later this leads to "poor" performance. However, when the bonus depends upon profits and fulfilling the planned output assortment, prices that are badly out of line will lead to severe shortages or gluts of the good in question. The planners can bring these back into the vicinity of equilibrium without converting to a basically market economy.

There are several kinds of efficiency, and Western critics of Liberman have had in mind the traditional notion dealing with the allocation of resources and goods among various producers and users. When a businessman speaks of efficiency, on the other hand, he is usually thinking about X efficiency, or how effectively a firm uses the resources at its disposal. We may argue, as well, that this is what Liberman had in mind.

Given the economic environment of a Soviet firm in the 1960s, a logical way to promote X efficiency was by introducing a simple but comprehensive set of success indicators, by encouraging direct contacts between customers and suppliers, and by reducing the detailed interference of higher authorities in the internal affairs of the enterprise. As a complement to the latter, the decision-making authority permitted most managers would have expanded appreciably. But perhaps most important of all was a need to make the economy more self-enforcing by tying managerial salaries to the incomes of their enterprises after all costs had been met. It is hard to imagine an easier way to motivate them to meet user requirements while keeping their costs under control.

The reasons why most of Liberman's proposals were not adopted probably relate to the desire of the vast planning bureaucracy to survive and maintain its power, as well as to the evident "bourgeois" implications of using "profits" as an incentive. Direct contacts between firms plus even minor increases in the decision-making autonomy of managers have always appeared to Soviet bureaucrats as a threat to their survival. In one sense, they have a point. If a command economy had already decided to decentralize, a preliminary step would be to switch over the Liberman incentive scheme, if this was not already in effect.[20] But we are likewise maintaining that this is the best incentive program when no abandonment of the command mechanism is foreseen.

Any formula for rewarding managers and lower-level bureaucrats is bound to have defects in a command-economy setting. The dialogue between planners

---

[20] See the discussion in Chapter 11.

and plannees, like most other phenomena, will probably conform to the cycle described by Gregory Grossman as "Routine, Inertia, and Pressure." [21] A certain kind of planning organization, mentality, and methodology entrenches itself and becomes part of the landscape. The economy develops a momentum based upon it. Then, when shortcomings become so serious that the EPC can afford them special attention, the system may change under pressure from the center. But without this, there is insufficient incentive to break out of the routine.

Thus, while central pressure is the initial *raison d'être* of a command economy, it is likely to become less efficient in pushing the system along a given development path as the economy complexifies over time.

[21] Grossman, op. cit.

Chapter 10

Multilevel Planning and Bureaucracy

The workers, having conquered political power, will smash the old bureaucratic apparatus, they will shatter it to its very foundations, they will destroy it to the very roots; and they will replace it by a new one, consisting of the very same workers and office employees *against* whose transformation into bureaucrats the measures will at once be taken which were specified in detail by Marx and Engels: (1) not only election, but recall at any time; (2) pay not exceeding that of a workman; (3) immediate introduction of control and supervision by *all*, so that *all* shall become "bureaucrats" for a time and that therefore *nobody* may be able to become a "bureaucrat."

Lenin: *State and Revolution*

Vital work we do is sinking in a dead sea of paperwork. We get sucked in by a foul bureaucratic swamp.

Lenin (*after the Revolution*)

For many purposes we can profitably pursue planning problems by considering the interaction between two different levels in the planning hierarchy. However, any real-life planning structure contains at least *three* stages. Intermediate officials and bureaus will always play the key role of translating broad directives and targets from above into action commands and incentives for producers. The same is true to a lesser extent when it comes to more decentralized planning. We need to probe inside the notion of bureaucracy and ask what the implications are for planning.

10–1   The Notion of Bureaucracy

If a law to transform all Western corporations into workers' cooperatives was to become a serious possibility, its most ardent opponents might well be neither stockholders nor managers, but many labor unions. Most managers could expect to be able to retain their employment and stockholders to receive "reasonable" compensation for lost property. By contrast, the jobs of labor union officials depend closely upon the present system of labor relations based upon collective bargaining and the socioeconomic class divisions that this entails.

Similarly, suppose that in the year 2075, a proposal to sweep away the maze of overlapping welfare programs, which sometimes work at cross purposes, seriously threatens to pass the United States Congress. In its place would come a guaranteed annual income, with built-in work incentives, which puts a "decent" income floor under every household. This would be a more efficient program which is much cheaper and easier to administer. But it would likewise require fewer administrators. Consequently, a portion of the federal bureaucracy which handles existing programs is threatened with a decline in the demand for its services. We would expect it to fervently oppose the reform.

Finally, let us suppose that the world's major trading nations were to seriously consider following the lead of Canada and switching to a system of more flexible exchange rates between national currencies. This would probably bring opposition from the International Monetary Fund. The IMF is the nominal guardian and administrator of the current system of fixed exchange rates (although it has little enforcement power) and would either cease to exist or play a much diminished role in world of flexible rates.[1]

The above are but two of an endless list of examples that we could use to show that bureaucracies often tend to resist change, whether it is for better or worse. Any bureau is built around the idea of a chain of command whose essence is differentiation by rank or status. Every bureau thus has its own "bureaucratic elite," which occupies its higher echelons. This elite has a vested interest in maintaining the status quo whenever reforms are proposed that risk diminishing the demand for the bureau's services.

The lower echelons will feel that they also have a stake in the status quo if they view their chances for advancement within the bureau as being significantly greater than outside it. In a world where seniority per se counts,

---

[1] The exchange rate between any two currencies is the amount of one that will exchange for a unit of the other. Thus about $2.61 U.S. currently (1972) exchanges for one British pound. We live in a world of fixed exchange rates where normally the price of each currency in terms of gold or U.S. dollars is held within very narrow limits. The only exception is Canada. The price of the Canadian dollar in terms of the U.S. dollar and all other national currencies is allowed to respond to the forces of (long-run) supply and demand.

this will often be the case. Bureaus do not *always* oppose "reform," however. They will favor changes that promise to enhance their prestige, size, and power. The net result will often be that bureaus are much more likely to grow than to decline, even when their areas of control or responsibility are shrinking.

Bureaucracies exist in every kind of economic system, but they are most prevalent in command economies, where a complex chain of command is needed to translate broad directives from the EPC into action orders for firms. Not only will bureaus proliferate in such a system, but we can think of the entire planning network as constituting a single giant bureau. Later, we shall argue that it makes a difference whether bureaus are linked through the market mechanism, or themselves form a large parent bureaucracy. Indeed, many firms in any developed market economy will resemble bureaus in their internal organizations.

The presence of hierarchies is the most visible sign of bureaucracy, but when we try to give a formal definition of a bureau, it proves more useful to take a different approach. Every bureau produces a "product" of some kind, which it exchanges directly or indirectly for other goods and services. The intermediate bureaucracy of a command economy produces "administration," "enforcement," and feedback information to the EPC concerning the system's production possibilities. There are two basic ways of exchanging any product. The supplier may agree to part with x units of a good for a specified sum of money or for specified amounts of other goods. Toothpaste selling for $1 per tube, an automobile that is a bargain at $4,000, and Manhattan Island traded for a few trinkets are examples of this. But we can also imagine exchanges in which the number of units to be provided by the supplier cannot be precisely determined in advance or even where the product itself cannot be well defined.

Of course, a barter transaction could occur in which one ill-defined package is traded for another—for example, two vague promises. However, we wish to focus upon one-sided transactions in which a definite command over resources is provided by the user to the supplier in exchange for something much harder to specify. Among the difficult-to-quantify goods are those produced by a command economy's intermediate bureaucracy, along with certain staff functions necessary to administrators, such as banking and information gathering, processing, and analyzing. The right to provide a relatively ill-defined product puts the supplier in a more powerful position vis-à-vis his customers than he otherwise would be.

A transaction cannot occur unless each party makes a well-defined commitment of some sort. When the package to be "purchased" is imprecise, it is natural to reward the supplier for specific time periods of production. In a market economy this gives rise to the notion of a budget, which rewards the activities of universities, hospitals, government agencies, and a host of other organizations, usually on an annual basis. Budgets will also exist in command economies, but they are less likely to correspond to the actual reward such organizations receive, if only because prices are less likely to be rational.

To begin with, a bureau is a producer selling or exchanging most of its output by the time period rather than the unit. By this criterion, there may be both very large and very small bureaus. However, we want them to be hierarchical to some extent, and we shall add the requirement that a bureau contain at least one internal chain of command. In particular, this rules out one-man bureaus. Finally, every bureau must have a chief or director at its apex who ultimately takes responsibility for all the bureau's actions. (A sign on President Truman's desk read, "The buck stops here.")

We shall be most interested in bureaus that are so large that most of the employees at the bottom of the chain of command are not personal acquaintances of the agency's director. This we call an impersonal bureau. Within it, "the initial hiring of personnel, their promotion within the organization, and their retention are . . . theoretically based upon some type of assessment of the way in which they have performed or can be expected to perform their organizational roles . . . ." [2]

Following popular usage, we shall say that a bureaucracy is a collection or network of bureaus, but we shall also reserve the term for very large bureaus such as the Pentagon, Whitehall, or the Soviet Ministry of Chemical and Petroleum Industries. In any planned economy, the planning bureaucracy is that collection of bureaus participating in the planning process.

10–2 Some Elementary Economics of Bureaucracy

The best way to approach the theory of bureaucracy is to set out and justify its principal conclusions as these apply to planning. In more-or-less logical order they are as follows. [3]

1. In a market economy a bureau will try to maximize its size and growth and hence its budget. A bureaucrat's welfare depends upon his salary, power, prestige, patronage, and public reputation. Moreover, any bureau chief will want to minimize internal conflict, by parceling out additional duties, responsibilities, prestige, and income to his subordinates, and to ensure the survival of his operation. Within a command economy, bureaucrats may not try to maximize their budgets, but they will wish to increase the scope and importance of the areas under their control and the sizes of the staffs working under them.

Recalling a famous forecast by Marx, I think it may be worthwhile here to cite another quotation from Professor Smolinski: "Failing a radical reform

2 Anthony Downs, "A Theory of Bureaucracy," *American Economic Review*, May 1965, pp. 439–440.

3 These conclusions are mainly due to Anthony Downs and to the German Social philosopher Max Weber (primarily the former). See Anthony Downs, *Inside Bureaucracy* (Boston: Little Brown, 1967), especially Chs. 1, 2, 3, 4, 6, 7, 8 to p. 88, 9, 12, 13, 18, 19, 22; "A Theory of Bureaucracy," op. cit. (entire article). S. N. Eisenstadt, ed., *Max Weber on Charisma and Institution Building* (Chicago: U. of Chicago, 1968). Max Weber, *The Theory of Social and Economic Organization*, ed. by Talcott Parsons (New York: Free Press, 1968). With great effort, the author has prevented himself from including *The Peter Principle*, by Lawrence J. Peter and Raymond Hull (New York: Bantam, 1969).

in planning methods, the planning bureaucracy [of the U.S.S.R.] [will] grow 36-fold by 1980, requiring the services of the entire Soviet population." [4] In 1968, about 15 per cent of the total population held administrative jobs. This is not an action portrait of the state withering away. Administrative bureaus may also obey Parkinson's Law, which says that the size of a bureau bears no relation at all to the size of its administrative burden. [5]

2. The director of a bureau has at least three potential bargaining aces to aid him in his quest for more resources. The first stems from the intangible, difficult-to-quantify nature of his product and the resultant need to sell or exchange it by the time period. In a sense this product is indivisible. A command-economy EPC cannot choose between $(x - 1)$, x, and $(x + 1)$ units of administration from its ministry of ferrous metallurgy in the way that a household can decide how much soap or toothpaste it wishes to buy. By definition, a bureau will exchange its product once a year or so on something of an all-or-nothing basis. Ultimately, the EPC must buy a year's worth of administration or sack the minister and get a new one. Then it will have to work out a new administrative package with the new minister.

Second, competition between different bureaus will often be wasteful. If there were two defense departments, two central statistical offices, two ministries of ferrous metallurgy, or two state planning bureaus competing with one another, considerable duplication of effort would result. This could not be made up by any increase in efficiency that competitive pressures might bring. Thus the bureau is left with a "natural" monopoly.

The third factor is less obvious, but it may be the most important of all. There is some evidence that the size of bureaus in Western countries, where governments are chosen by majority voting, is a simple function of original size at birth and age. The older a bureau is, the larger it is. (This is called *Wagner's Law*.) One suggested explanation is that the demand for a bureau's services is a function of their supply. [6] This demand comes from the country's legislative and executive branches in the form of appropriations that ultimately translate into bureau budgets.

Politicians seeking reelection will respond to the bureau's lobby and raise its appropriation enough to enable it to expand, if they think they can gain votes by doing so. A bureau's political clout depends in the first instance upon

---

[4] Leon Smolinski, "What Next in Soviet Planning?" *Foreign Affairs*, July 1964, p. 602; reprinted in Morris Bornstein and Daniel R. Fusfeld, eds., *The Soviet Economy* rev. ed. (Homewood, Ill.: Irwin, 1966), p. 329. The prediction was made by Victor Glushkov, a Soviet cybernetician.

[5] For a Soviet comment about Parkinson's Law at work in the Soviet context, see Vasily Selyunin, "The Inverted Pyramid," *Moskva*, Jan. 1968. The 15 per cent estimate was supplied by Selyunin.

[6] This argument is due to Gordon Tullock, although spatial limitations have forced us to considerably oversimplify his discussion. See Tullock's review of W. A. Niskanen, *Bureaucracy and Representative Government* (Chicago: Aldine-Atherton, 1971) in the Spring 1972 issue of *Public Choice*, pp.119–124. The Niskanen book is also worthy of attention.

the number of people with votes whose jobs are affected by an expansion of its services. More precisely, it depends upon the number who will directly profit from such an expansion through employment, promotion, and higher pay or prestige relative to what they could get elsewhere. These will include employees of the bureau—and, perhaps, their relatives—along with employees, relatives, and stockholders associated with government contractors and other firms who can profit from the bureau's activities.

Of course, taxpayers must ultimately bear the cost of expansion, but these costs are spread over many times the number of people who benefit. Except under special circumstances, these people will not be sufficiently aroused to prevent a net vote gain from expansion to a size far beyond that consistent with economic efficiency.

Command-economy leaders need not worry about general elections, but they are always in some danger of a coup d'état, an assassination, or a limited-participation revolution. They must have support from at least the upper echelons of the Communist Party as insurance against this. These supporters will, in many instances, be top bureaucrats in the command planning hierarchy. They, in turn, will usually seek insurance in the form of support further down this hierarchy. The leaders may also find it prudent to seek such support directly. This is why the command planning bureaucracy becomes a political power base, and the need for support gives bureaucrats a bargaining card in their quest for expansion.

Khrushchev's 1957 reorganization of planning in the Soviet Union from a partition by branch of industry to a geographical partitition appears to represent an effort to put men loyal to himself in key decision-making posts. When Khrushchev fell from power, another thorough reorganization followed soon afterward.

The three factors listed above give bureau directors scope for maneuvering and for the acquisition of power. We would expect to find that large bureaus occupying key positions are important centers of power in a command economy, and this is particularly true of the highest organs in the intermediate planning hierarchy. Ministers will have an incentive to use their power to their own advantage, which will not always harmonize with the priorities chosen by the EPC.

Our discussion in Chapters 1 and 2 indicates that bureaus will also eventually tend to become internally inefficient as they grow larger. As spans of control widen and chains of command grow longer, the information cost of operating the bureau rises—eventually, much more rapidly than its size. This cost has two interrelated components: (1) the cost of supervision, or of enforcing commands, including the cost of operationalizing responses; and (2) the coordinating cost of determining how inputs must be efficiently combined to produce different combinations of outputs. The difficulty of measuring these outputs makes both kinds of costs even higher.

More specifically, we have the following conclusions regarding the internal operation of a bureau:

3. Bureaus inevitably involve information losses. Orders become distorted as they flow down a chain of command, and responses are sometimes twisted to the point where they do not reflect an accurate picture to top echelons of what goes on below. One basic reason for this has already been advanced in Chapter 1. A small information loss—say 5 per cent, on the average, at each level in a chain of command—multiplies to become a much larger loss—about 23 per cent when there are five levels—for the entire chain. This assumes that the chain in question behaves like a *team* whose members all have the same basic goals, while allowing for the fact that no one is perfect.

However, we also saw that some divergence of interests, and therefore some goal conflict, would inevitably arise in the operation of a hierarchical organization. Nor will all members of a bureau be above promoting their own interests. When there is room for interpreting an order being passed down a chain of command, it may be phrased so as to enhance the position of the official who handles it or to minimize the risk that he will appear unsuccessful. In particular, a bold call from the top to innovate, explore new areas, or otherwise drastically break with past routine may be considerably watered down by the time it reaches the level where action occurs. This helps explain why command economies tend to get into ruts, except when extreme pressure is applied from above, often bypassing one or more levels in the usual hierarchy.

Feedback information also risks being slanted toward telling senior officials what they are believed to want to hear and toward otherwise reflecting junior officials in a favorable light. For example, we would expect the latter to be more likely to report successes than failures and to prepare analyses suggesting that the bureau should expand rather than contract. In a command economy this implies some built-in tendency to exaggerate production performance.[7]

Leeway for interpreting orders will exist, at least in large bureaus, because of the specialization of function, which increases as we go down various chains of command. Down says,

As the bureau grows, its internal division of labor tends to embody ever more intensive specialization. This creates more difficult co-ordination problems because more people are involved in each decision. Also, there is often a loss of over-all perspective because each task is fragmented into tiny parts. Consequently, individual specialists think less about making the whole operation work well, and more about increasing the sophistication of their own fragments . . . since each specialist deals with only a small fraction of the entire project, authority rises to

---

[7] Western economists have long argued that the Soviet Union's growth claims are exaggerated, particularly for the 1930s. See, for example, Robert W. Campbell, *Soviet Economic Power*, 2nd ed. (Boston: Houghton-Mifflin, 1966), Ch. 6. See, as well, the Appendix to Chapter 6.

a high enough level that the efforts of many specialists can be coordinated by one superior.[8]

The ability to accommodate an extremely fine division of labor among specialists who could not efficiently exchange their products through a market mechanism is a major advantage of hierarchical forms. But to the upper echelons of a large bureau, the information cost of handling anything other than aggregate data will be prohibitive, except in cases of extraordinary importance.[9]

Orders will therefore start out in aggregated form at the apex of the bureau and become progressively disaggregated as they move down its various chains of command. Each official who disaggregates has some leeway to choose the exact order he passes on, and skillful bureaucrats will improve their chances for survival and advancement in this way. Feedback information becomes more aggregated as it moves up a chain of command, and there will again be room for "interpretation." But an even greater degree of distortion may arise because of the ability of lower-level officials to select what to report. Since it is never feasible to pass every piece of information upward, the opportunity is created to withhold data that might be useful to senior officials but which lower authorities feel will not ultimately advance their own interests.

The other side of this coin is that a scrupulously honest lower-level functionary will on occasion risk putting himself in the figurative position of the messenger who brought bad tidings in olden days. He may *lose* his job or normal chance of promotion.

4. To combat behavior from below that may be wasteful or run counter to the goals of upper-level bureaucrats, the latter will use a number of "anti-distortion" devices or checking procedures. Whatever form these may take, they will always combine two principles, which Downs calls "redundancy" and "bypassing."

Occasionally and perhaps at random, the top brass will make on-site inspections (bypassing) or duplicate the efforts of lower-level officials by having reports submitted directly to them (bypassing and redundancy). Alternatively, informers can be placed at various checkpoints whose own feedback lines bypass several links in the official chain of command. Finally, different departments of a bureau can be asked to cooperate on several projects or be given overlapping jurisdictions generally. Thus their reports should check up on one another to an extent. Jurisdictional disputes will have to be referred above, increasing the control functions of the upper echelons.

---

[8] Downs, *Inside Bureaucracy,* op. cit., p. 159.

[9] The reasons such coordination would often fail to work efficiently through the market relate to the difficult-to-measure nature of the product each individual produces, the fact that his output may have some of the qualities of a public good (to be discussed in Chapter 15), and other factors that would make the transactions costs involved extremely high. See the discussion above in Chapter 2.

There is, however, a "law of countercontrol": *"The greater the effort made . . . to control the behavior of subordinate officials, the greater the efforts made by these subordinates to evade or counteract such control"* [Down's italics].[10]

The classic story of the informer found floating in the river gives an exaggerated indication of the social pressures on these individuals. In all likelihood, however, lower-level officials will cooperate to form a kind of "early-warning system" on inspections and other "surprise" moves to bypass regular channels. The more lower-level officials are able to cooperate, help one another, and present a united front to their superiors, the more effective countercontrol will be.

Conversely, it will pay top officials to encourage competition at lower levels in situations where goals above and below are likely to conflict. The upper levels will also want to profit from the natural tendency of intermediate echelons to "pass responsibility up and work down" and intervene in decision making at key moments.

Thus, although the term "bureaucrat" usually carries a negative connotation, a top-level bureau official will need all the qualities of a superadministrator. Even if it possesses these qualities, however, the leadership of a large bureau is almost certain to get out of contact with what is going on at the bottom. It is not inconceivable that less than half of all the time spent on the job by the employees working for such an organization would go toward furthering its ultimate objectives. The rest would be spent in control and countercontrol, information handling, and other routine administrative matters.

We would thus expect a large bureau to be inefficient when measured against any sort of absolute standard for much the same reasons that a command economy is likely to be inefficient. Because shakeups in its organizational hierarchy will not usually reduce the size of the bureau significantly and because its leadership is partly out of touch with what is going on at the bottom, we would predict a poor-to-mediocre efficiency improvement record for organizational changes.

The various reorganizations in the Soviet and East European economies which have left the command structure intact tend to bear this out. If upper-level officials are clever, they will understand the various problems that are likely to exist in their operations and protect themselves by exaggerating the need for secrecy and opposing outside investigations. Indeed, although they will want to keep the bureau under control, their pay depends upon its size rather than a profit residual after all bills have been met. Thus their incentive to keep costs low is mitigated and even reversed in some instances.

The difficulty of controlling lower-level officials can sometimes be reduced if top authorities make proper use of the external environment. Outside

---

[10] Downs, *Inside Bureaucracy,* op. cit., p. 147.

sources have been known to act like bypasses between upper- and lower-echelon bureaucrats. Downs says: "Merely by reading several good newspapers a day and letting all his subordinates know that he does, a top official can (reduce) the distortion practiced by his own bureau. . . ." [11]

It is no accident that the Soviet press, which does not usually dare to touch political controversy, is laden with reports of plan failures and fulfillments, economic controversies, and other aspects of economic performance. As long as matters do not get out of hand, economic exposé is viewed as a major task of the journalistic profession. Nonetheless, when the goals of external sources collide with the aims of a bureau's top management, the presence of these sources is more likely to prove a nuisance than a benefit. Downs therefore argues that the effort to control extremely large bureaucracies would require the creation of new bureaus (such as the bureau of the budget in the United States) or watchdog agencies, whose tasks involve control and little else.

5. Finally, any hierarchical organization will have trouble evaluating the contributions of some of its personnel to the over-all success of the organization. Like a bureau, itself, these employees produce something intangible and difficult to measure. Most professors fall into this category, as do generals, statesmen, administrators, clerks, and a host of others.

Often the result is that superiors evaluate subordinates on the basis of input characteristics as well as of performance. A professor is promoted or dismissed because of his "agreeableness," his habits and tastes, or even how he holds his cup of tea. A junior executive can promote his own cause by dressing properly, by engaging in the "right" sort of conversation, by having a lovely wife and children, and, on occasion, by losing to his boss at tennis but not by too much. Both the professor and the executive stand to rise or fall on the basis of their ideological convictions, their connections, and their family backgrounds. Any frequent author of letters of recommendation knows that these characteristics are at least as important as competence.

10–3 Bureaucracies, Ideology, and Efficiency

The need for goal homogeneity within a bureau is likely to lead it to identify with ideology and indoctrination and to accept new members on condition that they conform. Thus, perhaps ironically:

6. A society in which production is largely organized along bureaucratic lines is likely to be *more* discriminatory and *more* ideologically oriented than a market economy in deciding who should succeed and who should fail. (This is aided and abetted by the difficult-to-measure nature of the contributions of many employees within a hierarchical organization.) Although we may not like the specific criteria for success in a particular market economy, the market test is at least semiobjective. Most goods and services will sell pri-

[11] Ibid., p. 119.

marily on the basis of how badly buyers want them rather than who is providing them.[12]

The use of ideology can be a powerful mobilizing tool. In China, individuals are evaluated for promotion and other purposes by committees rather than examinations so that the weights assigned to competence and to ideological factors—mainly devotion to and enthusiam for party ideals and programs—can be assigned independently in each case. We have indicated that a human error or poor performance will often be assessed as disloyalty, requiring the individual in question to prove over and over that he is basically committed to the regime.[13] Moreover:

> Changes in political policy [in China] are more disruptive to bureaucratic organization than in Western countries where the bureaucracy is more insulated from political considerations. All officials in the bureaucracy of any consequence are expected to express strong commitments not only to the over-all Party but to the main outlines of current policy. . . . As a result . . . when a new policy comes down, not only must everyone study the new policy, but all those closely identified with the old policy must criticize themselves for their errors. This is true even for such a simple matter as the adjustment of local production quotas. . . .[14]

The Chinese EPC enforces this politicization of the intermediate hierarchy with what Donald Klein has called the "semi-purge":

> Disciplinary measures are applied to ensure political reliability. Communist China's bureaucracy has not undergone the severity of the violent purges in Russia in the 1930's, but. . . . Cadres who are not responsive to political leadership are sent away for study or physical labor (including tedious farm chores) for periods of time and then returned to work, although often at a somewhat lower position. This practice tends to maintain a high degree of responsiveness to political pressures from above. . . .[15]

All Chinese bureaucrats must spend some time doing physical labor so that the cost of such a penalty will not be lost on them. Speaking generally, Chinese bureaucracy obeys Lenin's "three commandments" much more closely than do its counterparts in the U.S.S.R. and Eastern Europe.[16]

Predictably, however, the use of ideology and indoctrination will not com-

---

[12] Of course, discrimination can also be practiced—indeed, can be rampant—in a market economy. But the reader should ask himself to what extent this stems from the fact that markets are used vis-à-vis the inevitable presence of hierarchical organizations in any system.

[13] See Ezra F. Vogel, "Politicized Bureaucracy: Communist China," in *Newsletter of Comparative Studies of Communism*, May 1971, pp. 28–30. Children of the "wrong social classes"—the bourgeois and landlord classes—are automatically considered to be ideologically suspect. Their level of competence must be considerably higher than those of their rivals to have the same chance for promotion.

[14] Ibid., p. 29.

[15] Ibid., p. 28.

[16] These commandments appear on the first page of this chapter.

pletely succeed in making the bureau into a team. Instead, areas of disagreement will tend to be confined within an ideology or cloaked over by it. During the Chinese cultural revolution, all contesting factions proclaimed loyalty to Mao Tse-Tung and his thought. Each side insisted that it had the only true version of Maoism and that its rivals were heretics.

7. The larger a bureau and the more diversified its activities, the more likely it is to avoid innovation and to routinize all aspects of its behavior. The reasons for this are legion, but three appear to stand out. First, the identification of a bureau with an ideology and indoctrination will probably derationalize it in some ways. A rational accounting of costs and benefits is bound to threaten certain "cherished" beliefs, and the larger a bureau is, the more officials there are to uncover conflicts between doctrine and rationality—quite possibly in the hope of furthering their own promotion chances. Routine then becomes an alternative to rational behavior.

Second, and working hand in hand with this, the information cost of thoroughly considering alternatives may often become prohibitive. In a large and diversified—yet centralized—bureau, it becomes impossible to give this type of attention to any decisions except the most important. Without internal markets to break up large problems into smaller ones, "the use of extensive rules [is] a rational response to a bureau's problems of decision-making and communicating." Once a large bureau has sunk into established behavior patterns, it becomes quite expensive to change these.

Third, innovation means change, the costs and consequences of which are always impossible to foresee perfectly. Thus any specific innovation is likely to endanger the status of at least one official, a tendency that increases with the size and diversity of the bureau. For the same reason, the lower-level employee who displays too much initiative may be passed over or dismissed rather than promoted. Barring special incentives from still higher officials which can substantially improve the material well-being or status of ambitious bureaucrats, a mentality of "live and let live" is therefore likely to prevail. Each official will try to carve out a sphere of influence for himself, and a tacit agreement is likely to evolve among bureaucrats at more or less the same level to respect one another's spheres in whole or part.[17] For the alternative would be to threaten someone's vested interests and invite retaliation.

All this presupposes that a kind of power balance will establish itself within the bureau (which may partly result from aversion to conflict) that everyone respects. Otherwise, if one group gains enough power and is sufficiently dedicated to a cause or otherwise motivated, it can provoke sweeping changes in the bureau's personnel and, perhaps, in its structure and mode of action. Normally, however, bureaus will only accommodate a gradual pace of modification.

[17] It is with this in mind that the Soviet press has complained about the tendency of Soviet ministers and managers to try to lead "quiet lives." See Alec Nove, *The Soviet Economy* (London: G. Allen, 1968), Chs, 6, 7, and Joseph Berliner, *Factory and Manager in the U.S.S.R.* (Cambridge, Mass.: Harvard U.P., 1957), especially Ch. 14.

It is also true that the more centralized the decision making within a bureau, the slower it is likely to be in responding to a perceived need for change. More messages will have to pass between more officials, on the average, and more decisions, each one dependent upon the others, will have to be taken at various levels in a chain of command before the actual execution of any change can occur.

Rigidity, routine, inertia, and lack of creativity are the images that the word "bureaucrat" often conjures up. However, they are more likely to apply to intermediate and lower-level officials than to a bureau's top management.

8. The inertia of complex and well-entrenched bureaus makes them ill-suited to tackle urgent problems without a structural modification imposed from above. Consequently, special departments or "task forces" often come into being whose own internal organizations are more informal and less centralized than the bureau proper. Typically, task-force members will be chosen for creativity, dynamism, and a reputation of not being routine-oriented. We would expect them to enjoy a special status vis-à-vis the rest of the bureau, both regarding their obligations and their access to higher officials.

Once the project for which the task force was created comes to an end, pressures will arise to dissolve it, inasmuch as its favored position will have antagonized other bureaucrats. Dissolution may, in fact, be the normal outcome, but sometimes the task force will survive and split apart to become a new bureau. According to Downs, bureaus usually come into being through "routinization of charisma, splitting off from an existing bureau, entrepreneurial development of a new idea by zealots . . . or creation out of nothing by powerful social agents." [18]

Thus bureaus often arise in a charismatic atmosphere of optimism, creativity, and enthusiasm. For awhile they learn to perform their functions more effectively. Eventually, however, routinization sets in and the initial exuberance wanes. They "develop more numerous and more extensive rules and regulations, shift their goals from performing their functions well to maintaining their organizational structures, become increasingly subject to inertia, and expand the scope of their functions. As with politicians, few die and none retire." [19] A study of the Ukrainian Communist party apparatus during the 1960s, for example, revealed that many of the "men of 1938" were still in power despite numerous purges and reorganizations.[20]

Nevertheless, in his article on Chinese bureaucracy, Ezra Vogel says, "One of the impressive features of Chinese Communist bureaucratic organization, the largest the world has ever known, is the remarkable speed with which it can be mobilized for effective action. To be sure, the effectiveness derives partly from a very large propoganda network, but it is immeasurably aided by the

---

[18] Downs, "A Theory of Bureaucracy," op. cit., p. 445.

[19] Ibid.

[20] Paul Hollander, "Politicized Bureaucracy: The Soviet Case," *Newsletter on Comparative Studies of Communism,* May 1971, p. 18.

high degree of politicization of the bureaucracy which makes it responsive to campaigns, pressure, and commands from above." [21]

The price for this is an even greater reluctance to report unfavorable results higher up a chain of command or to take any initiative beyond immediate and direct orders from above. Unrealistic orders are less likely to be questioned, and during mobilization drives:

> Forms and reports may be dispensed with, leading bureacrats sent to work in factories and farms without replacement, and remaining bureaucrats may devote most of their energies to the current campaign. Indeed, this was precisely the problem with the Great Leap Forward . . . routine administrative tasks were neglected and in the end it proved the undoing of the mobilization efforts." [22]

The leaders also prevent rival power centers from developing within the intermediate hierarchy by systematically "sending in outsiders and transferring out insiders" whenever a rudimentary clique forms. The Soviets have used the reorganization technique on a somewhat grander scale in efforts to promote efficiency, flush out hidden reserves of capacity and inventories, improve the political power base (or control) of higher authorities, and mobilize the economy. Since the death of Stalin, Soviet leaders have reorganized the planning hierarchy three times. From a partitioning by branch of industry, it went to a geographical partitioning in 1957 and back again in 1965. By 1971 a new organization by branch of industry, the production association or giant trust, was beginning to take over some of the powers of the ministries.[23]

9. Finally, whether we are talking about the Peace Corps, Housing and Urban Development, or the U.S.S.R. Ministry of Ferrous Metallurgy, the main task of most large bureaus is to facilitate the pursuit of certain social goals. But the effectiveness of any bureau depends partly upon its ability to rationally calculate and compare costs and benefits of alternative courses of action. Although large bureaus are not likely to be efficient, they will have to develop some kind of efficiency calculus to be successful at all. The ability to do so will often depend upon whether and how often (approximately) rational prices are available to use in the calculations. Thus a bureau should operate most efficiently in a market economy, other things being equal.

It also follows that calculating skills and attitudes are definite assets. A shortage of same may explain why bureaus are apt to be ineffective in certain environments—for example, an underdeveloped nation. The calculating attitude is bound to conflict on occasion with predispositions toward ideology

---

[21] Vogel, op. cit., p. 31.

[22] Ibid., p. 32.

[23] Production associations are essentially associations of geographically separate plants producing the same commodity. They are more specialized than ministries whom they remain nominally below.

and indoctrination and toward judging employees on the basis of input characteristics. (Bureaucracies may therefore be least effective of all in underdeveloped command economies with strong ideological orientations, where nepotism abounds.) When the cost of *not* using some kind of efficiency calculus because of ideology becomes prohibitive, an exercise in inventiveness is necessary to reconcile it with existing doctrine, which is likely to alter in consequence.

A case in point is the long series of debates among Soviet economists, planners, and engineers about whether and how to charge for the use of scarce capital and natural resources. A particularly narrow interpretation of Marx had insisted that these goods were free, leading to some of the distortions in pricing and resource allocation mentioned in Chapter 8.

If the potential information flow is "large," a bureau will also be hampered in applying rational accounting methods by a lack of internal markets. This is yet another problem of bureaucracy which stems from sheer complexity, as measured by the number of a bureau's employees, the diversity of its tasks and goals, and the lengths of its various chains of command. Where possible it will pay society to restrict the growth of bureaus along each of these dimensions. The ability to do so, in a particular set of circumstances, will depend heavily upon the development of techniques and machinery to gather, transmit, and process large amounts of information. Conversely, the greater a bureau's information-handling capabilities, for any given complexity, the more effective it is likely to be in comparing alternatives and in keeping top officials informed of what goes on below.

But Parkinson's Law is apt to play a negative role here. The computerization of a bureau, for example, can wipe out whole departments and bring many serene and lucrative supervisory positions to an end. The officials who feel threatened by a data-handling innovation will resist it in the way they would resist any other "dangerous" new idea.[24]

10–4   The Command-Planning Bureaucracy

The basic problems of a large bureau resemble those facing a command economy and vice versa. Both revolve around chains of command and vertical messages which are more or less the antithesis of markets and horizontal information flows. In such a context we may think of a command-economy planning hierarchy, including enterprise managements, as comprising a single giant bureau. This will accentuate both the advantages and the defects that we assigned to command planning in earlier chapters.

Like any bureaucracy, the command planners may launch their program in an atmosphere of exuberance and charisma which permits them to steer the system along a course of rapid development which a more marketized econ-

---

24 Alternatively, they may try to subvert efforts to computerize the bureau's activities.

omy could not achieve. In the process, however, vested interests arise with a stake in the status quo. The system eventually loses its exuberance—barring recurring phenomena such as a cultural revolution—and its defects become more costly and evident. These include "built-in" difficulties in rationally comparing alternatives and tendencies to routinize economic decision making, to suppress initiative, and to promote autarky.

The reaction to increasing difficulties, actual or anticipated, may then be to shake up personnel and programs without really decentralizing the economy very much. Over an extended period of time, on the other hand, a succession of these "reforms" could conceivably bring decentralization to pass.

The watchdog of the planning hierarchy in all current command economies is the Communist Party. In the U.S.S.R., one official Communist Party representative sits in every firm of any size and serves as a liaison between the enterprise and the Party. Although this representative works for the firm, he is not directly responsible to its manager. The latter engages in counter-control by trying to win the representative's allegiance, and this is sometimes possible because both have a stake in the overall statistical success of the firm. The Communist Party also uses outside agencies, such as youth groups, who visit factories and construction sites to encourage the workers, while publicizing failures, successes, and irregularities. In a political environment of rigid control over press commentary, newspapers have an obligation to air production failures and disputes, subject to the qualifications noted earlier. The Communist Party is, itself, a bureau and so is the state banking system, which likewise exercises a control function.

The intermediate planning authorities are best viewed as bureaus in their own right which are also "levels" in the giant, over-all planning bureau. As bureaus, they are likely to display many or all of the characteristics developed above. For example, we would expect them to contain a number of built-in rigidities, and we would predict that their goals will be expansionary and empire building. But as elements within a bureau, they are likely to show some mutual respect for each others' spheres of influence. A plausible outcome of both these tendencies, bolstered by observation in Eastern Europe, is autarkic behavior within ministries and considerable duplication of effort between them.

Our discussion above also predicts that an ideological framework will surround a command economy and be used both to galvanize it and to justify it. In recent history, most command economies have professed to be the embodiments of one version or other of Marxism, and this has served from time to time as a rallying cry. But it has also led to problems—notably, arising from a rather narrow interpretation of the labor theory of value, which maintains that natural resources and borrowed funds for investment purposes should be free goods.

The result has been enormous misallocation and waste, which, in turn, has finally forced the introduction of interest and rental charges through the back door. Natural resources have proved to be a particular problem because often they are obviously not produced with the aid of labor.[25] Within the ideological framework applying to the command economy as a whole we would expect intermediate authorities to expound subideologies favorable to their sectors—for example, priority expansion of heavy industry.

They will also have an incentive to interpret directives from above to their own advantage, to feed back reports from below that conceal poor performance, and to emphasize those favorable results most likely to please their intended audiences. Indeed, an oft-noted phenomenon of a command economy is that everyone in the planning hierarchy from the plant manager to the EPC derives benefit from statistical indications of success. Thus exaggeration through selectivity, altered definitions, and biased interpretations could work its way right up into the statistical yearbook.

Managers in sectors of the economy whose priorites most urgently demand outstanding performance in fact as well as in claim will probably be able to bypass a part of the normal command structure. In the Soviet Union the atomic energy ministry (called the Ministry of Medium Machine Building), along with space and defense industries, has enjoyed special status, and key industrial complexes have nearly the rank of ministries. The idea in each case is to avoid ossification and to encourage innovation while maintaining the ability to respond quickly when the need for moving in a new direction arises.

Nevertheless, we have already seen that three major over-all weaknesses of a command economy will be its inability to innovate, compare alternatives, and keep out of ruts. The intermediate authorities are likely to make things worse here because they will be particularly keen on preserving the status quo in just those areas where this can do the most harm. Earlier, we indicated that bureaucrats would protect their jobs by resisting the computerization of planning. More generally, they are apt to oppose the introduction of radical new production and distribution methods and the building of whole new industries. Such continuing renovation is part of the lifeblood of every developed economy. Yet, if adopted, any new idea may lead to new vested interests and spheres of influence that will compete with one or more old ones. It will threaten the jobs or the pay or prestige of some officials, who will therefore have an incentive to try to prevent it from being adopted.

Any specific innovation project should be undertaken if and only if the

[25] For a Soviet discussion of this problem, see N. Fedorenko, "Natural Resources Being Used Wastefully," *Voprosy Ekonomiki*, Mar. 1968. Also, Yu. Sukhotin, "Evaluations of Natural Resources," *Voprosy Ekonomiki*, Dec. 1967, and Ye. Karnaukhova, "The Economic Evaluation of Land in Agriculture," *Voprosy Ekonomiki*, Aug. 1968. Low rents and interest charges encourage managers to waste capital, materials, and natural resources and to use too much of these relative to labor inputs whenever they are able. Thus it becomes a problem of managerial "success indicators." Soviet press comments on the problem of waste are frequent. For samples, see *Current Digest of the Soviet Press*, Apr. 6, 1966, p. 29; Mar. 31, 1970, p. 4; Mar. 31, 1970, pp. 16–18, and Aug. 25, 1970, p. 23. In the next-to-last reference it is estimated that "almost as much lumber is lost as waste, burned, or left on the felling site as is worked by [enterprises of the Ministry of Lumber and Woodprocessing Industries]."

required investment has an expected yield that is at least competitive with other claims on available resources—perhaps after an adjustment for the unusual risk involved has been made. Unfortunately, it is also in the area of new activities that calculations of expected social benefit are most complex and problematical. Hunches will normally play a role, and conclusions will be open to interpretation and even outright manipulation. This is particularly true in a system without rational prices from which calculations of expected return might be made.

Thus expansion-minded coal, steel, or other entrenched interests may succeed in using a variety of statistical means to exaggerate the expected yields on investments in their own areas relative to plastics or the peaceful uses of atomic energy. Because rival new industries are likely, at first, to be heavily reliant on outside funds for development, it will be somewhat easier to stall their birth and early expansion. If a proposed project can be shelved soon enough by one means or other, no one will know what its return would have been—unless, perhaps, it is tried out in another country later. The sort of mentality which these officials would seek to promote would be one requiring new ventures to have a fairly certain expected payoff soon after inception.

This tendency is reinforced by the prevalence of irrational prices, which make investment alternatives difficult to compare even in the absence of uncertainty. It will reinforce, in turn, any tendencies of the command economy to avoid risky undertakings and tread familiar paths. Except in those sectors deemed so crucial that they are specially administered on a permanent basis, this is a mentality from which command economies will always be in danger.

Figure 10-1 shows what we mean. The vertical axis indexes output in established industries, such as steel, machine tools, mining, electric power, and defense. The horizontal axis indexes output in newer industries, such as plastics, peaceful uses of atomic energy, petrochemicals, electronics, data processing, and consumer durables. The curve PP', bowed out away from the origin, is the economy's production-possibility frontier over, let us say, a five-year horizon. This will be largely unknown to the EPC, owing to difficulties met in comparing the productivities of alternative investment programs.

The indifference curves bowed in toward the origin depict the EPC's preferences. The higher the indifference curve, or the farther it is from the origin, the higher the EPC's welfare. Its optimal pattern of production is at A. However, by diverting investible resources, the established industries are able to move the economy away from the center's preferred path of economic development through A toward the one through B. Because there will be some production inefficiency, the economy winds up at a position such as C. The outputs of established industries are greater and those of new industries smaller than the central planners would prefer. They have effectively lost some of their power to steer the economy.

There are partial antidotes for this. A plastics industry or atomic energy plant can sometimes be placed under the same ministry as a steel mill or a coal power station. Similarly, a water resources ministry that is presently

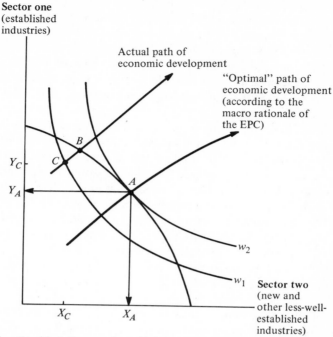

Figure 10–1. Possible influence of established industries on the command economy's path of economic development.

responsible for irrigating arid farmland by conventional methods could receive control over the development of a new supply source, such as a desalinization plant. In each case, the hope would be to make the new idea sufficiently attractive to some vested interests that the latter would push for its adoption.

This would also fit in with a more general "countervailing-power" strategy by which an EPC could seek to prevent too much power from shifting down to the ministerial level. The idea would be to distribute tasks and incentives among intermediate and lower-level decision makers so as to leave the center with a substantial backing on any given issue, although its supporters will vary from one issue to another. On some occasions this support will arise simply because intermediate authorities constitute a portion of the EPC's present and potential membership. In Eastern Europe it is current practice to grant membership in the EPC to top intermediate officials and to otherwise try to make them identify with "top management's" goals.

In all likelihood, though, the problem will remain partly unsolved because construction of countervailing power has its limits and also because ministries, as bureaus, will have built-in biases again innovation. On top of this, we again run into the problem of demand pressures. Intermediate officials will be judged on performance within their sectors. Unless they can receive unusually large rewards for doing so, they will not wish to interrupt production to introduce new products or techniques. These rewards would be on a scale that existing command economies have so far been reluctant to pay. As noted previously, most innovation in a command economy is a direct or indirect result of pressure from the top. To apply this the EPC will sometimes find it necessary to bypass several links in the usual chain of command and, on occasion, to create special task forces charged with implementing or exploring particular ideas. Later these may become independent parts of the planning bureaucracy.

It is a tribute to the theories of bureaucracy developed by Downs and Weber that much of the detail written since 1930 about particular aspects of existing command economies can be viewed as case studies of their analyses. We have tried to indicate some highlights of this application, although spatial limitations preclude anything like a thorough treatment. It would be inappropriate, however, to close without noting two effects which a bureaucracy may have upon the environment within which it is implanted. Writers from Adam Smith to René Clair and Charlie Chaplin have maintained that assembly-line workers tend to become automatons themselves to whom a life of adventure or even variety would be abhorrent. Likewise, bureaus can ossify individual behavior and build a bias against innovation and change into a society's mentality.

In an entirely different dimension, an economy that is essentially one big bureaucracy is unlikely to be a classless society. Those higher upon any given chain of command will usually occupy positions of greater pay and prestige than those below, and it is impossible for these distinctions to remain without social implications. In addition, the mere existence of chains of command will created vested interests that hinder progress in order to preserve their spheres of influence. Those at the top may be able to rule and maintain their power by virtue of the sheer weight of the bureaucratic mass beneath them.

It is ironic that Marx's criticisms of the capitalist societies he encountered were much along these lines. Capitalism breeds vested interests and a social superstructure, according to Marx, which eventually impedes social and economic progress. We have little evidence, however, that command economies will satisfy his criteria for a society without social classes. Later we shall discover a "revisionist" theory which tries to build an efficient, classless economy based on markets combined with workers' management of productive enterprises.

Chapter **11**

Systemic Change in Centralized Economies

Here they are, trying to put as many more items as possible into production, without thinking about whether the consumer needs them today and whether they are finding a market. The principle of "produce, produce" clings tenaciously.

Literaturnaya Gazeta (Feb. 1, 1966)

11–1 The Advantages of Command Economies Revisited

We have argued that when command economies have a comparative advantage over more marketized systems, from a (prospective) planner's viewpoint, some combination of the following conditions is likely to prevail:

1. The economic environment or the planner's preference function is relatively simple. In the latter case, a few key socioeconomic goals stand out above all others.

2. A firmer grip over the economy's path of development is desirable than the EPC can achieve within a basically marketized framework. This may include a drastic goal reorientation, such as a jump in the growth rate which requires pressure from the center to realize. For example, commands will sometimes permit the planner to mobilize resources which would respond sluggishly to market signals. They can prove useful in overcoming bottlenecks and also in promoting extensive development, whose prerequisite is a massive shift of inputs

from one sector of the economy to another. However, we would expect market economies to have an over-all advantage where intensive development is concerned.

3. An especially acute need has arisen to get the most out of scarce managerial talent. (However, a command economy provides a poor training ground for expanding this talent pool.)
4. The political power base that a command planning bureaucracy provides may prove attractive.

Much of our discussion so far indicates that a command planning mechanism will not have a permanent advantage over basically marketized forms in an economy where tastes and potential technology are constantly changing. Indeed, of the eight largest East European economies, seven (all but Albania), began reforms aimed at some degree of decentralization in economic decision making during the early to mid 1960s. (The eighth, Yugoslavia, dismantled its command economy during 1950–1953.) Table 11–1 shows the status of the reform movement in 1970.

By 1972, Hungary was the only country of the seven to have passed beyond command planning. The other six countries were content mainly to strengthen intermediate links in the chain of command (that is, the production or industrial associations lying between the ministries and the enterprises) and to allow small increases in enterprise autonomy. Thus, the transition period may be long, but let us suppose that reform is in the air in the sense that proposals to decentralize are coming up for open debate and discussion. It becomes appropriate, therefore, to ask how to conduct the reform so as to maximize the chances for success, while minimizing transition costs. It may be best to begin by contrasting market and command planning briefly.

11–2 A Bird's-Eye View of Centralized and Decentralized Planning

When we turn to mixed economies, planning becomes a low-key operation in which the central planners concentrate on determining the broad path of economic development. If an economic plan exists in quantitative terms, it is likely to be as much a synthesis of partly independent plans of individual enterprises and lower-level planning agencies as a creation of the center. However, the center will try to influence goals at lower levels by changing the environment within which micro decision makers operate so that individual interests harmonize more completely with the interests of society (regardless of) how the latter are defined. The contrast was described in 1968 by a Czech economist, who, at the time he spoke, was outlining the expected transformation of his own country:

We are aware . . . that the reform [that is, the proposed transition from a command to a mixed economic system] represents a far-reaching measure affecting social life, comparable to the revolutionary changes that occurred in Czechoslo-

Table 11–1. Main features of economic reforms in Eastern Europe.

	Hungary	Czechoslovakia	Bulgaria	East Germany	Poland	Romania	U.S.S.R.
1. Substantial increase in enterprise autonomy	x	(x)	(x)				
2. Primary performance indicator(s)							
a. Sales							
b. Profits	x				x		x
c. Profitability				x	x		x
d. Value added (wages and profits)					x		x
3. Price reforms							
a. Centralized calculations on traditional cost-plus lines		x	x				
b. Introduction of capital charges	x	x	x	x			x
c. Greater role for decentralized price setting in response to market forces	x	x	x	x	x		x
4. Shift toward financing investment via credit and self-finance instead of budget grants	x	(x)					
5. Use of profits taxes to regulate behavior of firms	x	x	x	x	x	x	x
6. Greater role for enterprises or production associations in conduct of foreign trade	x	(x)	(x)	x		x	
7. Introduction of workers' management							
8. Decollectivization of agriculture		(x)			x*		

Source: Morris Bornstein, "East European Economic Reforms and the Convergence of Economic Systems," *Yearbook of East European Economics*, Vol. 2, 1971.

Blank, no significant change from traditional Soviet-type command-economy model; x, change adopted after 1965; x, change adopted before 1965; (x), change adopted was subsequently curtailed or eliminated.

vakia in the years 1945–1948 [that is, when communism took power]. . . . Let me present several problems and changes which the reform will bring to economic life:

(a) A fundamental change in the role of prices. . . . In place of the system of fixed prices—which served above all as an instrument of measuring costs and the volume of output [that is, as accounting prices]—prices and profitability become a fundamental guide for enterprises in deciding what and how much ought to be produced. Price thus becomes a basic element of the system. It becomes flexible as a function of supply and demand, including foreign trade.

(b) The incomes of enterprises . . . become fully dependent on the financial situation of the enterprise, i.e., on the degree of success of entrepreneurial activity. The enterprise, therefore, acquires complete jurisdiction over decisions concerning the utilization of its income, its allocation between investment and compensation of employees, and the direction of its investment and wage policies.

(c) In this connection the entire nature of the activity of enterprises is changed. Whereas in the past the management of enterprises aimed only at the fulfilling of output targets . . . while supply, sales, and investment policy were handled on behalf of the enterprises by central organs—under the new system enterprises are forced to engage in entrepreneurial activity in the fullest sense of the word, i.e., including marketing, project-designing activity, technical research, foreign markets, etc. Industrial enterprises are now becoming organizations engaged in many-sided productive and commercial activities.

(d) The role of the plan is changing; and by the same token—the central organs of management of the economy must completely revise their methods of directing the economy. In place of a set of directive indicators and orders, arises the role of instruments of economic policy, such as the state budget, credit policy, tariff policy, tax policy, and other indirect instruments. From the point of view of planning there occurs a transition from a monocentric to a polycentric system; i.e. in place of a single central plan—in which the plans of enterprises were merely a detailed breakdown of centrally established targets—we shall have a spectrum of enterprises planning on their own. Vis-à-vis the enterprises, the central planning body performs two functions:

(1) supplying information concerning future development, which is to serve the enterprises as a basis for their own development and planning decisions;

(2) formulating basic objectives of central economic policy and determining the role of economic instruments with whose aid these objectives are to be attained and which also influence very strongly the plans of enterprises.

Within a command economy the EPC, together with its technical divisions and staff organs, directly controls the rudder of economic performance. Within a mixed economy it adjusts the tiller. As decision making decentralizes, even more of the EPC's harmonizing of individual and social interests consists of designing an incentive system to make that which is profitable to society profitable to producing enterprises as well.

11–3 The First Steps in Transition

In proceeding to reform the economy, we must bear in mind that political pressures both at home and abroad may oppose change, perhaps decisively, if we push too far too fast. We particularly have in mind the bureaucratic elite of a command economy, which may feel a severe threat to its status and prestige.

Moreover, society may be legally oriented away from the use of markets, along with contract respect and enforcement. The switch from commands to markets involves radical organizational changes that may plunge society into chaos if the groundwork is not properly prepared.[1] Consequently, a multi-stage transition period appears to be appropriate. Although we cannot specify it too closely in the abstract, the following general guidelines suggest themselves.

Perhaps our first thought would be to introduce markets simply by having the EPC manipulate prices instead of quantities. The planners already control prices and, on some occasions, will be adjusting them to keep supply and demand from getting entirely out of balance. It is not impossible to imagine this adjustment mechanism becoming more finely tuned while enterprise managements receive increased freedom to decide what and how to produce. The EPC would change thousands of prices simultaneously at irregular and unannounced intervals in an effort to keep most prices close to their equilibrium levels most of the time.[2] The general rule will be to raise prices of goods in short supply and to lower prices of goods in surplus.

The reform would normally begin in low-priority sectors and spread "upward." [3] Within these sectors the firms best able to benefit from the specialization and cooperation which marketization should bring and which have the best potential all-around management teams ought to go first. In all likelihood these will be among the larger companies. Some smaller and less efficient firms may either have to disappear or merge in order to realize economies of mass production, research, and management. As a part of this, specialization is bound to increase in the sense that many plants will be turning out a narrower range of products than before.

Conceivably, the most important sectors—sometimes called the "leading links" of the economy—would remain subject to commands and direct allocation of resources after the reform was complete. Similarly, the government will still be the principal buyer of goods such as highways, jet aircraft, and education, and the principal supplier of police protection, national defense, mail service, and, perhaps, railroad transportation and utilities. Quantitative targets need not be abandoned altogether in every reformed sector, but when they are retained, they should become increasingly indicative in nature as firms are allowed to play greater decision-making roles.

[1] An examination of the Soviet press leaves little doubt that the limited watered-down decentralization being pursued there has sometimes been traumatic, both for managers and bureaucrats.

[2] The basic reason for changing prices at irregular and unannounced intervals is to prevent speculation and anticipation of price changes.

[3] The EPC will try to test the reform and iron out difficulties in low-priority sectors while retaining its grip on the path of economic development.

As outlined above, our transition period recalls the most famous models of market socialism, due to Oskar Lange and Fred M. Taylor. Their distinguishing feature is widespread central price adjustment of intermediate goods and natural resources with a view to simultaneously balancing supply and demand in every market.

However, we shall discover later that these models contain serious weaknesses. In particular, widespread central price manipulation has a high risk of failure, except, perhaps, when maintained for a short period of time.[4] The best the EPC can hope to do on a long-term basis is to manipulate prices of a few goods and services within each commodity group. Moreover, the planners will probably have to go one step further and establish a *central marketing agency*. Wherever feasible, intermediate goods which are produced in large amounts will have to be marketed through this agency as soon as their production is no longer governed by commands. (The internal organization of CMA would follow the command principle.)

Every command economy will maintain a wholesale distribution network, and, basically, the central marketing agency is an outgrowth of this. It will operate inventory depots and marketing centers throughout the economy, where, by law, all trading in specific types of intermediate goods must take place at prices set by the EPC. The latter, in turn, must guarantee that firms are able to buy and sell all that they wish of each centrally marketed good at going prices. Where necessary, losses will be absorbed out of taxes, and goods will be imported or destroyed to maintain this guarantee. However, the crucial role played by the EPC is to change prices at various intervals in an effort to keep inventories at desired levels—that is, to balance supply and demand. It is this function which signals that a market mechanism is operating.[5]

One drawback of this system is that many goods, such as consulting services, construction projects, and custom-built machinery, cannot be centrally marketed. In these cases decentralization of production will have to go hand in hand with decentralized prices set in bargaining between buyers and sellers. This will also mean decentralized marketing, although a central agency can assist in bringing buyers and sellers together.

Nevertheless, the centralized marketing scheme has several points to recommend it wherever it is feasible. Perhaps the most important is that command-economy managers will normally rise from the ranks of engineers and foremen. They should be excellently acquainted with the technical details of production, especially in their own factories, farms, or mines, but they are likely to be novices when it comes to tackling the problems involved in marketing. (They will be the opposite of managers in the West.)

In *no* command economy will centralization be so complete that managers

---

[4] This is true, partly for reasons mentioned in Section 2-3.

[5] Local marketing centers will be responsible for keeping the prices of some goods close to their equilibrium levels. Even where prices are centrally determined, local centers ought to be given ranges rather than exact levels.

are denied jurisdiction over all decisions. Moreover, prior to decentralizing, the EPC should launch a (mini) reform, if necessary, to accomplish two purposes. First, it should align managerial incentive payments on the "optimal" Liberman incentive plan outlined earlier. Second, and hand in hand with this, it should allow managers some increased freedom to choose their own assortments of inputs and outputs, in direct consultation with users and suppliers. (This will imply the right to make some investment decisions.)

Thus, when decentralization comes, managers will be best qualified to take over the entire responsibility of deciding what and how to produce in response to given price signals, but less acquainted with the problems of selling their goods and otherwise establishing and exploiting relations with prospective buyers and suppliers. The latter includes demand forecasting—or predicting and understanding user requirements—and innovating, inasmuch as new products must be sold as well as invented.

We may also take another viewpoint. For a given range of products and production technologies market economies function most efficiently when the appearance of monopoly profits is followed by increased competition. If investments in the auto industry are earning 20 per cent or better while the normal return elsewhere on investments with this degree of risk is 10 per cent, society is signaling that it wants more autos.[6] Efficiency requires production to expand and prices to fall until the excess profits disappear. A key factor in this process will often be efforts by additional firms to enter the industry and share in the excess profits before they vanish.

However, a command economy is more efficiently organized when many firms are in strong regional monopoly positions. Under command planning, a major consideration is to minimize the burdens on the communications and transportation networks, even at the expense of competition, because the latter is of secondary importance.

In these circumstances, it is not surprising that command-economy firms are sometimes accused of overpricing in those few instances (for example, in the manufacture of custom-built goods) where the opportunity arises to do this. (In a more general sense, low quality is analogous to high price.) Furthermore, experience with decentralization in Czechoslovakia and Yugoslavia suggests that, as markets replace commands, monopoly power may become a serious problem. (This does not turn out to be the private property of capitalism.[7])

---

[6] This supposes that external effects are being internalized. If the 20 percent return in auto manufacturing is partly due to the costs of pollution being shifted by automakers onto others, part of the solution is a combination of controls, penalties, taxes, and incentives to correct this.

[7] For example, during 1967 and the first half of 1968, many wholesale prices were freed in Czechoslovakia. Firms raised their prices, sometimes by 30 to 40 per cent. When the government tried to get this money back, the enterprises refused to return it. According to *Fortune* magazine, some enterprises became so profitable that they did not have to go to the state banks for investment loans. Thus an important instrument for steering a mixed economy was blunted. See *Fortune,* June 1, 1968, p. 62. The Soviet

Once again, the adverse effect on performance can threaten the reform by strengthening its critics. Some competition may be introduced by splitting up existing firms, but an overzealous use of this tool will leave many enterprises too small to realize economies of mass production. The competition so created will then be wasteful.

It follows that the EPC will often have to rely upon creation of new firms and expansion of the market areas served by old ones so that they invade one another's territories.[8] This, in turn, means relying upon the skill and initiative of entrepreneurs in expanding their product lines, diversifying, and moving into new areas whenever profit prospects are lucrative enough. Because command-economy managers are apt to fall short here, the EPC must, at first, substitute its own authority for the power of potential competition by controlling prices and marketing.

Centralized marketing also takes a step toward operationalizing the system. The central marketing agency is in a better position to spot and reject goods of inferior quality, as well as those which arrive late or in bad condition, than any agency in a command economy. Likewise, as a seller, it should be better acquainted with user requirements. Finally, as an organ within the planning hierarchy, it should be reasonably well equipped to enforce the contracts that it makes with producers for purchase and sale. Thus it can help society become acclimatized to a contract law that must ultimately replace the legal authority of the yearly plans and whose most important provision is the right of the injured party to claim recourse.

The main disadvantage of a centralized marketing economy is that it is still partly bureaucratized. Requests for many price changes will have to travel up at least one chain of command, and approval will then have to come back down. We would therefore not expect prices to adjust as quickly to permanent shifts in supply and demand as in a system in which competent decentralized pricing prevails. The marketing centers should gather and spread nonprice as well as price information—in particular, information about new products and techniques. Nevertheless, such a system may experience problems with innovation similar to those of a command economy.

11–4   The Conclusion of the Reform

When all is said and done, centralized marketing is not the ultimate goal of the decentralizing reform, and both it and most of the direct central pressures characteristic of command planning will ultimately have to disappear.

---

reform has freed a few prices, notably for custom machinery and machine tools where certain units may be produced to fill a specific order and never again exactly copied. This has given rise to complaints of (in effect) monopoly pricing, and firms have also been charged with illegal price manipulation. See, for example, *Current Digest of the Soviet Press,* July 21, 1970, p. 17, and Aug. 25, 1970, pp. 12–13.

[8] Of course, this may have been fostered to some extent by the minireform discussed in Chapter 9. Such a procedure would then be continued and pushed farther.

In the mixed economy that finally emerges, managers, households, labor unions, and other decentralized actors will take command of the vast majority of production, distribution, and pricing decisions.

Consequently, the reform divides naturally into two or three stages. Stage I, described above, decentralizes most production. We may, in turn, break this into stage Ia, the decentralization of most short-run production decisions, and stage Ib, the decentralization of most long-run or investment decisions. In any event, stage II, the decentralization of most marketing (or distribution) and pricing, must eventually follow.

By the time stage II is complete, the economy will be relying upon the initiative of lower-lever decision makers—and principally of enterprise managements—for its dynamism. This will largely replace the direct pressure from above. Stage II must see the emergence of a whole new breed of managers, who will be exposed for the first time to the full range of survival tests that a market economy has to offer.

It has been said that good entrepreneurs are born rather than trained, but a competent modern manager still needs a modern education to develop his innate skills. Therefore, during or prior to stage I, a (former) command economy should set about organizing schools of business administration and educating this new breed. Traditionally, such schools have not been part of command-economy higher-education establishments. At the same time, many bureaus in the intermediate planning hierarchy will have to be dissolved or else undergo personnel cuts as their duties are reduced. These employees are potentially strong opponents of the decentralization, but many among them will have skills that can prove useful to firms in their expanded roles, perhaps after some retraining. Such a program therefore recommends itself as another part of stage I.

Stage II should again proceed upward from low- to high-priority sectors, with the somewhat paradoxical result that the "new breed" of managers will be installed in high-priority sectors last. (The reason is that these sectors should not bear the brunt of experimentation.) Now the speed and direction of the reform will depend upon how efficiently, in the broadest sense, liberated managers perform and also how rapidly the planners learn to steer without relying primarily upon commands.

Prices will probably be freed from central control in two or three steps rather than all at once, the aim being to minimize the effect of monopoly power on price and to give managers time to adjust to greater freedom. Step 1 might abolish centralized marketing and establish upper and lower boundaries within which given prices are allowed to fluctuate, while step 2 eliminates the floors and keeps the ceilings. Only at step 3 would pricing become entirely decentralized. At any particular point during the reform, some products could easily be in each category, so that all three kinds of pricing are simultaneously present. Thus an economy in the process of decentralizing presents a hodge-podge, reflecting a desire by the EPC not to let performance get out of control.

Among the prices to be ultimately freed is the complex of long-term interest rates that govern the availability of investment funds. This can be viewed as a major step that will eventually transfer most investment decision making to managers, along perhaps with some intermediate authorities. At first the EPC will probably retain the right to step in and establish direct ceilings on the amounts that low-priority sectors may invest. But in the end this becomes another control, which must be at least severely curtailed before decentralization can be considered to have been achieved.

At the same time, maintenance and repair facilities can be shrunk to something like "normal" size, and manufacture of spare parts and inputs for the plant's basic product can be reduced. Offsetting this in some cases will be increased product diversification to accommodate seasonal fluctuations in demand.

The exact nature of any decentralizing reform will depend greatly on the environment within which it is carried out, and without doubt the reader has formed many reservations about our discussion above. Rather than speculate further, therefore, let us close by noting that a key distinction between planning in command and mixed forms shows up in the roles played by the banking and financial systems in each. In a command economy these are basically instruments for control and enforcement of the physical plan. But one measure of decentralization in planning is managerial freedom from obligatory quantitative targets. In a mixed system banks and other financial institutions become major instruments for steering the economy, internalizing social costs and benefits, and realizing economies of mass production.

REFERENCES

(For Chs. 7–11)

The command economy that has generated the most internal discussion about its own institutions, structure, and functioning is the Soviet Union. The nonreader of Russian has a wealth of translated material at his disposal—most notably the *Current Digest of the Soviet Press* and the *Current Abstracts of the Soviet Press.* These translate selections from both newspapers and journals. Material of a more scholarly or academic nature is translated in *Problems of Economics.*

Readers of Russian will also find a wealth of material in the Soviet journal *Voprosy Ekonomiki* and in the newspapers *Pravda* (official Communist Party organ), *Izvestia* (official government newspaper), *Ekonomicheskaya Gazeta,* and *Literaturnaya Gazeta.* Other sources, cited in the footnotes, are also useful.

Balassa, Bela. *The Hungarian Experience in Economic Planning.* New Haven, Conn.: Yale University Press, 1959.

Baran, Paul A. "National Economic Planning." In Bernard F. Haley, ed., *A Survey of Contemporary Economics.* Homewood, Ill.: Richard D. Irwin, Inc., 1952.

Bergson, Abram. *The Economics of Soviet Planning.* New Haven, Conn.: Yale University Press, 1964.

Bornstein, Morris, ed. *Comparative Economic Systems: Models and Cases.* Homewood, Ill.: Richard D. Irwin, Inc., 1969, Chs. 3, 7–10, 15–19, 20.

Campbell, Robert W. *Soviet Economic Power.* Boston: Houghton-Mifflin Company, 1966.

Djilas, Milovan. *The New Class.* New York: Praeger Publishers, Inc., 1957.

Dobb, Maurice. *An Essay on Economic Growth and Planning.* London: Routledge & Kegan Paul, Ltd., 1960.

Donnithorne, Audrey. *China's Economic System.* London: George Allen & Unwin, Ltd., 1967.

Downs, Anthony. *Inside Bureaucracy.* Boston: Little, Brown and Company, 1967, especially Chs. 1–4, 6–9, 11, 13, 18, 19, and 22.

———. "A Theory of Bureaucracy." *American Economic Review,* May 1965.

Evenko, I. A. *Planning in the U.S.S.R.* Moscow: Foreign Languages Publishing House, 1961. (A Soviet economist's view of planning in his own country.)

Granick, David. *The Red Executive.* New York: Doubleday & Company, Inc., Anchor Books, 1960.

Grossman, Gregory. "Notes for a Theory of the Command Economy." *Soviet Studies,* Oct. 1963.

Hunter, Holland. " 'Optimal' Tautness in Development Planning." *Economic Development and Cultural Change,* July 1961.

Huberman, Leo, and Paul M. Sweezy. *Socialism in Cuba.* New York: Monthly Review Press, 1969.

Leeman, Wayne. "Bonus Formulae and Soviet Managerial Performance." *Southern Economic Journal,* Apr. 1970.

Levine, H. S. "The Centralized Planning of Supply in Soviet Industry." In F. D. Holzman, ed., *Readings on the Soviet Economy.* Chicago: Rand McNally & Company, 1962. (This book contains many other worthwhile readings.)

Montias, Michael. *Central Planning in Poland.* New Haven, Conn.: Yale University Press, 1962.

———. *Economic Development in Communist Rumania.* Cambridge, Mass.: The MIT Press, 1967.

Nove, Alec. *The Soviet Economy.* London: George Allen & Unwin, 1968, especially Chs. 6, 7.

———. "The Problem of Success Indicators in Soviet Industry." *Economica,* Feb. 1958; reprinted in Holzman (see Levine).

Raitsin, V. I. "Planning the Standard of Living According to Consumption Norms." *Problems of Economics,* Oct.–Nov. 1968.

Sharpe, Myron E. ed., *Planning, Profits, and Incentives in the U.S.S.R.* New Brunswick, N.J.: Rutgers University Press, 1967.

Wiles, P. J. D. *The Political Economy of Communism.* Oxford: Basil Blackwell, 1962.

Part **THREE**

Marx and the Labor Theory of Value

12–1   Marx's Economic Forebears*

We generally identify Marx with the "labor theory of value." In fact, the labor theory of value was the establishment value theory of the Classical School of Economics, which prevailed from 1775 to around 1870. We may view Marx as the last of the classical economists, and in this context it is not surprising that he adopted a labor-value theory.[1] However, the mainstream of classical economic thought did not view their value theory as part of a broader theory of exploitation. Marx did, and it is here that his economics takes its revolutionary turn. In fact, Marx has more than a theory of economic behavior, but it appears easiest to work our way into his broader analysis by first examining the mainstream he inherited from his classical forebears.

His most famous forebear was David Ricardo, who brought the classical

---

[1] Economics is usually said to have blossomed as a full-fledged discipline with the publication of Adam Smith's classic, *The Wealth of Nations,* in 1776. See Adam Smith, *The Wealth of Nations* (New York: Modern Library, 1937).

* For a bibliography of the most relevant works by Marx, see references at the end of Chapter 13.

model to its highest degree of logical perfection in his *Principles of Political Economy and Taxation*.[2] For Ricardo and all the other classical economists, there could be no supply-and-demand theory of value because they were unable to develop a satisfactory theory of demand. Why, they asked, should diamonds be worth a fortune and water be nearly free, when water is necessary for life itself while diamonds are merely ornamentation?

Later, the Neoclassical School was to resolve the paradox by introducing the notion of marginal quantities. A millionaire trapped in the desert might indeed be willing to give a fortune for a drink of water. A manager of a diamond mine may not be willing to pay anything to get one on the market. But in an environment where water is plentiful, individuals are only willing to pay a small price to get more of it. The *marginal* utility of additional water is low relative to the marginal utilities of other goods, even though the *total* utility assignable to water may be relatively high. Similarly, suppose that diamonds are scarce and that the basic needs of life are satisfied well within the budget constraints of some households. Then at least a few among them may expect to derive great satisfaction from the purchase of a diamond. Thus it can command a high price.

While the demand for glasses of water may be far greater than the demand for diamonds, the supply of the latter is also far less. With more refined tools, the Neoclassical economists were able to resolve the famous water–diamonds paradox, and Figure 12–1 shows the paradox untangled. The Classical School never achieved a resolution, however. For Marx, a good had to be useful before it could have exchange value, but it could be useful *without* possessing exchange value—for example, "air, virgin soil, natural meadows," and other natural resources.

As we shall see, one version of the "contradiction" between value in use and in exchange becomes a central tenet of Marx's theory of capitalist exploitation. Interestingly enough, we can introduce exploitation into the Neoclassical framework via monopoly restrictions on output or "artificial" scarcity. In Figure 12–1, suppose that there are monopoly elements in the diamond industry which restrict the supply. Without these restrictions the supply curve would be $S'_d S'_d$, we assume, and the price P'_d, below P_d. Part of this higher price goes into monopoly profits, but we should note that P'_d is still considerably higher than P_w.

Because they were unable to build a theory of demand, the Classical economists had to rely entirely on a supply or cost of production theory of

[2] David Ricardo, *The Principles of Political Economy and Taxation* (New York: Dutton, Everyman, 1911). See, as well, the version edited by Piero Sraffa. This is Vol. I of *The Works of David Ricardo*, P. Sraffa and M. Dobb, eds. (New York: Cambridge U.P., 1951). We should point out that Ricardo did not hold an *analytical* labor theory of value. Ricardo felt that, over time, relative prices of different goods tend to approximately reflect relative labor costs in most cases. This is an *empirical* labor theory of value. Because direct labor costs dominated total production costs in most industries, relative prices more closely reflect these, say, than relative capital costs.

Price

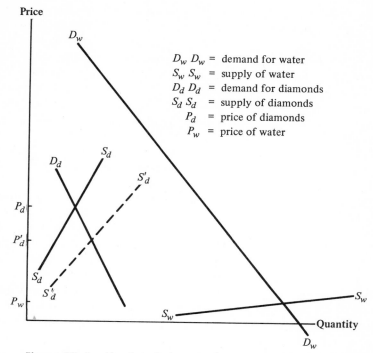

$D_w D_w$ = demand for water
$S_w S_w$ = supply of water
$D_d D_d$ = demand for diamonds
$S_d S_d$ = supply of diamonds
P_d = price of diamonds
P_w = price of water

Figure 12–1. The (seeming) water–diamonds paradox untangled.

value. Because labor is, in a sense, the most fundamental input, this often turned into a labor-value theory. We shall see shortly that no logical contradiction exists between the Marxian labor and the conventional supply-and-demand value theories. Basically, they reflect different emphases.

The Classical school also assumed a famous postulate known as *Say's Law*.[3] In its crudest form, it maintained that "supply creates its own demand." Its thrust was to assert that there could be no permanent problem with an aggregate demand for goods and services that is too low to absorb a full employment level of output. Whenever production occurs, incomes must be paid to those who assist in creating the goods and services involved. Individuals only seek money in order to spend it on more goods and services, according to the spirit of Say's Law, and these incomes immediately result in an increased consumption and investment demand whose value matches that of the increased production (or supply).

In these circumstances, there can be overproduction of particular goods and underproduction of others, relative to demand. This can cause temporary dislocations and also the phenomenon known as a business cycle. But the

---

[3] J. B. Say, *Letters to Thomas Malthus on Political Economy and Stagnation of Commerce* (London: G. Harding, 1936).

value of the *total* demand for goods and services must be equal to the value of the total supply, regardless of how much is produced. There cannot be a recession as a result of an aggregate demand that is too low. Moreover, both the Classical mainstream and their Neoclassical heirs often emphasized the flexibility of wages and prices and the ability of markets to return to equilibrium positions at which supply and demand are in balance. Occupational entry barriers were implicitly presumed not to exist. If unemployed workers were willing to work at a wage below the existing rate, they were assumed to bid the wage down.

Consequently, unemployment appeared as a transitional or temporary problem in most of the Classical-mainstream literature. With the technology taken as given, or at least not discussed, the Classical theory became one of distribution rather than of output and employment. Ricardo distinguished three major socioeconomic classes—laborers, capitalists, and landlords—and tried to explain how a full-employment level of income and output would be divided up among them. To do this, he needed the famous Malthusian population dilemma which, after Say's Law, became the second pillar of Classical-mainstream theory.[4]

According to Malthus, the natural tendency of mankind was to increase its members without limit unless a natural check was imposed. The check in question was man's ability to increase the food supply, which, Malthus argued, fell short of his propensity to reproduce. Specifically, according to Malthus, while the food supply would grow in an arithmetic progression: 1, 2, 3, 4, 5, 6, . . . , the population growth, if unchecked, would follow a geometric progression: 2, 4, 8, 16, 32. . . . Unless other factors intervened, the population would be constantly pressing against the food supply, and the bulk of humanity would be forced to a subsistence level of living. Malthus calculated that unchecked population growth would be around 3 per cent per year, although the basis of his conclusion is far from scientific.

Other factors could indeed intervene to restrain population growth before the food supply became the ultimate check. Wars, epidemics, natural disasters, and genocide all perform this function from time to time. But, according to Malthus, these do not normally cause the bulk of humanity to rise above a subsistence level of living, and, in any event, are not especially attractive alternatives to famine.[5] "Moral restraint" could also provide a check, but here Malthus, essentially the victim of a generation gap, was deeply pessimistic.

---

[4] Robert Malthus, "An Essay on the Principle of Population," in L. D. Abbott, ed., *Masterworks of Economics* (New York: Doubleday, 1948).

[5] "Famine seems to be the last, most dreadful resource of nature. The power of population is so superior to the power of the Earth to provide subsistence . . . that premature death must in some shape or other visit the human race. The vices of mankind are active and able ministers of depopulation . . . . But should they fail in this war of extermination, sickly seasons, epidemics, pestilence, and plagues advance in terrific array and sweep off their thousands and tens of thousands. Should success still be incomplete, gigantic inevitable famine stalks in the rear, and with one mighty blow, levels the population with the food of the world."

Mankind was basically indolent and pleasure-seeking, he believed, and he failed to foresee the power and the possibilities of contraception.[6]

If the human race had begun in 10,000 b.c. with a single couple and had grown at a rate of 1 per cent per year since then, the world would now be a mass of flesh several thousand light-years in diameter expanding at a rate that exceeds the speed of light. This does not not refute Malthus, who was only telling us what would happen if population remained unchecked. Because it is checked, it may actually grow at a rate more closely approximating an arithmetic progression. The important thing is that it always tends to press against the food supply, and this pressure keeps the wage rate at a "subsistence" level. Indeed, we can reach this conclusion with much weaker assumptions than Malthus used.

Today, the Malthusian population dilemma does appear to confront much of that part of the world—comprising nearly two-thirds of the human race—that we sometimes call the "developing" nations. Here, an inadequate resource base helps to keep most people in abject poverty. But what of the developed world? Ricardo's answer was that the subsistence wage rate could be at a psychological or cultural rather than a physiological minimum. Differences in wage rates from country to country could thus be a function of "habit and custom." However, there would be a determinate subsistence wage rate within any country and at any point in time. Most of the population was condemned to live close to subsistence, however defined. More precisely, whenever the actual wage was greater than or equal to the subsistence wage, the population would tend to rise. Whenever the actual wage was less than subsistence, the population would tend to fall.

If we multiply the subsistence wage times the total number of laborers and then make an upward adjustment for the skill mix of the labor force, therefore, we get a very good approximation to the total wages bill. Dividing this, in turn, by a full-employment level of income gives us a good approximation to the wage share. We have yet to determine the shares of capitalists and landlords. To this end we first note that the mainstream Classicists generally viewed the capitalist as an entrepreneur who powered the engine of progress by taking the risks and responsibilities of investment decision making upon his shoulders. To attract able and innovative entrepreneurs, there had to be a profit reward for productive investments. By and large, the Classical economists assumed that competition would equalize the rate of profit throughout the economy.

[6] It was, however, a friendly generation gap. Malthus's father was impressed with the anarchist and Utopian ideas of William Godwin, who was all the rage of the drawing rooms of London toward the end of the eighteenth century. Godwin was horrified with the present, but looked forward to a future in which "There will be no war, no crime, no administration of justice, as it is called, and no government. Besides this there will be no disease, anguish, melancholy, or resentment." Poverty would likewise all but disappear. Godwin was a kind of matured and mellowed Abbie Hoffman of his day, and Malthus wrote his *Essay on Population* to refute this point of view. Godwin's daughter, Mary, eloped with Percy Bysshe Shelley; she later wrote *Frankenstein*.

The landlord, on the other hand, was viewed as an owner of renewable natural resources. His reward is rent, a payment for "the use of the original and indestructible powers of the soil." Should an entrepreneur exploit new deposits of mineral wealth, he would receive a profit for doing so. But the *owner* of the site would normally receive a rent over and above this profit just for the use of his land. The amount of rent that he can command is essentially determined by the demand for the land. The landlord was assumed to place his property in that use from which his rental income would be highest. The opportunity cost of using land in any given line of production is the highest rental income that it could earn elsewhere. However, if we consider all uses together, land was considered to be a "free gift of nature" which could come into production even though the rent was zero, provided there was a sufficient incentive to the capitalist to get production organized.[7]

A single individual may play the roles of both capitalist and landlord, and even that of laborer. Ricardo wished to explain the rewards earned by each socioeconomic *role* rather than the distribution of income among specific individuals or households. (That is, he wished to explain what is sometimes called the *functional* distribution of income.) He also wished to describe the long-run evolution of functional shares and the implications of this for the long-run growth of income and output.

If we are to explain long-run distribution in the conditions just outlined, it appears worthwhile to look at agriculture, inasmuch as this industry becomes a long-run constraint on the rest of the system. Wheat was the staple food in Ricardo's day. We shall therefore consider the production of wheat to see how the income which this activity generates is distributed among laborers, capitalists, and landlords associated with its production. Following Ricardo, we compute this distribution in terms of bushels of wheat, or value equivalents, rather than pounds sterling. Such a procedure is simply convention. As long as there are well-defined and accepted exchange rates prevailing between all goods, it does not matter which one we use as our unit of account.

In the spirit of Ricardo, we shall assume that wheat is being grown on four grades of land, A, B, C, and D, with declining yields as we go from A to D. The division of these yields into wages, rent, and profit is as follows:

Grade of Land	Average Yield (bushels) per Labor Week	Wage (Subsistence)	Rent	Profit
A	500	100	300	100
B	400	100	200	100
C	300	100	100	100
D	200	100	0	100

[7] The supply of any natural resource is taken to be a vertical line. That is, the quantity supplied is fixed and completely independent of the prevailing price (or rent). The rent on a renewable natural resource is therefore entirely determined by the demand for it in its most lucrative use.

Ricardo implicitly supposed that the ratio of capital to labor was the same on all four grades of land. (In effect, he assumed that labor could not be substituted for capital or vice versa.) Consequently, the capital outlays required to bring and maintain each grade of land into production are the same. Because competition equalizes the rate of profit, total profits are the same on each grade of land.

To get the profit share, we therefore go to the no-rent land, where profit is a residual equal to total yield minus subsistence wages. One hundred bushels of wheat become the amount of profit on each grade of land (on, let us say, a per acre-week basis). Rent is the total amount left over after *both* profits and subsistence wages have been subtracted. Rent is highest on the best land and falls off from there. In more modern terms, the demand for the best land per acre-week is greatest. Thus the price of using an acre for a week, or the weekly rent per acre, will be highest there.

Because the population tends to press against the food supply, population increases will occur, but they will eventually be reversed unless the food supply expands. We can and will get more production from land already under cultivation, but production on each grade of land is subject to the *law of diminishing returns*. As we keep adding fixed doses of labor and capital to any given plot of cultivated ground, the resulting increments to output eventually become less and less. (If this did not happen, in fact, it would be possible to grow the nation's entire food supply on a few acres of good farmland, provided sufficient labor and machinery were available.)

As technological progress is not allowed for, grade E land must come into production sooner or later if output is to continue to grow. We suppose that it would yield but 150 bushels per acre-week, subject to the same dose of labor and capital applied above. However, before grade E land comes into use, further doses of labor and capital will be applied to grades A–D land, thereby raising output subject to the law of diminishing returns. The result is a table such as the following:

Grade of Land	Average Yield (bushels) per Labor Week	Wage (Subsistence)	Rent	Profit
A	550	140	350	60
B	450	140	250	60
C	350	140	150	60
D	250	140	50	60
E	200	140	0	60

Once again the worst grade of land yields no rent. It is assumed to have no alternative uses outside of wheat farming, and its owner–manager will put it into production for a normal profit return on his investment. However, because profits are the residual on the no-rent land, the per acre profit, measured in wheat equivalents, must be lower. Rents, on the other hand, must be higher since they are a residual after profits and wages are deducted.

The main feature of Ricardo's model, therefore, is rising rents and a falling rate of profit. The latter, first formalized by Ricardo, became a key feature in the theories of capitalist development by Marx, Schumpeter, and Keynes, even though all four theories are as different as they could be and no two scholars would even agree on a definition of profit.

Of course, grade E land will not even be brought into use until the economy-wide profits, measured in terms of wheat, reach 60 bushels on the outlay needed to bring and maintain another acre of land into wheat production. If the supply of wheat does not increase over a fairly long period of time, the price of wheat will rise relative to the prices of other goods and, in particular, relative to the prices of tools and implements used in producing wheat. This will encourage more acreage to go into wheat farming. The profit from wheat farming, valued in wheat, may well then fall as Ricardo suggested.

However, it is not clear that the *rate* of profit will fall in our example above. If the price of wheat rises more than twice as much as the prices of tools and implements needed in producing wheat, the rate of profit in wheat farming will have risen. Thus it was necessary for Ricardo to argue further to show that, ultimately, the rate of profit would indeed go down. This is possible if we (1) assume a labor theory of value; (2) abstract entirely from technical progress, *either* in the wheat industry or anywhere else; and (3) suppose that there are very limited ways for most people to substitute goods *not* subject to long-run diminishing returns on natural resources in production for those which are. If individuals can achieve high levels of material welfare by consuming additional quantities of the first category of goods, the importance of food in determining the "level of living" will no longer be paramount.[8]

Making these assumptions for the moment, we reach Ricardo's conclusion that the rate of profit will fall until there is no further incentive for capitalists to expand the food supply. Beyond this point, population, income, and output would remain largely stagnant. The country in question would have entered the famous "stationary state." To Ricardo, this state was both gloomy and imminent. Because of his dire outlook, economics became known as the "dismal science." Yet, nothing in his decidedly long-run analysis suggests that England would enter into the stationary state in 10 to 15 rather than 500 years hence. According to Ricardo's theory, rents would rise, the rate of profit would fall, and real wages would remain the same. (In fact, profits were rising and rents were falling in post-Napoleonic England. "Ye Gods," exclaimed a fellow MP, "did this man just descend from Mars?")

Neither need the stationary state be dismal if we allow, as Ricardo did, for

---

[8] For a proof, see Mark Blaug, *Economic Theory in Retrospect* (Homewood, Ill.: Irwin, 1962), Ch. 4. Blaug's discussion of Ricardian theory is superb. Interestingly enough, the emphasis of the classical economists on diminishing returns to land made them strong advocates of free trade. Through trade, England and other densely populated countries could import cheap food from abroad—for example, from countries further removed from their stationary states and thereby postpone the march into the stationary state at home.

a cultural or a psychological concept of subsistence. When the food supply suffices to maintain most of the population in good health, it probably will prove possible to increase welfare significantly through increased nonfood consumption (provided it can be raised through *some* form of increased consumption). For John Stuart Mill, another classical economist, the stationary state became the benign achievement of man's striving and sacrifice. Having maximized income per capita, it would become possible for man to curb his acquisitive instincts and turn toward a higher form of self-realization.

Prior to the stationary state, according to Mill, capitalism was necessary to translate the acquisitive drive into social progress in the form of increasing output. By giving entrepreneurs the rights to the earnings of their investments and by subjecting their performance to a market test, the desire for wealth could be harnessed and made into a creative force. (Under favorable conditions, an entrepreneur would be judged solely according to whether he brought a product to market that was wanted at a price rational customers were willing to pay. However, competition would have to be relied upon to eliminate entrepreneurs whose investments were unproductive.)

As we approach the stationary state, on the other hand, and the "subsistence" wage nears its maximum level, the importance of the acquisitive instinct and of competitive relationships among society's members begins to fade. Cooperative relationships begin to rise in importance. When the stationary state reaches full bloom, a kind of "socialist harmony" ought, in Mill's view, to prevail. The economic problem ceases to be of prime importance, along with the need for large incentives to motivate entrepreneurial behavior.

The results of the classical model will withstand some technological progress—which, in agriculture, would raise the yields on one or more grades of land above. They will not withstand a succession of Green Revolutions or, more generally, technological progress sufficient to offset the effects of diminishing returns to land. They are also vulnerable to technical progress, which does not affect food production, but does raise the output of goods which can be substituted for food to maintain or raise the standard of living. It is vulnerable to technical progress in the production and distribution of contraceptives.

There are a number of defects in the basic Ricardian analysis. However, many economists would argue that technological change has been the most important factor in preventing the Malthusian population dilemma from pushing the world's developed nations into a stationary state.[9]

And yet, we are today reviving some of what were once considered the most unrealistic ideas of Ricardo and Malthus. Ricardo's emphasis on diminishing returns to reusable or "inexhaustible" natural resources is quite like the modern tendency to view the world as a spaceship. The standard of living on "spaceship Earth" depends heavily upon population control and the ability to reuse resources, including the recycling of all kinds of waste products. The

---

[9] For a broader discussion of the merits and demerits of the "Ricardian engine," see Blaug, op. cit., Ch. 4 and the references cited there.

natural-resource endowment of the ship has a definite finite limit and is therefore subject to diminishing returns.

Technological progress can occur and become embodied in new products,
notably new capital goods. Much of the difference between the Classical emphasis and the more recent emphasis on permanent growth of output per head
over time stems directly from the kinds of inputs which each school uses in
its description of production. The Classicists stressed labor and land as fundamental factors of production. More recent models have substituted capital,
which is both reproducible and augmentable, for nonreproducible and non-
augmentable land. One could argue that this is the most fundamental distinction between them.

Yet, it is at least conceivable that much of man's recorded technical
progress over the last 100 years or so consists of new ways to exploit ex-
hustible or *non*renewable natural resources more quickly. If so, this represents
a transfer of welfare from future to present generations, rather than an absolute
efficiency gain which makes some generations better off and none worse off.
Until now, mankind has been fairly successful in discovering new technologies
which have enabled it to use new or lower-quality nonrenewable resources as
old reserves have disappeared. But this activity may, itself, be ultimately subject
to diminishing returns.

In order to turn the mainstream Classical theory into a theory of "capitalist
exploitation," Marx had to deny the Malthusian population dilemma, at least
as a general law applying to all societies. Marx denounced the Malthusian
doctrine, in fact, as an insult to the working class. In its place he substituted
a phenomenon that he thought would result in a subsistence wage solely under
conditions of capitalist exploitation.

In the third edition of his *Principles,* Ricardo added a chapter entitled
"On Machinery," which came as a kind of afterthought to his principal theme.
There he concluded that "the subtitution of machinery for human labor is
often very injurious to the interests of the class of laborers. [Investment may]
render the population redundant and deteriorate the condition of the laborer."

For the first time Ricardo explicitly acknowledged the possibility of substituting capital for labor in production. A machine can replace laborers in the
sense that it becomes possible to produce the same amount of output with
fewer workers.[10] The introduction of new machinery can therefore throw men
out of work. Of course, it can also permit society to expand its income and
output because it enables output per worker to rise. If Say's Law holds, the
economy should find a new long-run equilibrium at a higher level of production
and with full employment restored.

The factory that installs the machinery may find it so profitable to expand
output, given the lower cost of production or higher quality that it is now
able to sustain, that it ultimately reabsorbs all laborers initially laid off. Other-

---

[10] In fact, output falls in the example given by Ricardo, which is also confusing in
several other ways. Interested readers should consult Ricardo, op. cit, and Blaug, op. cit.,
starting with the latter.

wise, unemployed workers may be able to find new jobs elsewhere in expanding sectors. Even if no such sectors exist, workers can always find employment, given Say's Law and flexible wages, by offering to work at a wage below the going rate.

However, Marx denounced Say's Law, and even if we believe in it as a long-run phenomenon, we must admit that the reabsorption of unemployed workers will take time. The greater the required mobility of labor from one geographical region to another and the higher are effective job entry barriers, the longer reabsortion is likely to take. Because some time will be required in any event, the adjustment to one labor-saving innovation could well be incomplete when another comes along. A succession of labor-saving changes in technology could well maintain a permanent "reserve army of unemployed." Wage rates might then remain close to subsistence because of the resulting competition for jobs.

Marx held that an increasing capital-to-labor ratio characterized technological progress under capitalism and that an industrial reserve army did indeed arise to maintain a near-subsistence wage. Once we have a determinate wage rate in the Marxian model, the functional distribution of income is determined, because Marx essentially collapsed the landlord and capitalist classes into one. The reward of this class, the members of which are called capitalists or bourgeoisie, is profit, which is now expanded to include Ricardian rents.

Marx would divide the 550 bushels of wheat harvested on grade A land above into 140 bushels, or value equivalents, of subsistence wages and 410 bushels of profit. However, all output is created, according to Marx, by living labor inputs. The 410 bushels of profit are therefore viewed as an expropriation from labor and as a manifestation of "capitalist exploitation."

Marx believed that most of any expansion in output and income due to technological progress would accrue to capitalists, whose propensity to consume is much lower than that of the working class. Consequently, technical change is accompanied by a slower expansion in consumption demand than would occur if the working class reaped most of the benefits. Investment demand is also sluggish because technological progress tends to lower the rate of profit, which is the capitalist's motive to invest.[11] The upshot is that an expansion through technological progress of the economy's ability to produce is not immediately followed by a corresponding expansion in aggregate demand, a result that tends to create or prolong unemployment; hence the reserve army of the unemployed.

Marx was also more akin to modern growth theorists than to other Classicists in stressing the productive power of laissez-faire capitalism. For him, capitalism was the culmination of a series of property-right forms which had made it possible to subordinate nature to man. The price of this, however, was exploitation of one social class by another. For example, in the *Communist Manifesto,* he writes: "[Capitalism] has been the first to show what man's activity can bring about. It has accomplished wonders far surpassing Egyp-

---

[11] Marx believed that this conclusion followed from his labor theory of value. We shall discuss the matter later.

tian pyramids, Roman aqueducts, and Gothic cathedrals. . . . The Bourgeoisie, during its rule of scarce 100 years, has created more massive and more colossal productive forces than have all preceding generations together." [12]

Nevertheless, as capitalism matures, the benefits of this productivity are concentrated in fewer and fewer hands. A principal advantage of socialism, to Marx's way of thinking, would be its ability to accommodate laborsaving technical progress, while maintaining full employment and redistributing the resulting benefits. Once "objective conditions" are ripe for revolution, the emerging socialist state would be able to accommodate an even higher level of productivity than capitalism.

Unfortunately, Marx did not leave a set of blueprints to describe the socialist system that would bring these wonders to pass, but socialism is in any event only a transitional phase along the road to full communism. The latter replaces the classical stationary state in Marx's thought.

12–2   The Labor Theory of Value Versus Modern Value Theory

Perhaps the dimension of Marxian economics that has drawn the greatest amount of criticism from economists is his labor theory of value. Some have maintained that it cannot be reconciled with modern Western supply-and-demand value theory, and others have simply claimed that it is incorrect. (A few have even argued that Marx evenutally abandoned the labor theory of value, although the author can find no justification for this position.)

Our purpose in this section will not be to defend Marxian value theory from its critics, for this discussion ought best to occupy the pages of treatises on the history of economic thought. Rather, we shall show that a labor-value theory in the spirit of Marx is also quite consistent with Western value theory. The latter does not imply that, in a broad sense, only human labor can create value (or be "creative") or that labor is the most essential factor of production. This is, however, a difference of emphasis. Marx focused on what he believed to be the exploitive nature of capitalism; Western value theory provides no such filter. On the other hand, Marxian value theory does not uniquely determine the relative exchange values of different goods and services until we appeal to some notion of supply and demand.

As a naïve first approximation to Marxian value theory, we may assign a value to each good which equals the quantity of living labor that went into its production. This would be exchange value of the good. (Having noted that the exchange and use values of a good may differ, Marx sets out to explain the former.) The more living labor, measured in labor hours or some other time unit, that is necessary to produce a good, the higher its exchange value. We may divide this living labor input into an amount, V, of wages and

---

[12] Karl Marx and Friedrich Engels, *Manifesto of the Communist Party* (New York: International Publishers, 1948), pp. 11, 13.

salaries and an amount, S, of surplus value or profit expropriated by the capitalist.

We may go so far as to apply the labor theory of value to labor itself. The pressure of the industrial reserve army of unemployed causes wages and salaries to show a long-run tendency toward physiological or cultural subsistence levels. (Marx is ambiguous as to which notion of subsistence is most appropriate. However, since wages and salaries are allowed to differ according to talent and skill, the latter is the most logically consistent.) The average of all wages and salaries thus tends toward a level that will just enable the laboring classes to reproduce themselves, while more or less maintaining their standard of living.

The value of this subsistence wage, in terms of purchasing power over food, clothing, shelter, and other items in the workingman's budget, is the exchange value of the laborer. This is what the capitalist pays to hire him. According to Marx, however, the capitalist does not pay for a laborer. Rather, he pays for an abstract commodity called labor-power. The capitalist supposedly views the laborer, not as a creative human being but as a source of profit. Marx felt that labor was the fundamental form of human expression and creation. Because the workingman must sell his labor to the capitalist, he is robbed of "the natural spontaneous activity to which he is entitled as a member of the human race . . . and [degraded] to working for mere existence, like a horse." [13] In this way he is dehumanized.

Because living labor can create goods and services worth more than the wages it is paid, the capitalist actually receives more value than he pays for. He receives the right to use labor, and this "use-value" of labor is greater than the exchange value or labor power embodied in it. Hence exploitation, according to Marx; part of the laborer's effort goes toward earning an income for the capitalist, and this "surplus value" may be looked upon as unpaid labor.

The above discussion ignores the presence of capital in production. Capital cannot create value, but it does embody value, since labor was previously used to help produce it. We may think of capital as coming in two basic forms. *Circulating* capital, such as cloth, flour, tin cans, or sheet steel, becomes a part of the product it assists in producing. It thereby imparts its own value to the product. For example, the value of sheet steel is imparted to the values of refrigerators and automobiles when sheet steel is fashioned into doors, fenders, and so on, of which the autos or refrigerators are made. *Fixed* capital, such as plant, machinery, and other equipment, does not become a part of the goods and service it assists in producing.

However, fixed capital does wear out in the process of production and, as it depreciates, its value is imparted to these goods and services. A part of the value of each good or service produced consists of this depreciation flow. Thus the value of a machine tool on an automobile assembly line is slowly im-

---

[13] Dirk Struik, "Introduction" to Karl Marx, *The Economic and Philosophical Manuscripts of 1844* (New York: International Publishers, 1964), p. 45.

parted, a tiny amount at a time, to each of the thousands of cars manufactured there every year.

Let C stand for the combined values of the depreciation flow and materials used up in producing a particular good. Then the total Marxian value of the good equals C plus the wages (and fringe benefits) bill V plus the surplus value created by labor but expropriated by the capitalist S. We usually denote Marxian value by W. Therefore,

$$W = C + V + S$$

for every good or service. The principal difference between labor and capital, according to Marx, is that living labor alone can *create* value. The value already embodied in capital goods can be imparted to goods that capital assists in producing. But in the process, no *new* value is created.

We can perhaps see this even better by using a *value-added* approach. The total value which an automobile assembly plant adds to its inputs is $(S + V)$. The amount of value, C, was already in existence in the form of material inputs and fixed capital. [The sum of $(S + V)$ over all the production processes in the economy would give us net national product.[14]] Current Western value theory departs from Marxian theory in (also) permitting fixed capital to make a productive contribution to value added, $(S + V)$. The contribution of labor is the value of labor's marginal physical product times the amount of labor used. The contribution of capital is the value of capital's marginal product times the amount of capital used. The sum of these contributions of all kinds of labor and capital will equal the total value added, $(S + V)$. This is true for each production process, subject to certain considerations of a technical nature.[15]

Suppose that all kinds of labor, including management, are receiving wages and salaries equal to the values of their marginal products and that property owners are receiving a price for the use of each kind of fixed capital equal to that capital's VMP. Then S gives the net income of property owners and V the total wage and salary bill in any production activity.

Then, within the context of Western theory, there would be no "exploita-

---

[14] There is, however, a difference between Western and Marxian national income accounting theories. Marx was consistent with the classical school in distinguishing between "productive" and "unproductive" labor, the latter working mainly in the service industries. The output of the service sector (created by "unproductive" labor) is not included in net material product, the Marxian concept of value added, which the socialist countries calculate in place of Western NNP. The Western view is that a good's ability to create utility, either directly or indirectly by helping to produce other goods, is the sole criterion for inclusion.

The value of a haircut would count as part of Western NNP but not as part of Soviet net material product. The value of a lawyer's services would count as part of the latter if he was working for a metallurgical firm but not if he was working for a supervising office in the intermediate planning bureaucracy. This is a second difference (besides the one given below) between Marxian (or classical) and Western value theory. For a discussion see Smith, op. cit., Ch. III.

[15] Each production process would have to operate under constant returns to scale— a doubling or halving of all inputs would have to double or halve total output.

tion." Exploitation of labor, or of any input, for that matter, is said to occur when the price of the input is *less than* the value of its marginal product. Exploitation of labor would therefore occur when V is less than the VMP of labor times the amount of labor employed. Exploitation of capital would occur when S is less than the productive contribution of capital—perhaps because of the power of labor unions or because property owners are effectively exploited by managers.

Moving back to Marxian theory, we might say that exploitation of labor always occurs in the above sense because the "full" value created by labor, $(S + V)$, is always greater than the bill of wages and salaries, V. In effect, Marx supposes the value of capital's marginal product to be zero. Capitalists who are also owner–managers do create value in their technical function of coordinating production. But these functions can be delegated to a hired manager for modest "wages of superintendence." Moreover, according to Marx: "It is not because he is a leader of industry that a man is a capitalist; on the contrary, he is a leader of industry because he is a capitalist. The leadership of industry is an attribute of capital, just as in feudal times the functions of generals and judges were attributes of landed property." [16]

In modern Western theory, "exploitation" has a purely technical connotation. There is no moral implication that each input *should* be paid the value of its marginal product. The value of labor's marginal product depends on how much capital labor has to work with in any event (generally speaking, labor is more productive when it has more and better capital to work with), and vice versa, so that such a moral pronouncement would not make sense. However, Marx definitely argues that capitalists are getting an income they do not deserve—that they are effectively robbing the working man. We shall return to this matter shortly.

From Chapter 3 we recall that the value of capital's marginal product in the manufacture of any good equals the price of the good times capital's marginal physical product. A zero VMP of capital therefore implies that capital's marginal physical product is equal to zero. If we add more fixed capital to any production process, we do not get any more output (or, at any rate, we do not get more value) beyond that needed to compensate for depreciation. According to Marxists, "bourgeois" value theory, by justifying payments for nonlabor factors of production, is rationalizing the exploitation of man by man.

Nevertheless, we must add an important qualification. Capital is productive in the sense that labor becomes more productive when working with the technology embodied in better plant and equipment. Likewise, labor may become more productive when working with better-quality natural resources or resources that have been newly discovered or for which new uses have been found. The difference between natural resources and capital here is that nature embodies technology into the former, whereas man embodies it into the latter.

[16] Marx, *Capital* (Moscow: Foreign Languages Publishing, 1965–1967), Vol. I, p. 332.

Therefore, according to Marx, natural resources do not themselves have exchange value, whereas capital does. But both make labor more productive.

Consequently, the value added in each production activity depends, not only upon its living labor inputs, but also on a broad definition of technology, called the "mode of production." The mode of production, in fact, comprises not only the techniques used in production and distribution, or what Marx called the "productive forces," but also the aggregate of socioeconomic relationships between individuals which defines the current organization of production and distribution. According to Loucks and Whitney:

> In a given situation in which certain natural resources, human resources, and technical knowledge of processes prevail, the economic processes of production, exchange, distribution, and consumption will come to be organized into certain institutions, primarily of a social sort, since they involve relationships among men. The totality of these relationships, including innumerable interactions among them, constitute as a whole the 'mode of production' which will set the form and content of all other social institutions.[17]

We shall consider the role played by the mode of production more thoroughly below. For now we simply note that any improvement in technology will be a combination of better organization of production, broadly understood; better capital, both fixed and circulating, for labor to work with; and better use of natural resources. With this in mind, economists often talk about embodied and disembodied technological progress, meaning that some technical changes are embodied in new and inproved capital, whereas others are not. *Dis*embodied technological progress is the same as an improvement in what we earlier referred to as "X efficiency." [18] Both kinds of technology can be looked upon as direct or indirect contributions of labor.

Thus both embodied and disembodied technological progress represent the fruits of labor spent in research and development. It is through the efforts of managers, foremen, consulting personnel, and, on occasion, ordinary workmen that disembodied progress is implemented. Technological change is physically embodied into capital by labor working with other material means of production, which already contain their own embodied technology. Whenever labor works with fixed capital or natural resources, we can think of it as unlocking the technology within and thereby imparting adidtional value to goods and services being created. It is not hard to reconcile this approach with Marx:

> If the productivity of labor is increased . . . for instance, if weaving with power-looms becomes no longer exceptional, and if the weaving of a yard with the power-loom requires only half the labor time required with the hand-loom, the twelve hours' labor of a hand-loom weaver is no longer represented in a value of twelve hours, but in one of six, since the socially necessary labor time has now become six hours. The hand-loom weaver's twelve hours now only [represent]

17 W. N. Loucks and W. G. Whitney, *Comparative Economic Systems,* 8th ed. (New York: Harper, 1969), p. 75.
18 In Section 3–7 we pointed out that X efficiency complements the more conventional notion of production efficiency which deals with the allocation of inputs among different production activities.

six hours of social labor-time, although he still works twelve hours as he did before.[19]

Suppose, then that we set up a standard (Neoclassical) growth model in the manner of modern Western economists. In it the level of technology and the inputs of both capital and labor all make contributions to the value of output. The rates of technological change and of change in capital and labor inputs all contribute to the rate of growth in value added. But there is no unique way of separating the contribution of capital to value added from the contribution of technology.

In particular, we may assign the entire combined contribution to technology. This, in turn, becomes an indirect contribution of labor, completing the basis of a labor value theory that is quite in the spirit of Marx. The full contribution of labor to value creation now consists of a direct plus an indirect component, at least part of the latter being assigned to capital in conventional Western value theory.

Such an approach eliminates several of the problems that have plagued adherents of a labor theory of value in the past. For example, followers of Ricardo were occasionally driven to distraction by the thought of grape juice maturing into wine and thereby rising in value with no application of labor. However, labor is used to bottle the wine, place it into proper storage facilities, maintain the right environment for fermentation, and remove the fermented wine at the right time. In the process, labor unlocks the technology already embodied in the bottles, storage facilities, temperature-control apparatus, and so on. It thereby enables the value of the grape juice to rise even when it is not physically present.

Nevertheless, a complete value theory must explain the relative values of different goods and services to one another. As we have seen, Western value theory does this on the basis of demand and supply. The higher the demand for one good relative to others, the higher its relative price, for any given supply, and vice versa. The higher the supply, or the more plentiful the good, the lower its price, for any given demand, and vice versa. Neither determinant of value is more important than the other. In the words of Marshall, both blades of the scissors do the cutting.

Either supply or demand may contain elements of monopoly power, a point on which Western and Marxian economists can presumably agree. In particular, monopolistic restrictions on supply can force up the price. However, supply is also determined by costs of production, which, in turn, reflect input prices (and thereby the availability of inputs) and the technology of production. In the case of labor, the supply depends upon work–leisure preferences and the availability of other job opportunities. The demand for produced goods depends upon their productivity in further production or the preferences of households for them vis-à-vis other commodities.

To a conventional Western economist relative value is partly subjective. It depends upon tastes or preferences, as well as "objective conditions of pro-

[19] See Marx, *Theories of Surplus Value*, Pt. I, op. cit., Vol. IV, p. 381.

duction." Marxian economists, on the other hand, claim that they have an entirely objective value standard, the amount of labor embodied in a commodity, whether bestowed by living labor or past labor already embodied in some form of capital. For example:

A use value, or useful article therefore has value only because human labor in the abstract has been embodied or materialized in it. How, then, is the magnitude of this value to be measured? Plainly, by the quantity of value-creating substance, the labor, contained in the article. The quantity of labor, however, is measured by its duration, and labor time in turn finds its standard in weeks, days, and hours. A commodity has a value, because it is a crystallization of social labor. The greatness of its value, or its relative value, depends upon the greater or less amount of that social substance contained in it; that is to say, on the relative mass of labor necessary for its production. The relative values of commodities are, therefore, determined by the respective quantities or amounts of labor worked up, realized, fixed in them. . . .
Every commodity is a symbol, since, insofar as it has value, it is only the material envelope of the human labor spent upon it.[20]

Yet, all labor is not identical with respect to skill and ability; different individuals possess differential comparative advantages in performing various jobs, duties, and tasks. Moreover, some labor has better capital equipment to work with than other, and we have just seen that the value added by workers in any line of production will depend upon this. Finally, Marx did not claim that more labor applied to the production of a given commodity *automatically* made it more valuable. Only *socially necessary* labor time is value-determining.

Labor time is socially necessary in Marx to an extent determined by the quality of the technology that labor works with (as in our earlier example of the weaver) and by the skill and ability embodied in it. However, the demand for the good being produced is also a determinant. Marx describes a market in which there is an excess supply of linen as follows:

suppose that every piece of linen in the market contains no more labor-time than is socially necessary (given the current state of technology). In spite of this, all these pieces taken as a whole may have had superfluous labor time (i.e., labor time not socially necessary) spent on them. If the market cannot stomach the whole quantity at the normal price of 2 shillings a yard, this proves that too great a portion of the total labor of the community has been expended in the form of weaving. The effect is the same as if each individual weaver had expended more labor time upon his particular product than is socially necessary.[21]

Later he maintains:

For a commodity to be sold at its market value, i.e., proportionate to the socially necessary labor contained in it, the total quantity of social labor used in

---

[20] These quotes come from the following sources (in sequence): Marx, *Capital,* op. cit., Vol. I, p. 38; Marx, *Value, Price and Profit,* (New York: International Publishers, 1935), p. 31; and Marx, *Capital,* op. cit., Vol. I, p. 90.
[21] Ibid., Vol. I, p. 107.

producing the total mass of this commodity must correspond to the quantity of the social want [or demand] for it, i.e., to the effective social want.[22]

When we say that the relative values of two goods equal the relative quantities of labor embodied in them, we must be speaking in terms of "standard" socially necessary labor units. We would standardize labor for skills and abilities, for the quality of the capital made available, and also for product demand. Marx emphasizes the influence of habit and custom in assigning different values to different skills and also the costs of education and training. However, in the final analysis, labor can only be standardized by supply and demand, where the demand for any kind of labor is derived from the demand for the goods it assists in producing. That is, the relative values of two different kinds of labor working under different conditions are determined by their relative supply and demand. There is no other universally operating mechanism to relate them. Marx says:

when we bring the products of our labor into relation with each other as values, it is not because we see in these articles the material receptacles of homogenous human labor. Quite the contrary: whenever, by an exchange we equate as values our different products, by that very act, we also equate, as human labor, the different kinds of labor expended upon them. We are not aware of this, nevertheless, we do it.[23]

By now, we can begin to see the outline of a reconciliation between Marxian and Western theories. The relative values of the labor inputs into two different industries (that is, relative $S + V$) are determined by the relative demand for and supply of labor in those industries. The demand for labor in each industry, however, is derived from two sources.

The first is the product demand, which mirrors household preferences for the good or goods being produced. The second is the industry's access to technology, both embodied and disembodied. For example, the *more* capital that labor has to work with, the higher will be labor's VMP, and the greater will be the industry's demand for labor, for any given product demand. Similarly, better management will lower a firm's costs and enable it to meet any given level of demand with a higher rate of output. This will normally cause it to hire more labor and more capital.

The supply of labor, in turn, becomes an ingredient of the supply of the product. Given the rate of depreciation and the input of circulating capital (Marxian c), the remaining ingredient, in fact, is the industry's access to embodied and disembodied technology. Thus the factors that determine the relative (direct and indirect) values of labor going into the production of two different goods are also the factors that determine their relative supply and demand.

We would, in particular, argue that the relative values of different com-

[22] Ibid., Vol. III, p. 192.

[23] Ibid., Vol. I, p. 74.

modities are no more objective in Marxian than in conventional Western theory. Household preferences for consumer goods, leisure, and work are a major determining force in both cases.

12–3   Distribution Versus Allocation

Marx's labor theory of value is largely a complaint about income distribution. A major objection to the bourgeoisie (capitalists, including Ricardo's landlords) is that they receive a large income, but make no contribution or sacrifice in return. This income is earned by the worker, but expropriated by the capitalist. Thus Marx viewed surplus value as "unpaid labor." Unfortunately, the question of income distribution is intimately bound up with another question, that of the allocation and use of capital and natural resources in production. This points to a key difficulty or misunderstanding in Marxian theory.

Let us return, for a moment, to the notion of rent. In Ricardo's theory, this is a payment to landlords as owners of renewable natural resources, notably farmland. Such land is completely fixed in supply, and the amount forthcoming at a zero rent is the same as the amount that would be available if the rent were extremely high. According to Marxian theory, we would expect the exchange value of natural resources to be zero, and Marx directly affirms this.[24] Clearly, no direct or indirect labor becomes involved in its production.

For a long time the Soviet Union and other Eastern European countries did officially consider the value of land to be zero. In practice, rent was sometimes extracted, but this was far below the value of the land's marginal product (VMP). (We once again view land as productive in the sense of making labor more productive, a possibility explicitly acknowledged by Marx.) This approach ran headlong into the problem of resource allocation. Land is scarce; it has many alternative uses, and it is in the best interests of any society to allocate it to those uses where the value of its social marginal product is greatest.

If the price of land is set *below* its greatest possible VMP, an excess demand will arise for it. Low-value as well as high-value users will be able to "afford" it. Then the land will be rationed, not among those uses in which it is most productive but on some other basis, perhaps to those users who get in line first. We would expect to find land with a social VMP of $40 when $60 uses are unfulfilled. Because they are not valued highly, these resources will also be used wastefully. The undervaluation of air and water resources, not only in the U.S.S.R. but virtually everywhere in the world, for example, is the major cause of pollution. The Soviet economist Yu. Sukhotin writes:

For a time . . . the natural resources . . . [of] the Soviet Union might have seemed inexhaustible. This situation has changed. The use of natural resources has often been wasteful, causing irreplaceable losses of valuable

[24] Ibid., pp. 40–41.

natural riches. Examples: 50 to 60% of surveyed reserves of coal, petroleum and potassium salts are lost in the extraction process, and the percentage is even higher in the case of other minerals; waste heaps at ore pits, beneficiation mills and metallurgical plants are rich in mineral content but go unprocessed; sulphuric acid plants throw out pyrites that contain 45% iron, and this goes unused by metallurgy plants; 60% of the casing-head gas is lost during petroleum extraction; lumber is used with low efficiency largely because of under-developed chemical processing; agricultural land is insufficiently productive, and inordinately large amounts of it are appropriated for other purposes; vast amounts of smoke and fumes discharged into the air contain valuable substances that are recovered in infinitesimal quantities, leading to deterioration of hygenic conditions.[25]

Later Sukhotin makes it clear that water pollution is a major consequence of the fact that both planners and producers have been able to treat water as a free good. Thus, even if we do not wish to say that natural resources have a "value" from the standpoint of society as a whole, we must still assign a price to them in order to ration them among those uses where the values of their marginal products are greatest.

If the rent on land is set equal to zero, this will dry up a source of "measured" income and may thereby equalize the distribution of wealth. But at the same time, land will not always go into its most productive uses and will sometimes be used wastefully. This reduces present and future income and output. In trying to distribute society's wealth more equally, we end up by reducing it. Although such a tradeoff is probably inevitable to some extent, we should try to minimize the wealth loss resulting from a given move toward equality.

Sukhotin continues:

The attitude of some theoreticians toward the economic evaluation of natural resources is defined by the solitary argument that such resources, not being the products of labor, cannot possess value. Here, value itself more often than not is incorrectly understood as the input of labor actually expended in the manufacture of the given product. This notion contradicts the sense of Marx's theory of value, which consistently draws the distinction between the individual expenses of particular enterprises and socially necessary expenditures. . . .[26]

He then argues that the "value" of land, for the purposes of allocating and using it efficiently, should be determined essentially on an opportunity cost basis. The cost of using land for pasture is the highest earnings foregone from not using it to grow, for example, cotton or citrus fruits.

The land should then be assigned to pasturage if and only if the additional earnings received from doing so are greater than this cost. Few Western economists, if any, would disagree. The famous Soviet economist N. Federenko goes one step further. He maintains, in effect, that the value of a piece of land in any use should equal the sum of its expected future contributions to

[25] Yu. Sukhotin, "Evaluations of Natural Resources," *Voprosy Ekonomikis,* Dec. 1967, pp. 87–98.

[26] Ibid.

society's output, suitably discounted back to the present. Land should then be allocated to its highest-value uses. With some refinement, this is essentially the Western version.[27]

We may generalize our discussion of natural resources to say that *any* input is earning a rent whenever its supply curve becomes vertical. For example, if an entertainer such as Tom Jones or a superathlete such as Jean-Claude Killy or an outstanding manager earns $1 million per year but would be willing to do the same work for $250,000, he is receiving a rent of $750,000. Figure 12–2 captures this idea.

Suppose now that the government sets a price ceiling on the manager's services which is so low that he could only earn $100,000 by working 20,000 hours. This will lead to an excess demand for his services. Unless the ceiling is virtually ignored, only by chance will he allocate them to those uses where the value of their marginal product is greatest. Once again, the resource is partly allocated or rationed by some mechanism other than its price. This becomes a source of inefficiency, as before. But the $100,000 income ceiling also acts as a work disincentive. His *total* provision of services falls below the socially efficient level, and this becomes a second source of inefficiency.

On the other hand, suppose that someone were to invent a tax that takes away the entire rental portion of every income and *only* the rental portion. This tax could be gathered—for example, as a progressive income tax—in such a way it does not interfere with the allocation of any input among its alternative uses. In the underground economic literature this is often called a "single tax" because it is a tax on rental income only. The proceeds from the single tax could pay the operating expenses of government and also serve to subsidize some incomes. For example, it might finance a family-assistance plan, unemployment insurance, or medicare.

Under ideal conditions, a combination of a single tax with subsidies could be used to achieve the most socially "desirable" of a wide range of income distributions without adversely affecting efficiency. This helps to explain its popularity among populist leaders in North America and among underground economists.[28] It also helps to explain the presence of progressive-income-tax structures that try, to some extent, to capture rental incomes.

Yet a practical single tax is virtually impossible. We cannot tell by looking at a musician, a plumber, a manager, or an athlete where the rental portion of his income begins and the nonrental portion ends. It is in his interest to conceal this fact—assuming that he himself knows—whether we are prospective employers, government tax men, or just plain nosy.

Nor can we easily find a simple formula that leaves nonrental income untaxed. For example, suppose that Figure 12–2 applies to an engineering consultant and that the government is extracting exactly $750,000. Then the

[27] N. Federenko, "The Economic Evaluation of Natural Resources," *Voprosy Ekonomicki,* Mar. 1968.

[28] Principal among them is the 19th-century American economist Henry George. See his *Progress and Poverty* (New York: Doubleday, 1926).

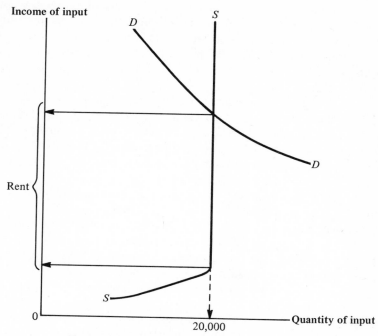

Figure 12–2. The rental portion of an income.

demand for his services falls, so demand crosses supply at $900,000. The rental portion of his income also falls by $100,000, to $650,000.

However, the income tax must fall by less than $100,000 when his income falls by that amount. Or, to say the same thing, the tax must rise by *less* than any rise in his total income. Otherwise, the consultant will not have an incentive to allocate his services to the highest value users who can pay the highest consulting fees. (The resulting increase in his income would all be taxed away.) Since his income tax falls by less than $100,000, it now takes *more* than rental income.

Likewise, we have no sure-fire way of separating rents from profits in the property incomes of each capitalist–landlord. But it is important to note that this would make little difference to Marx. The capitalist is anything but the engine of progress who takes the challenges and risks of economic development on his shoulders through his investment decisions. Rather, he is a parasite with all the qualities of a Ricardian landlord. He does not invest intelligently, but blindly, in response to forces he does not understand and over which he has no control.

For Marx, the optimal mode of production advances through time with an "inner logic of its own." It is no less than the force of destiny and operates with the inevitability of natural laws. The optimal set of productive relations and level of technology are determined independently of man's will. He has absolutely no control over them. By the same token, we may view the optimal mode of production as a free gift of nature, much like natural resources in Ricardo's model. The best the capitalist can do is to make the actual level of technology correspond to the optimal level. But this will naturally occur when the socioeconomic relations corresponding to laissez-faire capitalism are the currently optimal set.

As technological progress occurs, society's optimal socioeconomic relations change automatically. If the relations corresponding to laissez-faire capitalism persist, according to Marx, the actual level of technology will fall below the optimal level. Laissez-faire relations will also contribute to unemployment, poverty, business cycles, and low growth, not to mention an "unjustifiably" unequal income distribution.

To view profit as a necessary magnet for investment and innovation in these circumstances would be tantamount to mistakenly viewing the social and legal infrastructure of laissez-faire capitalism as permanent rather than transitory, in the opinion of Marxists. According to their view, we should regard profit as a "rent" the bourgeoisie can extract as long as it is able to preserve the superstructure of laissez-faire capitalism in which it has a vested interest. However, society as a *whole* experiences lower levels of productivity and income as a consequence.

Nevertheless, it is worth noting that most existing socialist countries have eventually come to introduce profits as an incentive to better managerial performance. They have also established special bonuses to stimulate innovation, which has been in notable undersupply. Even if we take the supply of entrepreneurship, along with the stock of capital goods and the quantity of funds for investment, as given, we still need a price to ration these items among their most productive uses.

In the case of investment funds, such a price is called an interest rate. Any economy, capitalist or socialist, will need a positive interest rate that mirrors the expected VMP of these investments in the following way. Suppose that a new plant initially costing $100 million is expected to raise future national income and output by $8 million per year, on the average, over the relevant future, because of the technology embodied in it. Then we say that it has a yield of 8 per cent. Subject to considerations of risk, society will want to obtain the highest possible yields on its investments. It will not want to invest in projects yielding 5 per cent when projects that would yield 15 per cent are going begging.

But this is what will happen if the government of a socialist state sets the effective interest rate (or, more generally, the cost of investment credit in whatever form it may appear) too low. Insofar as they are guided by these costs, decision makers compare the prospective yield on an investment with the interest cost of borrowing the necessary funds. When the prospective yield exceeds the cost of credit, subject to risk considerations, the investment appears to be desirable, and the decision maker will try to obtain and invest the funds. Thus the interest rate balances the demand for investment funds against their supply. When it is set too low—let us say, at 3 per cent— the demand for funds will be greater than the supply. Some projects yielding 5 per cent may then be undertaken while others yielding 15 per cent are left in the queue.

The Soviet Union and other East European countries did pass through periods in which required investment yields were much too low, resulting in efficiency losses due to misallocation and misuse of investment funds. The situation has since improved, although several serious problems remain. For example, there still seems to be a severe regional misallocation of investment funds.[29] Managers are still hoarding equipment, materials, inventory, and plant capacity—as a reserve against difficult-to-fulfill plan targets—partly because the interest charges for tying up these resources are still too low. (Since the July 1967 price reform in the Soviet Union, most firms pay an effective 6 per cent interest charge per year on the book value of their fixed and circulating capital.)

Finally, since the July 1967 price reform, land and underground natural resources are no longer treated as free goods in the U.S.S.R. But they are still undervalued, causing waste and environmental disruption.[30]

---

[29] See M. Vilenskii, "Determining the Efficiency of Territorial Distribution of Production," *Problems of Economics,* Sept. 1967. The classic article on Soviet investment decisionmaking up to the early 1950s is Gregory Grossman, "Scarce Capital and Soviet Doctrine," *Quarterly Journal of Economics,* Aug. 1953.

[30] The most thorough account of environmental disruption and waste of natural resources in the U.S.S.R. is given by Marshall Goldman. See his *The Spoils of Progress: Environmental Pollution in the Soviet Union* (Cambridge, Mass.: MIT, 1972).

Chapter **12**

Section **B**

Marx and the Economic Theory of History

12–4 Marx on Historical Determinism

Marx held an economic interpretation of history. The evolution of the optimal mode of production is the force of destiny which determines all other change and operates outside the influence of man. It is therefore the ultimate force of history.

The general conclusion I arrived at—and once reached, it served as the guiding thread in my studies—can be briefly formulated as follows: In the social production of their means of existence, men enter into definite, necessary relations which are independent of their will, productive relationships that correspond to a definite stage of development of their material productive forces. The aggregate of these productive relationships constitutes the economic structure of society, the real basis on which a juridical and political superstructure arises, and to which definite forms of social consciousness correspond. The mode of production of the material means of existence constitutes the whole process of social, political, and intellectual life.[1]

[1] Karl Marx, "Preface" to *A Contribution to the Critique of Political Economy*, in Emile Burns, compiler, *Handbook of Marxism* (New York: Random, 1935), pp. 371–372.

It must be emphasized that, although their effects are often quite indirect, economic forces embodied in the mode of production—and, more fundamentally, in the "optimal" production technology—are the sole ultimate determinants of history. We say, therefore, that Marx had a theory of *economic determinism*.

He was also a dialectic. Basically, he believed that history moves forward through a clash of opposing forces called "thesis" and "antithesis." The result of the clash is a new thesis, called the "synthesis," which borrows elements from both the original thesis and its antithesis. A new antithesis is likewise born in the clash, or else the new thesis (old synthesis) will eventually create its own antithesis.

For example, we know that in Western Europe, capitalism evolved out of feudalism. Under feudalism, we can distinguish at least three major socio-economic classes—the feudal nobility, including the church, plus the serfs, and the rising commercial classes.[2] The feudal lords (thesis) were the rulers, but as the optimal mode of production evolved, they inevitably came into conflict with the rising commercial classes and the upper strata of the peasantry and urban craftsmen (antithesis). These forces clashed, and feudalism declined. However, the victorious capitalist or bourgeois class embodied elements both of the fallen feudal aristocracy and of the former merchant and "embryo capitalist" classes, as well as elements not present in any of these. The bourgeoisie constitutes the new thesis, and it largely created the class of workers or proletariat (new antithesis) which it exploits, and who will ultimately respond by seizing the reins of power (new synthesis).

Marx learned his dialectics from the German philosopher Hegel, of whom he was a follower in his youthful days and a lifelong admirer. However, for Hegel, the only reality existed in the human mind. The material world was only an imperfect reflection of the ideas of man. "The universe and all events therein existed and transpired only in the mind, and all change was a change in ideas. Therefore, to account for these changes in ideas was to account for change in the universe." [3] For Hegel, history was generated by changing ideas in the minds of men—notably great men—which caused changes in the material world. Ideas changed with their own inner logic, and man is the carrier of ideas. Great men, the carriers of great ideas, inevitably influenced history the most.

But according to Marx, "With [Hegel], [the dialectic] is standing on its head. It must be turned right side up again if you would discover the rational kernel behind the mystical shell . . . with me on the contrary, [ideas are] nothing other than the material world reflected by the human mind, and translated into the forms of thought." [4] Thus Marx concluded that in the very long

---

[2] There were also craftsmen, artisans, urban laborers, and so on, who grew more numerous and important as the Middle Ages progressed.

[3] W. N. Loucks and W. G. Whitney, *Comparative Economic Systems,* 8th ed. (New York: Harper, 1969), p. 69.

[4] Karl Marx, *Capital* (Moscow: Foreign Languages Publishing, 1965–1967), Vol. I, pp. 20, 19.

run, the world evolves independently of human consciousness, although the latter can temporarily slow down evolution. He sought his universal explanation of all phenomena—including what men thought—in the material world, finally settling on the mode of production.

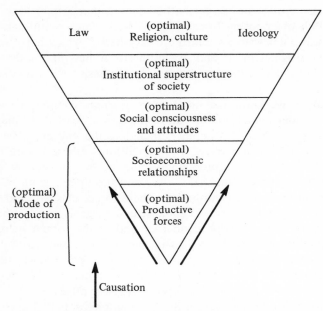

Figure 12–3. The Marxian causal chain.

We may better understand the Marxian causal chain by means of the inverted pyramid in Figure 12–3. We first break the mode of production into two parts—the "productive forces" or technology of production, and the prevailing socioeconomic relations in society's various production and distribution processes. The latter correspond to what we have called the structure or the organization of the economy. (For example, we may speak of the socioeconomic relations corresponding to specific kinds of laissez-faire, command, or mixed economies.)

However, it is technological progress—more precisely, the evolution of the "optimal" technologies of production and distribution—which becomes the ultimate motor force of history. These optimal productive forces evolve autonomously, and we place them at the base of our inverted pyramid. Causation will work its way upward from there. We should make it clear now, however, that "optimal" here means in the very restricted sense of enabling an economy to get as close as possible to its production-possibility frontier. In particular, the stronger meaning assigned in Chapters 2 and 4 does not apply. (In subsequent chapters, however, we shall return to this meaning.)

Thus defined, the optimal technology determines an optimal set of socioeconomic relations. For example, at particular points in time in France, England, Germany, and other Western countries, the optimal "productive forces" were such that the optimal socioeconomic relations were those corresponding to laissez-faire capitalism. Earlier, specific types of feudalism were optimal. The optimal set of socioeconomic relations then determines an optimal social consciousness and optimal social attitudes which, in turn, determine the optimal institutional superstructure of society. Finally, the latter determines the optimal law, religion, ideology, and culture.

As we move down the inverted pyramid, we may imagine ourselves stripping away layer after layer of *apparent* fundamental determining forces until we, at last, discover the true one. Marx himself appears to have followed this road, first exploring the roles of the top two layers in his early philosophical manuscripts, then social consciousness, attitudes, and relations in his historical works, and, finally, the mode of production in *Das Kapital*. Marx tends to ignore feedback down the pyramid, and this, together with the primacy that he assigns to economic forces, has given rise to much criticism of his entire view of history.[5]

There is a kind of feedback, however, which plays a fundamental role in the Marxian causal machinery. The actual technology of production and distribution in any economy need not be optimal, and the same may be said for every layer of the inverted pyramid. Corresponding to the optimal pyramid just examined is another proceeding from *actual* productive forces to *actual* socioeconomic relations, to *actual* social consciousness and attitudes, and so on. Causation will again run upward, although the causal forces are not as strong, and operate with a lag. Although the actual technology keeps falling behind the optimal, it always eventually catches up, and the same is true of the other layers of the "actual" pyramid.

The key question is: What causes the actual "productive forces" to fall behind? On this point, Marx is unequivocal: Throughout history, society has always been partitioned into classes along economic lines. At least through the flowering of capitalism, the optimal organization of the economy has embodied some sort of socioeconomic class structure in which some groups are exploited and others dominant. However, as the optimal mode of production changes, the optimal class structure changes with it. The dominating classes find their roles being made obsolete by technological progress.

This dominance goes hand in hand with a privileged position in society. Thus the socioeconomic elite has a vested interest in using its power to preserve existing socioeconomic relations. Because these are no longer optimal, the new optimal technology cannot be achieved. The new optimal technology must be accommodated by a new optimal set of socioeconomic relations before it can realize itself. Consequently, the actual socioeconomic relations and productive forces both become suboptimal. By impeding technical

---

[5] See, for example, M. M. Bober, *Karl Marx's Interpretation of History* (Cambridge, Mass.: Harvard U. P., 1962).

progress and in other ways, vested interests prevent the economy from achieving its production potential.

> At a certain stage of their development, the material productive forces of society come into contradiction with the existing productive relationships, or, what is but a legal expression for these, with the property relationships within which they had moved before. From forms of development of the productive forces, these relationships are transformed into their fetters. Then, an epoch of social revolution opens. With the change in the economic foundation, the whole vast superstructure is more or less rapidly transformed.[6]

More bluntly, when the development of productive forces outstrips the development of socioeconomic relations, the ruling "exploiter" class always has a stake in preserving the existing property relations. Although impeded, the actual technology has a built-in tendency to follow the optimal. Moreover, groups will exist or emerge in society which have a vested interest in technological progress. They will become the new elite, once the optimal productive forces reassert themselves.

These groups inevitably come into conflict with the old established interests. While technological progress is the motor of historical change, therefore, class conflict is its external sign. "The history of all hitherto existing societies is the history of class conflict" wrote Marx and Engels in the *Communist Manifesto.* Nor is the present era different in that respect:

> In the earlier epochs of history, we find almost everywhere a complicated arrangement of society into various orders, a manifold gradation of social ranks. In Ancient Rome, we have patricians, knights, plebians, slaves; in the Middle Ages, feudal lords, vassals, guildmasters, journeymen, apprentices, serfs; in almost all of these classes, again, subordinate gradation. . . .
> Our epoch, the epoch of the bourgeoisie, possesses . . . this distinctive feature: it has simplified the class antagonisms. Society . . . is more and more split up into two great hostile camps, into two great classes directly facing each other—bourgeoisie and proletariat.[7]

Thus Marx set out to explore the last great class conflict in an environment in which, in his view, laissez-faire capitalism was becoming increasingly hostile to further evolution of society's productive forces.

12–5   Pre-Capitalist Evolution

Before considering the development of laissez-faire capitalism in more detail, however, let us briefly outline the unfolding of history up to the time when the modern bourgeois sprouts from the ruins of feudalism. The "com-

---

[6] Karl Marx, "Preface" to *A Contribution to the Critique of Political Economy,* in Burns, op. cit., p. 372.

[7] Karl Marx and Friedrich Engels, *Manifesto of the Communist Party* (New York: International Publishers, 1948), p. 9.

plete" evolution of history is as follows: primitive communism → slavery → feudalism → capitalism → state socialism → full communism.

Primitive Communism

The history of all civilized races dawns with a mode of production—or, more precisely, a set of socioeconomic relations—that we call primitive communism. Under it, most material means of production and distribution are communally owned. That is, all members have the right to use these means in specified ways, and they may exercise their rights as they wish. The rights to hunt and till the soil would be the most obvious examples. M. M. Bober describes primitive communism as follows:

> Agriculture and crafts are the chief occupations. The land is held and tilled in common by members of the tribe, and the yield is divided among the producers for consumption (directly without going through an exchange intermediary). The other needs are supplied by each family through handicraft labor. The patriarchal industries of the peasant household furnish the illustration: spinning, weaving, cattle raising, and the preparation of clothing are functions performed by the whole family; division of labor within this unit is based on age and sex, and on natural conditions varying with the seasons.[8]

Such a society would have its tribal or communal elite, chosen according to accepted political procedures. There might also be a comparative "handful of people, charged with duties of public interest and maintained at the expense of the community; like the smith, the carpenter, watchmen and judges." [9] We see here the origins of private property. Moreover, different tribes may be differently endowed with natural resources. It will pay them to specialize somewhat and to engage in limited trade according to comparative advantage. This is the origin of exchange.

Marx praises these simple societies as "Communit[ies] of free individuals, carrying on their own work with the means of production in common, in which the labor-power of all the different individuals is consciously applied as the combined labor-power of the community." [10] Because exchange is limited, most production takes place directly for use. Use value rather than exchange value tends to guide production. However, primitive communism "can arise and exist only when the development of the productive power of labor has not risen beyond a low stage." [11] As technological progress proceeds, it inevitably leads to a new economic order, for reasons which we shall examine shortly.

It is quite significant, on the other hand, that the cycle ends where it began, with communism. Full communism thrives in an era of superabun-

[8] Bober, op. cit.

[9] Ibid., pp. 46–47.

[10] Marx, *Capital,* op. cit., Vol. I, p. 78.

[11] Ibid., p. 79.

dance, after technology has risen to such a level that an efficient organization of production and distribution is no longer critical. Economic forces no longer determine the evolution of history, and the rule "to each according to his needs" prevails.

Indeed, this role of the mode of production ends with the demise of capitalism. Under state socialism—which features state rather than communal ownership of the means of production—the economic problem remains. Employees are still paid at least partly on the basis of contribution, although a spreading of what were incomes from private property under capitalism may substantially reduce income inequality.

However, the major socioeconomic class distinctions will have been abolished. Therefore, state socialism can accommodate technological progress without class antagonisms and without the resulting conflict between society's productive forces, on one hand, and its socioeconomic relations and institutional superstructure, on the other. As the economy becomes more and more productive, the role of the government diminishes. By the time full communism is in bloom, the state will have withered away.

Although Marx did not identify the major cause of the evolution of primitive communism into ancient slavery, Engels emphasized the appearance of private property.[12] We may supply a more fundamental rationale as follows. The problem with communal ownership in a world where scarcity counts is that the resulting external effects may have a disastrous impact on the organization of production (e.g., on communally owned land) or on the incentives to produce and invest.

In fact, communal ownership of the means of production is never guaranteed to be satisfactory from an efficiency standpoint because one producer (call him B) cannot be involuntarily excluded from activities that may interfere with those of another producer (call him A). If producer A bribes producer B to prevent the latter from interfering, A has no guarantee that a third producer, C, will not come along and interfere. For example, let A be a group of farmers and B and C be hunters whose shortest path lies across land planted by A. Alternatively, let A, B, and C be farmers, all of whom wish to farm the same plot of land.

Even the threat of interference and resulting damages will reduce the incentives of producers to invest or to maintain property. In effect, such threats must be avoided through the mutual consent of all parties who might become involved. The required transactions costs will be great enough to shorten the time horizons of most producers. On top of this, any organization of production or division of labor must be entirely through unanimous mutual consent. Hence specialization in production may be largely according to age and sex and limited to roles that have been established through accepted custom. Even so, the inability to involuntarily exclude individuals from certain activities may make communal production somewhat anarchic.

---

[12] Friedrich Engels, *The Origin of the Family, Private Property, and the State* (New York: International Publishers, 1942), Ch. IX.

Furthermore, in principle, anyone has the right to milk a communally owned cow, to hunt communal game, to fish in communal waters, or to harvest the wheat from communal fields. Within limits, these freedoms are automatically implied by communal property rights. The consequence is a reduced motive for particular individuals or groups to invest their time and money in the upkeep, expansion, and improvement of communal resources. Most of the fruits of their outlays would probably go to others. There will probably also be a reduced incentive to experiment or innovate on this account, and, in general, the effect will once again be to shorten time horizons.

There are, however, at least two situations where basically communal production may be tolerable from an efficiency standpoint. The first is when a low level of technology or a sparse population keeps the demand for a communally owned resource so low that it is not scarce and when the resource requires little or no upkeep. Among the North American Indians, communal property rights in land traditionally prevailed in many areas for hunting, fishing, trapping, and even farming.[13]

Predominantly communal property rights may also be desirable when the economy has become so productive that scarcity is no longer a problem. This is the "full communism" referred to above. It is the avowed aim of every present-day socialist country, and it occcurs under conditions that are exactly the opposite of those conducive to primitive communism. It is a time when "Leisure increases to almost intolerable proportions, money falls out of use, and we can all go and help ourselves in the shops. Choice and scarcity cease to be a problem and economics to be a worthwhile study." [14] Individuals work and invest from an inner need to create, as a means of self-expression, out of a wish to serve the community, and to relieve the boredom of too much leisure.

For the foreseeable future, however, full communism remains a utopian ideal. It is the crucial role of the noncommunist modes of production—particularly capitalism and state socialism—to raise productivity to a level that will permit later generations to enjoy the luxury of self-realization that full communism brings.[15]

Returning to primitive communism, we should note that communal property rights in farmland will become relatively less efficient with the discovery

---

[13] However, in agriculture, some individuals must have specific rights to the *crops* being grown. Otherwise, there will not be sufficient incentive to plant, care for, and harvest them. Regarding property rights among the North American Indians, see Harold Demsetz, "Toward a Theory of Property Rights," op. cit., and John C. McManus, "An Economic Analysis of Indian Behavior in the North American Fur Trade," *Journal of Economic History,* March 1972, and the references therein. See, as well, Abraham Rotstein, "Fur Trade and Empire: An Institutional Analysis," unpublished Ph.D. dissertation, University of Toronto, 1967.

[14] Peter Wiles, "Growth vs. Choice," *Economic Journal,* June 1956, p. 245.

[15] A second version of the communist ideal, due to Mao and Guevara, has been explored in the Appendix to Chapter 7. Instead of material abundance, it stresses the transformation of human nature so that man is no longer self-seeking.

of crop rotation. This increases the need for formal organization and for exclusion of specific activities on specific plots. A similar result holds for the invention of better tools, of fertilizers, and of improved farming methods. These are likely to increase the potential productivity of a given individual or small production team on a particular plot of land, thereby making it more important to grant that individual or team exclusive use of the land. At the same time, the need for investment of time and money to bring the land to its full production potential will increase. Hopeful beneficiaries of this investment will then press for private (or perhaps state) property rights to emerge.

For similar reasons, the discoveries of metals and of new ways to fashion wood and stone may set the stage for the decline of communal production in other areas. Such discoveries can easily lead to the development of tools, weapons, and simple machinery capable of raising the productivity of labor in several occupations. This in turn raises the optimal capital-to-labor ratio in production and makes optimal production processes more roundabout. Once again, investment, maintenance and protection of property will become more important, and, potentially, more lucrative. Pressure for more private or state property rights will then arise in order that the actual incentives and rewards for these activities will more closely approximate their potential levels.

The same discoveries raise the skill requirements for some kinds of labor and also increase the skill differentials between occupations associated with the most efficient technology. The optimal degree of specialization in production grows, as does, to a lesser extent, the optimal division of labor. Consequently, the optimal amount of exchange *within* the tribe rises. This again creates pressure either for markets or for a command economy to emerge. If a command economy cannot arise, perhaps because it requires too large an economic surplus to support its power base, this becomes pressure for markets and for at least semiprivate ownership of the means of production.

In any event, communal socioeconomic relationships are strained, ultimately to the breaking point. M. M. Bober adds:

during the [highest stages of primitive communism], progress is "irresistible, less interrupted, and more rapid." Agriculture develops and yields new products like oil and wine. Handicraft industry becomes increasingly diversified, especially in textiles and metals. The town and the artisan are more and more divided off from the country and the agricultural laborer. Wealth is sought after. Production for exchange increases, and commerce advances.[16]

At the same time, the growing productivity of labor means that most workers will be able to create a clear surplus value over and above their physical subsistence levels of consumption. This makes ownership of labor power—as well as of land and other resources for labor to work—more attractive, and leads to war for the purpose of capturing slaves and enlarging the territory under a particular tribes control.

[16] Bober, op. cit., p. 49.

Slaves come not only from conquered tribes, however, but also from among the indigenous population. Because of bad luck, exploitation, or lack of skill, some individuals may find bondage the only alternative to starvation or imprisonment. Almost inevitably, the appearance of private property eventually led to a division of farmers into a small aristocracy of large landowners, on one hand, and a large class of owners of medium- to small-sized holdings on the other. Most slaves worked on the large estates, and the poorer farmers gradually came to be dominated by the aristocrats, because of the former's competitive advantages or power, as exercised, for example, through harsh debtor law. Often, small farmers or their heirs would sink into slavery.

Nevertheless, improved transport and communications facilities do become a final course of primitive communism's rise and slavery's demise. Simple inventions such as the wheel, an efficient alphabet or ships able to ply the seas will bring more tribes into more meaningful contact with one another and increase the probability of merger, either peacefully or through conquest. Not only plunder, but a desire for protection and cooperation, or for more or better fishing, farming, or hunting grounds, could motivate union. In addition, many tribal kings or chieftains doubtless measured their strength or prestige by number of subjects, and also, eventually, by accumulation of material wealth and number of cattle and slaves.

Thus tribes began to grow into city-states. This hastened the decline of primitive communism, for the larger the community, the more unwieldy communal production becomes and the greater the comparative advantage of other organizational forms. In permitting private and semiprivate property, along with slavery, and in expanding their realms, tribal chieftains were often guilty of what Marx called "false consciousness." That is, they failed to perceive the dynamic consequences of their actions.

Consequently, their short-run gains in wealth, prestige, and protection were purchased at the expense of a long-run undermining of the system in which the roots of their power lay. In trying to enhance their domains, they set in motion a chain of events whose outcome they could not control and thereby assisted in their own or their heirs' overthrow. This paved the way for a slave-based aristocracy of wealthy land owners, traders, or cattle growers to eventually assume command.

Later, the great plantation owners of Rome would use their political power and, to a lesser extent, their ability to produce on a large scale to crush the lower and middle classes of free citizens. The upper clergy and senatorial classes were largely exempt from taxes and other obligations. But small, independent craftsmen, traders, and farmers were forced out of business and frequently into effective serfdom by them. Others were ruined by the subsidized competition of big producers or by imports from abroad, collected as a tribute and distributed free or at low cost to ultimate consumers. In this way, wealth and power became even more concentrated, but the lower and middle classes were Rome's chief source of military and moral support. As they declined or fell into bondage the Roman Empire weakened and eventually crumpled before the onslaught of barbaric invaders.[17]

Subsequently, the feudal lords and capitalist bourgeoisie would give repeat performances, effectively helping to destroy themselves, according to Marx, by their false consciousness.

Ancient Slavery

In any event, slavery was to a large extent the basis of the glory that was Greece and the grandeur that was Rome. "It was slavery that first made possible the [specialization in production] between agriculture and industry on a considerable scale. . . At the time of greatest prosperity . . . there were at least 18 slaves to every adult male citizen [of ancient Athens]. . . . In Corinth, at the height of its power, the number of slaves was 460,000; in Aegina, 470,000. In both cases [this was] ten times the number of free citizens." [18] The large agricultural estate, worked mainly by slaves, became the economic backbone of the Roman—and to a lesser extent, the Greek—Empire. This evolved into the feudal manor, also largely an agricultural estate and worked mainly by serfs, which was the basic production unit of the medieval period.

Historically, in fact, slavery began declining in Western Europe before the fall of Rome, although it persisted or reappeared in various forms and guises until well into the 19th century. A clear forerunner of the medieval economic order, based on the *latifundia,* and to a lesser extent on the Roman guilds or *collegia,* was fairly firmly established in much of the Roman Empire prior to the fall of Rome. (In frontier areas, the declining power of Rome and the consequent rising need for protection effectively decentralized authority, another important feature of medieval society.)

It is also true that many nominal serfs or freedmen of medieval times were less free than many Roman slaves, especially since the master of a Roman estate or *latifundium* was more likely to be an absentee owner. In medieval Europe, as well as in ancient Rome and Greece, slaves, serfs, and many nominally free men were attached to the land they tilled or the shops in which they worked. As ownership of an estate was transferred through death, exchange, war, or seizure, its labor force was often transferred along

---

[17] A similar phenomenon was probably the chief cause of the downfall of ancient Greece. We would suggest the following sources to the interested reader: Herbert Heaton, *The Economic History of Europe* (New York: Harper, 1936), Chs. III–V; M. M. Knight, *Economic History of Europe Until the End of the Middle Ages* (Boston: Houghton, 1928); M. I. Rostovseff, *A History of the Ancient World* (2 vols.) (New York: Oxford U.P., 1928); Shepard B. Clough, *The Economic Development of Western Civilization* (New York: McGraw-Hill, 1959), Chs. 2–4. Note Clough's bibliography, pp. 501–503.

[18] The first quote is from Friedrich Engels, *Anti-Dühring* (New York: International Publishers, 1939), pp. 199–200. The second is from Engels, *The Origin of the Family, Private Property, and the State,* pp. 107, 153.

with it. When all is said and done, we cannot identify any violent break between ancient slavery and feudal serfdom.[19]

Nevertheless, in order to differentiate, we shall say that a slave is someone who owes at least 50 per cent of his labor *time,* measured as the residual after deducting minimal eating, sleeping, and recreation time, to his master. Moreover, his basic obligations would be defined more in terms of a time commitment than in terms of specific tasks to be performed or in terms of a tax, rent, or tribute to be paid the lord, at first in kind and later in cash. Eventually, the latter became more important and the former less so. By the end of the medieval era, serfs could buy their freedom, and a significant number of them did this.[20] In addition, serfs had rights of inheritance not generally granted to slaves.

On the other hand, whereas the master owes his slaves their food, shelter, and clothing—at least in theory—the lord must only provide his serfs with certain *means* of sustenance. The feudal lord was typically supposed to supply land, implements, draft animals, protection from external enemies, and a minimum of subsistence, only in times of food shortages. In return, the serfs had to work three or more days a week out of a normal six-day work week on the lord's land, although other members of his family, such as a grown son, could often acquit part of this obligation. This was in addition to taxes, rents, tributes, and military service.

We may extend the above distinction to define a whole continuum of relations between the owner or controller of the material means of production and the worker, who owns only his own labor power (to use Marx's simplification). Such a continuum will take us from ancient slavery to modern laissez-faire capitalism and cover most of the important forms of private-property relations, according to Marx. It also describes very unevenly the long-run evolution of private-property relations in Western Europe and North America, according to Marx and Engels.

As we move from slavery toward developed laissez-faire capitalism, the obligation of the employer to his laborer becomes less and less that of direct upkeep and more and more in terms of providing means with which the laborer tries to sustain himself. At the end of this transition, the capitalist employer can acquit his obligation with a money payment, prompting Marx and Engels to declare: "The bourgeoisie . . . has put an end to all feudal, patriarchal, idyllic relations. It has pitilessly torn asunder the motly feudal ties that bound man to his 'natural superiors,' and has left no other bond

---

[19] For discussions, see the references in footnote 17.

[20] Many Roman slaves were also emancipated for one reason or other. However, a number of these or their descendents found it impossible to remain independent in a climate of heavy obligations to the state and stiff competition from *latifundia* and large workshops that were owned by the wealthiest citizens and virtually tax-free. Freedmen became tied to their land or to their occupations and were thereby effectively transformed into serfs. It is no exaggeration to say, in fact, that the Roman middle class was effectively eliminated in this way during the third, fourth, and fifth centuries.

between man and man than naked self-interest, than callous 'cash payment.' " [21]

As the employer's direct (nominal) responsibilities for the well-being—or at least the survival—of his laborers declines, so does his nominal power to directly judge them in areas not related to their jobs and to mete out punishment other than firing. In fact, a slave would never be fired, although he could be put to death for relatively minor offenses by his employer. Neither would a serf be fired, although he could be severely punished and perhaps starved by denial of certain means of production.

The declining direct responsibilities and powers of the employer are, in theory, picked up by the state. Marx and his followers were emphatic in claiming that the state was an instrument and even an extension of the economic elite. Nonetheless, relations between individual laborers and employers or their representatives changed, with consequences to be described below. They may well have become less personal. Moreover, the alienation of labor became more complete, according to Marx, as the division of labor proceeded and as the laborer was more efficiently exploited.

Indeed, a strict interpretation of some remarks made by Marx would indicate no improvement in the workingman's lot from the institution of slavery to the maturing of capitalism. Instead, income differentials and class antagonisms have widened every step of the way by this view. At least regarding income differentials, however, Marx's claim is contradicted by historical evidence.[22]

Likewise, the means of judging the poor and of maintaining them through economic crises have probably become more generous, but quite possibly less personal and less sustaining of human dignity. At the same time, the laborer's obligation to his master or employer has become defined less and less in terms of labor time (or, more generally, of input time) and more and more directly in terms of his ability to generate utility or an income in cash or in kind. This, in turn, has become increasingly a cash income, stemming from the laborer's surplus value in production. Finally, as we move from slavery toward laissez-faire capitalism, the producer is judged more and more by the exchange as opposed to the use value that he creates. "[The bourgeoisie] has resolved personal worth [itself] into exchange value." [23]

Our task is therefore to explain how changes in society's "optimal productive forces" could plausibly have brought about the evolution just described. Once again, we shall have to fill in some of the gaps in Marx's and Engel's own writings. We would first note that the advantage of slavery to a master is the complete nominal control that he possesses over the labor time of his slaves. The corresponding *dis*advantage is the relatively high cost of

[21] Marx and Engels, op. cit., p. 9.

[22] That is, the historical evidence does *not* point to a long-term tendency for the ratio of wage and salary to property income to fall. See further discussion of this point in Chapter 13.

[23] Ibid.

enforcing a satisfactory level of productivity. Indeed, complete bondage is entirely based on supervision coupled with the threat of coercion.

As society's productive forces develop, it is reasonable to expect the optimal scale of any production activity and the optimal division of labor to increase. As the range of products grows for the economy as a whole, moreover, the heterogeneity of outputs from many particular production activities will also rise. These factors are likely to raise the cost of supervision (and, in particular, of enforcing commands). A Roman *latifundium* was probably never less than 1,000 acres and often many times that size. (There are records of estates in lands ruled by the ancient Greeks of more than 5,000 acres.) The optimal technology of production was still highly labor-intensive, and when one owner died in 8 B.C., he left over 4,000 slaves. His estate also included 3,600 yoke of oxen and 257,000 other animals.

Nevertheless, the average medieval manor was much larger. By the 12th century, the average estate size may have reached close to 10,000 acres and was constantly being built up through marriages, gifts, inheritances, and conquests. The heterogeneity of production was also greater because it was more self-sufficient, although the *latifundium* became more self-sufficient as the power of the Roman Empire declined and trade decreased. In both ancient and medieval times, the division of labor was primitive in comparison with 19th-century capitalism, but trusted slaves and serfs occupied most foreman-level supervisory roles.

There is also considerable evidence of supervisory difficulties. "Columella, a writer on agriculture about 50 A.D., reported that on large grain farms the slaves treated the oxen badly and stole whenever and whatever they could . . . the use of slaves was probably economical only so long as the supply was abundant and the price low. When the wars gave place to the *pax Romana* of the first two centuries AD., the stream dried up, the price rose, and slave cultivation of plantations receded in favor of tenant farming." [24] Many of these tenants came to have serf-like obligations.

Similarly, in medieval times, relations between lord and serf became most like those between master and slave during the busy seasons of plowing and harvesting. Then the peasant had to do extra work (called boon work) for the lord just when the opportunity cost of being absent from his own lands was highest. In return, the lord fed his serfs, and it was occasionally observed that some serfs ate up more than they produced.

Medieval Serfdom

Once the complexity of production under one master (defined in terms of scale, heterogeneity, and division of labor) has passed a critical point, it becomes more efficient to reduce supervisory efforts, while combining the carrot with the stick as a means of raising labor productivity. The slave is

[24] Heaton, op. cit., p. 52.

offered positive incentives tied to his productivity in specific tasks. If these incentives are to work, the slave needs some freedom to enjoy them—and, indeed, freedom itself is apt to prove a powerful incentive. Thus the successful slave is likely to find his absolute obligation effectively diluted, as some of his time becomes his own.

A second important incentive, as virtually every command economy has learned, is a plot of ground, along with a few implements and animals, for the peasant to farm on his own.[25] However, many serfs did not rise from slavery, but fell from the status of freeman, particularly that of small, independent farmer. Other freemen, relatively few in number, rose to become lords. (In either case, of course, the freemen may have descended from a slave.) The period from the 4th to the 10th centuries was one of continuing pillage, migration, and warfare, since no nation state could completely fill the power vacuum left by the decline of Rome. Land and serfs were often rewards for outstanding leadership and daring deeds in battle. Seizure and forfeit for various reasons were also common.

> If we look at the growth of lordship from above we see strong men gaining power, property, and privileges. If we look at it from below, we see weak men sinking into dependence or reaching up for protection. Some sank under the familiar burden of debt or taxes. Some abandoned freedom in order to escape military service or to secure protection in troubled times . . . if a strong state, able to defend its subjects from attack and keep the peace, was not available, other sanctuary must be sought, and many found it under the wing of some lord. To "commend" one's life and land to him, to accept liability for certain obligations, and in return to get protection and the secure use of some land was a wise, even if a hard bargain.[26]

Despite the loosening of bonds, the feudal lord needed enforcement power, and one relatively inexpensive way of getting this was to organize production on a partly communal basis. The commune became collectively responsible for many of the obligations of each member household—for example, in the manner of the Russian *mir* described in the Appendix to Chapter 7. If one household failed to meet its obligation, other members of the collectivity became liable to penalty. By coercing the communal organization, the lord could hope to force it to apply some coercion to individual members.

Indeed, within limits permitted by the lord, production decision making on a typical medieval manor was probably more communal than private. Forest and grazing lands were also in common, along with important operations such as plowing. Thus the commune was in a position to withhold valuable services from the individual serf if it chose to do so. Reasons for communal organization other than the enforcement advantage were a continuing low level of productivity, combined with a relative abundance of forest

---

[25] Conversely, when the peasant begins with serf status, the threat of removing some of his freedoms may act as a (negative) incentive.

[26] Heaton, op. cit., p. 76.

land and pasture and a low upkeep requirement. In addition, virtually no farmer could afford the eight oxen needed to pull a medieval plow.

By keeping cropland, animals, and implements mainly private, the medieval manor avoided some of the most obvious external diseconomies of primitive communism. Still, there was no lack of disincentive to accumulate and to innovate. Any capital equipment accumulated by a serf was at least partly subject to depreciation through communal use and abuse. Seizure and robbery were also serious threats (insurance was unknown) and wars, raids, and plunder were common. In fact, the latter was often a profitable enterprise in an era where the social surplus was still very low.

In addition,

Bitter disputes and litigations arose when farmers tried to enlarge their territory by stealing a furrow from their neighbours (often the only way that they could expand). Weeds flourished and scattered the seeds from the unplowed boundaries, and good drainage was impossible . . . without markets in which to sell surplus products, except in times of famine, the chief purpose for having more land was to increase one's supply of consumer goods. . . . Investment for more than a modicum of greater production was, therefore, almost unknown among peasants and for that matter among lords.

[As to innovation] Farmers could not introduce new crops into the rotation if the entire village (or manor) did not agree, because all crops had to be harvested at the same time. If the enterprising farmer had turnips in his field while his neighbors were harvesting wheat, his crop would be trampled. Besides, after the harvest, livestock were allowed to range over the entire field. Scientific breeding of livestock could not develop with the promiscuous intermingling of everybody's animals, and animal diseases spread rapidly.[27]

Under these conditions, it is not surprising that feudal bonds started to become fetters when innovations raised the productivity of individual serfs and reduced their dependence on lord and manor. The burden of these fetters increased when the growth of markets raised the profitable degree of specialization and scale of production of many particular commodities.

Starting in the 11th or 12th centuries, a parallel quickening of technological progress occurred in agriculture and in industry—at first in textiles and shortly thereafter in metallurgy, armaments, printing and papermaking, architecture, and construction. In food production, the primitive plow was greatly improved, and a harness was developed in the 10th or 11th centuries that enabled the horse to become a useful draft animal. To this, we should add iron shoes for horses and cattle, the hinged flail for threshing, and, above all, the widespread use of water and windmills for grinding grain.

By 1088, it is said, England had over 5,000 mills, most of which were water driven. If each mill did the work of a hundred men per day, as has been estimated . . . there was available . . . the work equivalent of one man to every four or

---

[27] Quotes from Clough, op. cit., p. 55, and H. E. Friedlaender and Jacob Oser, *Economic History of Modern Europe* (New York: Prentice-Hall, 1953), p. 27.

five members of the population. For the first time on any appreciable scale, the industrial capacity of man was being increased by the inorganic forces of nature.[28]

But the crucial economic change of this era was the commercial revolution, symbolized by the Crusades and the voyages of Marco Polo, and made possible by technological improvements in transportation and communication. Dramatic improvements in seafaring, coupled with slowly but steadily increasing surpluses in industry and agriculture—and the rising power of the nation state, itself made possible by better internal transportation and communication—turned ships from plunder to trade. The story of the latter Middle Ages is one of rising trade and expanding markets and consequently of greater specialization in production on a larger scale for sale rather than use. On the strength of this and of the corresponding decline in pillage and invasions, the population of Europe, long stagnant, began rising until temporarily checked by the famine and Black Death of the early 14th century.

At the same time, the services that the lord could provide for his serfs became less valuable. The growth of the nation state saw a shift in military power and in responsibility for defense from lords to kings, who hired a professional army for the purpose. With improved implements and tools, those peasants who planned better, worked harder, and were thriftier and luckier became less reliant on the services provided by the lord and commune. Famine also became less of an *ever-present* danger to these people and might become even less so were the constraints and disincentives of feudal relations affecting accumulation to be loosened.

It became more and more necessary for the lord to enforce his power at the very time that it was being competed away. (Not surprisingly, it was not until the 12th century that lawyers began defining exactly what the status of a serf was.) The serf who wanted to risk flight could take refuge in the rapidly growing cities, where life was based on commerce and industry, or to new lands, previously considered marginal, but now being cleared, drained, and brought into cultivation. The new agricultural lands offered favorable conditions to attract labor, and freedom was often granted to any serf—originally the property of another lord—who would work there for a year and a day. In fact, serfdom hardly existed in these areas. In the cities, production was being transferred more and more to hired or contractual labor, although semi-communal guild production and, to a lesser extent, independent craftsmen remained dominant.

With the rise of commerce and industry and the growth of exchange and the use of money, power tended to shift from countryside to city. The terms of trade came more and more under the influence of the rising merchant classes, who controlled trade. The lord who wanted the goods that only the merchant could supply had to have a money income. Consequently, he tended

---

[28] Clough, op. cit., p. 89. Clough's Chapters 4, 5, and 6 are excellent as a non-Marxian view of the transition from feudalism to capitalism. For the Marxist view, see Maurice Dobb, "The Transition from Feudalism to Capitalism," lecture delivered to the Institute of Statistics of the University of Bologna, Italy, Mar. 24, 1962.

to "play the game" by specializing more in his own production facilities for sale to the market. He also began to convert his serf's obligations into money, which meant that the latter had to produce partly for sale. Thus the entire manor was specializing more according to comparative advantage and reaping some of the resulting benefits. According to Dobb:

> The spread of commerce encouraged the demand among the aristocracy for imported luxuries; merchant caravans, forming permanent settlements at key points, stimulated a revival of town life and market exchange; feudal estates themselves were encouraged by the proximity of markets and of a thriving exchange to produce a surplus (of rural produce or of handicrafts) for sale outside the locality . . . feudal lords themselves became increasingly reliant on trade and obtaining a money income. . . .[29]

As the medium-of-exchange role played by money became widespread, it also gained prominence as a store of value. Of necessity, this affected fundamental relations—especially where the most enterprising, hard-working, and thrifty serfs, who were able to develop some entrepreneurial skills, were concerned. For *some* price many lords would be willing to free many of their serfs. Given the rising agricultural productivity, in fact, many lords with good land could reap a handsome profit by selling freedom to their serfs, renting the land and certain implements out to them, and living off the proceeds. And if the reduced status (in effect, that of Ricardian landlord) was too painful for a given nobleman, one of his descendants might not be so reluctant to lower his opportunity cost.

Even where complete freedom was not granted, the growth of specialization and exchange increased the lord's incentive to loosen feudal bonds enough to encourage serf initiative. Because a nobleman could share in the profits from his serf's investments, it appeared particularly worthwhile to many lords to encourage demonstrated entrepreneurial ability among their subjects. In this way, however, they showed themselves guilty of classic Marxian false consciousness. For a process of social differentiation began to develop within the serf classes, who slowly separated into an upper stratum of well-to-do kulak peasants and small producers vis-à-vis a much larger lower stratum of poor cottagers, artisans and handicraft workers, and landless squatters. It is here that we find the elements of capitalist society nascent in the feudal womb.[30]

From at least the end of the 14th century onward, we find serfs managing estates, large handicraft and cottage industries, and even a few factories, which produced almost entirely for the market and were worked by other serfs. "It was these more prosperous elements . . . both in agriculture and in the urban handicrafts, who not only had direct links with the market, but sought

[29] Maurice Dobb, "The Transition from Feudalism to Capitalism," op. cit.

[30] A splendid, essentially positive, and non-Marxist account of the serf-entrepreneur is given by H. Rosovsky in "The Serf Entrepreneur in Russia," *Explorations in Entrepreneurial History,* May 1954.

to improve and extend production, and as they expanded, became employers of wage-labor."

During the same period,

a main factor in the decline of feudalism in Western Europe . . . was the struggle of small producers to loosen the bonds of feudal exploitation. Particularly conscious of these bonds were the upper stratum of well-to-do peasants, who were in a position to extend cultivation onto new land and to improve it, and who accordingly tended to be the spearpoint of revolt. Such tendencies were both aided by and aided the spread of trade, [accumulation], and production for the market. . . . [As] disintegration of the old order proceeded and . . . production shook itself loose from feudal bonds and feudal exploitation, the process of social differentiation was accelerated. . . .

As social differentiation proceeded, the upper stratum was increasingly able to free itself from feudal bondage.[31]

The lord's position in society declined, not only relative to the emerging capitalist class, but also in absolute terms, as he faced what may be broadly termed a deteriorating labor market. The rising power and wealth of towns tempted more and more serfs to run away and made it harder for their former masters to recapture them. The competition for labor among lords in more recently cultivated lands tended to prevent them from cooperating in returning runaway serfs. On top of this and the serf revolts came waves of plague and pestilence, probably brought into Europe by rising commercial contact. By the time the Black Death had run its course in 1350, it had killed more than one-third of Western Europe's population and also raised the bargaining power of the laboring classes.

In the final analysis, the revival of commerce and industry in the 12th through 15th centuries marks first the high-water mark of feudalism, and then its long, slow, painful, and irregular decline. Concomitant with the latter came an equally long, slow, and painful rise of capitalism. We should not identify the growth of trade too closely or directly with the decline of feudalism and the rise of capitalism, however. Trade closely interacted with the rising productive forces in agriculture and industry, which, so to speak, tended to undermine feudal relations from within.

It appears, in fact, that the growth of trade per se was quite compatible with feudal relations and even accompanied a temporary reestablishment or restrengthening of serfdom in some areas (notably eastern Germany). We have noted that feudal lords often engaged in trade (this was particularly true of monasteries) and their sons would often be accepted as partners by the merchants in return for land or titles of gentility. Of course, the story of the marriage uniting the (relatively) impoverished but thoroughly reputable aristocrat with the wealthy, but clearly less reputable, merchant is a classic. While frictions certainly existed between merchants and lords—notably over

31 Dobb, "The Transition from Feudalism to Capitalism," op. cit.

the latter's desire to exact tolls and taxes—the two appear to have been quite compatible as long as the merchant remained a merchant and invested his capital in trade.

It was only when the merchant joined the upper stratum of urban crafts-men and relatively prosperous peasants in investing to expand production and the employment of hired or contractual labor that he came into competition with the feudal system. In this competition, the lord was at a disadvantage, both because he did not rise to his position on the basis of his entrepreneurial ability and because he was probably more affected by religious and social stigmas against accumulation than the initially lower socioeconomic classes. Nevertheless, some lords did become successful enterpreneurs, and more made the transitions to successful landlord or rentier.[32]

But in the more fundamental competition, laissez-faire capitalism won over feudalism when the system of hired and contractual labor finally domi-nated the system based on serf labor. In most Western Europe, this occurred during the 16th and 17th centuries, although it was delayed in France until the 18th century and in Russia until the late 19th or early 20th century. Besides the fact that the budding entrepreneur was usually limited in acquir-ing his own serf labor force, the wage-labor system had three basic advantages in meeting the demands of an ever-expanding market. (These would ulti-mately translate into a lower cost curve for the employer of wage labor or a wider or more efficient product line.)

First, employers had more freedom to shift laborers between jobs, includ-ing hiring and firing, and to reward them according to their contributions to exchange-value creation. Second, and the other side of this coin, the worker had more "freedom" to seek out the highest paying jobs—where his value of marginal product would be highest under approximately competitive condi-tions—or those jobs which he preferred. (Marx would deny, however, that any broader permanent freedom for the working class could be more than illusory under capitalism.[33]) Finally, as feudal bonds loosened, there was in-creasing freedom to experiment with and to market new ideas, products, and techniques. This, in turn, helped to loosen these bonds still further by speed-ing up the rate of innovation.

Once launched, the evolution of capitalism would mirror feudalism, ac-cording to Marx, in two ways. First, it would pass through two distinct stages, the first under which it would flourish, but the second to which it could not

[32] Marx denied the importance of entrepreneurial ability as a factor of production and preferred to think of the capitalist as having achieved his status through inheritance, or through luck, excessive greed, and hard-heartedness, or graft or theft. In this case, it is hard to see why the feudal lords were not the ones to principally succeed themselves as capitalist entrepreneurs. They were well positioned to do so, and many did not show themselves wanting for greed or hard-heartedness.

[33] In particular the working class largely remained the exploited class, no matter what occupation the laborer might choose; and, upward mobility into the capitalist class would be minimized once the bourgeoisie got matters under firm control. Marx put little faith in the classic "rags-to-riches" tale.

adapt. Second, it would reach its most productive hours during the second stage, in the very act of laying the groundwork for its inevitable decline and demise.

Table 12–1 summarizes the evolution of primitive communism, slavery, and feudalism.

12–6   Concluding Remarks

If we take the above theory too literally—as describing an inevitable historical evolution in any society—the weight of empirical evidence turns heavily against us. It is, for example, oriented toward Western culture and does not adapt well to Asian economic history. It is also more applicable to Western Europe than to North America. Although private property did sometimes emerge on the North American continent under conditions that Table 12–1 would lead us to expect, neither slave-based nor feudalist production was ever the dominant form in most localities.[34] And in the U.S. South, where slavery did predominate in agriculture, historians are presently maintaining that it was much more efficient in the decades before the Civil War than was formerly believed.[35]

In terms of actual history, therefore, Marx appears to have considered a rather special case. In addition, Marx and Engels may well have exaggerated the distinction between private and communal ownership in many primitive communities. According to one source:

Communism as a legal institution has often been read into primitive societies in cases where a closer study would have shown the joint ownership to be that of a kinship group [for example, where] the inhabitants of a village coincide exactly with a . . . clan of blood relations, jointly owning the arable and other lands.

[34] For example, many, although by no means all, historians feel that a historical and geographical relationship exists among North American Indians between the development of private rights in land and the development of the commercial fur trade. With the appearance of a market for furs, according to this thesis, the values, both of fur-bearing animals and of the lands they roamed, increased sharply. It became efficient to divide up the land and allow private owners the right to any income earned from selling furs. This reduced overly intensive hunting, permitted the introduction of more efficient hunting and trapping methods, and gave the owner an incentive to preserve the supply of fur-bearing animals as his principal source of wealth. However, private property rights were often not complete. Among Indians living in what is now Quebec, a starving man could kill and eat another's beaver—if he left the fur and tail. There was also a kind of "good samaritan" rule of income redistribution (in effect, a communal property right) among at least one tribe, which attenuated the incentive to maintain the beaver population. The latter, in fact, diminished. See Demsetz, op. cit., and references cited. Demsetz, however, overstates the argument for his case. See, as well, John C. McManns, "An Economic Analysis of Indian Behavior in the North American Fur Trade," *Journal of Economic History,* Mar. 1972.

[35] See, for example, Robert W. Fogel and Stanley L. Engermann, "The Relative Efficiency of Slavery: A Comparison of Northern and Southern Agriculture in 1860," *Explorations in Economic History,* Spring–Summer 1971, and references cited.

Table 12-1. Evolution of certain "primitive" property-right forms.

Form of Property Rights	Presumed Advantages	Changing Nature of Mode of Production	Hypothesized Cause of Downfall (Disadvantage)
Primitive communism	Relative lack of class antagonism and strife; communal sharing of fruits of production.	Growing productivity of land and labor and increasing population due to labor's ability to produce a surplus. Consequent rise in the values of land and labor. Growing roundaboutness of production so that incentives to invest become more important. Rising ability to travel, transport, and communicate. Beginnings of industrial production.	External diseconomies, which become more serious as technology improves. Consequent disincentives to invest and to maintain material means of production. Even a low-level division of labor and specialization in production sometimes proves difficult.
Slavery	Private property includes some right to income from investment, hence growing incentive to invest and maintain property. Right to coordinate and control labor so as to maximize surplus value it produces.	Optimal scale of production grows larger and, to a lesser extent, optimal division of labor increases. The heterogeneity of outputs from a given production activity also rises, as the optimal range of products grows for the whole economy. We may summarize this to some extent by saying that the optimal complexity of production grows.	As the complexity of production grows, the supervisory costs of slavery eventually grow rapidly, and the need for more positive work incentives becomes more acute.
Feudalism	Increasing autonomy of laborers and consequent reduced costs of supervision, combined with guarantees of some protection against violence and famine.	Growing ability to transport and communicate; rising productivity of labor in agriculture and industry causes sharp upswing in optimal degree of specialization and trade. The same rising productivity enables individual peasants and craftsmen to become more independent and raises the importance of experimentation and innovation.	As opposed to hired or contractual labor, serf labor has less flexibility in allocating itself or in being allocated to those jobs where its (marginal) contribution to exchange value is greatest. Feudal ties also permit less freedom to innovate and experiment.

. . . [Moreover] something akin to private property is nearly always present, even in groups which seem most communistic. . . .[36]

Finally, if we jump forward into state socialism, our earlier discussion tempts us to fill in a fourth row in Table 12–1 corresponding to a highly centralized command economy. Under "Presumed Advantages" (vis-à-vis a planned market economy) we may list the improved ability of a "respected" economic planning council to steer the economy, especially when a radical reordering of priorities is called for. Under "Changing Nature of Mode of Production," we may list a growing complexity of the economy, including a growing interdependency and an increasing range of products.

Under "Disadvantages" (vis-à-vis a planned market economy or the "reformed" command-economy model discussed in Chapter 9) we may list higher information costs, difficulties in accommodating technological change, supply breakdowns, and success-indicator problems. Nonetheless, a bureaucratic elite with a vested interest in preventing economic decentralization may prolong the status quo.

On the other hand, if we abstract the Marx–Engels theory from its specific historical setting and prognosis of the future, and strip it down to its essentials, we get the following basic components. First, the inevitable chicken-and-egg problem is solved by postulating partially autonomous technical change. Although this is not the only conceivable solution, economists have never been able to construct useful models in which the rate of technological progress is entirely determined by other factors. If we wish, however, we may broaden our definition of the prime mover so that it becomes autonomous environmental change in the spirit of Section 2–6.[37]

Corresponding to any given (multidimensional) level of technology, or to any given environment, will be an optimal economic system or range of systems, implying an optimal range of socioeconomic relations or property-right forms. This is the second ingredient, from which we may climb the inverted pyramid of Figure 12–3. Once again, we may define "optimal" in the restricted sense of permitting the economy to get as close as possible to its production-possibility frontier. However, we may also broaden this term to mean a kind of "equilibrium in harmony" between the three dimensions of an economic system.

By the latter, in turn, we shall mean that there is widespread acceptance of the existing political and economic decision-making processes and therefore no current impulse to adapt the system for better goal pursuit. In particular, the division of economic activity into an area covered by absolute property rights and governed by commands on one hand, and an area left

[36] Knight, op. cit., pp. 15–16.

[37] There we said that the environment of an economic system consisted of its resource endowment, its geography, its prevailing culture and technology, and its world position with regard to each of these factors vis-à-vis other economies. We have dropped the notion of the optimal (opposed to the actual) level of technology (or productive forces) because we do not feel that it really adds anything essential to the theory.

to individual choice and governed by contract law on the other is widely accepted. The political and economic decision-making processes are also well tuned to each other. By and large, the degree of success met in translating economic goals into achievements is least acceptable.

As technology, or the environment, changes, the old harmony erodes, and new frictions arise. Eventually, a new "optimal" economic system will emerge. However, the old socioeconomic relations created an institutional superstructure that is inevitably tied to the existing distributions of wealth, power, privilege, and prestige. This, in turn, has created a class—or, more generally, a group of economic actors—with a vested interest in preventing systemic change. These actors become our third basic ingredient.

At the same time, the new optimal economic system must be more efficient in the pursuit of *some* set of socioeconomic goals than the old. The chance will therefore arise for opportunistic elements in society to benefit themselves by promoting systemic change. In many cases, society's leaders would do this, seeking to improve economic performance. Alternatively, at least two kinds of friction may be generated by a technology that tends to evolve ahead of the economy's institutional superstructure:

1. External effects may arise that permit some economic actors to inflict part of the costs of their activities onto others or else to benefit from the activities of others without having to pay. Pollution, congestion, and shoplifting are all examples of this in a modern economy.
2. Barriers to entry may arise or grow more costly for various actors. Here we include barriers to various kinds of employment, to education or training, to invention and innovation, and to the production or distribution of particular goods and services. (The latter comprise barriers to new competition in an industry.) Such barriers will often be higher for some individuals and firms than for others. That is, they will go hand in hand with inequality of opportunity.[38]

When the tensions generated by external effects or entry barriers pass some threshold level, the affected actors will have an incentive to unite. Articulation leaders will tend to emerge who express the group's discontent and try to lead its efforts to influence society's decision-making processes. Whether they be opportunistic elements, ruling bodies seeking to improve economic performance, or articulation leaders arising under (1) or (2), economic actors will emerge to press for systemic change. They become the fourth and final basic ingredient of our neo-Marxian theory of systemic change.

If successful, the actors promoting change will probably alter the dis-

---

[38] The forms that these barriers may assume are too numerous to cover exhaustively here. However, they include housing and job discrimination, protection of privileged positions of all kinds—in particular, protection of monopolies and bureaucratic elites—and suppression of new products and new ideas in the sense of not allowing them to be fairly tested against the old.

tribution of economic power—not necessarily in the sense of centralizing or decentralizing it—but in the more general sense of changing the distribution of power weights. They are almost certain to alter the distribution of property rights and the structure of information flows. For this network facilitated the emergence of entry barriers, external effects, or "unsatisfactory" performance which caused the tensions in the first place.

Consequently, we shall see a new distribution of property rights, accompanied by changes in the nature and pattern of information flows, and new institutions to accommodate these changes. The respective areas covered by commands, markets, and taxation will probably alter, and new laws and regulations may arise or old ones be better enforced. At the same time, old institutions will diminish or die and old laws are likely to be repealed, to lapse, or to fall into disuse. In the event of complete success, a new harmony and unity will emerge between the three dimensions of the economy, relieving the original sources of tension. This is the classic Marxian outcome in which the forces promoting "optimal" systemic change win out over the old vested interests.

In practice, however, any movement may bog down short of its goals (perhaps because it is blocked or relentlessly opposed by more powerful groups), or, for some other reason, result in suboptimal systemic change. It may eventually die or give rise to a minority political party or fringe group. Such an effort may yet survive for a long time, and ultimately even come to prevail.

A third possibility is that, as a result of tension, "reforms" are made that may placate some groups or serve as a vehicle through which others consolidate their power. However, these changes actually turn out to be rather modest and leave the basic nature of the system alone. If made cleverly, they will improve performance for awhile or prevent it from deteriorating further. Eventually, the old problems and tensions return, and they may be met by a new series of reform measures—somewhat different from the old—which again leave the basic nature of the system unchanged. Thus we go through a repeating cycle of tension–reform–retrenchment–tension–reform–retrenchment. Over a very long time period, the system may well change in a fundamental way. That is, the cycle may not be entirely circular.

The recent history of the U.S.S.R. gives us an example. Successive reforms have uncovered many of the "hidden reserves" of productive capacity and inventories while not reducing by very much the importance of the role played by commands. One apparent reason is that the Soviet leaders believe much of their power to stem from the sheer weight of the bureaucratic mass beneath them. It is far from clear that an alternative power base could not be found in a market-planned economy, but the leadership has not wished to play Russian Roulette on this score.

In addition, we may wish to modify Figure 12–3 to permit all forms of feedback down the inverted triangle. This will considerably complexify the model, but despite this and the above, we may still be able to say that, in the very long run, an economic system's basic features are largely determined by autonomous changes in technology or in the environment. Moreover, the emerging system would be optimal for the technology or environment in question. As such, the theory is weaker because a particular system could now take so long to emerge that its appearance would no longer be optimal. Indeed, for this reason, it might never emerge. Nevertheless, many writers on economic history have used such a framework, often implicitly, for their discussions.

A final objection is that the prime mover of history is still defined too narrowly. Some economists would argue, for example, that the "optimal" system should depend upon social preferences, independently of technology or the environment. A change in social preferences could then, by itself, set systemic change in motion. If we interpret the basic motor force of history too broadly, however, virtually any observation becomes reconcilable with it. Such a theory would have no explanatory power.

Chapter 13

Two Theories
of Capitalist Development

13–1   Primitive Accumulation and Early Capitalism

To complete Marx's specific economic theory of history, we now turn to the evolution of capitalism itself. Historically, none of the transitions we described in Section B of Chapter 12 was either rapid, smooth, or regular. A feature of each one was a rise in the number of independent, small capitalists or "freemen"—farmers, craftsmen, artisans, traders, and the like—who employed, at the very outside, a handful of slaves, serfs, or hired laborers. At times this class took advantage of struggles growing at least partly out of the clash between the old and new property-rights forms.

Later it would be submerged when the new socioeconomic relations came to dominate. (Or, more accurately, class divisions would arise within it based on the emerging form of property rights. Most of the remaining "small fish" would be swallowed.) Although the class of small proprietors never entirely disappeared, its flourishing was always a temporary respite, usually between what Marx would call two different forms of bondage.

The rise of laissez-faire capitalism was no different. During the 12th through the 15th centuries in Western Europe, many freed serfs became small farmers and independent craftsmen. Together with guild masters, they began to employ hired laborers and thus emerged as a class of small capitalists. The guilds held monopolies in their respective crafts, but individual guild masters were not supposed to hire laborers except apprentices, who could hope to eventually become masters themselves. Nevertheless,

In spite of all regulations . . . economic inequalities did grow up among guild masters, especially where opportunities for expansion were great. The rich enlarged their shops, took on more apprentices and journeymen than the poorer masters, and made it practically impossible for journeymen to become guild masters. . . . Thus, the rich guildsmen became, in fact, industrial employers, hiring workers for money wages and producing for profit.[1]

The more prosperous among the class of small, independent producers were therefore moving into a position from which they could become large capitalists, employing many workers. Still, according to Marx, the infant bourgeoisie was forced to advance, at first, at a snail's pace.

The new productive forces and the rising bourgeoisie are handicapped at each step by the old [socioeconomic relations]—by feudal restrictions, guild regulations, absence of freedom of contract, local legal provisions, diverse schemes of taxation, and the arrogant privileges of the hierarchical nobility. There is an insistent call for hired labor [by capitalists wanting to expand], but labor . . . for hire is tantalizingly scarce. . . . Everywhere the worker possesses the means of production and works for himself.[2]

In a sense, there are two important prerequisites for "capitalist production"—"the owners of money and the means of production, eager to hire wage labor; and . . . masses of workers . . . divorced from the [material] means of production, owners of labor-power alone and eager to sell it for a wage." [3] Until at least the late 1400s, only the first was present in Western Europe; the other shoe was still waiting to drop. It fell, first of all, with the enclosure movement in Britain. The period in question was one of rapid growth in the European textile industry, both because of trade expansion and internal technological improvements. This led to a bourgeoning demand for wool and a rapidly rising price. Britain had a strong comparative advantage in supplying this principal raw material.

Big landowners began evicting tenants, or raising their rent and forcing them to leave, in order to convert small farms into large sheep pastures. This greatly reduced the labor requirement in comparison with tillage, and farmers and farm laborers were evicted from their land or found that they could not pass on their property to heirs. Robert Kett led a uprising against the enclosure movement in 1549, but, like subsequent rebellions, it was crushed, and the enclosures continued. The result was a genuine industrial reserve army, as much of the dispossessed peasantry found its way into crowded city

[1] Shepard B. Clough, *The Economic Development of Western Civilization* (New York: McGraw-Hill, 1959), p. 101.

[2] M. M. Bober, *Karl Marx's Interpretation of History* (Cambridge, Mass.: Harvard U.P., 1962), p. 56.

[3] Ibid., p. 57.

slums, and was forced to accept employment under adverse bargaining conditions.

In addition, "The impoverished feudal nobility disband[ed] the numerous retainers who had thronged house and castle . . . The Reformation impart[ed] a 'new and frightful impulse' to the process through the suppression of monasteries and the dispersion of the serfs attached to them." [4] The independent craftsman or artisan was gradually eliminated and then absorbed by the putting-out system.[5] In the process, his tools and equipment effectively passed into the service of the merchant–capitalist, often at bankruptcy prices. Harsh laws to combat idleness, reduce wages, and prolong the working day, combined with severe, sternly enforced penalties for thievery, completed the picture.

Marx called the expropriation of the individual peasant and producer *primitive accumulation.* He viewed it at accumulation by naked theft which granted the capitalist his first major source of surplus value. Once he had "stolen" the instruments of production, the capitalist could presumably borrow against them to invest and thereby to realize further surplus value in the form of profit on the investment. In this way, capitalists could expand their power and their empires, while pushing the laboring class into ever deepening dependency.[6]

Primitive accumulation thus marks the birth of laissez-faire capitalism for all practical purposes in Marx's view, but we should hasten to add that his characterization fits the facts in England much better than elsewhere. In other countries, notably France, the rise of early capitalism was slower and not accompanied by a gigantic uprooting of the rural population. In England, itself, it is clear that feudalism would have crumbled and the system known as laissez-faire capitalism risen to take its place without the enclosure movement.

Indeed, rising productivity in both industry and agriculture would likewise have resulted in a largely urban population, although the process would have taken longer and might have been less painful. Marx would nevertheless argue that, as the bourgeoisie gradually accumulated capital and reinvested its sur-

---

4 Ibid., p. 58.

5 Under the putting-out system, many handicraftsmen, weavers, artisans, or laborers would work for a merchant–capitalist, sometimes in their own homes. Typically, the merchant would supply tools, or the money to buy them, raw materials, technical instructions, and, on occasion, larger capital equipment to the workers. He would also advance the means for sustaining the worker and his family and any working-capital requirements. Then he collected and sold the finished production. (There were a number of variations on this theme; in mining, for example, the merchant would often simply advance capital to the producer and take care of sales. In any event, the merchant always financed the operation.)

The putting-out system allowed the division of labor to reach a much more advanced stage than hitherto. The merchant capitalist was also able to achieve scale economies unavailable to independent craftsmen in many instances, and he had better access to finance. Finally, he had more market and political power and a better knowledge of market conditions, both in buying and selling.

6 Karl Marx, *Capital* (Moscow: Foreign Languages Publishing, 1965–1967), Vol. I, Pt. VIII.

plus value, perhaps starting from a very small base, the gulf between it and the working class would widen. The latter would again sink into a kind of slavery whose bonds are simply far less visible and more sophisticated than in previous times. According to Marx, there is a key thread which links the worker under laissez-faire capitalism with the feudal serf and the ancient slave. This is the "alienation" or estrangement of labor from the product it produces.

To understand alienation, we must first give a more careful definition of the notion of "commodities" in Marxist theory. Commodities are goods that are traded on some kind of market place. Marx particularly emphasized commodities that were sold by someone other than the worker or workers who directly produced them. Such a seller would not interest himself directly in the use value of commodities, according to Marx.

Instead, whether he be a slave owner in Rome or a British capitalist many centuries later, he wants to know what price his products will bring. That is, he is interested in their exchange value, which will reflect not only use value, but monopoly power, faulty or misleading information, and the whole range of "market imperfections," discussed by modern Western economists. A particular villain in this piece is the merchant, who creates no use value at all, according to Marx. Instead he connects buyers and sellers through exchange, sometimes over great distances, and lives off the profit that he extracts from buying low and selling high.

The important point for our purposes, however, is that labor itself becomes a commodity as soon as slavery succeeds primitive communism, and this is the first source of alienation. Neither the slave nor the medieval serf nor the proletarian works out of an inner need to create or to express himself, but out of dire necessity, in order to make a living. The goods that he produces are not his but the property of his owner, lord, or employer. Human labor is therefore alienated from its product and is reduced to an abstract quality called "labor power," which forms the basis of its exchange value. According to Marx:

> It is true that labor produces wonderful things for the rich—but for the worker it producers a privation. It produces palaces—but for the worker, hovels. It produces beauty—but for the worker, deformity. It replaces labor by machines, but it throws a section of the workers back to a barbarous type of labor, and it turns the other workers into machines. . . .[7]

If anything, alienation grows worse as we move from the absolute slavery end of the private-property continuum toward modern laissez-faire capitalism. The first principal source, exploitation, may not be stronger under one form than under another. However, a second major source, the division of labor, becomes more and more pronounced. "The alienation [of labor] grows even deeper as the division of labor works its way into the workshop [and] the

[7] Karl Marx, *The Economic and Philosophical Manuscripts of 1844* (New York: International Publishers, 1964), p. 110.

factory and transforms the worker . . . into a detail worker who no longer creates the whole product, but only a part of it and carries out several tasks or even one partial task in which he specializes and acquires a degree of virtuosity. If human labor had a meaning earlier, man was the maker of use-value. [This] meaning is now lost. . . ." [8]

Marx divided the era of laissez-faire capitalism into two major periods based upon the use of mechanical (largely steam) power and associated machinery. The first phase, lasting in Britain from the middle of the 16th century to the last third of the 18th, largely precedes the industrial revolution in which steam power becomes dominant. By 1650 the use of labor-saving machinery would doubtless have awed the Rip van Winkle awakening after 400 years of slumber. But it was largely based upon a more efficient harnessing of wind, water, and draft animals. The major characteristic of the first phase of capitalism, moreover, was not the development of new and better machinery, so much as it was a rapidly increasing division of labor, expanding use of the factory system (as outlined in Chapter 5) and, to a lesser extent, a growing scale of production.

This phase

begins as a twofold development. First . . . the employer assembles in the workshop a number of [artisans], all of whom do the same work, and each one of whom goes through alone all the successive processes necessary for completion of the product. Second, the capitalist employs simultaneously various craftsmen who engage in successive handicraft pursuits which contribute to a final product; thus he engages wheelwrights, harness-makers, blacksmiths, painters, and so forth, to cooperate in making carriages . . . sooner or later, an elaborate . . . division of labor sets in, and what was previously performed by one handicraftsman [becomes] many elementary processes, one or more of which claims the full attention of the worker.[9]

As the division of labor develops, so does the improvement of hand tools to accommodate this. Indeed, laissez-faire capitalism both accommodates and encourages the division of labor, the introduction of the factory system, and the realization of scale economies to a far greater extent than either slavery or feudalism could do. It also encourages greater class divisions, but by the beginning of the 19th century, capitalism was firmly entrenched in Western Europe, and North America and the second or machine phase was well under way in Britain.

We could also call this the "modern industry" or even better, the "scientific" phase. For while its achievements were most impressive in industry,

[8] Radoslav Selucky, "Marketization and Democratization: Their Interdependence within the Reform Movement in the Soviet Bloc," paper presented to the Workshop on Economics Organization and Development, Ottawa, Carleton University, Feb. 1971, pp. 12–13. By an increasing division of labor, we mean the splitting of any particular production activity into a larger number of more specialized tasks.

[9] Bober, op. cit., p. 61.

the rise of scientific agriculture caused a second enclosure movement in Britain, which reached its height in the period from 1760 to 1820. In effect, big farming replaced small-scale tillage, to which there had been some reversion following the first enclosure movement, and turned loose another industrial reserve army. The same thing happened in Germany east of the Elbe River. With the introduction of modern technology, capitalism enjoyed its finest hour in terms of productivity, although the fruits of increased production went mainly to the rich, according to Marx.

Indeed, it is with this era that we begin "the story of the flaming Marxian indictments against the present system with its enslavement of man to machine, the remorseless grinding of surplus value out of the exploited wage-slaves . . . the increasing misery of the workers, and crises and panics." [10] It is, likewise, the machine era which Marx believed capitalism would not be able to accommodate. If so, even as it reaches its most productive hour, the forces to destroy it would be set in motion.

13-2   Marx's Theory of the Development of Modern Capitalism

A recurring theme in discussion of the evolution of capitalism is what we may call the "falling rate of profit." According to both Marx and modern Western economists, the capitalist (or, more accurately, the manager) invests primarily to secure a profit. If the expected profitability (or yield) on investments falls, so will his incentive to invest, until a full-employment level of income and output can no longer be maintained. The short-run result will be a crisis or depression, unless government policies can intervene to prevent this. A long-run tendency for the rate of profit to fall will cause secular stagnation or, as in Marx, a worsening sequence of crises.

Such a long-run tendency was inevitable in Marx's view, because of a rising capital intensity of production (that is, a rising capital-to-labor ratio or, in Marxian terminology, a rising organic composition of capital) against the backdrop of a labor theory of value. This is the basic characteristic of the changing mode of production, according to Marx, once the second or machine phase of capitalism gets under way. Ironically, it is the capitalists' own investments that cause the organic composition of capital to rise, and this is their manifestation of false consciousness.

From Section A of Chapter 12 we recall that the Marxian labor value of a commodity, W, equals $C + V + S$. C is the value of the fixed and circulating capital used up in producing the good, V the wages and salaries bill, and S the surplus value or profit which goes to the owners of capital. We may break up the income earned by a producing enterprise in the same way. Marx would define the average rate of profit in a firm, π, to be its total profits, S divided

[10] Ibid., p. 63.

by $C + V$, which we may view as the outlay needed to maintain its productive capacity, together with its labor force. That is,

$$\pi = \frac{S}{C + V}$$

Because only living labor can create value, the amount of surplus value which a *given* outlay, $C + V$, can produce falls when the capital intensity of production, defined as C/V by Marx, rises. Hence π falls.[11] Alternatively,

As capital accumulates in a capitalist society, proportionately more of the total will consist of machinery and tools . . . and proportionately less . . . will go into payment of current wages. . . . However, only the latter can yield surplus value, since only labor creates value. Thus, since a smaller proportion of the total outlay [$C + V$] goes into that use where surplus value is created, the surplus value realized [S] will tend to become a smaller and smaller percentage of total [$C + V$] as that total increases.[12]

The reason why managers increase C/V, given these results, is a bit obscure in Marx. However, he argues that "The battle of competition [between capitalists] is fought by cheapening of commodities. The cheapness of commodities depends . . . on the productiveness of labour and . . . on the scale of production. Therefore, the larger capitals beat the smaller. . . ."[13]

This appears to say that, as the modern industry phase of capitalism proceeds, the efficient scale of production grows. At a given point in time, some firms will be using more up-to-date technologies of production than others in the same industry. Presumably, the productivity of labor will be greater in the more advanced firms because laborers have better capital to work with. But one aspect of this is that these firms are achieving cost savings by realizing economies of scale or mass production. The three apparently distinct phenomena—more up-to-date methods of production, increasing economies of scale, and a higher organic composition of capital—are all assumed to go hand in hand, if our interpretation of Marx is correct.

Suppose, now, that the management of a firm expects its product prices to remain fixed—or to rise at least as fast as the prices of its inputs—over

[11] This is not the same definition of profit that Western economists now use, even after we sort out some confusion in Marx between stocks and flows. To the modern theorist, the rate of profit is defined as a yield on investments. The average yield during any particular year on past investments made in a particular firm would equal the firm's accounting profits (that is, S) divided by the value of its capital stock.

Under "reasonable" assumptions, the Marxian rate of profit will tend to zero if and only if the above version does. Nevertheless, the two could follow markedly diverse time paths, with one "approaching" zero long before the other. In these circumstances, the Marxian definition is the more misleading as an indication of the incentive to invest. It could fall, for example, simply because of a rise in the real wage rate. But this might increase the incentive to invest in labor-saving machinery.

[12] W. N. Loucks and W. G. Whitney, *Comparative Economic Systems*, 8th ed. (New York: Harper, 1969), p. 128.

[13] Marx, *Capital*, op. cit., Vol. I, p. 626.

some time horizon relevant to investment decision making. It therefore decides to undertake a large capital-spending project which will raise the productivity of labor, reduce its required labor input, and enable it to achieve greater scale economies. The minimum rate of output needed to achieve these scale economies also rises, as Figure 13–1 shows.

There, the dashed line, lac_1, describes the firm's old cost curve, and the solid line, lac_2, its anticipated new one after the proposed investment project begins to bear fruit. The minimum least-cost rate of output is 110,000 units before and 150,000 units after the modernization. At a present price of $4, management looks forward to substantially increased profits, inasmuch as its minimum average cost has fallen from $3 to $1.75 per unit of output.

In fact, when the firm expands its own production to achieve its increased mass production benefits, it may well lower the price at which market demand will absorb industry-wide output. If this drops to $3.50 in Figure 13–1, the firm is still better off after the investment because minimum average costs have fallen by more. However, matters are unlikely to end here. Managers of other firms observe that the highest rates of profit and the biggest shares of

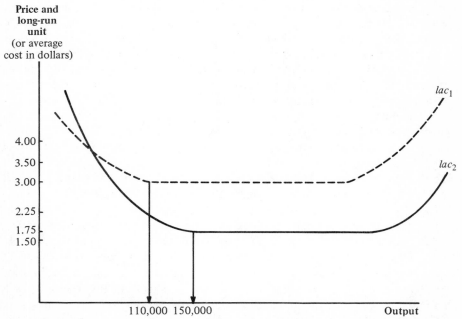

Figure 13–1. A downward shifting unit (or average) cost curve during the modern-industry phase of laissez-faire capitalism.

industry-wide profit are being earned in those enterprises which use the most up-to-date production techniques. Consequently, a more capital-intensive technology spreads throughout the industry, and the minimum lowest-average-cost scale of output tends to rise within each firm. The collective result of this, in turn, is an increase, perhaps substantial, in the rate of industry-wide output which market demand must absorb.

It can only do so at a lower price, which we therefore suppose to reach $2.25 in Figure 13–1. The firm whose cost curve we depict can continue to survive, but only if it produces more than 115,000 units. However, some less modern or less ably managed enterprises may find themselves taking losses at such a low price. If they expect it to persist, they will leave the industry, thereby increasing the immediate unemployment effect of the labor-saving technical change. This exit will raise the demand curves facing the remaining firms, *provided* market demand does not fall. Moreover, the capital equipment of the firms that leave the industry may fall into the hands of survivors or of new firms at bankruptcy prices. In this way, primitive accumulation is repeated many times on a minute scale.

Thus the profit prospects of remaining firms may improve, prompting them to raise output and, perhaps, increase price. Nevertheless, there may be a net decline of employment within the industry as a consequence of the departure of some producers and the growing capital intensity of production. In addition, it is far from clear that the market demand curve will remain where it was, because it depends upon the incomes of would-be buyers. If we assume that the above-described phenomenon repeats itself in several industries at once, the rate of unemployment would rise, thereby impairing the purchasing power of a number of households. Some market demand curves will fall. Those which are most elastic with respect to income—presumably durable goods whose replacement can be postponed—will fall the most.

Depending upon timing, therefore, the price could fall as low as $1.50 (instead of $2.25) in Figure 13–1, driving even more firms out of the industry. (The exact number to leave will also depend upon how long the low price is expected to last, how long it actually does last, and, perhaps, upon the financial resources of different firms.) Such a phenomenon could snowball into a crisis or depression, particularly if it is continually being fed by labor-saving technical change.

A specific failure of managerial foresight in the above example is its underestimate of the impact on price of a spreading labor-saving and increasingly indivisible technology. Yet, if we drop this assumption, our results may still hold. For it is not clear that any producer behaved irrationally from his own particular point of view. The initial investment (shown in Figure 13–1) will actually pay off, even though it forces down the rate of profit in the long run, if the firm in question can reap enormous profits before the technology spreads to other producers.[14] Once launched, its adoption may become a question of survival to the others.

---

[14] A disproportionate share of these profits goes to the owners of capital, whose own increased demand for goods and services could offset the decline resulting from unemployment. Marx would probably reply (in modern terminology) that the bourgeoisie has a low marginal propensity to consume. However, this does not explain why the

As with tribal chieftains, *latifundium* owners, and feudal lords, the false consciousness of the bourgeoisie is a class rather than an individual phenomenon. In particular, it relies on a failure of managers to collude efficiently, a point that may raise a few eyebrows.

In any event, crises and depressions become increasingly severe and each recovery more feeble than the preceding as the rate of profit continues its long-run downward course. The bourgeois class dwindles, and the laboring class grows as small capitalists are competed out of business and forced to sell out to their larger competitors at bankruptcy prices. Power therefore concentrates in the hands of an increasingly small elite until the pit of the last great depression arrives. Then the working class finds itself strong enough to launch the social revolution, eventually seize the reins of power, and establish a "dictatorship of the proletariat."

Additional details of this process appear on the left-hand side of Table 13–1. The reader should keep in mind the particular underlying assumptions, notably concerning the nature of technological change.

Table 13–1. Theories of Marx and Schumpeter paralleled.

Marx	*Schumpeter*
1. *Nature of Class Conflict* Capitalists versus workers or laboring class. The capitalists (bourgeoisie) own or control the material means of production. This gives them monopoly power over the workers (proletariat), who own only their own labor power. Consequently, the workers are subjected to exploitation.	1. *Nature of Class Conflict* Productive versus unproductive. The focus of the class conflict is on the intelligentsia versus the managers. The *productive* class consists largely of managers or entrepreneurs and workers with a "direct responsibility for practical affairs." Their efforts are largely market-oriented. However, the workers are passive, for the most part, in any class conflict except where this can win them better wages and working conditions. The *unproductive* class consists of intellectuals and others who do not have a direct responsibility for practical affairs. They are largely onlookers and, often, not market-oriented or dependent upon acceptance by buyers of the product they produce. The intellectuals are the active perpetrators of class conflict. *Note:* In contrast to Marx, class identification is subdued and does not play a principal role in the evolution and eventual demise of capitalism.

capitalists' savings are not invested, particularly in view of their own false consciousness. To complete the Marxian theory of cycles, we would probably need a Keynesian-type theory of liquidity preference or some sort of structural theory of unemployment. Examples of both of these appear in Chapter 14.

Table 13—1 (cont.)

Marx	Schumpeter
2. *Changing Nature of Mode of Production* Increasing organic composition of capital (rising capital-to-labor ratio) brought about by capitalists investing in labor-saving technology.	2. *Changing Nature of Mode of Production* Increasing automation and technical sophistication of production improving product quality, widening range of products—all brought about by "creative destruction." The expanding social surplus permits mass higher education to breed a large class of intellectuals. Ultimately, creative destruction also leads to increasing use of numerical calculation, in the form of cost-benefit analysis, as a tool of managerial decision making. The managerial function, itself, becomes increasingly standardized, routinized, automated, and bureaucratized.
3. *Profit Viewed As:* A surplus value created by labor and expropriated by the capitalist, whose ownership of the material means of production gives him monopoly power vis-à-vis his work force.	3. *Profit Viewed As:* A reward for innovation requiring the bearing or risk, particularly when this risk cannot be quantified to the extent of saying, for example, that, with 95 per cent probability, the rate of return will be 6 per cent or greater.
4. *Forms of False Consciousness* Capitalists observe that firms using the most up-to-date (meaning most capital-intensive) techniques within any given industry have the highest profit rates. Consequently, they invest in labor-saving technology, thereby causing the organic composition of capital to rise. Because only living labor is productive, and profit is a surplus value expropriated from labor, industry-wide rates of profit go down. This reduces the willingness of the capitalists to invest and eventually brings about crises. During any crisis, some capitalists go bankrupt and join the proletariat. The proletariat bears the brunt of each crisis, however, giving the workers an incentive to organize so that	4. *Forms of False Consciousness* (a) "Creative destruction" continually makes the economy more productive by rationalizing the process of production. Eventually, "innovation" begins to routinize, standardize, automate, and ultimately, to bureaucratize the entrepreneurial function itself. The entrepreneur appears to become obsolete and slowly becomes extinct on that account. (b) Capitalists turn upon and destroy or wear away institutions which sometimes fetter the innovative effort, but which could also protect the entrepreneurial class from hostile elements. "Capitalism creates a critical frame of mind, which after having destroyed the moral authority of so many other institutions, in the end turns against its own; the bourgeois finds . . . that the rationalist attitude does not stop at the credentials of popes and kings but goes on to attack private property and the whole scheme of bourgeois values." (c) Capitalism also creates mass higher education, from which entrepreneurs derive some short-term benefits but which likewise

Table 13–1 (*cont.*)

Marx	*Schumpeter*
they are better prepared to seize power when the time arrives. *Note:* In contrast with Schumpeter, Marx does not view the entrepreneur as playing a useful social role and certainly not as someone who shapes the course of economic development. Rather, he invests blindly, in response to forces beyond his control. He is seen as a kind of social parasite.	expands far "beyond the point determined by cost—[benefit] considerations." Thus capitalism breeds the intellectual class that will ultimately destroy it. (d) The intelligentsia may also be guilty of false consciousness, in part because its (latent or open) fears of underemployment may come closer to realization with the demise of the bourgeoisie. In addition, because the intellectuals are essentially onlookers, without the first-hand knowledge of practical affairs that only experience can give, they fail to perceive the importance of the entrepreneurial role. Thus, although the wealth and the faults of entrepreneurs are evident, their contribution, as the engine of progress, is not well understood.
5. *The Rate of Profit Falls Because:* As the industry-wide organic composition of capital rises, the industry-wide rate of profit falls, because only living labor can create surplus value. Wars result because capitalists of different nations agree to destroy one another's capital stock in order to raise the rate of profit. Colonial exploitation provides profitable plunder because production in developing nations is relatively labor-intensive.	5. *The Rate of Profit Falls Because:* As the enterpreneurial function gives way to standardization, bureaucratization, and cost-benefit analysis, risk bearing that cannot be quantified tends to be avoided. Consequently, the expected rate of return on more and more "creative destruction" projects is understated, and the probability that such a project will be undertaken becomes less and less. It is in this sense that the rate of profit "falls."
6. *The Cause of Business Cycles* The falling rate of profit impedes investment spending and combines with a sluggish expansion of consumer demand, as the economy's full-employment level of income and output rises. (This is due to technological progress.) The sluggish consumer demand results from the fact that the fruits of technological progress accrue mainly to the bourgeoisie, which has a low marginal propensity to consume. (*Note:* See foot-	6. *The Cause of Business Cycles* Business cycles result from alternating and unforeseeable floods and drouths of creative destruction-motivated investment spending. However, the ebb and flow of creative destruction can only be controlled by eliminating creative destruction as an innovating force. According to Schumpeter's theory, business cycles do not become increasingly severe as capitalism falters. Cycles ultimately start to dampen as creative destruction dies out. Nevertheless, recessions and depressions do generate hostility toward the managerial classes, and may lead to revolution before capitalism crumbles to the point where a peaceful evolution is both

Table 13–1 (*cont.*)

Marx	*Schumpeter*
note 14.)	possible and desirable to the prospective socialist leadership.

7. *The Depletion of the Bourgeois Class*

During each business-cycle trough, some capital is destroyed, reducing the organic composition of capital and causing the rate of profit to rise somewhat. In the process, some capitalists go bankrupt and join the proletariat. Capital is increasingly concentrated into the hands of fewer and fewer capitalists, who often expropriate the holdings of their fallen colleagues at confiscatory prices.

Normally, the small rise in the rate of profit, combined with the concentration of capital and the acquisition of some means of production through confiscation, would cause recovery from depression.

However, either war or fresh or intensified colonial exploitation can cause a recovery from each depression save the last. This culminates in the destruction of laissez-faire capitalism.

7. *The Depletion of the Entrepreneurial (and, therefore, the Bourgeois) Class*

(a) As the entrepreneurial function becomes routinized, depersonalized, and subject to mounting controls, its attraction to aspirants diminishes. To complement this, risk avoidance increases with rising incomes. (In technical language, this is a luxury "good.") Individuals become more willing to trade a certain income with a relatively low expected annual value for an uncertain stream with a higher expected annual value. These individuals may still join the bourgeois class, but they are no longer "hungry" would-be entrepreneurs.

(b) In addition to and reinforcing the above, as capitalism becomes increasingly productive, it supports a larger and larger intelligentsia for at least two reasons. First, the demand for higher education will probably rise relative to the demand for other goods. (It is also apt to be a "luxury" good.) Second, successful entrepreneurship requires an atmosphere of comparative tolerance, and this extends to intellectual ferment, even when directed against the "system."

Intellectuals are no longer burned at the stake for dissent; they may even enjoy substantial success within their own peer groups. Moreover they are often reasonably well off in material terms. Higher education itself becomes a large-scale industry, and is helped along by a favorable public attitude in combination with the fact that it need not meet a very stiff market test.

All this plus a rising hostility toward the managerial class implies that more and more prime candidates for the latter may opt to go elsewhere. Many may join the intelligentsia to put their critical minds to work there.

The net result of (a) and (b) is a dwindling supply of entrepreneurs, because the function is dehumanized, because of growing hostility and disaffection, and because of a willingness to pay a higher price to avoid risk.

Table 13-1 (cont.)

Marx	Schumpeter
	(c) The drive to standardize and to automate entrepreneurial decision making ends up by bureaucratizing it. Thus a falling demand for the services of "true" entrepreneurship complements the dwindling supply.

8. *Growing Hostility and the Demise of Capitalism*

As the rate of profit follows its long-term downward course—interrupted by cyclical fluctuations—the bourgeois class is depleted. The proletariat grows stronger, both in numbers and in terms of organization. It uses the strike with increasing effectiveness.

Finally, during the last great depression—the most severe of all—the proletariat takes advantage of the prevailing chaos and disaffection to seize the reins of power. Violent revolution replaces capitalism with an unspecified form of socialism.

8. *Growing Hostility and the Demise of Capitalism*

(a) Capitalism may end violently with some combination of a foreign invasion and revolution, perhaps following a particularly severe depression, or some other state of chaos in the organization of production. This would have to be combined with disaffection toward a still strong and influential bourgeois class. For Schumpeter, this would be a "premature" ending. Barring this, capitalism would still wither away naturally, and a revolution would become unnecessary.

(b) In the hands of the managerial class, the rational critical attitude which capitalism encourages, is productive, except insofar as it mechanizes progress and ultimately replaces the entrepreneur with the industry of invention. But in the hands of the intelligentsia, this attitude becomes destructive. The intelligensia must find some activity to occupy itself and to justify its own existence. So it engages in "social criticism," whose brunt is borne by businessmen for reasons already outlined. Working through the political process, this ultimately results in a rising number of restrictions and regulations which hamper entrepreneurs and reduce their potential rewards (through "wealth redistribution"). The obsolescence of the entrepreneurial function is thereby speeded up.

Because of rising hostility, controls, regulations, taxes, automation of decision making, and a dwindling supply of entrepreneurs, the role of creative destruction eventually vanishes. Risks that cannot be qualified and diversified are no longer taken. Stocks and corporate bonds become more and more like government bonds. The actual demise comes to pass when the government issues bonds to replace all securities of private firms, but by then capitalism is already a hollow shell.

427

13-3   Schumpeter's Theory of Capitalist Development

Colombo, Ceylon, Aug. 28, 1971—Ceylon faces the loss of $1.5 million in foreign exchange because the Soviet Union is to end its imports of Ceylonese tea. The U.S.S.R. had been negotiating to buy about 2,200 tons of the tea from Ceylon, but withdrew because the authorities here insisted that the sales be channeled through [Ceylonese] Government agencies.

The Soviet Union expressed concern that the government agencies might not give the standard of service offered by private exporters. [It was] afraid that shipments might be delayed by administrative dislocations and labor problems in state-controlled warehouses.

—The New York Times

There are at least two prominent theories of capitalist development, besides that of Marx, which forecast the downfall of laissez-faire capitalism on the basis of a long-run tendency for the rate of profit to fall. These are due to the Austrian economist J. A. Schumpeter and the British economist J. M. Keynes. To a degree, they compete with Marx, but we may also combine features of each into a composite theory of capitalist development.

Like Marx, Schumpeter saw the inevitable rise of socialism going hand in hand with the demise of laissez faire. For Keynes, any of the mixed economies discussed below could assume the succession, and many interpreters of Keynes have even maintained that laissez faire could survive as long as the government engaged in successful contracyclical policy. We shall consider Keynesian theory in Chapter 14 and devote the present section to Schumpeter, whose analysis appears side by side with that of Marx in Table 13–1. This is possible because the two use the same basic analytical framework.

In particular, Schumpeter accepted the dynamics and the dialectics of Marx and decried as irrelevant those theories of monopoly, oligopoly, and general equilibrium which attempt to depict a laissez-faire economy in static terms. "The problem that is usually being visualized," wrote Schumpeter of contemporary economists, "is how capitalism administers existing structures, whereas the relevant problem is how it creates and destroys them. . . . Capitalism is, by nature, a form or method of economic change and not only never is, but never can be stationary. . . ." [15]

But Schumpeter refused to accept Marx's characterization of the fundamental class conflict under laissez-faire capitalism. For Schumpeter, this took place between what we may call the "productive" and "unproductive" classes

---

[15] From *Capitalism, Socialism, and Democracy,* 3rd Ed., by Joseph A. Schumpeter, pp. 82, 84. Copyright, 1942, 1947 by Joseph A. Schumpeter. Copyright, 1950 by Harper & Row, Publishers, Inc. By permission of the publishers.

Schumpeter may be characterized as a modern Western economist. He died on January 8, 1950, shortly after delivering an address, "The March into Socialism," to the American Economic Association in New York. This is reprinted at the end of *Capitalism, Socialism, and Democracy* and in the *American Economic Review,* May 1950.

of society, and he insisted on allying the proletariat with many capitalists in the former. Indeed, what made a capitalist system progress, according to his doctrine, was the drive by enterpreneur–innovators to introduce and to exploit totally new products and methods of production and distribution. These effectively "destroyed" old ways of doing things by rendering them obsolete and replacing them with something new and better. Schumpeter called this process "creative destruction."

Creative destruction is investment that completely "revolutionizes" existing products and methods. The first assembly line was a creative destruction project, as was the airplane, the automobile, the electronic computer, the electric light bulb, the steam plow, the first fully automated production process, and subsequent major improvements in these. By undertaking creative destruction projects, Marx's social parasites become Schumpeter's dynamic entrepreneurs, who are the mainspring of progress. It was largely with this transformation that Schumpeter turned Marx's flaming indictment of capitalism into its most eloquent defense.

The fundamental impulse that sets and keeps the capitalist engine in motion comes from the new consumers' goods, the new methods of production or transportation, the new markets, the new forms of industrial organization that capitalist enterprise creates . . . the contents of a laborer's budget, say from 1760 to 1940, did not simply grow on unchanging lines, but they underwent a process of qualitative change. . . . The opening up of new markets, foreign or domestic, and the organizational development from the craft shop and factory to [the modern industrial concern] illustrate the process of industrial mutation . . . that incessantly revolutionizes the economic structure from within, incessantly destroying the old one, incessantly creating a new one. This process of "Creative Destruction" is the essential fact about capitalism. . . .[16]

Such men as Henry Ford and Thomas Edison would be the superstars of the Schumpeterian entrepreneurial class. However, they are cited mainly for their ability to successfully market new products or to introduce new ways of doing things. The successful entrepreneur is more an industrious businessman with keen foresight and a perceptive grasp of what goods and services the market is eager to accept than he is a successful inventor. He must also be somewhat of a gambler.

If we look at a payoff profile for a "typical" creative destruction investment project, its most important feature is that it is difficult to quantify. No one could say with any confidence that the yield on the first commercial airliner to cross the English Channel would be x per cent or higher with 95, or even 50, per cent probability. As a matter of fact, this venture went bankrupt, as do most would-be creative destruction projects. The second most important feature of such a payoff profile is a small chance of earning a very high yield, coupled with a high probability of losing one's shirt. The counterpart of this is that, while some entrepreneur–innovators eventually become rich, many

[16] Ibid., p. 83.

more go broke and drop out. As a class, they are a bargain, according to Schumpeter.

In some cases [creative destruction] is so successful as to yield profits far above what is necessary in order to induce the corresponding investment. These cases then provide the baits that lure capital on to untried trails. Their presence explains in part how it is possible for so large a section of the capitalist world to work for nothing: in the midst of the prosperous 1920's just about half of the business corporations in the United States were run at a loss, at zero profits, or at profits which, if they had been foreseen, would have been inadequate to call forth the effort and expenditure involved.[17]

Profits are therefore viewed by Schumpeter as a reward for innovation involving risk, and particularly nonquantifiable risks.[18] As such, they are also the earnings of entrepreneurship as a factor of production. However, most property income cannot be classified as profit by this definition, and most of the bourgeoisie are likewise not entrepreneurs. The latter constitute the cream of the capitalist class, both in skill and in daring.

Furthermore, entrepreneurial "profits" are not a rent in Schumpeter's view. The entrepreneurial drive stems, in part, from the satisfaction of creating or introducing something new and of building an industrial empire. But it also derives from the enormous profits that one can earn from success. As a prominent socialist economist recently remarked, "We are realizing more and more that entrepreneurship cannot be avoided in a modern economy and that in order to get it you have to pay for it." [19]

This point is crucial. When the rewards were attractive enough, would-be innovators would undergo incalculable frustration and endure physical hardship, if necessary, in gambling against enormous odds. Schumpeter would presumably not object very much to income redistribution schemes that struck only at non-"profit" property incomes, notably at inherited wealth. But he would probably suspect that the emerging egalitarian constraints, if effective, would risk decimating the entrepreneurial class by depriving it of fresh blood. This Schumpeter decidedly wished to postpone.

Business cycles for Schumpeter result from the ebb and flow of innovation, particularly of creative destruction projects, over time. An unforeseen and unexpected wave of innovations causes a boom, as during the early 1920s,

[17] Ibid., p. 90.

[18] Schumpeterian profits are also long-run *dis*equilibrium profits, within the context of Chapters 16 and 17. They are earned, for example, between the time an industry is shocked out of long-run equilibrium by an innovation and the time it returns. During this period, the innovator should have a better cost–price margin than his competitors or than he himself can hope to have when equilibrium is restored. Schumpeter believed these profits were much more important than long-run monopoly rents and would decry most of our static analysis in Chapters 16 and 17 as irrelevant. In practice, it is often difficult to distinguish between long-run disequilibrium profits due to innovation and long-run equilibrium monopoly rents.

[19] Alexander Bajt, "Property in Capital and the Means of Production in Socialist Economies," *Journal of Law and Economics,* Apr. 1968, p. 3.

which will sustain itself for awhile. But after the resulting products or methods have been exploited and have spread through the economy, creating jobs and generating income, a comparative dearth of fresh innovations may set in. Since the demand being generated by the old ones is now largely confined to replacement, a recession or depression will occur, to be interrupted later by another "revolutionary phase" of new products and techniques.[20]

In contrast to Marx, however, we would not expect a sequence of increasingly severe cycles to culminate in the destruction of capitalism. Opportunistic elements could take advantage of chaos, indecision, or a weakening of government caused by a severe depression to seize power and establish a "socialist" government. But Schumpeter believed that capitalism was doomed to die a "mature" death from natural causes even if this did not occur.

In the latter case, as the long-run power of creative destruction rises, so does the amplitude of accompanying cycles. Then, as creative destruction passes its zenith as a "revolutionizing force" and begins its inevitable descent, the severity of business cycles will also become less and less. The Schumpeterian "profit" share of property income will start into a long-run decline, and the supply of capable, dynamic innovators will start to dwindle.

Laissez-faire capitalism, itself, will then proceed downhill until, one day, the government replaces all corporate securities and other ownership certificates with government bonds. By then, an important distinction between managerial and property incomes on one hand, and "ordinary" wage and salary incomes on the other, will have become extremely blurred. We recall that managers and owners are normally viewed as residual claimants to the earnings of an enterprise after its debts, including its wage and salary bill, have been paid. This factor makes their incomes riskier and contingent upon the efficient operation of enterprises under their control. It thereby disciplines them to strive for efficiency, as well as offering them an incentive to innovate.

But for reasons we shall explore, the managerial function comes to be more and more the province of salaried personnel, whose incomes depend less and less upon the residual earnings of the organizations for which they work. These residuals also become more certain, with the decline of innovation, since established market positions are in less and less danger. Production becomes more bureaucratized, and government subsidies to rescue firms in trouble may become more frequent. By the time complete nationalization arrives, little difference will remain between the streams of earnings yielded by government bonds and various private certificates and securities. Consequently, widespread resistance to the exchange does not arise.

Capitalism ends not with a bang but a whimper, after much of the "real" transformation has already been accomplished over a long period of time. As in Marx, false consciousness abounds, and the system effectively self-destructs.

---

[20] Just as a sequence of random numbers will move up and down in cyclical fashion about a trend path, so will the stream of creative destruction projects ebb and flow in at least a partly random pattern.

At least two factors combine to bring this result to pass, both arising out of what Schumpeter called "the civilization of capitalism." [21] Whereas pre-capitalist man generally reached conclusions and made decisions at least partly on the basis of magic or mystery, and often spurned logic, capitalism must, by its nature, encourage a "rational attitude." A calculating, critical mentality is part of this, but so is an enquiring mind that makes every idea, individual, social institution, product, or technology justify itself according to a performance standard. Along with this goes a tolerance for new ideas and the necessary freedom to test or try them out.

Without freedom to enquire and to innovate, there would have been no Industrial Revolution, but also no Age of Enlightenment. A legacy of greater industrial freedom is a generally high level of social tolerance by historical standards. Here Schumpeter parts company with most Western intellectuals:

> Radicals may insist that the masses are crying for salvation from intolerable sufferings and rattling their chains in darkness and despair, but of course there never was so much personal freedom of mind and body *for all,* never so much readiness to bear with and even to finance the mental enemies of the leading class, never so much sympathy with real or faked sufferings . . . and whatever democracy there [has been through history], outside of peasant communities, developed in the wake of both modern and ancient capitalism. . . .[22]

(Although Schumpeter would acknowledge that capitalist societies sometimes wage war for profit, he would deny that a capitalist system was more likely to wage war or colonial exploitation, *in general,* than another type of society.)

When creative destruction is in its heyday, existing firms must constantly scramble to keep their positions in the market from being cut from under them. Managers must continually improve their product lines and production methods just to stand still in the face of dynamic competition. This, plus the rewards awaiting the first enterprise to introduce a successful innovation, puts a premium on the rational attitude and also on the freedom to innovate and to collect the rewards therefrom. Even a blackguard bourgeoisie cannot crush the freedom of which it disapproves without risking to crush the freedom on which it depends as well.

What could be more rational, in these conditions, than to mechanize innovation itself, by reducing it to a "scientific" routine based on cost-benefit analysis? To Schumpeter, it seems that

> Technological progress is increasingly becoming the business of teams of trained specialists who turn out what is required and make it work in predictable

---

[21] In addition to the forces of self-destruction described below, Schumpeter argued that the bourgeoisie began planting the seeds of its downfall in emancipating itself from and *completely* destroying the late medieval order. For feudalist institutions not only hampered the innovative effort, they were also capable of protecting the entrepreneurial class from hostile elements. See Schumpeter, op. cit., Ch. 12.

[22] Ibid., p. 126.

ways. The romance of earlier commercial adventure is rapidly wearing away, because so many more things can be strictly calculated that had, of old, to be visualized in a flash of genius. . . .

[Consequently] economic progress tends to [become] depersonalized and automatized. Bureau and committee work tends to replace individual action. . . .

[In this way] rationalized and specialized office work will eventually blot out personality [and] the calculable result, the vision. The leading man no longer has an opportunity to fling himself into the fray. He is becoming just another office worker—and one who is not always difficult to replace.[23]

The entrepreneur who first employed cost-benefit analysis to aid his investment decision making has therefore let a genie out of its bottle. An entire industry of research and development laboratories, think tanks, engineering and management consulting firms, and the like evolve to take over the entrepreneurial function. The individual entrepreneur finds himself in his own museum, alongside the horseless carriage, the hand loom, the silent movie projector, the horse-drawn plow, and the blacksmith's shop—his role seemingly made obsolete.

Yet, false consciousness is definitely the cause. To routinize and automate investment decision making is inevitably to bureaucratize it to some degree. Our earlier discussion shows that the risk aversion inherent in investment decision making is likely to rise, perhaps to skyrocket. But this may not be the worst. A cost-benefit calculus is helpless when the payoff profile of a proposed investment can scarcely be quantitfied, and those benefits not subject to quantification are likely to be ignored.

Consequently, cost-benefit analysis can often tell the management of a farm-machinery corporation which types of tractors to market under different geographical and economic conditions and how far to go in mechanizing or automatizing a particular tractor plant. It would have been far less useful to the man who first tried to market a tractor. If he had been an element in a bureaucracy, the idea might not have occurred to him or it may have been rejected by a superior somewhere up the chain of command. If pushed too far, therefore, the gains of cost-benefit analysis are not worth the cost.

At the same time that the individual entrepreneur is being phased out, the bourgeois class comes under mounting attack from what we earlier called the "unproductive" sector. As a capitalist, the entrepreneur encounters his share of growing hostility—in the form of egalitarian constraints, controls on his behavior, and social disapproval. As creative destruction gives way to the industry of invention, these attacks gather force. And as the resulting controls become more numerous and intense, they hasten the decline of creative destruction.

The notion of an unproductive sector, encumbering or fettering the productive one, appears in Marx and in the writings of classical economists, at least back to Adam Smith. However, these writers tended to identify the

23 Ibid., pp. 132–133.

unproductive sector with the service industries, whereas Schumpeter tends to identify it, perhaps unfairly, with the class of intellectuals.[24] More precisely, "unproductive" individuals are those who have no direct responsibility for practical affairs. In addition to intellectuals, more narrowly defined, this embraces malcontents and hangers-on of a variety of shades and hues, and others, notably many journalists, who make their living from social commentary.

Because capitalism fosters innovation, it gives rise to an economic surplus, which is immense by previous standards. For the first time since the dawn of history, the great mass of society does not have to preoccupy itself with the everyday tasks of production and distribution in order to keep the wolf away from the door. Consequently, a superstructure of Schumpeterian "intellectuals" arises and grows with the social surplus.

Indeed, higher education will eventually grow faster than gross national product, because the demand for higher education is probably elastic with respect to income (it is a luxury good, in other words) and because it benefits from some of the causes of bureaucratic growth outlined in Chapter 10. In addition, the public attitude toward higher education is generally benevolent. Suggestions that rate-of-return calculations can help determine when it should stop expanding will be viewed, at least initially, with alarm.

Thus higher education becomes a large industry, heavily subsidized, with significant power, which eventually begins to turn out a surplus of graduates for occupations that require university-level training. Consequently, the college diploma becomes a kind of union card, which sometimes prevents the best-qualified man from getting a particular job. College graduates also feed the growing public sector, likewise spawned by the economic surplus and by the factors discussed in Chapter 10. In some cases this sector may actually expand to keep graduates, or students, from becoming unemployed.

According to Schumpeter, the intelligentsia foments class conflict. Intellectuals court the laboring "masses" and embrace a variety of left-wing causes. The workers, in turn, sometimes use the intelligentsia as a cutting edge, either directly or indirectly, in their drive for better wages and working conditions. (As an unusually overt example of this, we would cite the riots of May 1968 in France.) But workers also have a vested interest in the existing system, which, far from leaving them at subsistence, has brought them the greatest gains in wages and working conditions in history. Thus the working class is not likely to become revolutionary unless intellectuals are sufficiently successful in egging it on. And yet, even in siding with the intelligentsia

---

[24] According to Adam Smith, labor is unproductive when its "services . . . perish in the very instant of their performance . . . and do not fix or [embody themselves] in any permanent subject or vendible commodity, which endures after that labour is past . . . . In the same class [of unproductive labor] must be ranked, some both of the gravest and most important, and some of the most frivolous professions: churchmen, lawyers, physicians, men of letters of all kinds [including university professors]; players, buffoons, musicians, opera-singers, opera-dancers, etc. . . ." There is some overlap with Schumpeter's definition, but the emphasis is clearly different.

from time to time, the proletariat is guilty of false consciousness because it helps to kill the goose that lays the golden eggs.

In the final analysis, the reason for the intellectual's dissent is that he is always in some ultimate danger of not having enough to do. This includes a risk of losing status, of lacking a sufficient challenge or creative outlet, and of being "unceremoniously told to mind his own business." The classical economists had been worried that a society confronted by niggardly nature would not be able to support a large service sector from the surplus earned in manufacturing and in agriculture. Now, the cycle has come full tilt. The intelligentsia tries to solve its problem by adopting for itself the role of social critic. At its worst, this leads intellectuals to "flatter, promise, and incite left wings and scowling minorities, sponsor doubtful or submarginal cases, [and] appeal to fringe ends. . . ." [25]

Nevertheless, we should really distinguish two strata of intellectuals, according to prestige, status, and income. The upper stratum—exemplified by the university professor of fine arts or social sciences—consciously commits itself to seek "constructive" social change. It quite naturally adopts the rational attitude for its tool kit, and having considerable time at its disposal, hones this to an ever higher degree of precision. Eventually, the "reshaping" of society becomes an obligation, enshrined in such requirements as "publish or perish." In the competition to criticize society, a growing tendency likewise emerges to compare the existing system with an absolute ideal, instead of a feasible alternative.

The second stratum consists of less fortunate individuals who become part of the excess supply of university graduates. Being psychologically unsuited for manual labor, they must take white-collar jobs (when they are employed) that offer less in terms of prestige, challenge, and income than they expect from society. From there, discontent breeds resentment which rationalizes itself into social criticism. Thus members of both strata often gain a vested interest in dissent.

With such a high propensity to criticize, the bourgeoisie finds itself the obvious target. Because the intellectuals are essentially onlookers, without the first-hand knowledge of practical affairs that only experience can give, they fail to perceive the importance of the entrepreneurial role. Thus, although the wealth and the faults of entrepreneurs are evident, their contribution is not well understood. More important to the intellectual will be the fact that in achieving his wealth and in passing it on to his heirs, the entrepreneur must probably violate some moral code or other somewhere along the way. In the final analysis, it is not difficult for the intellectual either to ignore those would-be innovators who fall by the wayside or who barely survive one crisis in time to confront another, or to rationalize away the contributions of those who succeed.

[25] Schumpeter, op. cit., p. 154.

To top everything off, while the entrepreneurial role is essentially one of individual leadership, it is also unromantic and antiheroic in nature. There is "no flourishing of swords about it, not much physical prowess, no chance to gallop the armored horse into the enemy, preferably a heretic or a heathen —and the ideology that glorifies . . . victory for victory's sake understandably withers in the office among all of the columns of figures." [26]

The bourgeoisie, and with it the entrepreneurial class, thus finds itself the prime target of the intelligentsia, which exercises an influence beyond its numbers and responsibilities. The public therefore becomes increasingly suspicious of private industry in general and more and more favorable toward a growing body of constraints, restrictions, and regulations, applied by a public sector whose expansion mirrors the progressive socialization of the economy. This expansion occurs both to nationalize private firms and to better control the private sector.

Finally, a point will be reached where the existing government finds it both feasible and desirable to nationalize all remaining private industry, save possibly firms employing no more than a handful of workers. For its role in the drama, the intelligentsia may well be guilty of false consciousness, in part because its (latent or open) fears of underemployment may now come closer to being realized. Additional details on the evolution appear in Table 13–1.

Because the private sector will have become a hollow shell of its former self by the final nationalization, Schumpeter felt that the emerging socialist economy would outperform its immediate predecessor. Not only would it be free of cyclical fluctuations and class frictions, but it would be able to combine satisfactory growth, albeit along relatively unchanging product lines, with a more equalitarian income distribution. But Schumpeter was also adamant in insisting that a socialist society "should embark upon its career . . . as richly endowed as possible by its capitalist predecessor—with experience and techniques as well as with resources—and also after the latter has sown its wild oats, done its work and is approaching a stationary state. . . ." Of the various blueprints, Schumpeter apparently preferred the command-economy model, at least for major industries.[27]

Nevertheless, it is not clear why we should continue to expect cycles under capitalism, within the confines of Schumpeter's theory, once creative destruction has died down. Although planning may account for increased growth, we have seen that this rules out neither markets nor private ownership. The introduction of a command economy *may* entail a spreading of property incomes, but it carries no guarantee of a classless society.

Generally speaking, Schumpeter appears to have dismissed the range of mixed-economy models too quickly. The tendency among most command economies today is to assign a growing role to market and semimarket mechanisms. Mixed economies can permit the entrepreneurial role to survive at the

---

[26] Ibid., p. 128.
[27] Ibid., Ch. 16. Quote is from p. 178.

managerial level and even rejuvenate this, while maintaining an overall strategic direction of the economy from the top. The post-World War II French economy appears to be a case study of such a phenomenon.

When we look at Schumpeter's prognoses from a perspective of the 1970s, he seems somewhat prophetic. Both the rapid expansion of higher education and the subsequent job difficulties and growing disaffection of an army of intellectual types appear to have been foreseen at least a quarter-century ahead of time. The same is true of a more general malaise and growing hostility toward the "system," and we should not overlook the decline in business-cycle intensity since the wave of innovations during the 1920s and subsequent crash.

Nevertheless, we are still quite close in time to these events. If we accept Schumpeter's thesis too readily, we may find ourselves repeating the mistake of those Marxists who proclaimed during the Great Depression that the revolution was at hand. It is not clear that any Western economy is headed toward a dominant public sector, and there are signs that the public romance with higher education as a potential panacea for all problems has begun to erode. Conceivably, a backlash could eventually develop which would hamper intellectuals in social criticism that even Schumpeter would find legitimate—for example, of the growing evidence of major corporate tax loopholes in the United States.[28]

At the same time, the entrepreneur in most laissez-faire economies has played and continues to play a role between Marx's social parasite and Schumpeter's somewhat romanticized (if unseeming) hero. The rate of innovation in laissez-faire—and, more generally, in market economies—is high, not only by historical standards, but also in comparison with command economies. Nevertheless, as the reader is undoubtedly aware, firms can enrich themselves by harming as well as helping society. Any economy is probably well advised to channel to some extent the entrepreneurial initiative it generates.

We shall indicate in Chapter 20 some guidelines for doing this. In particular, a "positive" financial-incentive program tries to channel initiative through incentives rather than controls where possible. But some prevention of otherwise profitable investment—for example, which has adverse environmental effects—will be desirable in any economy. It is not clear where we cross the border into what Schumpeter would consider to be "excessive" control.

Neither is there adequate empirical knowledge of the motives behind innovation and thus of the sacrifice in entrepreneurship required to get a given equalization of incomes or vice versa. In particular, we do not know enough about the rental components of property incomes or the power of pecuniary vis-à-vis nonpecuniary incentive. When we look at innovation within the

---

[28] It has also been alleged that many intellectuals are forced to engage in research, which is neither of much practical use nor very rich in social criticism, in order to meet their "publish or perish" requirements.

Soviet context, we find not only egalitarian constraints but also bureaucratic controls and an uncertain supply system hampering the innovative effect. (Indeed, incentives actually paid to "innovators" often work in this direction because the relevant "success indicators" do not force them to produce innovations with practical usefulness.) It is not clear which combination of these restricts innovation decisively.

In many cases, although certainly not in all, the satisfaction derived from creating or introducing something new or from building an industrial empire may provide enough motivation. If we knew beforehand which cases these were, we could largely redistribute the resulting profits. Unfortunately, no one has yet invented such a crystal ball.

Finally, Schumpeter readily agreed that the dominant form of industrial structure in contemporary capitalist countries is oligopoly or "competition among the few." (Indeed, this is true in socialist market economies as well.) He agreed enthusiastically that certain departures from static efficiency are inevitable in such a form. But we have seen that he regarded most of the discussion of competition in contemporary Western theory as irrelevant because of its largely static point of view. Perfectly competitive firms have neither the market position nor the short-run (as opposed to long-run) security needed to innovate successfully, and they often lack access to adequate financial resources.[29]

> In capitalist reality as distinguished from its textbook picture, it is not ["static"] competition which counts, but competition from the new technology, the new source of supply, [and] the new type of organization . . . competition which commands a decisive cost or quality advantage and which strikes, not at the margins of profits and the outputs of existing firms, but at their foundations and their very lives. This kind of competition is . . . so much more important that it becomes a matter of comparative indifference whether competition in the ordinary sense functions more or less promptly. . . .[30]

We shall explore competition "in the ordinary sense" in Chapters 16, 17, and 20. Here we note that Schumpeter, like Marx, appears to have underestimated the potential for collusion within an oligopoly that is well protected by barriers to new competition. In particular, firms in such an industry may tacitly agree to protect their profits on past investments from creative destruction by slowing down and smoothing out the flow of new products and techniques.[31] There would also be added danger of planned obsolescence.

[29] We recall that a perfectly competitive firm cannot influence the prices of the goods it produces or of the inputs it uses by varying the quantities it sells or buys. If it raises one of its product prices above the going level, for example, it will not be able to sell anything because its competitors will take all its customers at the old price. There can be absolutely no product differentiation of any kind under perfect competition, and each buyer or seller faces an unlimited market. The completely decentralized economy of Chapter 2 is one in which all buyers and sellers are perfect competitors.

[30] Schumpeter, op. cit., pp. 84–85.

[31] This point is due to Oskar Lange. See his article in Benjamin Lippincott, ed., *On the Economic Theory of Socialism* (New York: McGraw-Hill, 1964), pp. 110–121.

If these problems become especially acute after the process of disintegration described by Schumpeter has already set in, they would hasten the resulting demise. If they become serious earlier, they could make Schumpeter's model irrelevant. (By contrast, collusive managers within a Marxian framework should be able to keep down the organic composition of capital and thereby prolong laissez-faire capitalism.)

Schumpeter's thesis appears to require industries which are not perfectly competitive but which are also not too highly concentrated or too well protected by entry barriers. Later we shall describe these as "workably" competitive industries. What evidence is available, moreover, indicates that the innovators in an industry are usually not its giants. Rather, they are the medium-sized and even relatively small firms who have the least to lose from a radical change in technology (which renders existing production capacity obsolete) and whose informal organization is often more conducive to pursuing new and risky undertakings. Both high barriers to new competition and, beyond a point, high industrial concentration will reduce the rate of innovation.[32]

This again suggests "workable" competition. But largely because perfectly competitive firms often fail to realize important economies of mass production, our static analysis will also point toward workable competition as a desirable form for many, perhaps the majority, of a nation's industries. Perfect competition is a practical impossibility for all but a handful of industries in any event, so the optimal market-structure policies recommended by Schumpeterian and conventional static theory will often coincide.

13–4   Concluding Comments on Marx

After so brief an introduction to the writings of Karl Marx, it would be presumptuous at this stage to attempt very much by way of evaluation. The best we can hope for now is to put some of his thoughts briefly into historical perspective with the admitted benefit of 100 years and more of hindsight. To this author, the best of Marx is to be found in his economic theory of history. It is here that we find elements of sociology and philosophy combined with economics to get a dynamic theory of systemic change which, despite its weaknesses, remains without parallel. Nevertheless, we have discussed

[32] We particularly have in mind what we shall describe in Chapter 16 as *artificial* barriers to entry. The interested reader is invited to examine the following references for this paragraph: Joe S. Bain, *Barriers to New Competition* (Cambridge, Mass.: Harvard U.P., 1965); W. S. Comanor and T. A. Wilson, "Advertising, Market Structure, and Performance," *Review of Economics and Statistics,* Nov. 1967; H. Michael Mann, "Seller Concentration, Barriers to Entry, and Rates of Return in Thirty Industries," *Review of Economics and Statistics,* Aug. 1966; Edwin Mansfield, *Industrial Research and Technological Innovation* (New York: Norton, 1968); Dennis C. Mueller and John E. Tilton, "Research and Development Costs as a Barrier to Entry," *Canadian Journal of Economics,* Nov. 1969 (see also the references cited there); Donald F. Turner, "The Anti-Trust Chief Replies," in Edwin Mansfield, ed., *Monopoly Power and Economic Performance,* rev. ed. (New York: Norton, 1968).

Mark's theory of history in Section B of Chapter 12, although again all too briefly. We shall therefore confine our remarks in the present section to the labor theory of value and his specific theory of the evolution of modern capitalism.

Of these the labor theory of value is probably the weakest, partly for a reason that is no fault of Marx. Although the labor and supply-and-demand theories of value can be reconciled, the former also lends itself to an extremely narrow interpretation, which, among other things, requires interest and rent payments to be zero. When this happens, natural resources and investable funds are treated like free goods, with resulting waste, queueing, and resource misallocation.

At the same time that planning was impeded by this doctrine in the U.S.S.R. and, to a lesser extent, in the smaller East European countries, the development of economics as a science was also hampered. Not only was it forbidden to consider capital inputs as productive—for a time, even in a roundabout way—but the dichotomy between value in use and value in exchange, combined with the labor-value theory, prevented the development of demand theory. (Indeed, these areas are still relatively underdeveloped there.) This, in turn, appears to have made economics less useful than it might have been as a planning tool.[33]

Most Western economists would probably prefer the supply-and-demand value theory, largely on the grounds of broader coverage, greater determinacy, and greater empirical usefulness. A theory which says that value is determined by "socially necessary" labor time cannot function until we have an index of social necessity. To get this, we need to know something of the past, present, and expected future compositions of demand. If we wish to forecast quantities or prices, we must normally take both demand and supply into account, and both may be influenced, not only by preferences, but by availability of capital and natural-resource inputs. In the final analysis, the existence of a labor-value theory is based entirely on faith.

Nevertheless, the Marxist scholar may object that the labor theory emphasizes wealth inequities and alienation which derive from exploitation, and that this focus more than makes up for any defects that it may have. Although Marx deserves credit for developing the notion of exploitation, this concept is probably better handled within the framework of supply-and-demand the-

---

[33] However, by renouncing and denouncing marginal utility (and, hence, demand) theory, the leaders of these nations have spared themselves some political embarrassment. For it was possible to claim under a labor theory of value, both that the values of goods and services were somehow "objective" (in contrast to "subjective" marginal utility theory based on human preferences) and that there was a unique, objectively determined, optimal rate of development which the planners had chosen. This helped to get them around the need to explain the priorities resulting from their particular planners' preference function vis-à-vis the priorities that would emerge from some other preference function, for example, one more oriented toward present consumption. The interested reader is referred to Robert W. Campbell, "Marx, Kantorovich, and Novozhilov: Stoimost versus Reality," *Slavic Review,* Oct. 1961; reprinted as Ch. 8 in Wayne Leeman, ed., *Capitalism, Market Socialism, and Central Planning* (Boston: Houghton, 1963).

ory. To see why, let us take a classic case of exploitation, involving a giant corporation from a developed country whose supply of natural resources comes largely from a developing nation. Marx attributed colonialism to the enormous profitability of operations in countries with very low organic compositions of capital (or relatively labor-intensive production methods) which he also expected to be relatively poor.

Suppose, however, that our colonialist decides on a highly capital-intensive production technology. This may be because capital and labor are not very substitutible in his operation, because he feels that native workers are unreliable, unskilled, or undisciplined, or for a variety of other reasons. Marxian theory would then lead us to believe that his profit potential would necessarily be reduced, whereas supply-and-demand theory contains no such implication.

The ability of a producer, or of any actor, to "exploit" within a supply-and-demand framework depends solely upon his relative economic power. Thus, if the firm in question had to compete with other producers in bidding for access rights to the resource, we would expect him to pay a higher price and to be able to command lower monopoly profits than if he were granted an exclusive sphere of influence. But we would not expect his profit to depend upon whether the optimal technology for extracting the resource was labor or capital-intensive.[34]

In fact, power may ultimately derive from property via the earnings which the latter yields to its owners. But there can likewise be power without property—for example, of managers and labor unions. Any of these factors may engage in exploitation if they are powerful enough. The one essential prerequisite to preserving power, however, is the ability to erect barriers to regulation and to competition (or entry barriers) through the political process. Any study of exploitation must focus to some extent on ways in which these are erected. Marx appears to go overboard in identifying power and exploitation automatically with capital ownership.

Furthermore, if we confine our attention to wealth inequalities stemming from the distribution of property incomes, we need only note that the owner of capital does not automatically deserve to receive its earnings. (Indeed, there is virtually no country in which he could hope to keep all of them without taking sufficient advantage of tax loopholes.) The question of income distribution has nothing whatever to do with whether capital has a positive VMP, and the latter issue tends to be somewhat of a red herring. Instead, we must seek to learn social priorities for innovation and growth vis-à-vis equality, and something of the magnitude of the incentive needed to generate

[34] We recall that exploitation of an input in both Western and Marxian theory occurs, in effect, when its price is less than the value of its marginal product (which measures its productive contribution). For a technical discussion of exploitation within a supply-and-demand context, see any good intermediate microeconomic text—for example, Richard H. Leftwich, *The Price System and Resource Allocation,* 4th ed. (Hinsdale, Ill.: Dryden, 1970), Ch. 14, or C. E. Ferguson, *Microeconomic Theory,* 3rd ed. (Homewood, Ill.: Irwin, 1972), Ch. 14, especially pp. 435–449.

innovation in order to decide on an optimal distribution of property incomes.

Finally, our Marxist protagonist may insist on the labor theory of value as the generator of the falling rate of profit, which lends, in turn, to laissez-faire capitalism's demise. We should not assume a theory to prove a point (we might as well assume the point to begin with), however, and empirical evidence to directly demonstrate that the rate of profit has shown a long-run tendency to fall in capitalist countries is notably lacking. In addition, business cycles have not grown increasingly severe, as Marx had forecast, since the Great Depression more than forty years ago.

Nevertheless, the possibility of a future, even greater depression cannot be ruled out altogether, and the empirical evidence regarding profit rates over long periods of time may be subject to dispute. We shall therefore, try to get at the problem via a more indirect route. To begin with, we shall show that the falling rate of profit is, in fact, independent of the labor theory of value. It could arise under conventional value theory as, for example, a consequence of a falling VMP of capital, leading to declining investment yields. The declining VMP of capital, in turn, could stem from an increasing capital intensity of production—so that each unit of capital has less and less labor to work with it—which is partially but not entirely offset by technological advance.

Let us again write Marxian value as $C + V + S$, remembering that S may be viewed as a productive contribution either of capital or labor, depending upon which value theory one subscribes to. We also recall that the Marxian rate of profit, π, is defined to be $S/C + V$. The organic composition of capital, a measure of the capital intensity of production, is defined to be C/V. However, for convenience, we shall replace this with $C/C + V$ (both indexes will move in the same direction) and write

$$c = \frac{C}{C + V}$$

to be our new measure of the organic composition of capital.

Finally, we need a measure of exploitation of labor. This will be S/V, or the ratio of property to wage and salary incomes. Under the labor theory of value this gives the percentage of the average working day expropriated by capitalists. The greater the exploitation of labor, the higher S/V will be. We therefore define

$$s = \frac{S}{V}$$

to be the rate of exploitation.

With a bit of algebraic manipulation, we can derive a formula linking π, s, and c. This is

$$\pi = s(1 - c)$$

Not too surprisingly, the rate of profit rises with the rate of exploitation and falls when the organic composition of capital rises.[35] But the movement over time of each of the latter two variables has nothing to do with the labor theory of value. The same must therefore be true of the rate of profit itself.

In fact, a falling rate of profit means precisely that the organic composition of capital must rise at a more rapid rate than the rate of exploitation. Only if the latter fails to rise at all, therefore, does a rising organic composition of capital guarantee a falling rate of profit. But a constant rate of exploitation is not favorable to Marx's theory of capitalist development. For it implies that the proletariat shares at least equally in economic growth, a view that Marx specifically denied. Yet available empirical evidence tends, on balance, to support such an observation. That is, this evidence does not suggest a long-run tendency for the wage-and-salary share of national income to fall.[36]

Picking a constant ratio of property to wage-and-salary income, therefore, let us ask whether the organic composition of capital has, in fact, tended to rise since the Industrial Revolution. This turns out to be a subtle question. It is not enough simply for the value of the capital stock in use per man-hour to rise. $C/C + V$ could still fall if the quality of the labor force was rising fast enough. Marx makes it clear that a skilled labor hour is a multiple of an unskilled hour. Moreover, with a constant rate of exploitation, rising skills will find reflection in higher real wage and salary rates.[37]

Nevertheless, several economists have made measurements that we can bring to bear on our question. A French Marxist, Eliane Mossé, tried to chart the actual increase in C/V, or, more precisely, of an index that could be expected to move in the same direction as C/V over long periods of time.[38] She took estimates of the total fixed capital stock in all of French industry corresponding to four benchmark years over the period 1789 to 1913, and divided these by estimates of the total industrial wage-and-salary bill for each of the same years. Her results follow:

[35] To get the above formula, we note that

$$1 - c = 1 - \frac{C}{C + V} = \frac{C + V - C}{C + V} = \frac{V}{C + V}$$

Therefore,

$$s(1 - c) = \frac{S}{V}\left(\frac{V}{C + V}\right) = \frac{S}{C + V} = \pi$$

[36] In fact, the stability of S/V over time has been widely observed. Weintraub even goes so far as to label it, in effect, a "magic constant." See Sidney Weintraub, *A General Theory of the Price Level, Output, Income Distribution, and Economic Growth* (Philadelphia: Chilton, 1959). Alternatively, see his *Classical Keynesianism, Monetary Theory, and the Price Level* (Philadelphia: Chilton, 1961).

[37] Furthermore, unless we assume false consciousness, these additional skills must be rewarded with greater purchasing power, insofar as additional education or training is required to acquire them. For otherwise, no one would be willing to invest in the necessary education while foregoing present earnings.

[38] Eliane Mossé, *Marx et le problème de la croissance dans une économie capitaliste* (Paris: Librairie Armand Colin, 1956), pp. 178ff.

1789   2.4   1890   3.5
1845   3.4   1913   3.8

This led her to conclude that the organic composition of capital had indeed risen over the course of the industrial revolution.

However, her figures are crude, at best, and the comparatively large jump from 1789 to 1845 suggests an alternative hypothesis. During the height of the Industrial Revolution, as this converts production in a given nation, region, or industry to modern methods, we might expect the organic composition of capital to grow rapidly. Once this period is over, however, the growth of this ratio may slow down, cease, or even reverse itself. When Mossé examined specific French industries over roughly the same period, she found in each case that most of the growth of the organic composition of capital was concentrated into a period of forty years or less and that it was eventually followed by a decline.

This suggests that we examine a time series which clearly follows the peak of the Industrial Revolution. Robert M. Solow has estimated that employed capital per man-hour in the United States rose from $2.06 in 1909 to $2.70 in 1949, the latter figure representing a decline from higher ratios achieved during several intervening years.[39] This is an increase of about 31 per cent. During the same period, there appeared to be no long-run tendency for S/V (again as estimated by Solow) to rise or fall. However, the quality of the labor force, as calculated by Denison, grew by over 41 per cent.[40] Employed capital per constant (1909) man-hour, our proxy for the organic composition of capital, *declined* from $2.06 to $1.91.[41]

By contrast, Denison's measures of roughly the same proxy for the United States and several European countries for the shorter, more recent time space, 1959–1962, tend to *support* a rising organic composition of capital.[42] It remains to be seen, however, whether this trend has or will continue.

There are also two important corollaries about the evolution of a capitalist economy stemming from the falling rate of profit and the rising organic com-

[39] Solow also concluded that, on balance, technological progress was (Hicks) neutral —that is, neither labor- nor capital-saving. See Robert M. Solow, "Technical Change and the Aggregate Production Function," *Review of Economics and Statistics,* Aug. 1957, and references cited. The highest capital-to-labor ratios were achieved during the Great Depression and, more generally, during the 1930s, when unemployment of the labor force was abnormally high. Such a situation appears to have inflated these ratios above any level sustainable in the long run.

[40] Edward F. Denison, *The Sources of Economic Growth in the United States and the Alternatives Before Us* (New York: Committee for Economic Development, 1962), Ch. 9.

[41] In addition, "The combined increase in the quantity and quality of labor was the source of 54 per cent of the total growth . . . of national product from 1929 to 1957," ibid., p. 87. This contribution was about equally divided between growth in quantity and growth in quality.

[42] Edward F. Denison, *Why Growth Rates Differ* (Washington, D.C.: Brookings, 1967), Ch. 15.

position of capital which may help us to test this thesis. The first says that the middle class of such a country will tend to decline and eventually disappear as the wealthiest capitalists drive their smaller brethren into the ranks of the proletariat. However, the century since Marx's death has witnessed the rise rather than the decline of the middle class in virtually every Western capitalist society.

A second, and more contentious, corollary is that, over time, economic power will tend to become more concentrated within each industry. This is supposed to occur as smaller firms or their assets are absorbed by larger ones and as mergers occur among the latter. Within a Marxian context, we may view mergers as efforts by big capitalists to countervail the falling yield on each investment dollar and to maintain their incomes, both by increasing their monopoly power and by concentrating investible funds in fewer hands. Consequently, Marxist economists often point to bankruptcies and mergers as indirect evidence of the falling rate of profit.

Unfortunately, matters are once again not as simple as they may seem. At the same time that bankruptcies occur, new firms are being born to start their life cycles. And, while the net effect of births, bankruptcies, and mergers has been to increase average firm size, the size of the average market has grown at the same time, as a consequence of rising incomes, increasing population density, and improved transport and communications. Only if the largest firms in an industry have gained an increasing percentage of industry sales in a particular market can we say that monopoly power has become more concentrated there.

Once again, although the experts disagree, the available evidence does *not* support any marked tendency for concentration of power to increase. For example, Kamerschen's study of 205 U.S. industries over the period 1947–1963 showed a (net) reduced concentration in 40 per cent, an increased concentration in 38 per cent, and the remaining 22 per cent stayed the same.[43] Like our other bits of evidence, this one is open to challenge. But the cumulative weight of all the best available information known to the author tends not to support Marx's specific hypotheses about the evolution of modern capitalism.

Let us close this chapter with a word on Marx's theory of classes. Like most modern Western economists, Marx assumed that individuals were basically guided by self-interest. *Un*like most of them, including Schumpeter, he assumed that, under private-property relations, individuals were also intensely class-oriented in their behavior. It was, notably, in obedience to class interests that the mass of workers would combine to launch the revolution resulting in capitalism's overthrow.

---

[43] Specifically, the percentages of industry-wide sales made by the four largest firms behave in these ways. See David R. Kamerschen, "Market Growth and Industry Concentration," *Journal of the American Statistical Association,* Mar. 1968, and references cited.

However, such a theory of class action suffers from the same weakness that we encountered earlier in our study of moral incentives.[44] Just as a *single* worker cannot do much, in most cases, to raise the output of his nation, region, or locale, neither can he hope to have a significant impact on the success of an effort to overthrow the government. Moreover, if the government falls anyway, he will gain whatever benefit flows directly from this phenomenon without having to risk his life or make another form of sacrifice. Thus, the rational, self-interested individual will mind his own and ignore class interests unless he receives a private, selective incentive to do otherwise.[45] The latter may take the form of coercion or of promises by a revolutionary leader of personal reward, contingent upon both participation and success of the government. (Alternatively, such a reward may simply be expected by the participant.)

It is partly for this reason that successful revolutions almost never turn out to be mass, spontaneous uprisings. Usually they result from careful planning by a small, interwoven elite or from the ability of such a group to take intelligent advantage of an existing situation. In either case group members will feel that they can have a major impact on the outcome of their cause. Once initial successes have been scored, the costs or the foregone rewards to others of not supporting the movement will rise, and its base of support will grow. The October 1917 Revolution in the U.S.S.R. is no exception to this pattern.

REFERENCES

(For Marx)

Freedman, Robert, ed. *Marx on Economics.* New York: Harcourt Brace Jovanovich, Inc., 1961.

Loucks, W. L., and W. G. Whitney. *Comparative Economic Systems.* New York: Harper & Row, Publishers, 1969, Pt. III.

Mandel, Ernest. *Marxist Economic Theory.* New York: Monthly Review Press, 1970, especially Vol. 1, pp. 320–331. These two volumes are reputed to be the best modern development of Marx's thought, by a noted Belgian Marxist scholar.

Marx, Karl. *Capital.* Moscow: Foreign Languages Publishing House, 1965–1967 (four vols.). See especially Vol I, Ch. 7, Sec. 2, "The Production of Surplus Value"; Vol. I, Ch. 25, "The General Law of Capitalist Accumulation"; and

[44] We discussed moral incentives in the Appendix to Chapter 7. The discussion below derives from Mancur Olson, Jr., *The Logic of Collective Action* (New York: Schocken, 1968), pp. 102–111. See, as well, Gordon Tullock, "The Paradox of Revolution," *Public Choice,* Fall 1971.

[45] Even a self*less* individual (in the sense of the Appendix to Chapter 7) will not be rational to participate in class action unless he feels that he can significantly improve the chances of the class to achieve its goals. The selfish individual has a second reason not to participate—the costs that he must incur in the process—unless these costs are somehow turned into private benefits, including escape from punishment. For selfish individuals, the *principle of exclusion* (introduced in Section 2–3) applies here.

Vol. III, Ch. 52, "Classes." The latter gives Marx's last thoughts on the stratifi-
cation of society into socioeconomic classes.
There is also a Modern Library edition of *Capital* (or *Das Kapital*).
————. *A Critique of the Gotha Programme.* New York: International Publishers,
1933.
————. *Value, Price and Profit.* New York: International Publishers, 1935.
————. *Wage Labor and Capital.* New York: International Publishers, 1933.
————, and Freidrich Engels. *Manifesto of the Communist Party.* New York:
International Publishers, 1948.
Robinson, Joan. *An Essay on Marxian Economics.* New York: Macmillan Pub-
lishing Co., Inc., 1966.
Sraffa, Piero. *The Production of Commodities By Means of Commodities.* New
York: Cambridge University Press, 1960.
Sweezy, Paul. *The Theory of Capitalist Development.* New York: Monthly Review
Press, 1956.
Wilson, Edmund. *To the Finland Station.* New York: Doubleday Company, Inc.,
1955, Pt. II, Ch. 15.
Wolfson, Murray. *A Reappraisal of Marxian Economics.* New York: Columbia
University Press, 1966.

REFERENCES

(For Schumpeter)

Halm, George. *Comparative Economic Systems,* 3rd ed. New York: Holt, Rine-
hart and Winston, Inc., 1968, Ch. 7–9.
Schumpeter, J. A. *Capitalism, Socialism, and Democracy,* 3rd ed. New York:
Harper & Row, Publishers, 1950.

Part **FOUR**

Chapter 14

The Functioning of a Laissez-Faire Economy

14–1 Introduction

After Upton Sinclair's *The Jungle* appeared in 1906, quite a few people stopped eating meat. The novel was a story of the exploitation of poor immigrant workers, some of whom could barely speak English, in the Chicago stockyards around the turn of the century. It told of child labor, of unspeakable poverty and filth, of wives and daughters forced into prostitution, of workmen constantly losing their health, falling into debt, or landing in prison —and, incidentally, of men who fell into the machinery and came out as "pure leaf lard." Sinclair was seeking to transform America into a socialist industrial democracy. What he got was a pure food and drug law.

Later, at the bottom of the Great Depression, many socialists thought that they were passing through the last great crisis foreseen by Marx. They expected a revolution, but what they got were white papers on employment and fiscal policy. Laissez faire ranks high on anyone's scale of survival ability, at least until the past couple of decades or so. Moreover, when we view recent trends in Yugoslavia, we may be tempted to feel that its persistence is still underrated.

Those systems that continue to fly the laissez-faire banner today may be called "Keynesian" laissez-faire economies.[1] That is, their governments accept, with varying degrees of steadfastness, a commitment to use fiscal and monetary policies in pursuit of high employment and output levels.[2]

More traditional concepts of laissez faire do not permit even this, and in the libertarian version the government's role is limited to "preventing" one man from injuring another. Evidently, the values of most men would favor penalties for murderers and for managers who blow up their rivals' plants. Yet, if we extend our notion of "injury" beyond that of crude physical violence, a firm that pollutes the air or water is also "injuring" other firms and individuals who use these resources. Even according to the libertarian view, therefore, the government has an obligation to internalize social costs and benefits. When we extend this commitment to encourage efficiency by maintaining competition and realizing certain economies of mass production, we have already taken an important step away from laissez faire.

We shall postpone consideration of these matters for now, however, and begin our exploration of laissez faire with a probe into the nature of markets, both in theory and in practice.

14–2   Markets and Their Duties

There is a gulf between markets in theory and markets in practice that no one has yet been able to bridge. Let us go back to the completely decentralized economy of Chapter 2, which economists often call the "perfectly competitive model." In it there are many buyers and sellers for every good, and each firm and household is a *price taker* in the sense that it must accept every price as given. Yet prices do change in such an economy, and the embarrassing question arises as to "how," since no trader has the power to do this. To be logically complete, the thoroughly decentralized system requires at least one more actor—a kind of central gnome or auctioneer, a shadowy but incorruptible figure who raises and lowers prices according to one simple rule: Wherever there is a shortage of a good, he raises its price; wherever there is a surplus, he lowers the price. This is shown in Figure 14–1.

---

[1] For a more complete exposition of "Keynesian" economics than we have space for, see any good intermediate macroeconomic textbook, for example, Gardner Ackley, *Macroeconomic Theory* (New York: Macmillan, 1961). It is doubtful that Keynes himself was a laissez-faire economist by our use of the term; he certainly did not consider himself to be one, nor did he think that laissez faire had much of a future in the Western world. See J. M. Keynes, *The General Theory of Employment, Interest and Money* (London: Macmillan, 1951), especially Ch. 24, and *Essays in Persuasion* (London: Macmillan, 1931), Pts. IV and V.

[2] More specifically we shall say that a Keynesian laissez-faire economy is one that uses monetary or fiscal policies to promote a high level of employment and within which government revenues equal 20 per cent or more of net national product. Lately a school has emerged under the leadership of Milton Friedman, called the Monetarists, who claim that the scale of economic activity can best be controlled by automatically regulating the supply of money that firms, households, and governments have available to spend. This school is not Keynesian in the usual (post-World War II) sense of the term. See Milton Friedman, *The Optimum Quantity of Money and Other Essays* (Chicago: Aldine, 1969); Milton Friedman and Walter Heller, *Monetary vs. Fiscal Policy: A Dialogue* (New York: Norton, 1969).

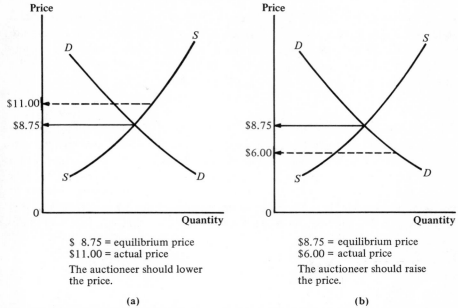

$ 8.75 = equilibrium price
$11.00 = actual price

The auctioneer should lower
the price.

(a)

$8.75 = equilibrium price
$6.00 = actual price

The auctioneer should raise
the price.

(b)

Figure 14—1.   The auctioneer should lower the price in diagram (a) to get rid of excess
supply and raise it in diagram (b) to get rid of excess demand.

Moreover, until supply and demand balance on *every* market in the
economy (that is, until there is no longer a shortage or surplus of *any* good),
the auctioneer forbids all trading. Instead, he revises his price list and requests
new bids from all would-be traders. Finally, when every market is in equilibrium, he permits buying and selling of equilibrium quantities at equilibrium
prices only.

How far this model departs from the real world can be imagined by asking how long it would take to bring such an economy to equilibrium and what
the corresponding information costs would be. The central gnome must be in
continuous contact with hundreds of thousands, if not millions, of firms and
households all the time. The latter send demand-and-supply information in
exchange for prices. Both center and periphery process the information they
receive before sending replies. We may well wonder whether they would
get anything else done or whether any trading at all will ever be able to occur.[3]

Interestingly enough, centralized pricing mechanisms have been proposed
for two important models of market socialism, which we shall encounter in
Chapter 18. Under laissez faire, however, most markets will not be run by
the auctioneer method. The simplest practical models will call for sellers or

---

[3] There is an additional problem, which we shall discuss in Ch. 19. The excess
demand-and-supply information being returned to the center is nonoperational and
therefore not completely reliable. The central gnome or auctioneer does not "see" the
excess inventories or production capacity, which are the physical signs of excess supply,
nor does he personally observe the unfilled orders, which signal excess demand. This
would not matter so much if producers had no motives to send him false or misleading
signals, but they sometimes will.

buyers to change prices (that is, for decentralized pricing). For example, if a seller is building up excessive inventories, he may lower his price; if buyers are queueing up, he may raise it. The notion of "price change" must be understood broadly. A firm may find it more acceptable or discreet to reduce the quality of its product or service rather than to raise price overtly.

14–3   The Cobweb Model and the Labor Market

As soon as we permit decentralized and uncoordinated pricing, we virtually assure ourselves that some trading will take place at disequilibrium prices (for example, at $11 or $6 in Figure 14–1), where demand and supply do not balance. Now there is no reason to expect, even in theory, that prices will ever adjust to their equilibrium values.[4] One simple example of this, called a cobweb model, appears in Figure 14–2. Suppose that producers initially

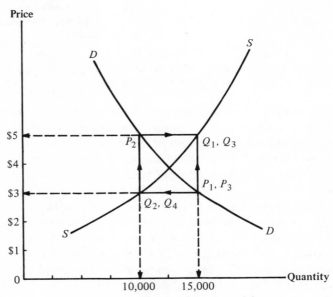

Figure 14–2.   The cobweb model.

expect a price of $5, which is above the actual equilibrium level of $4. Therefore, they bring 15,000 units of their product to market. However, at $5 buyers will only take 10,000, leaving a surplus of 5,000. This will put downward pressure on the price, and to keep matters as uncomplicated as possible, we assume (1) that the demand and supply curves do not shift, and (2) that

[4] In the discussion to follow we make a number of simplifying assumptions. Moreover, the demand and supply curves in Figure 14-2 are not defined in quite the usual textbook way. For details the interested reader should consult Mordecai Ezekiel, "The Cobweb Theorem," *Quarterly Journal of Economics,* Feb. 1938; reprinted in American Economic Association, *Readings in Business Cycle Theory* (Philadelphia: Blakiston, 1951), Ch. 21.

all units are sold at the same price. Then the price will fall to $3, where the demand curve cuts the vertical line representing 15,000 units.

The market is not in equilibrium because producers are forced to supply more at the $3 price than they wish to. From their supply curve we see that they would prefer to bring only 10,000 units to market at that price. Suppose that present production plans, and thus future supply, depend upon the currently prevailing price; then producers will supply 10,000 units during a forthcoming period. However, at a price of $3, buyers want 15,000 units, and a shortage of 5,000 would emerge. Instead, the price rises to $5, at which demand will absorb the 10,000 units. Now we are right back where we started. The $5 current price calls forth a future supply of 15,000, which can only be absorbed at the lower $3 price. Over time, price and output fluctuate up and down inversely to one another and never tend toward their equilibrium levels. If output fluctuations were to coincide in many industries, they would result in significant employment fluctuations and the phenomenon commonly known as a business cycle.

We shall call the above case 1; there are two more cases to consider, based upon the slopes and positions of the demand-and-supply curves relative to one another. If they retain roughly their positions of Figure 14–2 but the supply curve is relatively flatter, the fluctuations will grow in size (or amplitude) over time. This is case 2, the explosive cobweb cycle. On the other hand, if the demand curve is relatively flatter, the fluctuations will diminish over time, and sooner or later the actual price and quantity will approach equilibrium. Only in case 3, the convergent cobweb cycle, will the market mechanism eventually coordinate production, consumption, and distribution efficiently. On a purely a priori basis there is no reason to expect case 3 to be more common than the other two combined.

Admittedly, our implicit assumptions are a bit specialized. Producers base their future supply plans solely on the basis of current price. They do not forecast demand at that price, nor does an independent agency arise to perform this service. In effect we are still in the perfectly competitive market, with many buyers and sellers, each of whom provides a tiny fraction of total market supply or demand. Moreover, firms are inflexible in that they cannot reduce their supply when their price forecasts turn out to be overoptimistic, nor can they increase it in the reverse situation. More generally they cannot shift capacity out of slow-moving items into those which are in greater demand. The strict cobweb model therefore appears to be confined to a few sectors, notably certain agricultural commodities and, with some modifications, higher education.[5]

In the case of farming, once some crops are planted, they can only be harvested and brought to market, destroyed, or consumed by the grower.[6] This implies a certain inflexibility, and the cobweb is the brainchild of agricultural

---

[5] In the case of the latter, the cobweb dilemma is exacerbated by a shifting of the demand-and-supply curves around which the cobweb is woven.

[6] In fact, the supply curve of Figure 14–2 is the excess supply of producers over their own demand for the product.

economists. However, consider the budding engineer who, at current salary levels, decides he wants to become a part of the aerospace team. He is buoyed by rosy forecasts of unlimited horizons in aeronautical engineering and dire predictions of what will happen in the probable event that the Russians graduate more engineers than the Americans. He decides to invest in himself, but when he receives his degree, he discovers that his expectations are not borne out. The excess demand for engineers has vanished and because the salary scale is somewhat rigid downward, there is now an excess supply. When the graduate goes to join "the few," he is told that there are already too many. Consequently, he joins the ranks of the unemployed or takes a job not classified as aeronautical engineering.

Proper vocational guidance, including demand-and-supply forecasting, might have alerted the budding aerospaceman in time. A laissez-faire enthusiast would predict the emergence of this kind of counseling service on a profit-and-loss basis. For it will pay individuals to seek good vocational counseling as an insurance premium against bad investments in education or training.

Yet vocational guidance is information and, as such, is at least partly what we shall later call a "public good." For reasons to be explained in Chapter 15, it is far from obvious that society will invest enough in this kind of activity without some kind of government encouragement. Some actors will even have an incentive to be misleading in their forecasts. For example, a manufacturers' association might find it in their interests to overstate the probable demand for key employees—without whom important production processes cannot go on —in order to eliminate all risk of shortage. The uncertainty then shows up in periodic "reserve armies of unemployed" which act as shock absorbers should the demand curves for these skills suddenly shift upward.

Moreover, vocational demand and supply are notoriously difficult to forecast in any situation, so that some structural unemployment—or mismatching of labor-force skills and vacancies—is bound to occur. The question then arises as to who is responsible for retraining and reeducating people with obsolete or unwanted skills and recycling them into productive employment. We could put the entire risk upon the individual, but this is asking him to play an inhumane form of Russian Roulette.

On the other hand, our laissez-faire advocate would also suggest that insurance against structural unemployment ought to emerge on a profit-and-loss basis. Private vocational and professional guidance agencies would offer to insure advisees against unemployment for a fee by financing any necessary reeducation or training. In effect they would be giving advisees a steadier and more certain stream of income in exchange for one less certain and more variable from one year to the next. Individual agencies could then insure themselves against having to pay out large sums all at one time, and the result would be a kind of private unemployment scheme.

Unfortunately, the history of laissez faire in giving rise to comprehensive insurance of this nature is not good for several reasons. To begin with, there is the problem of determining liability. If the aggregate demand for goods and services is too low to absorb all who wish to work at going wage and salary rates, there will be unemployment on this count which is different from structural unemployment. The guidance agencies are only responsible for part of the latter, but it may be impossible to tell where one kind begins and another ends.

Second, insurance for human assets (or "human capital") raises legal entanglements. Imagine a company that, in effect, trades steady, certain income streams for uncertain, variable ones. When all these variable streams are pooled together, the result is a considerably less volatile and more certain *average* income stream. The losses of some individuals due to inaccurate forecasting by vocational-guidance counsellors will always be at least partly offset by the gains of individuals who earn more than the counsellors expected on the basis of aptitude and intelligence tests and type of education or training chosen. The insurance companies are effectively diversifying their investments in human capital.

If enough unemployment insurance is to be supplied, therefore, relative to the requirements of economic efficiency, the insurance company will have to be a kind of Robin Hood. It must collect a portion of the excess earnings of individuals who do better than foreseen and use these to honor the claims of policyholders who do poorly. However, the courts will never uphold a contract that requires an individual to pay a private agency whenever his income exceeds the level forecast by a guidance counsellor. Consequently, the insurance company would have to honor claims entirely from its earnings on fees. There would be no choice but to set the fee so high that it choked off demand below efficient levels. The result would be too little unemployment insurance which is too high-priced.

The government can fill the gap by subsidizing a comprehensive manpower program to reeducate and recycle potentially productive labor. It can pay comprehensive unemployment insurance, partly out of taxes collected from those who work. But when we add these to guidance and counselling, we are again taking an important step away from laissez faire.

14–4   Keynesian Unemployment [7]

While the strict cobweb model has limited application, the consequence of relaxing its special assumptions is an even more confused picture. And yet, provided factors of production are sufficiently mobile and prices are not overly rigid, approximate market equilibrium appears to be the rule rather than the

---

[7] In the discussion to follow we shall focus attention on group decision making within labor unions and professional associations, coupled with membership barriers, as a principal source of wage rigidity. Keynes did not stress this source. For his discussion, see *The General Theory of Employment, Interest and Money,* op. cit., Chs. 2, 19–21.

exception. This is so much the case that economists usually suppose prices to stay close to their equilibrium levels, even though they have no satisfactory theory to explain why.

Nevertheless, one explanation of the emergence of a command economy rests partly on the failure of markets to function properly when a drastic re-ordering of priorities is sought. We have just seen that unemployment may result because of inaccurate demand forecasting by prospective employers or employees. And finally, most theories of the business cycle or of unemploy-ment are anchored somewhere to prices that are unable to adjust rapidly enough to supply–demand imbalances. Consequently, the volume of output and employment adjusts instead. We now wish to explore the notion of rigid prices in more detail.

By price rigidity, we mean a reluctance of prices to adjust either down-ward in response to excess supply or upward in response to excess demand. Prices may be rigid because households or firms are uncertain or ignorant of the state of excess demand and sufficiently well satisfied with the present price not to risk a change. It is said, for example, that competition sometimes re-duces downward price rigidity. On the other hand, firms worried about their community images may be hesitant to raise prices too rapidly, preferring to allow customers to queue to some extent on a waiting list. Alternatively, the government may fix price ceilings (for example, on airplane transportation) or price floors (such as a minimum-wage law), which prevent prices from re-sponding to market forces.

However, Keynesian discussions of unemployment usually rely upon subtler reasons to explain why prices or wages may fail to respond to excess supply or demand. Let us say that involuntary unemployment exists whenever individuals are willing and potentially qualified to work at one or more occu-pations but unable to find employment in them at going wage or salary rates. Thus there is an excess supply of at least some kinds of labor.

The first potential cause of involuntary unemployment is then rigid interest rates on bonds or bank loans. These rigidities result simply from the existence of money. One way for a firm or a government to borrow money is to sell bonds to the public. The public accepts bonds and gives up money, but since it cannot directly spend the bonds on goods and services, it will exact a fee for this service called an interest charge. The interest charge on a bond, divided by the value of the bond, is its interest rate. This cannot go below zero, and the same is true on virtually all bank loans.

Indeed, during a period of inflation, we would be irrational to purchase a bond bearing a zero interest rate. For not only will we forego the use of our money, but by the time we get it back, its purchasing power will have shrunk. We should demand compensation for this and for any risk that the borrower (or seller of bonds) will have to be late with or default on some of his pay-ments of principal or interest because of his own financial condition. Conse-quently, the yield on most bonds may never be able to fall to zero. Indeed the floor may be very high when an inflationary psychosis prevails, such as in 1970, or when the future is clouded with uncertainty, as during the Great Depression.

Both the uncertainty about future demand and the high borrowing costs may serve to choke off investment demand and also the demand for durable consumer goods, such as autos and homes. Involuntary unemployment may then result as a consequence of an aggregate demand for goods and services which is too low. This is the first version of Keynesian theory.[8, 9]

The second version of Keynesian unemployment rests on rigid wages. Our underlying philosophy of markets must metamorphose when buyers or sellers decide to improve their market power by forming coalitions, such as labor unions and professional associations. A union will usually bring higher wages and salaries to some employees than they could get in individual bargaining with employers. However, one advantage of a market without coalitions is that each buyer and seller may decide for himself and only himself exactly how much of a good he wishes to trade at each price. In so doing he achieves a kind of personal freedom without directly coercing anyone else, unless his activities inflict external costs upon others.

The members of a labor union or of an independent truckers' association formed to negotiate with a teamsters' union are not in such a simple position. Now the decision to accept or reject a wage offer—and, in some cases, to make one—has become a collective or group decision instead of an individual one. Let us suppose that the group decision making is "democratic" in the sense that proposed contract agreements are rejected or accepted by majority vote, union officials are elected in the same way, and nomination is open to rank-and-file members.

There can still be a tyranny of the majority in the following sense. Suppose that a union ratifies a contract containing extremely attractive wages and working conditions by a $2:1$ majority. The terms, in fact, are so good from the union's viewpoint that employers are not willing to hire all who wish to work at the wage rate agreed to, and unemployment results. If a free market were operating, some who became unemployed would then offer their services at lower wages. Under favorable conditions the market would eventually find an equilibrium at rates below those set in the contract. However, the contract has the force of law, and it preserves wage-rate rigidity.

---

[8] For those who wish a bit more highbrow explanation of the foregoing, we may think of money as the most liquid of all assets, in the sense that it is the most widely and readily accepted in exchange for all goods and services. In particular, money is more liquid than any bond. Thus, to part with money and accept a bond of equivalent value, individuals and firms will ask a premium called interest. If we range all bonds in order or increasing liquidity, we shall have money at the top, and in this sense we may view money as a zero-interest bond.

[9] A more popular version of Keynesian rigid-interest-rate theory revolves around what is known as a "liquidity trap." Suppose that interest rates fall to levels that are historically low. Then, according to the theory, practically everyone expects them to go back up. Rather than lend money now (or purchase bonds or stocks) they hold idle balances in expectation that rates will rise again. Eventually, the demand for money becomes absolute in the sense that any increases in the money supply will go into idle balances. This puts an effective floor on interest rates below which no one will lend money for investment purposes. Nevertheless, Keynes denied the practical importance of the trap (*General Theory*, p. 207), and there seems to be no firm empirical evidence to support it.

The reader may well ask why a labor union, professional association, or other market coalition would ever behave in this manner. In fact, it may not. The textbooks are full of diagrams to show that when a labor union confronts a powerful employer, the union can raise both the wage rate and the level of employment in comparison with the situation where individual workers are left to fend for themselves. However, nothing prevents the same union from striving for still higher incomes, which actually reduce the number of employees that management is willing to hire. A number of motives for this have been advanced, most relating to the existence of an "inner core" of union members, which is less than its present or potential membership. (The latter would comprise all who wish to work at going wage or salary rates and who possess the necessary native capabilities.)

The inner core in question consists of men who have at least minimum seniority so that they are not first to be fired or last to be hired. Nevertheless, they constitute a majority of the present union membership and therefore predominate in any union election. Because of their seniority they may also, on balance, be the highest paid and the highest dues-paying members. Thus it is alleged that the union caters to the preferences of the core in terms of job security, protection from inflation, and over-all wages and working conditions, at the expense of other members or potential members. For example, it may seek a high wage rate which denies employment to all those without a minimum level of seniority.

Unions and professional associations cannot afford to have too many unemployed members, however, and this gives them a twofold incentive. On the one hand, they may try to raise the demand for their services by operating through the political process. They may also establish stiff requirements for membership, which become occupational entry barriers. It is sometimes alleged, for example, that the American Medical Association has controlled medical-school vacancies to this end. Some unions have been charged with refusing membership on the grounds that no employment was available or with imposing other requirements, such as kinship or "unreasonable" apprenticeships.

If true, these claims indicate that the organizations in question have stood between the demand for and the supply of labor. By filtering the latter and holding some of it back, they would have kept the incomes of their members above market equilibrium levels. The conventional textbook example assumes that labor unions and professional associations have no power whatever to prevent anyone from working, or from qualifying for work, who is willing to do so at going salary rates or below. The textbook example will not describe reality, however, unless market-structure policy successfully brings down job-entry barriers. In particular, no association can have the power to use educational, training, or apprenticeship programs to restrict the flow of potentially qualified personnel into any occupation or profession.

The above is one modern version of the Keynesian "rigid-wage" model. However, we have not yet generated any involuntary unemployment with it.

What we have done so far is to divide the labor force into two components. The first, protected by unions and professional associations, contains a relatively high proportion of skilled and other better-paying jobs. These are made even more lucrative by occupational entry barriers which restrict the supply.

The second component is not protected by unions and professional associations of any kind. It contains a relatively high proportion of unskilled and other poorer-paying jobs. By restricting the supply of labor into first-category jobs, unions expand the supply available here. This lowers the wages or salaries at which these markets will clear, making the jobs in question even less lucrative.

Figure 14-3 shows what we mean. Here DD gives the demand for one kind of category 2 labor. Without job-entry barriers into other kinds of work, the supply of this labor is SS and the equilibrium wage $1.75 per hour. With barriers elsewhere, more people crowd into this market, lowering the supply to $S'S'$. The market will now clear at $1.40.

The consequence is to widen wage and salary differentials, but we still have not necessarily put anyone out of work. Unemployment is finally generated by an effective minimum wage law, which prevents wages and salaries from falling far enough in nonprotected sectors to encourage the hiring of all those who wish to work there. By definition, a minimum wage that is effective must price some workers out of the market. Inevitably, these will be the most disadvantaged whose value of marginal product does not reach, for some reason, the minimum wage that employers must legally pay. If we set a minimum wage of $2 per hour in Figure 14-3, we put AC employees out of work. Note that the presence of occupational entry barriers elsewhere in the economy worsens the unemployment impact of a minimum wage. Without them it would only be AB.

By now the reader may feel a deep sense of shock and outrage at what we have just written, even though it follows from relatively straightforward analysis. Surely we should put pursuit of a decent minimum wage into the same category as the battle for motherhood and against man-eating sharks and sweatshop working conditions. Nevertheless, mounting empirical evidence shows that minimum wages, which inevitably rise over time, produce both inflation and unemployment, especially among relatively disadvantaged groups.[10]

A minimum wage is thus a two-edged sword, benefitting those who can work under its protection but hurting those who are priced out of the market. Although we usually think of Sweden as the archetype of a welfare state, it does not have a minimum wage. There is an alternative, possessing the bene-

[10] For an excellent survey of the theory and empirical evidence relating to minimum wage laws in North America, see E. G. West, "Toward a Comprehensive Theory of Minimum Wage Laws," Carleton University, Working Paper 72-08, Ottawa, May 1972, and references cited there. See also Ontario Department of Labour, "The Short-Run Impact of the Thirty-Cent Revision in Ontario's Minimum Wage in Five Industries," Toronto, Queen's Park, 1970. Interestingly enough, union lobbies often support minimum wage legislation strongly. We shall examine this matter in Chapter 23.

fits of a minimum wage without its harmful effects. This is a guaranteed annual income, also known as a comprehensive family assistance plan or a negative income tax. Here the basic idea is once again to put an income floor under every household, but without directly affecting the price of its labor services. Instead of forcing employers to pay a legal minimum, each potential income earner seeks work at whatever wage he can bargain for. If this is too low to assure him a "decent" standard of living, the government makes up the difference. The minimum income can be varied regionally to compensate for differences in price levels and escalated or deescalated over time by a consumer price index. There is no reason why its coverage cannot be at least as broad as that of a minimum wage law.

We may use the ideas developed above to show how unemployment can combine with inflation. Let us suppose that the aggregate, economy-wide demand for goods and services is high enough to absorb a full-employment level of output. (It need not be so high, however, as to create inflation on its own.) We may start from relative full employment, meaning that no more than 3 per cent of the labor force in North America and 1.5 per cent elsewhere are involuntarily jobless.

Even if we assume that aggregate demand remains high, we must realize that the composition of demand is constantly changing. As of any point in time, the demand curves for some goods will be rising, and by varying amounts. Other goods will experience declining or relatively stable demands. The same is true of the composition of aggregate supply. At the most basic level, this shifting stems from such forces as changes in tastes, technology, population, income levels, and known resource endowments and capabilities. As a consequence, markets are continually getting out of equilibrium, with excess supply appearing in some cases and excess demand in others. This transfers to the labor market through the mechanism of derived demand.

If we are to avoid unemployment, some combination of two things must happen. First, labor may move out of industries in which it is in excess supply and into industries in which it is in excess demand. To the extent that it remains in excess supply in some industries (or geographical regions), it must absorb wage cuts in order to restore labor-market equilibrium. Otherwise, there will be layoffs. But if wages are propped up by unions or by a legal minimum, they cannot fall.

At the same time, suppose that prices are rising more rapidly in industries experiencing excess demand than they are falling in industries with excess supply. (Demand pressures are more effective in pulling prices up than are supply pressures in pushing them down.) This may happen for a number of reasons. In particular, prices may be reluctant to fall in excess supply industries because of rigid wages. A general price index covering all goods will then be rising, and this is inflation by definition.

We can easily imagine variations on the above theme. Let us begin with a combination of two situations: (1) A high level of aggregate demand, perhaps temporary, has caused an inflation to begin; (2) large wage gains are awarded in an industry that has experienced spectacular increases in demand or productivity.

Then employees in sectors where neither productivity nor demand has been growing so fast may nevertheless wish to prevent their own incomes from falling too much relative to incomes elsewhere. Alternatively, they may expect further inflation in the months and years to come. This, in turn, can lead to increased wage demands and, ultimately, to inflationary pressures. Unions

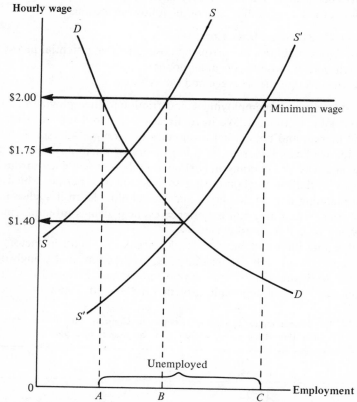

Figure 14–3. Possible unemployment effect of occupational entry barriers and minimum wage law.

or professional associations are risking unemployment in the process, but the majority voting rule again makes this possible, and indeed rational, for the individuals involved, although it is not rational for society as a whole.

Downward rigidities in both interest and wage rates, coupled with occupational entry barriers, have been cited as factors in creating or prolonging unemployment. Nevertheless, empirical evidence does not clearly indicate whether the actions of professional associations and labor unions have done more than other factors to cause involuntary unemployment since, let us say,

World War II. Even if they had, we cannot blame them for protecting the interests of their members, who might otherwise be exploited, within society's framework of rules and laws. But if market-structure policy is to promote both efficiency and full employment, it must prevent organizations from restricting access to jobs or to job qualification.

14-5   Some Standard Business-Cycle Analysis

We have discovered that involuntary unemployment may arise in a laissez-faire economy for some combination of the following reasons:

1. Inaccurate demand forecasting.
2. Downward rigidities in borrowing costs affecting potential investors and purchasers of durable consumer goods.
3. Downward rigidities in wage and salary rates.

We may add seasonal unemployment and frictional unemployment, or workers between jobs, to this list. We have already compared unemployment rates for several market and nonmarket economies in Section 5–3 (see Table 5–1).

Thus far we have explored the static theory of unemployment. It tries to show how and why an economy may show no inherent tendency toward a full-employment level of production during any specific time period, which we may view as a planning horizon for firms and households. Even if such a tendency does exist, the system may still experience cyclical swings in employment and output, which we call business cycles.

The dynamic theory of business cycles speaks of "built-in factors" which send the economy through expansion, peak, contraction, and trough over and over again. A theoretical business cycle appears in Figure 14–4 around a longer-run trend line of economic growth (AA'), and Table 14–1 compares

Table 14–1.   Business-cycle peaks and troughs in Canada, the United States, and the United Kingdom, 1870–1970 (by month and year).

Cycle Phase	Canada	U.S.	U.K.
P	11/73	10/73	9/72
T	5/79	3/79	6/79
P	7/82	—	—
T	3/85	5/85	6/86
P	2/87	3/87	— *
T	2/88	4/88	—
P	7/90	7/90	9/90
T	3/91	5/91	—
P	2/93	1/93	—
T	3/94	6/94	2/95
P	8/95	12/95	—
T	8/96	6/97	—
P	4/00	6/99	6/100
T	2/01	12/00	9/01

Table 14–1 (cont.)

Cycle Phase	Canada	U.S.	U.K.
P	12/02	9/02	6/03
T	6/04	8/04	11/04
P	12/06	5/07	6/07
T	7/08	6/08	11/08
P	3/10	1/10	—
T	7/11	1/12	—
P	11/12	1/13	12/12
T	1/15	12/14	9/14
P	1/18	8/18	10/18
T	4/19	3/19	4/19
P	6/20	1/20	6/20
T	9/21	7/21	6/21
P	6/23	5/23	11/24
T	8/24	7/24	7/26
P	—	10/26	5/27
T	—	11/27	9/28
P	4/29	8/29	7/29
T	3/33	3/33	8/32
P	7/37	5/37	9/37
T	10/38	6/38	9/38
P	—	2/45	—
T	2/46	10/45	—
P	10/48	11/48	—
T	9/49	10/49	—
P	5/43	7/53	4/51
T	6/54	8/54	7/52
P	—	—	12/55
T	—	—	11/56
P	4/57	7/57	9/57
T	4/58	4/58	9/58
P	1/60	5/60	—
T	3/61	2/61	—
P	N.a.	11/69 †	N.a.
T	N.a.	11/70 †	N.a.

Sources: K. A. J. Hay, "Early Twentieth Century Business Cycles in Canada," *Canadian Journal of Economics and Political Science,* Aug. 1966. Solomon Fabricant, "Recent Economic Changes and the Agenda of Business-Cycle Research," National Bureau Report Supplement 8, May 1971.
* No cycle.
† Tentative.

business-cycle peaks and troughs for the United States, Canada, and the United Kingdom over the period 1870–1970, utilizing data available by the end of 1970. Although the business cycle has toned down a bit since World War II, it still appears to be with us.[11]

[11] Although it has not yet been done to the author's knowledge (as of early 1973), a business-cycle peak may eventually be assigned to Canada for late 1969 or 1970. A peak and trough may be assigned to the United Kingdom for the 1960s.

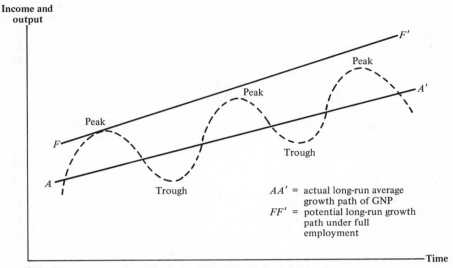

Figure 14–4. Hypothetical business cycles.

To begin our analysis of business cycles, let us suppose that a business cycle is in progress which we interrupt as the economy passes a trough and enters into a period of expansion. Recovery may occur for any combination of a number of reasons. A wave of optimism may result in greater investor confidence and demand. Or, a wave of technological innovations may improve cost–price relationships, expand certain domestic markets, or create new ones. Population growth may expand the markets for consumption necessities, or growth in foreign countries may expand export markets. Inventories, once grown too high, may become depleted and need rejuvenating.

Moreover, because of a principle known as the *accelerator,* the mere flattening out of the decline in income, output, and employment will eventually translate into an increased demand for investment in new plant and equipment.[12] To see way, let us divide net investment into two parts. When producers expand output, they may have to invest to install new productive capacity. Similarly, when output is declining, they may not only fail to invest, they may disinvest by letting capital equipment run down, wear out, or become obsolete. The first component of investment therefore depends upon ex-

_____

[12] The accelerator principle was discovered by J. M. Clark. His classic article "Business Acceleration and the Law of Demand" appeared in the *Journal of Political Economy,* Mar. 1917. It is reprinted in American Economic Association, *Readings in Business Cycle Theory* (Philadelphia: Blakiston, 1951), Ch. 11. See also James S. Duesenberry, *Business Cycles and Economic Growth* (New York: McGraw-Hill, 1958), and Robert Eisner, "A Permanent Income Theory of Investment," *American Economic Review,* June 1967, or "Investment: Fact and Fancy," *American Economic Review,* May 1963. Eisner's restatement of the theory is the most sophisticated and the best confirmed by statistical tests. It also indicates the accelerator to be a somewhat weaker factor in generating business cycles than Clark seems to have believed.

pected or realized changes in demand. If demand and, therefore, output and income were to level off for a sufficiently long period of time, this component of *net* investment would fall to zero. (*Gross* investment would still be going on as producers maintained their capital equipment to meet a steady demand. *Gross* investment would equal depreciation.)

The acceleration principle says that the *level* of the first component of investment depends upon *changes* in demand. When producers foresee increases in the demand for their products which, if they are to be met, will require additional capacity, the first component will be positive. Otherwise it will be zero or negative (in the sense that some existing capital equipment is not being replaced as it wears out).

A second component of investment spending is related to innovation in one way or other or else to an assortment of other factors which do not directly depend upon changes in demand. When decreases in demand are large, the first component is negative and at least partly offsets the second. As demand decreases level off, the negative first component eventually rises toward zero, and if the second (or autonomous) component does not happen to be falling just as fast, total net investment will rise.

We now observe a rather remarkable thing. Investment demand is one component of the aggregate demand for all kinds of goods and services. As the aggregate demand for goods and services begins to decline less rapidly, investment demand eventually begins to rise. This in turn can cause the total demand for goods and services to stop declining and start advancing. Thus the acceleration is capable of turning the economy around by itself. In practice, however, this effect is likely to be weak and certainly no substitute for well-timed government policy to stimulate demand.

Once the economy turns the corner and begins to wend its upward way, our attention shifts from the accelerator to another famous effect, known as the *multiplier*. Suppose that an initial increase in demand raises output, employment, and income. Individuals then spend part of their increases in income on consumer goods, thus raising demand still further. This second increase in demand generates a second increase in income which generates a third increase in demand, and so it goes in an ever-widening circle of income, output, and employment. The government can assist this process by generating further spending with continuing expansionary policies. Each increase in spending will be multiplied.

In the first phases of the expansion, firms may largely bring existing production capacity back into operation. But later, if demand continues to grow and business confidence is buoyed, acceleration-induced investment will increase and these increases will be multiplied. The accelerator and multiplier will then be working hand in hand.

To illustrate with an example, let us suppose that, during the expansion, the aggregate demand for goods and services grows every year by 10 per cent of its previous trough level until full employment is reached. If the trough level of income and output was $100,000,000 in prices of some base year, demand grows every year by $10,000,000 in constant prices. If one assumes a full-employment level of output worth $150,000,000, the expansion ends five years later, and the goal then becomes to maintain aggregate demand at its full-employment level. However, a problem of proportions has already arisen which threatens to develop into a crisis. The reason, once again, is that the *level* of investment responds partly to the *rate* at which aggregate demand is growing or declining. Thus the accelerator can now turn the economy down.

To see how, let us divide the total aggregate demand for goods and services into a demand for consumer goods and a demand for investment in capital goods.[13] The proportion of each component in aggregate demand will not be accidental as the economy approaches the peak of its business cycle. Both consumption and investment demand must be at levels that can continually support one another. Consumption ultimately gives rise to the derived demand for investment, and income earned by employees who produce capital goods helps to sustain consumption.

For simplicity, assume that by the last year before full employment is reached, the increase in aggregate demand equals $5 million worth of consumer goods and $5 million worth of investment goods. Once we reach full employment, further output expansion can only come from increases in the labor force and in output per worker. A slowdown in the expansion, which is also a reduction in the rate of increase of household incomes, must eventually occur. This, in turn, causes the demand for consumer goods to rise more slowly, which ultimately translates into a decline in the demand for investment goods. Unless a new source of expansion can be found, the economy will not turn onto its long-run full-employment growth path (*FF'* in Figure 14–4). Instead, unemployment will result as the system passes its peak and then turns down.

Along the full-employment growth path, national output and income are growing more slowly than during the cyclical expansion. Thus consumption demand, which is related to income, is also growing more slowly, and the derived demand for investment is lower. It follows that the share of investment in total demand must be lower than it was during the cyclical expansion. The share of consumption must become correspondingly higher. For every $10 million increase in aggregate demand, $7 or $8 million might typically have to be consumption, while only $2 or $3 million is investment if the system is to stay on this path. Just to maintain full employment, therefore, the economy will have to change directions.

Well-timed government policy—for example, an increase in spending on public consumption to supplement spending on private consumer goods—can stimulate the economy just before it starts to turn down. Alternatively, the mix of demand may itself adjust in response to changing market forces. The

---

[13] We have not allowed for government spending. However, we may divide this into spending on capital goods and (public) consumption. Then the essence of the text remains true.

latter requires both that prices be flexible and that responses to price changes be prompt. But in the absence of either of these, a recession will begin.

Once the downturn is underway, it is propelled along by the multiplier effect. Initial decreases in output and income lead to cutbacks in spending plans, which cause secondary declines in income, and so it goes. As output falls, the accelerator also begins to work backward, further reducing investment, and this reduction is again multiplied. The multiplier and accelerator are again working hand in hand, but in the wrong direction. If the level of business confidence also depends upon expected or realized changes in demand, this, too, will fall and reinforce the accelerator effect. A wave of technological innovation can stimulate the economy just as employment and output threaten to fall off, but a dearth of same can propel it downward even more rapidly. There is no obvious way to time this factor.

For awhile the rate at which output and employment are falling may actually increase as some combination of the multiplier, accelerator, lack of business confidence, and other factors continues to interact. However, there will be a floor (to be explored later) below which the economy is unlikely to slip for very long. As this floor is approached, the rate of decrease in output should slacken, permitting the accelerator effect, probably combined by now with expansionary government policies, to turn the system around. Thus our cycle is complete.

14-6   Additional Theories of the Business Cycle

Practically every economist would have some reservations about our description of a business cycle, and it is probably true that no two cycles have ever been exactly alike. To close, therefore, we will briefly cite six descriptions that do not refer to the acceleration principle. The first is the cobweb theorem, discussed earlier. Second, some economists have suggested that cycles are simply the reflections of a series of random shocks to the economy. Perhaps surprisingly, this is difficult to rule out on purely statistical grounds if we exclude the Great Depression. At the other extreme, Marx and Schumpeter believed in economic determinism. We have discussed their theories in Chapter 13.

Fifth, the monetarist school under Milton Friedman traces cycles almost exclusively to unexpected changes in the supply of money. An increase in the quantities of money available to businesses, households, and banks may make the former more willing to spend and the latter more willing to lend. Thus increases in the money supply tend to stimulate the economy, while decreases tend to be contractionary. A certain steady increase in the money supply is necessary to accommodate a system growing along its long-run path of full-employment potential. However, deviations from this steady increase produce business cycles, according to Friedman.[14]

[14] We refer the reader to the citations in footnotes 19 and 20.

Consequently, the monetarists favor a law regulating the annual increase in the money supply at a constant rate somewhere between 2 and 5 per cent. Eventually, they claim, the system would settle down close to its long-run growth path under these conditions. In their view the major reason for past cycles has been mishandling of the money supply by central banking authorities—specifically, an inability or unwillingness to achieve a steady rate of growth of this stock.

Finally, an important subthesis of the monetarists argues that the government cannot time the impact of its policies designed to stimulate the economy during a recession and to cool it off during a boom. Thus it is as likely to aggravate or even to cause a business cycle as to damp it down with its conscious fiscal and monetary policies. The monetarists therefore argue that contracyclical policies, other than a steady rate of growth of the money supply, ought to be prohibited.

14–7   More Keynesian Economics

To merge the above dynamic analysis with a Keynesian unemployment model, we rejoin the business cycle at its peak, just before the downturn. This is a critical point because it is now that the economy must adapt its mix of production to the mix of demand or else see the aggregate demand for goods and services fall below a level that will absorb a full-employment rate of output.

When aggregate demand threatens to fall, a decline in the interest rate, an easing of credit conditions, or a greater flexibility in the terms on which loans must be repaid can make investors and purchasers of consumer durables more willing to borrow. Thus it can correct the situation before too much damage is done. However, any interest rate has a floor reflecting the borrower's expectation of the rate of inflation and the risk that the loan will not be repaid on schedule. If a downturn is feared, the latter risk may be very high, and it will also make the lender less likely to offer easier credit or a flexible repayment plan.

From the investor's point of view, anticipation of a downturn will make him less likely to borrow at every interest rate—unless he can get such a repayment plan—because he is less optimistic about his own future demand. When interest rates and credit conditions have eased as far as they can go, aggregate demand may still not be high enough to keep the economy from turning down. Then some of the gloomy forecasts will prove to be self-fulfilling.

We may view the dilemma in a somewhat different way. All national output or income must either go into intended savings, including net taxes to the government, or intended spending on consumer goods. Individuals must intend either to spend or to save their incomes, and the retained earnings of producers are automatically classified as savings. On the other hand, aggregate demand (or intended spending) consists of consumption plus investment plus government spending. If this is large enough to absorb a full-employment level of output and income, intended investment (I) plus government spending (G) must be large enough to absorb the volume of intended savings (S) that this level of income will bring forth.

When $I + G$ is less than S, unemployment will result. Once the economy turns into a recession, it will continue its downward trend as long as intended saving exceeds intended investment plus government spending. Eventually, a floor will be reached at a level of income where the intentions of savers match those of investors and the government. This will normally occur by the time net savings have fallen to zero, although it may well happen before.[15]

The higher are the incomes of households and firms, the more they will tend to save. Thus, if a full-employent level of income is not achieved, society will collectively end up saving less. Ironically, if its members had planned to save less in the first place out of each given level of income, $I + G$ might have been high enough to ensure full employment. Then, from higher incomes, society could conceivably have ended up saving more than it actually did; this irony is called the "paradox of thrift." (If society had tried to save less, it would have achieved a higher level of income and therefore actually saved more.)

Let us agree with Keynes that his theories apply to a mature or developed laissez-faire economy. This is one whose average income and output per capita considerably exceed subsistence levels. Consequently, the horizons of many individuals have expanded beyond the present. Their economic decision making is based more upon a continuing desire to provide for their own future welfare and for the well-being of their heirs than upon a daily struggle to survive. Consequently, savings form an important percentage of national income and output, and such a society has a high propensity to save.

Suppose, now, that we start with an economy a bit below the developed stage and set it in motion along a long-run trend path of economic growth. As income-per-head rises, the propensity to save eventually starts to increase as well, and savings form a growing percentage of national income. This tendency does not permanently alter when interest rates paid to savers fall to very low levels (exclusive of risk and expected future inflation).[16] The capital stock is

---

[15] In practice this is only a broad constraint. If the business outlook becomes bad enough, firms will let their plant and equipment run down. Net saving could become negative, causing national income to exceed economy-wide consumption by the extent to which society is "eating into" its capital stock. During the Great Depression, negative saving occurred in both Canada (1930–1934) and the United States (1931–1934). We have seen that actual savings, including net taxes to the government, must always equal actual investment plus government spending. This is a national-income-accounting identity. However, the *plans* of spenders and savers need not match, and this is when unemployment —or inflation—may threaten. If planned savings are above planned investment plus government spending, aggregate demand will be too low to absorb the output that the nation is capable of producing. Firms will find themselves with excess inventories which count as investment, even though they are unplanned and unwanted.

[16] Technically speaking, savings tend to be both a luxury "good" and inelastic with respect to interest-rate changes.

also growing, and it becomes harder and harder for the private sector to profitably invest the entire available supply of savings. When the volume of profitable investment projects is exhausted *before* the full-employment supply of savings, full employment will not be achieved.

Thus we are again face to face with a falling rate of profit, here also referred to as a declining yield or marginal efficiency of investment. In effect, the growing propensity to save in Keynes plays the same role as the rising organic composition of capital in Marx and the routinization of investment decision making in Schumpeter. When we counterpoint this with cyclical swings in expectations and risk, we reproduce Marx's tendency for depressions to grow increasingly severe, *provided* government policies do not offset this. Rigid wages may then add to the gloom.

For Keynes, the expansion of time horizons meant that a laissez-faire economy was passing from one era to another. Formerly, the key economic problem facing mankind was symbolized by a daily wrestling match with the specter of scarcity. In the new era it becomes more important to learn to make the best social use of the savings that relative prosperity allows the community to enjoy. At the very least, this means an obligation of the government to maintain aggregate demand at a full-employment level.

Nevertheless, we should again note that evidence of declining investment yields over long periods of time is, at best, skimpy and contentious. Keynesian unemployment theory is a bit more convincing as part and parcel of a business-cycle theory than as a theory of capitalist evolution.

14–8 Government Policies to Promote Full Employment

In principle, a government can do many things to raise the levels of output and employment. It can try to loosen up the supply side, by breaking down occupational entry barriers, and it can try to stimulate the aggregate demand for goods and services. We may divide all policy measures into discretionary or deliberately undertaken policies on one hand, and automatic stabilizers (such as a progressive income tax) on the other. The latter are supposed to buoy the economy automatically in the event that recession threatens. We can also separate policies aimed at raising demand into two categories, commonly called *fiscal* and *monetary* policy. By fiscal policy, we mean changes in direct government spending or net taxes. Monetary policy refers to changes in the money supply, in credit conditions, and in interest rates brought about by the government.

Thus the government would follow an expansionary fiscal policy by raising its spending or by reducing net taxes, thereby leaving more spending power in the hands of firms and households. An expansionary monetary policy involves some combination of an increase in the money supply, a lowering of interest rates, and an easing of terms upon which loans must be repaid. A standard example finds the government buying back some of its bonds from banks, business firms, and the public on the "open market." This pumps money into the economy since the government, in effect, exchanges money for bonds. It also raises the demand for bonds, thereby raising bond prices and lowering interest rates.[17]

The theory of how to stimulate aggregate demand is therefore simple, but expansionary policy making in practice turns out to be exceedingly complex. Increases in the money supply, for example, may go largely into idle balances. An easing of credit may fail to stimulate investment demand appreciably when the business outlook is bleak. Perhaps most critical of all is the *timing* of policy measures. The underlying goal of contracyclical policy is to keep the system close to a long-run growth path of full-employment potential. Ideally, the full thrust of any policy should be felt just as the economy starts to turn down, and expansionary measures should certainly take hold before a recession ends and the succeeding boom begins. Unfortunately, no one will be able to forecast business-cycle turning points precisely or, for that matter, know just when they have occurred until some time afterward. The situation is further complicated by the existence of lags between a perception of need and the actual taking hold of expansionary policies.

To illustrate, suppose that the government decides to increase its spending. This decision-making process will itself take time, as will the drawing up of plans. Administrative orders are likely to have to go through some bureaucratic red tape before projects are set in motion. Even then, the entire increase in spending will not occur right away but will be spread over a period of time during which the project achieves fruition. Similarly, an expansion of money and an easing of credit conditions may not stimulate banks to lend and business firms and households to spend right away, especially if gloomy forecasts predominate. Once businesses decide to borrow and invest more, there may be a lag between orders, production, and construction responses.

Automatic fiscal policy, using built-in stabilizers, will have a shorter lag because no time is lost in perceiving a need and in taking and implementing decisions to buoy output.[18] The lag can also be shortened in the case of deliberate government spending by having a shelf of projects ready to go plus a speedy transmission belt, which bypasses usual bureaucratic channels, to put them into action. Yet, some lag will persist, and the same is true of monetary policy, where we have only a vague understanding of how an easing of credit

---

[17] Bond prices are inversely related to interest rates via the formula $r = \bar{y} \div p$, where r is the interest rate or yield of a bond, $\bar{y}$ the fixed interest payment (for example, the annual payment), and p its price.

[18] Ando and Brown divide the time pattern with which fiscal policy measures are transmitted to the economy into five steps. "The first stage is the period of recognition [of need]; the second is the taking of [decisions]; the third is the change in the flow of revenues and expenditures [which put some men back to work and raise individual and enterprise incomes]; the fourth is the change in the demand for output [resulting from this expansion of income]; and the last is the alteration in production in response to the change in demand. Automatic fiscal [policy measures] telescope the first three steps. . . ." Albert Ando and E. Cary Brown, "Lags in Fiscal Policy: A Summary," in W. L. Smith and Ronald L. Teiger, eds., *Money, National Income, and Stabilization Policy* (Homewood, Ill.: Irwin, 1965).

or an expansion of the money supply is transformed into increased output. Not only will lags exist, but they will vary in length from one use of policy to another, making it difficult to forecast exactly when a particular measure is going to take hold.[19]

Consequently, the government may still be fighting an inflationary boom with reduced spending, tight money and credit restrictions, high taxes, and even wage and price controls when the economy is threatening to turn downward. If so, any downward momentum will be intensified. The converse result also holds. According to the monetarist school, the lag between any change in the money supply or in credit conditions and its impact upon the spending decisions of firms and households is bound to be long and unforeseeable. Thus the authorities should undertake no deliberate monetary policy at all. For the same reason, they should undertake no deliberate fiscal policy, and they should not rely upon automatic policies, save for the constant annual increase in the money supply noted earlier, which is eventually supposed to solve the problem of business cycles altogether.[20]

In all likelihood a steadier growth in any market economy's money stock would act as a stabilizer on income and output. If the growth is not too rapid, it may restrain inflation as well. But more will probably be needed if we are to ensure a continuing full-employment level of output. At the same time, the monetarists' case for the imprecision of other policy tools, particularly automatic policies, appears less than solid to the present author.

By automatic policies we mean not only the customary ones such as progressive tax rates and unemployment insurance, but also several that are less conventional. The latter include automatic subsidies to retrain workers and to ease credit for would-be investors and house buyers as soon as the rate of unemployment rises above some predetermined (but not yet recession) level. Also included are the concepts of a full-employment government budget and the earlier-noted comprehensive family-assistance program.

The latter puts a floor under everyone's income whether he works or not. The government establishes this floor by supplementing any income that the employee may earn without removing his incentive to work. Thus it does not interfere with the operation of the labor market. When the individual cannot find work, it becomes unemployment compensation or compensation while retraining. Such a program is always an effective contracyclical tool in the

---

[19] For fiscal policy, see Ando and Brown, op. cit. For monetary policy, see the dialogue between Friedman and Culbertson. The references are J. M. Culbertson, "The Lag in the Effect of Monetary Policy," *Journal of Political Economy,* Dec. 1960; and Milton Friedman, "The Lag in the Effect of Monetary Policy," *Journal of Political Economy,* Oct. 1961. Culbertson's reply follows the Friedman article. See also the references cited by Culbertson and Friedman.

[20] See Friedman, *The Optimum Quantity of Money and Other Essays,* op. cit. For an alternative view, see Albert Ando, E. Cary Brown, Robert M. Solow, and John Kareken, "Lags in Fiscal and Monetary Policy," Research Study 1 in the Commission on Money and Credit, *Stabilization Policies* (Englewood Cliffs, N.J.: Prentice-Hall, 1963). Finally, see the references in footnote 19.

sense that it places a permanent absolute floor on individual income levels. It can, in principle, eliminate any risk of the worst forms of poverty.[21]

If we think of work not only as a means of earning a livelihood but as a source of psychological satisfaction or an expression of the individual, the second great tragedy of a recession is the loss of this kind of satisfaction. Manpower-retraining programs, and in some instances aid for embryo business firms, form a natural complement to the family-assistance program.

Finally, even discretionary contracyclical policies should not be ruled out, in the author's view, provided the transmission belt can be improved to a variety of sectors in the economy.

[21] The Nixon family-assistance plan, proposed but not adopted by the U.S. Congress during his first administration, had the right principle but the wrong figures, in the view of the author. The floor of $1,600 for a family of four probably was below the subsistence level in many parts of the country. The scale of a family-assistance program should be escalated by a suitable consumer price index. For example, suppose that a floor of $2,000 had been adopted in 1970. If by 1980 the price index is up 50 per cent, the floor of the plan should automatically be scaled up to $3,000. There should also be allowances for regional differences in the cost of living.

Chapter **15**

The Social Technology of a Laissez-Faire Economy: External Effects

15–1 Efficiency and the Harmony of Interests
15–2 Removing Externalities
15–3 Specific Solutions

15–1 Efficiency and the Harmony of Interests

Traditional economics tells us that we may investigate any economy from three points of view: its level of employment, the efficiency with which it allocates any given bundle of productive resources, and the way it distributes the fruits of production among households. We have spent considerable time examining the first problem, and we now wish to return to the second pair, focusing first upon the pricing rules for economic efficiency.

From Chapter 3 we recall that, when the economic problem is efficiently solved, the system achieves two important frontiers. One is the production-possibility surface along which production is efficient. (When we add the potential gains from international trade, this shifts outward to become the consumption-possibility frontier.) The other is the efficiency frontier itself.

These appear respectively in Figures 15–1(a) and (b). When the economy is *not* efficient, it is at a point like B in Figure 15–1(b). [If it is not efficient in production or international trade, it is in a position such as B' in Figure 15–1(a).] From B it could conceivably move onto the efficiency frontier in such a way as to make at least one person better off and no one else worse off. At *B*, in fact, the first individual is just twice as well off as the second, and the same ratio of U_I to U_{II} holds everywhere along the line we have drawn through *B*. By moving from *B* to *A* we make *both* individuals better off.

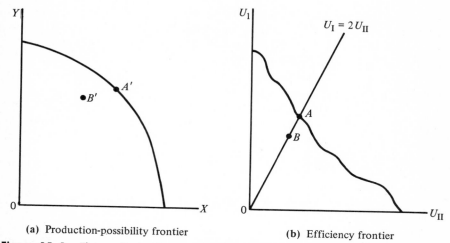

    (a) Production-possibility frontier   (b) Efficiency frontier

Figure 15-1. The production (or consumption) possibility and efficiency frontiers revisited.

If the difference between *A* and *B* was originally caused by a tariff (in a way to be explored in Chapter 16), there would be a "harmony of interests" in removing it. At first only consumers and export industries might benefit from lower prices and more open markets abroad. But if this caused a more efficient allocation of resources and realization of economies of mass production, a spurt of economic growth could result, making everyone better off in the long run. This was, indeed, the spirit of many arguments by laissez-faire enthusiasts in Britain during the first half of the 19th century, although we would be wrong to confine their views on laissez faire and the harmony of interests to economics. They wished to extend the same principle to "all aspects of man's social and moral life." The following passage, quoted by Scott Gordon from the *Economist,* gives the flavor of their philosophy:

    Examined in detail, or looked at under the most general aspect, all the great branches of human industry are found replete with order, which, growing from the selfish exertions of individuals, pervades the whole. Experience has proved that this order is invariably deranged when it is forcibly interfered with by the state; and thus not *laissez-faire,* not the undirected exertions of merchants, manufacturers, and farmers, but the interference of Governments, is anarchy. "Self-love and social are the same." [1]

    [1] H. Scott Gordon, "The London *Economist* and the High Tide of Laissez Faire," *Journal of Political Economy,* Dec. 1955, p. 479. Many readers who are interested in laissez faire will find this a fascinating piece.

Lying behind all of this is the notion of the "invisible hand" of the market mechanism efficiently coordinating production and consumption. As economics became a science and grew dull during the latter 19th and early 20th centuries, the harmony-of-interests thesis hardened and became more rigorous. Eventually it emerged as the "fundamental theorem of welfare economics," which we shall meet again in Chapter 16. Basically, this identifies efficiency with the completely decentralized economy described in Chapter 2 under some very restrictive assumptions. One of these is that no problems arise with external effects—that social costs and benefits always coincide, in other words. When they do not, it is *social* costs, *social* productivities, and *social* utilities that enter into the efficiency pricing rules.

However, the completely decentralized economy will substitute the corresponding *private* measure when its market mechanism is working smoothly. This destroys the harmony of interests. Indeed, we may associate external effects with involuntary production and consumption in the following sense. When external effects are present, some households or firms are not able to control the quantities of certain goods that they consume or use in production, or else they are unable to prevent others from gaining free access to goods which they own or have paid to use.

For example, a household may be forced to "consume" quantities of congestion, pollution, or noise. A fishery may see its catch diminish because of fouled water, which effectively becomes a destructive input (that is, with a negative marginal product) into its production process. A farmer whose livestock drink from a polluted river will have a similar problem. A taxicab company operating in Manhattan will experience congestion as a negative, uncontrolled input. Finally, an apple-orchard owner cannot regulate its contribution to the honey production of nearby beekeepers. By contrast, these enterprises can normally choose the amounts of labor and capital they use or of product they sell.

In each instance, the "involuntariness" arises because some households and firms succeed in shifting their costs onto others or else derive benefits from the activities of others for which they do not pay. External effects are also equivalent to changes in costs for firms and in incomes for households that are involuntarily affected. When pollution reduces an individual's welfare, he must spend part of his income on goods he enjoys (or goods like medical care to erase the effects of the pollution) simply to restore his level of well-being.

Whenever individuals choose for themselves and themselves only, the market mechanism is well suited to register their choices and weigh these against the production and consumption decisions of their fellow citizens. Markets permit each individual to choose exactly how much of each good or service he wishes to sell or buy, a degree of precision that no practical form of voting can hope to match. Moreover, a dollar vote on the marketplace always buys goods offered for sale there. That is, it is effective; it is never overruled like a vote for a losing political candidate. By the some token, a householder can divide his money income between many goods and services. He does not have to choose between mutually exclusive alternatives. The American voter who preferred three tablespoons of Nixon and two of Humphrey in 1968 had to settle for Nixon.[2, 3]

Added to the above advantages from individual's viewpoint are several more from the standpoint of society as a whole, which we explored in Chapters 2 and 5. In particular, markets can often break up the economic problem efficiently into numerous mini subproblems. When they do, there are some grounds for claiming that "self-love and social are the same." But the appearance of external effects, which bring with them involuntary production and consumption and divergences between social and private costs and benefits, partly removes this identity. When the economic problem is broken up, external costs and benefits persist, creating a loss of efficiency.

Pressure is then likely to arise for collective decision making and action on behalf of producers and consumers who suffer significantly. Let us briefly review the ways in which society can cope with the problems that external effects create.

15–2   Removing Externalities

From our discussion in Chapter 2 of ways to mix markets and commands, we may deduce three broad ways to internalize social costs and benefits within a basically market economy: [4]

1. In some cases, a group affected by an externality can act directly through the market mechanism—for example, to bribe a polluter to stop inflicting damages.
2. Alternatively, the affected group may prevail upon community, regional, or national governments to issue laws, decrees, regulations, and standards, backed up by penalties and bonuses, which seek outright prohibition of activities generating external effects.
3. Between (1) and (2), taxes and subsidies may encourage producers and consumers to generate smaller external costs (or discourage them from deriving such large external benefits). For example, the American environmental protection agency is now helping to underwrite the cost of a generator designed to produce electricity from solid wastes —without itself polluting the atmosphere. Most societies subsidize education because they feel that spillover benefits will result which the individuals being educated cannot themselves always capture.

[2] There is a partial offset to this. Because Nixon won by a slim majority, he probably behaved more like Humphrey and other liberal Democrats on domestic issues than he otherwise would have.

[3] To get an in-depth comparison of voting and individual choice, see James M. Buchanan, "Individual Choice in Voting and the Market," *Journal of Political Economy*, Aug. 1954.

[4] Removing external effects is sometimes called "internalizing" them.

In some cases, the group affected by an externality will comprise almost the whole of society; in others it will be only a small minority. In either event, if any of the above methods are to be used effectively, the individuals who participate in group action to remove externalities must bind themselves to a common course of action. Insofar as he affects the common course, each group member will choose by voting rather than through a market mechanism (even though the group may subsequently act through the market).

Unless the collectivity is quite small, members will lose some of the advantages of individual choice through the market, insofar as (internal) group decision making is conceived. As in the case of a labor union or professional association, individuals surrender some freedom of action in order to form coalitions that can improve their bargaining strength. But this is not all they give up.

Suppose, for example, that the externality is traffic congestion or over-crowded schools. Then the affected group does indeed comprise most of a community, and we shall imagine that a referendum is called to deal with the issue. Voters will not have a long list of prospective school sizes or alternative public transportation systems—each paired with an estimated cost—to choose from. Because referenda are expensive and voting and vote counting take time, they will face, at most, three or four simple alternatives. The choice procedure can be further refined by hearings, forums, and legislative compromise, but it never reaches the precision of individual market choice.

By the same token, when the collective decision making occurs within a special interest or political pressure group, such as the Sierra Club or an oil lobby, some compromise among individual preferences must occur before the group preference function can emerge. Moreover, if the group works through society's political processes, it will have to press for simple objectives, such as complete elimination of pollution, congestion, or pesticides, when the problem seen in all its ramifications may be quite complex. For instance, to reduce pollution, it is sometimes necessary to close down plants in the short run and create unemployment, or power or fuel shortages. The elimination of DDT will benefit fish and wildlife. But in some areas it will raise the incidence of human disease at the same time. Even in the best of circumstances, environmental disruption cannot be reduced or eliminated without cost.

Finally, let us imagine a market solution in which a group of fisheries bribe municipal governments to install a sewage-treatment facility to reduce the pollution of a bay. The *principle of exclusion,* introduced in Chapter 2, will be a problem among the fisheries because, once the sewage facility is in operation, each one will automatically benefit, regardless of his contribution toward the bribe. The fisheries must therefore agree collectively to tax themselves on the basis of a simple formula reflecting presumed "ability to pay" and "benefits received" from the facility.

More generally, the transactions costs of the above solution are likely to be high. For this reason, unless the "injured" group is quite small, *completely* market solutions to externality problems will not usually emerge.

(However, this does not necessarily rule out as unadvisable solutions in which the market mechanism plays a principal role, as we shall see below.[5]) Whenever market solutions require a bribe to be paid, moreover, there is an additional problem, aside from the issue of fairness.

Indeed, to encourage these "solutions" is tantamount to encouraging some individuals and firms to shift their costs onto others in order to extract bribes and other concessions. In spirit, such an attitude condones occupations of government and campus buildings, as well as the threat system formerly used by mobsters to extract "protection" from owners of small shops in large American cities. Any society must draw a line beyond which it refuses to tolerate the threat system, implying that this kind of use of the market mechanism is generally unacceptable.

By contrast, the difficulty with using taxes and subsidies to solve externality problems is that the information requirements of an optimal solution are usually too great for a laissez-faire government to meet. Suppose that we return to an earlier example in which a soap producer empties its waste into a river from which farmers' cattle drink. After lobbying by the farmers, the government may decide to tax the soap company and to pay the proceeds as compensation for cattle losses. The government's goal would be to reduce pollution largely by reducing the output of soap in the short run, while encouraging investment in purification facilities in the long run.

On a per unit of soap output basis, the tax ought to just cover the gap between the marginal private and the marginal social costs of the soap company's operations when both it and the farmers are producing their optimal rates of output. Yet a consequence of the soap producer's ability to shift costs onto the farmers is that the former produces beyond its optimal output level and the latter below. The government will not know what these optimal rates are or how much cost would be shifted were they to be achieved. For this reason alone, the gap which the tax must cover can only be guesstimated, although some tax may be better than none.

Indeed, the latter philosophy is apt to go a long way toward explaining a laissez-faire economy's approach to external costs. This is especially true if

[5] In addition, J. H. Dales has proposed an interesting combination of markets and commands to "solve" water-pollution problems. Essentially, the government would auction off licenses to pollute (or pollution quotas) to the highest bidders. The volume of licenses to be sold would be determined by the amount of pollution that society decided to tolerate. (This would be a political decision.) The proceeds from the auction would become available for whatever social purposes the government considered to be of highest priority.

The scheme is internally consistent and even ingenious. At present levels of technology, however, difficulties of monitoring, and even of defining tolerable pollution levels, would limit its practical usefulness. There is also a problem of equity—since a firm's economic power is an important determinant of how much it can bid—and of collusion in bidding among the largest polluters to keep the price down. These same firms may lobby through the political process to raise the over-all level of pollution which the government decides to tolerate. In this sense, demand creates its own supply. See J. H. Dales, *Pollution, Property, and Prices* (Toronto: University of Toronto Press, 1968).

it has a representative government with widespread powers to legislate and to enforce its laws and regulations. Even when the injuries are concentrated within easily identifiable groups—such as farmers or fishermen in a given locality—the latter may find it easier to get action through the political process than through the market.[6] If the group eventually succeeds, a genuine effort will be made to ultimately remove the externality altogether. Otherwise, the perpetrators of external costs will continue more or less unabated, perhaps having to incur a nominal fine as part of their operating costs.

Consequently, a laissez-faire economy tends toward an all-or-nothing approach to the problem of social cost. It will not seek coordinated tax-subsidy programs to encourage an optimal substitution of production and consumption activities which are externality-free for those which are not. Instead, its taxes will tend to become fines, in fact if not in name, which either have nuisance value or else force firms to choose between completely cleaning up production activities and shutting them down.

In extreme cases, this is often desirable. If air pollution does threaten the very existence of the human race, as some ecologists claim, it would be better to err on the side of harshness and to risk acting too swiftly rather than too slowly. By the same token, government decision makers may genuinely feel that there is a range of grants to education or to basic research, which is definitely better than no grant at all. Their concern will primarily be to give *some* subsidy from this range rather than an optimal subsidy.

However, an all-or-nothing approach to social cost is also probably likely to be more nothing than all, inasmuch as the actors who create external costs, and their supporters, often have considerable political clout. Moreover, in cases less extreme than air pollution, a laissez-faire economy may pay a high price for its inability to act with greater precision on the basis of a rational weighing of the costs and benefits involved in reducing external effects.

In the final analysis, virtually any market economy will be best advised to rely upon a hodge-podge of solutions to externality problems. The best approaches will depend upon cultural, political, and legal traditions, as well as purely economic criteria. However, we can say that an effective solution to the subproblems of pollution and congestion will probably involve the flexible use of carrots as well as sticks. Financial incentives tied to the development and adoption of more pollution-free technologies are likely to be a key ingredient in any efficient program designed to clean up the environment.

Indeed, if a judicious combination of commands and incentives can be found and enforced, a market system is likely to have the advantage here over a command economy. For the elimination of pollution, congestion, and several other related problems depends upon technological innovation as well as

---

[6] Nevertheless, these groups are likely to be less effective through the political process than representatives of large firms, industrial associations, and government agencies for reasons to be explored in Chapter 23.

national priorities.[7] The country that produces the first fume-free car may well be the one with the greatest ability to generate innovation in this area. As we have seen, command economies do not generally rank high on this scale.

15-3   Specific Solutions

Space prevents us from going too deeply into specific solutions for various kinds of externality problems, but we shall try to give their flavor. At the same time, we want to change our perspective somewhat. We have said that externalities are present in a market economy when actors derive benefits for which they do not pay or when they are able to shift some of the costs of their production or consumption onto others. We may also say that many externalities occur because state property rights are incomplete—that is, not sufficiently extensive in their coverage (see Chapter 2). From this standpoint we shall discuss *common property natural resources* and *public goods*.

Common property natural resources are resources that are scarce, and therefore valuable, to society but whose nature is such that they will be owned by no one or by everyone in common, even in countries with strong private-property traditions. Fresh air and ocean water are common-property resources, as are some inland waters, fish and wildlife, petroleum and salt in their natural states, and any other mineral not embedded in a specific locality. In medieval Europe and in certain tribal societies, the concept of private property was generally recognized, but land was often community property.

Historically, because no one could or would extract a sufficient rent for using common-property resources, they have been overexploited, often severely. Generally they have been free to all users, and both consumers and producers have overused them relative to other resources and used them wastefully as well. (To view the problem in a different light, suppose that we have a firm producing one output with three inputs: capital, labor, and a common-property resource. If the government mistakenly subsidizes the common-property resource, too much of it will be used.)

It is basically because fresh air, water, and space on city streets are free goods to all who wish to use them that we get as much pollution and congestion as we now have. These problems would be less severe today if there had been strictly enforced charges for driving on city streets during rush hours or for using up clear air and water by spilling pollutants into them. The same basic reasons account for overfishing, for the near elimination of entire species by hunters and trappers, and for the wasteful exploitation of oil reserves.

If the price of a mink or an alligator is zero in its natural habitat while the value of its hide runs into the thousands of dollars, there is a clear incentive to transform the living into the dead. A similar situation holds in the case of

---

[7] More specifically, these would be problems involving common-property natural resources and public goods, discussed below.

oil drilling. If I strike oil, the news is likely to spread quickly. I will not own all the land underneath which the oil flows, and so competitive wells will spring up. If they take oil from the same reserve that I am exploiting, it is a loss to me, although not to society. Every producer has an incentive to exhaust the reserve as quickly as possible, and care to prevent waste becomes a secondary consideration.[8]

Generally speaking, market prices reflecting the values of common-property resources to society are almost impossible to come by, except with good fortune, and this leads to at least partial reliance on fines and commands. It is now popular to speak of "user changes" for dumping wastes into inland waterways or emitting them into the atmosphere. These levies would not normally reflect social values but rather the philosophy that to charge something is better than to charge nothing at all.

Yet the use of commands has not provided an automatic cure-all. Restrictions on hunting and fishing seasons have simply led to more efficient and rapid means of catching the prey. Production controls on Texas oil wells have forced oilmen to adopt a less efficient and more wasteful technology.

We next turn to a consideration of public goods. If we wanted to find the total amount of bread consumed in a given city on a given day, we would simply add up the amounts consumed by each individual. But neither the broadcasts of a local television station nor the pleasures of an uncrowded, open-admissions public park can be divided up among consumers in this way. Each person who listens to the broadcast or uses the park can be said to consume the *entire* amount of good that is available. The same is true for many particular pieces of information unless they can be packaged so as to retain their secrecy. Public goods are such goods as broadcasts, uncrowded parks, and information that cannot be divided into pieces for each consumer. Purely private goods can be.

Figures 15–2(a) and (b) contrast the demand conditions for public and private goods. In each case d_1d_1 and d_2d_2 are the demand curves of two individuals, and DD is the total or market demand curve for the good. Thus DD is the sum of all the individual demand curves. For a private good such as bread, we add the individual demand curves *horizontally* along the quantity axis. The total amount of bread demanded at each price equals the amount demanded by the first individual plus the amount demanded by the second, and so on. But for a public good, we add the individual demand curves vertically along the price axis. Each individual consumes the same

[8] We do not mean that hunting or drilling for oil is a costless operation. However, the costs to society are understated because no price tag is put on these resources in their natural states. Moreover, this often makes it profitable for anyone exploiting them to be lavish in his purchase of capital equipment designed for the task. The classic article on common-property resources—written years before "ecology" became a household word or "Earth Day" a gleam in an environmentalist's eye—is H. Scott Gordon's "The Economic Theory of a Common Property Resource: The Fishery," *Journal of Political Economy,* Apr. 1954.

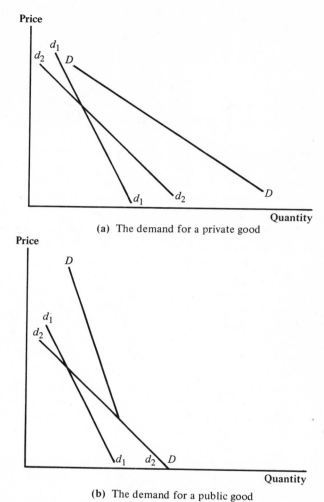

(a) The demand for a private good

(b) The demand for a public good

Figure 15-2. The demand curves for public and private goods compared.

radio broadcast or park space, and the price that society is willing to pay for these is the sum of the prices each individual would pay.

From another point of view, when one person consumes a loaf of bread, he reduces the amount available to everyone else by this loaf. When the same person listens to the radio or strolls through an uncrowded park, he does not reduce the amount available to others at all. On this account we say that bread is a private good, whereas the others are public. There is an important intermediate class of *joint public–private goods*—for example, a partly crowded city park or a public transportation network at rush hour—whose total availability falls, but not by the full amount consumed by each individual.

Conceptually, we may view a joint public–private good as a public good (or bad) in combination with a private good. For example, a city's public transport system provides two benefits: first, transportation, which is a purely private good; but second, it provides a public good by reducing traffic noise, density, and pollution. Everyone in the vicinity will automatically benefit from the latter.

Public and joint public–private "bads" also exist. Pollution will fall into this category, along with false or misleading information. More generally, anything that damages or destroys common property resources will be a public bad.

Some economists have suggested that most purely private goods ought to be financed (or purchased) entirely through the market mechanism on a profit-and-loss basis. The market is relatively efficient in adding up individual demand and supply curves horizontally, but it is not capable of summing them vertically. Many economists say that purely public goods should be financed entirely from public funds. Joint public–private goods would have their private components market financed on a profit-and-loss basis and their public components subsidized from tax monies or other funds. (In practice, these two components would be difficult to estimate, but there should be joint public–private financing of joint goods.)

Once a purely public good is made available to one citizen of a community, the marginal cost of supplying it to another is zero. Therefore, the rule for efficient pricing and production says that its price should be zero. In Figure 15–2(b) the efficient rate of output is 12,500 units—assuming that the good should be produced—where the total demand curve cuts the quantity axis. But if production is to be paid for entirely from market receipts, the price will have to be greater than zero.

The quantity demanded would then be less than the efficient rate, and the public good would be underproduced. (By the same token, it would not pay sufficiently to eliminate public bads, and they would remain in too-large quantities.) Joint public–private goods would be underproduced as well, because the market price will have to finance the public as well as the private component. For example, we have the familiar sight in North America of too little public and too much private transportation.

These tendencies are reinforced by the principle of exclusion. For example, suppose that once a radio program is on the air, anyone may tune in without charge. However, the program is offered for sale beforehand to prospective listeners. Most listeners would bear but a minute fraction of the total costs of putting the program on the air. Whether a particular listener pays will not normally influence the decision to broadcast the show. Moreover, no single prospective listener has any guarantee that the others will bear their fair shares of the cost. Consequently, many listeners would be rational to understate their desires for the program in the hope that others will pay. If the radio station tried to finance itself entirely by selling its fare to the public, it would almost certainly fold.

By the same token, as these lines are being written, marketing executives

in Canada are baffled at consumer resistance to low-lead and no-lead gaso-
lines. These pollute the air less than regular blends, but they also perform
less well in the engines of many automobiles. Because each automobile adds
virtually nothing to air pollution, a consumer using lead-free gasoline—with
no assurance that other car owners will emulate him—is not reducing air
pollution, but he is reducing the performance and perhaps the life of his car.

It is therefore the indivisible nature of public goods that prevents the market from working efficiently. We saw earlier that the market mechanism's chief
virtue was its ability to break up the economic problem into comparatively
tiny component parts by enabling the separate plans of many decision makers
to be coordinated. But what is needed here is a mechanism that will combine
plans rather than separate them.

Before he can be induced to pay an amount that reflects his true desire
for a public benefit, in fact, the rational buyer must usually receive a kind of
leverage over the behavior of other consumers. In our above example, the
household who buys lead-free gasoline must have some assurance that other
automobile owners will do the same. We associate this leverage with voting,
and in the case of public goods, it is an advantage of voting that will often
more than make up for its disadvantages vis-à-vis market choice.

The citizen who votes for new taxes to finance a school or to subsidize
the price of lead-free gasoline knows that, if the measure passes, his own
payment will be accompanied by many others according to an agreed-upon
formula. He is voting not only for his own contribution but for a much bigger
contribution from the rest of society; in any "democratic" choice process,
this applies to every voter. Leverage is not important, of course, in buying
bananas. But where collective choice is involved it helps the individual to look
at matters from society's rather than his own private point of view.

Thus, because of their indivisibility, each individual will be prepared to
pay more for public benefits when he knows that his own payments will be
tied through a general formula to contributions by many other fellow citizens.
The natural taxing authority is the government, which already has the necessary collection and enforcement mechanisms. In an era that has outgrown the
town meeting, a representative government based on elections and relying on
occasional referenda may come as close as possible to efficiently reading the
public's preferences for many public goods. There are exceptions, however,
where we may want to rely upon other solutions, even including the market
mechanism. Let us consider two examples in which other solutions appear
advisable.

At present, all television broadcasting is financed from advertising and tax
revenues. But a few economists favor market financing through a scheme
known as pay TV, perhaps to be combined with existing revenue sources.
According to this scheme, television-set owners would not receive broadcasts
in intelligible form unless they rented a device that effectively "unscrambled"
the picture. (This device removes the public-good nature of telecasts.)

By refining our technology, we can exclude any individual from watching any program until he pays for it. We now have a market for television programs which stands a good chance of proving viable in the sense that, if it were allowed to become widespread, many stations could probably survive from market receipts alone. Nevertheless, the result cannot be completely efficient because a positive price must be charged of program viewers to cover transmitting and production costs. The marginal cost of providing the program to one more viewer is still zero.

Yet, efficiency is not achievable under present arrangements either. While the price is zero, permission to telecast into any particular viewing area is rigidly controlled and is not awarded to everyone who guarantees to meet reasonable criteria for operating in the public interest. Because of the earlier-noted advantages of markets, introduction of pay TV would probably permit a wider variety of more flexible programming, resulting in more choice by the individual viewer at each point in time than is currently available.[9]

As our final example, let us look at *applied* research and development. Sometimes, research is classified according to the extent to which it is "basic" or "applied." Basic research delves more into the fundamental nature of things; applied research is directed more toward developing a specific product line or production technique.

Basic research also takes a longer time to materialize into something capable of increasing human welfare and, ultimately, is likely to affect a wider range of goods and services. It is therefore riskier, and the successful research worker will often find that his discoveries have many applications, some of which cannot even be foreseen when his work is in progress. Thus the value of basic research to other members of society often cannot even be measured.

Consequently, the successful research worker could not hope to capture the value of his marginal social product (or a "fair" percentage of this) from market sales. To ensure an adequate incentive, society will probably wish to purchase at least part of its basic research effort collectively, in the form of subsidies to universities and basic research institutes.

By contrast, our initial reaction as government policy makers might be to force applied research institutes to sell their products on a profit-and-loss basis through the market. One or more such institutes would do most of the

---

[9] Presumably, many programs would be financed both by subsidies or advertising and by sale to viewers. Some would continue to be free. The possibility of advertising makes it more lucrative for telecasters to increase audience size and thus to keep program prices lower. It will also pay telecasters to appeal to minority viewing groups. For this reason, and contrary to popular opinion, pay television will not necessarily lower the average quality of programming. Suppose that, at 11:00 p.m. on week nights, 10 million people would prefer to watch a popular variety show, while only 100,000 would watch a play or concert, if the price were 25 cents for either. Under present arrangements, there would be no concert or play in countries with mainly private telecasting. In fact, we would expect several competitive variety shows, each very much like the others.

In countries in which state financing of telecasts predominates, we would predict an overdose of culture. In neither instance would we expect the range of viewer preferences to be well served. Pay television would permit this, and it is worth noting that, if the variety show is sufficiently popular, it will probably continue to be free.

major applied research work in chemistry, for example, and the research activities of duPont, Monsanto, and Dow Chemical would be correspondingly curtailed. Subject to scale economies of management, we would then break up one or more of these companies into smaller, hopefully more competitive, enterprises. The latter would buy technology, expertise, and licenses to produce and use certain kinds of materials or products as inputs from the institutes.

Unfortunately, such a program is likely to create bigger problems than it solves. If applied research institutes are not to duplicate one another's work, they must specialize by area and so become at least partial monopolies. Even worse, it is unclear that methods and ideas can be efficiently marketed at all until they are embodied in a usable product.

Consider the case of a research institute that invents a wrinkleproof, fireproof, waterproof, dirtproof, stainproof, tearproof, and blastproof man-made fiber. The actual material must be produced outside the institute, which otherwise beomes an enterprise in the usual sense. Consequently, the institute sells licenses to use its formula, which must be protected by patent rights. However, the formula is a public good. The marginal cost of supplying it to an additional user is zero, but if a zero price is charged, the institute will not stay in business very long.

On the other hand, if the institute is completely subsidized from public funds, so that it need face no market tests at all, it will have no incentive to make useful inventions. The Soviet Union's experience (described above in Chapter 9) provides us with a case in point. The best solution is probably to permit most applied research to be done by producing enterprises, while trying to design patent laws that allow successful innovations to be copied, but not so soon or so closely as to overly discourage innovative activity. In effect we would be seeking an "optimal" environment for creative destruction and would have to accept at the outset that we could not succeed with much precision.[10]

We may sum up this chapter by noting that, when social costs and benefits fail to coincide, it will generally no longer be possible to solve the economic problem efficiently without sending some personally addressed commands, taxes, and subsidies to individual households and firms. Anonymously addressed price messages will no longer suffice to promote the "harmony of interests," and selected government intervention will be able to improve (as well as to reduce) efficiency. At the same time there is no pat formula for solving the problems that externalities raise. Specific solutions will depend upon specific circumstances.

The existence of a number of external bads, notably pollution and con-

---

[10] For example, patent and copyright laws in North America probably protect inventions for too long (17 and 68 years, respectively). Where effective, this protection results in monopoly power, but it is often possible to copy an innovation in slightly modified form at a fraction of the original development cost. Here secrecy will be the greatest protection, and to gain this, firms may actually refuse to patent an innovation, whose nature would then have to be made available to anyone requesting the information. Thus a patent may actually make a formula easier to copy with small changes.

gestion, also says something about the appropriateness of more libertarian versions of laissez faire. Because it relies upon and fosters individual initiative, laissez faire is likely to have many advantages in a country with a geographically sparse population not crowded into urban centers and whose technology is not extensively based on chemistry. If this "frontier laissez faire" spurs economic development and innovation, it will thereby sow the seeds of its own obsolescence.

However, we can also imagine a kind of mature or socially responsible laissez-faire economy whose citizens view pollution as a social taboo. The enterprising manager in such a society would no sooner build a plant without purification facilities or produce a good whose consumption caused pollution than he would destroy a factory belonging to one of his rivals or intimidate a salesman.

Such a solution would again be of the all-or-nothing variety, but it may be true that freedom from pollution is a kind of "luxury good" whose relative desirability grows with affluence. In a sufficiently wealthy society, therefore, this attitude may not be too expensive to be approximately efficient. Indeed, within a "Keynesian" laissez-faire economy, where the government's role can prove decisive in determining the path of economic development, such an ethic may even be essential to curb efficiency losses stemming from the political decision-making process.[11]

[11] Again, we shall explore this matter in Chapter 23.

Chapter **16**

The Social Technology of a Laissez-Faire Economy: Competition

16–1 A Fundamental Proposition

When the analytic eye of the economist scans the various forms that market competition and noncompetition can take among firms, labor unions, and other organizations, he comes up with what he calls market-structure theory. We have already encountered one type of market structure, which prevails throughout the completely decentralized economy. Since it is comparatively easy to analyze, economists call it *perfect competition*. Each perfect competitor always buys or sells a negligible fraction of total market quantities and has no power whatsoever to influence the prevailing price—except, possibly, to correct market disequilibrium.

Other market structures are often messier and harder to analyze. Therefore, economists call them collectively *imperfect competition*. An extreme form of imperfect competition is monopoly—in many respects the opposite of perfect competition—in which there is but a single buyer or seller called a *monopolist*. Between monopoly and perfect competition we have *oligopoly*, or "competition among the few," which many economists tell us characterizes most industries in the developed Western world.

Planned market economies should have a positive market-structure policy through which the economic planning council tries to shape the forms that competition takes in order to improve efficiency and facilitate pursuit of long-range socioeconomic goals. We shall discuss this matter in Chapter 20. Laissez-faire economies are likely to have a less comprehensive—and more negative—counterpart called antitrust policy. This is generally confined to competition among firms and, in principle, seeks to break up concentrations of market power when these threaten to "impede competitive forces." Sometimes, however, this behavior can be counterproductive, and in its worst form it amounts to a game of "cops and robbers."

According to this view, monopolistic practices represent the exceptional activity of a small minority of businessmen and are shunned by the law-abiding majority. Combines are thus viewed as constituting a *police* problem and a *legal* problem—not an *economic* problem. . . . [This] leads to a policy of enforcement which provides a few spectacular court cases to which the attention of voters can be directed, while leaving most business activity unmolested. Moreover, the high standards of proof required in criminal proceedings provide relative immunity to verbal agreements among a few large firms. . . .[1]

In any market economy—planned, unplanned, capitalist, or socialist—some forms of "monopolistic" behavior will be practiced by most firms. ("Monopoly" in the popular usage denotes any kind of imperfect competition, notably oligopoly.) Nor is this always bad. However, to begin with we want to return to a proposition introduced in Chapter 2 and called the "fundamental theorem of welfare economics," which relates to perfect competition. The fundamental theorem says that under certain assumptions, an economy in which perfect competition characterizes every market is efficient. It also says that a market economy within which the economic problem is being efficiently solved is one within which producers are following the rules for pricing, output, and input use associated with perfect competition.

We should note immediately that an economy can contain elements of oligopoly and even monopoly and still be efficient as long as producers follow the pricing and production rules that normally go with perfect rather than imperfect competition. As we shall see, this may happen and it is important because it keeps the fundamental theorem from being irrelevant. All-around perfect competition is impractical, but an economy containing a hodge-podge of competitive forms in which the perfectly competitive rules are approximated is by no means so far fetched.

A complete proof of the fundamental theorem is far beyond the scope of this book, although we shall be able to give some of its flavor. First we examine briefly the most important assumptions necessary if it is to hold.

[1] Gideon Rosenbluth and H. G. Thorburn, "Canadian Anti-Combines Administration, 1952–1960," *Canadian Journal of Economics and Political Science,* Nov. 1961, pp. 498–499.

1. Market prices must remain in the neighborhoods of equilibrium values which balance supply and demand. This is a prerequisite for any market economy to work efficiently; otherwise, price signals will reflect neither scarcity nor demand.

2. Efficiency in consumption must prevail. Relative market prices must reflect relative marginal utilities or "consumption prices" for each consumer. Households behave rationally; they are not fooled and not ignorant, either about employment opportunities or the menu of consumer goods and savings outlets available. This implies that households have easy access to reliable education and information about products and jobs.

3. Problems with external effects are being solved. Social and private costs and benefits must coincide, for otherwise decision makers will be guided by private rather than social indicators. By implication, the maximum decentralization consistent with economic efficiency is one where every decision is taken at a level barely high enough to make negligible the spillovers (or external effects) associated with it. We therefore rule out the completely decentralized economy, although, as far as the market extends, perfect competition may still prevail.

4. In an economy that does not have an "excess labor supply," there must be full employment.[2] If men are out of work who could add to the economy's income and output, efficiency cannot prevail. The same is true of any other factor of production.

5. Problems connected with economies of scale or mass production are likewise being solved.

To explore the fifth assumption further, let us divide all the inputs used by a firm into two categories. One kind, exemplified by most materials—wood, steel, cloth—and in some cases by labor services, can be divided into very small units. Moreover, the firm will only pay for what it uses. Another kind—for example, a railroad bed—is more indivisible. The amount that the firm uses is to some extent independent of its scale of output.

Thus, as the firm's output expands, it may be able to use better production methods, such as an assembly line or an automated plant, and also make better use of its indivisible inputs. If so, its average costs or costs per unit of output will fall as output expands (assuming fixed input prices), and we say that it is realizing economies of mass production.[3]

---

[2] By an "excess labor supply" we mean that the labor force could actually be reduced without reducing output. This situation is usually said to characterize many developing countries.

[3] In the final analysis there is no difference between making better use of indivisible inputs and using better production techniques at higher rates of output. At low rates of output it is impossible to make effective use of indivisible inputs such as assembly lines and automated plants. Therefore, we use hand methods.

This is shown in Figure 16–1, where we have graphed the long-run average or unit costs for a firm that experiences scale economies.[4] As output increases from zero to 100,000 units per month, average cost falls. Unit costs then remain at their lowest level between 100,000 and 350,000 units of output and thereafter start to rise. Beyond 350,000 units, the firm is using some of its indivisible inputs above their optimal levels of intensity. (For example, a railroad may be using its tracks so intensively that maintenance costs per unit of

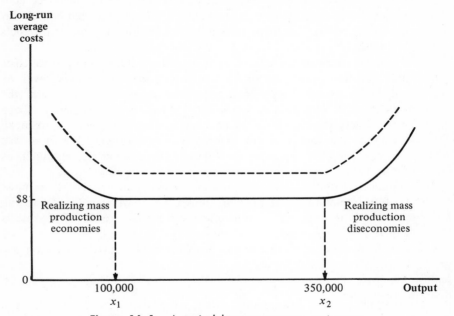

Figure 16–1. A typical long-run average cost curve.

output rise and some trains are delayed.) Eventually, the firm may add to its indivisible inputs and thereby cause unit costs to start falling again. We could conceivably get a string of ∪-shaped forms.

However, the efforts of economists who have tried to measure cost curves empirically indicate that Figure 16–1 is fairly reasonable as drawn.[5] More-

[4] Economists conventionally divide the planning horizons of firms into "long run" and "short run." Short-run planning horizons are so short that the firm has no opportunity to expand or contract its capital plant and equipment. The long-run planning horizon is long enough to allow the manager to change the amount of any input that he has available. Thus we can discuss his choice of an optimal rate of output and of *each* input within the context of the long run but not the short run. The long-run cost of each rate of output is the expected cost under the assumption that the amount of each input can be varied. The long run and the short run are both "here and now" in the sense that a manager or other official of the firm is planning today for what lies ahead.

[5] See, for example, A. A. Walters, "Production and Cost Functions: An Econometric Survey," *Econometrica,* Jan. 1963, especially Sec. 7 and the studies listed in Tables VI and VII. See, as well, G. J. Stigler, "The Economies of Scale," *Journal of Law and Economics,* Oct. 1958.

over, most firms appear to operate close to or along the flat or horizontal bottom portions of their curves, a point that will be important later.

Economies of scale take place on the production floor, but there are also mass-production economies in marketing, management, and other areas. In many industries a firm will have to achieve a certain size before it can support an efficient research establishment. The latter may be necessary to its long-run survival, and research is a prerequisite to a dynamically efficient economy.

Given the current state of managerial arts, there will be a range of firm sizes over which management's direction will be most effective. If many enterprises remain too small, managerial talent will be wasted or lie idle, and it may not get a chance to develop. On the other hand, if a firm gets too large and unwieldy, management will lose some of its power to direct, administer, and control. From one viewpoint our discussion of the command economy was an analysis of what happened when top management is overextended. Although the firm may decentralize its organizational structure, a point will eventually be reached where direction by the center grows less effective.

Risk can likewise lead to scale economies. The insurance company that writes the largest number of policies and best diversifies its risk of payout will have the smallest long-run unit costs, other things being equal. In some cases the most efficient way of supplying a particular type of insurance to a particular market may be through a single firm, which would become a natural monopoly. This would have to be regulated and, perhaps, made into a public utility.

Just to give an idea of the impact of scale economies not found on the production floor, Comanor and Wilson estimated that, among 29 U.S. manufacturing industries, the minimum efficient *firm* size was, on the average, 12.6 times greater than the minimum efficient *plant* size. The median was 5.6 times greater.[6] Although these estimates are probably biased upward by the influence of advertising (see the discussion below), they do support the thesis that the most efficient-sized firms are larger than the minimum efficient-sized plants. Inasmuch as all kinds of mass-production economies and diseconomies affect the firm's long-run average costs, all are reflected in the unit-cost curve of Figure 16–1.

There is no inherent contradiction between perfect competition and economies of mass production. However, the perfect competitor must be small relative to the size of the market in which he buys or sells. This may not permit scale economies to be realized. It is true that we are living in an era when markets tend to be larger than ever before, whether we measure them geographically, in terms of population, or by the incomes that buyers have to spend. But it is also an age when research is more important and more complex than ever before, and the "information revolution" has vastly increased

---

[6] William S. Comanor and Thomas A. Wilson, "Advertising and the Advantages of Size," *American Economic Review*, May 1969, p. 91. Wherever Comanor and Wilson have found the minimum efficient plant size to *exceed* the minimum efficient firm size, we have equated the two.

management's span of control. Moreover, because research is a prerequisite to dynamic efficiency, perfect competition on an economy-wide basis may preclude such efficiency.

16–2   Perfect Competition and Barriers to Entry

Next we make the five assumptions above and add a sixth, which says that managers try to maximize the long-run profits earned by their enterprises. Since the welfare of the owners of the firm depends directly upon its long-run profitability, this is like trying to maximize the owners' well-being. We now ask what could be so attractive about perfect competition. Basically, there are two factors, which we shall examine one after the other.

The perfect competitor is, first, a *price taker* in the sense that he has no influence over the maximum price that he can charge. Any attempt to charge more than the going price will cause him to lose all his customers to competitors whose products are viewed as perfect substitutes for his own. The *imperfect competitor,* by contrast, can offer to sell less of his product and, thereby, command a higher price. On that account we call him a *price maker.* Price taking is the most obvious characteristic of perfect competition, but in many ways a more important one is what we call *freedom of entry.*

Whenever "excess" profits appear in a perfectly competitive industry, additional firms will enter the industry until these are competed away. Potential competition thus helps to keep prices low and output high for consumers and is a key factor in making any market economy work efficiently. But potential competition is most effective when perfectly competitive market structures prevail. A similar situation holds in input markets where there can be no occupational entry barriers under perfect competition. Thus each individual is free to seek out that job which appears most attractive to him and to move any other inputs under his control in response to higher prospective earnings.

Because a perfect competitor is a price taker, the cost-benefit analyses that he will perform resemble those appropriate to society, given the six assumptions above. Figure 16–2 shows what we mean. In a perfect competitor's product market, the price measures the benefit to him as well as to society of expanding output by one unit. The constant price is the additional revenue that the firm will receive. On the other hand, the marginal cost is the additional cost that the firm will incur and also the additional cost to society. A cost-benefit analysis tells the firm to expand output when price exceeds marginal cost and to contract when price is less than marginal cost, as in Figure 16–2(a).[7] If he is rational—that is, if he succeeds in maximizing profits—he will stop about where price and marginal cost are equal.

---

[7] More precisely, the firm will decrease its profits by expanding output when price is less than marginal cost. But this implies that it will increase profits by reducing output. By "expanding" output here, we actually mean choosing a higher rate in preference to a lower one. By "reducing" output, we mean choosing a lower rate.

We may go through much the same drill for input markets. Using a particular type of labor as our example, the wage rate, including fringe benefits, measures the cost to the firm of hiring more labor. The benefit (revenue) is the value of the output or marginal product which additional labor will create in production and which the firm can then sell. As long as this value exceeds the wage rate, the enterprise will increase its profits by expanding its use of

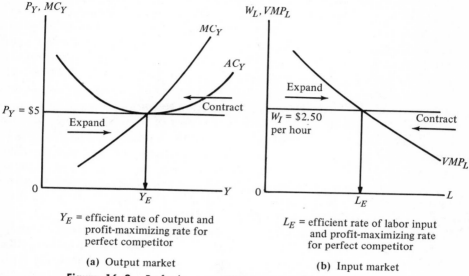

Y_E = efficient rate of output and
profit-maximizing rate for
perfect competitor

L_E = efficient rate of labor input
and profit-maximizing rate
for perfect competitor

(a) Output market

(b) Input market

Figure 16–2. Perfectly competitive output and input markets.

the input. Whenever the wage rate exceeds the value of labor's marginal product, the firm can increase its profits by reducing its labor input. This leads it to approximately equate W_L and VMP_L as in Figure 16–2(b). Our perfectly competitive enterprise will therefore set $P_Y = MC_Y$ and $W_L = VMP_L$ when it is maximizing profits.

When a perfectly competitive market is in long-run equilibrium, price and average cost are also identical for each firm. Since price is also revenue per unit or *average* revenue, the firm is now earning a zero economic profit. The question therefore arises: Why does he stay in business? The answer lies in the way economists define cost. From Chapter 3 we recall that this may be viewed as the cost of opportunities foregone. One opportunity that an investor in the firm foregoes when he sinks his capital into the enterprise is that of putting it someplace else. Thus he foregoes the return that he could have gotten elsewhere.

For an economist, average cost is therefore more than the out-of-pocket expense needed to hire inputs and get the production process rolling. It also includes a markup to cover a normal or "going" return on investments with the same degree of risk as those made in the firm. When an economist says that price equals average cost, he means that price is just high enough to give the owners a normal return on their investments (that is, what they could have gotten elsewhere) and no higher. Sometimes we say that there is no *economic* or *excess* profit when the owners are recovering exactly a normal return on their investment. (The accountant, however, counts this normal return as part of profits rather than costs. He would say that the firm is earning a "normal" profit.[8])

From an economy-wide viewpoint, efficiency requires investments to be made in those industries where their social return is greatest. Since we are assuming that social and private yields are the same, we may say that investments should go to those industries where excess profits—or above-normal yields—are being made. This is the function of freedom of entry. When a positive economic profit is being earned in an industry, it acts like a magnet to draw investments from firms who wish to enter. The bigger the excess profits, the bigger the magnet, other things being equal.

On input markets, efficiency requires factors of production to go to firms where the values of their marginal products are highest, provided the cost to the mover is not greater than the additional benefit society will receive. Here the essential thing is that higher productivities—and, more precisely, higher values of marginal products—should act like bigger magnets for inputs to move. Since the value of each input's marginal product is equal to the price paid the input, including fringe benefits, the condition is fulfilled.

Essentially, perfect competition is efficient because price signals accurately reflect marginal costs and benefits and because goods and resources move freely. We now switch the scene to imperfect competition to see how inefficiency can arise there. To keep matters simple, let us consider a monopolist who is the sole seller of a particular good or service. Once again we shall picture him maximizing long-run profits. However, the cost-benefit analysis that he will apply to determine how much of each output to produce and of each

---

[8] We can illustrate the way in which the economist's concept of profits (or "economic profits") diverges from that of the accountant (or "accounting profits") with the following example. Suppose that we have a firm whose opportunity cost of financing investment is 8 per cent. (This is the return foregone by not choosing the next best alternative to putting money into the firm.) Suppose that we have a board of directors sitting down to finalize a five-year capital-spending program. During the five years in question, the cost of financing investment is not expected to change. The board decides to build a new plant. Construction and installation will take one year, and the cost, to be paid out during that year, is $100 million.

We also assume that the board expects gross recipts to reach $30 million per year. Annual labor and materials costs, taxes, and depreciation are expected to amount to $20 million. This leaves a net of $10 million, which is 10 per cent of $100 million. Thus the board is expecting a 10 per cent return on its investment.

Nevertheless, according to the economist, the rate of profit is just 2 per cent, or $2 million per year. He calculates as follows: Total receipts are $30 million. Total costs equal $20 million worth of taxes, depreciation, labor, and materials plus $8 million (or 8 per cent of $100 million) foregone when the money is committed to the project in question. Thus total costs are $28 million and total profits, the difference between total revenues and costs, are $2 million.

The accountant, on the other hand, will lump the $8 million in foregone earnings into profits. (It does, after all, represent a flow of cash into the firm.) Thus accounting profits are larger than economic profits (here 10 per cent of the total investment) and accounting costs are smaller than economic or opportunity costs by the same amount.

input to hire differs from the cost-benefit analysis appropriate to society, even though no external effects are presumed to exist. More precisely, the price of a good no longer measures the benefit to the monopolist from producing and selling more of it. Consider the following example.

A perfectly competitive wheat farm faces a price per bushel of $1. If the farm brings 1,000 bushels to market, it can sell them for $1,000. Should it decide to produce and sell 1,100 bushels, the farm will earn $1,100. The gain from output expansion is $100, or $1 per bushel. This is equal to the price of the wheat.

By contrast, the sole seller of Chevrolets in a medium-sized community faces a downward-sloping demand curve. If he sets his price at $3,000, he can sell 1,000 Chevelles, we suppose, for a total revenue of $3,000,000 during a specified time period. On the other hand, if he wants to sell 1,100 Chevelles in the same market over the same period of time, he must cut his price to $2,800. This gives him a total revenue of $3,080,000, or a net gain of $800 per car.

This net gain will always be *less than* the price when the demand curve is downward-sloping. Conceivably it could become negative—that is, the gain could become a loss. This would happen here if, at a price of $2,600, the dealer could only sell 1,180 vehicles, for a total revenue of $3,068,000.

Economists call this per unit addition to total revenue at higher rates of output the *marginal revenue* of the firm. Marginal revenue measures the per unit benefit to the enterprise of choosing a higher rate of output. When we take the difference between marginal revenue and marginal cost, we get the firm's marginal profit or its per unit addition to total profits from choosing a higher rate of output as opposed to a lower one. When marginal revenue exceeds marginal cost, the firm should choose the higher rate of output. When marginal cost exceeds marginal revenue, it should choose the lower rate.

It will eventually find its profit-maximizing rate of output, X_π, where marginal revenue and marginal cost are approximately the same. Figure 16–3 shows this. Because marginal revenue is less than price (measured along the demand curve) the firm produces less than the efficient rate of output, X_E, where price equals marginal cost (or where the demand and marginal cost curves intersect). That is, X_π is less than X_E.

From a slightly different standpoint, as long as the firm is a price taker, price and marginal revenue are identical, as in our example with the wheat farmer. Since the price measures the per unit benefit to society while the marginal revenue measures the per unit benefit to the firm, there is no contradiction between the two. However, let us return to the auto dealer facing his downward-sloping demand. He can sell 1,000 Chevelles for $3,000 apiece or 1,100 Chevelles at $2,800. If he chooses the higher rate, he must accept a lower price—not only on the additional 100 units that he would sell—but on the previous 1,000 units as well.[9] The latter factor is not present under per-

---

[9] We assume, for now, that he does not price-discriminate—that is, he does not charge different prices for different automobiles sold to different customers. In practice he probably would discriminate to some extent.

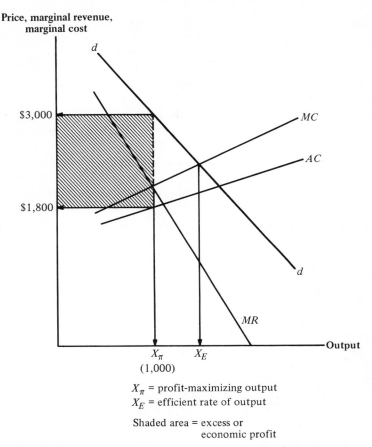

Price, marginal revenue, marginal cost

Figure 16–3. Monopoly price and output under profit maximization.

fect competition, and it makes the benefit to the enterprise from output expansion *less* than the benefit to society.

Consequently, the manager chooses an output that is less than the efficient rate and charges a price above marginal cost. We shall omit the analogous drill for the input side. Its outcome would show the monopolistic buyer hiring too little of the input—in comparison with the efficiency norm—and paying too low a price or wage for it.

However, this cannot be the end of the story because the firm is earning an excess profit above its opportunity cost. In Figure 16–3 the profit-maximizing price is $3,000 per unit, while average costs are $1,800, including a normal return on invested capital. Economic profits are $1,200 per unit, and with $1,000 units being sold, total economic profits come to $1,200,000. This is the area of the shaded rectangle in Figure 16–3.[10] These profits would

[10] We use the formula from geometry, which says that the area of a rectangle equals its base (or quantity) times its height (or profit per unit).

draw additional competition into the industry unless entry were too expensive or blocked for some reason. Our Chevrolet dealer above was undoubtedly the only retail outlet licensed by General Motors to sell Chevelles within his territory.

Other intermediate-priced cars will provide some competition, assuming that collusion between local dealerships is not complete. However, whereas farmer Brown's wheat and farmer Jones' wheat are perfect substitutes, Fords and Chevrolets are *imperfect* substitutes in the eyes of potential buyers. A rise in the price of Fords relative to the price of Chevrolets will not cost Ford dealers all their customers. They will retain some clientèle and are therefore free to do some price making.

Generally speaking, we say that there are barriers to entry into an industry when the firms already there can earn a higher return on their investments (within the industry) than firms who may consider entering. This higher return does not result from better all-around management but can be assigned just to the fact that the enterprise is already there. Not surprisingly, strong empirical evidence shows that high barriers to entry go hand-in-hand with persistent (monopoly) pricing above marginal cost.[11] We may divide entry barriers into two categories:

1. *Scale or "natural"* barriers. We have already mentioned that many firms must be large relative to the markets which they supply in order to realize all of their potential scale economies. Consequently, the average cost curves of these firms may fall over a range of output that is a significant fraction of the industry-wide total.

Returning to Figure 16–1, suppose that the entire industry is meeting demand at 500,000 units of output. Then at most five firms could operate in such an industry if all had about the same cost curves and all were to reach their lowest levels of average cost. If a sixth firm were to enter, he might have to produce at such a scale to realize his economies of mass production that he and at least one of the established firms would be driven into the red. Market demand is simply not large enough to accommodate six firms of efficient size. The scale at which a sixth firm would have to come in effectively keeps him out and thereby becomes an entry barrier.[12]

We normally associate natural or scale barriers with large firms, but technically they need only be large *relative* to the markets they supply. When scale economies are so great that the market has room for only one firm, we say that the industry in question is a natural monopoly. The usual examples

---

[11] See John Palmer, "Barriers to Entry as a Measure of a Firm's Monopoly Power," Research Report 7124, London, Canada, University of Western Ontario, Department of Economics, and references cited. Alternatively, see H. Mann, "Asymmetry, Barriers to Entry, and Rates of Return in Twenty-six Concentrated Industries, 1948 to 1957," *Western Economic Journal,* Mar. 1970, and references cited.

[12] It could happen that the newcomer was more efficient for some reason than an existing firm which he then "bumps" out of the industry. It remains true, however, that market demand is not large enough to accommodate six firms of efficient size.

of natural monopolies are public utilities and railroads, although any kind of mass-production economy can give rise to this phenomenon.

2. *"Artificial" barriers to entry.* An industry has an artificial barrier whenever a prospective entrant automatically has his long-run average cost curve shifted up by a premium that existing firms do not have to pay. Once again the premium can be assigned simply to the fact that some companies are already established in the industry whereas others are not. For example, in Figure 16–1 the dashed curve might confront newcomers while the solid curve describes the alternatives facing an established firm. More generally, there is at least one rate of output at which a prospective entrant will face higher costs simply because he is not already established in the industry.

The would-be entrant is penalized because he lacks access to specialized inputs, because the established firms control the best sources of supply or have easily recognized brand names, or because they are protected by special subsidies, patents, copyrights, licenses, tariffs, political influence, or agreements. The question of size of firms is not paramount in discussing artificial barriers. Rather, the established enterprises occupy a privileged position.

The privilege may arise because a steel firm owns all the available iron ore mines or all the transport facilities for moving the ore. It may also arise because a few firms have access to important information—for example, about the future economic activities of government—which is not generally available. Advertising and lobbying may create artificial barriers, as may agreements among firms to give one another regional monopolies.[13] By the same token, artificial occupational entry barriers will exist whenever there is discrimination among job seekers on some basis other than ability or aptitude. For instance, union members might be hired before nonunion workers. Within the union, discrimination will often occur on a seniority basis.

Artificial and scale barriers will coexist in many industries. If the established firms in these industries are profit maximizers, they will produce less, charge higher prices, and take home larger profits than if scale barriers alone were protecting them. When excess or "monopoly" profits are protected by entry barriers, we sometimes call these profits "monopoly rents." Firms would be willing to produce the same or even a higher rate of output at a lower price and a lower profit margin. Likewise, when professional associations or labor unions prop up wages and salaries behind occupational entry barriers, we sometimes say that these incomes have a monopoly rent component.

Finally, let us ask how we may identify the departure from efficiency caused by an oligopolist or monopolist with a corresponding departure of

---

[13] Bain divides artificial entry barriers into three categories: (1) *Product differentiation barriers* resulting from brand loyalty by users; (2) *absolute cost barriers,* resulting from special access to natural resources, patents, copyrights, important information, and so on, or due to trade barriers; (3) *imperfect competition among banks and other lenders of investible funds.* This may result in higher borrowing costs to new firms, especially if large amounts of capital are required to get started. See J. S. Bain, *Barriers to New Competition* (Cambridge, Mass.: Harvard U.P., 1956).

his price messages from complete anonymity. Here we can best think of the manager as sending one message, normally the price of the good, to outside parties and another, normally marginal revenue, to himself upon which he bases his own decisions and his orders to subordinates. Marginal revenue thereby becomes a kind of "internal price" which departs from the quoted price except in the case of perfect competition. In addition, imperfect competitors will often price discriminate in the more usual sense of charging higher prices of some buyers than of others for the same product. This must be inefficient because at least one of these prices will necessarily depart from marginal cost.

It is the fashion among economists today to think of any good or service as a bundle of "characteristics"—that is, as so much prestige, security, warmth, status, sex symbol, and juiciness. Using this idea we can also view misleading advertising in terms of a departure from complete anonymity. Advertising can be informative, and informative advertising, like any other activity, should be expanded as long as its marginal cost is less than the value of the marginal benefit it provides to at least one consumer.

However, firms will have an incentive to overemphasize the most desirable characteristics of their products and underemphasize those which they feel most consumers will find least desirable. Few beer commercials dramatize alcoholism or hangovers. Perhaps every reader can identify with the man who ordered "minced filet of beef" and then heard the waitress in the kitchen shouting for "one large hamburger." Consequently, many households will expect to get a somewhat different bundle of characteristics than the product actually embodies. The prices they pay for various characteristics therefore diverge from the prices they believe they are paying at the time of the purchase.

16-3   The (Shudder) Evil of Monopoly

An unregulated, profit-maximizing monopoly redistributes income in favor of itself; that is what those excess profits are all about. However, this is not the "welfare loss" from monopoly to which the mainstream of Western economic thought has generally referred, since most economists shy away from making value judgments. Such a monopolist also raises price and restricts output below the level consistent with economic efficiency. This is, in part, to what the welfare loss refers. However, the monopolist restricts output by reducing the flow of inputs going to work in his industry. If these resources do not remain idle, they go to work in more competitive sectors of the economy, where they raise output and partially make up for the monopolist's restrictive practices.

However, the increased output in the competitive sectors can only partly make up for monopolistic restrictions, and that is what the welfare loss is about. It is entirely an efficiency loss. Because of monopoly it would in theory be possible to make some people better off without making any others worse off. To give away the plot in advance, we may make the following statements.

1. *Monopoly in output markets for final use goods tends to cause inefficient coordination of production and consumption.* The pattern of aggregate supply does not correspond to users' preferences because the monopolist responds to demand by raising price above marginal cost. The condition for efficient coordination of production and consumption is that the ratio of marginal utilities or "consumption prices" for each consumer should equal the ratio of marginal costs for any producer. If we have two goods, X and Y, this becomes

$$\frac{MC_X}{MC_Y} = \frac{MU_X}{MU_Y}$$

However, the rational consumer equates his consumption tradeoffs with the ratio of market prices:

$$\frac{MU_X}{MU_Y} = \frac{P_X}{P_Y}$$

and we shall assume that Y is produced to the point where $P_Y = MC_Y$.

By contrast, good X is the product of a profit-maximizing monopolist who sets marginal revenue equal to marginal cost, as in Figure 16–3. Since the price is greater than marginal revenue, price is also greater than marginal cost. In particular, P_X and MC_X are not equal. Therefore,

$$\frac{P_X}{P_Y} \text{ does not equal } \frac{MC_X}{MC_Y}$$

and consequently,

$$\frac{MU_X}{MU_Y} \text{ does not equal } \frac{MC_X}{MC_Y}$$

The condition for efficient coordination of production and consumption is violated. In fact, consumers would prefer to get more X and would be willing to receive less Y in exchange.

In this sense resources are misallocated between production processes with too many going to the competitive and not enough to the monopoly sectors. Sometimes we say that this is allocative inefficiency, and allocative inefficiency is what the "evil" of monopoly, as conventionally interpreted, is about.

2. However, we may also have *monopoly in markets for primary (or nonproduced) inputs* which will tend to cause inefficiency in production, forcing an economy inside its production-possibility frontier. This is true of a profit-maximizing monopolistic buyer of an input, and it may also be true of a monopolistic seller, whether this be a labor union or a professional association. As a result of restrictive practices by either the buyer or the seller, some input prices will not reflect the values of their marginal products, being either greater or less.

3. *Monopoly in markets for intermediate goods* may cause inefficiency both in production and in the coordination of production and consumption because intermediate goods are the outputs of one set of production processes and the inputs to another.

Space allows us to explore just one case in detail, and we shall choose case 1 because it appears to have the most interesting applications. To do so we are forced by the two-dimensional paper on which we write to return to the little two-cylinder world of Chapter 3. This world, we recall, contains two people (or two identifiable groups of individuals) consuming two goods, wine (X) and bread (Y). To match the context above, we suppose wine to be produced by a profit-maximizing single seller while bread is manufactured within a competitive industry. This is a black-and-white world, whereas the real one consists of shades of gray representing various kinds and degrees of imperfect competition, notably oligopoly. Therefore, once we have run through the basic drill, we shall leap at the chance to modify our analysis toward greater realism.

We can take an early step in this direction by assuming that imperfectly competitive firms face average or unit-cost curves like the one drawn in Figure 16–1. Empirical studies show that, by and large, they tend to operate close to or along the flat bottom portions of their curves. Here it can be shown that average and marginal costs are at least approximately equal.[14] In Figure 16–4 they are the same between the parentheses on the long-run average cost curve. Without too much loss of generality, we can assume that the firm operates here.

In addition, when the demand curve facing the firm is a straight line, the profit-maximizing rate of output, X_π, will be just half the efficient rate, X_E, where price and marginal cost are the same. If the demand curve is a curved line, X_π will be either greater or less than half the efficient rate, but there is no harm in taking the simplest case for purposes of illustration.[15] Consequently, if the monopolist were meeting demand where price equals marginal cost, he would produce 100,000 cases of wine per year, but he decides instead to meet it at 50,000 cases, where marginal cost intersects marginal revenue. The 50,000 cases will sell at a higher price, $12 as opposed to $8.

The effect of this shows up on our little society's production-possibility frontier graphed in Figure 16–5(a). If the monopoly were to bottle, pack and sell 100,000 cases, the economy would achieve an efficient solution at E, where the ratio of marginal utilities for each consumer matches the ratio of marginal costs. That is,

$$\frac{MU_X}{MU_Y} = \frac{MC_X}{MC_Y}$$

[14] For a demonstration, see any good economic-principles text, for example, Lloyd Reynolds, *Economics: A General Introduction* (Homewood, Ill.: Irwin, 1966), pp. 175–180.

[15] For a demonstration of the relation between X_π and X_E, see C. E. Ferguson, *Microeconomic Theory* (Homewood, Ill.: Irwin, 1969), pp. 93–95.

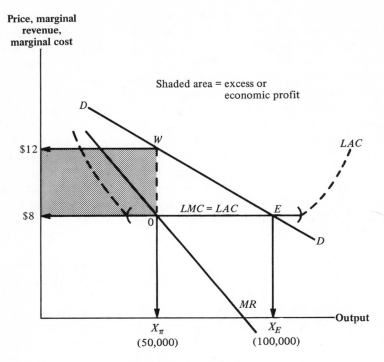

Price, marginal
revenue,
marginal cost

Shaded area = excess or
economic profit

X_π = profit-maximizing output
X_E = efficient rate of output

Figure 16–4. The efficient versus the profit-maximizing rate of output for a monopoly facing constant costs and a linear demand curve.

and efficiency in distribution prevails. Given the existing distribution of welfare, everyone is as well off at E as he can be made, subject to the economy's production (or, more generally, consumption) possibility frontier. Corresponding to E, there will be a position $\bar{E}$, along the efficiency frontier in Figure 16–5(b).

To analyze the purely efficiency impact of monopoly, we must keep the distribution of welfare fixed. Let us therefore assume that the first individual or group is twice as well off as the second, so that we are always somewhere along the line $U_I = 2U_{II}$ in Figure 16–5(b). (Any other distribution would serve the purposes of illustration equally well.) Every move we take along or inside the production-possibility frontier will mirror itself in a corresponding move along this line.

In fixing the distribution of welfare, we enable ourselves to index social welfare solely in terms of the global quantities of goods and services consumed. This leads us to the social indifference curves in Figure 16–5(a). The higher the indifference curve that society can achieve, the better off everyone is. Once

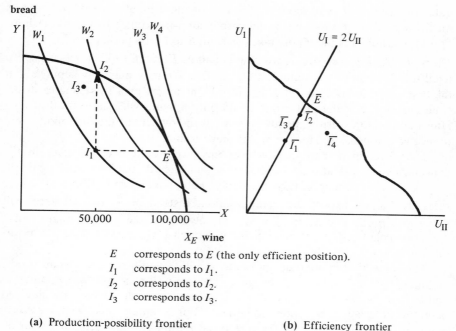

bread

E corresponds to E (the only efficient position).
I_1 corresponds to I_1.
I_2 corresponds to I_2.
I_3 corresponds to I_3.

(a) Production-possibility frontier   (b) Efficiency frontier

Figure 16–5. The welfare loss from monopoly.

again we see that E is the "best" point, where marginal costs and prices are equal in all industries and everyone's welfare is maximized.

If we start out from E and consider only the effect of the monopoly restriction on output, the economy would exchange its spot at E for I_1 inside the production-possibility frontier. This lies directly above the 50,000 units mark along the X axis. Some resources will be unemployed at I_1. The analogous move takes us from $\bar{E}$ on the efficiency frontier, down the line $U_{\rm I} = 2U_{\rm II}$, to $\bar{I}_1$. (To preserve the same distribution of welfare, we suppose that owners of idle resources, including labor, are being paid unemployment compensation.) However, if we suppose instead that these resources are at work in the competitive industry producing bread, the economy will move to I_2, directly above I_1. Because more bread is being produced than at I_1, and no less wine, the economy is better off at I_2 than at I_1. In Figure 16–5(b) it is at $\bar{I}_2$, above $\bar{I}_1$. Because of the inefficient coordination of production and consumption, it is still worse off than at E, achieving indifference curve W_2, below W_3.

Once again, the problem results because the monopolist responds to demand partly by raising price above marginal cost and restricting output. As a consequence, the pattern of production corresponds less well to consumer preferences at I_2 than at E. To return to E, it would be necessary to reallocate resources away from the competitive and into the imperfectly competitive industries. When we add monopoly in one or more input markets, the system makes a final shift to I_3 inside the production-possibility frontier. In short, (profit-maximizing) monopoly takes us from E to I_2 and perhaps to I_3.

At I_2 (or $\bar{I}_2$) everyone is worse off than at E (or $\bar{E}$). This is because we fixed the distribution of welfare at $U_I = 2U_{II}$. We may plausibly suppose that the first group is better off at I_2 because its members own more shares in the wine industry. But the first group could only remain twice as well off at E—after the monopoly firm expands output—if the owners of the monopoly were to receive compensation for the profits they sacrifice.

Therefore, in a many-person economy, we would find ourselves in the concentrated cost-scattered benefits case considered in Chapters 2 and 15. Any real-world monopolist knows that if he expands production and lowers price, he cannot expect full compensation. Instead of $\bar{E}$, the economy will move to a position such as $\bar{I}_4$, where the owners of the monopoly are worse off. An unregulated, profit-maximizing monopolist would try to keep the economy at I_2.

The same kind of analysis applies to subsidies and taxes—unless all goods, including leisure, are taxed at the same rate—as well as to price discrimination and to many kinds of external effects. In each case, resources are misallocated between different production activities. (For example, too few resources would probably go to sectors that are taxed the most.) The economy is again reoriented around its production or consumption-possibilities frontier away from the position where efficient coordination of production and consumption prevails.

To modify the above example, suppose that firms in both industries follow the marginal-cost pricing rule. However, the protestant ethic predominates, resulting in sales and excise taxes on wine amounting to 50 per cent. Bread receives only a standard 5 per cent sales tax. In each instance the tax will raise the average and marginal costs to producers of supplying their goods to market. But the increase felt by the wine producer will be far greater, and the mix of the two outputs will change toward fewer bottles of wine per loaf of bread.

Similarly, consider once again the case of the detergent company polluting a bay that has been a prime source of catch for a local fishery. For simplicity, we assume that both enterprises produce where prices equal marginal *private* costs. Since the detergent manufacturer kills some fish in the bay and contaminates others, it raises marginal costs to the fishery and forces the latter to curtail output. If Y stands for the volume of detergent production and X represents the output of ready-to-cook fish, the result of this cost shifting can easily be a reorientation from E to I_2.

Finally, to complexify our original argument slightly, let us divide the economy into three sectors. Producers of X will again restrict output and charge a price above marginal cost. Producers of Y will again produce to the point where price equals marginal cost. Z will index production in a bureaucratic sector, given our definition in Chapter 10. By making our analysis there a bit more rigorous and incorporating it into the above, we could show that too *much* Z will be produced in comparison with the efficiency norm.[16] That is, the bureaucratic sector will overexpand, *and* it will also charge too much for its product. Once again, the imperfectly competitive or monopoly sector will produce too little, and the production of Y may equal, exceed, or fall short of the efficient level.

16–4   How Great Is the Efficiency Loss from Monopoly?

How great, indeed? Many economists have tried to measure it, principally for the U.S. economy. From Chapter 5 we know that a key ingredient is the percentage gap between price and marginal social cost.[17] In the example above, the markup of price over opportunity cost was no less than 50 per cent. The percentage gap (or the percentage markdown of marginal cost from price) is a whopping 33 per cent. Under reasonable assumptions, the efficiency cost of monopoly power equals about 3 per cent.[18]

What evidence the "real" world provides, however, suggests that 8 per cent is a more reasonable markup figure. That is, price is marked up over out-of-pocket expenses to cover a normal return on the capital invested in the firm plus another 8 per cent, on the average, as a consequence of "monopoly power." [19]

The associated efficiency loss is on the order of *0.1 per cent* of GNP or less. In an economy whose real gross national product per capita is growing at approximately 3 per cent per year; this represents a loss of less than one month's growth. Although the estimates apply to the United States, there is no reason to expect very high efficiency losses due to imperfections in com-

[16] See W. A. Niskanen, "The Peculiar Economics of Bureaucracy," *American Economic Review,* May 1968. This conclusion depends upon the bureau's not being too internally inefficient. Otherwise, it would continue to absorb too many resources relative to the efficiency norm, but might actually produce a *lower* rate of output with these. We shall discuss internal or X inefficiency in Section 17–2.

[17] It is possible to show that the money value of the efficiency loss from monopoly equals the area of triangle *WOE* in Figure 16–4. This, in turn, can be shown to equal one-half of the total monopoly profit when long-run average costs are constant and the demand curve is a straight line. In practice, much lower efficiency losses have been measured, for reasons which we shall explore below.

[18] This assumes half the nation's output to be produced in industries where monopoly power is significant. It also supposes an average elasticity of demand equal to 1 for those industries.

[19] The most famous studies of this loss are the ones by Harberger and Schwartzman. The references are Arnold C. Harberger, "Monopoly and Resource Allocation," *American Economic Review,* May 1954; D. Schwartzman, "The Burden of Monopoly," *Journal of Political Economy,* Dec. 1960. Another article by Schwartzman worth examining in this context is "The Effect of Monopoly on Price," *Journal of Political Economy,* Aug. 1959. Finally, Gordon Tullock argues that these studies and others of the efficiency losses from tariffs (particularly the latter, in fact) understate the true costs involved. See Gordon Tullock, "The Welfare Costs of Tariffs, Monopolies, and Theft," *Western Economic Journal,* June 1967. In the author's view, the efficiency losses from monopoly would remain minuscule, even after allowing for Tullock's additions.

petition in other developed market economies. The exceptions, if there are any, would probably be confined to countries with small internal markets and producers who are protected from foreign competition. Smaller markets will permit of fewer sellers and thus imply higher concentrations of market power.

In countries whose efficiency losses from monopoly are low, the first policy implication is that other problems are likely to be more urgent. Insofar as regulation is extended to curb these losses, it should be confined to industries where the price markup above opportunity cost is much greater than average. (In the United States the drug and cosmetics industries have been mentioned in this light.) Otherwise, the recorded losses may represent the smallest price we can hope to pay to get firms large enough to realize all their mass-production economies. The losses from failing to realize these economies are *not* captured as part of the efficiency cost of monopoly. Nothing we have said dismisses the importance of scale economies. In countries, such as Canada, with limited markets, and hence potentially higher efficiency losses from imperfect competition, the problem of small-scale production may still be the greater of the two.[20]

Because the efficiency costs of imperfect competition appear to be low, some economists have speculated that economics may no longer be relevant. For example, R. A. Mundell once wrote: "There have appeared in recent years studies claiming that the welfare loss due to monopoly is small . . . . Unless there is a thorough . . . re-examination of the validity of the tools on which these studies are founded . . . some one inevitably will draw the conclusion that economics has ceased to be important!" [21]

People have questioned the relevance of economics ever since the British M.P. asked whether Ricardo had just descended from Mars. Perhaps economists have not always allocated their own resources among alternative activities in the best possible way, but it would be folly to suggest that nothing worthwhile remains for them to study. A 5 per cent unemployment rate is a disaster, even if we consider only the lost output which the idle resources could be creating.

Within the realm of inefficiency due to misallocated resources, we have yet to discuss tariffs, domestic taxes and subsidies and external effects. Here the losses often appear to be many times greater than those recorded for monopoly, notably in the case of environmental disruption. We should also add some X inefficiency to this list. Once again, the losses may be considerably higher.[22]

---

[20] See H. Edward English, *Industrial Structure in Canada's International Competitive Position,* Montreal, The Private Planning Association of Canada, 1964; H. C. Eastman, "The Canadian Tariff and the Efficiency of the Canadian Economy," *American Economic Review,* May 1964.

[21] Quoted by Harvey Leibenstein in "Allocative Efficiency vs. X-Efficiency," *American Economic Review,* June 1966, p. 394.

[22] We shall discuss X efficiency in Chapter 17. In connection with this paragraph, we would cite the following studies: Leibenstein, ibid.; Harry Johnson, "The Gains from

Applying the model of monopoly distortion developed above, in fact, we should conclude that there is too much food, clothing, and shelter on one hand (these are produced in relatively competitive industries) and too few automobiles, guns, and jet aircraft on the other. An economist reaching these conclusions may truly appear to have descended from Mars. One problem is that the effects of externalities and monopoly restrictions, insofar as the latter exist, often tend to work against each other. Any markup of price over marginal private cost by the automotive industry is likely to be more than offset by the ability of the same industry to shift pollution and highway-building costs onto others. The markup of price over marginal private cost is less than the markdown of marginal private from the marginal social cost of motor-vehicle production.

Ultimately the abilities of some actors to erect entry barriers and to persistently shift costs onto others represents a defect in an economy's *political* decision-making process. We shall explore this problem in Chapter 23. For now we note that the effects of monopoly power and of taxes and subsidies on the distribution of welfare and upon the pattern of production in a market economy are likely to greatly exceed their impact on efficiency. An efficiency loss on the order of 0.5 per cent or less may go hand in hand with a 10 to 20 per cent difference in the pattern of production [that is, a 10 to 20 per cent difference in Y/X in Figure 16–5(a)] and a corresponding shift in the distribution of welfare. Far from signaling the demise of economics, this opens new horizons.

We shall argue later that the political decision-making processes in some kinds of laissez-faire economies are likely to be neither completely "dictatorial" nor completely "democratic," according to conventional interpretations of these terms. Suppose, therefore, that we contrast the actual process of goal formation in a laissez-faire economy with two others, one more dictatorial and the other more democratic. Each will yield its own social preference function and thus its own solution to the economic problem in terms of the pattern of production (position on or inside the production-possibility frontier) and distribution of welfare (point on or inside the efficiency frontier). Let us call these solutions A (actual), B (more dictatorial), and C (more democratic).

When markets work well, the government will be able to use taxes and subsidies, including financial incentives for producers, to reorient the economy

Trade with Europe: An Estimate," *Manchester School of Economic and Social Studies,* Sept. 1958; A. C. Harberger, "Taxation, Resource Allocation, and Welfare," in National Bureau of Economic Research, *The Role of Direct and Indirect Taxes in the Federal System* (Princeton, N.J.: Princeton U.P., 1964) (see also "Comment" by William Fellner and Otto Eckstein, "European and U.S. Tax Structure," in the same volume); William Nordhaus and James Tobin, "Is Growth Obsolete?" paper presented to the National Bureau of Economic Research Colloquium, San Francisco, Dec. 10, 1970 (mimeo) (see the discussion of this paper in Chapter 6); Ralph C. d'Arge, "International Trade, Domestic Income, and Environmental Controls: Some Empirical Evidence," in "Pollution in the United States," prepared for the Atlantic Council by Allen Kneese, unpublished manuscript, Washington, D.C., Dec. 1970.

from A toward either B or C. If the positions are not too far apart, the resulting efficiency cost should be but a fraction of the reorientation achieved. (If the solutions do differ radically, we may have to rely upon commands.)

Moreover, it should be remembered that we are talking about, for example, a 10 to 20 per cent change in the distribution of welfare or a similar increase in the rate of saving and investment, accompanied by increased growth or decreased external costs. Thus the percentage gain in social welfare, as indexed by either the dictatorial or the democratic preference function—whichever is appropriate—may also be several times greater than the efficiency cost. This becomes one of the foundations on which the argument for a mixed economy rests.

16–5   Potential Competition

The real world contains few examples of completely perfect competition and probably fewer still of pure and unregulated monopoly. It is nevertheless useful to view the various observed departures from perfect competition as dimensions of imperfect competition in trying to understand entrepreneurial behavior. For our purposes there are three important dimensions—"natural" or scale barriers to entry, artificial barriers, and product differentiation. We shall consider the first of these here and the latter two in Section 16–6. We continue to assume that each firm tries to maximize its long-run profits.

In Section 16–1 we emphasized scale barriers as a reason for price to exceed marginal cost. When firms must be large relative to the markets they supply in order to produce efficiently, they will be able to raise their prices above marginal costs without immediately inviting additional firms into the industry. But, by the same token, established firms cannot normally raise their prices to any extent without inviting potential competition to come in. We may therefore view potential competition as limiting the freedom that an oligopolist or monopolist has to mark up his price. Let us try to establish a crude benchmark for this limit, assuming that scale barriers to entry are the only departure from perfect competition. We also suppose that the industry in question has become "full" in the sense that established firms are both willing and able to prevent further entry. In other words, all firms who could enter the industry at a price exceeding average cost, and thus make a normal return or better on the necessary invested capital, have done so. It is no longer profitable for additional firms to enter, and established enterprises plan to meet any increases in market demand.

It is therefore not profitable for a newcomer to produce *any* rate of output. In particular it is unprofitable to produce that rate of output—call it x_1—for which all mass-production economies are barely realized so that the firm has just reached the bottom of its long-run unit-cost curve. (This would be 100,000 units in Figure 16–1.) If a newcomer were to enter and add x_1 units to existing production, the industry-wide output would be so great that demand would only absorb it at a price *below* the newcomer's average cost and thus marginal cost (since the latter two are equal along the flat bottom portion of the average cost curve).[23] Consequently, if we add x_1 units to the existing industry-wide output, we get a volume greater than the efficient rate of output that demand could absorb at a price equal to long-run average and marginal cost.

As in Figure 16–1, suppose that the minimum level of average cost is $8 per unit of output and that the newcomer must produce at least 100,000 units to bring his costs down to this level. Assuming that private and social costs are the same, $8 will be the efficient price for this industry since this price equals both marginal and average social cost. Figure 16–6 shows the market demand curve facing the entire industry. The point on the demand curve corresponding to a price of $8 gives the efficient economy-wide rate of output, here 2,000,000 units. Because we are dealing with oligopoly, the prevailing price is above $8 and industry-wide output is less than 2,000,000 units. However, were an additional 100,000 units of output to be produced, price would fall below minimum average cost, to $7.75. Since the demand curve slopes down, a price of $7.75 corresponds to a rate of output above 2,000,000— say, at 2,025,000 units. Subtracting 100,000 units from this, we get the actual rate of output, 1,925,000 units.

This is less than 5 per cent below the efficient rate. Under reasonable assumptions the actual price will be about 2.5 to 10 per cent above the efficient price of $8.[24] We again take 5 per cent, giving us an actual price of $8.40. In some cases we may be able to think of this as a list price, and it is likewise a "stay-out" price, a price low enough to make entry unprofitable. Nevertheless, the results we have derived approximate the efficiency norm. The reason does not relate to competition among firms already established in the industry, however. In fact, we have not said whether these compete at all. Rather, price is kept lower and output higher by the threat of new competition coming into the industry whenever entry becomes possible at a price that will permit a normal return or greater on invested capital.

In our example, market demand was able to absorb a maximum of 20 efficient-sized firms, each producing 100,000 units of output, and the actual industry-wide output was, at most, 5 per cent less than the rate consistent

[23] We suppose that established firms would not contract output in the face of competition from a newcomer trying to enter the industry. This would be accommodating the would-be entrant, and we have assumed that the established firms no longer plan to do that.

[24] The actual price will exceed the competitive (here also the efficient price) by an amount that depends upon the elasticity of demand as well as the factors we have just considered. (See footnote 25.) If we assume an elasticity of 1, the actual price would be the competitive price ($8) marked up by 5 per cent (or $8.40). If the elasticity of demand equals 2, the markup will be just 2.5 per cent (that is, a price of $8.20); if the elasticity is equal to one half, the markup will be 10 per cent (giving a price of $8.80).

In contrast to Figure 16–4, the effect of potential competition is to make the demand curve facing each established firm concave to the origin (like d_2d in Figure 16–7). This can be shown to reduce the gap between the marginal revenue and demand curves and thereby to make the profit-maximizing output closer to the efficient one.

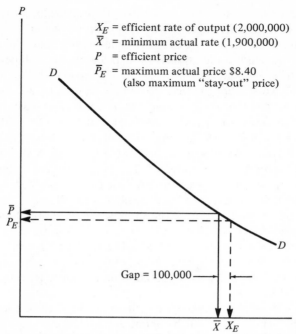

X_E = efficient rate of output (2,000,000)
$\overline{X}$ = minimum actual rate (1,900,000)
P = efficient price
$\overline{P}_E$ = maximum actual price $8.40
   (also maximum "stay-out" price)

Gap = 100,000

Figure 16–6. The effect of potential competition on industry-wide output.

with over-all economic efficiency. Alternatively, industry-wide output was short by the production of one firm barely able to realize all its mass-production economies. In a sense this is the "firm" that was prevented from entering.

We should emphasize that 5 per cent is a *maximum* deviation. If a firm could enter and establish itself at 75,000 units, without realizing all its scale economies, actual industry-wide output would be *more* than 1,925,000 units. Generalizing, if the *smallest* firm realizing all scale economies can produce 10 per cent of the efficient industry-wide output, then actual production will fall short of the efficiency norm by at most 10 per cent. If such a firm produces x per cent of the efficiency norm, actual output will fall short by, at most, x per cent.[25]

The threat of potential competition changes the shapes of the demand curves facing each firm already in the industry. (These should not be confused with the market-demand curve facing the whole industry in Figure

[25] We should emphasize that, in our example, there may be fewer than 19 firms in the industry. Since each enterprise can produce up to 350,000 units of output without encountering diseconomies of scale (see Figure 16–1), there may be only six. However, it remains true that a firm producing 100,000 units of output could enter the industry and realize all mass-production economies. Because of this, our analysis continues to hold. For further discussion and derivation, see Franco Modigliani, "New Developments on the Oligopoly Front," *Journal of Political Economy*, June 1958. See, as well, Roger D. Blackwell, "Price Levels in the Funeral Industry," *Quarterly Review of Economics and Business*, Winter 1967.

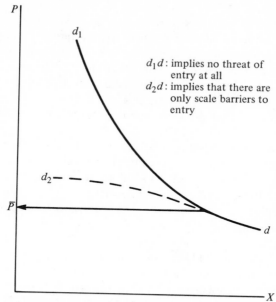

Figure 16–7. The effect of potential competition on the demand curve facing a firm.

16–6.) The higher each firm raises its price above the stay-out level, the more it will lose customers to newcomers. Thus the top portion of its demand curve is lower and flatter than the one it would face if no threat of entry occurred, as Figure 16–7 shows. Again the result more closely approximates perfect competition when the threat of new competition is present. Our analysis can only provide a crude benchmark, however, and we must now examine some problems with it.

The first is that we have said nothing about competition among established firms. Indeed, discussions of oligopoly fill literally thousands of pages in economics treatises and textbooks, and still no definitive theory emerges to explain the behavior and interaction of rival firms. The truth is we cannot say anything terribly useful about it.

However, suppose that the managers of all firms in an industry get together at a wine and cheese party and plot to keep price high and output low. If they also plan to keep out new competition, our analysis still holds; if they do not, additional firms will enter the industry, raising output and forcing price to fall. On the other hand, assume that collusion is less than complete. Some firms, for example, may give discounts below the stay-out price, or price competition may even be the rule rather than the exception. In either case average price will be lower and average quantity higher than in our examples. Thus the stated departures from efficiency still remain as outer bounds.[26]

---

[26] George J. Stigler has proposed a theory of oligopoly based on imperfect *collusion*. The imperfections result from difficulties in policing any (tacit or open) agreement among firms in an industry. See George J. Stigler, "A Theory of Oligopoly," *Journal of Political Economy*, Feb. 1964.

These boundaries do move farther out, however, when we allow both for uncertainty and for the fact that entry into an industry takes time. A newcomer cannot establish himself overnight, and he is bound to be a bit uncertain about how established firms will react, just what initial costs he will encounter, and how long it will take to make the operation profitable, assuming that it can succeed. The more uncertain and time-consuming entry is, the easier it is for established firms to maintain prices higher than the stay-out levels derived above.

If one or more newcomers try to enter, the established firms may allow this to go on until the former have committed a fair amount of capital to the undertaking but not until they are on solid ground. Then the established firms may strike back by lowering price and forcing the newcomers to leave the industry, although not before absorbing a healthy loss on their commitment. The greater an industry's reputation for being able to manhandle potential entrants in this fashion, the more easily its members can maintain a higher price and a lower total output than our example suggests.

On occasion a newcomer will succeed in entering by opening up new markets, deriving new methods of production or distribution, creating new forms of organization, or marketing new products that satisfy old needs in a superior way. Then some of the old firms may be forced out of existence while the entrant enjoys handsome profits for a considerable period of time until his idea can be duplicated or superseded by an even better one. According to Schumpeter, this "creative destruction" is the real motor force behind economic development under laissez-faire capitalism.[27]

However, we are no longer talking about profits in the sense of the shaded areas of Figures 16–3 and 16–4. The latter are the profits earned by a firm, owing to its monopoly or oligopoly position, *after* the industry has settled down to long-run equilibrium. "Schumpeterian" profits are disequilibrium profits earned by the innovator while the rest of the industry is recovering from the shock of his creative destruction.

16–6   Additional Dimensions of Imperfect Competition

The next departure from perfect competition, viewed as a dimension of imperfect competition, is *product differentiation.* We say that two products are differentiated when they are close but not perfect substitutes in the eyes of buyers. A ton of steel from Bethlehem may be the same to users as a ton from Kaiser. But a Ford is not a perfect substitute for a Chevrolet nor is a Frigidaire a perfect substitute for a Bendix. The incentive for a firm to differentiate its products from others in the same industry is twofold. First, a reduction in quality is often a more discrete and acceptable way of raising price. Second, the establishment of a brand name, favorable location, or friendly reputation is insurance that customers will not flock away to competitors whenever the latter charge slightly lower prices. In other words, the successful firm gains a clientele.

[27] See the discussion of Schumpeter's theory of capitalist development in Section 13–3.

Product differentiation is not necessarily bad. It is unlikely that consumers would want all automobiles to be alike, even in the absence of persuasion by ad men. In fact, economic efficiency requires product differentiation to take place whenever the value of said differentiation to at least one user of the good or service exceeds the cost. We did not allow for product differentiation in the above example, but the mere existence of such a phenomenon does little more than render our conclusions less exact. The trouble is that when we open the gates to advertising, quality variation, and other kinds of non-price competition, we also unlock a Pandora's box of possible sources of inefficiency not yet accounted for. The producer's hope in many quality reductions, for example, is surely that the buyer will not notice right away that he is getting less for his money. Similarly, advertising may mislead the consumer, and many selling costs are incurred by the firm just to keep pace with its rivals.

According to the famous "Red Queen" effect, each firm in an industry that is competitive in any sense must run just to keep pace with its rivals. Regarding innovation, this can be quite desirable, but it also applies to advertising. If one firm's competitors are keeping their brand names continually before the public while it chooses to be frugal and forego most of its selling costs, the management is also likely to find its market share slipping away. What is true within an industry is to some extent true among industries, all of whom are ultimately competing for the buyer's dollar.

Thus, of the more than 3 per cent of national income that is spent each year on advertising and other selling costs in the United States, the first question should be to what extent it all cancels out.[28] The television ban on cigarette advertising has not stopped the rise in consumption, despite the increased alarm over cigarette smoking. (It is still too early to assess long-run effects, but the volume of cigarettes sold in 1971 set a new record.) It appears that much of advertising's effects were canceling within the industry. If so, this resulted in swollen costs from society's point of view.

We have already indicated that advertising may mislead consumers. The cost of fraudulent advertising to the poor, who have the lowest access to protection and alternative sources of information and who are often the least rational decision makers, is particularly intolerable.[29]

In 1969 the U.S. government spent an estimated $154 million on consumer protection. This was approximately equal to the television advertising

---

[28] *Reported* direct advertising expenditures ran to $16.9, $18.1, and $19.5 billion, respectively, in 1967, 1968, and 1969. This was 2.6, 2.5, and 2.5 per cent of national income. The 1969 figure was also 2.1 per cent of gross national product, probably the highest in the world. Other estimates are Japan, 1.1 per cent; France, 0.7 per cent; West Germany, 1.7 per cent; United Kingdom, 1.2 per cent; and Sweden, 1.5 per cent. Socialist nations advertise as well, but data are unavailable. These figures understate true selling costs by omitting such major items as the salaries of salesmen. Source: Bureau of the Census, *Statistical Abstract of the United States* (1970) (Washington, D.C.: G.P.O., 1970), p. 756.

[29] For a series of horror stories on this topic, see Warren Magnuson and Jean Carper, *The Dark Side of the Marketplace* (Englewood Cliffs, N.J.: Prentice-Hall, 1968), especially Pt. I.

budget for laundry soaps, cleansers, and polishes, but considerably less than that for toiletries and toilet goods ($276 million) or drugs and home remedies ($216 million). (It was also considerably less than the *total* advertising budget for laundry soaps, cleansers, and polishes.) Income from sales of *Consumer Reports,* the major source of revenues for Consumers' Union, which, in turn, is the leading tester and rater of consumer products, rose fourfold in the period 1955–1970. Yet, at $10.7 million in 1970, it totaled a bit more than half of the combined television advertising budgets of the beer and wine industries.[30]

On the other hand, advertising may be informative. In particular, it may inform potential users about new products and thereby enable firms to enter an industry where, otherwise, entry might be blocked. If customers are not misled, advertising thereby performs a social service, and this undoubtedly does happen.

Nevertheless, advertising can also help to erect artificial entry barriers, and Comanor and Wilson discovered evidence to support this thesis. In another study of 29 U.S. manufacturing industries, they found "that product differentiation via advertising confers an advantage upon the very largest firms in an industry." For example, a firm selling 1,000,000 units of a given product per year is likely to be able to establish and maintain its brand name in the eyes of the public for a lower unit cost than a firm whose annual sales run to 100,000 units. More generally there appear to be increasing returns to scale in advertising, which will sometimes make it harder for firms to enter an industry beyond any "legitimate" economies due to production, research, and management. A number of studies, most notably of Canadian breweries, suggest this.[31]

The policy implication of our discussion is that flexible upper limits on advertising spending are probably desirable. Moreover, "objective" consumer information agencies ought to be subsidized with grants tied to more extensive and up-to-date services. There is also room for commands in the form of truth-in-advertising and unit-pricing laws. If done properly, each of these measures would help to validate the assumption of rational consumer behavior.

Next we turn to artificial entry barriers. There are 4,500 tobacco-growing

[30] Source: *Statistical Abstract of the United States,* op. cit., pp. 757–759. The consumer-protection figure is from Bureau of the Budget, *The [U.S. Federal] Budget for Fiscal 1971* (Washington, D.C. G.P.O., 1970), p. 148. The *Consumer Reports* figures are courtesy of Consumers' Union.

[31] See J. C. H. Jones, "Mergers and Competition: The Brewing Case," *Canadian Journal of Economics and Political Science,* Nov. 1967. Also, Lester G. Telser, "Advertising and Cigarettes," *Journal of Political Economy,* Oct. 1962. The references to Comanor and Wilson are William S. Comanor and Thomas A. Wilson, "Advertising, Market Structure, and Performance," *Review of Economics and Statistics,* Nov. 1967; and "Advertising and the Advantage of Size," op. cit., quote p. 98. For criticism, see Lester Telser's comments, pp. 121–123. Finally, for a partial defense of advertising, see Lester G. Telser, "Advertising and Competition," *Journal of Political Economy,* Dec. 1964.

farms in the province of Ontario, accounting for about 95 per cent of all Canadian output and the great bulk of Canadian consumption. No single farm accounts for a significant percentage of industry-wide output, and at first blush we might be willing to call this industry perfectly competitive. In particular we would expect the actual industry-wide output to approximate the efficiency norm. Nothing, however, could be further from the truth. According to D. R. Campbell, industry-wide output may be no more than one sixth of the perfectly competitive norm. The industry is, in fact, a legal monopoly controlled by the Ontario Flue-Cured Tobacco Growers Marketing Board. It appears reasonable to assume that it is a profit-maximizing monopoly.[32]

The Board controls production by allowing each farm a maximum acreage quota for tobacco planting which the farmer is forbidden by law from exceeding. As of 1970 the allotment acreage had not been increased for over 10 years despite rapidly rising domestic demand and virtually complete tariff protection. Thus output was sharply curtailed below the efficiency norm, resulting in a higher price, 50 to 70 cents per pound rather than 30 to 40 cents.

Such a high price could not prevail if additional farms were free to enter the industry. However, they are absolutely prohibited by law from entering unless the Tobacco Growers' Marketing Board permits this. Each farm either has a license to grow tobacco or is forbidden from growing it altogether. Normally, the only way to get a license is to buy a farm with one attached. Similar methods are used to control the outputs of tobacco, oil, taxi-cab rides, and restaurant meals, to name just a few, in the United States.

All this is by way of saying that when artificial barriers to entry are high, the analysis developed for scale barriers becomes irrelevant. Price can be considerably higher and output far lower than in our example. By implication, a principal goal of market-structure policy should be to keep down artificial barriers, into occupations as well as industries. However, difficult as implementing such a program might prove to be, this is only half the problem. A defect in the political decision-making process is usually behind the appearance of the artificial barrier in the first place. The ability of tobacco growers to acquire a legal monopoly exemplifies a departure from democracy that we shall examine later.

Finally, departures from perfect competition also occur because of price discrimination, interdependence of rivals within an industry, and uncertainty. We have explored these briefly, and we shall again encounter uncertainty when we discuss mixed economies.

[32] D. R. Campbell, "The Economics of Production Control: The Example of Tobacco," *Canadian Journal of Economics*, Feb. 1969.

Chapter 17

Concluding Remarks on Laissez Faire; Laissez Faire and Systemic Change

17–1 Competition Substitutes

We have been discussing imperfect competition and the efficiency loss from monopoly. We discovered that while a laissez-faire economy may or may not be highly efficient over all, the efficiency cost of monopoly appears to be low. One reason for this may be that potential competition from prospective entrants into an industry keeps output higher and price lower than would be the case if we had to rely solely on competition between established producers.

At least four more reasons exist to explain why the price markup above private marginal cost is often low. None of these relate to the classical notion of competition, either potential or actual. Instead they revolve around "competition substitutes." In market economies where the competitive tradition is not strong, one or more competition substitutes is apt to find extensive use. The most important among them are the following:

Direct Regulation

Direct regulation can take the form of direct interference in a firm's operations—which takes us part-way back toward the command economy—

or some form of price regulation. A price ceiling should be designed not only to give users of the product a better buy, but also to encourage expanded production. A firm facing an effective price ceiling cannot raise its profits by increasing price. It must do so by expanding volume. If an effective price ceiling is set just where the demand and marginal cost curves cross, the firm will be forced to produce to the point where price and marginal cost are equal, as in Figure 17–1.

However, the regulatory authorities will not normally know what exact price ceiling to set. It could remain too high or too low, and if it is too low a shortage of the good will develop. In Figure 17–1, suppose that we set a price ceiling of $11. Even if the manager sets his output where marginal cost equals this price ceiling, he will produce only 10,000 units, 23,000 short of demand and 18,500 short of the efficient rate. The low price here becomes a disincentive.

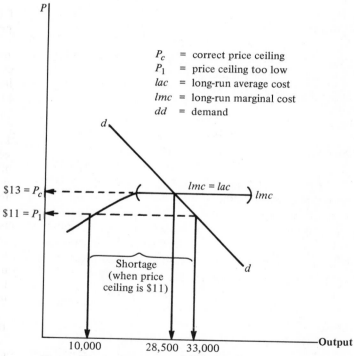

Figure 17–1. The impact of effective price ceilings.

The 23,000-unit shortage may simply mean that some buyers must go unsatisfied, as during the winter of 1970–1971, when a low price ceiling on natural gas caused a fuel shortage in the United States. Alternatively, a black market may arise on which suppliers, who have been able to obtain the good at the official price, then sell to unsatisfied buyers at much higher prices. Finally, some sellers will bypass a price ceiling with reductions in quality.

Often regulatory agencies are charged with setting prices that allow producers a "fair" return on invested capital. To the economist "fair" means "normal," and he envisages a price that will just yield investors the same return on their capital that they could receive elsewhere—that is, a price ceiling equal to average (opportunity) cost. If we are in the horizontal range of the average cost curve, average and marginal cost will be the same and thus the price ceiling will equal marginal cost. Production should take place where the demand curve crosses the average and marginal cost curves.

Nevertheless, there are conceptual problems in determining when firms are earning a normal return. To a buyer an investment is a purchase of assets that he hopes will earn him an income stream. The (annual) return on an investment to the buyer equals its yearly earnings divided by the value that he must pay to acquire the assets. Consider, then, a farmer buying some acreage in Ontario with a license to grow tobacco attached to it. During the late 1960s he would have paid $2,000 to $3,000 per acre and expected to earn a normal to a bit better than normal return on his outlays. Yet, at the end of Chapter 16, we said that this industry was a legal monopoly cartel in which price was considerably above marginal and average cost.

The apparent paradox is explained by the fact that the land, itself, was (and remains) valued above its opportunity cost because of the excess profits that could be earned from it. Similar land without tobacco-growing rights attached to it was going for $200 to $300 per acre. This was what the tobacco-growing land was worth in alternative uses such as corn and other crops. Thus $200 to $300 was approximately the value of the tobacco land in terms of *opportunity cost*. In effect the license to grow tobacco was worth $1,800 to $2,800, and this reflects nothing but the present value of expected excess profits. The prices of land, natural resources, and specialized plant and durable capital equipment will usually rise above their opportunity costs when these are principally used in industries in which excess profits are high.

In particular, a firm can earn monopoly profits without these going to its *current* owners. Previous owners could charge a higher price for the firm (or for its stock) because of its present and expected future monopoly position. This higher price would, or at least could, cover the discounted sum of expected future monopoly profits. Consider any individual or group which acquires ownership shares of a firm at a competitive price and then achieves a monopoly position. This "original monopolist" can realize tomorrow's expected monopoly profits today in the form of capital gains.[1]

If a regulatory agency permits a normal return to the tobacco farmer who paid $3,000 per acre for his farm, it would still be permitting price to be far above marginal or average opportunity cost. The farmer paid a price for his

<hr>

[1] Over time, a firm's monopoly power may either rise or erode. Presumably, there is some risk that it will fall, however, and the price of shares in such a firm may be discounted to allow for this.

land that exceeds its opportunity costs; consequently, his own costs of growing tobacco are higher than the opportunity cost to society of this activity. The farmer who owned the land when the tobacco license was granted could realize all the expected excess profits to be derived from it over the indefinite future by selling the land for much more than he paid.

As the reader probably suspects, the realizing of tomorrow's excess profits today is a standard way of avoiding regulation as well as taxation. If we are to put a permanent price ceiling on tobacco, there should be some compensation for farmers who subsequently absorb reduced land values.

Finally, the notion of a "fair" return on invested capital often receives a legal or moral interpretation rather than an economic one. The consequence is that price setting and other regulatory activities sometimes make little economic sense. Moreover, let us assume that a price ceiling is correct as of a particular point in time. Preoccupation with a morally or legally fair return will often preclude any changes in price until after a lengthy series of hearings and deliberations. The machinery for altering prices may also be bureaucratized and thus inflexible. Consequently, although we start out with the right price, adjustments over time will often lag behind changes in demand and opportunity cost.

It is worth noting that some sellers will inevitably succeed in bypassing a price ceiling with reductions in quality or servicing of the product, and so on. In the case of some goods—such as custom-built machine tools—there is almost an infinity of ways to make an implicit price increase. Consequently, widespread price ceilings (or price "guidelines") do not suggest themselves as a long-run means of combatting inflation or monopolistic restrictions. They are no substitutes for a market-structure policy that seeks to break down occupational and industrial entry barriers.

The Durability of Many Goods

General Motors does not only compete with Ford; it also competes with last year's Chevrolets, Pontiacs, and Buicks. The same is true of any durable-goods industry. If all firms decide to raise their prices in concert, some users will respond by keeping older products another year. In the extreme case in which current production capacity is but a tiny fraction of the total stock of a durable good and there is little difference between different vintages of the good, even a monopolist would become a virtual price taker. If he raised his price by a small amount, most customers would keep the models he produced in former years.[2]

There are ways of getting around this. Technological advance renders last year's models obsolete, and often such "creative destruction" will prove to be

---

[2] The definitive treatment of this phenomenon is the article of J. G. Witte, Jr., "The Microfoundations of the Social Investment Function," *Journal of Political Economy*, Oct. 1963.

a good thing. But obsolescence can also be built into a product through frequent style changes and by deliberately reducing its expected life. If successful, such "planned obsolescence" has the same effect on the demand for a firm's current production as artificial barriers to new competition. In each case established enterprises have more freedom to raise their prices and restrict output.

The existence or nonexistence of competition among established firms then becomes important. One auto producer has a limited power to reduce the expected life of his vehicles in isolation from the rest of the industry without eventually losing significant business to rivals. Such reductions will usually result from open or tacit collusion.

The policy implication is that built-in obsolescence in many industries can be as serious as artificial barriers to new competition. In some cases regulatory agencies can use commands, in the form of product specifications, to halt any decline in durability. However, for reasons to be explored later on, this method is cumbersome and costly and will have to remain the exception rather than the rule. A more fruitful approach is once again to keep artificial barriers low so that a decline in durability, which is analogous to an increase in price, will invite new competition. The success of Volkswagen in North America is largely due to its reputation for a lack of built-in obsolescence.

When it comes to business cycles, on the other hand, the durability of goods is definitely a two-edged sword. Suppose that firms or households desire a small percentage change in the stock of any class of durables they own. Because yearly production of most durables is but a fraction of the total stock in existence, this will amount to a much bigger increase or decrease in the demand for the kind of good in question. The demand for durable goods is typically more volatile from year to year than the demand for nondurables and thus more destabilizing to the economy.

Bilateral Monopoly or Countervailing Power

Bilateral monopoly or countervailing power occurs when strong buyers confront strong sellers. Except in our discussion of labor unions, we have so far assumed that at least one side of every market is perfectly competitive. Thus monopolists and oligopolists sell to much weaker buyers; monopsonists and oligopsonists buy from much weaker sellers. But when a large segment of the producing sector is not perfectly competitive, the strong are bound to confront the strong sooner or later. Suppose that a large producer of sheet steel sells to a large motor-vehicle producer. If both firms are profit maximizers, they will negotiate over price, and the outcome of their bargaining is indeterminate until we know their relative bargaining strengths and skills.

On the other hand, we can determine the quantity of sheet steel to be bought and sold if we specify that buyer and seller will maximize their combined profits from the transaction. The seller makes a profit equal to the price times quantity sold less his total cost of production. The buyer makes a profit equal to the value that he derives from using the input less price times quantity sold. The combined profit of buyer and seller equals the total value of the input to the buyer less the total cost of producing it to the seller. This does *not* depend upon the price at which the good changes hands.

Thus we may conceptualize the relationship between buyer and seller as follows. The two *collude* in determining a quantity to be bought and sold that will maximize their combined profits. Having made the total pie to be shared as large as possible, they then *compete* over how it is going to be split up. That is, they bargain over prices. A high price is relatively more favorable to the seller and signals that he has gotten the biggest piece of the joint pie. A low price signals relatively greater success for the buyer.

Countervailing power is therefore partly competition but also partly collusion across the market. Unlike collusion among buyers or sellers, however, this kind will produce not restriction but expansion of production and input use. The quantity that maximizes the combined profits of buyer and seller exceeds both the rate of output that would maximize the sellers' profits —if all buyers were perfectly competitive—and the rate of input use that would maximize the buyers' profits—if all sellers were perfectly competitive. The joint profit-maximizing rate is also closest to the efficient rate of output and input use.[3]

A detailed proof of the expansive nature of countervailing power lies beyond the scope of our analysis, but the basic reasoning is simple enough. A seller, facing some downward pressure on price from his buyers, will have to get his profits more by expanding output and less by raising price than he would if buyers were without market power. It therefore pays him to expand. A buyer, facing some upward pressure on price, has to earn more of his profits from expanding his use of the good and less from depressing its price. It also pays him to expand.

The policy implication for antitrust action is that by breaking up the concentration of power within one industry, the authorities may also destroy countervailing power. The industry in question may now be more subject to exploitation by strong buyers or sellers. It is no longer possible to view each industry as an isolated unit; rather, its place within the interdependent economic organism must be kept constantly in view.

Sometimes the problem can be handled by establishing organizations whose sole purpose is to bring countervailing power to bear. An independent truckers' association could conceivably be set up to countervail a powerful teamsters' union without impairing competition among truckers. If there are many small firms in the industry, such an association might not arise without some encouragement because of the costs involved in organizing them into a

[3] These results are shown by William Fellner in "Prices and Wages Under Bilateral Monopoly," *Quarterly Journal of Economics,* Aug. 1947. See also J. K. Galbraith, *American Capitalism: The Concept of Countervailing Power* (Boston: Houghton, 1956), especially Ch. IX.

common bargaining front. Generally speaking, such costs will impede the emergence of countervailing power.

Unfortunately, all the potential results of countervailing power are not beneficial for society. A firm can get together with its principal suppliers and try to influence them to cut off the flow of inputs to its rivals. This interferes with competition among buyers and should be prohibited. Countervailing power also presupposes a cooperative and workmanlike atmosphere between buyer and seller in which serious negotiations can materialize and bear fruit. In particular it assumes that buyer and seller can reach an agreement over prices or wages without a test of power that will disrupt production. Thus, if social-class antagonisms and distrust are added to the problems that such negotiations always involve, the system can literally be brought to a grinding halt.

We can generalize the kind of collusion inherent in bilateral monopoly to many industries that form supplier–user chains. For example, iron-ore mines supply pig-iron producers, which supply steel mills, which supply producers of durable capital and consumer goods. Some of the latter will then sell to steel mills, pig-iron producers, and iron mines. Suppose that we consider 25 or so leading industries which are interdependent in the sense of being plugged into one another through a table of interindustry (or intersectoral) flows.

We could imagine managers in these industries getting together and deciding to expand production to one another's mutual benefit, just as in the two-dimensional case, except that the transactions costs of such an arrangement may prove too high. However, under suitable conditions, the government can then take the lead as a mediator in these or similar negotiations and also use its role to implement its own growth priorities. With considerable qualification, this gives, in part, the rationale behind French planning.

If we add labor unions to the negotiations we have a framework within which a government might use moral suasion to promote full employment, along with reductions in wage and price increases. Regarding the latter, the principal goal will be to dampen the wage–price spiral through mutual agreement to avoid "excessive" wage and price increases. The principal incentive to agreement is the fact that one decision-maker's higher prices become another's increased costs. Thus labor unions would receive a lower rate of inflation from such an accord and thereby a lesser erosion in members' purchasing power over time. Firms would experience lower cost hikes for productive inputs.

Without such an agreement, many households in their roles as suppliers of labor may be able to use the monopoly power of labor unions and professional associations to win large pay increases from their employers. Firms might then use their monopoly power over households, acting as consumers, to raise prices. Once started, wages and prices could then spiral upward over long periods of time. The major losers would be those households that do not belong to any powerful decision-making bodies, but everyone's initial gains would eventually be eroded in part.

Moral suasion can become part of a broader program to control inflation known as an *incomes policy*. The success of an incomes policy depends upon the mutual trust of the various parties asked to agree to wage-and-price moderation, along with the ability and willingness of the government to penalize those who use their monopoly power to make "excessive" demands.[4]

Goals Other Than Long-Run Profit Maximization

Some real-life management teams are almost certain to pursue goals other than long-run profit maximization. The profit-maximizing goal stems from our assumption that managers try to maximize the welfare of the enterprise's owners. Management cannot neglect the owners, but in modern capitalist corporations, as well as in most socialist enterprises, there is some divorce between ownership and control.

A capitalist firm will often be owned by many stockholders, most of whom are out of touch with its day-to-day operations and even with its basic long-range plans. They are not aware of the alternatives that management rejects and only dimly aware of the alternatives accepted. The behavior of management is not visible to them. Any message to them describing managerial goals is partly nonoperational, and this dilutes their control.

In fact, within a laissez-faire economy, owners have two methods of control open to them. They can vote to remove the current management team at their annual meeting, and they can sell their stock. The actions of many sellers in concert will depress stock prices and make it more difficult for the managers to finance their operations through the sale of additional equities. When one corporation's value is falling *relative to* the values of rival firms, this is a signal for would-be management teams to seek out defects in the operation of the company and try to convince stockholders that it is time for a change. In more popular terms the aspirants will try to "raid" the firm by gaining a majority of stockholders' votes, and this process will often include efforts to buy shares. Even if they are unsuccessful, or even if stockholder dissent cannot crystallize around an alternative managerial team, the resulting pressure may force changes in current management practices and personnel.

Yet several factors warn us not to overemphasize the impact of this kind of pressure. Just as there will often be entry barriers into industries and occupations, so there is likely to be an advantage to current management just because it is established. It will control some stock and thus some voting rights that can constitute a deciding bloc in the event of an election. It may also be able to count on many votes from apathetic or inert stockholders or those who simply wish to preserve continuity and avoid any risks that a change in management might bring.

All stockholders will have some incentive to preserve continuity if, as seems likely, the new team will be less acquainted with the ins and outs of

---

[4] We shall give an example in Chapter 20.

running the firm and, initially, less effective on that account. As for the would-be raiders, they will probably find that a campaign to take over the firm is an expensive proposition.

Another source of control is the firm's creditors, notably its banks. They can raise interest rates and otherwise make it difficult for the company to borrow both on long and short term. Even an enterprise that tries to finance all its investment spending from its own (retained) earnings is likely to be vulnerable to restrictions that make short-term working capital more expensive to borrow.

When we put all these factors together, the following rough benchmark emerges. Most management teams will face difficulties if they cannot meet their debt payments, or else postpone them at a small cost, or when they cannot earn at least a long-run normal return on most of the equity capital invested in the firm. That is, management must give stockholders owning a majority of the shares at least the return they could have gotten elsewhere. This is the way in which the firm's profit residual impinges on managerial behavior.

Consequently, the firm must charge a price for its product which is at least high enough to cover its long-run average cost. Indeed, it may have to earn a positive minimum amount of (excess) profits because the expectation of these may have inflated the price of its stock when a majority of the currently held shares were bought. For simplicity, however, we shall suppose that the only hard-and-fast constraint that holders of debt and equity are able to put on the management is that price should cover long-run average cost. This will not constrain it to a unique rate of output unless there is only one rate at which the firm can avoid taking a loss.

In Figure 17–2, management can pick any rate of output between 50,000 and 135,000 units. To determine which rate will be chosen, we must inquire once more into management's success criteria. Profits are one such criterion, growth is another, sales constitutes yet another, and any combination of these is also a candidate. There are reasons, however, to suspect that on balance these motives will produce a rate of output greater than that associated with profit maximization. In describing the German economy around the turn of the century, Gustav Stölper writes:

> In this brief liberal era, the profit motive was never regarded, even by the ruling class, as either desirable or honourable. The tone was set by the bureaucracy and the army; in their opinion, the profit motive was something rather contemptible. The capitalist bourgeoisie regarded the life of the non-business strata of society as an ideal to which they tried to conform.[5]

We may view this as an effort to use ideological subversion—or as an early appeal to "corporate consciousness"—in order to degrade the profit

[5] Gustav Stölper, Karl Häuser, and Knut Borchardt, *The German Economy: 1870 to the Present* (New York: Harcourt, 1967), p. 47.

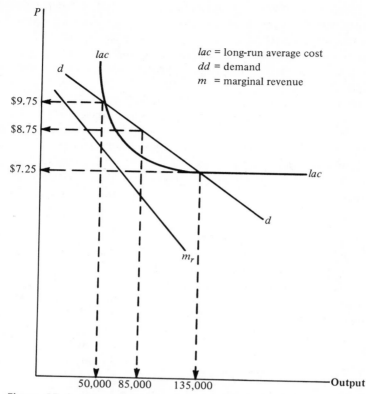

Figure 17–2. The sales versus the profit-maximizing rates of output.

motive and to replace it with some more expansive goal. More recently, economists have emphasized that even without such appeals, large, publicly owned firms will not strive to maximize long-run profits to the exclusion of other goals. Essentially, this is because managers will maximize their own welfares which the separation of ownership from control has partly divorced from the welfare of the stockholders.

Managerial success indicators will therefore reflect the way a manager is judged by owners, the public, and by fellow managers (since he wishes to be promoted). Profits are visible signs of success, but so are sales, growth, share of market, and improvements in each of these. This is particularly important when only insiders can estimate the amounts of profit foregone in courses of action not taken. The consequence is to shift the "optimal" output from the manager's point of view to the right of the profit-maximizing rate and to make him prefer the higher of any two rates yielding the same profit.

A manager who maximizes the total revenue that his firm can earn from selling a particular good or the total quantity of the good that it can sell, subject to an average cost constraint will normally produce 135,000 units in

Figure 17–2.[6] He cannot sell any more without price falling below average opportunity cost (135,000 units is also the efficient rate of output since the horizontal average and marginal cost curves coincide there). Since he must cover his opportunity costs in the long run, we shall pick the sales-maximizing rate as our outer bound to the range of production levels that the enterprise is likely to maintain.

The profit-maximizing output is less (85,000 units) and price higher. There is no reason to expect a smaller rate, and we pick 85,000 as the lower bound to the range of possible production levels. If every output in this range is equally likely, there is a 50 per cent chance that 110,000 units or more will be produced. Over many firms, the presence of goals such as growth, sales, or share-of-market maximization, will increase output, lower prices, and in many cases result in a more efficient allocation of resources than would occur under pure profit maximization.

Finally, J. K. Galbraith has argued that giant modern firms are dominated by their scientific and engineering elite, or "technostructure," upon which management is absolutely dependent for survival.[7] Consequently, according to Galbraith, the technostructure can impose its goals upon management much as management may impose upon the owners. Among the supposed goals of the technostructure is a display of technical prowess for its own sake. Although there may be some truth in Galbraith's contentions, we would expect that managers could better manipulate the goals of the technostructure by controlling its incentive pay than the owners could manipulate the goals of management.

17–2   X Efficiency

So far our discussion in this chapter and in the last half of Chapter 16 fits a bit too neatly under the heading, "Do you mean I get all of that for such a small premium?" The premium is the efficiency cost of imperfect competition, which can apparently be kept low with suitable restraints on barriers to entry and upon advertising and selling expenditures, coupled with incentives for more objective product information.

What we get in return are dynamic and scale economies plus whatever insurance for the user that brand-name identification can provide. The theoretical model of perfect competition would probably not accommodate the technological or organizational sinews of a modern industrial economy nor the varieties of haggling between buyers and sellers that characterize most market systems. The "industry of invention" would be out of place in it as

---

[6] There is an exception to this. A manager maximizing total revenue from sales will produce where marginal revenue is zero if this occurs at a *lower* rate of output than 135,000 units. For an explanation, see W. J. Baumol, *Economic Theory and Operations Analysis*, 2nd ed. (Englewood Cliffs, N.J.: Prentice-Hall, 1965), Ch. 13.

[7] See J. K. Galbraith, *The New Industrial State* (Boston: Houghton, 1967), especially Chs. II–VIII.

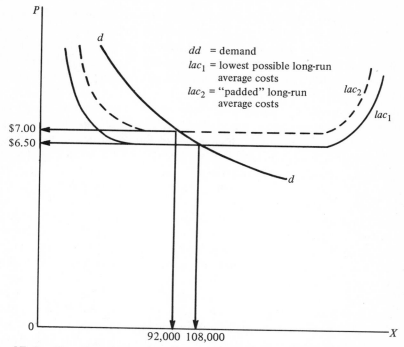

Figure 17–3. The effect of X inefficiency and other types of "padding" on the firm's long-run average cost curve.

would the automated factory and the practices of discounting from list price or negotiating contracts between industries and labor unions.

Nevertheless, we must now ask whether we have underestimated the premium. Unfortunately, what empirical evidence is available suggests that we have. There appears to be an inefficiency in the form of "padded" costs which many enterprises will experience, but which the welfare-loss-from-monopoly studies did not capture. Figure 17–3 tries to show what we mean. The solid average cost curve represents the lowest costs that the firm could achieve if its management hired optimal quantities of the best available inputs and combined these in the best possible way within the firm. The upper, dashed curve describes actual costs because management is not "best" in one or both respects. Consequently, for any given managerial goal, the firm will produce less and charge a higher price. The sales maximizer in Figure 17–3 turns out 92,000 units instead of 108,000 and charges $7.00 rather than $6.50.

It is important to realize that there are two reasons why such a firm's costs may become "padded." One relates to the kind of economic inefficiency already described—that due to a misallocation of resources between firms and between work on one hand and leisure on the other. On an economy-wide basis, too few resources may be devoted to research, to worker training, or to personnel relations. Firms may fail to take sufficient advantage of specialized services—such as consulting—thus creating a demand for these services which is too low. Because employees' pay is not related to the results they produce, they devote too much time to leisure and too little to productive labor. There is nothing new in all of this except that the studies of inefficiency cited earlier do not take these matters into account.

The second reason relates to the concept of X efficiency introduced in Chapter 3.[8] Just as resources may be badly allocated among firms, so a given firm may fail to make the most efficient use of the resources at its disposal.

We have no measurements of X inefficiency on an economy-wide basis. However, Leibenstein cites a number of case studies that try to measure the padding in the cost curves of specific enterprises, most of which is apparently due to X inefficiency. The majority of these cases occur within the developing nations, which are still "learning the ropes" of efficient management. Moreover, we shall argue that his method of measurement biases the loss estimates upward. Nevertheless, the figures given by Leibenstein are far above anything we have yet encountered. We shall summarize a few of the case studies he cites to give their flavor.

The most important are the results of International Labour Organization Productivity Missions. "In one of the ILO missions to Pakistan an improvement in labor relations in a textile mill in Lyallpur resulted in a productivity increase of 30 per cent. Nothing else was changed except that labor turnover was reduced by one-fifth." A vast number of these missions to firms in India, Burma, Indonesia, Malaysia, Thailand, Pakistan, and Israel obtained labor productivity increases of anywhere from 5 to 500 per cent without any increases in other inputs.

What they did do was to improve work methods, materials handling, workers' training and supervision, waste control, and machinery utilization. They also reorganized the plant layout in some instances, introduced or improved incentive pay, and made simple technical alterations. In India, productivity improvements ranged from 5 to 500 per cent, largely from improved work methods, while in Israel, which is not a developing country, the improvements ran from 30 to 91 per cent. In Britain, as a consequence of revitalized incentive pay plans, "the change in output per worker was found to vary . . . all the way from an increase of 7.5 per cent to one of 291 per cent, about half of the cases falling between 43 per cent and 76 per cent." [9]

X inefficiency arises because managers are inexperienced or ignorant of the best methods of organizing production, distribution, and research. But evidence also indicates that managers sometimes deliberately introduce other kinds of padding into their cost curves. The goals of management appear to include not only higher profits and sales, but "pretty secretaries, thick rugs,

---

[8] Harvey Leibenstein, "Allocative Efficiency vs. 'X-Efficiency'," *American Economic Review,* June 1966. See also references cited by Leibenstein.

[9] Ibid., pp. 400–401.

interesting colleagues, leisurely work loads, executive washrooms, a larger staff, relaxed personnel, job security, time off for statesmanlike community activities, gifts of company funds to colleges, out-of-town hotel suites," and so on.[10] In each case a manager may be willing to pad his costs a bit and sacrifice some profits or sales to realize more of these amenities, and there are two basic reasons for this.

To begin with, large firms will contain at least one hierarchy or chain of command with a number of levels in it. Parts of our theory of bureaucracy will therefore apply to them. In particular, markets will not directly value the outputs of some employees, notably administrators, making their productivities difficult to measure. Variables such as the size of a supervisor's staff will therefore play a role in determining his salary and chances for future advancement.

Second, no theory of managerial behavior can neglect the fact that, like all human beings, managers and their employees will derive pleasure from nonmarket goods. The theory of profit maximization says only that managers will try to maximize profits, *given* their consumption of nonmarket amenities, and the same is true of sales or growth maximization. It does not say that the manager will prefer a competitive rat race to leading a "quiet life" in an enjoyable work environment.

Consequently, in measuring X-efficiency gains, we must be careful to subtract the value of any nonpecuniary benefits lost from the value of productivity increases. This was not done in the studies cited by Leibenstein, which therefore overstated the actual efficiency gains and corresponding losses before changes occurred.

Nevertheless, Leibenstein's figures are impressive, and the net loss from X inefficiency may well be important on an economy-wide basis. One suggested remedy is to devote more resources to managerial education, research into organizational techniques, and diffusion of knowledge about technological and organizational advances. Government support for this kind of activity in some countries will no doubt pay off handsomely.

But another major cause of X inefficiency is simply that the firm's environment leaves management with a comfortable *potential* profit residual to play around with. Instead of maximizing profit or sacrificing profits for sales, management choses to sacrifice them for some of the amenities listed above. Empirical evidence indicates that firms begin cutting back on these "nonessential" costs when competitive pressures increase or when demand falls off due to a general recession.

Measures to break down artificial entry barriers again suggest themselves

[10] Armen A. Alchian, "The Basis of Some Recent Advances in the Theory of Management of the Firm," *Journal of Industrial Economics,* June 1965, p. 34. Alchian's article provides an excellent summary discussion of managerial goals. See also the references cited by Alchian, particularly Oliver E. Williamson, *The Economics of Discretionary Behavior: Managerial Objectives in a Theory of the Firm* (Englewood Cliffs, N.J.: Prentice-Hall, 1964).

as a remedy, along with antitrust activities designed to promote competition among established firms. What we are now after, however, is nothing so precise as our old notion of perfect competition. Instead, our basic goal is to maintain competitive pressures within most industries so that what several economists have called "workable competition" prevails there. Workable competition is an extension of potential competition.

According to one description, an industry is workably competitive if (1) artificial barriers to entry are low; "(2) the firms in the industry are . . . active rivals" and not overly collusive; "(3) the number of firms is large enough so that none is dominant. When competition is [workable], buyers have free choices among alternatives, and firms are under constant pressures to keep their costs low." [11] If we build market structures on the premise that workable competition is the basic guideline, to be replaced or supplemented by countervailing power and other competition substitutes where necessary, we may well be able to keep the premium on competitive imperfections low.

Yet our remarks suggest that success in promoting workable competition does not automatically signal the best of all possible worlds. Many of the goods that add the most to the quality of life are not bought and sold on any market. Moreover, the demand for nonmarket activities appears to rise faster than the demand for market goods as society grows more affluent. Every market economy will have to devote resources to maintaing optimal market structures. But excessive preoccupation with competition could become self-defeating.

17–3 Four Varieties of Laissez Faire

We have now accumulated enough tools to describe four kinds of laissez-faire economies, two of which we have already analyzed.

The Completely Decentralized System

The completely decentralized system is characterized by perfect competition on both sides of every market. This is a frictionless economy in which all resources move easily from one industry to another, with no industrial or occupational entry barriers to block the way. It will be an efficient economy only when external effects are not important and each market is large relative to the scale of output that enables mass-production economies to be realized. Such a system will probably work best in an environment where there is still plenty of "elbow room." That is, the population density has not yet become too high, and people are not yet crowded into congested urban centers. It

---

[11] D. S. Watson, *Price Theory and Its Uses,* 2nd ed. (Boston: Houghton, 1968, p. 266). We have altered Watson's second condition. He requires that firms in an industry not collude in any way, but such a requirement is unnecessarily harsh and would probably make workable competition as restrictive in practice as perfect competition.

would also help if the technology is still somewhat primitive and not extensively based upon chemistry since the use of chemicals in manufacturing becomes an important source of pollution.

Consequently, any real-world economy that approximates the decentralized norm would probably lead at best a limited life as an efficient instrument for realizing human welfare. With population growth and economic development, the potential disadvantages of this model would become more real. (Indeed, the system, itself, would almost certainly erode as imperfections in competition appeared.) Competition could remain as a major regulatory force, but it would have to be supplemented by competition substitutes and more centralized decision making in the area of externalities if efficiency was to be maintained. Moreover, potential competition would probably have to increase in importance.

The distribution of welfare in any economy characterized by all-around perfect competition need not be equal and would not be so except by chance. However, the absence of occupational and industrial entry barriers implies that a principal source of inequality in opportunity has been removed. Thus the notion of socioeconomic class division (for example, into "bourgeoisie" and proletariat) does not fit easily into this model.

One Part Competitive–One Part Monopoly Economy

The one part competitive–one part monopoly economy combines a frictionless sector with a monopoly sector whose artificial entry barriers are absolute. Resources cannot move into the monopoly sector from the competitive one, nor can they move from one monopolized industry to another except when established firms choose to hire them. Under the assumption of profit maximization, this barrier redistributes income in favor of those firms, labor unions, and other organizations with monopoly power. It also reorients the pattern of production so that too little output is produced in monopoly sectors and too much in competitive sectors, given users' preferences. This causes resources to be misallocated.

The case of bilateral monopoly is not normally analyzed in this context. However, we have said that it will usually reduce, although not eliminate, monopoly restrictions when two monopoly firms trade with one another. If a labor union is involved, on the other hand, the result could be more or less efficient, depending upon the union's goals. If it sets wages too high, the result will be less employment and, consequently, greater inefficiency.

The existence of monopoly power suggests a division of society into two socioeconomic classes, those with monopoly power and those without. Such a division does not mirror the Marxist one because a labor union may fall within the monopoly sector while a private farm or a textile mill produces under conditions of perfect competition. An unequal distribution of wealth will usually reflect a concentrated ownership of the material means of production. But it is also likely to reflect to some extent control over the acquisition of human capital and barriers to entry not obviously tied to ownership of material means of production.

Traditional or Customary Economy

Our completely decentralized economy is by no means the only or even the most likely system with small-scale production. Historically, the traditional or customary economy seems to predominate.

The principal identifying mark of this kind of system, in addition to the small size of production units, is widespread occupational entry barriers based upon custom. The town or neighborhood baker is likely to be the son of a baker who inherited his father's business, and similarly with the butcher, the blacksmith, the shoemaker, and so on. Most farmers will probably work land owned by their fathers and grandfathers before them and expect to pass it on to their heirs. In cases where the owner–manager has no sons or where for some reason one of his sons does not inherit the business, this would normally go to an apprentice. However, the apprentice would have trained under the direct personal supervision of the master for a long time and might be a virtual member of the family, perhaps by marriage.

Once a plumber has begun his apprenticeship or a doctor his formal medical studies, the probability of the former taking up the occupation of the latter or vice versa is low in almost any economy. For this reason we sometimes say that doctors and plumbers are *noncompeting groups,* and the same is true for any pair of occupations between which mobility is well nigh impossible. Within a traditional economy, most occupations are noncompeting groups. This is not because a baker is incapable of learning the shoemaker's trade, but because society tends in one way or other to preserve regional monopolies for established shoemakers and their designated heirs.

Because production is small in scale, occupational entry barriers translate into entry barriers on the product side. The restriction on the number of apprentices who can learn the cobbler's trade becomes a restriction on the number of shoe-making firms. In return for this protection, producers are not supposed to price-gouge other members of the community. The price charged would normally fall between that set by a profit-maximizing monopoly and that associated with perfect competition. We may think of this as a kind of "just" price to which there will correspond a "just" quantity supplied since the seller is expected to meet demand at that price.

Ultimately society is applying a loose notion of what constitutes a just income distribution to its members, and we would expect custom to play a role in this. Because the identification between producer and product is close, society is likely to attach a strong responsibility for quality craftsmanship. Medieval producers were sometimes forced to display shoddy and defective goods in prominent places around their shops or stalls.

Entry barriers may constitute an important source of inefficiency within a traditional economy. Labor and capital cannot move into those occupations where the values of their marginal products are highest. Consider a baker who has some money to invest. The opportunity cost of plowing this money back into his firm is likely to be almost zero. He cannot invest it in another industry, and no stock and bond markets will exist to absorb it. If he were to lend the money, this would probably be a personal event between friends. Consequently, if he can realize any positive return at all on his investment, he will usually put the money into his business, and the same is true of most firms.

In such an economy there is no reason for the return on investments in one industry or geographical region to bear any relation to the yields earned elsewhere. People tend to invest in their own businesses, to some extent regardless of how profitable other businesses are. From society's viewpoint, this is a waste because investment funds do not flow toward those sectors of the economy where they will be most productive.[12] The baker will invest in his own firm even though there are investment opportunities elsewhere with no greater risk attached and yielding several times as much.

In such a society, most established firms are making a profit over and above their opportunity costs because the latter are so low. However, the average economy-wide return on invested capital is lower than it would be if opportunity costs were higher, and investment funds moved easily into those areas where they could earn the highest yields. Because artificial barriers are high, the resulting efficiency loss may greatly exceed the efficiency cost of monopoly discussed earlier.

New Industrial State Economy

Finally, we have the new industrial state type of laissez-faire economy. The term was coined by Galbraith, although we shall adopt a somewhat different definition than his. For us it refers to any market economy characterized by large-scale production in many industries, a variety of competitive forms and competition substitutes, and strong reliance by firms, industries, and other production-oriented organizations upon political action.[13]

A new industrial state is therefore an economy of coalitions, formed along lines of common interest, which are active in both economic and political decision making. Inevitably, the government has some important leverage in a new industrial state type of economy. In all likelihood, it will also be a "Keynesian" economy—that is, one in which government receipts constitute 20 per cent or more of net national product.

If such a society has reasonably active and participatory political decision-making processes, political action becomes a virtual prerequisite to economic power. To obtain and maintain such power, organizations must participate directly in social goal formation. Normally, the most effective way of doing

---

[12] The yield on an investment measures the productivity of the capital the investment creates. The value of capital's marginal product will differ, perhaps spectacularly, from one sector to another.

[13] The reader wishing the Galbraithean version should consult J. K. Galbraith, *New Industrial State,* op cit., especially Chs. 6–9.

this is to exert pressure through special-interest groups, which then become lobbies or political pressure groups.

Lobbies advance the causes of labor, environmental protection, "consumerism," banks, chambers of commerce, tobacco growers, independent-coal-mine operators, automobile producers, textile mills, oil, steel, and practically every industry of any size or consequence. The political activities of key decision makers, working through special-interest groups or lobbies, are likely to be just as important as their economic activities.

Indeed, we cannot easily divorce the economics from the politics of a large firm or bureaucracy, of a labor union, or of a professional or industrial association. One complements the other, as our discussion of the "economics of democracy" in Chapters 22 and 23 will show. Moreover, in a laissez-faire economy, special-interest groups will tend to approach the political process in a rather negative way. That is, they will be mainly interested in protecting their constituents with barriers to entry, and in some cases with enabling them to inflict part of the costs of their activities on the rest of society or to derive benefits from others for which they do not pay.

The traditional class division between labor and capital can be fitted into a new industrial state, although a richer heterogeneity of causes is likely to blur this. Being a society filled with coalitions, on the other hand, it does rely upon the abilities of these groups to negotiate their differences and compromise without undue costs arising in the process. In particular, if negotiations bog down or drag out, or if tensions reach the point where serious bargaining breaks off, some people may be made worse off, with virtually no one improving his lot.

The general strike and rioting that occurred in France during May 1968 illustrate this, but so does the General Motors Strike of 1970 in North America. The lost wages and other benefits of most workers during the strike were less than the additional benefits embodied in the new contract (as compared with the old) over its entire three-year life.

When tensions become too great, a new industrial state bursts asunder in revolution like any other system. Yet the presence of many heterogeneous poles of power will often make it harder to overhaul in a violent manner. Perhaps ironically, a successful revolution is likely to be more costly than in a command economy.

By definition, there will be a range of competitive forms in a new industrial state, probably extending from approximately perfect competition to a few monopolistic single sellers. Let us suppose that competitive firms tend to earn a normal return, on the average, from their invested capital once they are established. Then we would expect imperfectly competitive firms to earn an average return which is greater than normal. Once again, most established enterprises will be making a profit over and above their opportunity cost, and investment funds will not always flow toward those firms whose productivity and earnings are greatest. This leads to an efficiency loss, but one that has been found, where measured, to be insignificant.

Nevertheless, there are other potential sources of inefficiency within a new industrial state type of laissez faire. These include external effects, X inefficiency, dynamic inefficiency due to a lack of explicit long-range goals, and inefficiency built into the structure of taxes and restrictions on international trade. The net loss from all sources together may well be large. Moreover, by introducing planning into the political decision-making process, it may prove possible to reduce this loss significantly.

REFERENCES

(For laissez faire)

Ackley, Gardner W. *Macroeconomic Theory.* New York: Macmillan Publishing Co., Inc., 1961, especially Pts, 2, 3, 4.

Adams, Walter. *The Structure of American Industry.* New York: Macmillan Publishing Co., Inc., 1961.

Alchian, A. A. "The Basis of Some Recent Advances in the Theory of Management of the Firm." *Journal of Industrial Economics,* June 1965.

Bornstein, Morris. *Comparative Economic Systems: Models and Cases,* rev. ed. Homewood, Ill.: Richard D. Irwin, Inc., 1969, Chs. 2, 3, 11.

Edward, Corwin D. *Maintaining Competition: Requisites of a Governmental Policy.* New York: McGraw-Hill Book Company, 1949.

Friedman, Milton. *Capitalism and Freedom.* Chicago: University of Chicago Press, 1962.

Galbraith, J. K. *American Capitalism: The Concept of Countervailing Power.* Boston: Houghton Mifflin Company, 1956, Ch. 9.

Grossman, Gregory. *Economic Systems.* Englewood Cliffs, N.J.: Prentice-Hall, Inc., 1967, Ch. 4.

Halm, George. *Economic Systems.* New York: Holt, Rinehart and Winston, Inc., 1968, Pt. 2.

Hoover, Calvin B. *The Economy, Liberty, and the State.* New York: Doubleday & Company, Inc., 1961.

Keynes, J. M. *Essays in Persuasion.* New York: W. W. Norton & Company, Inc., 1963.

————. *The General Theory of Employment, Interest and Money.* New York: St. Martin's Press, Inc., 1961, especially Ch. 24.

Köhler, Heinz. *Welfare and Planning.* New York: John Wiley & Sons, Inc., 1966, Ch. 4.

Mansfield, Edwin, ed. *Monopoly Power and Economic Performance,* rev. ed. New York: W. W. Norton & Company, Inc., 1968.

Modigliani, Franco. "New Developments on the Oligopoly Front," *Journal of Political Economy,* June 1958, Pts. 1, 2.

Schumpeter, Joseph A. *Capitalism, Socialism, and Democracy.* New York: Harper & Row, Publishers, 1950, Pt. 2.

Smith, Adam. *The Wealth of Nations* (Edwin Canaan, ed.). New York: Modern Library, 1937, Bk. II.

Weiss, Leonard W. *Economics and American Industry.* New York: John Wiley & Sons, Inc., 1961.

Part **FIVE**

Chapter 18

The Social Technology of Mixed Economies: An Overview

18–1 Introduction

The period between World Wars I and II produced one of the great economic debates of all time, a debate whose issues are still very much the subject of controversy. Two interrelated questions were raised: (1) Would an efficient solution to the economic problem exist in a socialist system, and (2), even if it would, could it be found in practice? In other words, could a socialist society actually hope to allocate inputs among its various production processes and distribute the fruits of production among society's various economic actors so as to solve the economic problem efficiently?

Arrayed on one side of the debate were the intellectual forces of the right-wing Austrian school led by Ludwig von Mises.[1] It was von Mises who initially flung the gauntlet with a charge that economic efficiency was logically impossible under socialism. His gauntlet was picked up by the Polish economist Oskar Lange,[2] and by the American Abba Lerner,[3] along with a number of their less

[1] L. von Mises, "Economic Calculation in the Socialist Commonwealth"; reprinted in F. A. Hayek, ed., *Collectivist Economic Planning* (London: Routledge, 1963).

[2] Oskar Lange, "On the Economic Theory of Socialism"; reprinted in Benjamin E. Lippincott, ed., *On The Economic Theory of Socialism* (New York: McGraw-Hill 1964).

[3] Abba P. Lerner, "Statics and Dynamics in Socialist Economies," *Economic Journal*,

conspicuous contemporaries. As a science, economics gained a number of external benefits from this debate. The contributions of Lerner and Benjamin Lippincott,[4] for example, are among the clearest statements on the nature and significance of economic efficiency ever made. Our main interest, however, will lie in the specific characteristics of Lange's model of socialism, the famous "competitive solution." Lange formulated it as a reply to von Mises, the latter having attacked socialism under the only guise that he knew, that of a command economy.

The most notable economic institution in Lange's model is a simulated market mechanism, hence the name "market socialism." With its aid, he succeeded in laying to rest any doubts about the existence of economic efficiency under socialism. Even von Mises capitulated on this point, and Lange punctuated his victory with the following famous ironic commentary:

> The merit of having caused the socialists to approach the problem [of economic efficiency] systematically belongs entirely to Professor Mises. Both as an expression of recognition for the great service rendered by him and as a memento of the prime importance of sound economic accounting, a statue of Professor Mises ought to occupy an honourable place in the great hall of the Ministry of Socialization or of the Central Planning Board of the socialist state. . . .[5]

Yet today we can discern a somewhat uncertain ring to Lange's triumph. From a practical point of view, it really makes no difference how question (1) is answered so long as the reply to (2) is negative. In Chapter 3 we saw that an efficient solution to the economic problem depends only upon an economy's production (or consumption) possibilities, along with the microoriented preferences of its individual actors. It will always *exist,* regardless of the information system used to coordinate economic activity. The important question here is what kind of economic system will lead to the highest level of social welfare in practice. This issue is far from being resolved, but it is quite likely that the system proposed by Lange will prove inferior to a number of capitalist and socialist alternatives in this respect.

Lange's "competitive solution" is the first mixed economy to make a full-fledged theoretical appearance. We shall study three others in Chapters 19–21. One was originally constructed as a model of market socialism, and another is a system of workers' cooperatives. The fourth, which we tentatively label Brand X, relaxes a constraint or two of the Lange model and, in consequence, could just as easily be market socialism or a form of "guided" capitalism. Many of the features of any particular form of market socialism carry over quite conveniently into a non-laissez-faire type of capitalism. France is in many ways the most interesting practical example of this, but Japan, Sweden, the Netherlands, and other nominally "capitalist" countries carry policy mak-

---

June 1937; reprinted in Lerner, *Essays in Economic Analysis* (New York: Macmillan, 1953), Ch. 1.

[4] Lippincott, op. cit., "Introduction."

[5] Lange, op. cit., pp. 57–58.

ing to the point where we may wish to say that they are planned. In fact, one could argue over whether some of these are basically capitalist or socialist.

The four theoretical mixed forms to be explored here and in the next three chapters fall into two convenient categories based upon the way prices for intermediate goods and natural resources are determined. In the competitive solution and in Taylor's model, these are set for domestic buyers and sellers by the economic planning council. But the Brand X and cooperative versions allow buyers and sellers to determine prices much as in Western capitalist society. In all four systems, prices are supposed to guide the decision making of individual firms and households.

18–2   Four Mixed Forms

Lange's Competitive Solution

Focusing on the short run, we begin by comparing pricing decisions in Lange's system with those in a Western capitalist economy. In both the interplay of supply and demand is supposed to determine market prices for consumer goods and services and for all kinds of labor inputs in approximately the same way. When it comes to intermediate goods and natural resources, though, an important difference appears. Markets exist for these items in a Lange system, and prices are supposed to respond to supply and demand. But these prices are set and manipulated centrally by the EPC according to certain rules.

Whenever a *surplus* of a particular good appears (that is, when quantity supplied exceeds quantity demanded at the current price), the EPC is supposed to lower price to choke off supply and encourage demand. When a *shortage* crops up, the planners are supposed to raise the price so as to produce the opposite effect. In this way the planners hope to keep supply and demand reasonably well balanced on the markets they control.

The EPC will also exercise at least some control over the distribution of wealth. In particular, it will pay the managers of socialist enterprises for their services, and decide the basis upon which this pay will be higher or lower than a standard amount. Normally, managerial bonuses will be geared to the profitability of the firms they direct, and it will be up to the EPC to ensure that the profitability of each enterprise is an accurate measure of its value to society.

This, in turn, implies that managers will have to maximize profits at rates of output where prices reflect marginal costs and at rates of input use where prices reflect the value of each input's marginal social product.[6,7] As we have

[6] A basic underlying assumption is that output prices measure the marginal benefits received by members of society from using the goods in question, while input prices measure the corresponding marginal sacrifices or costs. When an output price exceeds the corresponding marginal (social) cost, a cost-benefit analysis suggests expanding production. When marginal social cost is higher, the same analysis suggests contracting production. Similar rules apply to input use.

[7] Recently, many economists have argued that most managers should not set prices equal to marginal social costs or to the values of marginal social products. The reason

seen, these are both requirements of economic efficiency. However, we also know that these will be conditions of maximum profitability only if the planners are able to do three things:

1. Recognize all potential external effects and internalize these so that private and social costs and benefits always coincide.
2. Get managers to behave as if (a) all prices are completely beyond their ability to control, and (b) there will be no problems in hiring as much of each input as they need and selling as much of each output as they can produce at prevailing price levels.
3. Assure an absence of occupational and industrial entry barriers.

Conditions 2 and 3 are approximately the requirements for the institutional form known as perfect competition, hence the name "competitive solution." However, Lange realized that even approximate perfect competition might not be the rule in the system that he was designing. Thus he relied, in part, on the power invested in the "central planning board" or EPC to substitute for the power of competition.

Another feature of the competitive solution is that some taxes, notably on enterprise profits, will be available for distribution to households as a kind of "social dividend." In part, this will be like a corporate dividend in a capitalist country, but there are two major differences. First, the distribution of dividends is not to be connected with stock ownership. Indeed, in a socialist country, business firms are, at least in principle, owned by the public at large. Second, the EPC is supposed to achieve a "correct" allocation of productive resources independently of social dividend payments. Thus the latter must be carefully handled so that they do not affect productive activity in any way. They might, for instance, be paid as a family allowance or be related to such attributes as age and sex as long as occupation or number of hours worked do not enter through the back door.

Despite restrictions upon the ways in which they may be used, transfer payments like the social dividend will serve as an important means of reducing inequalities in the distribution of wealth. By spreading property income over the populace more evenly than would probably occur in a laissez-faire capitalist economy they will become important instruments for steering the system toward its distribution goals. They amount, in effect, to a program of income supplements designed to put a standard-of-living floor under every household.

The Taylor Version

The Taylor model resembles Lange's in that an EPC is responsible for setting prices and changing them when circumstances appear to warrant, but the following major differences also appear:

---

is that a *completely* efficient solution to the economic problem is unachievable. In trying for a second best, a different set of pricing rules ought to be followed. W. J. Baumol and D. F. Bradford give a second-best set of rules in their article, "Optimal Departures from Marginal-Cost Pricing," *American Economic Review,* June 1970. Such a substitution would not alter the rest of the discussion.

1. Taylor apparently wished the EPC to control all prices, not just those for natural resources and intermediate goods.

2. Just as in the case of a command economy, the EPC will make use of a *planning* year or year in which the plan is drawn up prior to execution in the *operating* year. While Lange was unquestionably aware of the need for advance planning, he makes no formal provision for a planning year nor for a systematic round of exchanges between planners and producers before production and distribution get underway.

3. During the planning year, the EPC will send target prices for inputs and outputs to producing enterprises accompanied by the following message: "Suppose these prices were to hold during the year to come. What levels of output would you expect to produce and what methods or techniques of production would you use if you were to minimize the per unit (or average) cost of producing each good or service?"

4. In reply, producers are to give the EPC lists of projected levels of output plus "production coefficients." These coefficients (which we have already encountered in our discussion of the command economy) indicate how much of each input the firm plans to use per unit of every good or service that it turns out, given the average cost is being minimized. From these coefficients plus the forecasts of expected rates of output, the EPC will be able to deduce how much of each input every firm will need. In fact, the planners could just as well ask each producer how much of each output he was going to produce and how much of each input he would need (given average cost minimization) and do the divisions themselves. In practice, they probably would.

5. The EPC then proceeds to alter its previous lists of target prices until the price of each product just covers the per unit cost of producing it in the *highest-cost* firm. This per unit cost has to include an interest charge for use of durable capital equipment (plant and machinery) and a rental charge for use of the production site. Ideally, better locations, superior endowments of natural resources, and more capital equipment will result in higher rent and interest charges. As in the Lange model, there must also be some provision for allocating investment funds to their most profitable uses and, in particular, for adjusting production capacity to demand in each industry so that prices and *long run* marginal costs always tend toward approximate equality.

6. When the revised price list is complete, it is sent to each firm a second time. Again, producers are to reply with production coefficients and projected rates of output. If the second set of target prices is significantly different from the first, some producers will find it necessary to alter their proposed input mixes in order to minimize per unit costs. This will lead them to send back a new set of production coefficients, and the series of exchanges will go on in this fashion until the EPC deems it necessary or desirable to stop.

When negotiations cease—probably after two or, at most, three rounds—there will be a set of target prices in existence, which we may call the final target prices. These may become the set that prevails at the start of the operating year, or the EPC may make some final adjustments on its own before the operating year begins. This will happen when the planners fear that supply and demand are still too badly out of balance. In connection with this, the EPC will have to make fairly elaborate forecasts of the various components of final demand and of supplies of basic inputs to supplement the input requirements and projected outputs sent to them by producers. On the basis of this information they will hope to have at least a rudimentary idea of supply and demand in every important market.

By introducing a planning year during which the EPC would manipulate target prices, Taylor consciously or unconsciously made his market mechanism resemble the theoretical textbook model. In Chapter 14 we saw that most of economic theory about markets revolved around an idealized model in which every good or service was effectively sold through an "auctioneer." The latter sent tentative price lists for all goods and services to all prospective buyers and sellers, who responded with quantities demanded and supplied. The auctioneer's staff then compared supply and demand for every good and adjusted prices where these did not match. Then it sent out revised price lists. Potential buyers and sellers would respond once more, and the process would continue until supply did equal demand for every good. Then and only then would exchange take place.

The Taylor system also resembles a command economy in that production coefficients are exchanged between planners and producers. However, in the latter, planners send target rates of output and of input use to producers, who, in principle, have no authority to change these. The role of counterproposals from below is simply to inform the EPC so that it can make a better plan. In the Taylor model, the producers advise, the EPC consents, and it is here that the decentralization of the system becomes most manifest. In any actual economy where output and input targets pass up and down the planning hierarchy, a measure of the degree of decentralization in decision making can be derived by observing how target production techniques are determined through bargaining between planners and producers.

Once again the economy's complex of interest rates will be among the prices that planners manipulate. Thus the first set of target prices sent to each firm would include a complete specification of the terms on which the enterprise could borrow money for various purposes. These terms may be contingent, in some way, upon "cooperation" with the EPC or its goals.

This is the essence of the Taylor model. Variations of its basic theme are not too difficult to imagine. Managers could be asked to maximize profits or sales, for example (which they are likely to try to do anyway), and send back the most efficient production coefficients resulting from these goals. But regardless of the set of instructions finally decided on by the EPC, the Taylor version of market socialism will be subject to many of the criticisms leveled at the command economy in Chapters 7–11. Specifically, managers will have an incentive to specify production coefficients that are too high (that is, those which call for more input per unit of output than is absolutely necessary). This is analogous to trying for an "easy plan" in a command economy.

Brand X

The architects of the traditional mixed-economy models keyed their analyses to central price manipulation because they were most anxious to show how a simulated market mechanism could coordinate economic activity in a socialist system. Neither Lange nor Taylor was much interested in developing the instruments by which the EPC could steer the system along a particular path of economic development.

Interestingly enough, Lange did not have to use central price manipulation to prove his point. He could as easily have used a conventional market with buyers and sellers setting prices. This leads us into the "Brand X" category of mixed systems, largely a composite picture emerging from the writings of post-World War II economists.

Within Brand X, managers play a role closer to that of a Western corporate manager than to the managerial function in either the Lange or Taylor versions. Decentralized pricing prevails, and firms take over many of the investment decisions relegated by Lange to the intermediate planning bureaucracy. The latter, in turn, can be reduced since firms require less direct supervision. The principal tasks of the planners are to promote efficiency and to steer the economy. These duties will overlap because steering implies that the economic planning council is influencing the distribution of welfare and the patterns of production and input use. It will do this partly with a view to internalizing social costs and benefits and helping to realize mass production economies.

We may say, in fact, that steering the economy in production space has two faces. On the *demand* side, the EPC must ensure that sectors given a high priority according to the index of social welfare that it wishes to implement have both the means and the incentive to expand. The *supply* side is concerned with realizing economies of mass production and internalizing social costs and benefits. Because incentives tend to replace commands and controls, in comparison with a command economy, a basic tool for both kinds of production steering is the financial-incentive program, which was introduced in Chapter 5. Financial incentives are subsidies in the broadest sense, firmly tied to selective expansion.

It is no exaggeration to say that the financial incentive program, as we use the term here, is an extension of the principal means of steering most West European economies, Japan, and, perhaps, Hungary. Financial incentives are also finding growing use in North America. If we extend the concept to comprise moral as well as material incentives, it even becomes an important tool in China, in particular to encourage local small-scale industry.

Ideally, a financial-incentive program will satisfy two basic requirements. First, all subsidies are tied to specific areas of expansion and must be justified within an over-all framework of priorities that effectively constitutes a plan. In this sense, there can be no such thing as a science policy apart from a program to encourage the spread of technology or a manpower-retraining program apart from a program of area development. All must be treated as interrelated parts of the planning process.

Second, it will prove possible to monitor each dollar spent in subsidy, both by destination and according to the purpose for which it is spent. In this way society retains firm control over the conditions under which incentives are granted. This will enable the EPC to continually assess the impact of the financial-incentive program and to redesign it in order to achieve a higher level of social welfare.

To give an example of what should not happen, a 1972 Canadian study showed that 11 of 18 firms receiving $34 million in industrial location grants simply reaped windfall profits.[8] They made no investment in depressed regions that they would not have made anyway. Chapter 23 will explore a political framework within which a better monitoring of grants is likely.

The planners will also foster a "positive" market-structure policy and, if necessary, consumer protection agencies and centers for information about producers' goods and production technology. One guideline for these agencies will be to *avoid* interfering directly in negotiations between buyers and sellers unless there are costs or benefits from these which spill over onto third parties.

Workers' Cooperatives [9]

A cooperative firm is an enterprise managed by its employees or by their elected representatives. We normally think of three economic roles in connection with a firm, those of labor, management, and owner. Usually the wages of labor are not *explicitly* tied to enterprise profits, and this constitutes an important dividing line between labor on one hand and owners and managers on the other. A producers' cooperative goes at least part way toward removing or blurring this distinction. More precisely, we are defining a cooperative to be a firm satisfying two conditions:

1. Its retained earnings are at least partly divided up among the majority of its employees, whose earnings will depend to an important extent upon the enterprise's profits and losses. Thus the personnel tends to sink or swim with it.
2. Its managerial decision making is shared to some extent by elected representatives of the employees who constitute a "workers' council."

[8] See David Springate, *Regional Development Incentive Grants and Private Investment in Canada,* unpublished Ph.D. thesis, Harvard University, 1972.

[9] The model of a workers' cooperative discussed here and in Chapter 17 is due to Benjamin Ward. See Benjamin Ward, "The Firm in Illyria: Market Syndicalism," *The American Economic Review,* Sept. 1958. For criticism and an alternative view, see Jaroslav Vanek, "Decentralization Under Workers' Management: A Theoretical Appraisal," *American Economic Review,* May 1970. The following books on the subject are also by Vanek: *The Labor-Managed Market Economy: General Theory* (Ithaca, N.Y.: Cornell U.P., 1970); *The Labor-Managed Market Economy: An Evolutionary Hypothesis* (Ithaca, N.Y.: Cornell U.P., 1970).

In particular, the decisions on how much of each output to produce, how much of each input to use, and what prices to pay and charge are at least partly collective decisions of the council. For this reason we often call an economy in which most firms are cooperatives a system of "workers' participation" in management.

The purpose of having a cooperative economy is twofold. On the one hand, its designers would hope to wipe out differences in economic goals among workers, owners, and managers—to make enterprises, in other words, more like teams. But at a more fundamental level their aim would be to make real progress toward the age-old dream of a classless society.

We want to explore the workers' cooperative form, both from the standpoint of efficiency and from that of eliminating socioeconomic class differences. At least in theory, the cooperative is the dominant producing enterprise in Yugoslavia, and the principle lies to some extent behind the practice of industrial relations in the United Kingdom, West Germany, Sweden, and France. Moreover, it has been proposed and seriously considered in nearly every other developed, capitalist nation, including the United States, where profit sharing is already not uncommon.

Some have speculated that if the convergence of different kinds of economic systems were to take place, this is basically the form to which they would converge, at least when the discussion is confined to developed, industrial nations. Hence our exploration in Chapter 21 should be of more than passing interest. Workers' management is quite consistent with laissez faire, but we shall view it within a context of market planning. As such, it becomes a special case of Brand X.

18-3 Capsule Comparisons

Let us close the chapter by briefly comparing the mixed forms just introduced. This is done from three different points of view in Table 18-1 and Figures 18-1 and 18-2. Table 18-1 is self-explanatory except, perhaps, for the middle column. In each version the sector of direction and administration, working through its economic planning council, will decide upon the method of taxation and influence, at least to some extent, the distribution of wealth and welfare in the economy. Beyond this the EPC will have particular jobs to do that will vary from one mixed form to another.

Figure 18-1 gives a bird's-eye view of the *pattern* of information flows in each model with the completely centralized and decentralized economies included as reference points. The solid lines denote information triggers; the dashed lines represent feedback. In each case we have oversimplified somewhat to emphasize the differences between systems.

Lange's competitive solution requires the EPC to send price signals both to firms and to households (denoted P and C, respectively). Consumers and producers then respond to these signals through the market with quantities

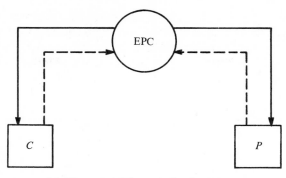

(a) The completely centralized economy

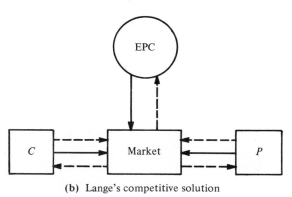

(b) Lange's competitive solution

Figure 18–1. A comparison of the pattern of information flows in centralized, mixed, and decentralized economies.

ordered or offered for sale. This is denoted by the top dashed arrow in Figure 18–1(b) between these actors and the market. The *net* feedback from the market to the EPC consists of surpluses or deficits (that is, of the differences between quantities demanded and supplied) where supply and demand fail to match. The EPC is then supposed to raise prices of goods in short supply or excess demand while cutting prices of items in excess supply.

The planners, however, only control prices of natural resources and intermediate goods. Other prices are market-determined in conventional fashion. Thus the bottom pair of arrows in Figure 18–1(b) between the market and households and firms represents price signals sent and quantities received of consumer goods and labor inputs. To make the diagram legible, we have made the oversimplified assumption that prices (solid arrows) are sent by producers through the market to consumers, who respond with quantities demanded and supplied (dashed arrows). The same convention has been followed in Figures 18–1(c) and (d). In practice, of course, consumers will sometimes send prices and producers will respond with quantities.

Within the Taylor economy, planners are required to send prospective

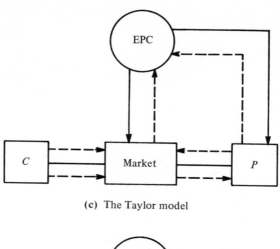

(c) The Taylor model

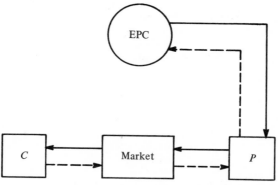

(d) Brand X and producers' cooperatives

(e) The completely decentralized economy

Figure 18–1 (cont.)

prices to firms and to receive production coefficients in reply. Our exploration of the Taylor system will also lead us briefly into *indicative planning*. This derives its name from the "indicators" which the EPC sends out to producers and consumers and which, like commands, express targets in terms of inputs and outputs. Usually indicators do not become as detailed at the microlevel

Table 18–1. The roles of central planners and managers in three mixed economies.

Type of Mixed Form	Particular Aspects of the EPC's Role	Role of "Representative" Firm Manager
Lange's "competitive solution"	Establish prices of intermediate goods and natural resources. Alter these prices where surpluses or shortages appear.	Maximize profits under assumption that prices are outside of their control. In the case of natural resources, and intermediate goods, these prices are set by the EPC. In the case of consumer goods and labor inputs, markets will, hopefully be competitive or nearly so.
Taylor version	1. Send "target prices" to firms during the planning year. 2. Alter prices upon receipt of production coefficients so that they just cover minimum per unit production costs. 3. Continue this series of exchanges for as long as possible and then set prices to prevail at the start of the operating year. 4. (Perhaps) manipulate current prices as in the Lange system.	1. Send production coefficients to the EPC upon receipt of target prices. 2. Fulfill targets set by the EPC with respect to productive inputs and outputs.
Brand X and producers' cooperatives	Manipulate bonuses, targets, taxes, subsidies, etc., so as to induce a system of checks and balances throughout the economy. Use the same levers to orient the system along a desired path of economic development.	Set prices, hire inputs, determine the assortment of goods to be produced. Very much the same role that a capitalist manager would have.

as command targets. There might be a planned output for the steel industry in 1975, for example, but there is less likely to be an explicit target for each enterprise.

Moving to the decentralized pricing systems, a whole raft of possible courses of action is open to the planners. They will probably continue to control a few crucial prices, notably interest rates. However, the keynote of these models is a withdrawal by the EPC from central price manipulation, and a consequent shift in emphasis from market to nonmarket interaction with the producing sector. The latter continues to interact with households through the market.

The second major characteristic of any system's information structure relates to the nature of the communications between different economic actors. We have seen that messages which trigger economic activity may be classified by degree of anonymity, while responses are graded according to their operationality (that is, whether or not they describe actions visible to those who receive them). Figure 18–2 compares the four theoretical mixed forms to be discussed according to what we would expect to be the average anonymity and operationality of the information flows in each. Both the completely centralized and completely decentralized systems (discussed in Chapter 1) are again included as reference points.

Of all these, the completely decentralized model (D) will have the most anonymous triggers and the most operational feedback. In both cases it will be followed by the Brand X and cooperative versions (BX), which are indistinguishable when one looks only at information flows *between* actors. We would expect to find less anonymity and operationality under BX for two reasons. First, such things as production targets may be used to supplement the market. Second, when prices are set in bargaining between small groups of buyers and sellers, they tend to lack the anonymous character of prices determined by supply and demand on markets with a multitude of participants. There may be some price discrimination if only in the sense that none

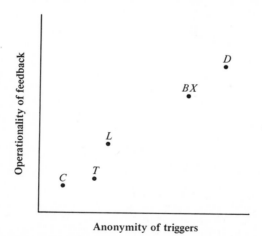

Figure 18–2. A comparison of the nature of information flows in centralized, mixed, and decentralized economies.

but "usual" customers or sellers are allowed to transact at established prices. Moreover, the response to any proposed price may well depend upon who quoted (or sent) it.

To run a Lange system (L) effectively, the EPC will continually need accurate, up-to-date information about supply and demand conditions for every good and service. These data are not likely to refer, in most cases, to events that are visible to the planners. Moreover, the reaction to price signals will depend, often in subtle ways, upon whether they are sent by the EPC or by someone else. For these reasons, we have ranked the Lange system below BX in terms both of operationality and of anonymity.[10]

Information triggers in the Taylor version (T) will be slightly less anonymous than in the Lange model since central control over prices is apparently extended to more sectors of the economy. As in the completely centralized case, feedback will be considerably less operational than in the Lange model. In both of the former systems a planning year is introduced during which exchanges of information occur between planners and firms "preliminary" to production or exchange of goods. The feedback from firms to planners and from lower levels of the planning hierarchy on up to the EPC gives each of these economies its low average operationality rating. On the other hand, we are supposing that the existence of a more comprehensive market system in T will make it more operational than C.

---

[10] A modified Lange model—the central marketing economy introduced in Chapter 11—separates the marketing and production aspects of managerial decision making. Production is decentralized, as in the original competitive solution, but firms in the centralized pricing sector must sell most of their output to a central marketing agency. Buyers of intermediate goods then make their purchase from this agency, which is organized according to the command principle and maintains inventory depots and marketing centers throughout the country. It also tries to guarantee managers that they may buy or sell as much of each intermediate good as they want at EPC-established prices.

We shall discuss this version further in Chapter 19. Here we note that it is somewhat less anonymous and either more or less operational than the original Lange model. Thus we would place it to the left and either above or below L in Figure 18–2. The decline in anonymity stems from the command organization of marketing, which may or may not increase the operationality—and more importantly, the reliability—of excess demand information reaching the center. One goal, however, is to deny this information to managers and their superiors in the intermediate planning hierarchy while keeping the EPC and its staff agencies continuously up to date.

Chapter 19

Traditional Market Socialism: Structure and Functioning

"Responding to the forces of Yugoslavia's market economy, sugar began to reappear this week on the shelves of . . . groceries. But the event produced few smiles from shoppers when they noted the new price, up 7.5 per cent.

"After months of controversy, the Cabinet decided Tuesday to raise the price not only of sugar, but also of bread, cooking oil, and margarine. As a result, sugar began to move out of the warehouses where producers had been storing it for months, waiting for the price increase. . . ."

The New York Times

19–1 The Competitive Solution: How It Is Supposed to Work

As in a command economy, the producing sector of Lange's system is organized into three basic tiers, with the economic planning council at the top and the firms, or executors of decisions about what and how to produce, at the bottom. However, the thousands of firms throughout the economy comprise too great a span of control for one central agency, even in a mixed system. Just the volume and variety of *non*market tasks whose responsibility belongs to the planners will require the EPC to partition the economy by industry or geographic region and assign a ministry to each sector.

Each ministry will have the job of spotting potential externalities and economies of mass production that occur wholly within its jurisdiction and, probably, the task of helping to internalize them. It will make forecasts of shifts in demand, technological change, and labor-force migration. Ministerial directors will also exercise many of the planning hierarchy's policing and checking powers plus much of whatever authority it retains to issue commands. In all likelihood these posts will serve as grooming grounds for future economic and political leaders.

The above is, in fact, a kind of minimum work load for the intermediate authorities, but within the competitive solution they are actually assigned a much wider role. Lange's principal partitioning is by branch of industry, and he called his ministers "industry managers." Each industry manager has responsibility for all important investment decisions within his sector—specifically, for investment decisions capable of affecting the production capacity of his industry.[1] Firm managements, in other words, can suggest additions to their existing plants, but the final decisions on these and on creation of new enterprises would normally rest with industry managers.

It follows that industry managers will play a key decision-making role. Capital is but one kind of productive input, and the optimal capital stock for any industry can only be determined in conjunction with an optimal output and optimal use of every other input. Thus industry managers will have to take charge of the bulk of all kinds of long-run planning and production decision making for the firms under their jurisdiction. They become analogous to managers of giant capitalist corporations and, in most cases, are likely to occupy even stronger monopoly positions.

Firm managers within a Lange economy will concern themselves mainly with short-run decisions relating to the efficient use of given plant and equipment, along with maintenance, repairs, and routine replacement. They are rather more like plant or division managers at General Motors, Armour, General Electric, or any other corporation where decision making has been decentralized.

Insofar as distribution goals are concerned, Lange, along with most other socialist writers, believed that market socialism should rest on the basis of "consumers' sovereignty" within the context of an essentially egalitarian social preference function. The planners are supposed to be "social engineers," charged with effectively translating the will of the people (with everyone receiving an approximately equal weight) into practical economic guidance.

With specific reference to the "competitive solution," however, we cannot agree that Lange entirely attained his goals, even in theory. To begin with,

[1] Oskar Lange, "On the Economic Theory of Socialism," in Benjamin E. Lippincott, ed., *On the Economic Theory of Socialism* (New York: McGraw-Hill, 1964), pp. 76–77.

what he called "consumers' sovereignty" is more like what we have called "consumers' sovereignty over (current) consumer goods" in the Appendix to Chapter 7. It is the central planners who are supposed to determine the tempo and, at least in part, the direction of economic development. In particular, it sets the minimal rates of return to be required on different kinds of investment, the interest rates to be paid for savings, and the economy's various tax-subsidy programs.[2]

Second, the competitive solution would probably be more egalitarian than most capitalist societies because of a spreading of property incomes. Yet noticeable departures from an equal distribution of welfare are likely to exist unless the economy can function largely on moral incentives. In particular, managers, technocrats, and other members of the bureaucratic elite are likely to be made better off by the material incentives given to induce them to improve their contribution to social welfare.[3]

Beyond this, at the micro level, Lange was particularly concerned that firms and industries should be efficient in the usual economic sense. Therefore, in order to investigate the operation of his model under ideal conditions, we shall assume throughout this section that managers determine their rates of operation so as to make output prices reflect marginal costs and input prices reflect the values of marginal products.

However, even if these rules are followed, economic efficiency is not assured unless private and social costs and benefits always coincide. Hence an important task of the EPC, besides price manipulation, will be to use taxes, laws, decrees, subsidies, and the like so that any potential external effects are always internalized. Lange felt that a socialist market economy would have an important advantage over laissez-faire capitalism in this regard. A key benefit from having a central planner, in his view, was its strategic position as an overseer of the whole interdependent economic process. Thus it would be in an ideal position to spot major actual and potential externalities and, at least in principle, have the power to internalize them.[4]

Throughout this section we shall give Lange the benefit of any doubt that might arise on this score. Managers of industries and producing enterprises will, therefore, produce output assortments that equate the price of each good with its marginal *social* cost and hire input assortments that bring input prices into equality with the values of their marginal *social* products.

To complete the supply-and-demand picture for the entire economy, then, we need to specify its endowments of natural resources, its level of technology, and a social preference function to steer it. From our discussion above we know that the latter is supposed to be a social guiding function—that is, it enunciates goals for the economy both in terms of the mix of goods and

---

[2] Lange, ibid., Secs. III and IV.

[3] It is quite possible that equality of welfares will prove to be incompatible with economic efficiency, as in Figure 3-2(b).

[4] Lange, op. cit., especially Sec. V.

services available to it and in terms of its distribution of wealth and welfare. Moreover, its distribution goals are basically egalitarian. Lange does not give us enough information to determine an exact social preference function, but whatever its form it will have to accomplish two basic tasks. First, it will have to express the national priorities that the EPC is *seeking* to implement (or the macro rationale of the EPC). Second, it will have to express the pattern of aggregate demand for goods and services, including leisure and capital goods, which *actually* emerges in the economy plus the actual distribution of welfare in the system.

It is quite important that the social preference function should simultaneously do both of these things, for only then can the EPC's priorities be translated into demand-and-supply votes that guide the economic activity of industries, firms, and households. Only then, in other words, can the EPC's social goals be translated into reality.

We mention this because Lange was a bit sparing in his discussion of how the EPC was going to steer the economy insofar as its output goals are concerned. In Section 19–2, we shall discover that firm and industry managers or other officials in the intermediate planning hierarchy may gain enough power to wrest control over the system's path of economic development from the EPC. But to begin with, we shall waive these problems and assume a consistent and unambiguous social preference function whose weights are consistent with EPC preferences.[5] Its interaction with society's production (or consumption) possibility frontier will determine "optimal" price ratios or terms of trade for every pair of goods.

The EPC's basic task is then to bring the economy to this optimum, and a principal tool will be price manipulation. It will be guided in changing prices by supply and demand. At specified or unspecified intervals, the central planners will cut the prices of goods that are in excess supply and raise the prices of goods in excess demand. As in our discussion of laissez faire, we must assume that transactions completed at disequilibrium prices will not significantly interfere with the pursuit of economy-wide equilibrium. Hopefully, after a reasonable length of time, approximate supply–demand balances will be achieved in nearly every market. It will then be up to the EPC to keep track of shifts in demand and supply over time.

Just to illustrate the basic operation of the competitive solution, let us confine our attention to two goods. Since we are interested in the way a Lange system departs from the more usual kind of market economy, we shall assume that these are goods whose prices are manipulated by the EPC. Such commodities do not normally enter directly into the social preference function. Indeed, since they must be intermediate goods or natural resources, they can do so only to the extent that they also become a part of final demand in the form of net exports, net inventory accumulation, or net capital formation during the current time period. But even if this is not so, the social preference

---

[5] We would remind the reader that the EPC may either be an economic dictatorship or a would-be "voice of the people."

function will assign them values indirectly through the mechanism of derived demand.

We shall call these commodities good 1 and good 2—or, if the reader prefers less abstract names—sheet steel and steel girders, respectively. Sheet steel will be used mainly in manufacturing such consumer durables as autos and refrigerators; steel girders will find application in heavy industry and construction. Let X_1 and X_2 be the quantities of sheet steel and steel girders produced in tons and let p_1 and p_2 be the prices of a ton of each. Moreover, let MSU_1 and MSU_2 be their marginal social utilities, defined as follows: MSU_1 will be the per unit change in the index of social welfare caused (directly and indirectly) by a small increase in the production of good 1. Similarly, for MSU_2 and good 2. Finally, let MSC_1 and MSC_2 be their marginal social costs.

From Chapter 3 we know that MSC_1 and MSC_2 may be viewed as production "prices" of these goods and that the ratio MSC_2/MSC_1 gives the production terms of trade between them just as p_2/p_1 gives their market terms of trade. By analogy, MSU_1 and MSU_2 can be thought of as their consumption prices and the ratio MSU_2/MSU_1 as their "optimal" consumption terms of trade. An "optimal" solution to the economic problem will require that MSC_2/MSC_1 and MSU_2/MSU_1 be approximately the same. In the special case where both the indifference curves of the social preference function and the production-possibility frontier are smooth, their slopes must be exactly equal, giving

$$\frac{MSC_2}{MSC_1} = \frac{MSU_2}{MSU_1} \tag{19–1}$$

Figure 19–1 shows why Equation (19–1) must hold. There U is the index of social welfare, and U_1, U_2 and U_3 are three ascending levels of social welfare, represented by three different indifference curves. Point A gives the optimal combination of the two goods to be produced since U_2 is the highest achievable level of social welfare. The EPC therefore will try to coordinate supply and demand through the market mechanism so that (19–1) (or its equivalent when some curves are not smooth) comes to prevail. Not surprisingly, this will involve equating both the consumption and production price ratios to the market terms of trade. When an optimal solution to the economic problem has been found, in other words, we must have

$$\frac{MSC_2}{MSC_1} = \frac{p_2}{p_1} = \frac{MSU_2}{MSU_1} \tag{19–2}$$

and Figure 19–1 also shows this. In the real world, with many goods and services, we would need a similar equality for *every* possible pair of commodities, and the EPC would have to simultaneously manipulate many prices so as to bring this about.

In order to understand the meaning of (19–2) more fully, let us begin with a situation where the economy has not yet found its optimum and try

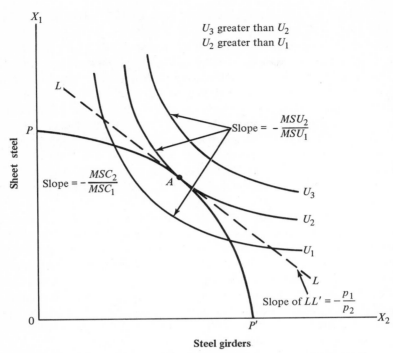

Figure 19–1. The social welfare maximum in a Lange economy.

to discover how the EPC can use the market mechanism to help achieve this.[6] The first thing to notice is that buyers and sellers will try to adjust their own internal tradeoffs to the prevailing market price ratios. Sellers will try to adjust their output mixes so that $p_2/p_1 = \text{MSC}_2/\text{MSC}_1$; buyers will try to regulate their purchases so that $\text{MSU}_2/\text{MSU}_1 = p_2/p_1$. For sellers, such behavior is a consequence of marginal (social) cost pricing of outputs. Buyers, however, will actually tend to set $p_2/p_1 = \text{MSPP}_2/\text{MSPP}_1$, where MSPP denotes marginal social product. [See equation (3–3a).] But the marginal social utilities of intermediate goods are simply reflections of the values of their marginal social products to users.

In these circumstances suppose that the EPC at first sets prices for the two goods which are *not* optimal. To be concrete, let the optimal price ratio, as

[6] Because the subject is extraordinarily complex, we shall implicitly assume below that all prices except those for sheet steel and steel girders are sufficiently close to their optimal levels that we can concentrate on the movement of p_1 and p_2 in isolation. Otherwise the subject would be manageable but beyond the scope of this volume.

To see how it can be managed in its full complexity, the following works are rated M, recommended for mathematically mature audiences only: Kenneth J. Arrow and Leonid Hurwicz, "Decentralization and Computation in Resource Allocation," in Ralph W. Pfouts, ed., *Essays in Economics and Econometrics* (Chapel Hill, N.C.: U. N.C., 1959); Kenneth J. Arrow and Leonid Hurwicz, "On the Stability of the Competitive Equilibrium, I," *Econometrica*, Oct. 1958; Kenneth J. Arrow, H. D. Bloch, and Leonid Hurwicz, "On the Stability of Competitive Equilibrium, II," *Econometrica*, Jan. 1959.

yet unknown to the planners, be 1. Instead, the EPC guesses a best price of $2 for good 2 and $1 for good 1, so that $p_2/p_1 = 2$. Firms will respond to the relatively high value of p_2 by overproducing good 2 and underproducing good 1, in comparison with the optimum. Buyers will react in just the opposite way, leading to a shortage of good 1 and a surplus of good 2, as Figures 19–2 and 19–3 illustrate. In Figure 19–3 producers have tended to direct the economy toward point B on the production-possibility frontier, where $MSC_2/MSC_1 = 2$. However, the pattern of demand has concentrated around a point such as C, where $MSU_2/MSU_1 = 2$. The optimum, as in Figure 19–1, is at A.

Managers will notice the disparities between demand and supply, for they will build up unwanted inventories of steel girders and have unfilled orders for sheet steel. According to the "rules of the game" they are supposed to communicate all excess demand information to the EPC. These communications are normally nonoperational, however, because they describe phenomena which the EPC or its representatives are unable to observe directly. For now we ignore any problems to which this may give rise.

Thus the EPC becomes aware of the discrepancy between positions B and C in Figure 19–3 and moves to raise p_1 and lower p_2. Let us suppose that

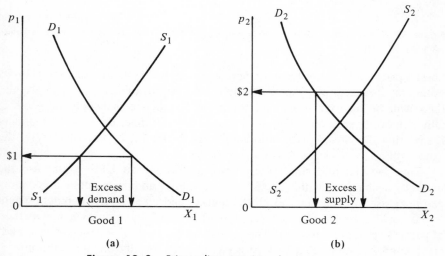

Figure 19–2. Price adjustment in a Lange economy.

it overshoots the mark and sets $p_2/p_1 = \frac{1}{2}$. Using an argument similar to the one set out above, we see there will be a surplus of good 1 and a shortage of good 2. Once more the planners know that they will have to step in and change prices, but they also have knowledge that they previously lacked—that the optimal price ratio lies somewhere between $\frac{1}{2}$ and 2. In fact, the aim of the whole process is to progressively narrow down the range within which the

Sheet
steel

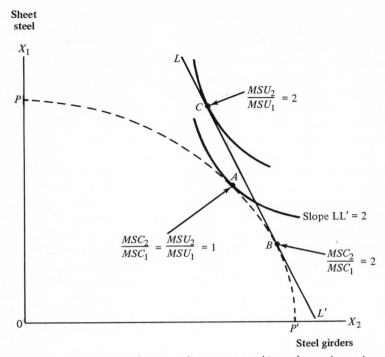

Figure 19–3. A global view of price adjustment to achieve the optimum in a Lange economy.

"best" price ratio must lie and thereby bring the system ever closer to its optimum. For example, the EPC might next try a price ratio of 1.5. Again, there will be an excess demand for good 1 and excess supply of good 2, although not to such an extent as appeared the first time. By now the planners realize that the "best" price ratio is between $\frac{1}{2}$ and $1\frac{1}{2}$. If they then try $\frac{3}{4}$, the range will be narrowed to $\frac{3}{4} - 1\frac{1}{2}$, and so on.

Thus we can find similarities between the way an EPC would use the market mechanism within a Lange economy and a command-economy planner's use of computers. Both the market and a series of computers would try to solve a complex set of supply-and-demand equations via the method of successive approximations. This consists, as above, of a series of trial-and-error approximations that seek to zero in systematically on the optimum.

In fact, when L. V. Kantorovich, the Russian mathematician-turned-economist, first discovered linear programming in 1939, his solution was of this type. What he did, in attacking a problem much like the one above, was to try a collection of numbers that he called "resolving multipliers" one after another. Each set had associated with it an approximate answer to his problem. Under favorable conditions these approximations would eventually get closer and closer to the true answer until, at last, the latter was found. Although he did not then realize it, Kantorovich's resolving multipliers were nothing more nor less than prices. Kantorovich had not only discovered linear programming, he had partially rediscovered the laws of supply and demand in a world where they were not supposed to exist.[7]

In reality an EPC will find itself manipulating hundreds of thousands of price ratios rather than just one. Yet the basic principle remains the same. The planners must try to simultaneously narrow down the intervals in which all the "optimal" price ratios lie until they have found the "best" solution to the economic problem. In all probability they will encounter some insensitivity of demand and supply to price changes, in which case it will only be necessary to get price ratios within optimal ranges. Like the market mechanism in a laissez-faire economy, the EPC would have a margin of error in which to operate.

This completes a rudimentary analysis of the way a Lange model is supposed to work. Perhaps the most remarkable thing about it is that, under ideal conditions, an optimum can be reached without a single command being issued to producers telling them how much of any good or service to produce or how much of any input to use. No single economic actor directly interferes with or observes the internal transformation processes of any other. Moreover, the amount of information needed by the planners is minimized. The optimum could theoretically remain completely unknown to the EPC until it is reached. This would occur as soon as demand and supply were equal on every market.

Unfortunately, in any realistic setting, the planners will need to know more. To close this section we want to illustrate this by posing two problems implicitly assumed away in the previous discussion. In the first place we invoked the law of diminishing returns to guarantee that the production-possibility frontier would be bowed out away from the origin, while all the social indifference curves were bowed in toward it. In the case of the latter, we ultimately implied something like the following: the *relative* priority attached to the heavy industrial products that use steel girders, over the durable consumer goods using sheet steel, will decline as heavy industrial output becomes more plentiful relative to durable consumer products. The reverse would also have to be true. (It would still be possible, however, for heavy industry to receive a much higher or lower *over-all* priority than durable consumer goods.) Thus when the economy is relatively saturated with girders, we would expect that 100,000 tons of girders would have to be traded abroad for a relatively smaller amount of sheet steel in order for the index, U, to remain at exactly the same level.

It was by virtue of the law of diminishing returns and the resulting shapes of the production-possibility frontier and indifference curves in Figures 19–1 and 19–3 that we were able to derive the following results:

---

[7] L. V. Kantorovich, "Mathematical Methods of Planning and Organizing Production," *Management Science,* July 1961; this is R. W. Campbell's translation of Kantorovich's historic 1939 article. See also Benjamin Ward, "Kantorovich on Economic Calculation," *Journal of Political Economy,* Dec. 1960.

1. There is just one "optimal" solution to the economic problem (at A). Moreover, this is the *only* place where an indifference curve is tangent to (touching but not crossing) the production-possibility frontier.
2. At all price ratios below the optimum, there is always an excess demand for good 2 and an excess supply of good 1. At all price ratios above the optimum, there is always an excess demand for good 1 and an excess supply of good 2.

Without these conditions, the EPC might not have been able to narrow down the range containing the optimal price ratio in a systematic fashion. If we look through the eyes of supply–demand analysis, the law of diminishing returns tells us that demand and supply curves are well behaved, as in Figure 19–4(a). Without this law, a situation such as that depicted in Figure 19–4(b) could easily develop. Correspondingly, both statements 1 and 2 could become untrue, leaving us with a messy state of affairs such as the one shown in Figure 19–5.

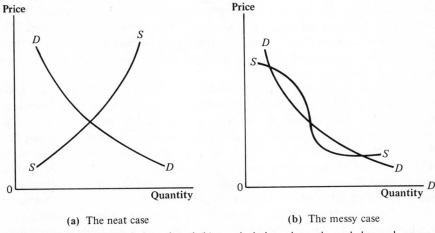

(a) The neat case   (b) The messy case

Figure 19–4. (a) Well-behaved and (b) poorly behaved supply and demand curves.

There the optimal solution to the economic problem occurs at A_3, and the indifference curve, U_3, represents the highest level of social welfare that we can hope to achieve. But if the EPC follows the same rules as above, it may fail to lead the economy to A_3. Indeed, if it starts out anywhere above A_1, it will probably take the system to A_2 and the lower level of social welfare, represented by U_2.[8] The problem here is that there are substantial "economies

---

[8] The demand and supply curves in Figure 19–4 and the production-possibility frontier in Figure 19–5 would best be interpreted as applying to the long run. In other words, industry managers have the opportunity to decide in which direction they wish to expand production capacity. It can be shown that the economy will not fall back to the still lower level of social utility U_1, which passes through A_1. The reason is that any departure from A_1 in either direction will lead to still greater departures in the same direction.

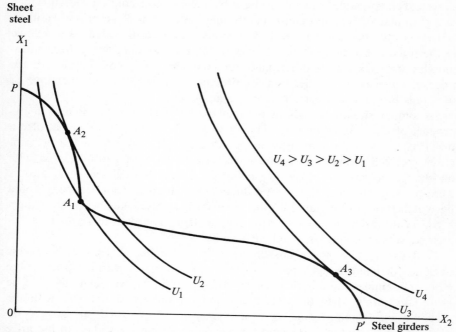

Figure 19–5. An example in which nonmarket information is required in order to optimize.

of mass production" to be had in producing steel girders, which will not be realized until the system undertakes their production on a large scale. These economies offset and nullify, to some extent, the law of diminishing returns. But we may not know that these economies exist at all until we actually guide the system, production-wise, into the vicinity of A_3. Since this may not happen, we might never succeed in finding an optimal solution to the economic problem.

Here the EPC cannot find the optimum solely by adjusting prices. There are points along the PP' curve near A_2 where the slopes, and hence the ratios of marginal social costs, are exactly the same as at output combinations around A_3. Consequently, we have found a situation where inexpensive information about excess supply and demand becomes an imperfect substitute for expensive, direct information about the nature of society's production and consumption possibilities. The EPC must seek out the optimum, in part, through detailed studies of a nonmarket character. Research and development efforts, engineering and technical explorations, and surveys of resource endowments and world production techniques constitute the only means of throwing daylight on the latent possibilities around A_3.

The second problem arises from the fact that the quantity demanded of any good responds not only to its own price but to the prices of other goods as well. Tea and coffee are said to be substitutes in consumption because they satisfy similar desires and consequently may be used in place of one another. We expect the demand for tea to rise when the price of coffee rises relative to the price of tea because people will drink more tea and less coffee. Automobiles and tires, on the other hand, are complements in consumption. If the price of autos rises, the demand for tires may fall even though the price of tires falls by a much greater percentage amount.

A similar situation holds in production. Gasoline, for example, is a by-product of the refining process. Thus it is complementary to other petroleum products in the sense that these are produced jointly. A rise in the price of diesel fuel will probably result in an increased supply of gasoline, even with no change in gasoline prices. By contrast, our sheet steel and steel girders were presumably substitutes in production inasmuch as some capacity could be switched out of one and into the other fairly easily. Thus we would expect a rise in the price of sheet steel relative to that of girders to result in a decreased supply of girders, and vice versa.

Let us say that two goods are *gross complements* whenever the excess demand (demand minus supply) for one varies *inversely* with the price of the other. (Examples are automobiles and tires.) Similarly, we define them to be *gross substitutes* when the excess demand for one varies *directly* with the other's price. (Examples are coffee and tea.) When two goods are gross complements, and the excess demand for one has a stronger response to the price of the other than to its own price, problems may arise in seeking out the economic optimum, even when no economies of mass production are present. To illustrate, suppose that the price of tires lies above its optimal level. Yet the demand for tires may exceed the supply because the price of autos is too low. If the planners did not know this, they would raise the price of tires still higher, and this particular move would take the economy *farther* from its optimal position. Thus the basis of the trial-and-error search procedure outlined above is partially undermined. The ranges within which the "best" prices must lie are not all being narrowed progressively down, and the consequence will be at least a longer time period required to find the optimum.

The planners can speed up the search, however, with a more sophisticated procedure which relies upon knowing in advance which goods are likely to display strong gross complementarity. In a system with decentralized pricing, tire producers would presumably gear their own output to the projected demand for cars as much as to any other single variable. Within a centralized pricing framework the idea would be to estimate the demand for tires as a function of both tire and auto prices, along, perhaps, with aggregate indexes of household purchasing power, such as disposable income. Then the influence of factors other than the price of tires could be netted out before deciding how to adjust tire prices.

The duties of an EPC within any mixed form, therefore, must include many activities other than price manipulation, and the examples above are an indication of this.[9] When centralized pricing prevails, a certain division of labor will be imparted to the process of planning or policy making. On one hand, the EPC must use activities other than price manipulation to move the economy within some neighborhood of the optimum. Price manipulation will then zero in on the precise optimal point (which, in practice, would lie on a second-best frontier). A risk will always remain that the first step will be unsuccessful and that price adjustments will consequently move the system toward a worse solution to the economic problem.

The presence of tasks beyond price manipulation necessarily requires a more extensive planning apparatus than would be otherwise necessary. In all likelihood the EPC will need a number of staff agencies for this purpose in addition to regional and industrial intermediate authorities, who will require their own staffs. Lange foresaw the need for such bodies, and he was also aware that "overbureaucratization" constituted a serious potential threat to the efficient operation of his system.[10]

Some socialists have drawn an analogy with external economies and argued that one advantage of a planned market system over an unplanned one would be the existence of a central body able to discover potential economies of mass production and to exploit them. Whatever their theoretical merit, however, there are some historical grounds for questioning these claims. Economic expansion under laissez-faire capitalism was, by and large, a story of the discovery of latent large-scale economies, like the assembly line, and their exploitation. One factor that has been important in this and has, so far, been largely absent in socialist countries is the freedom to seek out mass markets, combined with the possibility of earning enormous rewards for doing so. A market economy relies on this kind of initiative from below as much as a command economy depends upon pressure from above.

19-2   Criticisms of the Competitive Solution

We may divide our criticisms of the competitive solution into two parts, representing the two major problems such a system would probably encounter if it were ever to be tried. The first problem is one of statics and dynamics. The theoretical foundations of the competitive solution guarantee at best that an economic optimum will be found and maintained under completely static conditions. In reality, both the consumption-possibility frontier and the social preference function which guides the system will be shifting over time. Rather than shooting at an unknown stationary target, the planners are aiming at an unknown moving target which may be moving in unknown directions over time.

[9] For those who care, we are essentially repeating the well-known result that an optimal solution to the economic problem (and thus a position where all markets are in equilibrium) is more likely to be stable locally than globally. We have given two examples of this, and more could be cited.

[10] Lange, op. cit., pp. 109–110. See the discussion in Section 19–3.

We must therefore give a high priority to making quick and accurate responses as soon as excess demand or supply appears. The less bureaucratic the decision-making process that fixes prices, or the shorter the chain of command that price information must descend before it is applied, the more flexible are prices likely to be. Moreover, decentralized decision makers on the spot will better comprehend their own environments than the EPC or than a ministry, which, by nature, is divorced from the myriad of details surrounding each local situation. Managers will be best able to determine when their product prices are out of equilibrium.

Hayek has commented that

the difference between a system of regimented prices [that is, prices set by an EPC] and a system of prices determined by the market [that is, prices set by buyers and sellers] seems to be about the same as that between an attacking army where every unit and every man could only move by special command and by the exact distance ordered by headquarters and an army where every unit and every man can take advantage of every opportunity offered to them.[11]

We can imagine an attacking army running into ambush and having to send to headquarters before taking evasive action. Generally speaking, if EPC-manipulated prices are going to be further from their optimal levels than we could hope to get in a more decentralized pricing scheme, as seems likely, the cost of such a scheme may be high. This is particularly true when it comes to projects that take a long time to materialize. Steel mills may be located in the wrong places or, once started, have to be abandoned. A railway line may be built with a capacity that is too low or too high or where a canal would be a more efficient means of transport. Similarly, industry may be located on sites best suited for farm land, or vice versa.

The second problem concerns how well managers of socialist enterprises producing or using intermediate goods and natural resources are going to obey the "rules of the game." As it turns out, prices will not be entirely independent of their individual production and market behavior. This factor alone, combined with the nonoperationality of excess demand and supply feedback information, is enough to upset an otherwise well-tuned system.

In any planned economy, the key task of the EPC is to harmonize the goals of individual firms and households with its own set of social goals. Insofar as Lange considered this problem, it was a question of allocating productive inputs efficiently, that is, of getting both enterprise and industry managers to produce output combinations that equate output prices with marginal social costs and to use input assortments that cause input prices to reflect the values of their marginal social products. In the case of investment decision making, industry managers should undertake a potential capital-spending project when and only when at least a normal return can be earned from it, with risk taken into account.

However, Lange failed to explain what would motivate or enable man-

[11] Friedrich Hayek, "Socialist Calculation: The Competitive 'Solution'," *Economica*, May 1940, pp. 130–131.

agers to follow the efficiency rules. In Figure 18–1(b) we omitted any direct (or nonmarket) links between planners and producers in a Lange economy. This was meant to imply that Lange paid too little attention to these ties—in particular, when it came to appropriate incentives for lower-level decision makers. We shall now ask whether we can repair this defect.

One way to achieve goal harmony might simply be to ask or command managers to obey the competitive rules. But because they have complex implications for the daily conduct of production and distribution activity, even the most loyal and dedicated managers will sometimes find it necessary to be magicians in order to understand and interpret them. In this respect the planner who would ask producers to set prices equal to marginal costs is a little like the economist who reportedly went up to the head of an African state and asked, "What is your social welfare function?".

For managers who are less dedicated, it will be even harder for the EPC to monitor and to enforce efficient managerial behavior. Whether material or moral incentives predominate, both the top and the bottom of any decision-making hierarchy will need simple criteria to measure success by. This is, in part, why profits are almost certain to appear as the dominant managerial success indicator in a mixed economy. The other half of the story is that if all potential external effects are internalized and if managers believe that (1) prices are entirely outside their control, and (2) they can sell as much of each output and buy as much of each input as they wish at prevailing prices, maximum profit levels will be found by obeying the efficiency guidelines.

At the same time, let us view profits as a return to society on the capital it has invested to build firms and to install and maintain the tools and machinery in them. Then, after standardizing firms for size and risk, differences in profit levels year in and year out will tend to reflect differences in the return that society is earning on the capital invested in different enterprises. In maximizing their profits, managers are maximizing the yields on the portions of society's investment that are entrusted to them. Under a regime of material incentives, with managerial bonuses based on profit, managers could only earn higher incomes by increasing these returns, that is, by being better managers from society's point of view.[12]

Yet, equality between the profits earned by a firm or by an industry and its contribution to social welfare is only guaranteed when (1) and (2) *both* hold. Under laissez faire, we saw that one or both rules might be violated. A firm can often gain a measure of control over its price, either by cornering a significant percentage of a given market or by differentiating its product. If it is a profit maximizer, it will then raise its profits by raising its price above marginal cost and restricting its output correspondingly.

This action lowers the welfare of the consumer, who pays both for the

[12] We would remind the reader that costs of production, as the economist defines them, include a "normal" return on invested capital. The EPC will determine what this normal yield is to be, and it will also be the same as the charge on loans for investment purposes. (The normal return may vary with the risk of an investment and also to help implement a financial-incentive program.)

producers' monopoly profits and for any inefficiency in resource allocation that the monopoly restriction on output causes. In a Lange economy, no enterprise manager is supposed to be able to raise his own prices. Whereas the EPC has power to adjust prices as it sees fit, managers are supposed to treat price lists as fixed data around which their production plans revolve. In principle, therefore, monopoly restrictions on output will not occur.

At the same time, we recall that command-economy planners have nominal power to fix all quantitative targets. Nevertheless, a clever producer can sometimes use the nonoperationality of his feedback to the EPC to get himself a plan that he is able to fulfill with a margin of safety. At the same time, by continuing to overstate his input needs slightly, he can hope to build up reserves of scarce, essential inputs. By so doing, managers keep valuable inputs idle and thereby reduce the economy's production potential. A realistic EPC will have to set lower output targets. In short, managers can exert some indirect control over the EPC's output targets by manipulating the information regarding their own production requirements and capacity which they send back up the chain of command.

We have seen that excess demand and supply information in a Lange economy also tends to be nonoperational. We should therefore ask whether managers can take advantage of this to influence the effective prices which the EPC sets for their products. In fact, they can, in two different ways.

Suppose, first, that the market for steel ingots in a Lange economy is dominated by a few large firms. One company thinks that its demand is strong enough to bear a price increase which it would like to have. Consequently, it deliberately fails to meet demand by producing short of the point where price equals marginal social cost. If one or more competitors follows suit, a pronounced shortage of ingots could emerge which would be "artificial" in the sense that it results solely from violating the efficiency guidelines.

If the EPC goes by the rules of the game, it will then raise ingot prices. Thus, by restricting supply short of the point where price just covers marginal cost, producers can hope to keep price permanently above marginal cost. In binding itself to its own rules, the EPC may actually delegate this power unintentionally to enterprise management.

We should note here that a good manager will know his production capabilities and the unit costs associated with each possible rate of output better than anyone else. Thus there will be significant costs of monitoring and enforcing his excess demand reports. He will also be able to conceal excess inventories, on occasion, both from higher authorities and from his customers. He can use either of these variables to restrict the flow of goods going to market. From time to time daring managers will even try to build up their inventories while creating artificial market shortages in the hope of disposing of their inventories later at higher prices.

The second way that managers may influence the effective prices of their products is by varying quality. A quality decrease is an implicit price increase, and producers in Western market economies sometimes find it more palatable to "raise" their prices in this way.

A detergent manufacturer may cut the percentage of active ingredient in his product and raise the amount of filler. A textile mill can lower the thread count in its fabric. The quality of rabbitskin fur coats may deteriorate, with no increase in price, while the coats become scarce; but simultaneously there appears on the market a new fur, "peau de lapin," which naturally costs much more. Thus new brands can be marketed at higher prices with no increase in quality over previously existing brands. Cheaper materials can be substituted for more expensive ones, and so on.

A Lange economy may be subject to the same phenomenon. In our previous example, the price of steel ingots may remain fixed while the outlay made by a user of steel to get an ingot of a given size and quality into his warehouse is rising. The product can be varied in several ways by the manufacturer, and his quoted price may sometimes include and sometimes exclude transport costs, depending upon the strength of demand. A number of companies found this a useful way around the U.S. price freeze, which began in 1971.[13]

In short, if a firm has some monopoly power, the chances are not bad that it will be able to exercise this, even though the EPC nominally controls prices. In this sense, EPC control over prices will often prove illusory. Some experts would argue, however, that monopoly power at the enterprise level will be less in a Lange economy than under laissez faire. Reasons for the existence of corporate giants in North America and Western Europe often relate neither to production nor to research or managerial efficiency, but to consideration of market and financial power, international competition, and a desire to control one's sources of supply. These are motives which, it is argued, can be subdued or transferred away from the jurisdiction of the enterprise under socialism. (*Industry* managers, of course, retain complete monopoly power.[14])

This may reduce the extent to which firms can depart from marginal-cost pricing. Nevertheless, enterprise managers will retain some ability to differentiate their products. Earlier we noted that the work of one dentist might not be a perfect substitute for another's because the second dentist has a favorable location or a reassuring smile. A small candy-making company may package its products differently and, to some buyers, more attractively than its rivals. In either case, the firm has gained a clientele in the sense that it can raise its

---

[13] Let us view each good as a bundle of characteristics or intrinsic properties. We may think of a ton of coal in this vein, as so much heat or energy or of a ton of steel as a certain amount of strength and durability. Ability to resist heat or cold, juiciness, firmness, drilling power, and horsepower are other intrinsic properties that goods may have, and the reader can probably think of many more.

Although the planners will be able to assign prices to each good, they are unlikely to be able to price the characteristics upon which the value of a good to its buyers depends. By changing the nature of what they produce and sell, therefore, producers can hope to supplement and add flexibility to whatever power they have to affect centrally set prices through manipulation of supply.

[14] We recall that industry managers control the long-run expansion and contraction of their industries. Given their monopoly power, we cannot make them profit maximizers. We shall discuss their incentives below.

price without losing all its business. That is, it faces a downward-sloping demand curve.

For some firms in a Lange economy, then, the best strategy will be as follows. First, management should try to gain some monopoly power by differentiating its product. It should then try to raise price above marginal cost by a combination of the methods outlined above. (In practice, it may accomplish the two goals by a single stroke, such as the "creation" of a nominally "new" product or brand.)

To combat both undesirable product differentiation and quality reductions, the EPC can attempt to issue, keep up to date, and enforce a detailed list of product specifications. However, there would be many more standards to police than in an economy with decentralized pricing, where, according to contemporary Western experience, the costs of protecting users, the environment, and the general public are likely to be serious enough. We must remember that literally millions of different intermediate goods and services are being turned out and that new products should always be entering and old ones leaving. Some of these will be extremely intricate and in certain cases— for example, consulting services and custom-built machinery—no two orders will be exactly alike.

A cumbersome bureaucracy would therefore be needed to enforce the required standards. This will be expensive to operate, and the officials responsible for enforcement are certain to be biased in favor of product uniformity as of any point in time and unchanging standards over time. Such practices will work against product differentiation where this is necessary to satisfy user requirements. They will also help to stifle technological progress and initiative from below whenever this must bear fruit in the form of new products offered for sale. To the costs of control, we should add those of counter-control. As in a command economy, the two efforts are likely to intensify together.

The planners may be helped in the enforcement task, however, by the dedication of lower-level decision makers to the regime and its goals. The greater the willingness of managers to sacrifice income because of this dedication, the more feasible it will be to replace precise standards with guidelines spelling out in general terms what kinds of product differentiation and quality variation are permissible.

Without dedication, a Lange economy could easily succumb to something analogous to French mercantilism under Colbert, where "an edict covering the dyeing of cloth (had), for example, 371 articles." [15] It would not be entirely impossible for a command economy to eventually (re)establish itself.

---

[15] To cite an even less desirable alternative, the Roman emperor Diocletian decreed in 301 A.D. that merchants who exceeded his price controls would lose their heads.

The quote in the text is from Shepard B. Clough, *The Economic Development of Western Civilization* (New York: McGraw-Hill, 1959), p. 219. Regarding Colbertism, see, for example, Charles W. Cole, *Colbert and a Century of French Mercantilism* (New York: Columbia U.P., 1939).

Finally, we should note that, even when managers act as if they had no control over prices, they may still tend to restrict output below the point where price and marginal cost are the same. A problem of uncertainty arises because the EPC will sometimes set the wrong prices. When these are too high, producers will find that they cannot sell all that they wish and be stuck with excess inventories. If the EPC is playing the rules of the game, it will lower price, and managers will take losses on these inventories. (By unloading them at the new price, they may also spoil the EPC's calculations of excess demand and supply at this price.[16]) After one or two such experiences, managers will stop assuming that their markets are unlimited, and this is enough to cause the marginal-cost pricing rule to be violated, as Figure 19–6 shows.

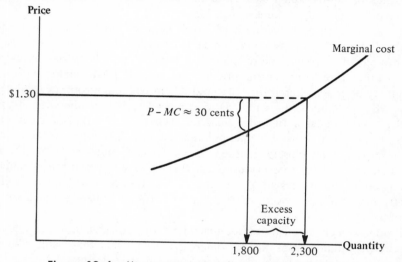

Figure 19–6. How uncertainty may cause output restriction.

There the manager takes the current EPC-set price as being beyond his influence but also fears that his market may prove to be limited. To keep from getting caught with excess inventories, he produces 1,800 units of output, 500 short of the rate that equates price and marginal social cost. Here, in fact, price is 30 per cent greater than marginal cost, and if many firms follow this practice, supply will fall significantly short of the efficient level. The counterpart of this will be a tendency of firms and industries to hoard inputs that managers have found to be in short supply because prices were set too low.

[16] Suppose that the new price would balance supply and demand were producers to start from zero-excess-inventory levels. Then, if producers have inventories that are too high, and if they unload these after the price falls (perhaps in anticipation of yet another price reduction), it will appear as if an excess supply exists. Consequently, the EPC will mistakenly lower price once more (thereby rendering the producers' forecast self-fulfilling). This indicates how actual trading at disequilibrium prices can distort feedback signals and prevent any convergence toward an eventual balancing of supply and demand.

19–3   Centralized Marketing

If firms do not possess too much monopoly power, the central marketing agency outlined in our discussion of command-economy reforms may provide an answer to most of the problems outlined above. There, most intermediate goods must be bought and sold through a central marketing agency, which maintains marketing centers throughout the economy. These are also centers for nonprice information concerning new products and technologies and, more generally, the characteristics of goods demanded and offered for sale. Ideally, marketing-center agents should be able to seek out potential suppliers for new kinds of inputs which users would like to be able to buy, as well as to market products and, in some cases, ideas.

Thus, the central marketing agency will help to "bring buyers and sellers together." Nevertheless, all goods whose prices are set centrally must also be bought and sold through one of the marketing centers, whose task is, in part, to "operationalize" the central pricing mechanism. Each center will judge the quality of goods offered for sale, grade them where appropriate, and reject goods whose quality it finds too low or which it feels are otherwise ill-suited to users' requirements. In order to deny each producer the information he needs to influence price by manipulating supply, inventory levels at each center must remain closely guarded secrets.[17] The counterpart of this is a guarantee by the EPC to every producer that he may buy and sell as much of each good as he wishes at going prices. Where necessary, goods will be secretly imported, destroyed, or transferred between centers to back up this guarantee.

Products such as custom-built machine tools or consulting services that are so differentiated from one *customer* to the next that they cannot be centrally marketed probably should not be centrally priced either. However, the central marketing agency can still act as a clearing house for nonprice information and help to bring buyers and sellers together. To increase price flexibility among goods that are centrally marketed, the EPC should also allow local marketing centers to adjust many prices. One general rule would require the EPC to set prices or price intervals for key commodities and one more-or-less standard item (for example, a standard spark plug or lathe) from every product group. All other prices would come under local jurisdiction. As a consequence, the number of simultaneous prices to be centrally manipu-

---

[17] Consequently, as a minimum requirement, there should probably be more than one buyer and more than one seller for each centrally marketed good. At the level of the firm, this condition is easy to meet, but industry managers will have monopolies. It is not clear just what the effect would be, since the latter will be mainly involved with investment decisions. Most capital-construction projects cannot be centrally marketed because they are too differentiated from one customer to another. Nevertheless, if some industry managers are willing and able to interfere with decision making at the enterprise level, they could cause the firms under their jurisdictions to buy and sell like monopolies. This is one reason why profit is unlikely to be an industry manager's dominant success indicator.

lated could fall from a few hundred thousand or a few million to several thousand or tens of thousands, still an awesome task.

Price changes for centrally marketed goods should be irregular and unannounced to avoid the consequences of speculation about when they will be made. Indeed, the most successful changes will come as surprises, much in the manner of the most successful devaluations of national currencies, and we should not underestimate the difficulties this will involve. Unless many thousands of prices are all maintained reasonably close to their equilibrium levels, firms will avoid buying and selling—or else engage in speculative selling or hoarding of goods whose prices they expect to change. The greater the volume of excess demand for or supply of any commodity, the harder it will be to conceal efforts to cover this by transporting goods or destroying them. Thus the more likely there is to be speculation, and, generally speaking, the danger of this will probably be greater than in a straight Lange economy.

The central marketing agency will necessarily be organized according to the command principle. Thus it constitutes a step back toward the command economy and the command-planning bureaucracy, and it is probably here that its biggest disadvantages lie. Among these, we would cite the nonoperationality of excess demand information relayed from the marketing centers and eventually reaching the EPC. If the central marketing scheme is to work, the marketing centers must act like appendages of the EPC. But the possibility remains that they will give some of their loyalty to producers or to the industrial ministries.

Whether or not this happens, industry managers are likely to become major poles of economic power in any Lange economy. They will play a role that we have so far neglected in our discussion of managerial incentives, and we now wish to fill this gap.

19–4 The Role of Industry Managers

We recall that industry managers are responsible for all major long-run decisions—notably for investment decision making—and that they are to set sector-wide outputs at levels where prices reflect long-run marginal costs.[18] Like everyone else in the system, industry managers will have goals reflecting whatever they believe to be their most important "success indicators" in terms of salary, prestige and advancement. If they draw paychecks based upon the profits earned by the firms in their sectors, profit maximization will be one of their goals. In all likelihood, however, if this is one goal, it will not be the only one, and it will usually be in the EPC's interest to see to this.

To begin with, it is easy to see that industry managers will normally be in far better monopoly positions than any enterprise manager. The more powerful

---

[18] Lange, op. cit., pp. 76–77. Lange assumed that these officials would be industry managers. There is no explicit statement of "success criteria" for industry managers, any more than there is for managers of firms. Thus we shall have to infer what these criteria should be.

among them may be capable of restricting their outputs so much that the "efficiency cost of monopoly" becomes serious. Moreover, under profit maximization for industry managers, the competitive solution would become vulnerable to one of Lange's most serious objections to laissez-faire capitalism.

In highly concentrated industries under laissez faire, profit-maximizing managers will have an incentive to tacitly agree to protect the profits from their investments by slowing down the flow of new products and techniques.[19] As long as previous investments are yielding handsome profits, they will avoid introducing any innovation capable of rendering these investments obsolete.

Ironically, Lange's industry managers are perfectly positioned to do this very thing. Normally, they will control the expansion or modification of existing firms and the creation of new ones within their jurisdictions. In other cases, for example the creation of new products or industries, they are likely to wield some influence over the initial decision on whether to go ahead and at what scale to produce.

In addition, there is the earlier-noted necessity of harmonizing goals at lower levels in the planning hierarchy with the social goals formulated by the EPC. When profit-maximizing enterprise managers seek to restrict output, it make sense to countervail this by giving intermediate authorities more expansionary motives. This could produce capacity which is simultaneously overexpanded and underutilized because of the difference in areas of decision-making responsibility. But there is also no reason why industry managers could not sometimes receive a variety of carrots and sticks—ranging from moral suasion to financial incentives to commands—to use in prompting firms to increase their output from given plant and equipment.

It is true that, for a number of reasons, industry managers are more likely than managers at the firm level to voluntarily try to harmonize their goals with those of the EPC. In the first place, some of them will comprise part of the EPC's present or potential membership. Others may simply feel "closer" to the top echelon of society's economic leadership. And it will, in any event, be easier for the center to directly scrutinize a few ministers than many firm managers.

But while recognizing this possibility, we still feel that the rewards of industry managers (including their promotion potential) will usually have to be tied at least partly to performance in their sectors. Whether the principal "success indicator" turns out to be sales, growth, or something else, this opens up the range of potential bureaucratic abuses discussed in Chapter 10.

Suppose, for example, that sales maximinization becomes an industry's principal goal. Then we may liken it to a giant, sales-maximizing corporation under laissez faire. If the corporations's cost constraint represents the costs to society of its activities, and if its demand curve measures their social benefit, the firm may well produce in the "public interest," given any reasonable inter-

[19] Lange, ibid., pp. 110–121.

pretation of the term. But when the corporation is able to lower its own costs, by shifting some of them onto other members of society, or raise its demand by lobbying, it is often able to destroy any identity between its private and its social costs and benefits.

Lange's industry managers are probably even better equipped to manipulate their own internal costs and benefits. In particular, industries threatened with declining demand will try to maintain their status by relying increasingly on government contracts or by overstating the expected yield on investments in their sectors.

As in a command economy, there is also a serious risk that intermediate officials will use their influence against innovation whenever this appears to threaten their vested interests. They will be aided by what is likely to be a frequent difficulty in a Lange system of knowing when a new product line, enterprise, or infant industry has failed or how to assign blame when failure becomes apparent.

Suppose, for instance, that a new atomic power plant is constructed. The industry manager who decides on this capital spending project will not normally be the enterprise manager who operates it. Therefore, should it prove unprofitable, the cause may lie with the plant manager, the industry manager who pushed for its undertaking, or with the EPC, if the prevailing set of prices has not been optimal. More generally, the division of responsibility between industry and firm managers creates a problem of assigning credit or blame for success or failure. This may further reduce some industry managers' taste for innovation.

Further, in a world where scale economies, along with external costs and benefits, are potentially present, many enterprises will be socially justifiable which appear to earn less than a "normal" return on the capital invested in them. Such an enterprise would find it possible to produce a positive output that would equate price and marginal social cost, at least approximately, and yet would require a subsidy to keep its books in the black. This kind of subsidy will be an essential part of any program to internalize external effects as or before they arise, but it will also be relatively easy to prevent by successful lobbying.

Contrary to the beliefs of some socialist writers, therefore, a Lange model, or any version of socialism for that matter, may choose a path of economic development that is inefficiently conservative. This tendency may be heightened by the egalitarian nature of such a system in contrast with capitalism. We recall that many writers have tried to justify the existence of property incomes, and of the gross inequities to which they often lead, as potential rewards for entrepreneurial risk taking.

In socialist countries, the mentality so far has been to deny these earnings in one way or other. Since they often come out of profits, a failure of centralized pricing may have the same effect, if profit controls are substituted for price controls. It is far from unlikely, then, that differences in salaries, both at the ministerial and managerial levels, will not be sufficient to serve as adequate incentives for risk bearing.[20]

The upshot of our discussion so far is that the "competitive solution" is likely to be saddled with problems of imperfect competition and bureaucracy. As in a command economy, ministries may become rigid and inert empire builders. If centralized marketing is largely absent, there is, as well, a risk of excessive product differentiation, excess inventories and production capacity, and costly measures of control and counter control relating to implicit price changes. Finally, prices may remain significantly above and below those levels which will balance demand and supply throughout the economy.

As centralized marketing becomes more widespread, most of these problems should lessen. However, the central marketing agency is only an intermediary buying on behalf of users whose preferences and requirements it must try to reflect. This it will do by laying down quality standards and other product specifications. But being both a third party in all transactions and a bureaucracy, it is apt to change these standards too slowly to keep pace with changing user preferences over time and to be a bit rigid and arbitrary in enforcing them. This, combined with a slow or reluctant marketing of new products and ideas, may stifle initiative and innovation.

In addition, we can neglect neither the interaction between industry and enterprise managers nor that between industry managers and marketing officials. We have already pointed out that industry managers can be motivated to countervail tendencies by firms to produce short of the point where price equals marginal cost. Nevertheless, the bias of industrial ministries against innovation may have an effect on firms which is complementary to that of the central marketing agency, and the two together can easily constitute a serious problem.

It is also possible for periodic power conflicts or jurisdictional disputes to erupt between marketing and intermediate planning authorities. On these occasions, some power will descend to the level of firms whose managers will have more influence on the path of development that the economy follows than they would if either central marketers or industry managers were removed from the scene.

In the final analysis, much of the functioning of any Lange economy must remain a matter for academic speculation. Two factors, however, do appear to stand out. First, inefficiency in at least one of the forms just mentioned is likely to be a constant headache for the EPC. Second, it is far from clear that the EPC will be able to steer the economy. There will be a number of power centers, some large and some small, and corresponding "spheres of influence" beneath the EPC, and there is no reason to expect that the vast majority of these will turn out to be mutually offsetting. Rather it appears that at least some intermediate authorities, firms, or marketing officials will be able to alter

---

[20] Of course, profit controls may remove some incentives for firms to be internally efficient (X efficiency) even without taking risk into account.

the economy's distribution of welfare, its pattern of production and specialization in international trade, and its rate and direction of investment and technical change.

Thus the most powerful actors below the EPC may gain control over the path of economic development. Then the prevailing pattern of aggregate demand—or the social preference function actually guiding the economy—will largely synthesize the preferences of these actors. The danger of this appears greater than in a command economy. Indeed, several economists have argued that the central planners will increasingly turn to commands, if they are able, to reassert their own social preferences.

Interestingly enough, the mixed forms which have arisen and which might be expected to emerge in the future depart significantly from the "competitive solution" along several dimensions. Most importantly, they make more provision for systematic advance planning than did Lange, and they do not try to simultaneously clear large numbers of markets through central price manipulation.[21] Decentralized pricing generally enables prices to remain closer to their equilibrium values, reduces the incentive toward product differentiation that is not use-oriented, and cuts down on the need for intermediate planning and marketing authorities.

Thus Lange's contribution was not to finalize the blueprints of a socialist market economy or of any other mixed system. It was to point out that planning and decentralized decision making are not inherently contradictory. A nation might be able to use the market mechanism and yet consciously control its economic destiny.

19–5   The Basic Taylor Model

When we talk about a "Taylor model," we are really speaking of a set of blueprints that have been more or less deduced from a brief and sketchy presidential address delivered by Fred M. Taylor to the 1928 meeting of the American Economic Association.[22] Lange himself was aware of Taylor's remarks and seems to have looked upon his own model as a considerable elaboration of what Taylor had to say. To some extent this is correct, but important differences exist between the two models in the way planners and producers divide the task of planning. These we now wish to explore.

As in the Lange model, a basic task of the EPC is to bring about economic efficiency. Once again the planners will try to achieve an economy-wide balance of supply and demand by manipulating many prices simultaneously. Indeed, Taylor appears to have foreseen that the planners would control virtually all prices. Thus our discussion and criticism of centralized pricing in the competitive solution will also apply here. It was also Taylor's belief that

[21] However, they do make frequent—and, generally speaking, not too successful—use of "temporary" price controls to combat inflation.

[22] Fred M. Taylor, "The Guidance of Production in a Socialist State," *American Economic Review,* Mar. 1929; reprinted in Lippincott, op. cit.

problems involved in converging to the optimum via a trial-and-error process, and of motivating socialist managers and ministerial directors to "play the rules of the game," would not, in practice, turn out to be difficult.[23] This may help explain why the Taylor model is the least operational of all the mixed forms that we discuss.

Taylor confined his discussion almost entirely to the series of information exchanges between planners and producers. Therefore, let us begin by seeing what sort of process he had in mind. During the planning year the EPC sends out target prices to firms and asks production techniques or coefficients plus projected levels of output in return. These replies are supposed to reflect production methods that would prevail if the system were going to operate at what Taylor believed was its maximal economic efficiency.

For every good or service, this meant finding a rate of output for which average or per unit production costs were at a minimum. In Figure 19–7, any rate of output between 500,000 and 900,000 units would be efficient, according to Taylor. However, planners wanting to promote efficiency would presumably choose the *lowest* rate of output at which scale economies are realized. They would therefore request the production coefficients that the firm would use at T, along with the associated rate of output. As is shown in elementary textbooks, T is a point at which marginal and average costs are the same, since it lies on the flat, bottom portion of the average cost curve.

When the plan has been put into operation, the question arises as to what tactics to follow in the almost certain event that some prices turn out to be too high or low. To the extent that excess demand and supply appear to be temporary fluctuations around a long-run trend line, the EPC will be reluctant to alter the *current* price, provided surplus goods can be stored. But in cases in which equilibrium prices are volatile from one year to the next and where goods cannot be easily preserved (for example, raw agricultural produce), the EPC will have little choice but to do this.

Nonetheless, other things being equal, the planners will prefer to adjust as few current prices as possible. For one thing, knowing that prices will remain stable over the course of a year or so will aid managers in their own planning of production. Perhaps more importantly, current price manipulation will tend to accentuate the danger already inherent in the nonoperationality of the Taylor system. If firm managers feel that their product prices may fall or that their input prices may rise during the course of the operating year, they will have increased incentive to try to get themselves some insurance in the form of an "easy" plan. As in a command economy, they would tend to inflate the production coefficients which they report back to the EPC, thereby gaining themselves more inputs per unit of output than they really expect to need. If the planners can be persuaded to go along with these padded estimates, the projections of minimum average costs will likewise be too high, as will the prices that firms are permitted to charge.

[23] Ibid., Sec. II.

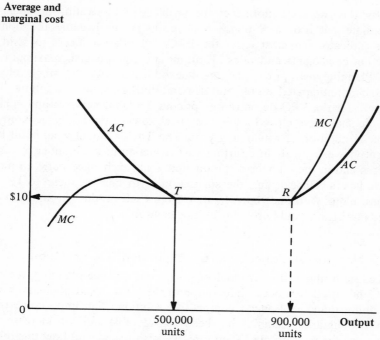

Figure 19–7. Average costs and efficient production in a Taylor economy.

In cases where a permanent change in the relationship between demand and costs appears to be occurring, the planners should expand or contract the industry in question. As in the Lange model, intermediate authorities are primarily responsible for predicting the evolution of demand and costs and for changing production capacity. Once again we would expect these officials to be overly optimistic about the desirability of expansion within their own sectors.

Taylor does not give us an interim pricing rule for the period when capacity is being adapted to demand and, in fact, this points up a fundamental weakness in his pricing policy. Suppose that the price is set equal to $10 in Figure 19–7. The firm in question will supply 500,000 units if it is obeying EPC directives, and other firms in the industry will produce analogous rates of output. The sum of all these outputs is the industry-wide supply at $10.

The problem is that demand may not match supply at this price. Generally speaking, the price that corresponds to minimum average cost will not always equate demand with supply *during any given time period,* unless the planners *always* have capacity exactly adjusted to demand. No EPC will be good enough to ensure that this is done continually in every industry.

Moreover, whenever there is a significant discrepancy between the two, economic efficiency requires prices to equal marginal costs rather than minimum average costs. Upon adjusting the Taylor model, where necessary, to allow for this, we once more face the problem of motivating producers and intermediate authorities. Suppose that profits again become the dominant success indicator. In most cases the EPC will ask producers to send back production coefficients and rates of output corresponding to maximum profit levels. Planning-year prices can then be adjusted with the single objective of balancing anticipated supply and demand during the year to follow.

Finally, if the EPC decentralizes pricing for labor services and consumer goods, we shall have moved a long way back toward the Lange economy with the crucial addition of a planning year. The Taylor model would still be impractical, however, without a further vast reduction in the number of centrally set prices and in the number of production goals exchanged between planners and producers. Once again, the suggestion is to confine these to key commodities, along with one representative from each product group. Some centralized marketing would probably also be advisable.

19–6   Nonmarket Aspects of an Expanded Taylor Model

Because it makes more formal provision for advance planning, the Taylor model lends itself to a better integration of the market and nonmarket aspects of planning than did Lange's competitive solution. The importance that we attach to nonmarket planning has been considerable and will increase as this chapter and the next unfold. Therefore, we wish to indicate how this might be integrated into a kind of two-stage approach to horizon or long-term planning. The same example will serve to contrast horizon and operative planning in a mixed-economy setting. In what follows we shall assume that we are dealing with two goods or categories of goods, X and Y, between which the optimal long-run demand tradeoffs (that is, the slopes of the social indifference surfaces) are known to the EPC with a fair degree of certainty. The future production possibilities in these commodities, on the other hand, can only be estimated.

In Figure 19–8 the curve PP' depicts the economy's production possibilities for a period, let us say five years hence. (In practice this would be a second-best frontier.) As it turns out, there are important economies of mass production to be had in good Y if the planners will devote sufficient resources to developing the industry that produces it. The EPC may suspect this from its own program of exploration, research, and development, but the precise curve, PP', remains unknown to it.

Therefore, we suppose the EPC to have divided the production space for X and Y into two large regions. The area enclosed by the boundary, EUREKO, contains all the output combinations that the planners believe might possibly be feasible (that is, all the points that they feel could conceivably be on or inside the production-possibility frontier). EUREKO, in turn, is split into smaller subregions. The more promising of these have been ranked according to some combination of desirability, as measured by the social preference function, and the probability that *all* output combinations

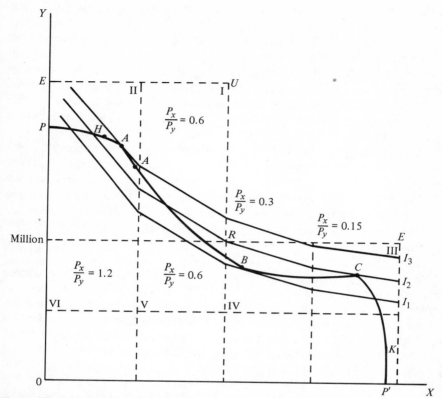

Figure 19–8. The combining of market and nonmarket information to approximate the social welfare optimum under conditions of uncertainty.

within them lie on or inside the unknown production-possibility frontier.[24] Other things being equal, the smaller each subregion can be made, the better. However, two different output combinations cannot be placed in different subregions unless there are strong grounds for ranking one significantly above the other along the scale of feasibility and desirability chosen by the EPC.

The basic idea in all of this is to devise a partitioning of the production space so that, as a minimum requirement, the subregion containing the optimal output combination (*A*) will contain no nonoptimal assortments at which supply and demand are going to balance on both markets. In other words, within each subregion there should be only *one* point of tangency between a social indifference curve and the production-posibility curve. For when the EPC maneuvers the economy into a given subregion (such as II in

[24] For example, we could assign each box a number equal to this probability times the average value of all output combinations within it. If we were basically conservative, we might then adjust those numbers downward which are the product of a high level of social welfare and a low probability.

Figure 19–8) it will have to be content with *any* equilibrium solution it finds there.

Next the social indifference curves will be approximated by kinked curves like, I_1, I_2, and I_3 in Figure 19–8. These curves consist of straight-line segments and have the same slope, representing identical consumption terms of trade, throughout each subregion. This enables us to identify a single price ratio with each subregion. For example, everywhere in Sector I, the price of X will be just 60 per cent of the price of Y because all kinked curves have a slope of 0.6 there.

With this setup, the EPC is ready to begin a series of price exchanges between it and the producing sector. Here the planners will be forced to manipulate future as well as present planning prices. Or, more accurately, they will have to project the evolution of the relative prices for X and Y over the five-year planning period, an operation in which intermediate authorities are likely to play a major role. Thus in Figure 19–8, P_x and P_y refer to target prices or price indices for X and Y, five years hence, but only their *relative* values are important for our purposes.

Because of the nature of the production-posibility frontier, price signals alone will not move the system into the vicinity of its optimum—they must be supplemented by less anonymous messages. The first goal of the EPC will be to steer the system into the subregion with the highest rank—sector I in Figure 19–8. If this turns out not to contain any point where supply and demand balance on an economy-wide basis, the planners will try sector II, and so forth. Thus the EPC in our example might send out a price of $6 for X and $10 for Y inasmuch as $P_x/P_y = 0.6$ in sector I.

In addition, producers of Y will receive a minimum output target of 1,000, 000 units. The key role played by this guideline is to make sure that the economy does not drift into sectors with the lower ranks, III, IV, V, and VI. Because we are in a mixed economy, this target will usually be an indicator, probably reinforced by some kind of incentive, rather than a command. However, its importance is underscored by the fact that sectors I and II become unachievable if firms fail to meet it. Thus a certain amount of persuasion may reinforce the incentive.

Suppose, in any event, that managers go along and reply with projected outputs of X and Y corresponding to H and thereby take system into sector II. The EPC would then set the price of X at $6 and the price of Y at $5.80 (so that $P_x/P_y = 1.2$), which would take the system toward A'. Finally, as the operating year approaches, the central planners can, if they wish, try to bring the economy closer to the true optimum at A. In any practical situation, both the EPC and lower-level decision makers will also be learning more about production possibilities as the operating year approaches. Thus some provision for reshaping EUREKO, reranking subregions, and retracing steps in the planning process may be included.

For the above arrangement to work well, we must assume that (1) accurate forecasting and research are taking place at all three basic levels of the planning hierarchy (producers, intermediate authorities, and EPC); and that (2) firms and intermediate authorities are playing the rules of the game. The scheme may be particularly vulnerable to the fact that estimates of the payoffs of proposed investment projects made by intermediate officials are not operational. Consequently, these officials may be able to bias the path of development which the system takes by affecting the EPC's ranking of subregions. Returning to Fig. 19–8, suppose that a high rate of production of Y runs contrary to what intermediate officials believe to be their vested interests. Consequently, they succeed in reversing ranks II and III. Then, when the EPC receives a proposed production response at H, it will conclude, correctly, that the optimum does not lie in subregion I. However, it will then proceed to move the system to the vicinity of C' by dropping the output target for Y and substituting one for X. Generally speaking, the ranking of subregions is the most critical function in the nonmarket stage of planning. Although it may not always be done explicitly, it cannot be avoided altogether.

The situation will become much more complex in a realistic setting where many prices have to be manipulated simultaneously and where the production space is multidimensional. Nevertheless, any two-stage integration of market and nonmarket planning will involve some variation on the above discussion. The nonmarket stage will always identify more closely than the market stage with horizon planning. It will have the basic task of ruling out certain undesirable alternatives in advance so that the market mechanism cannot lead the system off in an unwanted direction.

19–7   Concluding Remarks: Centralized Pricing and Mixed Economies

The critics of Lange's competitive solution, to give a particularly acrid summary of their views, have argued that it is neither competitive nor a solution. Even if each decentralized decision maker rigidly observes the rules of the game, dynamic problems may prevent an optimal set of prices from emerging, partly because central price manipulation is likely to prove more clumsy and rigid than manipulation by individual buyers and sellers. However, incentives to misbehave at lower levels will, in fact, abound, and either of these faults suffices to lead the system away from the optimal path of economic development according to the macrorationale of the EPC.

Hence some economists have argued that the competitive solution constitutes and unstable form that would sooner or later begin to evolve back toward the command prototype as the EPC seeks to reinforce its control. Similar comments apply to the Taylor model, and we may wish to view the central marketing economy as a stepping stone in this process.

But while such a forecast may appear to follow from what has been said above, it must sound a bit out of place to anyone who has observed evolution in the socialist world over the past quarter of a century or so. Change there ultimately seems to press toward more, not less, decentralization in deci-

sion making, despite the increasingly sophisticated computer complexes which
are available to serve the needs of centralized planning, and an ideological bias
in favor of centralization. Moreover, one reason appears to be that, eventually,
as centralized decision making becomes less manageable, the EPC begins to
lose control.[25]

An important difference between mixed economies in practice and the
models we have considered is that the former do not use economy-wide
central price manipulation to achieve supply–demand equilibrium. Price controls, where used, are generally on-again-off-again devices to combat inflation or else to countervail monopoly in particular industries. In Chapter 18
we noted that mixed-economy planning is largely "a question of molding market structures and of designing an incentive system that will motivate managers to produce efficiently and to harmonize their goals with those of the
center." By this definition both Lange and Taylor tended to ignore planning,
choosing instead to devote their attention to balancing the economy.

Yet our analysis has seriously questioned the wisdom of widespread central price manipulation. Not only may this promote rather than prevent
monopoly power and bureaucratic controls, but it will probably prove to be
clumsy and even illusory. In any event, less anonymous signals will be required
to steer the system satisfactorily. We can easily imagine either the Lange or
Taylor model just as it was proposed except that buyers and sellers establish
most prices in bargaining among themselves and never bother to send excess
demand information to higher authorities.

If we go back to Figure 19–8, for example, there was no inherent need
for central price control in that model. The crucial flows of information were
all quantities—projected rates of output and input from producers and intermediate officials to the EPC, and output goals moving in the opposite direction. We can generalize on this idea, in turn, to derive an expanded Taylor
model with decentralized pricing which bears some resemblance to planning
in the French economy.

If we put considerations of operationality aside, the division of function
between planners and producers is in many ways an ideal one in Taylor's
model. Although the planners can exploit managers' knowledge of local conditions, the EPC is much better placed to get an overview of the system as a
whole. An exchange of quantitative information is possible which can benefit
all parties and to which each decision maker contributes that data which he
is best able to gather and process. Enterprises will trade their own forecasts
of input requirements, output goals, and any other locally observable data
that the EPC finds relevant for information about the state of the nation, region, or industries within which they operate.

In this way individual data will move up the planning hierarchy. Along

---

[25] More specifically, as the importance and difficulty of making rational economic
calculations increases, power shifts down the planning hierarchy toward intermediate
authorities and firms. A macrorationality emerging from the interaction of these decision
makers replaces the macrorationale of the EPC.

the way, they will be aggregated, adjusted, and supplemented with information (for example, on research developments) that originates elsewhere. Finally, they will move back down.

If for no other reason than the law of large numbers, the EPC should be able to make the aggregate return information more reliable than most of the individual forecasts from which it was fashioned. The planners can also adjust their estimates up or down on the basis of their own previous experience with lower-level forecasting errors. Finally, they can often check different lower-level forecasts against one another or against independent predictions made entirely at more aggregated levels.[26]

Individual firms will translate EPC forecasts into (revised) predictions of their own rates of output and of input use by forecasting their market shares. When managers tend, on balance, to overestimate their shares of output markets and to underestimate input availabilities, they will likewise tend, on that account, to propel the economy toward overfulfilment of its plan. This would notably favor greater X efficiency and some increase in competitive behavior, as firms try to maintain the market shares that they project.

If the EPC can establish a record of competence, the data it produces will be highly prized by firms. The French manager in 1970 needs an over-all picture of his economy in 1975 if he is to comprehend his own role during the intervening years. It will make a difference to steel firms, for example, whether steel output is to grow by 3 per cent or 6 per cent and whether the trend will be to structural steel girders and beams or to cold-rolled sheets. Managers will also be interested in research developments and in such items as manpower-training programs and expected migration of labor from one geographical region to another. The planners can trade this information for more effective and reliable cooperation with the plan.

The other tools of indicative planning can be inserted into this context. Instead of simply exchanging information with producers, the planners would try to persuade them on to a more satisfactory performance in the light of EPC goals. Indeed, if the plan is reasonably consistent, its predictive power for any one industry or firm is greater the better other firms conform, on balance, to their input and output targets. Each firm or industry's compliance to the plan provides an external cost or benefit to others. One purpose of a financial-incentive program, for example, is to internalize these effects.

Suppose that, after bargaining between planners and producers, the EPC sets the output target for an industry about 15 per cent above the collective initial projects of individual firms. If managers nevertheless try to maintain or to increase their market shares, the output target will tend to become self-fulfilling. This is the most favorable case in which the plan's information externalties are self-internalizing. Suppose, on the other hand, that managers

---

[26] For further discussion of the role of data gathering, processing, and use in different kinds of planned economies, see Robert W. Campbell, "The Changing Role of Statistics in the Soviet Economic System," in Vladinier Treml and John Hardt, eds., *Soviet Economic Statistics* (Durham, N.C.: Duke U.P., 1972).

are more cautious or willing to discount the EPC's forecast. To induce the planned output increase, the planners may then offer carrots in the form of reduced borrowing costs or tax incentives. In extreme cases it will apply sticks, including its ability to ostrasize those who do not cooperate with the plan from those who do.

Consequently, although output targets in a mixed economy are less obligatory than commands, they are not "pure" indicators, nor are we likely to encounter the latter in practice. It is probably still true, however, that indicative planning will work best in an economy such as that in France, where cooperation has traditionally dominated competition in relations among producers. The planners' task is then to infuse dynamism and entrepreneurial spirit into management, while turning its collusive efforts away from restrictive practices. If they can make the economy more competitive in the process, this will generally be desirable.

We would, nevertheless, remind readers that, although producers of a given product can often get together and raise profits by increasing price and restricting output, this behavior is directly contrary to the interest of users. If *both* users and suppliers of a product collude, the result will be an expansion of output under bilaterial monopoly or countervailing power. More generally, suppose that we consider 25 or so leading industries which are interdependent in the sense of being plugged into one another through a table of interindustry (or intersectoral) flows. Managers in these industries could get together to expand production to one another's mutual benefit as in the two-dimensional case, except that the transactions costs of such an arrangement may prove too high.

However, under suitable conditions, the EPC can then take the lead as a mediator in these or similar negotiations and use its role to implement its own growth priorities. With considerable qualification, this indicates, in part, the rationale of French planning.

When all is said and done, our analysis suggests an important modification to the Lange and Taylor models before their contributions can be realized in real-world market economies. It is not prices that ought to be centrally manipulated but incentives of all kinds and, in some cases, indicative targets as well. In such a system, planners or policy makers will experiment with different combinations of incentives and, perhaps, indicators in an effort to find the best set to implement their own priorities. On the basis of a variety of feedback, they will adjust a specific set during the next round or planning period in order to improve it. Their objective is not to fashion economic performance from the ground up but to correct deviations from a best achievable norm.

Chapter **20**

Brand X:
Structure and Functioning

20–1 Introduction to Brand X

The mixed form we have christened Brand X could well be looked upon as a logical extension of laissez faire. It continues to rely upon horizon planning to move the economy into a broad neighborhood of its optimal solution and market activity to zero in on the precise optimum. However, it also features decentralized pricing and a "low-key" approach to planning. A basic idea is to interfere as little as possible in day-to-day managerial decisions, while giving producers increased autonomy, notably to make their own investment decisions.

Consequently, those planning bureaus which, in a Lange or Taylor economy, arise directly or indirectly out of the need to make centralized pricing work effectively will be dismantled. In addition, many bureaucrats will have their jurisdictions broadened as decision making is decentralized. Instead of manipulating market signals, the EPC will rely upon its ability to influence the environments within which decentralized decision makers operate.

The central marketing agency may be replaced by two agencies or by a single agency serving two distinct functions.[1] One, a consumers' union, would provide information to households about the safety, quality, and other characteristics of consumer goods. It or a sister agency would also become involved in legally protecting consumers. At the same time, a need may arise to limit the amounts which firms and other organizations are allowed to spend on advertising and other selling costs. Otherwise, they may undo much of the work of the consumers' union and proceed to differentiate their products in an "undesirable" fashion.

The second type of agency would be a center for information about producers' (or intermediate) goods and production technology. In particular, it would push the spread of technology, probably working hand in hand with a model firms' program whose principal task is to develop new products and techniques. The basic goal of each agency is to help validate the assumption of rational market behavior upon which many of the desirable properties of markets ultimately depend.

Of course, if any need exists for planning, it must be true in the final analysis that the system would not automatically perform satisfactorily, given the social preferences that an economic planning council wishes to implement. Assuming this to be so, planning within a Brand X economy breaks down into two interdependent stages.

Stage 1, which we may call the *conditioning* process, tries to create a favorable climate, both for production and economic efficiency and for efforts by the EPC to steer the economy along its optimal path of development. This is an outgrowth of antitrust or industrial structure policy. It turns out to be necessary in both socialist and capitalist market economies because all or part of the range of problems we associate with imperfections in competition may arise in either. Stage 2, the process of *steering,* then deals with the EPC's efforts to guide the economy along its optimal path. We shall explore each stage in turn.

20–2 Conditioning the Economy

A chief goal of conditioning is to eliminate both allocative and X inefficiency.[2] An EPC would attack both kinds in the first instance by trying to keep output higher and prices and costs lower than profit-oriented entrepreneurs would do under laissez faire. There are at least two ways of doing this, and we are thereby led to distinguish two polar Brand X forms.

The *cooperative* version is essentially the Taylor economy, including in-

---

[1] However, the scope and perspective of these agencies would clearly not be the same in India, for example, as in Canada. If we were to implant the consumers' union we have in mind into contemporary North America, it would be better endowed than the present consumers' research organizations. A method of finance is outlined in Chapter 23.

[2] However, in the very process of steering the EPC will introduce some inefficiency. See Section 5–5.

dicative planning, but with central pricing largely abandoned. Thus the planners will try to ensure efficiency by prodding producers with indicators, accompanied by moral suasion and by applying other carrots and sticks (including financial incentives) discussed in the latter part of Chapter 19. In particular we would expect a continual exchange of information between planners and producers. To the former this would be designed to provide a proper perspective on how the economy, as an interdependent organism, is evolving over time. In return, producers would receive the outlines of their own roles as integral units in the grand scheme of things. A feature of the cooperative version is that indicative planning becomes an important instrument to accomplish both stages of the planning process.

The *competitive* polar form, by contrast, will rely on shaping industrial or, more generally, market structure so as to keep artificial barriers to entry low and to provide mutual checks and balances upon economic power. It will seek to foster a policy that promotes as well as discourages large firms when efficiency appears to require this. Nonetheless, the planners will want workable competition to prevail where feasible as a first line of defense against inefficiency, and countervailing power to arise where needed to supplement this. Any practical version of Brand X would synthesize features from both polar versions. Having already discussed the Taylor economy at some length, however, we shall confine most of our attention here to the competitive model.

In both forms the basic requirement for economic efficiency is some mobility of management, labor, and capital into different production processes whenever this will cause the values of their marginal products to rise. We saw earlier that mobility has two requirements. First, higher marginal productivities must translate into higher prices and wages or other inducements offered to the inputs in question. Otherwise, these signals are distorted. Second, these inputs must have the opportunity to move in response to higher offers if their owners wish. Movement must be allowed to continue until no one wishes to transfer inputs any more.

When inputs cannot move in response to offers of higher rewards, we speak of artificial barriers to entry. Discrimination, control over sources of supply, or licensing agreements may prevent firms and their managements from entering certain industries where they could earn higher than normal rates of return on their invested capital. Alternatively, entry into trade unions or professional associations may be restricted on the basis of race, creed, sex, or religion or even to those whose fathers were members of the same union. The principal goals of market-structure policy in the competitive version of Brand X will be to break down all kinds of artificial barriers to entry, while keeping the concentration of power within most industries below a maximum level.[3] This would be the EPC's method of promoting workable

---

[3] Each economy must determine such an upper bound based on its own conditions. For the United States, G. J. Stigler has suggested an antimerger law rooted in the following considerations:

competition—on input as well as output markets. In the cooperative version, removal of artificial barriers remains a prominent goal, although some traditional barriers based on custom may have to be respected.

To make input markets competitive, the competitive version will require strong equal-opportunities legislation plus an information clearing house on employment opportunities and occupational characteristics. The latter complements the consumers' union in supplying households the information they need to make rational choices.[4] In addition, society will have to prevent labor unions and professional associations from gaining control over occupational mobility.

Under such a plan, a labor union would be allowed the same collective bargaining rights that unions now enjoy in most Western countries. But it would also have to accept any qualified new personnel as members and pay all or part of their compensation when they are unable to find work at going wage or salary rates for their professions.[5] Unions and professional associations would also be denied any responsibility for or control over educational or apprenticeship programs that prepare individuals for their professions.

All this will not prevent a union from eliminating "exploitation" of workers by powerful employers. If it was able to exercise countervailing power in the first place, it will still be able to increase both the employment of its members and their wages, in comparison with a situation where exploitation would have occurred.

---

1. Every firm that will have less than 5 to 10 per cent of an industry's output after the merger should be allowed to engage in the merger. Within this range the percentage should be lower, the larger the industry.
2. Every merger by a firm that will have 20 per cent or more of an industry's output after the merger should be made illegal.
3. Between the limits described in 1 and 2, a merger should be investigated if the total annual sales of the merging firms will exceed an absolute level, say 5 million dollars, after merger.
4. Where a firm has 20 per cent or more of an industry's output, its acquisition of more than 5 to 10 per cent of the output capacity of industries to which it sells or from which it buys in appreciable quantities, should be made illegal.

The first three rules apply to horizontal mergers between competitors; the last applies to vertical integration between buyer and seller. Some economists would disagree with Stigler, claiming, in particular, that he has downgraded the roles played by potential competition and countervailing power. Source: G. J. Stigler, "Mergers and Preventive Antitrust Policy," in G. J. Stigler, ed., *The Organization of Industry* (Homewood, Ill.: Irwin, 1968), Ch. 22.

[4] Counseling programs of all kinds and computerized job banks are examples of potential ingredients in this information flow. "The job bank is . . . a list and description of all job offerings in the area of a local employment office—fed into a computer and printed out by category in book form each day. These books are then used . . . in local offices to find jobs matching the needs and qualifications of job applicants," *The New York Times*, No. 8, 1970, Sec. 3, p. 3.

[5] Although we can hold a union or professional association responsible for permitting full employment of its members under an umbrella of adequate aggregate demand, we cannot hold it responsible for maintaining aggregate demand. Thus the percentage of compensation that it is required to pay ought to go down as economy-wide unemployment, or a related measure such as unemployment minus job vacancies, rises.

However, suppose that an economy does succeed in reducing occupational entry barriers. Then unions and professional associations will have less power to push up wages and salaries for a select core of members, while potentially willing and able workers are unemployed or forced to take other jobs because they cannot gain membership. Ultimately, such an economy should succeed in reducing both inflation and unemployment.

We can increase competition on output markets in two basic ways. First, we can enlarge the market within which a given product is distributed so that firms invade one another's territories. Second, we can increase the number of firms serving a given market. The first way may call forth several measures designed to modernize distribution facilities and otherwise lower distribution costs, or to encourage regional expansion and decentralization within enterprises.

It likewise implies a bias toward freer international trade, a mutual lowering of trade barriers, and even multinational free-trade areas. This, in turn, will sometimes mean subsidizing domestic producers to compete with foreign firms both at home and abroad. Sweden, for example, has a relatively open economy, and foreign companies find it comparatively easy to establish branch plants there. But when the government wishes to prevent foreign firms from gaining too large a foothold in domestic markets or to expand export sales, it offers the home producer a financial incentive.

In line with the second method of increasing competition, policy makers might try, as a (naïve) first approximation, to make separate production facilities into separate firms whenever these either trade with one another or potentially compete. In part the idea is to keep industrial concentration low by restricting the number of multiplant firms (except, in some instances, where these plants engage in unrelated lines of production). But the government would likewise hope to resist vertical integration when this leads to one firm controlling a significant portion of the potential supply sources for its rivals.

If these policies are successful we would rely upon competitive cost–price relationships to encourage X efficiency and to discourage both the building of pygmy production facilities and "gigantomania," or constructing plants that are too large and awkward to be efficient. The government's role will again be to keep down artificial barriers that might prevent firms from taking up a given line of production. This will mean, in particular, that borrowers can not be discriminated against solely on the basis of size, even if the consequence is that the EPC has to maintain a separate investment bank specializing in loans to small producers.[6]

---

[6] It is sometimes argued that small producers do not have access to credit on terms as attractive as those available to large "blue-chip" corporations. This is said to result often not so much from the inefficiency of small firms as from their lack of collateral. Loans to them are therefore riskier. A laissez-faire supporter might argue that "special-purpose" banks would automatically arise to specialize in lending to small producers.

If successful, the measures described thus far should be about as conducive to workable competition as we can hope to get through market-structure policy. Our one plant–one firm approximation can only be efficient, however, when each firm is able to realize most of its potential scale economies within a single optimal-sized production facility. We have already seen that scale economies in research and management will not permit this in all industries.

Nevertheless, empirical evidence exists to indicate that these economies still do not normally preclude workable competition, except in small markets. This reinforces the bias toward freer international trade. In some cases, large firms will subdivide on a regional or national basis into "profit centers," each having its own manager, who is accountable for the profits and losses of his division. The chief executive retains direct control over key investment decisions and supplies both research and development and technical expertise to each center. When a large firm wants to invade another's market, it often does so by establishing or acquiring a profit center. Potentially, therefore, such an organizational form combines economies of scale in research and management with workable competition in small markets.

A second argument for larger decision-making units stems from the role played by countervailing power. It may happen that a country's export industries face huge foreign monopolies. If domestic producers still bid competitively on foreign trade markets, the country will face unfavorable international terms of trade, having to pay too dearly for its imports and getting too little for its exports. Consequently, industrial associations and other kinds of cartels may have to be brought into being for the express purpose of bargaining with foreign buyers and sellers.

The strongest part of the countervailing-power argument, however, relates to domestic production and exchange. Workable competition will probably not succeed in generating all the checks and balances that (competitively based) Brand X will require. The basic problem is a risk that strong sellers will often face weak buyers, whom they are able to exploit, and vice versa. For example, not only will economies of mass production sometimes make the optimal size of a firm large relative to the total size of the markets in which it buys or sells, but the optimal scale will vary considerably from one industry to another.

Thus it will become necessary to reverse anticombines policy when strong sellers would otherwise face weak buyers or vice versa. In general the planners should try to establish a distribution of economic power so that, as minimum requirements:

1. Each economic actor has at least two independent customers or suppliers with whom he can deal on every market.
2. Although there may be relatively strong and relatively weak actors in

---

These banks would spread their loans over many kinds of firms, and thus diversify much of the risk away. Competition will then force the banks to pass on much of these savings to small borrowers. Unfortunately, experience shows that this kind of lending institution will often not come into existence without special encouragement.

the system, the strongest and weakest do not have to deal directly with each other.

We would hope to avoid confrontations such as those in North America where a strong Teamsters' Union can often dictate terms to small, independent businessmen, or where a Ford or General Motors buys from infinitely smaller and weaker producers of auto parts. This might mean splitting up GM and the Teamsters or uniting producers of auto parts. Alternatively, it could mean creating special-purpose organizations such as a bargaining unit for truckers possessing only the powers necessary to negotiate labor contracts with a truck-drivers' union.

When all is said and done, countervailing power and other competition substitutes ought to supplement competition as a regulatory force within the competitive version of Brand X, rather than vice versa. Although bilateral monopoly may be more satisfactory than monopoly or monopsony from the standpoint of resource allocation (or allocative efficiency), there is no reason for it to work better in terms of X efficiency.

The force that combats output restriction is not competition between buyers and sellers, but collusion, as when the two decide to maximize their joint profits. (Each firm has less power to gain additional profits by manipulating price. Therefore, each must raise its profits by expanding the quantity of the goods bought and sold.) If competition cannot be relied upon as the principal regulatory force, something more closely resembling the cooperative version will probably prove advisable.

With this in mind, we can view statements 1 and 2 above as a weak condition to place on market structure. A strict requirement that firms be as small and numerous as is consistent with economies of mass production would be a strong condition. The specific guidelines for workable competition outlined in Chapter 17 define one possible middle ground, among many. Other things being equal, the stronger the version that can be applied, the better.

When neither competition nor countervailing power can be made to work, the residual tool is some form of direct price regulation. We may view this as countervailing power by the government. It may take the form of price and wage ceilings, "strong" wage and price guidelines (for example, with tax penalties tied to disobedience), or compulsory arbitration (that is, compulsory settling of labor–management disputes by a third party, supposedly representing society's interests). The goal here will often be to combat inflation, but successful wage and price controls can substitute for competitive pressures, especially in the short run. For example, if it is not too low, an effective price ceiling will induce a profit-maximizing monopoly to expand—once again, because it must raise additional profits by expanding volume rather than by raising price.

Because the EPC will seek price ceilings that equate supply and demand, the widespread use of this device will take us partway back into Lange's competitive solution. The discussion in Chapter 19 therefore applies. In particular, as Americans found out during the early 1970s, firms will sometimes raise prices implicitly by reducing product quality or service. Thus in the long run, the planners would be best off confining direct price controls to natural monopolies—where there may be no feasible alternative means of regulation—and to commodities whose quality standards can be easily quantified and enforced. Even here, the bureaucratic nature of price controls makes them ill-suited to goods, such as agricultural produce, whose equilibrium prices are often volatile.

Price controls may also work better in smaller countries with fewer enterprises and smaller industrial product lines. The only two bona fide socialist market economies, Yugoslavia and Hungary, are both small economies, and both rely extensively on price ceilings to combat inflation. In addition, these ceilings are used in place of stiff import competition from foreign producers or a developed machinery to enforce competition at home. In both countries price controls are likely to endure for a long time—at least on an on-again-off-again basis. Yugoslavia, in particular, has used them as a measure of last resort ever since abandoning her command economy in 1953.

A final way of motivating managers to expand production in some cases will be to change their goal orientations by changing their success indicators —for example, away from profits and toward sales maximization. Such a measure could also be part of a financial-incentive program.

20–3   The Problem of Inflation

Inflation appears to have two causes, which may work together in a manner described in Chapter 14. *Demand-pull* inflation results when the aggregate demand for goods and services is greater than the maximum achievable supply at current price levels. There is too much money chasing too few goods, so to speak, and since output cannot rise enough, prices go up instead in response to a net excess demand over the whole economy. *Cost-push* inflation occurs when suppliers of inputs use their monopoly power to push up input prices in excess of increases in demand. This will create or worsen an excess supply for these inputs, but is still possible because an intermediary has gotten control over the supply and established entry barriers.

For example, a labor union decides to accept or reject a wage offer on the basis of a majority vote and elects its members in the same way. Some would-be employees may not even gain union membership or voting rights. Thus cost-push inflation can be cured in part by breaking down occupational entry barriers and, on occasion, by breaking down product-market entry barriers as well. Indeed, any mechanism, including price controls, capable of expanding output over the long or short run, can also reduce inflation over the same horizon. Any tool capable of improving market structure may combat inflation at the same time. (However, the reservations about price controls expressed earlier continue to apply here.)

Because inflation and unemployment have often gone hand in hand in the post-World War II era, a special premium attaches to measures that can reduce both simultaneously. Traditional fiscal and monetary policy tools may reduce the aggregate demand for goods and services and thereby reduce inflation. But they will *increase* unemployment. Alternatively, they may raise the aggregate demand for goods and services and thereby reduce unemployment, but also increase inflation.

Consequently, when inflation and unemployment appear together, a different set of policies is called for. These include the reduction of entry barriers, the replacement of minimum wages with a comprehensive family-assistance plan, manpower-retraining programs, and selective use of financial incentives in depressed areas. They may also include price controls—preferably used temporarily to break an inflationary psychology. Finally, they include a wide range of measures aimed at binding together productivity and pay increases (or, more simply, with holding down pay increases) and known collectively as *income policies.* An example, apparently successful at controlling both inflation and unemployment, is Hungary's constant average wage rule.

The basic idea is to keep the rise in the average of all wages and salaries within each enterprise—in the economy as a whole or in a particular sector —less than or equal to a target figure. The latter can be made to depend upon tolerable inflation plus expected productivity gains. To enforce the plan, enterprise profits or managerial bonuses become subject to a steep fine whenever the average wage gain is too high. This gives managers a strong incentive to resist wage demands, but it likewise motivates them to hire marginal employees whose wages will be less than the enterprise average. (Without doing so, in fact, the firm may be unable to bid competitively for the highly skilled and professional workers that it needs.)

Once hired, it will normally pay management to use these new employees as productively as possible. Consequently, it will expand output and lower price.[7] Nevertheless, the constant average wage rule is no substitute for a market-structure policy. Moreover, if full employment is going to prevail anyway, it may lead to a misallocation of labor resources. If it is difficult to penalize workers with lower pay for poorer performance, as appears to be the case currently in Hungry, the constant average wage rule may become a productivity disincentive. (These become costs of reduced unemployment and inflation.) But to the extent that it creates jobs, it is likely to increase efficiency.

It is also possible to concern ourselves not so much with eliminating inflation as with making it painless through the use of cost-of-living escalators.

---

[7] More precisely, the firm will expand output, provided it is producing at least one good in which the marginal physical product of these employees is greater than 0 and whose elasticity of demand is greater than 1. (Normally, it will operate in the elastic ranges of all its demand curves, where marginal revenues are all greater than 0.) This is provided, of course, that management has an incentive to raise the firm's revenues.

Rather than create an inflation-*free* economy, we would try to establish what Amotz Morag has called an inflation-*proof* system.[8] This idea has been practiced for many years in Chile, although it has not been applied as comprehensively as it could be. In a completely inflation-proof economy, virtually everyone's income would be inflated or deflated by a suitable consumer price index, insofar as it consists of contractual payments.

Suppose that a labor union signs a contract calling for a wage of $5.50 per hour during the first year and $6 during the second. By the time the second year arrives, we assume, prices of goods in a representative workers' market basket have risen by an average of 10 per cent. Then the wage rate rises automatically to $6.60. If prices had fallen by 10 per cent, the wage would fall to $5.40. Subject to the impossibility of finding a perfect index to escalate or deescalate by, a $6 wage in the contract means $6 of constant purchasing power.

Virtually all income payments, earned and unearned, would be protected in the same way, as long as they are contracted for in advance. In particular, pensioners and other persons on normally fixed incomes and receivers of income supplements such as unemployment insurance, would be protected against erosion of purchasing power. Most interest, principal, and dividend payments would receive the same protection. Thus the majority of stocks and bonds would become "constant-purchasing-power" securities, the only possible exceptions constituting an allowance for speculation about the future course of prices.

The consumer price indexes used as deflators should vary by geographical region—so that postal workers in the Toronto area, for example, will not be escalated on the same basis as workers in Montreal—and they may also reflect relative income levels. That is, the higher the income payment to be deflated, the greater would be the presence of luxury goods in the market basket from which the price index was constructed.

20-4   The Need to Steer

Our Brand X conditioning program could fit into the framework of a liberal laissez-faire economy whose basic social goals are not implemented by an economic planning council. It is in viewing this as a background for steering the system, as well as a mechanism for achieving efficiency, that we depart from laissez faire. If the EPC must steer the economy, it follows that the system has different goals than would arise under laissez faire. Thus the political process of goal formation must depart in some ways from that which characterizes laissez faire.

On the other hand, when there is a quantitative production plan under

---

[8] The scheme outlined below is essentially due to Morag. For an elaboration, see Amotz Morag, "For an Inflation-proof Economy," *American Economic Review*, Mar. 1962.

Brand X it will almost certainly be less detailed than in a command economy. Moreover, direct and precise orders sent to the producing sector are largely replaced by indirect inducements and penalities. Thus the preferences of the EPC for different categories of goods and services cannot be nearly as detailed under Brand X as they can, in principle, within a command economy. However, our earlier analysis suggests that the ability to implement detailed priorities is often illusory under command planning, so that the sacrifice on this score may be more apparent than real.

Assuming a need to steer, a fundamental task of the planners is to determine the system's basic goals and constraints, as well as the tradeoffs between different goals. An extremely distribution-oriented government might decide that it would only tolerate minor departures from complete equality of welfares, regardless of the cost in terms of lost output and growth. At the other extreme, the planners would opt for all-out growth, regardless of the necessary sacrifice in present consumption and of the inequities that resulted. More likely they will choose some middle ground. For example, they may try to establish constraints on the distribution of income or upon certain measures of growth performance which they are reluctant to violate, but which are also loose enough to permit some flexibility in goal pursuit.

As a consequence, a Brand X economy may present a somewhat schizophrenic appearance. On the one hand, it may undertake some "welfare-state" commitments to assure reasonably full employment and guaranteed minimum living standards for all its citizens. However, competition between individuals and organizations is likely to persevere, even in the cooperative version.

As part of the "discipline of the market," for example, bankruptcy must remain a distinct possibility for firms that fail to combine inputs efficiently or to keep pace with user preferences. More generally, competition can provide part of the spark necessary to keep an economy efficient and growing. But it will also create winners and losers and partly determine the distribution of income within whatever constraints society lays down.

The government must therefore reach a range of decisions about how to cushion the blows to losers and about whether and how to recycle them into new competition (for example, through retraining) in areas better suited to their abilities. It will have to decide what kinds of constraints to put on income or wealth inequality and how to use differentials as incentives to better performance. In particular it will have to establish a policy of gift and inheritance taxes and subsidies and rewards for risk taking. It must also try to ensure that income inequalities arise on the basis of contribution rather than exploitation. In effect, this is a principal goal of market-structure policy.

Assuming that the conditioning program goes well, a Brand X EPC will have three broad tasks remaining:

1. To achieve a high level of economic activity—to balance the system, in other words, at a rate of employment and output which is close to potential.

2. To steer the economy in production space—that is, to ensure the expansion of priority sectors, realize economies of mass production, and internalize social costs and benefits.
3. To steer the economy in distribution space—more specifically, to implement measures affecting the distribution of wealth among different socio-economic groups and different geographical regions in the country.

It is not too difficult to imagine a single project capable of achieving all three goals simultaneously. Let us suppose that the planners are thinking of industrializing a particular "depressed" geographical region. We shall assume that egalitarian motives and political liabilities give the project a reasonably high priority in any event, but that to make it even more attractive, substantial economies of mass production and external benefits lie dormant there.

For example, certain facilities, such as a transportation network, storage space, and filtration plants, are common to the production of goods with widely varying uses. The kind of warehousing that a steel mill would prefer will probably differ from the optimal storage facilities for automobiles, coal, or lumber, but presumably we could build structures that would adapt to each of these uses and many more. Similarly, firms will usually find it cheaper to locate closer to their major markets or suppliers. It follows that we can sometimes internalize social benefits by causing industrial complexes of firms, with each enterprise buying from or selling to at least one of the others, to be built in the same general location. As a final touch we could attempt to space the emerging production facilities and the population centers that arise around them so as to reduce problems of congestion and pollution.

The entrepreneurial effort needed to realize these economies may not be forthcoming without encouragement from the center. To begin with, certain activities such as road building and measures to avoid congestion produce goods with public qualities that cannot be efficiently bought and sold on the marketplace. In addition, enormous risks are involved, the problems of coordinating the activities of diverse firms are likely to be great, and, to top matters off, there may be a shortage of entrepreneurial talent within the economy or this talent may be blocked by some kind of artificial barrier to entry. At the extreme, a command-economy type of solution would then call for the EPC to assume the full entrepreneurial role itself, building a transportation infrastructure, clearing plant sites, and ordering firms to go there or starting new ones. But this solution is less likely within a mixed-economy framework.

Nevertheless, the government may well build a transportation infrastructure and handle such problems as coordination itself, while offering financial incentives or lowering barriers so that "desirable" firms will be more inclined to choose to locate in the area. Among the measures of desirability will be the likelihood that the presence of one firm will induce others to settle in the region.

A steel mill will normally be more attractive on this basis than a milk-processing plant employing the same number of men or producing the same value added. Steel is a basic input for a vast number of commodities, and its presence in a given area will make the area a more attractive location for users than it would otherwise be. If both firms will locate in the region for the same amount of subsidy, the government will be able to buy more area development per dollar by bringing in the steel firm. Generally speaking, intermediate goods producers whose outputs are key inputs for a number of subsequent manufacturing processes or which constitute major markets for earlier stages of production will form the most desirable core for an area development program.[9]

20–5   The Financial-Incentive Program

The planners' complete steering tool kit will include everything from indicators, in the form of production targets and coefficients, through taxes, subsidies, and laws down to direct government purchases of goods and services. But because they are the most subtle and complex—and among the most important—we are going to pay most attention to financial instruments, taxes and subsidies in the final analysis, which the government will use to stimulate the economy selectively.

We can illustrate this by going back to Figure 19–8. There the EPC could have tried steering the economy into the optimal subregion by making investment credit easier to come by, provided it was earmarked for expanding production facilities in Y. Alternatively, it could have subsidized expansion in industries that use Y, thus raising its derived demand. Finally, the planners could have tried influencing managerial "success indicators" within the industry producing Y so that managers would be more willing to trade an increase in profits for an increase in growth or sales.

Any of these approaches could also have been combined with indicative planning and guarantees by the government of some direct purchases of Y. In the latter event, the government would either use Y itself or else take the responsibility for marketing the good. (Thus we revive the idea of a marketing agency on a partial basis as a device through which the planners can subsidize expansion in priority sectors.[10]) If the government stockpiles significant quan-

---

[9] Yet, area development will be just one among a number of priorities that the EPC will have. Conceivably, for example, the EPC might be interested in expanding the dairy-processing industry. It could then decide to locate new plants in depressed areas.

[10] These subsidies would take several forms, some of them rather subtle. Suppose, for example, that the government guarantees a steady demand for a good whose sales are normally quite volatile on a seasonal or cyclical basis. Then the firms in question are having a part of their risk burden removed. They will also find it easier to plan internally. Depending upon what prices the government charges, it may also assume part of the inventory costs of storing the good and some or all of the distribution costs. Finally, if it signs a contract guaranteeing a steady demand for the good over an extended period of time, it is foregoing its right to shop around and compare values like any other customer. The first and last of these subsidies will have the disadvantage of being hard to measure, although their leverage factors (in the sense of Section 20–7) may be relatively high.

tities of some of the goods it buys, it can also use these to relieve temporary shortages and to keep prices from skyrocketing.

Regardless of which methods are used, the important point is that when we last discussed this example, we implicitly assumed that the emerging pattern of demand would automatically mirror the relative priorities attached by the EPC to X and Y. In practice these priorities will only be mirrored by accident unless it is here that financial incentives and other steering instruments become useful. Let us examine the problem, both from the standpoint of a firm receiving a financial incentive, and from that of the economy as a whole.

First, consider Figure 20–1. Here Y and X are either two different goods or one good produced in two different locations. Parts (b) and (d) apply to X; parts (a) and (c) apply to Y. With no financial-incentive program, the prices of Y and X are indicated by the solid horizontal line in all four graphs, while the solid, upward-sloping curves depict marginal costs.[11] If the conditioning program is working rather well, the prices of both goods will remain close to their marginal costs. For simplicity we shall assume that prices equal marginal costs. Thus, without a financial-incentive program the firm or firms in question would turn out 100,000 units of Y and 50,000 units of X. The EPC, however, wishes to reorient the economy toward Y, and it has two basic ways of achieving this goal.

To begin with, it can directly subsidize the production of Y, perhaps in the form of a tax *rebate* or accelerated depreciation writeoff, and tax that of X. This is shown in Figures 20–1(a) and (b). The subsidy reduces the marginal cost of Y at each rate of output from MC_y to the dashed line, $(MC_y - S)$. With lower costs and no change in demand, firms will be motivated to expand their production of Y from 100,000 units to 125,000. For X the situation is just reversed. The tax raises marginal costs at every rate of output, and production declines from 50,000 units to 40,000.

The planners can hope to achieve similar results by indirectly raising the demand for Y and lowering that for X, so that P_y rises while P_x falls. This is shown in Figures 20–1(c) and (d). For example, the planners may decide to subsidize firms that use Y and tax those using X. Or, if X and Y are substitute inputs for a number of prospective buyers, the government may subsidize the specific use of Y over X.

Figure 20–2 shows the economy-wide impact of these financial incentives. There PP' is a two-dimensional cross section of society's production-possibility frontier. The set of indifference curves labeled I gives the emerging pattern of aggregate demand in the absence of financial incentives. As noted above, this does not correspond to planners' preferences. The system would settle down at A if an efficient allocation of resources prevailed, or, more likely, at B inside the PP' curve. By giving financial incentives to producers of Y, we try to give them the means and the motive to expand their output

---

[11] The solid horizontal lines simply indicate price *levels*. They are not necessarily demand curves. That is, we are not necessarily assuming the institutional form known as perfect competition.

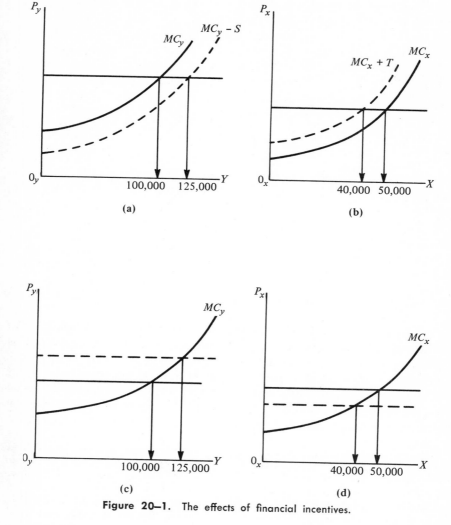

Figure 20–1. The effects of financial incentives.

and to bid resources away from other industries, including producers of X.

This will reorient the economy toward C, the optimum according to the EPC's macrorationale. In all likelihood, however, the best that can be hoped for is a solution like D, embodying some economic inefficiency but clearly preferable to A or B. If successful, the financial-incentive program will have the effect of adjusting the pattern of demand to EPC priorities.

A familiar example of goal reorientation with financial incentives occurs when a growth-oriented EPC pays a high interest rate to attract savings and charges a lower rate on long-term loans earmarked for investment, subsidizing the interest differential from taxes. It can also make tax monies directly available for lending and discriminate among borrowers by industry and geographi-

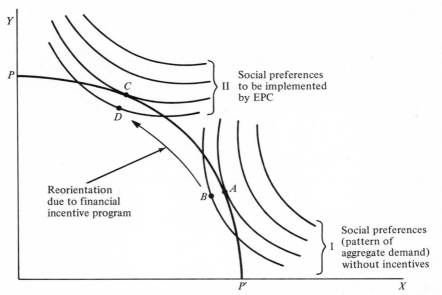

Figure 20–2. The change in priorities brought about by a financial-incentive program.

cal region, granting the lowest rates of all on loans destined to heavy or to export-oriented industries. Alternatively, the incentives may be packaged as a tax rebate or an easy repayment plan.

Alternatively, financial incentives can be used to realize economies of mass production, as in connection with Figure 19–8 or to internalize social costs and benefits. Location taxes and subsidies are also examples of financial incentives.

In the United Kingdom, the Board of Trade must approve the location of large new establishments and can provide tax incentives to encourage location in certain areas. In Sweden, the National Labor Market Board has the authority to approve tax exemptions and loans to influence the location of industry. A system of loans and grants is used in West Germany for the same purpose, and in France, subsidies and loans are offered to firms that locate in the areas of surplus labor, while firms trying to move into tight labor-market areas may find it impossible to obtain building permits and are also often subject to special high taxes.[12]

More generally, some systematic use of financial incentives characterizes virtually every country in Western Europe, Hungary, Yugoslavia, and Japan.

20–6 Guidelines for Using Financial Incentives

Any financial-incentive program will consist of rather delicate measures which must be applied subtly and, to some extent, inconspicuously. The planners will particularly want to avoid the "big brother" image, with its

[12] Daniel B. Suits, *Principles of Economics* (New York: Harper, 1970), p. 140.

implications of coercion, paternalism, and a lack of self-reliance or initiative among firm managers. Given this goal plus a desire to get the most out of every dollar spent on financial incentives, there are four guidelines that such a program would ideally follow. (In practice, of course, something less than the ideal will be found.)

1. Since effective market coordination of production and distribution requires supply and demand to balance, taxes and subsidies should not cause market disequilibrium. This often rules out such incentives as price supports, which prop up the price to the producer but also lead to goods piling up in inventory without current use. As a fairly general rule, financial incentives should be tied to transactions (that is, to goods and services bought and sold) rather than to production per se. Similar statements apply to controls.

2. For psychological reasons, steering ought to be accomplished as much as possible through subsidies rather than taxes or other financial penalties. The EPC should try to implement its priorities, for example, by offering such inducements as tax concessions, borrowing costs below going rates, easy repayment plans on loans, or accelerated depreciation. It should not explicitly use taxes, fines, or other levies to discourage production in low-priority sectors. Rather, it should directly encourage managers in high-priority sectors to produce more. Consequently, a financial-incentive program will result in more specific subsidies designed to achieve specific goals, combined with higher over-all tax rates and borrowing costs, which, in effect, endow the program.

Because any market economy must rely heavily upon initiative from lower-level decision makers, particular provision will have to be made for incentives to innovate. It should be possible for an individual to launch a new enterprise in a Brand X economy, even if it is entirely socialist, without running through a maze of red tape. The new venture would be owned by the state, but it could still be arranged for the founder to share substantially in its profits, or losses, for a specified time period. He should also have an avenue to use in applying for a financial inventive to aid his efforts.

Yugoslavia gives us a partial example of this. There individuals receiving the approval and encouragement of regional (communal) governments can often start enterprises with a minimum of their own capital and borrow the rest on attractive terms. In the Soviet Union, by contrast, the vast majority of all enterprises of any significance are created by edict from the intermediate or top-level planning authorities.[13]

On the other hand, it is equally important to tie incentives to performance

---

[13] Once the new enterprise has more than five full-time employees, it must become a producers cooperative, governed in principle by a workers' council. In particular, it will be a profit-sharing firm, a fact that will sometimes act as a disincentive to would-be founders. (See the discussion in Chapter 21.) A financial incentive can overcome this at some risk of subsidizing enterprises that really ought not to be started in the first place.

For a brief case history of five men who started a hotel on the island of Korcula (with a loan of $300,000 from a Belgrade bank), see *The New York Times,* Sept. 8, 1969, p. 36.

and to retain the right to abolish or even replace them with financial penalties when the funds in question are not used for priority investment.

3. In the long run, we may view society as investing in the activities which the financial-incentive program sponsors. Those managers who receive financial subsidies or incentives are the executors of this investment program. They should not be able to profit from it at society's expense. Both for morale reasons and to avoid misallocating managerial resources, the same quality of entrepreneurial effort should not consistently earn a higher reward in industries and geographical reasons favored by the financial-incentive program than elsewhere. Financial incentives should not become tax loopholes.

Ideally, subsidies would be completely nondiscriminating. That is, they should be awarded so as to increase the recipient's production activity in some way without redistributing income in his favor. To the reader, this guideline may seem like a contradiction in terms unless the planners can rely upon purely moral incentives. Otherwise, the incentive to output expansion must surely be a subsidy that will raise the manager's paycheck at the same time. In practice, we cannot usually divorce the latter from the former completely. But we can often go at least part way in this direction, even when material stimuli predominate. There are three cases to consider.

Case 1: Suppose that an EPC establishes profits as the dominant managerial success criterion. Certain priority sectors, however, may have their targets switched to maximization of sales or growth. Our discussion of laissez faire showed that, under imperfect competition, a sales maximizer would often produce and sell more than a firm maximizing profits, given comparable demand and cost conditions. There, a switch from profits to sales or growth maximization in priority sectors will give firms an expansion incentive.

Nevertheless, when it works, goal switching is basically nondiscriminatory. Varieties in the quality of managerial leadership will emerge in sales vis-à-vis profit-maximizing sectors. But the EPC will not automatically be making it easier for sales-maximizing entrepreneurs to earn higher salaries. Moreover, if mass production economies are present, the planners will be encouraging expansion in industries where monopoly restrictions on output might otherwise prevent an efficient scale of operation. Unfortunately, goal switching won't always be feasible, especially under capitalism, and even when it is, it won't always be enough. Then the planners must lower the cost curves facing one or more firms [as in Figure 20–1(a)].

Case 2: In some cases, however, we may be able to view the incentive as a payment for a service which a variety of firms in different industries are eligible to render. Thus it is quite normal to offer inducements to invest in specific geographical regions in the form of a semianonymous message (such as an official announcement and then invite applications. These inducements are, in effect, a price that can be varied over time in an effort to produce an optimal annual flow of new investment into the area.

By the same token, we can imagine the EPC holding investment auctions. That is, it would establish a commission to examine applications for investible funds on easy credit terms and make awards on a project basis to those applications deemed most "in the national interest." Awards would inevitably become a function of priorities embodied in the EPC's social preference function, but they could also depend upon the quality of managerial and engineering expertise that goes into the proposal. They then become, in part, prizes for this kind of excellence. Variants of this method have been used in several countries, notably Yugoslavia and Belgium.

To the extent that it is possible for different firms in different sectors of the economy to compete in these auctions, the degree of discrimination among managers is reduced. Moreover, the applications received become valuable feedback, giving the EPC an idea of what a particular incentive fund can "buy" in terms of performance. As a consequence of these responses, the planners may decide to adjust the size of this fund, to change some of its incentives, or to devise new ones.

We can also combine this idea with a Lange or Taylor-type trial-and-error methodology. Suppose that the response, in terms of actual or projected output, to one set of incentive awards yields a growth performance which the EPC would like to improve. To this end, it may enlarge its incentive fund and offer more attractive inducements to expand. It may also devise new incentives and revise others. If the lag is concentrated in export industries, depressed regions, or other identifiable sectors, the biggest increases in incentive awards can be concentrated here. Alternatively, if the production response to offers of incentive awards is more enthusiastic than the planners feel is desirable, they can scale down some grants and either reduce the size of the new incentive fund or else increase the number of awards. Finally, as in the now-defunct Yugoslav auctions, managers could be asked to include their own credit and repayment terms as part of the bid.

Such a procedure is theoretically much cruder and clumsier than the trial-and-error process discussed in Chapter 19 and also suffers from several of its drawbacks. However, it should be more feasible to implement, and it can also take advantage of competition for incentives across industries. This factor will make it harder for each manager to coax a higher subsidy by withholding output.

Case 3: Finally, cost-cutting incentives must sometimes be earmarked for specific firms. Then, we face the greatest danger that managers in priority sectors, whose salaries are increasing functions of profits or sales, will be able to raise their paychecks without a commensurate improvement in performance. One way out, largely restricted to publicly owned firms, is to reduce the percentage of a firm's profit, growth, or sales paid out as managerial bonuses, when increases in these indicators are made easier to achieve by incentives.

We can get a more general approach along the same lines, however, by noting the difference between *fixed* and *variable* costs. Over any planning horizon, some costs will be fixed to each firm in the sense that they do not vary with the rate of output of a particular good over the range of outputs that management is considering producing. Interest charges on outstanding debt are usually an example of fixed costs. Costs that depend upon the rate of output are called variable costs. In deciding how much to produce, the firm's management will be guided solely by variable costs. Strictly speaking, the cost curves in Figure 20–1 therefore measure only variable costs.

Therefore, the greater the percentage of a firm's total costs that are fixed, the more it will tend to produce. In Figure 20–1(a) suppose that A and B are two firms each producing the same good with the same technology, and each facing identical demand and supply conditions. If we then assume that a greater proportion of A's costs are fixed, it will face lower variable costs than B—for example ($MC_y - S$) rather than MC_y. When both managers have the same goal, firm A will produce more than B. (We can think of A as spreading his greater fixed costs over a larger output if we wish.)

The fact that firms in Western Europe, Hungary, Yugoslavia, and Japan find it more expensive, for a variety of reasons, to lay off workers makes a greater percentage of labor costs there fall into the fixed category than in North America. This gives them an incentive to run any given production capacity at a relatively high rate. Over a business cycle, output and employment will fluctuate less and prices more in response to changing demand conditions than in North America.

In these conditions, planners seeking to observe guideline 3 would try to shift relatively more costs in priority sectors into the fixed category without reducing total costs there by very much. For example, the government may impose higher basic tax rates on these firms than prevail generally throughout the economy. The same firms would then be allowed to earn tax credits, lower borrowing costs, direct subsidy payments, and so on, by expanding output sold.

Such a strategy will probably work best when the EPC can establish a business climate where prestige and expansion go hand in hand. In particular, this may enable the planners to persuade firms in favored industries to semi-voluntarily "opt in" to the scheme. French planners have found that, often, it is only necessary to persuade one or two managers within an industry to go along with an expansion program. Competitive pressures will soon force the others to follow.

A similar situation emerges when the planners can persuade managers in priority sectors to finance capital-spending projects with borrowed funds rather than from retained earnings or sale of stock. The interest and principal due on a loan are much closer to being fixed costs, independent of a firm's rate of profit and thus of output, than are dividend payments. The higher a firm's debt-to-equity ratio, the higher the percentage of its costs which tend to be fixed over certain ranges of output and the greater its incentive to use any capacity that it has installed.

Nevertheless, to induce managers to borrow, the planners will probably have to lower interest costs or else allow the firm a moratorium on repayment in years when its (accounting) profits are very low. This will reduce its total costs and may also make interest charges more of a variable cost, although still not as variable, in many cases, as dividends.

4. Even leaving aside the above considerations, a mixed economy will normally work best when firms must borrow a significant portion of their investment funds. The EPC's ability to steer the economy rests to no small extent upon its ability to influence investment spending. The outstanding debt of a Japanese corporation, for example, is typically more than four times as great as the total value of its equity. Working through the banking system, the Japanase government has a leverage over the capital-spending programs of these firms which no regional or federal government in North America could duplicate. Although the Japanese case is extreme, enterprise taxation should encourage or even force firms to finance some of their investment through borrowing.

There is a subtler reason for external financing, especially within a socialist economy. Let us briefly return to our sales-maximizing model. Since we don't want producers to ignore costs, this must be sales maximization subject to the constraint that prices cover average opportunity costs. However, consider a socialist manager with a large fund of retained earnings at his disposal after paying all salaries and bonuses. The private opportunity cost of investing these in his own enterprise may be nearly zero because the manager has no alternative use for them. Consequently, he will sometimes plow funds back even though the return to society from investing them elsewhere in the economy would be much greater. (He may also pay out additional bonuses when the EPC would prefer to have the money go elsewhere.)

More generally, the private opportunity cost to a manager of investing in his own enterprise will be less than the social opportunity cost when there is no way of transferring funds from one enterprise to another. The average return to society from all its investments will be less than if yields tended to be equated by a mechanism that caused investible funds to flow toward those sectors in which the marginal productivity of capital was greatest.

We need a transfer device that will transfer funds from low- to high-productivity sectors. The government budget and financial (or stock-and-bond) markets, along with the banking system, are candidates for such a role.

20–7 Concluding Comments

All in all, we have three reasons to expect that a financial-incentive program will often be able to withstand a cost-benefit analysis, as indeed it must if it is to be undertaken or continued:

1. As outlined earlier, the efficiency cost of a financial-incentive program should be much smaller than its impact upon the economy's output mix, provided the incentives are tied to expansion or technical progress and are sought after by managers.

2. In a modern economy, where government activity is bound to have a powerful effect on the system, the alternative to a financial-incentive program

is likely to be a similar, but less desirable program, from several points of view (for example, because different incentives work against one another).

Given the presence of government, it makes sense to try to use these instruments within an over-all framework designed to achieve reasonably well-defined economy-wide goals. By coordinating the efforts of all policymakers, by keeping inefficient subsidies (such as price supports and import quotas) to a minimum, and, finally, by reducing their canceling effect, a government can hope to reach a higher level of social welfare while reducing its participation in the economy.

3. The alternative to a financial-incentive program is, likewise, not a completely efficient economy. In some instances, financial incentives will combat monopoly restrictions. A well-managed program should succeed in realizing a number of economies of mass production and external economies.

On the other hand, nothing that we have said in this chapter gives an EPC unbridled license to grant differential taxes and subsidies. An important measure of the effectiveness of an incentive is its "leverage" factor. A net subsidy that is equivalent to $1 million per year and is expected to create $15 million worth of priority output annually for as long as its effects endure has an expected leverage factor of 15. Other things being equal, higher leverage factors are desirable, and this gives us one dimension along which to rank alternative incentive packages.

Finally, let us say a word about earmarking funds for the program. The EPC should be able to direct each incentive that it awards to a precise target —ideally, to a particular production process, distribution network, or construction project. And, except possibly where the planners operate by changing managerial success indicators, it should be possible to determine the total subsidies paid out. Otherwise, it will be impossible to calculate a return on the investment which these subsidies represent. A cost-benefit analysis could not take place even after the effect of the subsidy on output was known.

A workable way of administering the program might therefore be to first split all incentives into two categories. Category 1 would consist of tax credits and other grants which allow firms to forego repaying certain monies owed to the EPC (or sector of direction and administration). Most of these grants will probably be paper transfers in the sense that no funds actually change hands. Even so, they should go on the books as if a subsidy had been paid out, with the amount and exact destination duly noted.

Category 2 payments—roughly, everything else included within the financial incentive program—should be administered through a central banking or trust account and be made from a *revolving fund* managed by a staff agency of the EPC. A revolving fund is essentially a fund, set up by an initial endowment, from which loans of one kind or other are made and subsequently repaid into the fund to circulate again. Several revolving funds (called "counterpart funds") were established in western Europe during the late 1940s with Marshall Plan money.

Such a fund starts as a permanent endowment which may be raised or lowered from time to time as the EPC authorizes further subsidies to be paid into it or taxes to be deducted from it. But an even more important feature is that the fund constantly renews itself, in the absence of disaster, as loans made from it pay off and are then paid back. It thereby serves as a continuing catalyst of development.

Most of the money paid out of the fund will be in connection with loans to enterprises on terms more attractive than the market is currently allowing without any subsidy or guarantee. Either the full amount of such a loan will be forthcoming from the fund, or the fund will be used to back up guarantees made on specified loans by the commercial banking system.

We can hope that the subsidies paid into the fund will be less than the benefits which firms receive from it. For the government can, in effect, invest in diverse sectors of the economy and thereby reduce the risk to itself below the average risk embodied in the loans it guarantees. Consequently, the subsidy component of these loans might be difficult to estimate in the absence of a revolving fund. However, the EPC can measure the net subsidies paid into the fund itself.

Presumably, accounting needs will also require the fund to be split into two parts at the start of every accounting period. One part would be earmarked for taxes to the government, outright grants to enterprises, and a kind of reserve that represents a flexible lower bound to the size of the fund during the period. The other would be earmarked for current loans, and authorized transfers between the two parts would be allowed if the need arose. The government would have to reserve the right to tax the fund to ensure that all of society's resources are used as effectively as possible. Suppose, for example, that loans from the fund prove fabulously—and unexpectedly—successful. Then it eventually will start to grow and easily could become larger than is really necessary to steer the system. In these circumstances some of the monies being paid back into the fund are needed more urgently elsewhere and should, therefore, be taxed away.

Appendix to Chapter 20

Capitalism and Socialism: The Thin Edge of the Wedge

We next turn to a rather subtle and delicate issue which we have largely ignored up to now. We have never treated the distinction between capitalism and socialism as irrelevant and, indeed, it is not. Yet we have implied that, for many purposes, such a distinction oversimplifies and misleads the analyst attempting to compare different kinds of economic organization. Other related dimensions—specifically, the distribution of economic power and the centralization or decentralization of decision making—are more fundamental to our understanding of how different economies work. We saw in Chapter 1 how our three-dimensional spectrum of economic systems generalizes the conventional dichotomy between capitalism and socialism.

Despite this, we now wish to explore a technical but potentially important aspect of the capitalism versus socialism issue. Earlier in this chapter we indicated that implementing economic plans under capitalism was likely to be a more difficult and delicate operation than economic planning under market socialism, where the government will, of course, have more leverage over individual enterprise investments and also over the distribution of income. Opposing this is a potential advantage of capitalism which we now wish to explore.

No matter how comprehensive a socialist market mechanism may be, there will always be one type of commodity that cannot be traded and, consequently, for which no price will exist. This is a share in a producing enterprise. By definition, a stock market cannot exist under socialism. Every producing enterprise belongs in theory to all the people and thus cannot be bought and sold, either in whole or in part. The same is likely to be true of worker-managed firms. True stock ownership implies voting rights which, in theory and sometimes in practice, enable shareowners to overrule or to discard current managerial personnel. True workers' management, on the other hand, implies that at least this much power ultimately rests with the elected representatives of the workers.

Moreover, largely on ideological grounds, firms have been forbidden to borrow money by selling bonds directly to the public in all socialist countries except Yugoslavia, where the practice is not yet widespread. Consequently, securities markets, as any citizen of a developed Western nation knows them, are virtually nonexistent.

In a sense this is ironic, for one can, in the U.S.S.R. and in other socialist nations, open a private savings account and earn interest on his personal savings. Although large accounts are frowned upon, wealthier individuals get around this, as in other entirely different environments, by opening several accounts. The only risk that a citizen shoulders to earn his (rather meager) interest income is that the government will confiscate his account. This has been done on a wholesale basis in the past.

One consequence of not permitting stock and bond markets or other forms of property ownership is that most socialist governments are able to achieve a greater spreading of property incomes than usually occurs under capitalism. Wealth in the form of productive assets tends to become concentrated in the hands of successful entrepreneurs and their heirs.

To prevent this, many proponents of a "new capitalism" have advocated steeply progressive income taxes and stiff inheritance taxes, thereby hoping to redistribute much of society's rental income.[14] (Rental components of property incomes are often presumed to be greater for the heirs of entrepreneurs who have "struck it rich" than for the entrepreneurs themselves.) But to the extent that these redistributed incomes are not rents, but serve instead as incentives for innovation and better management, society will have to accept less of these commodities, and the same is true under socialism.

A second consequence of state ownership of productive assets, and the one to be explored here, is a greater likelihood that managers will be judged on the basis of short-run rather than long-run performance. Joseph L. Bower once noted that, "Almost every manager, at some time in his career, finds that the measures of his actions cover a much shorter time span than the results of his actions." [15] We would argue that this is more likely to be the case under public or cooperative than under private ownership.

Suppose that yearly profits, sales, or gross value of output become the principal success indicator in a socialist economy. Many managers will then have an incentive to run down their plant and equipment in order to improve current performance and simultaneously improve their chances for promotion while raising their annual bonus payments. Later their successors may have to take the blame for premature breakdowns or excessive replacement and

---

[14] This presupposes the power to bring about the required tax changes through society's political decision-making processes. We shall see what problems are involved here in Chapter 23.

[15] Joseph L. Bower, "Planning Within the Firm," paper delivered to the I.R.R.A. Conference in New York, Dec. 1969, pp. 9–10.

maintenance requirements. This would be less likely if an index of the firm's expected future profitability were available, and this is what financial markets provide.

Up to now, in fact, we have implicitly supposed that the goals of profit, growth, and (constrained) sales maximization are exactly the same for a socialist manager as for his capitalist counterpart. But unless we can assign some kind of value to a producing enterprise, such goals have a time dimension and are therefore ambiguous. Does a profit-maximizing entrepreneur maximize his profits today and fly by night or take a much longer time horizon into account? Does a sales maximizer look at anticipated sales for next month, next year, or over the entire decade to come?

We can remove the ambiguity either by specifying a time period or by translating these goals into other goals which involve no time dimension. But some firms will, in fact, maximize profits today and fly by night while others will have a much longer horizon. We cannot fix the same time period for all producers. We must take the second route and find a timeless (or stock) variable to replace profits.

Let us define the value of a capitalist corporation to be the market value of all its stock less the value of its outstanding debt. Basically, this value will reflect two interdependent elements, one purely speculative and the other depending upon how the market evaluates the present and future earnings potential of the firm. If we call the second element the *intrinsic* value of the enterprise, the goal of maximizing profits turns out to be the same as maximizing the present intrinsic value of the firm.[16] Or, viewing the corporation as the property of its stockholders, maximizing profits turns out to be equivalent to maximizing the present intrinsic value of this property.

Indeed, if long-run profits are to have any meaning at all, they must be defined as the intrinsic value of the firm times an appropriate discount rate, just as the annual interest payment on a perpetual bond will equal its market value times the interest rate. Such a profit concept will apply simultaneously to a fly-by-nighter as well as to a pillar of the community. The essential difference is that the fly-by-nighter will discount the future at a much higher rate. For him, long-run profits will identify more closely with the earning he anticipates over the near future.

Because of the speculative component, the net market value of a company's stock will not usually equal its intrinsic value. There may be no quoted figure to reflect the latter, and opinions will differ about it. A profit-maximizing management will presumably maximize what it believes to be the corporation's intrinsic value. However, it cannot entirely neglect any divergence of views with present and potential investors in its earning assets.

In particular, when the market value of their own shares shows a per-

---

[16] For a good discussion of how the goal of profit maximization translates into value maximization, see Franco Modigliani and Merton H. Miller, "The Cost of Capital, Corporation Finance, and the Theory of Investment," *American Economic Review*, June 1958, pp. 261–267 and references cited. A criticism of Modigliani and Miller is that they treat the intrinsic and market values of a corporation as identical.

sistent tendency to fall *relative* to that of rival firms, managers will review their over-all operations and, above all, their capital-spending programs in an effort to correct such a tendency. If they fail to do this or if they subsequently fail to find ways of correcting the relative decline, they will risk losing their jobs. Although the market and intrinsic values of a corporation need not coincide, the management will not be consistently able to avoid using relative market values as performance indicators.[17]

Hopefully, in any given society, most producers will not be fly-by-nighters. For them, intrinsic values will reflect three basic factors: current profitability, growth potential, and the uncertainty attached to the anticipated stream of future earnings. A manager may be penalized for failing to pay attention to any one of these. In particular he must look at his enterprise as an entity whose life span may exceed his own stay with the organization.

In a socialist market system, by contrast, there is no market index that amalgamates growth potential and uncertainty with current profitability. Whatever profit maximization might mean to a socialist manager, it cannot, except by accident, mean the same thing as in an economy where shares in firms can be bought and sold. Consequently, within any particular time period, a profit-maximizing socialist manager will not be likely to produce the same output mix of goods and services as his profit-maximizing capitalist counterpart.

As noted above, managers under market socialism will often have an incentive to concentrate on current indicators, since their pay and promotion will depend upon these. Like their command-economy counterparts, they will sometimes be led to neglect both the upkeep of plant and equipment and the introduction of improved technology because this may adversely affect short-term profit and production levels.

Nor is there any reason to limit the above analysis to profit maximization. For a wide range of goals, a manager is apt to find that socialist or cooperative ownership shortens his time horizon.[18]

REFERENCES

(For Chs. 18–20)

Allen, G. C. *Japan's Economic Expansion.* New York: Oxford University Press, Inc., 1972.

[17] This is less true if the firm is a single proprietorship, a partnership, or a cooperative. Then a market value for it may be quoted rarely, if at all. However, management may still try to maximize some subjective notion of long-run profitability that will take into account the three basic factors listed in the next paragraph. Moreover, the majority of single proprietors may expect to remain longer in their current managerial posts than most corporate managers. This will lengthen the time horizons of the former relative to the latter.

[18] The problem will exist under private ownership, however, especially in multiplant corporations in which plant managers may be judged on a current performance basis and accounting systems may overemphasize current performance by their reporting methods. See Rensis Likert, *New Patterns of Management* (New York: McGraw-Hill, 1961), Chs. 1–6, 13, 14.

Bergson, Abram. "Market Socialism Re-Visited." *Journal of Political Economy,*
Oct. 1967.
Cohen, Stephen. *Modern Capitalist Planning: The French Model.* Cambridge,
Mass.: Harvard University Press, 1969.
Galbraith, J. K. *The New Industrial State.* Boston: Houghton Mifflin Company,
1967.
Hayek, Friedrich. "Socialist Calculation: The 'Competitive Solution,' " *Economica,*
May 1940. Reprinted in Morris Bornstein, ed., *Comparative Economic Sys-
tems.* Homewood, Ill.: Richard D. Irwin, Inc., 1969, Ch. 6. Excerpts from
Lange and von Mises also appear as Chs. 4 and 5 in this volume.
Lippincott, Benjamin, ed. *On the Economic Theory of Socialism.* New York:
McGraw-Hill Book Company, 1964.
Lutz, Vera. *Central Planning for the Market Economy.* London: Harlow Long-
mans, Institute of Economic Affairs, 1969.
Oxenfeldt, A., and V. Holubnychy. *Economic Systems in Action.* New York: Holt,
Rinehart and Winston, Inc., 1965.
Pejovich, Svetozar. *The Market-Planned Economy of Yugoslavia.* Minneapolis:
University of Minnesota Press, 1966.
Schnitzer, Martin. *The Economy of Sweden: A Study of the Modern Welfare
State.* New York: Praeger Publishers, Inc., 1970.
Shonfield, Andrew. *Modern Capitalism.* New York: Oxford University Press,
1965.
von Mises, Ludwig. "Economic Calculation in the Socialist Commonwealth," in
F. A. Hayek, ed., *Collectivist Economic Planning.* London: Routledge &
Kegan Paul, Ltd., 1963.

Chapter **21**

Workers' Management:
Structure and Functioning

21–1   Definition of Workers' Management [1]

A producers' cooperative, by the definition we shall use, is a profit-sharing firm in which the elected representatives of all employees come together to form a workers' council. The workers' council decides what the basic goals of the enterprise will be, how much of each good it will produce, which basic production methods it will use, and what prices it will charge. In a fundamental sense, the elected representatives of the workers manage the enterprise. Consequently, we call such a system "workers' management."

In the first instance, workers' management is distinguished by the par-

---

[1] The model of a producers' cooperative discussed here is due to Benjamin Ward, "The Firm in Illyria: Market Syndicalism," *American Economic Review,* Sept. 1958. For a reply to Ward's conclusion, see Jaroslav Vanek, "Decentralization Under Workers' Management: A Theoretical Appraisal," *American Economic Review,* Dec. 1969.

We would emphasize that communal property relations (as defined in Chapter 1 and discussed in Chapter 13) do *not* generally prevail within such a firm. However, collective rights to income from investment are a fundamental feature of such a system, with consequences to be explored below.

ticipation of workers in the profits of capital. To some extent, everyone connected with the enterprise sinks or swims with its fortunes in the sense that everyone's paycheck depends at least partly on its residual income after all its bills have been paid.

Here, however, we are going to be more interested in employee participation in managerial decision making. If the cooperative form predominates on an economy-wide basis, we speak of a participatory, a cooperative, or a *worker-managed* economy. We shall assume that we are also dealing with a planned system. Workers' management becomes a special case of Brand X, although we could also view it within a laissez-faire context.

In discussing the internal organization of the enterprise, we are actually departing from our general framework, which has so far concentrated on relations between firms, households, and administrators. To an extent, we are now treating the firm rather than the economy as our system whose internal organization we wish to explore.

We have already seen that the organization of a firm can spectacularly effect its X efficiency. An important goal of workers' management is to raise this by harmonizing the economic goals of workers, owners, and managers. It is less obvious, but still true, that a switch to workers' management will probably change the economy-wide allocation of resources, and thus have an impact upon allocative efficiency.

We shall begin by exploring the relationship between workers' management and both kinds of efficiency. Important efficiency *dis*advantages may stem from cooperative employees' inability to claim future profits after leaving the firm or retiring;[2] from the tendency of cooperatives to maximize long-run profits *per employee* instead of the *total* long-run profits, growth, or sales of the enterprise; from the relatively cumbersome nature of communal goal formation within the firm; and from difficulties met in shifting the burden of risk-bearing onto those most willing and able to assume risks. A second potential advantage, in addition to goal harmonization, comes from a larger degree of external financing than in a conventional market economy. However, this financing may likewise be inflationary, making the blessing by no means a pure one.

At the same time, we would be sadly neglectful to confine our attention to efficiency. The architects of workers' management claim that their system makes important strides toward the age-old dream of a classless society by blurring the traditional class distinctions among owners, managers, and workers. They have also sought to give the worker more control over the conditions under which he works and the kind of product he produces, thereby making his work a more meaningful extension of his life. In Marxian terms, they have

---

[2] Most employees will probably consider that there is at least some possibility of their leaving or retiring from the firm during, for example, the next ten years. This will shorten the time horizon of the workers' council in the sense of creating a higher discount of future vis-à-vis present profits. It will also reduce the council's willingness to invest from retained earnings, a factor to be examined below.

sought to reduce the *alienation* of the worker from his product and from the production process.[3]

Finally, several socialist writers have considered "democracy" in the management of producing enterprises (often called "industrial democracy") to be at least a partial substitute for democracy in national and regional government. It is not clear to the present author how to compute the relative likelihood of dictatorship in a worker-managed vis-à-vis some other type of market economy. Moreover, once established, it would appear that dictatorship could inflict costs upon the citizens of a worker-managed society as well as upon any other.

We should note, however, that under ideal conditions, a worker-managed economy might be able to achieve a "democratically determined" income distribution without going through the tax-subsidy schemes envisaged by many advocates of market socialism. For example, it could conceivably achieve the effect of Lange's social dividend simply by letting workers' councils democratically decide how profits should be divided among the employees. These councils will also have an incentive to see that efficient work rules are enforced in order to maximize the employees' total profit pie. Thus we might get a better tradeoff between equity and efficiency than with conventionally managed enterprises.

Unfortunately, a serious flaw in this scheme is that an unequal distribution of profits may arise between different producing enterprises, which are protected by artificial entry barriers. We shall explore tendencies in this direction below.

21–2   The Flow of Funds in a Worker-Managed Firm

Let us say that the "pure socialist" model of Brand X is one in which firms must hand over to the state all profits except that portion which becomes wage and salary bonuses. All financing of investments in the pure socialist model will come from borrowing. Because it can dispose of a firm's profits as it wishes, the EPC can control the goals and, to an extent, the opportunity costs of each enterprise by manipulating incentive payments, interest rates, and other borrowing terms.

Under the pure socialist model, a switch from conventional to workers' management of the enterprise will not have any *automatic* effect upon the allocation of resources. The demand curve facing each firm remains the same. The EPC has complete control over enterprise goals, and no change will occur in these unless the central planners decide that a change is in order. After the switch, firms may experience differential X-efficiency gains and therefore differential cost reductions. This will lead to differential rates of

---

[3] We have identified two sources of alienation in Marx (see Chapter 12). First, as soon as there is division of labor, each worker creates only a small part of the end result of any production process. Workers' management may be able to remove a part of this source by helping to reidentify the worker with the total product. The second source is exploitation.

expansion (and probably to output contractions by some firms), causing changes in resource allocation. But all this is contingent upon the gains in X efficiency actually coming to pass.

On paper, workers' management performs best under the pure socialist model. Several proponents of cooperatives have argued for its adoption, one or two even going as far as to claim that the ability of the state to tax away profits (that is, to capture the income from capital) is the very essence of socialism. If so, the socialist sheep has appeared to many East European workers to wear the capitalist wolf's clothing. One prerogative of a workers' council would normally be to decide how profits shall be divided among the employees and the various investment alternatives open to the firm. The relations of the "pure socialist model" make the state appear to workers as an agency that undermines their sovereignty and exploits them by expropriating their surplus value. This reduces the ability of such a system to remove alienation.

Thus the pure socialist model does not characterize Yugoslavia, where workers' management is most predominant, nor does it prevail elsewhere in countries making some use of the basic idea. Moreover, in Yugoslavia, the state's power to directly tax enterprise profits has steadily eroded until rates are far lower than in Western capitalist nations.[4]

We shall accordingly assume that in most years workers' councils have at least some retained earnings to distribute or to invest as they see fit. The flow of funds in a "typical" Yugoslav firm circa 1970 appears in Figure 21–1. From gross receipts, largely consisting of sales revenue, we first subtract out-of-pocket expenses. These notably exclude labor costs, which are considered part of profits. The latter are therefore divided into a wages fund, from which employee earnings are paid, and three internal funds.

The latter include the investment fund, covering investment from retained earnings, the collective consumption fund to finance such things as worker housing and recreation, and the reserve fund. Yugoslavia has not one, but several minimum wages for various skills and types of labor. Enterprises are expected to pay these, even in low-profit years. The reserve fund therefore becomes a sinking fund channeled through local (or communal) governments, which is built up during good years from obligatory donations and then drawn down whenever this becomes necessary to ensure that minima are paid.

The basic tax on enterprise profits is a tax on the wage fund. This varies from one enterprise to another; the 12.5 per cent in Figure 21–1 may be taken as illustrative. (Occasionally, specific investments, for example in office buildings, are also taxed to discourage their proliferation.) This gives some disincentive to pay out high wages and salaries at the expense of the investment and collective consumption funds. However, the fruits of investment ma-

4 See Branko Horvat, "Yugoslav Economic Policy in the Post-War Period: Problems, Ideas, Institutional Developments," *American Economic Review,* June 1971, Suppl. Also E. G. Furubotn and Svetozar Pejovich, "Property Rights and the Behavior of the Firm in a Socialist State: The Example of Yugoslavia," *Zeitschrift für Nationalokonomie,* 1970, Nos. 3–4, pp. 431–454.

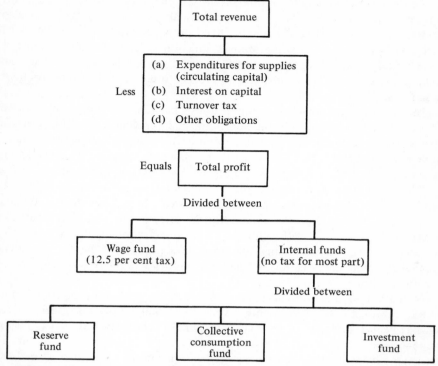

Figure 21–1. The distribution of funds in a worker-managed firm (circa 1970).

terialize in the form of higher future profits as the cooperative's labor acquires more and better capital to work with. That is, the attraction of higher future wages and collective consumption provides the basic incentive for workers' councils to invest. Insofar as the tax on the wages fund has any significant effect, therefore, it probably encourages collective consumption. Of course, the firm may also invest from borrowed funds.

21–3   Workers' Management and Allocative Efficiency: The Short Run

When workers' control is real, some economists have suggested that, as its basic pecuniary goal, a cooperative will try to maximize average long-run profits per employee rather than total long-run profits. That is, it will try to maximize the average long-run profit share or wealth of each employee. To begin with, therefore, we want to ask whether a firm maximizing profits per employee will behave any differently, on that account, from a firm maximizing total profits. For reasons that will become apparent as we proceed, we shall assume that the latter firm does not face a rigid wage dictated by a labor union or a professional association.

At the outset, we assume a firm producing one output, wine, in the short run with three variable inputs—labor, chemicals, and grapes. We shall also suppose that these are used in roughly fixed proportions so that we may treat them like a composite input. Moreover, the single type of labor can plant, harvest, and squash the grapes underfoot or do any of the other chores, and every laborer is a perfect substitute for every other in performing each of these tasks.

In addition, the firm uses land, tools, machinery, and plant, whose amounts will be fixed during the short run and for which the EPC charges $100,000 per year. Finally we assume that each laborer must receive a minimum wage of $5,000 per year even if the cooperative takes a loss and that the cost of chemicals and grapes will add a final $5,000 per man-year.

The firm's basic costs for the year to come will therefore equal $100,000 plus $10,000 times the number of workers hired plus any explicit taxes and less any explicit subsidies. Its revenue will be price per liter of wine times the number of liters sold. It will try to choose a rate of labor input, and, thereby, of output which maximizes this difference on a per worker basis. To understand the consequences of this, let us take another look at the straight profit-maximizing firm.

Whenever such a firm can increase its profit by expanding or contracting output, it will do so. Consequently, when the (total) profit-maximizing output has been found, the additional or marginal profit from further expansion or contraction should be approximately zero. If we write marginal profit as marginal revenue minus marginal cost, this means that the two should be approximately equal. Such, however, is not necessarily true for a cooperative.

Let us suppose that we are in an economy where firms tend, on the average, to earn some economic profits over and above their opportunity costs. This may happen because some barriers to entry exist in a number of industries (almost inevitable in any market economy) or because of continuing innovation.[5] Each act of innovation can lead to economic profits, which do not disappear until the idea is successfully copied in other firms.

In these conditions, an enterprise maximizing profits per employee will normally contract output when the marginal profit from doing so is positive (or when the marginal profit from expansion is negative). But it will not necessarily expand output when the marginal profit from expansion is positive. Rather, to keep average profits per employee from falling, it will take on a new man only when the additional profit that he will bring in equals or exceeds the present average. For only then will the old hands benefit by having newcomers in their midst.

As long as there are some levels of output at which a positive economic profit can be earned, therefore, a coop will not go on expanding output until marginal profit is zero. Instead, it will stop short of this, while marginal profit is still positive. Therefore, it will produce and hire less than a straight

[5] It may also happen simply because firms that take long-run losses tend to go out of business.

profit maximizer facing the same demand and cost conditions for nonhuman factors of production.

In particular, when the profit maximizer would equate price with marginal cost, the cooperative will restrict output and keep marginal cost below price. One consequence will be some contribution to economic inefficiency, although this may not be large. However, those cooperatives that achieve the greatest success in raising profits per employee will likewise be the ones to restrict output and employment the most. These are just the firms that the EPC will usually want most to expand because the high profits will normally indicate a high yield to further investment.

Consequently, the planners will have to carefully design tax-incentive packages, based on fairly detailed knowledge of each firm's demand and cost conditions, to ensure expansion. These packages should also be nondiscriminatory, and it appears that the information cost of steering a Brand X economy is likely to rise because of workers' management.

Next, let us ask how a cooperative will react to a change in the price of its product. If a market system is to be effective, a rise in the price of a good must normally lead to an increase in quantity supplied, and a fall in price must usually have the opposite effect. But a cooperative, in our simple model, will tend to do the opposite. A price rise means both an increase in average profits per employee *and* in the marginal or extra profits that would be foregone were an employee to be laid off or several employees put on shorter hours and lower profit shares. We can show, however, that these marginal profits per employee would rise by less than average profits.[6]

Since the cooperative wishes to choose rates of output and of labor input that approximately equate average and marginal profits per employee, let us assume that these were about the same just before the price increase. Afterward, the average will be less than the marginal, and it will pay the cooperative to *reduce* output, either by laying off men or by putting some men on shorter hours and lower profit shares. The profit-maximizing cooperative's short-run reaction to a price increase is the reverse of what we would normally expect. It will reduce rather than increase supply. The short-run supply schedule for the wine industry in our example will slope downward rather than upward, as shown in Figures 21-2(a) and (b).

In Figure 21-2(a), $\bar{p}$ and $\bar{q}$ are the equilibrium price and quantity of wine produced. In Figure 21-2(b), by contrast, where the supply curve is flatter than the demand curve, there is no stable equilibrium solution. To see why, suppose that the price rises momentarily above $\bar{p}$. As a result, quantity demanded exceeds quantity supplied, and there will be pressure for yet another price increase, coupled with further cutbacks in supply. If the cooperative

---

[6] See Ward, op. cit. As it turns out, this is equivalent to saying that the cooperative will always produce in what is variously known as the "economic region" or relevant range of production. This is the region within which every input has a positive marginal product or production price. For further discussion, see C. E. Ferguson, *Micro-economic Theory* (Homewood, Ill.: Irwin, 1969), Ch. 6, Sec. 3c.

responds to market pressures, the shortage will become worse, intensifying the pressure for yet a third price rise, and so it goes.

The result will either be creeping or galloping inflation, depending upon how rapidly the cooperative responds to excess demand pressures and what additional inflationary or deflationary forces are at work. Our analysis, therefore, shows a greater potential for short-run market instability in an economy where firms maximize profits per employee.

Several economists have objected, however, that this discussion pushes profit maximization too far. In the short run, they argue, any cooperative will

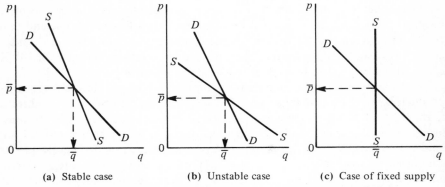

(a) Stable case   (b) Unstable case   (c) Case of fixed supply

Figure 21–2. Three possible supply curves for a worker-managed firm.

be constrained by both humanitarian and technological considerations from laying off workers or putting them on shorter hours (and, consequently, lower profit shares). The planners are likely to raise these costs a bit in an effort to keep down the unemployment rate.

On the other hand, let us stay with strict profit maximization and assume that most firms produce at least two commodities, whose demands are not highly correlated over time. Suppose, furthermore, that the firm can shift some production capacity between the two goods. Then it will always have an incentive to shift some capacity into production of the good whose excess demand is greatest. This will countervail any tendencies to reduce the supply of this good.

The short-run supply curve for a cooperative is therefore more likely to be approximately straight-up-and-down, as in Figure 21–2(c). Increases and decreases in demand are largely spent in price changes rather than in changes in output and employment. A decline or an increase in demand causes the cooperative to lower or raise price rather than production. In comparison with the conventional firm, prices are more flexible and output and employment more stable.

Because shifts in demand do not call forth large changes in output and employment, an EPC should find it easier to free a cooperative economy from seasonal and cyclical bouts with reduced output and employment. Cooperatives will also be more willing to cut price and maintain output on world markets in the face of increased competition or restrictions from foreign countries. This organizational form may therefore be especially attractive for export industries.[7]

Since we have raised the notion of cycles, let us take a closer look at the labor market. Suppose that the quantity of labor that workers supply depends upon the money wage being paid, say $5 per hour, divided by a price index of goods workers buy (that is, upon workers' real purchasing power). This wage will include each worker's share of profits.

Under these conditions, let there be an excess demand for labor at the wage rates that cooperatives are currently paying. Then both employment and the real wage would normally have to rise in order to bring supply and demand back into balance. However, firms are already paying their maximum wages (because they are maximizing profits per worker). Thus wages cannot rise and, in the short run, the labor market cannot adjust to a new equilibrium. Firms unable to hire all the labor they wish will have to remain short-handed.

Next, suppose that we are faced with unemployment. This is an excess supply of labor, so real wages should fall and employment increase. But employee–managers will be reluctant to expand output and cut their own profit shares in order to absorb new men. This reluctance will be reinforced by any government measures that may make it harder to lay off men later. Thus unemployment remains.

Wage rates are therefore downwardly rigid here just as they may be in a laissez-faire economy with strong labor unions and professional associations, and for basically the same reason. It is a group decision, in this case of the workers' council, rather than individual decision making which determines acceptable wages and working conditions. Here only members of the workers' council, whose constituents are already employed, may vote. They will have an incentive to respond to supply-and-demand conditions in the product market, while ignoring the presence of an excess supply of labor.

One partial way around labor-market rigidity would be to differentiate wages on the basis of seniority so that new employees are paid less than present staff for the same work. To be hired, a new employee would no longer have to create an additional profit equal to the existing average profit per employee, because his share of profits would be less than the average. However, he would still have to expand total profit by some minimum amount greater than zero, whereas, in a straight profit-maximizing enterprise, zero is the effective lower bound. In other words, a (modified) cooperative would still require a larger profit expansion as a precondition to expanding employment.

It follows that this device will not be able to completely eliminate unemployment. When it cannot, workers will remain idle, at least until new

---

[7] If the supply curve is upward-sloping, as in Figures 21-1(a) and (b), the cooperative would actually try to export more in the face of a lower realized price on world markets.

enterprises can be built or old ones expanded. In the short run the labor market cannot adjust supply and demand to one another except through wage discrimination. Moreover, it will not efficiently allocate labor between producing enterprises.

Assume for a moment that a group of sheet-metal workers would become more productive if they transferred jobs. If this requires them to change firms as well, they would become "new" employees. However, the enterprises in which the values of their marginal products would be higher may not offer them higher wages. Such could easily be the case if these firms practice wage discrimination based on seniority, but otherwise the jobs might not be offered at all. Movement toward higher productivity jobs will therefore not always occur in a cooperative economy.

This may remain true in the long run. A feature of a cooperative economy is that product market entry barriers, which create high profit shares for employees, also translate into job entry barriers. An EPC can alleviate both problems by promoting workable competition and by trying to ensure that the opportunity cost of investment to each firm approximately reflects the maximum yield obtainable elsewhere.

Nevertheless, we have a suggestion here, to be reinforced by the discussion below, that force of circumstances will often cause employees to attach themselves to particular firms over fairly long periods of time, somewhat independently of economic forces. The enterprise would then become a kind of club in which each employee was a member, and it would not be surprising to find a range of social and recreational activities centering around it, at least as broad as would be undertaken by a labor union in North America. Indeed, Yugoslav experience confirms this.

Thus the effect of cooperatives may well be to alleviate work alienation and perhaps thereby to make workers more productive. But they will also foster some labor immobility.

21–4   Workers' Management and Scale Economies

With the above results under our belt, we can now proceed toward greater realism by allowing inputs other than labor to vary. As decision-making horizons expand, our previous conclusions must be modified. A cooperative can now respond to an increase in demand by investing in new production capacity. If the increase is viewed as permanent, it will have an incentive to do this, and its long-run supply curve is practically certain to be upward-sloping or even horizontal. Both the EPC and would-be enterpreneurs can establish new firms, which will help to absorb involuntary unemployment.

Nevertheless, the EPC will be harder pressed to time and locate the construction of new firms so as to absorb potential unemployment before or soon after it appears than would be the case in a conventional market economy. To compensate for this, the planners may find it expedient to make it easier for enterprises to arise than to disband and to enter an industry than to leave it. Such a policy has the added advantage of discouraging artificial entry barriers, but if pushed too far, it can also subsidize the existence of inefficient firms. (This may be desirable, on balance, if no other way is found to keep unemployment low.)

In a completely decentralized (or perfectly competitive) economy without troublesome external effects, scale economies, X inefficiency, risk, or market breakdowns, the long-run cooperative model is every bit as efficient as its conventionally managed counterpart. When such an economy is in long-run equilibrium, firms are making zero excess profits. Both cooperatives and straight profit maximizers will be willing to hire an extra employee whenever he is able to raise profits by any positive amount (since the previous average was zero). Conceivably, the long-run equilibrium for cooperative and conventionally managed economies would be identical.

We wish to compare them, however, in a somewhat more realistic setting where risk and barriers to entry are important. Because of the latter, we would expect firms to earn *positive* excess profits on balance in long-run equilibrium. In these circumstances, cooperatives will still tend to produce less and charge higher prices than straight profit maximizers under comparable demand and cost conditions. There are four factors inhibiting the growth of worker-managed firms. First, both a cooperative and a straight profit-maximizing firm will want to expand by adding to their capital stock as long as the required investment raises the enterprises' total profits by any amount. (This will be an increase in profits per employee for any given number of employees.) But the cooperative will still hire another employee only when his contribution to economic profits exceeds the preceding average, less any discount for seniority discrimination. In the absence of risk considerations, this will also tend to make the cooperative more capital intensive than the straight profit-maximizing firm.

Second, the nonpecuniary benefits of participatory management may decrease as the firm grows larger. Many employees may be reluctant to see the the firm expand and grow more impersonal, while they are increasingly forced to share and to delegate their decision-making authority. Antimerger feelings among Yugoslav employees have prevented firms in different regions from merging in order to realize scale economies in management and research.

Third, and probably most important, there will be scale diseconomies inherent in the cooperative organizational form itself. We shall discover that as the process of goal formation within a firm becomes more democratic, it also becomes more expensive. Moreover, the difference in cost between participatory and authoritarian goal formation rises with the number and complexity of decisions to be taken.

Finally, we shall also see below that the cooperative is likely to be biased against investments, a large percentage of whose profits are expected to take a long time to materialize and also to be expecially risk averse.[8] (This will reinforce any disincentive to bear risk burdens caused by egalitarian princi-

---

[8] It is not clear, however, that a cooperative will be more biased against capital-spending projects with long gestation periods than some conventional socialist market managements (see footnote 16).

ples.) At least the third and fourth factors will also operate to discourage entry
into many industries making excess profits.

Furthermore, suppose that we have an enterprise starting from scratch,
as opposed to an old firm entering a new industry. Then the founders may not
be able to capture many of the excess profits to be earned there, if the firm
comes in at an efficient scale. The latter will be distributed by a workers'
council to employees who do not have to bear a commensurate share of the
risk involved in getting the business going. The result will be a disincentive to
entry. (A financial incentive can overcome this at some risk of subsidizing
firms that really ought not to be started in the first place.)

In particular, we have no guarantee that the short-run immobility and misallocation of labor cited above will disappear in the long run. The principal
mechanism to eliminate this is entry by firms into industries where a high
VMP of labor results in large profits and departure of (presumably the least
efficient) firms from industries where a low VMP of labor results in low
profits. This is, in any event, a blunt instrument.[9] It is certainly possible for a
particular kind of labor to have a high VMP in a low-profit industry, or vice
versa. Moreover, the factors just cited will reduce the attraction of expanding
into or within many industries making excess profits. To complement this, the
government is likely to be subsidizing some inefficient firms as a protection
against unemployment.

Our principal question here, however, is whether cooperatives will be
able to realize economies of mass production. To investigate this problem,
let us assume that we have two hypothetical industries, one inhabited by
cooperatives and the other by straight profit maximizers. We shall also suppose that both *industries* face the same demand curves and all firms use the
same technology of production and face the same supply conditions in input
markets. Finally, we shall suppose at the outset that no artificial barriers to
entry exist in either industry.

Under these conditions, we saw in Chapter 16 that the production of
straight profit-maximizing firms was generally close to the bottom of their
long-run average cost curves, provided the size of the scale barrier to entry
was not too large relative to the size of the market. In particular, they realized
most of their potential economies of mass production if the empirical studies
that are available to us can be believed. However, cooperatives will be smaller,
and we must therefore ask whether they are likely to be as fortunate.

In fact, a purely technical argument shows that a firm maximizing profits
per employee will produce at the bottom of its long-run average cost curve,
provided that it faces fixed product prices. That is, if its demand curve is
horizontal, it will produce at a point such as *A* in Figure 21–3. Under the
more likely assumption of downward sloping enterprise demand, however, the
same argument shows that it will produce *less* than is necessary to realize

---

[9] At the same time, it is an instrument not operating in a conventionally managed
market economy with rigid wages and occupational entry barriers.

Price

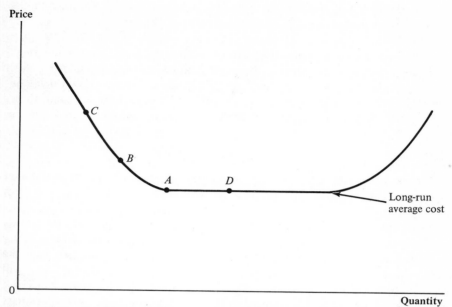

Figure 21–3. Possible rates of output for a cooperative vis-à-vis a straight profit maxi-mizer.

its potential scale economies. The important question, then, is whether it will continue to realize most of them, for example, producing at B in Figure 21–3, or retreat to a much less efficient position such as C.

In fact, supporters of workers' management would argue for B. They claim that, because cooperatives will be smaller than straight profit maximizers, there will be room for more of them in the industry, which will therefore be more competitive. Consequently, this point of view maintains that coopera-tives will face highly elastic (or nearly horizontal) demand curves, and by an extension of the technical argument just referred to, will produce close to A. The larger, straight profit maximizers would produce at a point such as D. Because they are more competitive, cooperatives could conceivably charge lower prices than straight profit maximizers, even though the latter face slightly lower unit costs and tend to accept lower price markups for any *given* elasticity of enterprise demand (because of their more expansive goal). In any event, we would not be able to say, à priori, which industry would charge the lower price and produce the greater total output.

Unfortunately, the technical argument under consideration takes into account the first but by no means the remaining factors restricting the size of the cooperative listed above. When we introduce any or all of these, we can-not rule out position C in Figure 21–3—where many scale economies remain unrealized—as the long-run equilibrium position of the cooperative. Indeed, in the presence of scale diseconomies inherent in the cooperative form, we cannot assume that it faces the same cost curve as the straight profit maximizer, except to the left of the point where these diseconomies appear.[10]

Finally, if excessive natural or artificial barriers to entry prevent straight profit maximizers from realizing their potential economies of scale, the effect on cooperatives of the same barriers is likely to be worse. Only when conventionally managed firms are too large and cumbersome to be efficient, therefore, could we hope for significant scale benefits from the cooperative form.

21–5 Saving, Investment, and Growth

When a workers' council votes an additional 1,000 dinars for investment out of current profit, it expects the employees to derive benefits in the form of higher profits later. The added capital equipment should make other inputs more productive on balance if it is worth purchasing. If the yield on investment is 10 per cent, profits will increase by 100 dinars, on the average, over at least the next several years.[11] Let us take the simplest case, in which the new capital equipment (and subsequent replacements as it depreciates) will raise annual profits permanently by 100 dinars over what they otherwise would have been. This is the reward to the workers for sacrificing 1,000 dinars in current wages or collective consumption.

Employees may also put part of their own incomes into private savings accounts. Suppose that the yield on such an account is 10 per cent. Then a 1,000-dinar deposit would also generate a perpetual annual (interest) income of 100 dinars. (Ultimately, this will come from taxes or from interest earnings on loans.) On balance, there may be no preference between the two income streams except on grounds of risk. If the workers' council tends to be risk averse, it may always prefer to pay higher wages in lieu of investing *internal* funds unless the yield on private savings falls below the expected yield on investments within the firm by a minimum amount.

No one keeps money in a savings account forever, however, and most

---

[10] We may also treat increased risk aversion as an upward shift in all or part of the long-run average cost curve. In addition, some economists, notably Vanek in *The Labor-Managed Market Economy: General Theory* (Ithaca, N.Y.: Cornell U.P., 1971, pp. 120–123, have argued that a cooperative economy will engage in less advertising, which, as far as it goes, will be more informative. The present author does not feel that this point has been established. Short of perfect competition, there is little empirical support for the claim that less concentrated industries do less advertising per unit of output. It is hard to see why a cooperative would especially want to be more informative, unless we argue that a truly classless society would emerge. We discuss this point below.

[11] More precisely, if P_1, P_2, P_3, . . . , are the expected profits from the investment 1, 2, 3, . . . , years from now, the yield on the 1,000-dinar outlay will be 10 per cent if:

$$1,000 = \frac{P_1}{1.1} + \frac{P_2}{(1.1)^2} + \frac{P_3}{(1.1)^3} + \cdots$$

That is, the stream of expected future profits, discounted by 10 per cent, will add to 1,000 workers will not expect to work forever for the same firm. An employee who keeps 1,000 dinars in a savings account at 10 per cent and lets it grow will have 1,100 dinars after the first year, 1,210 dinars after two years, and so on. If he withdraws after 10 years, he will take away his 1,000-dinar principal plus 1,579 dinars in accumulated interest.

Now let the same employee sacrifice 1,000 dinars in foregone wages to investment in his cooperative. After 10 years, we suppose, he leaves the firm to retire or join another enterprise. In the meantime, we may assume that he gets back the equivalent of 1,579 dinars in higher wages as his return on the investment. But he cannot also withdraw his original 1,000-dinar sacrifice to take with him, nor has he any right to the cooperative's future profits. By law, *this capital remains in the firm.* He has therefore lost the principal of his investment forever, and this is bound to make investing in the cooperative less attractive than private saving when the yields on the two are the same. (The fact that the departing worker loses all or part of his rights to future collective consumption in the enterprise, even though his own previous wage sacrifice with help to make this possible will also reduce his willingness to contribute to this fund.[12])

If a worker expects to remain with the collective for just one year, it will take a yield of 110 per cent on an investment in the cooperative to just compensate him for a yield of 10 per cent on his private saving. After one year, a saved 100 dinars will become 110. An invested 100 dinars will have to result in 110 dinars in higher wages over the course of the year if the worker is to be indifferent between these alternatives (with risk considerations aside).

If a worker expects to remain with the same collective for 10 years, or if a workers' council reflects an average 10 year horizon for the employees, it will take a yield of 15.5 per cent on an investment in the cooperative to just compensate for a 10 per cent yield on savings accounts. This continues to assume that 100 dinars worth of capital outlay will bring in 15.5 dinars in added profits every year.[13] If the bulk of the yield is expected to accrue several years after the outlay, however, the council will require *more* than 15.5 per cent to compensate for a 10 per cent return on private savings. For some members there will be a greater risk of leaving the firm before collecting a given percentage of their profit shares. Conversely, if most of the profit from an investment is expected during the early years of its life, less than a 15.5 per cent yield will compensate for a 10 per cent return on private savings.

---

[12] We would remind the reader that present Yugoslav tax policy will favor the collective consumption fund. Of course, when a worker moves from cooperative *A* to cooperative *B*, he begins to benefit from past wage sacrifices made by *B*. But he played no part in *B*'s decisions to undertake the associated investment or collective consumption spending.

[13] That is, the present value of 15.5 dinars per year received for 10 years and discounted at 10 per cent per year is 100 dinars. With a 20-year horizon, the equivalent yield becomes 11.2 per cent. With a better-than-30-year horizon, the equivalent yield is virtually the same as the return on savings accounts.

Part of the above discussion does not apply to investment from borrowed sources because, by definition, the principal comes from outside the cooperative. Risk considerations aside, a cooperative is no less willing to borrow for investment purposes than a conventionally managed firm. Its bias for investment projects with short gestation periods, however, will remain.[14]

With these ideas, let us now consider a simple economy in which all savings are voluntary and always equal to (planned and unplanned) investment. We suppose that the volume of savings depends both upon income and a single interest rate paid on all loans. Desired investment will likewise depend upon this rate because firms will seek to invest when and only when they have a project with a higher expected yield. (We continue to brush aside risk considerations.) As both the reward to savers and the cost of investible funds, the interest rate is the price that tries to equalize planned saving and investment. In Figure 21–4, 10 per cent is an equilibrium rate.

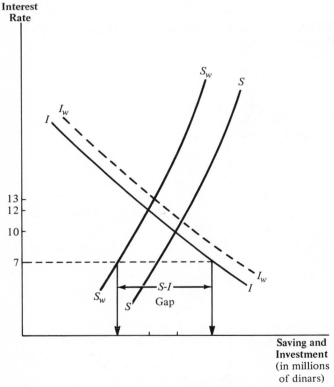

Figure 21–4. Saving and investment under conventional and workers' management.

[14] This bias is in addition to the success-indicator problem discussed in the appendix to Chapter 20 that we said would shorten the horizon of a socialist manager vis-à-vis a capitalist one. On balance, we cannot really say, however, whether a conventional socialist profit-maximizing management would have a longer or shorter horizon regarding the gestation of investment projects than a cooperative.

If we have two societies which are nearly identical except that the firms in one are workers' cooperatives, there is no reason why the same saving and investment schedules could not apply to each. We would expect more investment to be externally financed in the cooperative model. We have seen that individuals would prefer to put their savings in private accounts (from which money would then be lent out) than plow them back into their firms when the yields on these alternatives are the same. This leads to what Yugoslavs call the "privatization" of savings, but there is no reason to expect smaller savings in toto. We have seen that external financing can help to give the planners the leverage they need to steer the economy.

Nevertheless, when we make our assumptions a bit more realistic, the cooperative form does affect society's propensity to save, invest, and thus grow. Let us again contrast the cooperative economy with a similar system, filled with straight profit-maximizing firms, and go back to our presumption that firms are normally able to earn positive profits over and above their opportunity costs. We saw earlier that, under these conditions (and in the absence of risk) cooperatives would try to maintain higher capital-to-labor and capital-to-output ratios than straight profit maximixers for any particular prices of capital goods and interest rate. This will tend to produce a higher rate of desired investment for any given rate of interest.

However, cooperative management is likely to be more averse to risk. Ideally, the directors of a conventionally managed firm will reach their posts partly because they are more willing and able to assume business risks. If the market is functioning properly, it will allocate individuals to management who have dynamic entrepreneurial qualities.[15] The cooperative, by definition, obliterates this specialization of function when worker control is genuine. For any given cost of investible funds, we would therefore expect a cooperative to seek out safer investment alternatives, and since most investment involves some risk, to invest less over-all.

The net effect of the two offsetting tendencies above is unclear, and we therefore assume initially that there will be no change in the investment schedule of Figure 21–4. It appears, however, that the savings schedule will shift up from SS to S_wS_w. In other words, at any particular interest rate, the cooperative economy will tend to produce a *lower* level of voluntary savings than its more conventionally managed counterpart. In every Western country, business saving greatly exceeds saving by households, and saving out of property income is much greater than saving out of wage and salary earnings. In these conditions, the tendency to "privatize" savings will probably also be a tendency to reduce them. Some funds that would be retained by a conven-

---

[15] This also depends to an extent upon individuals being promoted within hierarchies largely on the basis of merit. In Chapter 10 we outlined several reasons why such an expectation may prove overoptimistic. However, we would argue that, the more stringent the market test (or the competition) that the firm must face, the less it can afford to promote managers for reasons other than competence and still survive. Similarly, a management post may be effectively inherited. But in a workably competitive market, this manager will be shunted aside if the firm is to survive.

tionally managed firm for investment will be taken home, if the workers' council holds sway, and consumed rather than saved.

The result is a higher equilibrium interest rate, 12 rather than 10 per cent, and a lower equilibrium rate of saving and investment, 9.25 as opposed to 11.25 million dinars. In effect, the higher equilibrium interest rate in the cooperative economy would reduce planned investment and, thereby, the growth rate. Such a system would not necessarily have low growth by international standards because its people may be relatively thrifty by nature. But the cooperative form would cost the economy some growth, at least over the long run. This leads us to expect that the government of a cooperative economy will not allow the cost of investible funds to rise to its equilibrium level. Instead, it will probably set a low effective rate—for example, 7 per cent in Figure 21–4—in an effort to stimulate investment and growth. Ideological considerations may help to keep the interest rate down.

The result will be a gap between desired investment spending and voluntary saving. If this gap is not filled, realized investment will fall to the level of voluntary saving at this rate, and growth will be even lower than in equilibrium. The filler will be some form of involuntary savings—either taxes or a requirement that the cooperative devote a minimum amount of profits to the investment fund. Indeed, we already know that any growth-oriented planner will combine investing tax monies outright with their use to subsidize low rates for borrowers combined with high rates for savers.

But worker resentment of taxes on cooperative profits may put the government of such a system at a relative disadvantage in trying to close the savings–investment gap this way. The same resentment may make it more difficult, in general, for a growth-oriented planner to harmonize the goals of a workers' council with its own than he would the goals of a conventional enterprise management. This is particularly true in view of the fact that a workers' council is less likely to voluntarily adopt such goals as growth, sales, or share-of-market maximization. An individual worker's chances for advancement are not likely to depend upon whether he is associated with a large and growing enterprise to the same extent that a manager's are. Nor is the former likely to derive as much nonpecuniary benefit.

Each cooperative will have a manager or director responsible for at least the technical coordination of the firm's factors of production. This manager, nominally subordinate to the workers' council, may nevertheless aspire to some kind of promotion and, for other reasons, more readily harmonize his own goals for the enterprise with those of the EPC. If he, in fact, dominates the workers' council, and if his success indicators include such criteria as sales, growth, and market share, our conclusion will not hold. Managerial control may mean a *higher* propensity to save and invest out of internal funds than in the case of long-run total profit maximization.

Under workers' control, a lower propensity to invest results from the inability of individual employees to reclaim the principals of their investments. But under managerial control, the director is able to invest revenue that would otherwise go mainly into the current paychecks of *other* employees.[16] If his own lifetime earnings can rise while the long-run profitability per worker of the cooperative is falling—because it expands beyond the profit-maximizing rate(s) of output—he will not have to bear his full share of the consumption sacrifice which this investment entails. The director may be more willing to save and invest the cooperative's profits because he may be able to derive more benefits from its sheer size or rate of growth. Paradoxically, the economy may then become more efficient and have a higher growth rate.

But if workers' control is real, the EPC of a growth-oriented cooperative economy will still be looking for a way to finance the savings–investment deficit. If the gap is substantial, it may have to turn to credit creation. Here the government will expand the money supply by offering low-cost loans earmarked for investment. Such a policy will be inflationary unless it generates a sufficiently rapid growth to absorb the expanded purchasing power. In effect, it would force involuntary saving through inflation, which transfers real purchasing power over goods and services from consumption to investment.

The circle could then become complete with price ceilings which convert some of the open inflation into repressed inflation, coupled with shortages and, possibly, black markets. (In the former case, forced saving occurs because goods in demand are not available to absorb purchasing power.) In addition to the costs of policing price controls, outright resource misallocation between industries or geographic regions would probably result if these ceilings endured for fairly long periods of time. In Yugoslavia today (1972) more than one half of all prices are frozen, and the proportion of output subject to "temporary" price controls has been rising irregularly since the inception of workers' management in 1953. Nevertheless, open inflation—at times rapid— has persisted. Although the cause is in dispute, the evidence appears consistent with the above hypothesis.[17]

Finally, let us view the cooperative as a vehicle through which the government of a developing country tries to generate growth. On the negative side,

---

[16] If the director and his staff are able to dominate the workers' council, using a method to be outlined in Chapter 22 or some other means, they will effectively be able to tax most of the workers. That is, management will succeed in putting a greater percentage of current cooperative income into the investment fund and a smaller percentage into other funds than most workers would prefer. See E. G. Furubotn and Svetozar Pejovich, op. cit. A growth-oriented EPC may be tempted to try to make use of such a taxing instrument.

[17] The inflation described above is basically demand-pull—that is, too much money chasing too few goods. But note that it might be hard to tell from a basically cost-push inflation caused by the monopoly power of cooperatives to push up wage rates (by pushing up the prices of their products). In either case, product prices and wages in money terms may go up simultaneously because a higher price caused by demand pull may become a higher profit and thus a higher profit share in the wage bill. This is particularly true, given a preference for external financing, coupled with a high credit availability at low rates. In the limit, nearly all profits would be allocated to the wages fund while the firm was borrowing extensively to finance investment, a practice often criticized in the Yugoslav press. See Branko Horvat, op. cit., and George Macesich and Frank Close, "The Comparative Stability of Monetary Velocity and the Investment Multiplier for Austria and Yugoslavia," *Florida State Slavic Papers*, Vol. 3, 1969.

we would have to note a possible bias against innovation involving risk—in comparison with a conventionally managed firm in a market economy—and against investment projects with long gestation periods. A lowered rate of voluntary saving and possible increased difficulties in raising involuntary savings through taxation are additional drawbacks.

On the other hand, suppose that the cooperative economy largely overcomes its bias against risk taking, causing the investment schedule in Figure 21–4 to shift out to I_wI_w. This will enlarge the savings–investment gap for any rate of interest below equilibrium. However, if this gap can be filled, the cooperative economy will have a higher rate of investment than the conventional market system. (During a period of rapid growth, moreover, any resulting inflation may be quite tolerable.[18]) The increased external financing of the cooperative then becomes a distinct steering advantage to the planners.

But this additional investment will not support a *permanently* higher growth rate. Instead, it will go first to achieve and then to maintain the higher capital-to-labor ratio characteristic of a cooperative making positive economic profits and not bothered by risk. (The high growth rate will only last while the higher capital-to-labor ratio is being built up.) If such an economy can employ its entire labor force, on the other hand, GNP will be permanently higher because this force will have more capital to work with.

The trouble is that implanting such a model into a developing country may actually make it harder to efficiently employ the entire labor force. Many of these countries suffer from *under*employment—that is, they are unable to find enough capital to employ the entire labor force before the marginal product of labor reaches zero. If the wealthier firms in such a system were to begin eating up its necessarily meager supply of savings in order to raise their capital-to-labor ratios, the problem of underemployment would probably become more acute.

This is especially true if, as is usual, the potential labor supply is growing, while underemployment is concentrated in the least profitable sectors. Normally, developing economies are best advised to seek labor rather than capital-intensive technologies, so that a given capital stock may stretch over more workers.

The cooperative's bias toward capital intensity, in the absence of risk aversion, may also make it more difficult to overcome already existing unemployment in *any* country. This is especially true, once again, when the labor force is growing or when technological progress tends to replace labor with capital. By contrast, too much risk aversion can, owing to inadequate aggregate demand, create Keynesian-type unemployment, which we encountered in Chapter 14. (This would presumably arise in an economy *not* strongly growth-oriented.)

We may sum up this section, for the most part, by noting that a growth or

---

[18] This is true provided the method of filling the gap does not reduce desired investment. In practice this will place some constraint on the tolerable level of inflation.

development-oriented government will probably have more difficulty harmonizing the goals of a cooperative than of a conventional enterprise management with its own. The bias of the cooperative toward external financing provides an offset, particularly when the populace is naturally thrifty or the economy inflation-proof. (Self-financing of gross investment in Yugoslav firms averaged about 36 per cent over the period 1959–1970, versus a typical 60 to over 80 per cent in Western firms.) A second pontentially offsetting factor is X efficiency, to which we now turn.

21–6   Workers' Management and X Efficiency

Because workers' councils replace labor unions and professional associations, as well as management, the cooperative is also a substitute form of labor relations. In the final analysis this may be its trump card. We have seen that labor unions will often have an incentive to erect artificial barriers to membership while pressing for wage and salary increases in excess of productivity gains. The result will be restrictions on labor mobility and possible unemployment for those who find it difficult to gain membership or sufficient seniority. There is no way of knowing, a priori, whether workers' councils would do better or worse on either of these counts. Moreover, workers' management should lead to greater product price flexibility (downward as well as upward.)

But the biggest gains from workers' councils may come in the internal operating efficiency of the firm, that is, in the realm of X efficiency or what the businessman often thinks of as efficiency. We should note immediately that these gains will not automatically come from the profit-sharing side of workers' management except in fairly small firms. Otherwise, most individual workers will not be able to significantly raise the total profits—and thus the profits per employee—of their enterprises. In larger firms, much of the discussion of moral incentives in the Appendix to Chapter 7 therefore applies. In all likelihood, the director of a large enterprise will have to use a familiar package of controls, incentives, penalties, success indicators, and direct supervision to help assure employee productivity, although a favorable attitude by the personnel toward the enterprise will help him out.

Earlier, we saw that X inefficiency could arise within a conventionally managed firm when the separation between ownership and control diluted the link between managerial remuneration and the enterprise's profit residual. This reduced management's incentive to enforce cost controls. Likewise, the fact that the cooperative's profit residual is spread over all employees, rather than concentrated on the director and his staff, may dilute the latter's incentive to control costs. For this reason the workers' council will want to make sure that the director's salary is a function of profits per employee, and it may seek to supervise his activities directly.

The source of X efficiency gain stems instead from the cooperative as a form of labor relations. Workers' council meetings will handle many of the problems now tackled by collective bargaining in Western countries. By its very nature, the latter tends to split labor and management somewhat artificially into antagonistic and mistrustful camps. This split carries over into the political decision-making arena, where business-oriented groups often appear to feel bound to oppose policies put forward by labor, and vice versa.

By contrast, workers' councils will seek to harmonize the goals of different categories of employees. Time lost from work due to strikes should decline, along with the need for officials directly concerned with negotiations and management–employee relations. There should be less interest in direct or indirect "sabotage" or vandalism, which adversely affects the production process.

More importantly, a number of studies have accumulated to indicate that worker efficiency rises when employees begin to participate in decisions affecting their activity and receive commensurate responsibilities. The same sort of improvement is noted when employees feel that they are their own bosses or that they are not being interfered with by bosses. A study by Herzberg, for example, concludes that 81 per cent of all factors contributing to job satisfaction are associated with these motivators. On this basis, the most fruitful way to increase worker satisfaction would be to allow workers more responsibility and decision-making leeway rather than to bribe them with greater security and wages.[19] If Herzberg is correct, we might expect the attitudes of employees toward their work to improve and their pride in doing a good job to increase under workers' management.

Jaroslav Vanek, one of the staunchest supporters of workers' management, adds:

> Without any doubt, labor-management is—among all the existing forms of enterprise organization—the optimal arrangement when it comes to finding the utility-maximizing effort—i.e., the proper quality, duration, and intensity of work —by the working collective. Not only is there no situation of conflict between management and the workers that might hinder the finding of the optimum, but the process of self-management itself can be viewed as a highly efficient device for communication, collusion control, and enforcement among the participants.[20]

Furthermore, suppose that the profits of a cooperative are distributed among its employees once each quarter (or four times a year). When an increase in productivity causes profits to rise, the employees will receive a

[19] F. Herzberg, "One More Time! How Do You Motivate Employees?" *Harvard Business Review,* Jan. 1968. We would also cite the following relevant studies: D. McGregor, *The Human Side of Enterprise* (New York: McGraw-Hill, 1960); F. J. Roethlisberger and W. J. Dickson, *Management and the Worker* (Cambridge, Mass.: Harvard U.P., 1939); P. Blumberg, *Industrial Democracy: The Sociology of Participation* (London: Constable), Chs. 1–3; Ely Chinoy, *Automobile Workers and the American Dream* (Garden City, N.Y.: Doubleday, 1955); and Donald Roy, "Quota Restrictions and Goldbricking in a Machine Shop," *American Journal of Sociology,* Mar. 1952.

[20] Vanek, "Decentralization Under Workers' Management: A Theoretical Appraisal, *op. cit.,* p. 1011.

bonus soon after. Thus they should associate increased productivity with higher wages. Under present collective-bargaining systems, wage and salary rates change less frequently and productivity is usually just one of a number of variables affecting negotiations for a pay increase. By the same token, poor work performance will lead more quickly and directly to salary decreases in a cooperative economy, and employees should be less willing to put up with featherbedding and incompetence.

In short, there is every reason to believe that the personnel of a cooperative will be better motivated than they would be in a conventional Brand X or laissez-faire economy. They may also be less resistant to adopting a new technology which increases the profitability of the enterprise but eliminates certain jobs. Consequently, technical change may spread more rapidly.

If we suppose that managers of conventionally organized firms will often lack the feedback information they need to assign jobs and determine the wage rate appropriate to each job, given differences in tastes and skills among employees, a cooperative ought to do better in this respect. In any event, when workers and managers are one, the management should have access to much better feedback information than when these functions are separated.

It is well to pause at this point and consider a balance sheet of the efficiency advantages and disadvantages of a worker-managed economy vis-à-vis a more conventional form of Brand X. Table 21-1 provides this. We would

Table 21-1. Efficiency advantages and disadvantages of workers' management (vis-à-vis a Brand X economy in which long-run profit maximization is the principal managerial "success indicator.").

Advantages	*Disadvantages*

1. Greater price flexibility.
  (a) Prices fluctuate; output and employment are relatively stable.
  (b) Export industries more competitive on world markets.
2. (Possibly) greater X efficiency.
3. Larger percentage of external investment financing.
	1. Greater immobility and resulting misallocation of labor, at least in the short run.*
	2. Greater difficulty in absorbing unemployment, at least in the short run.*
	3. (Possibly) greater difficulty in realizing scale economies.
	4. Collectivization of entrepreneurial function, notably resulting in greater risk aversion of management.
	5. Greater inflationary bias when growth-oriented.

* Assuming that wage rates are *not* rigid in the conventional Brand X system. If they are, these disadvantages may well disappear altogether.

add that higher X efficiency can compensate both for a failure to achieve scale economies and for any difficulties involving investment and growth. Indeed, if greater X efficiency raises the productivity, and hence the yields, of investment spending, neither problem may arise in the first place.

Still, the cooperative also means a rise in the cost of goal formation per se as this becomes less authoritarian, which may reduce the net X efficiency gain. At the same time, we may achieve some of these gains without adopting the full-worker-managed form. Such statements remind us to look once again at the cooperative as a system.

21–7   The Cooperative as a System

If we apply our three-dimensional spectrum of systems to a firm, we may say that workers' management corresponds to decentralization of power or of the process through which goals are formed. This is one reason workers' management may not have a fair chance to compete with other forms of enterprise organization in economies with strong labor unions, bureaucracies, or ownership elites. All those groups will have a vested interest in preventing an erosion of their power to workers' councils.[21]

Nevertheless, within existing cooperatives there has been confusion between political and economic decentralization. In Yugoslavia workers' management passed through an efficiency crises (which may not be over) because "a rather naïve ideology contained in legislation and political propaganda advocated direct participation in administrative work as indispensable (to) safe-guarding the interests of workers."[22]

Within any enterprise, professional managerial expertise is required to efficiently coordinate factors of production and to maintain work discipline. The cooperative is no exception. According to Horvat,

> The basic problem in building up the organization of the self-managed enterprise is maximizing democracy in [political] decision-making along with maximizing efficiency in carrying out decisions. In poor organizational solutions, these two goals appear mutually contradictory and that is a rather frequent case in Yugoslav practice. Adequate organizational solutions not only harmonize these two goals, but make them complementary. . . .[23]

To solve the crisis, a number of Yugoslav economists and sociologists have tried to design an optimal organizational scheme. We shall borrow a few basic ideas from Horvat and others, while warning our readers that the system to be outlined below is still on an experimental basis. The first idea is to subdivide the enterprise into smaller units, called "work units" by Horvat. A machine shop may become a work unit, as may a repair facility, an assembly line, the personnel department, or the top managerial staff.

We would then set up a workers' subcouncil for each work unit. Ideally, these units will be sufficiently small that every worker can sit on his respective

---

[21] Otherwise, we should have to explain why workers' management is so rarely found in most market economies, where it is a fully legal form of enterprise organization.

[22] Branko Horvat, "The Labor-Managed Enterprise," paper presented to the Workshop on Economic Organization and Development, Ottawa, Carleton University, Mar. 1972.

[23] Ibid., p. 8.

subcouncil and feel that his opinion is important. (That is, each subcouncil would embrace the entire membership of the work unit.) Ideally, as well, the interests of different employees within the work unit would be sufficiently homogeneous at this stage that the probability of seriously overriding minority viewpoints remains quite low.

The work units become the basic political divisions of the enterprise, corresponding to geographical regions or localities of a nation. All decisions that concern only the daily life and work of workers in one work unit, without having significant spillover effects onto other units, are made in the work unit with the direct participation of all those interested.[24] Each work unit will also elect a chairman, who leads its delegation to the workers' council. As in a representative national legislature, each member of the workers' council is then responsible to a definite constituency.

The council will determine the goals for the entire enterprise. These include hiring and firing policies, output and employment levels, desired rates of investment, and the basis for distributing profits. Exceptionally important decisions may be subject to ratification by referendum. The interests of different workers are bound to diverge at this stage, but a possible "tyranny of the majority" can be at least partly averted through a phenomenon known as vote trading, to be explored in Chapter 22.[25] The firm must also pay going wage and salary rates for its personnel, and its pricing policies depend upon what the market will bear (or what the government can enforce). These factors restrict the council's decision-making authority.

We can also imagine additional tiers between the work unit and the workers' council. For example, representatives of work units in each branch plant may unite to form a workers' council for that plant. Each plant council would take decisions relating to the daily life and work of the employees it represents which do not have significant spillover effects onto other plants. Representatives of workers' councils for each plant would then unite to form a workers' council for the entire firm.

In part, this design seeks to increase the individual worker's feeling of participation and influence in a multiplant cooperative large enough to realize major scale economies. As an additional step in this direction, the production divisions can be made into semiautonomous profit centers. (Indeed, such a move may recommend itself, purely in terms of efficient goal implementation.)

The political and economic decision-making functions come together in the relationship between the workers' council and the firm's director. The latter has final responsibility for implementing the basic goals determined by

---

[24] This sentence is paraphrased from Horvat, ibid., p. 11. The development below departs slightly from his version.

[25] The same phenomenon can, of course, operate in the work unit. In addition, work units that obviously have more than one subconstituency, for example skilled and unskilled workers, can be required to send at least one representative for each to the workers' council.

the former. The manager thus sits at the apex of the economic decision-making or goal-implementing hierarchy, and he will appoint an executive board, also consisting of experts, to assist him. From there, the chain of command depends upon the degree of centralization in the economic organization. Under a completely centralized scheme, the hierarchy would reach back down to the work unit, whose foreman, again chosen on the basis of expertise, may be, but need not be, the same as the elected chairman.

In a firm with decentralized decision making, the executive board will co-ordinate semiautonomous profit centers. Each will have its own director beneath whom a chain of command will again reach back down to the work unit. Regardless of the degree to which economic decision making is decentralized, each cooperative will have two distinct and coexisting organizations (representing goal formation and goal implementation) reaching from top to bottom. Some employees will probably wear hats in both organizations, although we would probably want to bar the manager from also sitting as a representative of his department on the workers' council.

A number of specific relationships are conceivable between the director of a firm and its workers' council. Basically, the council charges the director with implementing the firm's goals, and the executive board prepares a plan of work for the year (or years) to follow under his supervision. "When that program—with possible modification—is accepted [by the council] . . . *the executive board has a free hand to carry it out and the workers' council the obligation to provide full support in its implementation*" (Horvat's italics).[26]

This support must extend all the way down to the work unit. Workers must obey the foreman's orders, even though they may grumble. Later, at a meeting of the work unit, the foreman must be at least partly accountable, but the work unit has no power to dismiss or to overrule him on the spot. It can make recommendations up to the workers' council, which may then decide to pass these on to the manager. At the end of the year (or whatever time period is deemed appropriate), the manager must submit a thorough report on the year's performance to the workers' council. The council can then refuse to accept the report, which amounts to a vote of no confidence. The manager, his executive board, and, perhaps, other officials will have to resign. Horvat writes: "The workers' council can replace the manager—and in that way, the entire executive board—but it can not [arbitrarily] interfere in the operative implementation of the [cooperative's plan of work] once adopted. . . . Because the executive board bears full responsibility for operations . . . [it] must also have complete freedom of action. . . ."[27]

As a final safeguard, the council may hire a specialized consulting firm to audit the business and report back to the council. If the auditors can be induced to serve as "a watchdog for society," a secondary benefit may come in the form of a reduced possibility of collusion between firms who are supposed to be competitors.

26 Horvat, "The Labor-Managed Enterprise," op. cit., p. 13.
27 Ibid.

We may also argue, however, that many of the X-efficiency gains ascribed to workers' management in the literature relate specifically to a kind of decentralization of *economic* decision making. Figure 21–5 shows more precisely what we mean. In Figure 21–5(a) we have diagrammed a completely centralized plant in terms of implementation. Every employee has his position along a chain of command, but the management, $M,$ at the top may or may not be a workers' council.

Figure 21–5(b), by contrast, shows some decentralization below the foreman level (F). (This may occur at the level of Horvat's work units or among even smaller groups of employees.) Once again, top management may be a workers' council or a conventionally chosen managerial team. In effect, the team of workers at the bottom of the diagram receives certain "success criteria" and is told to organize their work as they wish, subject to fulfilling these. Superiors will rely upon the small size of these teams and the com-

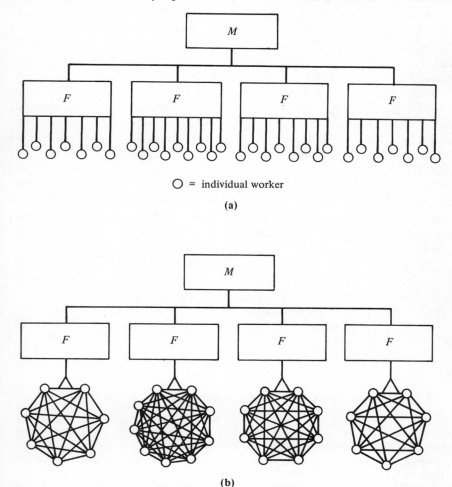

$\bigcirc$ = individual worker

(a)

(b)

Figure 21–5. The completely centralized (a) versus the partially decentralized (b) firm.

parative ease of checking their work to avoid the problem of success indicators, discussed in Chapter 9.

We may be able to realize most of the gains in X efficiency through the shop-floor decentralization shown in Figure 21–5(b). This allows many lower-level employees to be their own bosses insofar as immediate tasks are concerned. From current evidence, it is not possible to break X-efficiency increases into components resulting from decentralization of power and from an optimal decentralization of implementation. But when profit increases can be achieved by shop-floor decentralization, a conventional management is probably as likely to realize them as a workers' council. However, a workers' council may be more likely to give up profit to get a "more humane workplace," when these goals collide, and to choose shop-floor decentralization.

21–8 A Classless Society?

In fact, the chief social purpose of a cooperative society is to obliterate socioeconomic class distinctions. Its architects rejected both the traditional market economy with its managerial and, under capitalism, its ownership elite. They likewise rejected the command economy with its bureaucratic elite. Instead, they dreamed the age-old dream of a classless society.

In an article appearing about a year and a half before the August 1968 invasion, Kocanda and Pelikan, two Czech economists, viewed the cooperative "as the socialist enterprise envisaged in the final shape of the Czechoslavak economic model." [28] The gravest danger to the obliteration of class distinctions which they foresaw was that firms would become analogous to social clubs. The short-run immobility of labor resulting from an unwillingness to spread profits over more workers could turn into a long-run or even lifetime attachment of workers to their enterprises. Over time, the amount and quality of capital per worker and thus the profits per worker earned by this capital might grow throughout the economy. If so, either barriers to labor mobility or wage and salary discrimination, or both, would also be rising.

But even if this does not happen, the dispersion in profitability per employee between different firms is almost certain to increase over time. Some firms will do poorly and fail. Others will just manage to scrape along or improve their performance modestly. Still others will perform spectacularly for one reason or another and become extremely profitable on a per employee basis. Through a combination of luck, persistence, dynamism, ingenuity, and influence with higher authorities, some cooperatives are certain to become increasingly wealthier than others as time goes by. [29]

[28] Quoted by Ivo Moravčik in "From Command Economy to Market Socialism: The Czechoslovak Economic Reform," unpublished paper, 1968, p. 280. A later version was published in the *Canadian Slavonic Papers,* Winter 1968. The paper by Kocanda and Pelikan is also reprinted in English: "The Socialist Enterprise as a Participant in the Market," *Czechoslovak Economic Papers,* 1967, pp. 49–64.

[29] In Yugoslavia, interindustry wage differentials have increased over time, apparently largely because the more profitable firms have also reinvested a larger percentage of their profits. See Howard M. Wachtel, "Workers' Management and Interindustry Wage Differentials in Yugoslavia," *Journal of Political Economy,* June 1972.

The wealthiest enterprises, in turn, will have the highest barriers to entry by new workers. According to Kocanda and Pelikan, "this could lead to the emergence of closed castes of workers employed in certain prosperous enterprises . . ." [30] in the midst of unemployment. Thus, old class antagonisms between "bourgeoisie" and "proletariat" might simply be replaced by new ones. We could wind up with a "country-club" hierarchy *among* cooperatives, supplemented by further differentiation *within* firms based partly on seniority. Instead of removing class distinctions and antagonisms, the end result of a cooperative movement may largely be to redefine them. Potentially, this is the greatest social danger that such a movement faces.

Established employees in the wealthiest firms would occupy the highest social rungs in this society, and cooperatives prospering in the midst of unemployment cannot be ruled out. The lowest levels would consist of the hardcore unemployed, and in between would lie income earners with varying degrees of job security and volatility in take-home pay. Insofar as wages and salaries are concerned, we would expect, by and large, that those who receive the highest average incomes will also experience the greatest job security and, therefore, the least year-to-year variation in incomes.

To combat this, Kocanda and Pelikan proposed wage discrimination based on seniority. This might, indeed, alleviate the burden on the EPC to time the building of new enterprises so as to absorb excess labor whenever it appears. But wage discrimination is unlikely to remove the "club" effect. This may even be augmented in some ways with the reduced wages to new members serving as a kind of initiation fee.

Likewise, some of the more traditional class distinctions may infiltrate the labor-managed economy. Income differentials in a capitalist economy partly reflect past willingness to incur risk. When an enterpreneur, an athlete, or an entertainer rises rapidly through the income distribution, the chances are good that he is accepting a relatively high risk of failure in the process.

Once he has achieved the top part of the distribution, he can invest his earnings in diversified assets. Thus he can normally maintain a respectable income flow on a more-or-less permanent basis without encountering so much risk. Most individuals have an aversion to risk. Unless they are fortunate enough to inherit considerable talent or a privileged position that can be converted later into an income stream, they are less likely to rise so fast.

The income of an athlete or an entertainer is likely to be more volatile than that of a tradesman, and property income (or profit) is more volatile than wage and salary earnings. The cooperative economy seeks to spread the greater risks associated with profit as it spreads the profits themselves among the working members of the community. However, there is some scattered evidence to indicate that, when they get the opportunity, many workers will exchange their rights to future profits for a steadier, but smaller, expected

[30] Ivo Moravčik, "The Czechoslavak Economic Reform," *Canadian Slavonic Papers,* Winter 1968.

income stream.[31] In these conditions, some of the risk takers who effectively sell insurance against future income variations will become wealthy. Thus the cooperative economy will probably have to choose between accepting a more unequal income distribution than it would like and forcing its workers to tighten their belts when their firms experience lean-profit years.

An even greater danger of infiltration arises because of the specialized nature of modern management. Managing a firm has become a complex, highly technical and highly specialized task in a market economy which often requires the services of a team. If we are to combine the skill of professional management with the democratic principle of self-government, we shall need a fairly complex arrangement such as the one outlined above.

But such an arrangement can lead to the traditional management versus labor frictions, including strikes, and this has happened in Yugoslavia. For example, the professional managers may succeed in effectively reducing the actual range of decisions left to workers' councils and, thereby, in gaining some control over pricing and output. In Yugoslavia, once more,

an industrial sociologist . . . has come up with the staggering . . . conclusion that only two or three per cent of all decisions actually taken represent a democratic "self-management" judgment. The worker in Yugoslavia is not in fact king.

To whom do the workers think that they are losing their power and influence? To the educated, smooth gentlemen within the firm, is the most frequent reply— the managers, the technical chaps, the administrators who know the complicated law inside out and can talk the poor worker out of anything.[32]

Workers' councils can countervail this, at least in principle, by controlling the incentives and thereby the success indicators of professional managers. Nevertheless, the outcome of this interaction is impossible to forecast on an a priori basis. Clearly, it has not always favored the workers in practice, although the long-run tendency in Yugoslavia has been toward more power for the workers' councils and less for the director and his staff.

At present, the workers' council must reelect the director (every) four years and may dismiss him for cause in the interim. (However, local government representatives still have some voice in selecting the manager, including veto power.) There seems to be little doubt but that the workers' council usually exercises more countervailing power over management than would the stockholders of a representative Western corporation.[33]

[31] See, for example, J. M. Montias, "Discussion" in *American Economic Review,* May 1970, pp. 322–323.

[32] Chris Cviic, "Another Way: A Survey of Yugoslavia," *The Economist,* Aug. 21, 1971, p. xxii. Cviic makes it clear that he does *not* conclude that workers' management has failed in Yugoslavia. The workers themselves made it clear during what was, in effect, a strike that they were not against workers' management as such, but only the practice of workers' management in Yugoslavia. Such an expression raises as many questions, of course, as it answers.

[33] The power of the workers' councils has particularly expanded following a reform in 1965 (since which time problems with inflation and reduced growth have also ap-

Nevertheless, suppose that the presence or threat of unemployment leads to wage and salary discrimination based on seniority—which, we have seen, will make firms more willing to expand employment—and to a situation in which firms can deny newer employees certain rights to workers' council representation. If it becomes possible to make seniority qualifications increasingly severe over time, a cooperative could evolve toward a dual power base (workers' council and professional management) from which the majority of employees are effectively excluded. It might then pay these power poles to collude, thereby reviving the traditional division of function, and, ultimately, of class.

Until that day arrives when scarcity ceases to be important and we can all "take what we like in the shops," we may have to face the fact that socioeconomic class distinctions are inevitable. If we seek a rational allocation of resources, we must design our incentives so that good performance is rewarded and bad performance is discouraged. We must attract resources into those occupations where they are most productive. Unless we can largely rely on moral incentives to do this, income differentials large enough to produce socioeconomic class distinctions are likely to emerge. The problems faced by the government of a cooperative economy in this regard are quite like those faced by the government of any market economy. It must tie differences in wealth to differences in social contribution rather than to differences in social exploitation.

We have noted, for example, that some cooperatives are likely to grow much wealthier than others over time. The EPC's role is first to keep down artificial barriers to new competition and otherwise guard against restrictive practices. It should then determine what maximum income differentials it can tolerate as efficiency incentives, and design its tax-subsidy programs partly to keep the economy within these boundaries. Within this framework, the cooperative form provides the potential for combining greater price flexibility and X efficiency with a reduction both in traditional class distinctions and in work alienation. Thus in some sectors it may rank highest on a dual basis of efficiency and equality.

The net result of our discussion is neither to portray workers' participation as the cure for all economic evils nor to say that the cooperative idea is inadvisable. We have isolated both inherent weaknesses and prospective gains, and the cost-benefit analysis derived from balancing these will probably differ from one society—indeed, from one industry—to another.

---

peared to become more acute). In principle, the workers' council now makes all major decisions concerning employment, the rates of investment and output, and the division of profits among the wages, collective consumption, and investment funds. The director cannot ignore the workers' council, but he may be able to control it in subtle ways—for example, by playing various factions against one another, as in the example in Chapter 22.

REFERENCES

Blumberg, Paul. *Industrial Democracy: The Sociology of Participation.* London: Constable & Company, Ltd., 1968.

Broekmeyer, M. T., ed. *Yugoslav Workers' Self-Management.* Dordrecht, Holland: D. Reidel Publishing Co., 1970.

Furubotn, E. G., and Svetozar Pejovich. "Property Rights and the Behavior of the Firm in a Socialist State: The Example of Yugoslavia." *Zeitschrift für Nationalokonomie,* 1970, Nos. 3–4, pp. 431–454.

Horvat, Branko. "The Labor-Managed Enterprise." Paper presented to the Workshop on Economic Organization and Development, Ottawa, Carleton University, Mar. 1972.

———. "Yugoslav Economic Policy in the Post-War Period: Problems, Ideas, Institutional Developments." *The American Economic Review,* Supplement to June 1971 issue.

Kocanda, R. and P. Pelikan. "The Socialist Enterprise as a Participant in the Market." *Czechoslovak Economic Papers,* 1967, pp. 49–64.

Kolaja, Jiri. *Workers Councils: The Yugoslav Experience.* New York: Praeger Publishers, Inc., 1966.

Kyn, Oldrich. "The Rise and Fall of Economic Reform in Czechoslovakia." *American Economic Review,* May 1970.

McGregor, D. *The Human Side of Enterprise.* New York: McGraw-Hill Book Company, 1960.

Moravčik, Ivo. "The Czechoslovak Economic Reform." *Canadian Slavonic Papers,* Winter 1968.

Pejovich, S. "Toward a General Theory of Property Rights." *Zeitschrift für Nationalokonomie,* 1971, Nos. 1–2, pp. 141–155.

Roethlisberger, F. J., and W. J. Dickson. *Management and the Worker.* Cambridge, Mass.: Harvard University Press, 1939.

Sturmthal, Adolf. *Workers' Councils: A Study of Workplace Organization on Both Sides of the Iron Curtain.* Cambridge, Mass.: Harvard University Press, 1964.

Vanek, J. "Decentralization Under Workers' Management: A Theoretical Appraisal." *American Economic Review,* December 1969.

———. *The Labor-Managed Market Economy: General Theory.* Ithaca, N.Y.: Cornell University Press, 1970.

———. *The Labor-Managed Market Economy: An Evolutionary Hypothesis.* Ithaca, N.Y.: Cornell University Press, 1971.

———, and Peter Miovič. "Explanations into the Realistic Behavior of a Yugoslav Firm." Paper presented to the Workshop on Economic Organization and Development, Ottawa, Carleton University, February 1971.

Walters, A. A. "Production and Cost Functions: An Econometric Survey." *Econometrica,* January 1963. (*Note:* A simplified discussion of this paper appears in Edwin Mansfield, *Microeconomics,* New York: W. W. Norton & Company, Inc., 1970, pp. 178–184.)

Ward, Benjamin. "The Firm in Illyria: Market Syndicalism." *American Economic Review,* September 1958.

———. "The Nationalized Firm in Yugoslavia" and comments by G. Macesich and H. Gruble. *American Economic Review,* May 1965.

Part **SIX**

Chapter **22**

Some Economics of Democracy

Democracy is the worst of all possible forms of government—except, of course, for those others that have been tried from time to time.

Sir Winston Churchill

22–1   Introduction

Last of all, what about comparative systems and "democracy"? Economists have traditionally ignored the political or power dimension of our spectrum of economic systems because of a widespread belief within the profession that social goals should be taken as given. Economists as citizens may question the goals of the society in which they live, but economists in their professional roles should confine themselves to finding more efficient ways of implementing given priorities. A prominent Canadian economist once maintained in this spirit that "economists should be efficient garbage haulers."

Certainly, the economist has no more inherent right than anyone else to dictate goals for a society. But he need not ignore the procedures through which goals are determined any more than he ignore the way they are carried out. The economist can have no professional opinion about whether a given conception of democracy is good or bad. But he can try to formulate criteria for democracy which appear to capture popular ideas on the subject and also to design political processes that satisfy these criteria. Instead of taking society's goals as given, he would be taking as given the norms for deriving these goals. This, indeed, is how we shall proceed.

Much of our discussion will stem from the pathbreaking work on the economics of democracy by Anthony Downs and Gordon Tullock.[1] We shall accept the broad spirit of their notion of democracy as our norm and ask how this may be approximated in practice. We would warn our readers at the outset, however, that this will make our discussion to some extent oriented toward Western culture.

22–2 Political Decision Making

We should first recall that, conceptually, a society's political decision-making processes, including explicit and implicit decisions to preserve the status quo, formulate its socioeconomic goals, while its economic processes implement these goals. We may think of the political process as a kind of synthesizer which transforms the preferences of various individuals and groups, including those of a country's rulers, into a social preference function that prescribes goals for the economy.[2]

Let us imagine two societies which are quite similar in virtually every respect. Upon closer inspection, however, we discover that society A has a more unequal distribution of wealth than society B, along perhaps, with a higher growth rate, largely because B relies upon steeply progressive inheritance taxes which cut off "the sons of papa" and prevent the transfer of wealth from one generation to another. Society A, we assume, relies largely upon indirect taxes, while a third country, society C, makes use of progressive direct taxes on consumption and has a wealth distribution lying between the other two. These differences in tax structures quite likely reflect different goal-forming procedures, or different political decision-making processes, which lead to different sets of social goals and goal tradeoffs.

In the case of dictatorship, the synthesis of individual goals into a social preference function is comparatively simple because the dictator's preferences

---

[1] We particularly have the following works in mind: Anthony Downs, *An Economic Theory of Democracy* (New York: Harper, 1957) and "An Economic Theory of Political Action in a Democracy," *Journal of Political Economy*, Apr. 1957; Gordon Tullock, "Entry Barriers in Politics," *American Economic Review*, May 1965.

[2] In Chapter 2 we cited three categories of social preference functions: (1) The social welfare function phrases society's goals in terms of its distribution of welfare; (2) the commodity preference function phrases goals in terms of aggregate or per capita quantities of goods produced or consumed; and (3) the social guiding function combines the goals in (1) and (2). In some circumstances, we may wish to distinguish other goals, such as a desire for power or freedom from uncertainty.

dominate everyone else's. More generally, the relative weights attached to the goals that society pursues will reflect its distribution of economic power.

Roughly speaking, we may classify political decision making according to the degree to which it is (de)centralized. More decentralized decision making is more participatory. It implies that the preferences of more individuals will count more often in social goal formation. These preferences are less likely to be overruled, and administrators and legislators are more likely to have to rely upon popular support. Consequently, society's leaders will consult their constituents' preferences more often and leave open more channels for expression.

We also identify concentrated (diffuse) economic power with centralized (decentralized) political decision making. Although democratic decision making must be participatory, democracy is a stronger condition, as we shall see.

An important feature of *economic* decision making is that decentralization often goes hand in hand with efficiency. Except in special situations, we expect markets to be more efficient than commands. Markets also work best when complete anonymity prevails, implying just one price common to all buyers and sellers and also used by firms and households for their own internal decision making.

Price discrimination is not possible in these circumstances nor (as can be shown) are monopoly pricing and output restrictions.[3] There is no room for false or misleading advertising. Each buyer is able to choose the exact amount of every good that he wishes to buy at every price. Each buyer's preferences count in directing production and price formation. The same is true for sellers. Moreover, the efficiency with which a market operates does not decrease as the number of buyers and sellers rises.

The reverse is true when it comes to political decision making. There is no instrument, analogous to a market mechanism, available to simplify the problem of social goal formation by breaking it up into many subproblems which can be solved simultaneously and independently by each economic actor. Instead, the political process complexifies rapidly as the number of participants in any given decision rises.

The most efficient way to form social goals is usually to have them originate with a small group of like-minded men—and in the extreme case with a single dictator. More participatory processes are more complex, more cumbersome, more fraught with danger of tension, uncertainty, and breakdown and in the final analysis less efficient. If for no other reason than this, power will tend to centralize over time unless elaborate checks and balances

---

[3] This is because an output-restricting monopolist will use a different measure than price for his own internal decision making. For example, a profit-maximizing monopolist will equate marginal cost with marginal revenue. It is marginal revenue rather than price which guides his own production decisions. We may think of marginal revenue as his internal price, which is lower than the price to the buyer. Because of this difference, the monopolist attaches a lower value to output expansion than does the buyer. This is why he decides to restrict output.

to forestall this can be written into a nation's constitution and enforced in practice. Desire for power and prestige by (potential) leaders can, of course, accelerate the centralization process.

Nevertheless, it is worth our while to spend some time exploring the possibility of building workable democracy. This is particularly true when applied to mixed economies, where, for many, the principal interest relates to the likelihood that democracies can plan successfully. Ever since mixed systems were first a gleam in the eye of Pareto and Barone, this has been an overriding consideration.

In both command and laissez-faire economies, the seats of economic power also tend to be the principal economic decision makers, be they planners, firms, or labor unions. The powers to determine socioeconomic goals and to decide directly what and how to produce and how to reward the various factors of production lie in the same hands. In mixed economies, an economic planning council, acting within the framework of predetermined social priorities, at least partly controls the incentive systems that motivate micro decision makers. This leaves open the question of who controls the incentives of the planners, however, and besides planner–dictator, two possibilities suggest themselves.

One is that key micro decision makers, who are almost always motivated by their roles as producers rather than consumers, ultimately control the planners' incentives. Speaking loosely, market power and political power go hand in hand. For example, the biggest corporations, labor unions, and professional associations may control the government's powers to steer the economy and its market-structure policies. Likewise, they may control the regulatory agencies that nominally control them. Once again, the seats of power and economic decision making tend to coincide.

However, we can also conceive of societies whose political and economic decision-making processes are both decentralized, but where the implementation of economic goals is separated from the power to make them. Here the economic government tries to synthesize and then respond to a "will" of the the people. If successful, it will determine an index of social preferences, which embodies this will, along with a "best" set of policies to maximize the index. Thus it serves as an intermediary between the origin and implementation of socioeconomic goals. This case will interest us most because it has a better chance of being more democratic.

Nor do we rule out democracy in a command economy. We have seen that the command planning bureaucracy tends to become a political power base—to absorb political power, in other words—if it is not one initially. But there is no a priori reason to assume that this power base could not be eroded or countervailed or eventually disbanded.

Finally, we shall have to investigate the question of democracy under laissez faire. Here, we shall confine our attention to modern laissez-faire economies, which meet two conditions.

1. They are Keynesian—that is, their governments have a significant leverage over the economy and purport to use monetary or fiscal policies to achieve levels of output and employment that are close to potential. (We shall somewhat arbitrarily say that the former requirement is fulfilled when government revenues equal 20 per cent or more of net national product.)

2. They are characterized by large-scale production in many industries and strong reliance by firms, industries, and other production-oriented organizations upon political action.

22-3 An Analogy with Monopoly Regulation

Despite what we have said above, we can get an insight into one of the meanings of "democracy" by drawing an analogy with market competition. Following Tullock, let us approach the problem by forgetting all about the explicit notion of government for a moment and suppose that we are dealing with a special problem of monopoly regulation.[4]

Once upon a time there was an island kingdom with a small economy. One day, at a party on the mainland, the king of the island overheard an executive tell a young college graduate that the future lay in plastics. So the king called a general meeting of all his subjects in the large community square to announce his plans to bring a plastics industry to the realm. "Not only will the populace enjoy a wide variety of plastics products, ranging from toothbrushes, toys, and baby bottles to space suits and oil pipelines," said the king, "but hundreds of my subjects will find employment and higher incomes. As these are multiplied, great will be the rejoicing in the land."

Then the grand vizir rose to speak. He was a wise man who was often observed scratching his head while reading a big brown book filled with multicolored graphs. "O Sire," said the grand vizir, "our market is very small, and the economies of mass production and research in plastics are very great. If we are to have an efficient plastics industry which realizes these scale economies so that it can mass produce at low cost and employ many of your subjects, there will be room for just one firm in the industry. This firm will then be in a position to raise prices, restrict output, reduce quality, and, perhaps, to restrict its product line. Our dilemma is that, in order to have a modern, efficient-sized firm, we must give it a monopoly. But as a monopoly, it may exploit us, and take away many of the advantages of mass production and employment from your subjects."

Upon hearing these words, the king was sorely distressed. "But do not fear," said the grand vizir, "for I have a plan to regulate the monopoly." "Proceed with your plan," cried the King. "To begin with," replied the grand vizir, "society must build its own plant to manufacture plastics products. The public will own this plant, but its operation will be put up for auction every

---

[4] Tullock, op. cit.

four or five years to prospective management teams from far and wide. The management team submitting the best bid will receive the right to operate the plant for a specified period of time and to keep all the profits, or pay all the losses. As bids, each contender will submit a list of the products he proposes to produce in the plant, along with the maximum prices he would charge.

"Other things being equal, the low price bid wins, but consideration must also be given to the range of products proposed. If two management teams each propose lower prices on two different sets of products, the evaluation will become even more difficult. Finally, your majesty's subjects cannot ignore research and development or technical change at the plant, nor can they allow management to cut costs and expand output by running down the facilities through undermaintenance. Each bid will therefore have to include guarantees of proper maintenance and partially binding statements about proposed new products and programs of expansion and of technological improvement.

"By now, the bids will be very difficult to judge indeed, and your Majesty may wish to hire experts for the purpose. But while we may not live happily ever after, public ownership of plant and equipment and periodic auctions will make (potential) competition possible in a situation where monopoly would prevail under laissez faire. The consequence should be a lower cost for a wider range of higher-quality plastics products.

"At additional expense, barriers to competition can be lowered even further. Society may decide to award consolation prizes for one or more runner-up bids which subsidize the formation of 'shadow' management teams by the firms submitting them. These shadow teams would duplicate the top management of the plastics facilities and be privy to some of the details of day to day managerial problems and decision making. This puts them in a position both to criticize the mistakes of present management and to ensure continuity should management change hands at the next auction. To further ensure continuity, society may decide to grant certain kinds of job security to employees below the level of top management.

"Each of the above measures will also reduce the advantages accruing to an incumbent management just because it gains daily experience from running the firm and is constantly exposed to buyers, suppliers, and the public. Advertising expenditures may be controlled as an additional means to this end."

By now the reader has seen through our allegory. The plastics plant is a representative government; its managers are the rulers of a nation, region, or community, the periodic auctions are elections, and the scale barrier to competition derives from majority voting or some other decision rule which can only permit one set of rulers at a time. (In this sense, when it comes to government, every nation has a very small "market.") The bids are platforms and campaign promises of the candidate.

In practice, a number of more-or-less qualified and unbiased "experts" will try to evaluate both platforms and candidates in terms intelligible to the public. Each political party or candidate will notably contrast what it believes are the popular aspects of its own platform or record with the unpopular aspects of those of its rivals. In addition, a qualified and impartial press will ideally play the role of a consumers' union by informing the public about the affairs of politics and government.

Such an approach also points to the role of government as a provider of goods and services. (Even under laissez faire, it provides courts, police protection, national defense, and various administrative services.) We may view elections as a rather ingenious device to introduce competition into an industry—government—that would otherwise be a monopoly. Insofar as this industry is concerned, in fact, laissez faire implies monopoly, which is nothing more or less than dictatorship (that is, no elections and no regulation by the public), no matter how high-minded or devoted to a cause the dictators may be.[5]

Increased competition among potential leaders should make government more responsive to the preferences of those who are ruled just as increased market competition will often result in a better product selection at lower prices for the consumer. The same is true of an increased flow of information about the affairs of government. A few major implications of our allegory for "democratic" government are as follows.

First, there should be at least one organized opposition with a recognized leader who has the privilege of taking an alternative stand on any issue to that of the government, thus serving as a kind of counterweight to the actual ruler. This, in turn, probably requires the existence of more than one organized political party. Ideally, each opposition leader would have his own shadow government and be sufficiently informed about the details and current problems of governing that he could take over the reins of government at a moment's notice.

To further ensure continuity, a civil service, which is immune from politically motivated hiring and firing, should occupy the middle and lower levels of the government's decision-making bureaucracy. Finally, our earlier discussions of market-structure policy suggest some ceilings on advertising or campaign spending which are flexible enough to allow unknown candidates to get their names and their platforms before the public.

Without measures such as the ones just outlined, the practice and experience gained from running a government plus the daily exposure of the governors to the public may pose formidable entry barriers. Expressions of dissent in these circumstances would often appear to be ill-informed or naive. While the incumbents will retain certain advantages, even over well-organized opposition parties, the latter have advantages of their own. Because they do

---

[5] However, a monopolist may maximize sales rather than profits and consequently produce an efficient rate of output. By analogy, a ruler dedicated to his people and to "higher ideals" may provide a number of benefits for them. Yet, if he has absolute power, he is still a dictator, just as a single seller is still a monopolist. Nothing per se is wrong with either, but a danger exists that the dictatorial powers will endure beyond the dedication and idealism of those who rule.

not actually have to govern, for example, they can more easily avoid taking unpopular stands or force the government to take a stand first which they can then criticize from a distance.

22–4 Additional Conditions for Democracy

Other things being equal, increased competition for the positions of leadership signifies a more democratic government. But this is not the only dimension along which we should measure democracy. Another is the range of decisions on which the electorate is allowed to vote, and a third is the number of governed individuals who are allowed to vote. Downs defines democracy to be a political system satisfying the following four conditions [6]:

1. Two or more parties compete in periodic elections for control of the government apparatus.
2. The party (or coalition of parties) winning a majority of votes gains control of the governing apparatus until the next election.
3. Losing parties never attempt to prevent the winners from taking office, nor do winners use the powers of office to vitiate the ability of losers to compete in the next election. (This is simply another way of saying that competition for leadership will be "fair" and will continue.)
4. All sane, law-abiding adults who are governed are citizens, and every citizen has one and only one vote in each election.

For Downs, democratic decision making is an orderly process in which every individual who is governed has one vote. We shall adopt his conditions 1 and 2, and 3 is implied by our previous discussion. Condition 4, on the other hand, imposes an undesirable constraint. An election is likely to give citizens an imprecise way of registering their preferences in comparison with a market. At each price, an individual decides not only whether, but how much, he wishes to buy or sell of each good. Thus he has an opportunity to register the intensity of his preferences, which is denied the voter who must either abstain or cast a single ballot for one of the candidates running for a given office.

Other things being equal, more democratic processes will allow individuals to express the intensities of their preferences. One way of introducing this opportunity into elections is to allow every voter to cast as many ballots for each office as there are candidates for the office. He may then distribute these ballots among the candidates as he sees fit. This includes the right to refuse to cast any or all of them. Downs' condition (4) now reads:

4. All sane, law-abiding adults who are governed are citizens, and every citizen has an equal number of votes to cast in each election.

A question next arises as to what we are to do when one candidate or

[6] Downs, "An Economic Theory of Political Action in a Democracy," op. cit., p. 137.

slate of candidates fails to win a majority of the ballots cast (condition 2). At one extreme, the slate receiving the most votes would be declared the winner. This is the most common procedure in North America, but it violates condition 2. The other polar case would require a series of runoff elections. Each time, the slate receiving the fewest votes would be eliminated until one slate received a majority.

Strictly speaking, this is what condition 2 implies, although it is an extremely rare phenomenon to find in practice. Runoff elections are common in Western Europe, but the usual procedure there is to eliminate all slates except the two top ones after the first election, so that not more than one runoff election will have to be held. The reason for having runoffs is that they allow citizens who originally vote for the least popular candidates to have some voice in the final outcome. If we agree that every citizen should have such a voice, an electoral process will become more democratic as we approach the maximum number of runoff elections.

In short, we have linked democracy to voting, as the principal way in which most individuals participate in choosing their government. We have also identified democracy with the majority voting rule as the method of determining an outcome to the voting process.[7] Almost inevitably, the direct costs of democratic decision making, as we have defined it, are higher than the direct costs of authoritarian goal formation. This is part of the price we pay for the broader participation and protection which democracy involves.

The problem with giving a dictator laissez-faire carte blanche to impose his preferences on society is that he is in a position to inflict excessive costs upon the public to be governed. Such a ruler may demand collective farms, a high rate of "forced" saving, military adventures, or zoning of large tracts of residential land for industrial use. Alternatively, he may force society to tolerate a high level of pollution and congestion because he does not want to slow down measured economic "growth." It is to escape these costs that individuals and groups in society push for more responsive government.

We do not mean to imply, however, that there is no latent tyranny in the model of democracy we are trying to build. To ferret this out, we shall temporarily shift our emphasis from voting for candidates to voting directly on issues. The voters may be representatives who have, themselves, been elected, or citizens participating in a town meeting or some other form of direct democracy.

22-5   The Voting Paradox

To be definite, in fact, let us suppose at first that we are dealing with a worker-managed firm or producers' cooperative. We shall soon see that our discussion generalizes to any situation where the majority voting rule applies.

[7] When voting takes place on issues rather than candidates, some measures may be designated as "important questions" and require more than a simple majority to pass.

A producers' cooperative we recall, is a profit-sharing enterprise in which the elected representatives of all employees come together to form a *workers' council*, which, in principle, makes the basic production and pricing decisions of the enterprise. Workers' management is most prominent in Yugoslavia, where nearly all firms are of this type, but the phenomenon is both worldwide and growing.

In Yugoslavia, the net income of a cooperative is divided between four funds (Figure 21–1)—a wages and salaries fund, a collective consumption fund, an investment fund, and a reserve fund, which we do not consider in this example. Several rules and guidelines will govern the way in which earnings are divided among the former three funds. Nevertheless, we may imagine a workers' council with some leeway on this matter trying to choose a production and investment strategy to follow during the year ahead. Strategy *A* will concentrate on short-run wage and salary maximization, strategy *B* will emphasize building up the collective consumption fund, and strategy *C* will focus on long-run growth, thus maximizing the investment fund. These strategies are mutually exclusive.[8]

We may imagine that the workers' council is also divided into three groups. Group 1 will represent the relatively young and untrained workers. Group 2 will represent largely middle-aged and semiskilled workers, while group 3 represents the managerial elite, engineering staff, and many of the other white-collar or highly skilled blue-collar technical workers. We place no constraints on the relative sizes of the three groups, except that none of them is bigger than the other two put together. This is reasonable because, in practice, the largest and least skilled body of workers is usually underrepresented on the council. We also assume that every member of each group will rank the three strategies above in the same way—perhaps because a prior caucus has agreed on a united front.

In asking how each group would rank these strategies, then, we must recall two features of workers' management. First, the benefits of the collective consumption fund will often be spread more equally among the workers than will wages and salaries. Thus group 1 will prefer to emphasize this fund, choosing strategy *B*. Second, a worker who leaves the firm or retires loses most or all of his claim on its subsequent profits. This is true even though the wages he foregoes today help to make possible the investments, which, in turn, will help to create these profits. He may also lose part or all of his right to receive benefits from the collective consumption fund. Group 2 will therefore choose strategy *A*, which emphasizes short-run wage and salary maximization. Finally, the director and his staff will often find that growth is their principal

---

[8] Each of these strategies may be consistent with maximization of profits per employee because the three funds in question all come out of profits. Strategy *C*, however, may also represent a more expansive goal because, as we shall see, it is preferred by the director and his staff. The example below is derived from Egon Neuberger and Estelle James, "The Yugoslav Self-Managed Enterprise: A Systematic Approach," in Morris Bornstein, ed., *Plan and Market* (New Haven: Yale University Press, 1973).

success indicator, particularly if they are promotion-conscious. They will prefer strategy C.

It is not unreasonable to suppose that group 1 will rank the three strategies open to the firm in the order BCA. Group 2 would be expected to rank them ABC, and group 3 might initially rank them either CBA or CAB. However, group 3 will ultimately rank them CAB for strategic reasons, as we shall see, to enable C to win.

Given these rankings, suppose that alternative A is paired against B in an election. Groups 2 and 3 will vote for A, enabling A to win. When B is paired against C, groups 1 and 2 will vote for B, enabling it to win. The majority voting rule therefore ranks A over B and B over C. Logically, it should then rank A over C. However, when we pair A against C, we see that groups 1 and 3 will vote for C, giving it the win. Thus we have A over B, B over C, and, yet, C over A.

No single alternative is clearly preferred over the other two. In fact, no consistent ranking of the investment strategies open to the firm emerges at all, even though each individual member of the council has a perfectly consistent ranking. The majority voting rule, as the instrument of democratic choice, has failed to yield a clear choice. In this sense it has broken down. This is what we mean by a voting paradox.[9]

It is easy to find many examples of voting paradoxes from widely diverse sources. Canada has a program of "equalization" payments or subsidies from richer provinces to poorer ones designed to equalize the distribution of income on a regional basis. Suppose that under the present program of income redistribution, the per capita distribution of income in 1975 is expected to be $5,000 in Ontario, $3,750 in Quebec, and $3,200 in Nova Scotia. Call this alternative A. Also possible, we assume, are proposals to change this program so that the expected distribution becomes

B: Ontario, $5,150; Quebec, $3,900; Nova Scotia, $2,900

or

C: Ontario, $4,850; Quebec, $4,050; Nova Scotia, $3,050

When the three provincial premiers vote, alternative C will be preferred over B, B over A, but A over C. Once again, majority voting will not lead to a decision.

How, then, will a decision be reached? We can imagine several ways, none of which can automatically be ruled out. A long debate may break out, for example, which ultimately results in victory for those able to hold out longest—or preservation of the status quo. Or, suppose that the director has some control over the way that alternatives are paired in the workers' council

---

[9] We cannot resolve the paradox by introducing a runoff election. Suppose that group 2 is the largest, followed by group 1, with group 3 smallest. Then alternative C will be eliminated in the first election and A will beat B in the runoff. But the majority prefers C to A.

meeting and that he has a good idea of how different groups rank them. Then he will try to pair alternative A against B, using A, in effect, to beat B. Afterward, he will pair C against A, ensuring the victory for his favorite strategy.

Regardless of the way in which a decision finally emerges in each of the above cases, there is a clear risk that it will not turn out to be very democratic by our above criteria. When our basic instrument of democracy breaks down, a strong possibility emerges that a more dictatorial method will be substituted for it. This pessimistic conclusion holds true, not only for majority voting, but for *any* substitute social choice procedure that satisfies "reasonable" requirements to be democratic. Any such procedure may give rise to the same paradox discussed above.

The result is sometimes called the "impossibility" theorem on democratic government. In its strongest form it says that even partial democracy is logically impossible. This is too strong, however, because while voting paradoxes are always possible, they are never inevitable. It is also possible to blunt the effects of a voting paradox when it does arise.[10] Returning to our workers' council meeting, suppose that an alert opposition among the representatives of older, semiskilled workers smells out the director's strategy and begins a filibuster to forestall the initial vote. The result may be an endurance test, but it is likewise possible that both sides will find it to their advantage to compromise.

If so, three new alternative strategies—which we call A_1, B_1, and C_1—will emerge to replace A, B, and C. The former are modifications of the latter and continue to emphasize wage and salary maximization, collective consumption, and investment, respectively. However, A_1, B_1, and C_1 will be closer together than were A, B, and C, involving relatively less emphasis on their respective funds. That is, if C_1 were adopted, the costs to members of groups 1 and 2 would be less than those associated with C. Similar statements hold for A_1 and B_1. Therefore, while a voting paradox will still occur, its costs are lower.

When these costs are nevertheless still too high, so that the debate again bogs down, we would expect a third set of alternatives—A_2, B_2, and C_2—to emerge which are still closer together. In practice, much of this compromising will probably take place in committees or informal sessions outside the main

---

[10] The impossibility theorem is originally due to K. J. Arrow; see Arrow's *Social Choice and Individual Values,* 2nd ed. New York: Wiley, 1963. See, as well, Arrow's bibliography of other works on the subject. The "reasonable" requirements for democracy mentioned in the text include all of Arrow's conditions except the one on "independence of irrelevant alternatives." The *least* restrictive set of conditions known to the authors under which the voting paradox is guaranteed not to arise are given by A. K. Sen in his article, "A Possibility Theorem on Majority Decisions," *Econometrica,* Apr. 1966. Finally, the line of discussion that follows immediately below is essentially due to Gordon Tullock. See his "The General Irrelevance of the General Impossibility Theorem," *Quarterly Journal of Economics,* May 1967.

meeting. Once proposals reach the floor, only a small number of actual votes is likely to be necessary. By the time the final voting occurs, either the paradox will have been removed or else the three alternatives will be quite close together—so close, in fact, that a unique compromise may be selected without a vote.

All this does not rule out the possibility of dictatorship. However, given rational behavior and sufficient opportunity, there is good reason to believe that this kind of compromise will ultimately emerge under majority voting. Let us go back to our original example, in which the director was able to push through strategy C by first using A to eliminate B. We implicitly assumed a procedural rule banning the reintroduction of defeated motions. Supporters of B can nevertheless introduce a new strategy, B', which resembles B closely enough to defeat C. This possibility raises the likelihood that indecision inherent in the voting paradox will be largely eliminated.

22–6   Tyrannies of the Minority and Majority

Until now we have wrestled with problems stemming from a potential "tyranny of the minority" or danger that a collectivity may be dominated by the preferences of a small group of like-minded men. This is not, however, the only threat to the spirit of democracy inherent in majority voting. We must also contend with a potential "tyranny of the majority." A minority that feels intently about an issue—much more intently, let us say, than the majority—is in danger of having its preferences completely overruled, simply because it is a minority. The majority voting rule contains no built-in safeguards for minority interests.

Such safeguards can be built in, however, through a phenomenon known as vote trading. Each representative in a legislature or citizen at a town meeting has the right to the same number of votes on every issue that arises. Of these issues, any particular legislator will be strongly in favor of some and strongly opposed to others. But there will be a third set, perhaps the largest, about which he and his constituents do not feel so strongly.

Consider now two legislators and two proposed pieces of legislation, A and B. The first legislator strongly favors A and the second strongly favors B. Moreover, we suppose that neither bill seems favored to pass, given the initial views of all legislators. The first legislator then agrees to support B if the second will support A. Through such vote trading on an assembly-wide basis, either bill or both may pass.

Generally speaking, we may view each legislator as holding a stock of votes or voting rights on all issues. He will be rational to trade away his voting rights on those issues about which his constituents do not feel strongly in favor of support on issues which they consider to be more vital to their interests. In this sense, a legislature, a town meeting, or a workers' council in which vote trading is permitted can be viewed as a kind of market.

Despite its ill repute in some quarters, a reasonably rational market for votes is an essential safeguard for minority interests. When vote trading proves difficult, the resulting tyranny of the majority may be a principal source of unequal opportunities for various minority groups. We shall therefore make allowance for vote trading and other forms of compromise an additional requirement for democracy.

Unfortunately, even in the best of circumstances, such a market will not be perfect. It is, in particular, a barter market. The "price" of a vote is not defined according to a common denominator of value. The phenomenon of monopoly can also arise in the sense that a few representatives will sometimes succeed in blocking a measure that nearly everyone wants or in passing a bill that very few want.

What is required is that the minority in question feel much more intensely about the bill than the majority and that it be well placed to sell its votes on other issues for a high "price." This can also be looked upon as a new version of our old "tyranny of the minority." To block it we must build various checks and balances into government to establish a kind of countervailing power.

For example, the U.S. Congress consists of two legislative branches, a House of Representatives and a Senate. Each member of the Senate represents an entire state, and there are two senators from each state. Each member of the House comes from a particular district within a particular state. Illinois has 24 such representatives, about half coming from districts adjacent to or within Chicago. On the average, each representative has $\frac{1}{24}$ of the population from Illinois as his constituents.

Suppose, then, that two or three Illinois representatives wish to steer a bill through the House which benefits their constituents only and is undesirable on the grounds of efficiency. This could be a bit of protection for local industry from foreign or out-of-state domestic competition. Or it could be a public works project—such as a four-lane highway, a giant office building, a dam, or a bridge—whose return to society is much less than another project could earn elsewhere. (This is sometimes called "pork-barrel" spending.) If the representatives in question are in a good enough position to sell their votes on other issues, they will obtain passage.

Such mutual backscratching does indeed go on, but the presence of a Senate, which must pass the same bill, provides a partial check. Senators from Illinois will be less inclined to vote for the measure or to "buy" outside votes for it unless they feel that it is popular on a statewide basis. The executive veto and the abilities of the courts to interpret legislation or to declare it unconstitutional provide additional checks.

Within a parliamentary system, the same kinds of checks may appear in different guises. A member of the British or Canadian Parliament has far less ability to originate and to modify legislation than does his counterpart in the U.S. House of Representatives. He is also bound by tighter party discipline. The party in power is subject to votes of confidence and a strong tradition that serves to check the unbridled wielding of power by the majority party (which elects the executives branch from its ranks).[11]

The tyrannies of the majority and of the minority are both present to some degree in virtually any form of democratic government that has ever been designed. Unfortunately, efforts to protect against one will often increase the danger of the other. The art of building workable democracy is to no small extent the art of finding a precarious balance between them.

22–7   Democracy and Representative Government

An important result of our discussion to date is that majority voting is not by itself sufficient to guarantee democracy. Compromise, vote-trading, discussion, and debate are at least as important, and it is these activities which are most costly and time-consuming. Consequently, the technologically advanced society that has mastered the problem of providing "instant referenda" is no substitute for the small-community town meeting at which every citizen is able to have his say. The costs of voting paradoxes and tyrannies of the majority will both be higher under referenda. Voters are also likely to be less well informed about issues because they feel that they have a less important role to play in government.[12]

Because decision making consumes time, the number of issues that require decision is usually far greater than the number which can be discussed and voted on directly by the whole populace. This converts any government aspiring to be democratic into representative government. The nation is divided into geographical districts (states, provinces, departments, etc.) which may be subdivided several more times in turn. The people living in each subdivision elect representatives who will directly participate in decision making on their behalf. These representatives form the legislative and, in some cases, part of

[11] Under a parliamentary system, only the party or parties which form the government (that is, which elect the premier or chief executive) can propose major legislation. Individuals, as such, cannot do this, nor can the other parties. Party discipline is also stricter than under a presidential system. What vote trading does occur usually takes place between parties, in effect. Thus the "tyranny of the minority" is less likely under a parliamentary system.

However, the tyranny of the majority poses a greater potential danger. Suppose that one party has an absolute majority in parliament and can count on enough party loyalty to preserve this majority when most of its bills come up for passage. Then the party in power may have no automatic incentive to trade votes. What does act to protect minority interests is a strong tradition against deliberately overriding them without some mutually agreed-upon compensation. Thus the government may agree in effect not to introduce a measure that would receive less than a two-thirds majority, often after some vote trading has occurred. In this way, minority parties can have some influence over legislation.

[12] This is an additional problem with voting directly on issues in a referendum. Suppose that a vote is called on a proposal to build a new school. Almost an infinity of alternatives present themselves regarding the size and plan of the building and the method of financing it. At most, three or four of these can appear on a ballot, so many people will not get a chance to accurately express their preferences.

the judicial branches of government. These are needed to supplement the functions of the executive, and also to check its power.

In addition, regions and localities will have their own governments, largely responsible for internal affairs. Often the decisions taken by one region or locality—regarding education, construction of transportation and communications facilities, and sewage disposal, for example—will have spillover effects on others or on society as a whole. Thus the reluctance of Ontario to complete a four-lane highway begun by Québec from Montreal to Ottawa— despite the high accident death toll along the two-lane strip on the Ontario side—reportedly stems, in part, from the knowledge that many Québec residents would benefit. The reluctance of Québec to support English-language schooling and university education in some parts of the province stems partly from a belief that the beneficiaries have a greater-than-average likelihood of emigrating. The central government has the task of producing or negotiating a formula that will enable these effects to be internalized.[13]

A basic principle of representative government holds, then, that representatives rather than the people themselves will meet, debate, and vote on most of the issues of the day. The system thrives on the fact that the number of representatives is a miniscule fraction of the number of people whom they represent. One consequence of this, however, is that no representative can perfectly mirror the preferences of each of his constituents, even though being from the same geographical region gives them common interests.

Looking at matters from the other direction, the number of candidates running for each office during any given election is generally far less than the number of issues on which that candidate will have to decide or take a position. Thus, even though no two candidates agree on all the issues, most citizens are likely to find that they do not exactly agree with any candidate on every issue.

Despite this problem, we may view a representative legislature as a model of the whole population debating, voting, compromising, and vote trading. The main difference, of course, is that if the populace tried to do this, the

---

[13] We customarily distinguish two kinds of central government vis-à-vis its relations with the various regional governments. A *unitary* central government has the power to overrule lower governments on any occasion where externalities arise. France and the United Kingdom both have basically unitary governments. A *federal* central government lacks this extensive power and must negotiate compromises in at least some instances.

Thus unitary governments are nominally more efficient in the sense that they can more readily and inexpensively internalize most kinds of interregional social costs and benefits. Federal governments are necessary, however, in countries whose citizens have strong regional ties. The ethnic minorities of Canada and Yugoslavia, for example, have a regional basis. Groups in both countries would fear to be dominated and suppressed under a unitary form of government. This might strain the bonds of nationhood, even to the breaking point.

The Soviet Union is an example of a multinational state with a unitary government, and there have been periodic complaints of suppression of regionally based ethnic minority groups.

result would eventually be chaos or else a system of committees that would amount to a form of representative government.

What is perhaps remarkable is that under extremely ideal conditions, the legislature will accurately reproduce the preferences of its constituents regarding the passage or failure of a series of bills that are presented to it. That is, if a bill would pass (or fail) a vote of the whole population, after efficient vote trading and compromise had occurred, it would pass (or fail) a vote of the legislature after efficient compromise and vote trading. Let us call this likelihood the fundamental theorem of representative government.[14] Then the importance of the fundamental theorem stems from the fact that much more efficient compromise and vote trading are possible in a legislature.

We may recall that the fundamental theorem of welfare economics says, in effect, that it is possible to break up the gigantic unmanageable economic problem facing society as a whole into many infinitely smaller subproblems. Under extremely ideal conditions, this can be done efficiently. Although these ideal conditions do not prevail, we can still use the basic idea as an aid in designing a practical system that is reasonably efficient.

The fundamental theorem of representative government plays roughly the same role in the realm of political decision making. It says that, under ideal conditions, we can replace unworkable direct democracy with representative government, without altering inherent social priorities in a fundamental way.[15]

One of these conditions is that each legislator must represent the same number of constituents. If rural representatives are elected by 50,000 citizens, on the average, while city legislators are elected by 200,000, rural preferences will predominate in the legislative. In addition, legislators must have a good knowledge of the preferences of their constituents so that they can respond to these. Finally, each citizen must either be able to forecast the stands that the candidates will take on the issues that arise or else feel that he can trust the judgment of a particular candidate.

More generally, if the system is to work properly, every citizen should assess the costs that each candidate is likely to impose on him while in office, as well as the benefits each candidate will provide for him. He should then vote for that candidate or slate of candidates from whom he will receive the highest net benefits (or who will impose the lowest net costs on him). This is the procedure for deciding which candidate's "bid" he prefers, and by how much in cases where multiple ballots are allowed.

Unfortunately, the need for rational behavior on the part of voters creates serious problems. Many citizens will find the judging of bids difficult, often to

[14] See Edwin T. Haefele, "A Utility Theory of Representative Government," *American Economic Review*, June 1971.

[15] The exact "ideal conditions" under which this will happen are not yet fully known, insofar as the author is aware. Indeed, they are only beginning to be investigated, and a "fundamental theorem of representative government" has not (apparently) even been stated in a completely rigorous way.

the point of impossibility. Voters will not know what stand each candidate is going to take on every issue, nor even the range of issues upon which a given candidate will take a stand. Some decisions will remain secret until long after they are taken. Neither will most voters know how much influence each candidate is going to wield within the political decision-making process. Finally, voters will have only an imperfect knowledge of how specific policies or pursuit of particular goals will affect them.

Nevertheless, the reader may wonder why we have suddenly become so concerned about rational behavior. If we assume a citizen to be rational in buying a house or a used car, why should we not suppose him to be rational in voting? The reason is that the welfare that he will derive from buying a house, a car, or any other private good is directly tied to his own personal decision. If he picks a lemon, he pays the consequences. If he chooses a "best buy," he enjoys its benefits.

But this is not true when he votes. Virtually, no election will ride on the vote-casting power of a single citizen. It would therefore be rational for every citizen to assume that, with his own vote(s), he can have no effect whatsoever on the outcome. As long as his ballot is his only influence, therefore, it is irrational for him to go to considerable expense or to spend a great deal of time and energy becoming an informed voter.[16] This fact profoundly influences the nature of viable democratic processes in two ways.

The first is that candidates for public office who hope to win must make it easy for large numbers of voters to identify with them. Political parties and ideologies will assist in this simplification, whose thrust is to collapse multidimensional differences between candidates into a spectrum of one or two dimensions, often running from left wing to right wing. One consequence of this is that citizens are likely to vote on the basis of labels. Candidates and parties will have to avoid credibility gaps. In taking positions, they must concern themselves with ideology as well as merit, thus limiting the extent to which they can take left-wing stances on some issues and right-wing stances on others.

The political choice spectrum itself then tends to collapse (for example, into a left wing–right wing dimension). When voters cluster at different points along it, as in Figure 22–1(a), or polarize at either end, stable and efficient democratic government becomes difficult to conduct. In Figure 22–1(a), we would expect political parties to take up positions close to A, B, C, and/or D along this spectrum. No party would be able to hold a permanent majority of the voters.

Instead, stability would require the bulk of the citizenry to cluster their views around one particular point along the spectrum, as in Figure 22–1(b). Here one political party would likely settle close to A and the other close to B. They may even get so near to one another that charges of "no major differ-

---

[16] He may still vote out of a sense of civic pride or duty, because of identification with a candidate or his views, and so on.

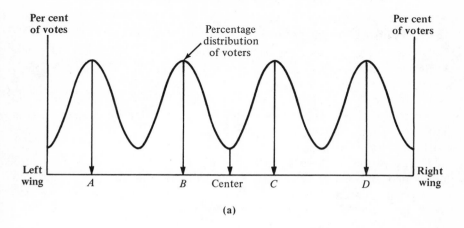

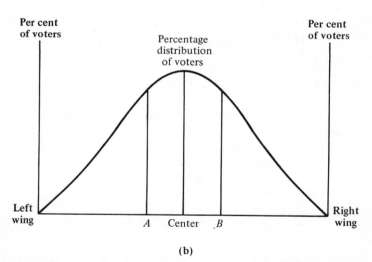

Figure 22–1. (a) Unstable distribution of voters; (b) stable distribution of voters.

ences between the major political parties" proliferate. Speaking generally, ideology oversimplifies issues, thereby sharpening conflicts and reducing the number of dimensions along which compromise in the form of give in one area and take in another can occur.[17]

The second influence of the small impact which individual voters can make is that "single-stage democracy" becomes "multistage democracy" with the appearance of political pressure groups.

---

[17] On some occasions, this will actually make secrecy in democratic government desirable because compromises can more easily be reached.

22–8   Political Pressure Groups

Let us, in fact, define a one-stage democratic process to consist of voters, elections, candidates, and an emerging government. The role of elections is to synthesize the preferences of voters for candidates and, in some cases, on issues directly. The goals of most incumbents will include reelection—if not of themselves, then of successors sharing party affiliation or some other common bond—and this will influence the index of socioeconomic preferences which they try to maximize.

Such a process will work quite imperfectly because voters will tend to be uninformed and also because politicians will often be unable to spot consensuses emerging within the population and to rationally weigh one consensus against another. To become workable, therefore, democracy will have to add at least one additional stage.

Citizens whose welfares are most affected by the differences between alternative government policies will often join together to form or support special-interest groups. These coalitions (or "embodied consensuses") then become political pressure groups or lobbies. Virtually every industry will have its own lobby, as will labor unions, professional, veterans', and consumer associations, conservation clubs, women's action groups, and a host of others. Some 269 organizations reported lobby spending at the federal government level in the United States in 1969, and many more were in existence that did not report.

We can also consider political parties and the campaign organizations of candidates for major offices to be pressure groups. (In particular, office holders or candidates may start political action groups to perpetuate their power.) Sometimes, special-interest groups will arise around one or two major issues and then disband. By contrast, some big-city political machines will control local governments for decades.

Pressure groups play no official role in government, nor can they vote, aside from the votes of their members and supporters. Yet their impact on the functioning of government is profound. They provide politicians with information about the preferences of their supporters and the public with information about politicians and programs, along with justifications of their own positions. Like successful advertisers, special-interest groups will help to shape and crystallize preferences at both ends. According to E. G. West, "Simple but persistent propaganda put out by them aims to create public opinion at the same time that it attempts to persuade governments that it exists." [18]

The ultimate objective of pressure groups is to influence government decison making. The relative effectiveness of different groups will thus depend upon their ability to deliver votes, whether through persuasion, violence, prior

[18] E. G. West, "Toward a Comprehensive Theory of Minimum Wage Laws," Economics Department Working Paper 72–08, Ottawa, Carleton University, May 1972.

conviction, campaign contributions, or friendly reminders such as a turkey dinner at Thanksgiving or Christmas.

Any citizen may support several special-interest groups, although the number of active groups must remain a small fraction of the number of citizens. The potential gains to supporters of pressure groups result from the leverage which these individuals acquire over the political process. The successful lobby influences goal formation by revealing its preferences for various programs, policies, and public goods provided by the government. The citizenry as a whole can also gain from two-stage political decision making because it is potentially a more flexible procedure.

A disadvantage is that pressure groups will sometimes influence voting habits by coercing citizens or because they are able to exert a significant impact upon the flow of information reaching prospective voters. The almost certain invasion of the information media by special-interest groups puts an additional strain on a competent and unbiased press. It also argues further for flexible ceilings on campaign spending and lobbying budgets.

The emerging two-stage process thus begins with special-interest groups synthesizing preferences, often in areas where individual differences are not too large to begin with. In the second stage the preferences of various pressure groups are synthesized during debate and discussion with government representatives. The more intense the lobbying for or against a given measure, other things being equal, the greater the respective probabilities of passage or failure.

The resulting index of social welfare then reflects both special-interest-group preferences and individual preferences as expressed in elections and referenda. A complicating factor is the ability of special-interest groups to manipulate voting patterns.

Figure 22–2 contrasts the one- and two-stage democratic processes. In the former, individual preferences ($u_1, u_2, \ldots, u_n$) are synthesized directly into a social preference function, W. The latter adds a synthesis of individual preferences into group preferences ($w_1, w_2, \ldots, w_m$), which then enter into an index of social preferences. Individual preferences continue to enter this index as well because individuals continue to vote in elections and referenda. We can increase the number of stages further by introducing multilayer special-interest groups or by adding different levels of government.

We may view the emergence of elected representatives, lobbies, and other special-interest groups as efforts to simplify political decision making. Rather than participate directly, most individuals allow others to represent them in a variety of ways, official and unofficial. Representative government and lobbying may thus enable the participatory base of political decision making to broaden.

In the final analysis, workable democracy cannot usually hope to be more than an interaction between elected government decision makers, special-interest groups, and, in many cases, technical experts. However, every repre-

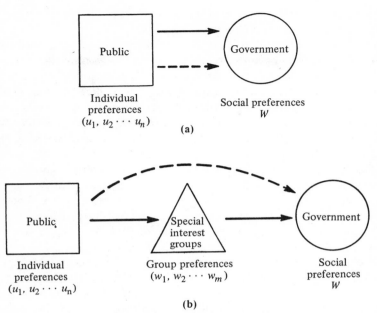

Figure 22–2. The one-stage (a) and two-stage (b) democratic processes. (The solid arrows indicate goal formation through direct participation, including political pressure, while the dashed arrows indicate goal formation through elections and referenda.)

sentative and most lobbies will have many constituents and cannot perfectly represent the preferences of most. For this reason alone, complete democracy is impossible.

Nevertheless, more democratic processes will be able to accommodate more special interests, reflecting a wider range of viewpoints in social goal formation. On any given issue, fewer segments of society which stand to gain or lose will be left without an effective voice. We shall, in fact, adopt this as our final criterion for democratic government.

Some economists say that a minimum requirement for consumers' sovereignty is that each individual's preferences should count—whenever he chooses to express them—in determining the mix of goods and services to be made available to society. Moreover, he should be permitted to "cast a vote" for every purely private good or service offered for sale by deciding whether and how much to buy.

In the same spirit, we can speak of "citizens' sovereignty" with respect to the political process. On any given issue or series of issues that can inflict costs upon him or provide benefits for him, he would ideally find easy access to one or more special-interest groups which have an incentive to take some interest in his freely volunteered opinion. This "citizens' sovereignty" motivates our final criterion.

Chapter **23**

Economic Planning in a Democratic Society?

. . . what we are doing right now is flying the most powerful economic machine in the history of mankind . . . and we are flying it by luck, by instinct, with almost no instruments at all in the cockpit. . . .

> Former U.S. Secretary of Labor,
> **Willard W. Wirtz**

23–1 The Financing of Lobbies[1]

Because the social priorities of purportedly "democratic" governments are bound to depend upon lobbying, we must now ask what causes political pressure groups to arise and fall. Clearly, they must represent well-defined special interests, but this will not guarantee an effective voice in goal formation. Pressure-group activity is expensive and demands both an awareness and fairly intense feelings within a recognizable segment of the public.

---

[1] The central idea of this section comes from Mancur Olson, Jr., *The Logic of Collective Action* (New York: Schocken, 1968).

The costs of lobbying will rise with its intensity on any given issue. Moreover, because it is probably possible to enhance the effectiveness of a given amount of lobbying on any particular issue by maintaining an "image," continually in front of elected representatives, we would expect economies of scale as well. These scale economies will probably prevent a number of (potential) special interests from having a significant voice in social goal formation.

We would expect the relative effectiveness of different groups in lobbying on a proposed measure to depend upon the magnitudes of the costs and benefits at stake for their constituents. (That is, relative effectiveness will depend upon the value of a tariff, an import quota, a legal cartel, a license, or other industrial or occupational entry barrier.) But effectiveness will also depend upon

1. The distribution of wealth—or, more precisely the distribution of control over purchasing power—among potential gainers and losers.
2. How easily the potential gainers and losers can be made aware of the benefits or costs involved.

For example, 1 and perhaps 2 lead us to predict that owners of large farms will have more political "clout" than migrant farm workers, a prediction that practice appears to bear out. These are not the sole factors, however, which affect the financing and hence the effectiveness of pressure groups. There is also a "public good" problem, whose implications will often be even more important.

Suppose that 1 million citizens each stand to benefit substantially if they can form an effective lobby. Yet each citizen would benefit from the actions of the lobby whether he supports it financially or not. Moreover, the effectiveness of the lobby will scarcely be affected at all by the decision of a particular individual to support it, even though it depends vitally upon the financial support of all affected individuals together.

To illustrate, the citizens in question could be residents of an urban community viewed in their role as consumers. The benefits comprise better consumer protection and information, a reduction of pollution and congestion, more stringent health and safety standards, construction of pedestrian walkways over intersections, and other measures designed to reduce the number of street accidents. If each individual gave $1 to maintain a "consumer lobby" and half or more agreed to support its position through their voting habits, the lobby might well return benefits to each household worth many times the dollar cost. But households will receive any benefits whether they contribute or not, and the decision of any particular citizen to withhold his "dollar votes" will not noticeably impair the lobby's effectiveness.

Because its effectiveness is independent of the individual household's efforts and because it provides him with a "public good," the consumer lobby is likely to be underfinanced, given its potential benefits. To offset this, it may successfully compete with charities and other worthy causes for donations motivated by a community or philanthropic spirit.

If it is extremely lucky, an entrepreneur with a Ralph Nader-like skill and zest for consumerism will take charge of its campaigns. Here the basic financing formula calls for translating the public good that the lobby provides into a series of private goods for individuals. Thus Nader and associates try to raise funds—through the sale of books, newsletters, or magazines and public appearances—which are then channeled into pressure-group activity. It also helps if the entrepreneurs enjoy what they are doing or get some kind of satisfaction from the results of their activities per se.

Nevertheless, even under favorable circumstances, consumer lobbies will probably enjoy mixed success. Their gains come partly at the expense of business firms, in the form of higher costs or lower revenues, partly at the expense of property owners, given the municipality's probable tax base, and, perhaps, partly at the expense of labor unions or professional associations. These groups are likely to be much better organized for lobbying purposes because they do *not* have to rely on the same financing formula.

Suppose that a tough new antipollution law threatens to impose heavy costs on local manufacturing or that a proposed anticongestion ordinance will discourage taxi rides in favor of mass transit. Unlike our households above, some of these threatened firms will probably be big enough to make contributions satisfying two criteria. The total sums involved will be less than the potential costs inflicted on them by antipollution or anticongestion laws and, at the same time, large enough to influence the success of lobbying on their own behalf. This gives adversely affected firms a direct incentive to pay for lobbying activities designed to sway lawmakers, and, perhaps, for publicity aimed at influencing the public.

Such is not necessarily the case where a labor union, a professional association, or a group of property owners is likely to bear the brunt of a particular consumer lobby success. An individual doctor, lawyer, labor-union member, or property owner will not usually be big enough to affect the political process personally at an acceptable cost. However, these groups are much more susceptible than consumers to organizing activity financially based on the sale of private benefits to members or dues collection. The latter, in turn, may be based partly on coercion. Once organized, a labor union or a professional or property owners' association will often be able to make large contributions which satisfy the above criteria.

It follows that the effectiveness of a (potential) lobby depends partly on the presence of large beneficiaries, each of whom has an incentive to make a significant contribution to the lobby's financing. To this we would add the need to overcome some scale economies before effective lobbying can occur at all. Finally, the more thinly spread the costs (or benefits) of a proposed government action among the citizenry, the lower its weight is likely to be vis-à-vis other government decisions in determining how those who bear the costs (or receive the benefits) will vote. Putting all these considerations to-gether, we get a third determinant of lobbying effectiveness:

3. How concentrated the benefits are relative to the costs among the individuals and organizations that stand to gain or lose from particular government decisions.

The more concentrated are the benefits or costs on side A relative to side B, the more successful would we expect A's political pressure-group activities to be on the issues involved. As a corollary of the three determinants of lobby-ing success just outlined, we would expect an oversupply of some public goods and an undersupply of others, relative to a "democratic" social welfare opti-mum. This contrasts with some claims that a laissez-faire economy will inevitably generate private opulence amid public squalor.

These determinants will often reinforce one another. Suppose that his-torical circumstances, together with 2 and 3, have built up a number of entry barriers into industries and occupations over time. These barriers will protect both monopoly profits and monopoly elements in wages and salaries, which can, in part, be converted into union or professional association dues. By reinvesting a portion of their monopoly rents in pressure-group activity, those who benefit the most in the first place can perpetuate and even increase in-equities in the distributions of wealth and power.

Later we shall argue that the impact of criteria 1, 2, and 3 may result in a kind of "tyranny of the minority" which constitutes a departure from demo-cratic decision making. We have seen, in fact, that the purpose of lobbies in a democratic government is to give individuals a voice in social goal forma-tion that they cannot get at the ballot box. Although the outcome of virtually every election will be independent of each particular vote that is cast, the outcomes of proposed legislation, hearings, potential executive orders, and so on, will not usually be independent of the efforts of every particular political pressure group.

Ideally, individuals get this clout by aligning themselves with others who are like-minded on one or more issues under the special interest group's umbrella. This can help to make workable government more democratic by making it more representative. Some economists have even argued that the representatives of different special interest groups should serve as the effective legislature of the nation, replacing the Parliament or Congress conventionally elected from geographical districts.[2]

The problem is that successful lobbying is more likely to occur when the principal benefactors are, at most, a few wealthy organizations or individuals. The organizing and entrepreneurial talents of a Ralph Nader or a Caesar

_____
[2] Such an assembly would correspond to Horvat's workers' council (Section 21–7) at the economy-wide level. If the problem discussed below can be overcome, it does appear promising as a relatively efficient link in democratic goal formation. However, it should probably be combined in a bicameral legislature with an assembly based on conventional geographical representation as an additional check on tyranny of the minority.

Chavez are needed to mobilize consumers and migrant farmers. Even then, success is painfully slow in coming. The high degree of organization and power of business interests, on the other hand, results largely from the fact that the business community is divided into a number of (generally oligopolistic) industries, each constituting, at most, a few large firms. A similar situation prevails for skilled and professional workers. These lobbies are likely to dominate the political process, thereby making it *less* representative.

Our dilemma, then, is that many lobbies that will be hardest to organize are also most essential if truly representative goal formation is to prevail. Consequently, a laissez-faire attitude toward pressure-group formation will not be very democratic, particularly when the government has a powerful leverage over the economy. Before exploring an antidote, however, we want to document the above discussion with some examples, notably relating to criterion 3.

23–2   Some Examples

Perhaps the most evident consequence of criterion 3 is that lobbying will be much more effective in protecting individuals in their roles as producers than in their roles as consumers. Most individuals consume a vast heterogeneity of products while deriving their livelihoods from just one or two sources. A particular good will normally be consumed by many more people than assist directly in its production. Thus the benefits or costs of (proposed) economic measures involving the good will tend to be much more concentrated among those affected on the production side than among those whose consumption is primarily affected.[3]

In North America the lobbies for consumer protection and advocacy, including those for environmental protection, were either nonexistent or completely drowned out until recently by the representatives of business, labor, farmers, and professional associations.[4] Even today, after the "consumer revolution," it is still difficult to shift a significant proportion of the costs of cleaning up the environment or of removing unsafe products from the market onto large firms or well-organized industries.[5]

[3] By "economic" measures, we mean laws, rules, and so on, which affect the production, distribution, or consumption of one or more goods and services. Reflection will show that most of any government's output has some economic impact.

[4] Referring to the United States, Epstein says that "almost all business corporations, even those which are small, engage in *some* forms of political activity. See Edwin Epstein, *The Corporation in American Politics* (Englewood Cliffs, N.J.: Prentice-Hall, 1969, p. 100). The 269 organizations reporting lobby spending at the level of the federal government in the United States in 1969 were classified as follows: business, 143; employee and labor, 30; farm, 16; professional associations, 16; military and veterans, 6; and citizens, 57. However, at the very outside, only about a dozen of the latter groups could be classified under consumer protection, including environmental preservation. See *Legislators and Lobbyists,* Congressional Quarterly Service, 4th ed., July 31, 1970, Washington, D.C.

[5] For an example, see *The New York Times,* May 7, 1972, Sec. 3, p. 3, on cyclamates.

The most frequently cited results of the power of production-oriented pressure groups in social goal formation are tariffs and other restrictions on international trade. The benefits of protection for one industry are paid for by millions of consumers in the form of higher prices. For example, import quotas provide the American oil industry with an annual subsidy of about $5 billion. Although only a few companies benefit, more than 200 million consumers each pay anywhere from $11 to $57 as their "shares." [6]

In fact, opposition to tariff legislation is most likely to rise in the event of expected retaliation from abroad whose costs would be confined within a few export industries. Regarding tariffs and import quotas, L. W. Weiss asks:

if trade restrictions are so awful, why do we have them? The answer is that the gain from tariffs is concentrated on a small group of people, but the loss is diffused throughout the whole country. If the woollen tariff were removed, the general public might have its over-all level of living increased by maybe one-half of one per cent. (The export industries might likewise benefit marginally.) For most consumers or exporters it would not be worthwhile to even write their congressman. On the other hand, the congressmen from New England would be deluged with letters, telegrams, and delegations from the mill owners and workers who felt that their lives were at stake. . . .[7]

And, we might add, the textile lobby would be hard at work. This lobby was quite active in 1971, pressing for new import quotas on textile and footwear. If passed, they were expected to be costing U.S. consumers $3.7 billion annually (in higher prices) by 1975.[8]

This phenomenon is not, unfortunately, confined to trade. Millions of Canadian buyers subsidize the Ontario tobacco industry, which has a legal monopoly cartel, by an infinitesimal amount every time they put money into a cigarette machine. The total subsidy comes to perhaps half of the $130 million that the 4,500 Ontario tobacco growers earn every year.

Production controls on tobacco have a similar effect in the United States. In addition, they are so worded as to keep tobacco-growing plots too small to realize scale economies. Both resulting increases in cost are passed along to consumers.[9] Oil-production quotas in Texas also encourage inefficient production methods. The cost in higher prices to consumers probably exceeded $1 billion over the period 1948–1970.[10]

The U.S. government spent between 3 and 5 billion dollars per year on

[6] See Cabinet Task Force on Oil Import Control, *The Oil Import Question* (Washington, D.C.: G.P.O., Feb. 1970), pp. 26–27.

[7] L. W. Weiss, *Economics and American Industry* (New York: Wiley, 1961), p. 161. The entire passage, pp. 150–161, is worthy of the reader's attention.

[8] See *Consumer Reports,* Feb. 1971, pp. 118–121.

[9] D. R. Campbell, "The Economics of Production Control: The Case of Tobacco," *Canadian Journal of Economics,* Feb. 1969.

[10] *Consumer Reports,* op. cit.

farm subsidies during the latter 1960s. Consumers paid for these in the form of taxes and higher prices. Much of the aid, however, did not go to sustain a class of hardy, independent farmers with holdings of small to medium size. They went to wealthy farms, including agro-businesses, which were driving out the family farm with their hired labor and "factories in the fields." At the same time, crippling inheritance taxes were forcing large numbers of relatively small farmers to sell their land to suburban real-estate speculators.

Pollution, congestion, waste and depletion of natural resources, and other external "bads" will often fall into the same category because they are frequently costs that large producers shift onto smaller ones as well as onto the public at large. The costs of water pollution arise mainly from the operations of oil refineries, chemical plants, detergent manufacturers, metallurgical industries, and local governments.

But they are largely borne by fishers, farmers, swimmers, sportsmen, and anyone else who derives pleasure or profit from fresh water. Rights to pollute are effectively acquired or maintained by lobbyists representing large firms, municipalities, industrial associations, and government agencies. In this way the demand for pollution often creates its own supply.

Similarly, we may argue that there is a component in the social cost of automobile production which auto manufacturers do not have to bear. Besides air pollution and auto graveyards, we should note the intense lobbying by the U.S. auto industry for highway construction. The federal government appropriated nearly $70 billion from tax revenues to build toll-free interstate (or federal) highways during the 1950s, 1960s, and 1970s while expecting other modes of transport to operate on more of a profit-and-loss basis. This almost certainly caused a greater expansion of automotive relative to rail and public transportation than would otherwise have occurred. (Of the $80 billion spent by the federal government on transportation over 1964–1972, only about 1 per cent went to mass transit.)

The value of the efficiency losses due to pollution and congestion is extremely difficult to measure. Insofar as the author is aware, only one rigorous effort has been made to compute them. This is by Nordhaus and Tobin, who estimate a loss that varied between 5.3 and 5.9 per cent of the entire U.S. gross national product between 1929 and 1965. Although their technique is ingenious, it almost certainly understates the true costs of pollution and congestion, and we can conservatively pick a figure of 6 per cent for 1970. This amounts to nearly $60 billion, or $290 for every man, woman, and child.[11]

The principle of concentrated benefits and scattered costs can work just as well when consumers are not directly involved. A U.S. author writes:

---

[11] William Nordhaus and James Tobin, "Is Growth Obsolete?" a paper presented to the National Bureau of Economic Research Colloquium, San Francisco, Dec. 10, 1970 (mimeo). See the discussion of this paper in Chapter 6.

Assuming that the costs of pollution and congestion do run into the tens of billions of dollars annually, national income and output in the United States is overstated by that amount. No subtraction is made for pollution and congestion "disamenities."

Businessmen have traditionally held a dual attitude toward making their voices heard in . . . the Federal Government. Where there has been a specific impact on a specific company—what seemed to be a heavy tax, a burdensome regulation, an unreasonable restriction—business executives have not hesitated to march on Washington personally and also to hire top legal, lobbying, and other talent to get their views across.

[But] where the impact has been less specific . . . business executives have generally stayed at home rather than tangle with the politicians and the bureaucracy. . . . Thus . . . business executives have hardly ever testified before Congress on such matters as education, welfare, or space budgets. They left the expression of business opinion on such issues to such organizations as the chamber of commerce, which . . . often has less impact than one identifiable, plain-spoken corporate executive.[12]

The burden of labor-union-sponsored legislation is often borne by relatively unskilled workers, those living in depressed areas or urban ghettos, or those who are most difficult to organize. Perhaps the best example of this is the minimum-wage law, which puts a legal floor under the hourly earnings of all workers covered by it. Unions usually lobby heavily for minimum-wage legislation and for regular increases in existing hourly minima once the basic law is passed.

On occasion, union members will benefit directly from higher legal minima. Weaker unions will occasionally find that the minimum wage exceeds the wage they could win for some of their members at the bargaining table. More importantly, since there must be pay differentials by skill and rank in any hierarchical organization, a whole series of higher floors effectively accompanies a legal floor under the least skilled workers. Relatively skilled union or even professional workers may benefit from these.

However, unions may also feel that they benefit indirectly. An effective minimum wage, by definition, prices some workers right out of the market. Inevitably, these will be workers whose value of marginal product falls below the minimum wage that employers must legally pay. They are therefore the least skilled—the teen-agers, the residents of depressed areas or urban ghettos, or others whose productivity is for some reason unusually low.

The benefits of this for union members are not guaranteed, but they may come (or members may believe that they come) from two sources. First, less skilled, nonunion workers may be partially substitutable for skilled, union employees in some production activities. If employers could pay less than the minimum wage, they would hire relatively more unskilled and relatively fewer skilled workers in these activities—unless unions lowered their own wage demands. Second, and perhaps more likely, goods that are produced with relatively large inputs of nonunion labor may be substituted for and thus compete with goods produced with relatively large inputs of union labor.

In this case, lower wages for nonunion workers will enable their employers to charge lower prices for the goods they assist in producing. To remain com-

---

[12] Eileen Shanahan, "The Reluctant Statisticians," *The New York Times,* Oct. 10, 1971, Sec. 3, p. 5.

petitive, prices of union-produced goods must also be lower, thus raising employer resistance to union wage demands. The same argument holds if we consider a single good which could be produced in two alternative locations. One site, we suppose, is a depressed area or an urban ghetto. It is at cost disadvantage because of transport problems to markets or sources of supply, because of a high crime rate, or simply because the available (nonunion) labor supply is short of skills or "work discipline."

However, by accepting lower wages, these workers may overcome their critical cost disadvantage. If employers must pay a minimum wage, on the other hand, the depressed area will look less attractive, and more plants will locate elsewhere. The area in question will become even more depressed relative to the rest of the economy. If instead of a depressed region we are dealing with a foreign country, the domestic union will not find minimum-wage legislation any advantage (although foreign unions may do the job for them). Nevertheless, it can join with the industry lobby to demand tariff or import quota protection from "cheap foreign labor." [13]

Of course, unions do not generally argue for minimum-wage laws on the grounds we have just described, and they may, indeed, view such legislation as basically compassionate. But mounting evidence shows that the *effect* of rising minimum wages is to produce both inflation and unemployment, especially among the relatively disadvantaged.[14]

In Chapter 14 we noted that a comprehensive family-assistance plan or a guaranteed annual income is a superior alternative to a minimum wage. The only things "wrong" with a guaranteed income are that it does not appear to benefit wealthy organizations or individuals, and what benefits it does provide may well be more scattered than in the case of a minimum wage. Consequently, it is likely to receive less favorable publicity, being portrayed as a subsidy rather than a "fair day's pay for a fair day's work." (In the broadest sense, however, those who benefit from a minimum wage are receiving a subsidy from those put out of work. This is unquestionably far more painful to give than a guaranteed annual income.) In the final analysis, the guaranteed annual income is less likely to become the law of the land.

We should not forget to include government bureaucracy in a discussion of lobbying influence. The fact that a bureau is public rather than private will not keep it from lobbying, usually to get an expanded demand for its services. Its political clout comes in the first instance from the votes it can control. Here we include the votes of employees and, perhaps, of their relatives, along with those of employees, relatives, and stockholders associated with govern-

[13] Nothing said in the text advocates the demise of unions per se. We can and do argue that unions and business firms should be denied the power to establish occupational and industrial entry barriers.

[14] For an excellent survey of the theory and empirical evidence relating to minimum-wage laws in North America, see E. G. West, "Toward a Comprehensive Theory of Minimum Wage Laws," Economics Department Working Paper 72-08, Ottawa, Carleton University, May 1972.

ment contractors and other firms that can benefit from an expansion of the bureau's activities.

Taxpayers will ultimately have to bear the costs of expansion, but we would again expect these to be much more scattered than the benefits. In most cases, the vast majority of taxpayers to whom there is a net cost of expansion will not base their votes on this fact. They may not even be aware of which of the bureau's activities are expanding, by how much, and what this expansion is going to cost them.

Bureaus may also align their lobbying strength with industry, farmers, or labor unions. In the United States a guaranteed annual income could replace not only a minimum wage, but a maze of overlapping welfare programs which sometimes work at cross purposes. It would also be cheaper to administer and require fewer administrators. Consequently, the affected bureaus will probably oppose such a proposal, and some may back the minimum wage as an alternative.

The military industrial complex is basically an alliance of business, labor, and bureaucracy whose combined forces, at their height, may have represented the most powerful political pressure group of all time. Not only did they achieve a rapidly rising defense budget, but the share of total government spending devoted to defense continued to increase long after it became the largest budget item. Many defense contracts guaranteed the producer a profit over and above his cost, regardless of how high these might be, and cost overruns were frequent. (A similar type of contract was common in highway construction.)

Eventually, the public became more aware of the costs associated with this bureau's operations and more willing to vote for politicians who promised to restrict their expansion. These costs also became concentrated among some segments of the population, notably war veterans and their relatives. But by then the defense bureaucracy may well have absorbed more than an efficient share of the nation's economic resources.

Unfortunately, a number of solutions often proposed to the problems outlined in this section will not usually work. Powerful interests will often use their political leverage to dominate or muzzle regulatory agencies (including the press) or to prevent them from arising. A simple switch to widespread public ownership may change the structure of special interest groups, but the problems of concentrated costs and benefits and of public awareness will remain. (Of course, if elections are abolished, awareness will not be nearly enough.) The U.S.S.R. has its own military–industrial complex, whose enthusiasm for expansion appears to equal or exceed that of its U.S. counterpart. Presumably, in fact, they have helped one another.

Generally speaking, industrial ministries have maintained a powerful voice in social goal formation in Eastern Europe. They are guilty of many of the same abuses, notably of pollution and waste of natural resources, that we attribute to major corporations in the West. They have added a few of their own, such as overexpansion of the traditional heavy industries at the expense of newer substitutes and production of consumer goods.

If we wish to build on the foundation of democracy constructed in Chapter 22, therefore, we shall have to look further.

23-3   Equity and Efficiency

We have studied enough examples to see that under a laissez-faire approach to pressure-group formation, some micro decision makers are likely to find it fairly easy to act through special interest groups to control their own reward structures. Three basic methods are open to them:

1. They can try to reduce their tax burdens while benefitting more from government subsidies and spending on goods and services.
2. They can create externalities by shifting some of their own costs onto others or benefitting from the activities of others without paying.
3. They can try for protection in the form of occupational or industrial entry barriers.

Point 3, in fact, complements 1 and 2 because, without it, the benefits provided by the first two activities would ultimately be competed away. For firms, success in a market economy will mean higher demand curves or lower cost curves. For a labor union, it will mean a restricted supply of labor, perhaps coupled with a public-works spending program which raises the demand.

The "products" of such a political process will therefore include a series of laws, regulations, agreements, and understandings which constitute the fruits of 1–3. Among these we would list international trade restrictions; price and wage supports; patent and copyright protection; monopoly positions for firms, bureaus, labor unions, and professional associations; resale-price maintenance; production quotas; "rights" to produce pollution, congestion, misleading advertising and labeling, and to exhaust natural resources; and lax enforcement of quality and safety standards. We may look upon most or all of these as manifestations of inequity brought about because some individuals have access to better political-pressure-group representation than others.

We may also look upon these products as sources of economic inefficiency. Pollution, congestion, monopoly power, and minimum-wage laws distort the allocation of resources or force them to remain idle. Cost-plus government contracts also encourage production inefficiency *within* firms (X inefficiency). Indeed, any sort of industrial entry barrier leaves room for cost padding in the form of expense accounts, higher executive salaries, pretty secretaries, and other nonpecuniary benefits which management may choose in lieu of higher profits. If the same firm succeeds in reducing its unit costs through political influence, the net result could be no change in its private costs. However, society would pay twice, once for the X inefficiency and once for the subsidies or externalities which cause private costs to fall.

We can view tariffs and input quotas (or controls) as implicit subsidies to domestic producers. In some ways these are among the most inefficient subsidies imaginable. In the first place, they restrict competition and guarantee domestic producers a substantial share of the market. The protected firms have no incentive to innovate or to become more internally efficient in any other way. Second, they provide protection alike to firms that do and do not need it. Third, it is difficult to estimate how much subsidy a given tariff embodies and therefore how much the protection costs. That is, nobody knows exactly how much money firms would have to receive in the absence of the tariff or quota to leave them as well off as they are under its umbrella.

Import quotas have become perhaps the major means of reducing "foreign competition," but they are likely to be even less efficient than tariffs. Moreover, the cost of an import quota to the nation that imposes it exceeds the efficiency loss—often, by many times. Suppose that I am a Japanese manufacturer of textiles or footwear competing in the United States. I know that I will eventually have to accept a "voluntary" quota in the form of a maximum percentage of the market based upon my sales in a previous year. My strategy, therefore, is to grab as big a chunk of the market as I can now, perhaps accepting losses in the process. Later, once quotas have been agreed to, and prices rise as a consequence of the restricted foreign supply and higher costs of American firms, I can enjoy my ensuing profits.

In the case of a tariff, the increase in price paid by the consumer goes to his government, which may use the proceeds to benefit society. In the case of an import quota, the increase in price goes abroad to the foreign producer or government.

Of course, we may be willing to sacrifice efficiency to get more democratic social goal formation. But in nearly all the examples cited so far, the evidence is that we are getting less of both. The most noteworthy thing about tariffs, import quotas, price supports, cost-plus government contracts, legal monopolies, and "illegal" businesses (such as gambling and prostitution), which are nevertheless permitted behind high entry barriers, is that the protection involved is particularly inconspicuous or unembarrassing.[15]

In every case it would be more efficient to abandon the protection and to pay a direct subsidy, should a decision be taken to benefit the firms involved. Although the added loss due to each particular kind of departure from efficiency may be small to insignificant, the net loss from many can easily be large. Moreover, some costs are hard to measure. It has been alleged, for instance, that the gun lobby in the United States has raised the crime rate by blocking controls over the distribution of firearms. The U.S. government has been accused of allying itself with American controlled oil interests to fix prices, allocate markets, and control production in the Middle East. This has caused frictions with governments in the area.

In other instances, because the political process is not well coordinated

---

[15] For a vivid discussion of these "illegal businesses," see Lincoln Steffens, *Autobiography* (New York: Harcourt, 1931), especially Pts. II and III.

under a laissez-faire approach to pressure-group formation, government "assistance programs" will actually work at cross purposes.

In both Canada and the United States, state, provincial, and local governments frantically compete for new industry through tax rebates. At present, they often duplicate or work against one another and thus cancel out. When Ontario, New York, and Pennsylvania all give tax reductions to attract industry, the first question must be to what extent the net change is merely a higher rate of after-tax corporate earnings. During the U.S. fuel shortage over the winter of 1970–1971, no fewer than nine uncoordinated agencies and departments were regulating the production and pricing of fuels at the federal level of government. There were also import quotas and price controls which allegedly contributed to the shortage.[16]

Or, we may imagine the New Republican Party sweeping to power in Utopia on a promise to build the Relevant Society by sweeping away unemployment, inflation, urban blight, and pockets of poverty in depressed areas. Its first act is to raise the minimum-wage rate by 25 per cent.

The conclusion seems inescapable that democracy has not only an equity but also an efficiency component. Certainly, the cost of more democratic decision making is initially higher. And, we may look upon this as an efficiency loss in the sense that resources are tied up in the actual process of social goal formation which would be freed for other uses under a more authoritarian regime. (Of course, the cost of enforcing social goals may be greater, the less democratic the process that evolves them.) But restricted participation in specific political decisions often results in barriers, in discrimination, or in freedom for some actors to inflict costs upon or to exploit others. These become sources of inefficiency.

The reader who finds our conclusion surprising will recall that we symbolized equity (in a political system with majority voting) by equal access to political-pressure-group representation. Let us now consider an individual who is relatively well represented in a country with a laissez-faire approach to pressure-group formation because he belongs to a strong labor union. Nevertheless, he breathes polluted air, drives on congested city streets, pays higher prices for goods protected by trade and industrial entry barriers and price supports, endures inflation, and pays taxes, some of which go to provide favors for other well-represented groups in society. He also contributes indirectly to compensation for the unemployed.

On balance, this individual hopefully receives a relatively large benefit

---

[16] For an example of such a program, see "Tax Credit in N.Y. State Spurs Plant Investment," *The New York Times,* Nov. 30, 1969, Sec. 3, p. 13. One paragraph from the article reads: "Among the incentives that have been offered by other [than New York State] areas are . . . corporate tax forgiveness of up to 50 per cent for specified periods of time, the issuance of industrial revenue bonds [that is, loans at low interest rates backed by government guarantees] to construct new factories and the availability of a large pool of low wage labor." New York officials then decided to practice their own brand of "forgiveness" with a tax credit on capital spending.

provided by his labor union in the form of a higher real wage and better working conditions than he could earn if his company or trade were not unionized. He endures many relatively small costs, which stem from the activities of other pressure groups trying to protect their supporters. It is far from clear that the total cost he endures is smaller than the benefit he gains. For society as a whole, in fact, there is a net (efficiency) loss referred to above.

Of course, no individual would choose a reduction in welfare such as the one just described. The point is that he cannot choose. Where his job is concerned, his interests are well represented by a group with an effective voice in social goal formation. But his representation on other issues is weaker to nonexistent. This is why we include citizens' sovereignty as one of our indexes of democracy. More democratic governments will give individuals an effective voice on more issues that affect them.

Nor is it hard to see that lapses from citizens' sovereignty are often the other face of a kind of tyranny of the minority. Suppose, for a moment, that we have a representative in the legislature whose constituents will not benefit from a proposed import quota to protect the textile industry. However, they will not suffer very much, on the average, and he will therefore be willing to sell his vote for a relatively low "price" in terms of support on other issues.

But under a laissez-faire approach to pressure-group formation, he may not even do this. Lobbying may induce the representative to give away his vote and even to solicit the votes of others. Such will be the case if his own constituents are not paying much attention to the issue, while the textile industry or a labor union is able to apply pressure or offer inducements. These include campaign contributions and direct publicity. (For example, the representative may run the risk of being declared "antilabor" or "anti-free enterprise" if he votes against protection.) In addition, political party discipline will often serve as a pressuring device.

By now, many skeptical and perceptive readers will suspect that we are faulting the real world for not achieving the perfection that can only be associated with a theoretical ideal. It is high time indeed that we began exploring a practical alternative.

23–4   Remedies

Let us now suppose that a government agency—to be further identified shortly—defines the rules under which special interest groups may emerge and earn the right to participate in social goal formation. Here the principal goal is analogous to keeping down market barriers to entry. That is, every identifiable community of interests that can benefit from or be hurt by government policies ought to be represented when those policies are decided upon. At the same time, the government should avoid subsidizing lobbies that fail to efficiently represent genuine special interests. Political pressure groups should succeed or fail on these grounds.

At the same time, we wish to change the basic formula for financing lobbies. We recall from Section 23–1 that there are two basic ways of financing lobbies under a laissez-faire approach. Formula A applies to pressure groups with a few large benefactors who have an incentive to support the lobby solely because of the benefits which it provides them. A large oil refinery may find that an import quota would substantially increase its expected profitability. By donating a sum that is less than the expected increase in profit, it can noticeably affect the lobby's chance of success. Consequently, it may voluntarily contribute, even though some of the benefits go to rivals who refuse to contribute.

Formula A will fail unless at least one firm, household, labor union, or other organization can influence the success of the lobby by donating an amount less than the benefit which it will receive. A consumer lobby is unlikely to be financed by this formula, even though it would prove a wise investment for millions of households, considered collectively.

When formula A fails, we turn to formula B. This comprises charitable and philanthropic gifts, along with the provision of private benefits or coercion to organize group members. We usually associate formula B with some form of dynamic entrepreneurship, whether it be a Ralph Nader organizing consumers or Samuel Gompers or Caesar Chavez organizing workers.

In the first instance, funds for a consumer lobby have generally been raised from public appearances, books, articles, and similar sources. In the second, the political and economic success of labor unions has notably depended upon their ability to tie jobs to union membership. A portion of the dues payment can then go toward financing a lobby. Medical associations have maintained financial support by selling technical advice and expertise, in the form of journals to members.[17] We can imagine formulas A and B being combined. Large steel mills may voluntarily support a lobby and then coerce their smaller rivals to contribute as well.

Here, our goal is to shift financing away from formula A toward formula B. We wish to design a system in which such crusaders as Nader may be more effective, but also one in which their constituents can better monitor and control their activities, hold them responsible, and replace them if this seems desirable. The best way to do this is to subsidize pressure groups on the basis of each citizen's preferences.

We would therefore require the government to set aside a small sum of money, say \$10 to \$20, for every citizen which can be earmarked to the financial support of lobbies according to any formula that the citizen may choose. Each citizen would be required to spend his sum on lobby support. For example, suppose that every citizen must fill out a tax form, whether he pays taxes, receives an allowance, or does neither. On such a form, he can also indicate how his lobbying donation is to be spread among pressure groups. [18]

To supplement this procedure, the ceilings on spending by all lobbies can

[17] Olson, op. cit., Pts. III, V, and VI. The existence of a dynamic entrepreneur (such as Nader) also provides a focus for receiving charitable and philanthropic donations.

[18] Such a proposal therefore dovetails with the plan for a guaranteed annual income for all citizens.

be coupled with tax-exempt status, which provides an effective subsidy common to all, provided a minimal cash flow is received. We would expect consumer and environmental lobbies to receive more dollar votes than most production-oriented lobbies because of the wider appeal of the former. In this way, we hope to partially get around the problem of scattered costs and concentrated benefits mentioned earlier. The production-oriented lobbies can continue to rely largely upon formula A financing, although some might have to merge to remain effective.

Under this or similar financing arrangements, we can be more certain that the financial decline of lobbies or their failure to arise reflects a failure (or an expected failure) to efficiently represent genuine special interests. When certain "legitimate" interests are still unrepresented, it is still possible to establish specific special interest groups as government agencies or departments. However, elections or direct referenda should be relied upon to determine whether these agencies ought to be created.[19]

Finally, to combat lack of awareness of issues, the government can publicize the positions taken by various groups for the benefit of present and potential constituents. It will have to do this judiciously, paying particular attention not to ruin possibilities for compromise between groups by publishing too many details at the wrong time.

Let us now suppose that the above proposals have gone into effect and take the emerging composition of political pressure groups as given. We must next explore the likely interaction between lobbies on one hand, and elected representatives and their staffs on the other, from which social goals will emerge. In particular, it will make a difference whether we are dealing with a planned economy. While we have abandoned a laissez-faire approach to pressure-group formation, we may still be dealing with a basically laissez-faire economy.

Perhaps the major difference, in fact, is that a plan could conceivably serve as a focus for this interaction. By a "plan" here we mean a series of measures, collectively designed to decisively influence the pattern of production and resource allocation and/or the distribution of welfare. The measures in question will not be primarily physical targets, except in a command economy, where these have the force of law. In mixed economies, they are certain to represent some or all of the various tax-subsidy programs discussed earlier which are designed to improve and supplement the market mechanism. These can still be legally enforced.

For example, a government agency may propose an initial financial incentive program or changes in market structure policy and receive counterproposals to be followed by discussion, negotiation, and compromise. Under favorable circumstances, an altered set of policies will emerge to be included

---

[19] Examples are a department of consumer affairs or of environmental protection. Presumably, these would be brought into being by vote of a representative legislature as well as by direct referenda.

in a final plan handed over to an economic planning council for implementation.

In a laissez-faire economy, on the other hand, there is by definition no agency charged with implementing society's principal economic goals and no plan embodying these. We must therefore ask what happens when this focal point for pressure-group interaction disappears.

Conceivably, the effect would be minimal. Special interest groups could meet on their own to negotiate, free of government "harassment," after which they would try to influence lawmaking and other government decision making on the basis of mutual agreement. The result could then be efficient goal formation, although goals would probably emerge piecemeal rather than as a unified block.

However, such a procedure would not be good strategy from the viewpoint of each individual lobby. In order to derive maximum benefits for its own interests, a pressure group is best advised to concentrate its forces where resistance is least. This is just the opposite of confronting those groups whose interests are diametrically opposed to its own. Such confrontations would tend to be minimized. Different groups representing a multiversity of special interests would normally *not* negotiate among themselves until they arrive at an efficient package of economic policies (that is, one which could not be altered so as to make one group better off without making another worse off).

Thus it is not in the private interests of a textile industry, threatened by foreign competition, to propose and publicize a general formula for protection under which it and several other industries would benefit at a cost to consumers (in the form of higher prices) and export industries (in the form of retaliation). Neither would it be in the private interests of the industry to initiate a debate on the matter. Instead, textile representatives should lobby legislators or other decision makers to get specific protection for their industry with a minimum of publicity and fuss. They should try to hide the benefits they receive and spread the costs of these as thinly as possible. By making the protection specific, they minimize the danger of retaliation. By making it inconspicuous and scattering its costs, they minimize the awareness of those who pay.

This takes us back to the problem of concentrated benefits and scattered costs, although many special interests in society are now better represented than previously and therefore less likely to be fooled or taken unaware. However, the role of the government in promoting or retarding political-pressure-group interaction remains crucial. Because it lacks an explicit definition of social welfare to implement, it is likely to concentrate on minimizing apparent conflict between special interests, while appearing to provide something for everyone at small costs to others. This, in turn, leads it to try to scatter the costs of benefits received and, on occasion, to conceal their extent. There will also be a tendency for (semi)clandestine agreements to emerge between government and those special interests it most wishes to please.

Different pressure groups will also tend to be compartmentalized, and various policies affecting the same problem area will often not be coordinated. Especially if it is Keynesian, a laissez-faire economy tends to pursue different goals in isolation, even though all are interdependent, at least in the sense that progress toward some inevitably comes at the expense of progress toward others.[20]

All this comes in lieu of an integrated plan, designed to chart a consistent long-range path for the economy in output and welfare space. From our discussion in Chapters 7–11 we know that fragmentation of *economic* decision making occurs within a command economy between bureaus and between different levels of the same chain of command. Each bureau tends to pursue its own output targets, partially handed down from above, working too much in isolation from the others. The interdependent efforts of several bureaus are not well coordinated. (The same may be true of government bureaus in a market economy.)

Consequently, no one may know the optimal production tradeoffs between two different kinds of machine tools or between machine tools, petrochemicals, data-processing equipment, and consumer durables. No market exists to evolve rational prices which would give these tradeoffs, and efforts to compute them directly are likely to prove inadequate. To say the same thing differently, no one is likely to be able to adequately compare investment yields between industries, especially if they are unrelated. In the long run, no one will know the marginal opportunity cost of increasing the output of one good in terms of the lost outputs of others that the same resources could have produced. This information cannot serve to coordinate production.

There will probably be less fragmentation of economic decision making in a market economy, but under laissez faire, the political process becomes fragmented in much the same way. No forum is likely to exist in which compromises determining social tradeoffs between different goals are hammered out in direct negotiation. We have just seen that it is not in the private interests of each pressure group to seek such a forum.

As a result, piecemeal policy making corresponds to piecemeal implementation under command planning. In an economy populated with coalitions, the government tends to deal separately with each one, providing benefits in such a way as to minimize conflict between them. This, in turn, reinforces any tendency among particular special interest groups to view their own interests apart from those of society as a whole.

However, consider the following method of building in countervailing power against this fragmentation. Instead of separately debating 50 different

---

[20] The cost of this will clearly depend on the share of national income and expenditure that goes to the government. Comparing scandals then and now, *The New York Times* editorialized, "The opportunities for government benefactions were relatively small in the Harding era compared to . . . Today, with enormous growth of the public sector dealing with national defense, housing, real estate, highways, railroads, airlines, shipping, mining, health, education, welfare, agriculture, and virtually every other facet of society."

trade-protection packages for 50 different industries, let us imagine a comprehensive protection law being discussed. This law would give a definite and
usable formula according to which any industry does or does not qualify for
protection. Only a few well-defined exceptions would be permitted.[21]

Moreover, let us specify in advance that the usual form of protection will
be direct subsidies to industries hit by foreign competition rather than tariffs
or import quotas that raise prices to consumers. Usually this will be more
efficient, and the total of amount of subsidy for each industry can easily be
monitored and publicized to make consumers aware of the costs they are
paying.

Each household will have a major stake in a comprehensive protection
bill. Whereas it may pay only a few dollars here to protect the textile industry
and a few dollars there to protect oil, it will pay hundreds or even thousands
of dollars to protect *all* industries combined. Similarly, each household will
be much more concerned with a comprehensive market-structure policy than
with increasing concentration in peanut manufacturing, production quotas for
oil and tobacco, and farm price supports considered separately.

The same is true of a guaranteed annual income, a comprehensive consumer protection law, or a general rule that makes the salaries of bureau
directors decrease with the sizes of their staffs beyond a well-defined limit.
In each case, we shall have reduced the scattering of costs and the concentration of benefits.

The ultimate way of doing this is to consider all the central government's
measures to supplement the market mechanism or to improve its performance
as parts of an integral economy-wide plan. The basic task of economic planning in a democratic society is to permit more democratic government to function more effectively in the economic sphere.

We shall now have a go at sketching a framework that we feel holds some
promise along these lines. As mentioned earlier, the key to success lies in
creating a mechanism that will perform roughly the same coordinating service
for the political process that the market mechanism performs for the economic
process.

However, it is not the job of the "political marketplace" to break up a
gigantic problem into millions of tiny ones. Rather, different special interests
should be combined and coordinated within a framework that makes it most
productive for each group to increase its own welfare by sharing in an expansion of social welfare from which other segments of society also benefit. This,

---

[21] This need not prevent us from treating each case on its merits. Such a law would
define fairly precisely what "merit" is by specifying fairly precisely the conditions under
which a firm could expect to receive a given amount of protection.

An alternative approach (followed, for example, in Canadian antitrust policy) is to
let each case be investigated and judged by an impartial tribunal of experts. The use of
general guidelines would presumably help to ensure that the tribunal is both expert and
unbiased. This approach is potentially more flexible, but also more expensive for a
given degree of effectiveness. (In practice, this may make it ineffective.) The two approaches can also be combined.

in turn, suggests some kind of multidimensional collective bargaining from which the plan will emerge as a social contract.

23–5   Economic Planning in a Democratic Society: General Observations

Let us continue to call the economic government of a country its sector of direction and administration. Rather than identify this with the economic planning council, however, we now note that it is potentially divisible into three bodies. The economic planning council would continue to ensure that plans and policies are implemented. It can be joined by a *council of social values* (CSV), which has responsibility for goal formation, and by an executive branch, which presides over the other two. The CSV will notably define the rules under which political pressure groups emerge and participate in social goal formation.

A democratic economic government must be one ultimately based on elections. However, we shall see that, by its nature, the CSV must consist of a battery of highly skilled mediators. Likewise, EPC will consist of specialists in planning and administration. This is why, within the economic administration as we conceive of it, the executive branch must be the elected body if there is to be one. Ideally, the executive body would be elected, but cost considerations may force it to be nominated by the political executive. Nevertheless, provision should be made for an opposition whose alternative plans and policies are well publicized. The need for alternatives is illustrated by the following story: The board of directors of a major corporation once met to approve its investment program for the coming year. The biggest project involved an expenditure of 1 million dollars, but after the chief engineer had explained it in rather technical terms, most members of the board didn't really understand it, so they passed it without any discussion. The second project involved an expected outlay of $750,000 and met the same fate. Finally, at the bottom of the list, was a proposed expenditure of $1,000 for washroom facilities. This was understood, and a two-hour debate ensued. The request was pared to $872.75 and approved.

The French plan, for example, must always receive the approval of a Parliament whose elected representatives span the political spectrum. The French planning authority can also exist independently of the rise and fall of political governments (which is desirable from the standpoint of efficient long-range planning). But when the plan comes up for approval, one suspects that Parliament is not unlike the Board of Directors above. Its job is to approve or disapprove of the social priorities that the plan embodies. It cannot do this completely, however, without a detailed knowledge of what alternatives are really available—which it does not have. Add the fact that each plan will contain a few unrealistic targets to capture the legislator's fancy, and we can see that Parliament often will not be in a position to pass intelligent judgment on it.

This is why democratic planning requires the presence of an opposition, with access to its own technical expertise, which will propose alternatives to some or all parts of a plan. The existence of this competition will force each side to make its programs more comprehensible to the layman and more open to the press. It will also make planning a more expensive proposition.

The question next arises as to what the relationship between the political and economic administrations will be. If we are to have efficient democratic planning, we must give the policymakers some room in which to operate. For this reason, it is not a good idea to throw the existing sector of direction and administration out of office every time the political government changes hands.

If this were to happen, the policies of one group of planners would always risk clashing with those of their successors. The economy might fail to chart any consistent course over time on this account, and thus lose many potential benefits from planning. Each set of planners could, at best, hope to establish some broad precedents without any guarantee that these would be picked up. Each would find that, for many purposes, its planning horizon could cover only the period prior to the next election. Each would therefore have to occupy itself overly with short-term problems and would often find it necessary to give them a sedative rather than to try to cure them. During the waning months of any outgoing political administration, the economic planning council would find that it could do virtually nothing at all, lest any measure be upset by the incoming planners, whose identity may not even be known.

Consequently, a country's economic administration should be at least partly independent of the political government. If the latter appoints the executive branch of the former, the terms of the two executives should not coincide. Indeed, the need for long-run, economy-wide planning probably dictates a longer term of office for the economic executive. The terms of economic executives can also be staggered as an additional means of promoting independence and, perhaps, of lengthening the acceptable term of office to the voters.

Any set of planners should remain as politically uncommitted as possible, and any political administration should be required to deal with whichever economic administration happens to be in power. Society will have to make some hard choices about what its long-run relative priorities are going to be, and these priorities ought then to become politically nonpartisan.[22] Finally, the economic administration in power should have the authority to initiate plans, programs, and policies which are not always subject to veto by the executive branch of the political administration.

This suggests that the respective areas of (economic) responsibility between the economic and political governments of a country should be complementary rather than competitive. As a first approximation, the political

---

[22] It also follows that each succeeding economic administration cannot receive carte blanche to undo long-range programs or to override basic goals determined by its predecessors, although these should be subject to periodic reviews even when the economic government does not change hands.

administration could be charged with determining the current *scale* of economic activity while the economic administration determines and implements the long-run *path* of economic development. Thus the political government would determine the *level* of government spending plus average tax rates. The economic administration would decide how to differentiate incentives and commands.

Nevertheless, as envisaged by the present authors, the economic administration would have no authority to legislate. Thus basic long-run plans (and alternatives) will have to be referred back to the political administration for some kind of legislative approval before taking effect, providing a major exception to the separation of economic and political authority. As compensation, safeguards should exist to prevent the legislature from blocking action simply by refusing to come to a decision. (For example, a plan passed by the economic administration might automatically go into effect in such an instance.)

It is hard to imagine successful democratic planning in operation without a collaborative spirit and a continuous dialogue prevailing among the planners and the various special interest groups which play a role in social goal formation. In a sense democratic economic planning requires "broadening the base of collusion." Instead of having a few steel magnates agree to prop up steel prices, we hope to get them and their suppliers to agree to increase production and lower price while labor unions are reducing their wage demands, an exchange that can prove beneficial to all concerned.

The idea is that society's basic economic goals can emerge as the result of a social contract between these groups in which all of them moderate their private aspirations to some extent in order to reap less direct benefits from an improved state of the economy.

The theory underlying participatory planning is a generalization of countervailing power from two decision makers to many. It says that up to a point, interdependent actors can mutually benefit from agreements to expand, especially within a context where society is able to keep artificial barriers to entry low. The ensuing negotiations need a catalyst and an impetus to expansion, quality improvements, technological progress, or whatever social priorities may emerge from the bargaining. This is provided by financial incentives, commands, moral suasion, government contracts, and the other planning instruments. The plan, of course, will also embody these priorities in some way.

On the implementation side, democratic planning has also been described as a mutual confidence game—confidence being the other face of cooperation.[23] Suppose that the economic planning council advises automobile producers to expect an average annual increase in demand of 4 per cent over the next five years. If the automen have faith in the EPC's forecasting powers, and

[23] Harry G. Johnson in *Economic Planning in a Democratic Society,* 9th C.I.P.A. Winter Conference (Toronto: U. of Toronto, 1963).

if they have sufficient incentive to expand output rather than to raise prices, they will invest for this amount of increase.[24]

The planners will also predict the evolution of demand facing steel firms, auto-parts producers, and other suppliers of the automobile industry. All these forecasts are interdependent. If everyone takes the planners' word as a competent guide to the future and if the EPC has correctly estimated the changing structure and growth potential of the system, it may grow smoothly. But the planners' forecasting activity depends, in turn, upon nonoperational information gathered from producers, regional and local government representatives, labor unions, chambers of commerce, manufacturers' associations, and so on. Thus the circle of confidence is complete.

Some economists have emphasized the self-fulfilling nature of economic projections when these are widely expected to come true. This is provided they are achievable and mutually consistent, and that firms do not substitute price for output adjustments. James Tobin once noted that "If businessmen individually have confidence that the markets will be there, they will make the investments which collectively help to provide those very markets." [25] Writing on the Japanese economy, Christopher Johnson says:

> There is a self-perpetuating element in the Japanese growth process . . . each company knows that it can double its sales every few years because it reckons that all the other companies with which it is doing business are also advancing at the same rate.
>
> In this fast moving situation, it is the cautious firm failing to invest in new and more efficient production capacity which is taking the risk . . . that it will become uncompetitive and thus go under.[26]

If the auto industry invests to grow at a projected 4 per cent per year, this will help provide the expected market for its suppliers and enable them to grow at their projected rates of increase. We may then go back one more stage, and so on. In the final analysis, the self-fulfilling property results from the interdependence of different sectors of the economy as described in an input–output table or a table of intersectoral flows.

23–6   Economic Planning in a Democratic Society: The Goal-Forming Process

We now wish to anatomize social goal formation under "democratic" economic planning. We cannot hope to characterize every possible democratic

---

[24] These incentives come from competition or from competition substitutes, including financial incentives. See Section 17–1.

[25] James Tobin, pp. 17–24 in *Economic Planning in a Democratic Society?* Symposium of 9th Winter Conference of Canadian Institute of Public Affairs (Toronto: U. of Toronto, 1963).

[26] Christopher Johnson, "Firms in Japan Prefer to Aim at Maintenance of Market Share Rather Than Rise in Profits," *Toronto Globe and Mail,* Sept. 18, 1971, p. 83.

plan-forming procedure, but we shall outline an alternative which suggests itself from our previous discussion.

In sorting out our ideas, it is once again useful to divide economic planning into two stages, one associated with goal formation and the other with implementation. The economic planning council is responsible for implementation, using tools such as those discussed in the preceding chapters, and also trying to produce the kind of coordination just described.[27] The responsibility for ensuring that economic goals are formulated, along with the plans and policies which embody these, will go to the council of social values.

Figure 23–1 conceptualizes the basic procedure we have in mind from one point of view. The CSV presides over the process, occupying the top rung of the chart, which chooses priorities and tradeoffs among different goals. The output of this process is a series of policy objectives. Once priorities are defined, we move to the second rung. Here the CSV also presides over the formulation of broad strategies or policies to use in reaching goals. In practice, these two stages are usually combined. For example, a decision may be taken to aid a depressed area or certain "growth" industries and a sum of x dollars earmarked for financial incentives to achieve this goal. The amount set aside helps to define the urgency of the priority in question.

Once formulated, the entire set of policies and policy objectives constitutes a plan which is submitted to the political legislature for approval and, ultimately, to the EPC for implementation. We then move to the third rung of Figure 23–1, where policies become specific programs. The x dollars become specific financial incentives offered under specific terms. A formula for market-structure policy receives a more specific interpretation each time it is applied to a specific product or job market.

Finally, each stage of the planning procedure generates feedback information in the form of results achieved. The EPC may consistently discover that some kinds of financial incentives work better than others or that the most productive kind depends in a systematic way upon the type of problem being tackled as well as the problem environment. (EPC will also be carrying on direct information exchanges with firms.) This is the bottom rung in Figure 23–1. As it gathers experience, the economic planning council will increasingly be able to advise the CSV on the best guidelines for policy formation and on the expected productivity or effectiveness of different policies in attaining goals. In this way, the CSV will eventually get a more accurate picture of the set of goals that are achievable.

The principal modification here to social goal formation under laissez faire, then, is that a council of social values presides over the construction of a plan. The plan will be submitted to the political legislature for approval and, ultimately, to the EPC for implementation. It will embody *all* policies

---

[27] The EPC will also take responsibility for implementing policies passed by the political government designed to affect the scale of economic activity.

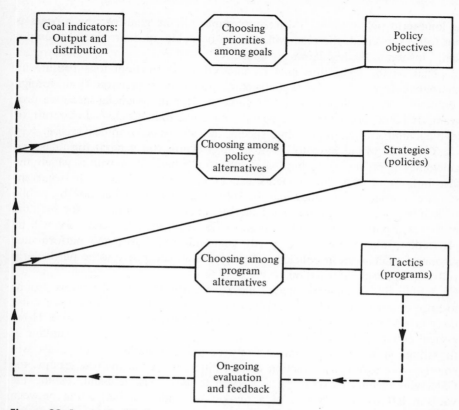

Figure 23–1. A simplified view of government decision making for planning. Source: Economic Council of Canada, *Design for Decision-Making* (8th annual review), Ottawa, Information Canada (Sept. 1971), p. 65.

that are potentially legally binding and fall under the jurisdiction of the economic administration.[28] Thus additive commands will be of primary importance only in a command economy. In cases where the plan seeks to preserve the status quo, the prevailing rule or law is understood to be part of the plan.

Most likely, CSV would submit a comprehensive long-term plan once every several years—five years has become a popular interval based on the needs of horizon planning—and less comprehensive, but in some cases more detailed proposals annually.

The legislature would have limited powers to modify the plan once it was submitted. For example, inefficient forms of subsidy, such as tariffs, import quotas, and price and wage supports or ceilings, could be ruled out

---

[28] The economic administration, like the political government, may have an important division of powers between a central unit and various partly autonomous regional bodies. If so, negotiations between these levels will become an important part of the goal-forming process.

as long-term policy tools.[29] More importantly, if the goal-forming process is not to be subverted, the plan will have to be made up of irreducible components, insofar as the legislators are concerned.

That is, the legislature may be allowed some freedom to substitute an alternative formula for market-structure policy or protection from foreign competition or an alternative set of guidelines for the financial-incentive program. It could *not* propose legislation covering only Lockheed Aircraft or textile manufacturing or any other specific industry or geographical region.

The CSV would have to insist, in other words, on general formulas and guidelines applying to each of a number of broad areas within which the distributions of costs and benefits will more nearly coincide. (In some instances, alternative formulas may be subjected to a direct decision by public referendum.) Each formula or set of guidelines should come up for periodic review as a part of the goal-forming process. Both the EPC and CSV will be proceeding and learning on a partly trial-and-error basis, and performance responses to changes in policies and programs should prove to be particularly valuable feedback information.

Within this framework, ample incentive exists for special interest groups to arise and join in political decision making. As in the case of laissez faire, these groups will lobby the political government, notably the legislature. However, it now pays them to lobby CSV as well. The latter can take advantage of the situation to involve them directly in plan formation. Then goals will emerge from a direct interaction among different special interest groups, the CSV, and technical experts. The CSV acts as a "visible hand," filling the vacuum left by the absence of a market to guide the bargaining between special interest groups.

In some respects, we may view the CSV as an outgrowth of the central auctioneer, who raises and lowers prices in a decentralized market economy. The auctioneer's job is to find a set of prices which balances supply and demand throughout the economy and to disallow trading at disequilibrium prices. In this way he guides the economy to an efficient equilibrium, provided certain assumptions, discussed in Chapter 16, are met. Thus he is a kind of social engineer who represents society in the bargaining process.

One of the assumptions referred to is that no need arises to internalize the costs of pollution or congestion or other external effects. If it does, the

---

[29] There are exceptions to this rule. If a country is a monopoly seller on the world market, it could decide to capitalize on this position by imposing a tariff on exported goods, thereby raising the price to foreign buyers, who effectively pay most of the tariff. Similarly, a nation that is a monopolistic buyer on world markets may decide to capitalize on its position by introducing a conventional tariff on imported goods. Because of its buying power, such a nation will be able to force foreign sellers to absorb most of the tariff payment.

In either case, therefore, the nation with monopoly power can collect a payment from foreign nationals or governments to use as it sees fit. (A nation may also try to organize its exporting and importing industries to achieve this monopoly; Japan is an example of this.)

social engineer has a wider role to play, and his decision-making function becomes more complex. He will need to gather nonprice information and to supplement the workings of the market mechanism with incentives and penalties, including controls. Finally, some goods will be at least partly public in nature, and some "markets" will be such that neither buyer nor seller is a price taker.

In such instances the auctioneer must become a mediator in bargaining between groups, as well as a guardian of the "collective interest." One of his duties will be to ensure that all parties bargain in good faith and that the negotiations make reasonable progress. This comes closest to describing the role played by CSV in social goal formation. First, and foremost, it will provide a forum for active bargaining, compromise, and vote trading (or exchange of support) between diverse economic interests and regions of the country.

Such interaction may be viewed as a much more complex version of collective bargaining or of procedures whereby insurance agencies decide how to settle mutual claims by clients of one company against those of another. However, decision-making requires information, and CSV must also "provide the right sort of locus for the integration of information contained in economic (studies and) reports, budget papers, and social policy statements." [30] In addition, CSV will gather data and engage in forecasting on its own, including committee hearings to gather expert opinion relating to policy alternatives.

The psychological advantages of such a framework over goal formation under laissez faire are potentially threefold, provided diverse special interest groups find it an effective context within which to express themselves. First, it enables them to see their own aspirations within a perspective based upon economy-wide alternatives. A better knowledge of constraints facing all groups representing all of the basic economic roles in society will cause some groups to moderate their demands and put them into a negotiating frame of mind, or so it is argued. Second, it provides a creative outlet for ideas and ambitions, as well as frustration, discontent, and so on, in the form of continuing dialogues.

Third, the output from this dialogue should be more than a series of measures designed to protect various groups from the rigors of the marketplace or to enable them to inflict external costs upon, or to receive external benefits from, other segments in society. Even a half-baked plan ought to be a positive program of social improvement, in which all groups can share. Planning should also enlarge the options open to economic decision makers and make them less likely to have to respond to contingencies of the moment.

If we think of plan and policy formation as a kind of multidimensional and multistage collective bargaining among special interest groups, the CSV

[30] G. Paquet, "The Economic Council as Phoenix," in W. E. Mann, ed., *Social and Cultural Change in Canada*, Vol. II (Toronto: Copp Clark, 1970), p. 60.

will play a role somewhere between that of arbitrator and conciliator. What it must do, in fact, is analogous to latent compulsory arbitration in that a solution (that is, a policy or plan) must usually emerge within a time constraint. The rules of democratic decision making do not permit the CSV to impose its own version of a plan except as an absolute last resort when collective bargaining fails to produce a mutually acceptable plan. However, the threat of last-resort arbitration both ensures that a plan will emerge and gives special interest groups an incentive to bargain efficiently and in good faith.

Nevertheless, the CSV's primary responsibility is to ensure that the rules and procedures of bargaining, along with ancillary activities such as information gathering, are such that a consensus has a good chance to emerge. It will therefore reserve the right to arbitrate efforts to define these rules. Like the auctioneer of a textbook laissez-faire economy, it is process-oriented (that is, oriented toward designing procedures that will work) rather than outcome-oriented.

For example, by withdrawing altogether from the negotiations, one special interest group may be able to sabotage them. In such a case, CSV must either be able to penalize a group which pulls out, to an extent that this tactic proves unprofitable, or else reserve the right to represent the group's interests in its absence.

A major goal of participatory plan construction is also to reduce the ideological content and polemics involved in goal formation. The idea is to make it less necessary—and less possible—for groups to crusade and to take simplistic and extreme positions in order to attract enough attention and support to participate in the political process.

Yet, in the final analysis, we would be naive to presume that any of the actors in the administration we are outlining will automatically be Platonic philosopher–decision makers. It is the architect of a workable democratic economy in the real world who must combine the dedication and genius of a William Pitt, Thomas Jefferson, Pericles, or Solon.

REFERENCES

Downs, Anthony. *An Economic Theory of Democracy.* New York: Harper & Row, Publishers, 1957.

———. "An Economic Theory of Political Action in a Democracy." *Journal of Political Economy,* Apr. 1957.

Economic Council of Canada, *Eighth Annual Review,* Ottawa, Information Canada, 1971, Chs. 1–5, 10.

Haefele, E. T. "A Utility Theory of Representative Government," *American Economic Review,* June 1971.

Malles, Paul. *Economic Consultative Bodies,* Ottawa, Information Canada, Jan. 1971.

Niskanen, William. *Bureaucracy and Representative Government,* Chicago, Aldine-Atherton, Inc., 1971.

Olson, Mancur, Jr. *The Logic of Collective Action.* New York: Schocken Books, Inc., 1968.

Paquet, G. "The Economic Council as Phoenix." In W. E. Mann, ed., *Social and Cultural Change in Canada,* Vol. II, Toronto: The Copp Clark Publishing Corporation, 1970, pp. 47–63.

Thorburn, H. G. "Pressure Groups in Canadian Politics." *Canadian Journal of Economics and Political Science,* May 1964.

Tullock, Gordon. "Entry Barriers in Politics." *American Economic Review,* May 1965.

Index